A History of the Formation and Development of the Volunteer Infantry: From the Earliest Times

Robert Potter Berry

Lieut. Coll. Sir George Armytage, Bart. 1796–1816.

A HISTORY

OF THE

FORMATION AND DEVELOPMENT

OF

THE VOLUNTEER INFANTRY,

FROM THE EARLIEST TIMES,

ILLUSTRATED BY THE LOCAL RECORDS

OF

HUDDERSFIELD AND ITS VICINITY,

FROM 1794 TO 1874,

BY

ROBERT POTTER BERRY,

(Late) Lieutenant 6th West York Rifle Volunteers.

———::———

LONDON:
SIMPKIN, MARSHALL, HAMILTON, KENT & Co., LIMITED,
4, STATIONERS' HALL COURT, E.C.
HUDDERSFIELD:
J. BROADBENT & Co., HIGH STREET AND ALBION STREET.

—

1903.

W.

TO

SIR THOMAS BROOKE, BART.,

OF ARMITAGE BRIDGE,

FORMERLY AND FOR MANY YEARS LIEUTENANT COLONEL

COMMANDANT OF THE

FIFTH ADMINISTRATIVE BATTALION OF THE WEST RIDING OF

YORKSHIRE RIFLE VOLUNTEERS,

THIS HISTORY

IS (BY PERMISSION) DEDICATED AS A RESPECTFUL TRIBUTE TO HIS

SERVICES TO THE BATTALION,

AND

IN GRATEFUL REMEMBRANCE OF HIS UNVARYING KINDNESS AND

CONSIDERATION TO HIS OFFICERS AND MEN,

AND NOT LEAST TO

THE AUTHOR.

TABLE OF CONTENTS.

PART I.

SECTION I.

SECTION II.

SECTION III.

SECTION IV.

Secretary Herbert's Circular, July 13th, 1859—Nature of the Instruction at Hythe—Memorandum, July 13th, 1859—Committee on Volunteer Rules and Regulations—Its Report, August, 1859—Committee on Military Organisation, August, 1859—Colonel Cooper King on the Volunteers of 1859—Correspondence as to Sashes, Swords, Goldlace—Dress Regulations—Salutes—The popularity of the movement in 1859—Circular of Secretary Herbert, December, 1859—Memorandum as to Drill Instructors, Feb., 1860—Green Book, 1859—Battalions become general—Memorandum as to Adjutants, 1860—War Office Circular, March, 1860—Memorandum as to Administrative and Consolidated Battalions, Sept., 1860—Royal Warrant as to Adjutants, June, 1860—Official Memorandum as to same, Sept., 1860—War Office Circular as to Reviews, July, 1860—Circular Memorandum as to Field Exercises, May, 1860—Volunteer Regulations, 1861—Circular as to Brigade Camps at Aldershot, &c., October, 1861—As to Local Camps, March, 1862—23 Vic. c. 13—23 and 24 Vic. c. 140—24 and 25 Vic. c. 126—Royal Commission on Volunteer Forces, May, 1862—Its Report—Strength of Volunteers, 1862—Volunteer Act, 1863—Order in Council, July 27th, 1863—Regulations, Sept., 1863—Volunteer Returns, 1863-1889—Circulars as to Enfield Rifles, 1867—Visit of Volunteers to Belgium, 1866—Of Belgian Volunteers to England, 1867—Report of Committee of Volunteer Officers on Capitation Grant, March, 1867—War Office Circular, April, 1870—War Office Circulars, August 29th and 30th, 1870—Circular, Sept., 1st, 1870—Auxiliary and Reserve Forces Circulars, Nov., 1870, Dec., 1870, Jan., 1871—Jurisdiction of Lord Lieutenant transferred to Secretary for War, 34 and 35 Vic. c. 86—Issue of Commissions, 25 and 26 Vic. c. 4—Regulation of Forces Act, 1871—Auxiliary and Reserve Forces Circular, May, 1872—Earlier Volunteer Levies contrasted with those of 1872—Order in Council, October, 1872—Auxiliary and Reserve Forces Circular, April, 1873—General Regulations, July, 1873—Army and Reserve Forces Circular, 1873—Short Account of the Office of Ensign—Letter of General Wolfe—Auxiliary and Reserve Forces Circular, April, 1874—Volunteer Regulations, 1878—Departmental Committee, 1878, and its Report—Abstract of Volunteer Returns, 1863-1878—Volunteer Regulations, 1881—Regulation of the Forces Act, 1881—Territorialization—Lord Stanley's Committee, 1876—Volunteer Regulations, 1884—Lord Harris' Committee, 1886—Its Report, 1887—Regulations of 1887—and of 1890—Army Order, 1890—Volunteer Regulations, 1891-1892—Army Order, 1893—Regulations, 1893—Army Act, 1881—Military Lands Act, 1892—Volunteer Regulations, 1894-1895-1896-1897-1898-1899—Provisional, 1901—Army Order, April, 1902—Order in Council, August, 1902—The Arms of the Force.

SECTION V.

The future of the Volunteer Force—Or its Alternative—Debate at the Royal United Service Institution on Essay by Mr. George Shee—The Chairman—Other Speakers—Report of the Debate—Do we require an Auxiliary for Home Defence?—Letter of Rev. John Freeman—Opinions of Major General Strange—Of Captain S. L. Murray—The strength of Germany in Transports—"Universal Service" recommended by Captain Murray—French opinion as to the feasibility of invading England—German opinion—The circumstances that will favour such invasion—Baron Maurice on the necessary force for invasion—Captain Wilkinson on the same subject—The German and French facilities for mobilization—What force could we oppose?—The Rt. Hon. J. Chamberlain, M.P. on the Volunteers as Marksmen—The Volunteer strength, 1902—Lord Wolseley on the Shooting of Volunteers—Shooting Competitions no test of general efficiency—General Mackay on Prize Shooting—Lieutenant Duncan Watson on defects in Volunteer Training—Lieutenant-Colonel Mayhew on Volunteer Officers—The German System of Universal Service—The inefficiency of Volunteer Training—What actual warfare would mean to the Volunteer—Is he prepared for the strain?—A Test Case—The vital defects of the Volunteer Principle—Inadequacy of certain suggested remedies—The revival of the Local Militia suggested—Service in the Regular Army not affected by proposal—The Population available for the Local Militia—Census of 1891—Number of males of the recruiting ages—and of the Military ages—The Population roughly classified by occupations—The professional classes—The domestic class—Commercial classes—The agricultural class—The industrial classes—Summary—The Local Militia Act, 1808—How its revival would operate—The number of men required annually under a system of Local Militia—Arguments in its support—Some objections considered—A further argument in its favour—The cost of a Local Militia—Sir R. R. Knox, K.C.B., on the cost of the Infantry Private.

PART II.

SECTION I.

Meeting of West Riding Magistrates at Pontefract, 30th April, 1794—Further Meeting, May 24th, 1794—Resolutions at these Meetings—Meeting at Huddersfield, June 28th, 1794—Resolution to raise a Corps of Volunteer Infantry—List of Subscriptions—First Officers of Corps—The rank of Captain-Lieutenant—Personal Notices of some Officers—Lieutenant-Colonel Nichols—Captain Joseph Haigh—1st Lieutenant Joseph Scott—1st Lieutenant Horsfall—2nd Lieutenant W. Stables—2nd Lieutenant T. Atkinson—Captain Seaton—1st Lieutenant Woolley—The Chaplain—Uniform—The Colours—Their Heraldic descriptions—Presentation Cups—Pay—Clothing Allowance—Military Festival, May 26th, 1795—Leeds Officers—Bradford Officers—Wakefield Officers—Halifax Officers—Loyal Addresses, Sept., 1796—Inspection, May, 1797—Officers of Huddersfield Corps, 1800—Strength of Corps, 1798-1802—Huddersfield Armed Association—Meeting at Huddersfield to form, April 23rd, 1798—Names of Committee—Rules and Regulations—Officers—Colours—Local Returns of men liable to serve in Armed Association—Uniform of Leeds Armed Association.

SECTION II.

The Upper Agbrigg (Huddersfield) Volunteers, 1803—Public Meeting to promote same—Loyal Address—Resolutions of Meeting—Further Meetings and Resolutions—Note as to the Drummers—List of Subscribers to the Volunteer Funds—Pay of the Volunteers—The Officers of the Corps—Text of one of the Commissions—Personal Notices of some of the Officers—Inspection, 1803—Presentation of Colours—Proceedings thereat—Annual Trainings, 1804-1805—Inspection, 1805—Official Returns, 1806—Meeting of Magistracy, 1806—Resolutions thereat—Postings of Officers, 1803-1807—Upper Agbrigg Militia—Its Uniform—The Colours—Their Heraldic descriptions—Some records of the Corps—Notice calling up Local Militia for Annual Training—The Annual Trainings and Inspections of successive years—Embodiment contemplated, 1804—Resolution of Magistracy thereanent—Votes of thanks of Parliament to Local Militia—Inspection of Corps—Mess Book of Local Militia—Huddersfield Armed Association, 1820—Watch and Ward Act—Local Disturbances—Officers of the Huddersfield Armed Association, 1820—Personal Notices of certain Officers—Complimentary Banquet.

SECTION III.

1859. Rifle Club first contemplated—Proposed Honorary and Acting members thereof—The Constable of Huddersfield's Proclamation—Town's Meeting summoned—Proceedings thereat—Meeting at Mr. Battye's office, June, 1859—Founders of the Huddersfield Volunteer Corps—Inaugural Meeting in Riding School—Resolutions thereat—First Roll of Volunteers—Negociations as to Exercise Ground, Drill Hall, &c.—Selection of Arms Magazine—and of Drill Hall—Presentation of Silver Bugle—Acceptance of No. 1 Company by the Crown, Nov. 3rd, 1859—Correspondence as to Establishment—First Muster Roll of No. 1 Company—First Drill Sergeant—Motto of Corps—Its History—Subscribers and amounts to Corps Funds—The first Uniform—Cost—Summer Uniform—Sashes and Plumes prohibited—Honorary Members' Uniform—No. 1 Company to be self-supporting—Regulations of the Corps—First Annual Meeting, Dec. 1st, 1859—First Parade—State and Establishment of Corps, Jan., 1860—Visit to Holmfirth—Muster Rolls, 1860—Correspondence as to further Companies and formation of Battalion—No. 2 Company formed—Inspection, 1860—No. 3 and No. 4 Companies formed—Muster Roll of the four Companies, 1861—Hon. Sec. of Companies 3 and 4—Mr. Chas. Mills—Battalion constituted—The First Adjutant—Annual Charges—Instruction of Officers at Hythe—Levée at St. James's, Banquet and Ball—New Designation of Corps—Field Day, Bradford, 1860—Review at York, Sept., 1860—Banquet at Guildhall, York—Prize Shooting Sweepstakes, 1860—Shooting Casualties—Inspection, 1860—Secretary's Report, Nov., 1860—Strength of the several Companies at this period—Volunteer Ball, Jan., 1861—Lieut.-Colonel Freeman's first connection with Corps—Presentation to Mr. Battye—General Annual Meeting, 1861—Changes of Commissions, 1861—Captain and Adjutant H. B. Chichester—York Review, 1861—Resignation of Major H. F. Beaumont—Appointment of Lieut.-Col. T. P. Crosland—Captain Batley's letter to his Company—Annual Meeting, 1862—Cadet Corps formed, 1862—Review at Doncaster, 1862—Presentation of Challenge Cup by Mr. and

Mrs. Bentley Shaw—Review at Huddersfield, 1862—First Prize Shooting Meeting—Changes in 1863—First Military Interment—The Armoury acquired and adapted—Subscriptions to cost of—Review at Doncaster, 1864—Simultaneous Enfield Rifle Contest, 1865—Presentations to Captain Joseph Batley—Committee of Enquiry into Corps finances, 1865—No. 5 Company formed—Review at York, 1865—Resignation of Colonel Crosland—Appointment of Lieut.-Col. Thos. Brooke—Resignation of Captain Batley—Formation of Companies Nos. 6, 7 and 8—Promotion of, and presentation to, Lieut.-Col. Greenwood—Death of Col. T. P. Crosland—Presentation of Band Instruments, 1868—and of Colours—The Huddersfield Enfield Rifle Club—Strength of Huddersfield Corps and united Corps in 1869—Presentation to Lieut. William Laycock—Death of Sergt.-Major Hunnybell—of Hon. Quarter-Master Eddison—Wakefield Review, 1870—Officers' Examination, 1871—Review at Doncaster, 1871—Memo. of Col. Brooke, 1871—Officers' Classes formed—Circular of Colonel Brooke to Corps—Resignation of Colonel Brooke—and of Colonel Greenwood—and of Captain and Adjutant Chichester—Death of Surgeon John Dow—Major Day appointed Lieut.-Col. of 5th A. B., and Captain Freeman Major of 6th Corps—Appointment of Captain and Adjutant Percy Bingham Schreiber—Reduction in number of Companies, 1873—10th Sub-district Brigade—9th ditto—Appointment of Captain and Adjutant W. S. Hardinge—Camp in Greenhead Park—Report thereon—New Uniforms and subscriptions towards cost of—Inspections and Strength, 1861-1874—War Office Returns, 1859 to 1881—Government Capitation Allowances—Summary of the Commandants and Staff of the 5th A. B.—Prize Winners of Challenge Medal and Cups, 1861 to 1874—War Office Postings of Officers from formation to consolidation—Lieutenancy Postings of Officers from formation to 1871—War Office Statistics of the 32nd Holmfirth Corps—41st Mirfield Corps and 44th Meltham Corps.—Conclusion.

Appendix.

War Office Circulars, May 12th and July 13th, 1859—Memorandum regarding the formation and organization of Corps, 1859—Rules—Volunteer Regulations, 1861.

ILLUSTRATIONS.

PREFACE.

"An historical account is to be kept in every Corps of its services, &c.; stating the period and circumstances of the original formation of the regiment; the means by which it has, from time to time, been recruited; the stations at which it has been employed, and the period of its arrival and departure from such stations; the badges and devices which the regiment has been permitted to bear, and the causes on account of which such badges and devices or any other marks of distinction were granted, are to be stated; also the dates of such permission being granted. Any particular alteration in the clothing, arms, accoutrements, colours, horse furniture, &c., are to be recorded and a reference made to the date of the Orders under which such alterations were made. The various alterations which may be made in the establishment of the regiment, either by augmentation or reduction, are also to be stated in this Book."—Queen's Regulations and Orders for the Army—Section 23, para. 44.

IN view of the importance now attached by men of all parties in the State to the existence and perfectioning of [illegible] Forces and the recognition that the War [illegible] ose Forces, as an indispensable [illegible] pology seems to me to be needed [illegible] plea for its claim to the approval [illegible], be found in the indefiniteness [illegible] ailing amongst men usually well [illegible] nting with some to mischievous [illegible] nigh to blank ignorance. I am [illegible] enlightened and patriotic citizens [illegible] ow something exact and reliable [illegible] Force of which this volume treats, [illegible] ed from acquiring that knowledge [illegible] e works, whose excellence I would [illegible] y justly be regarded as appealing [illegible] to the professedly military mind. [illegible] onsiderable reorganization of the [illegible] tended to turn the attention of politicia[illegible] Reform and no study of that question can be [illegible] hat does not embrace the history, constitution, and past se[illegible] the Volunteers of former days, services little noticed and apparently lightly appraised by the general historian. I have been further encouraged to a task of no slight difficulty by the hope that the perusal of these pages may stimulate the youth and manhood of these isles to a warmer and more appreciative interest and a personal participation in the Volunteer Movement.

With these convictions and in this hope I have endeavoured to present to the public a continuous narrative of the inception and progress of the various Volunteer organizations of successive epochs from the earliest period down to the present time; and in so doing have sought to establish the fact that there has been a gradual but persistent evolution, if I may borrow a term from natural and social science, of the principle of voluntary service. I have also, towards the conclusion of the work, been hazardous enough to contribute my humble quota to the many suggestions for further military reforms.

I have also added to the more general tenor of the work by appending a very detailed account of the various Volunteer Forces of Huddersfield and district from the year 1794 to a comparatively recent period. Though it may be confessed that this portion of the work is calculated to appeal more particularly to the inhabitants of that neighbourhood, yet, I am confident that alike the Volunteer and Antiquarian of other localities will find therein something not only to interest them, but possibly to direct their own attention to a like enquiry in their own districts. Though I am far from saying *ex uno disce omnes* I am persuaded the annals of my native town will serve, even to the reader in other districts, as a living commentary on the history of the Volunteers at large.

I have alluded to the difficulty of this undertaking. At the head of this Preface the reader will have observed the quotation from the Queen's Regulations and Orders for the Army of the day. A perusal of its terms would seem to justify the expectation that regimental records would be abundant, accurate, detailed, and zealously preserved. My own experience does not conform to that expectation.* In my own neighbourhood and in connection with our local levies I found, after exhaustive enquiry, no official records anterior to 1803. I have had to rely on the files of newspapers and such fragmentary information as private papers, collected from various sources, supplied. This observation, it will scarcely be

---

*Probably the Regulations were not considered to apply to the Volunteer Forces. They were originally issued in 1822 when the only bodies of that kind in existence were the Honorable Artillery Company and the Duke of Cumberland's Sharp-shooters, afterwards the Royal Victoria Rifles.

credited, applies with peculiar force to the local levies of 1859 of which no complete minute-book or muster-roll seems to exist. The same deplorable lack of official guidance was also found in connection with the corps of outlying districts associated with the Huddersfield body in the Administrative Battalion. I have had perforce to rest content with the Returns of the War Office and somewhat scanty gleanings from old members of those allied corps.

My thanks for assistance in my task are due to many, but perhaps more especially to the following and to them and to all who in whatsoever way have lent their aid those thanks are very cordially tended :

To the Royal United Service Institution which has much facilitated my access to the books of its invaluable Military Library.

To Sir George J. Armytage, of Kirklees Park, Yorkshire, Bart., who kindly favored me with the inspection of the ancient Mess Books and other old papers preserved by him and permitted also the reproduction of the portrait of his great-great-grandfather, Lieut.-Colonel Sir George Armytage, Bart. ; of the presentation Cups in his possession, an account of which will be found in the text ; and of certain Regimental Colours.

To Lieut.-Colonel Sir Thomas Brooke, of Armitage Bridge, Yorkshire, Bart., who lent me valuable and useful papers.

To Sir Jas. T. Woodhouse, M.P., who has much facilitated my necessary correspondence with the War Office.

To S. Milne Milne, Esq., of Calverley House, Calverley, Leeds, for reproducing the illustrations and description of the Colours of 1794 and 1808 and furnishing their heraldic descriptions, also for reproducing the uniforms of 1794 and 1808 and the silver medal of 1812. Mr. Milne, it is scarcely necessary to add, is the author of that unique and authoritative work "The Standards and Colours of the Army."

To Lieut.-Colonel Carlile, of Helme Hall, Yorkshire, the present Commanding Officer of the 2nd Vol. Batt. Duke of Wellington's West Riding Regiment, formerly the 6th West Yorks Rifles, (Huddersfield Corps), for allowing me the use of the archives of the Battalion under his command.

To Miss Lucy Hamerton, of Elland, for permitting the reproduction from a miniature in her possession of a portrait of her great-grand-uncle, Colonel Northend Nichols.

To S. J. Chadwick, Esqre, F.S.A., of Dewsbury, for the loan of an ancient Minute and Drill Book.

To Captain J. Edward Cooper, the acting Editor of the *Volunteer Service Gazette*, for the loan of the volumes of that Journal and otherwise assisting me.

To T. H. Fry, Esq., of The Elms, Belmont Hill, Blackheath, formerly of the London Rifle Brigade, who furnished me with much valuable information relating to the 1859 movement. Mr. Fry has for the last 15 years prepared the Volunteer list for the *Volunteer Service Gazette*, been a constant contributor to that excellent Journal for a much longer period and has also prepared a large number of valuable and interesting statistics relating to the Volunteer Force.

To the Rev. John Freeman, Vicarage, Woodkirk, Yorkshire, a former Officer of the 6th West Yorks Rifles, for information as to the uniform of 1859 and other assistance.

To Lieut.-Colonel Greenwood, J.P., and Lieut.-Colonel Liddell, both of the 6th West Yorks Rifles, for the loan of photographs and other matter enabling me to reproduce the uniforms of 1859 and 1863.

To James Priestley, Esq., J.P., of Huddersfield, a former Captain of the 6th West Yorks Rifles, for the loan of accoutrements of that Corps.

To Charles William Keighley, Esq., J.P., of Newhouse Hall, Huddersfield, a former officer of the 6th West Yorks Rifles, for the loan of a uniform of 1863.

To the Leeds Philosophical and Literary Society for allowing me an inspection of and to take extracts from the early files of the *Leeds Intelligencer*.

And to the Proprietors of the *Yorkshire Post*, *Leeds Mercury*, *Huddersfield Chronicle*, and *Huddersfield Examiner*, for the use of the files of their Journals.

To conclude a preface too long drawn out, I plead in extenuation of its faults that this is the first essay of the untried pen of one engrossed in professional duties. It has been a labor of love. It has relieved the tedium of a lawyer's chamber and enhanced the charm of his leisure hours.

ROYAL UNITED SERVICE INSTITUTION,
WHITEHALL,
October, *1903*.

R. P. B.

PART I.

SECTION I.

"Let any Prince or state think soberly of his forces except his militia of natives be good and valiant soldiers. And let Princes on the other side that have subjects of martial disposition know their own strength unless they be otherwise wanting in themselves. As for mercenary forces, which is the help in this case, all examples show that whatsoever estate or Prince doth rest upon *these*, he may spread his feathers for a time but he will mew them soon after."

Bacon.

You, you, if you shall fail to understand
  What England is, and what her all in all,
On you will come the curse of all the land,
  Should this old England fall
    Which Nelson left so great!

Tennyson.

WE of these latter times are so accustomed to the existence of a regular and standing army, our minds are so familiarised with the idea of a professional military class, so habituated to regard the soldier as a man apart, a costly servant rather than a citizen of the State, that it is difficult for us to realize that our present dispositions for national defence and for armed aggression are of comparatively recent creation, and that the existence of a class of men, exclusively devoted to the profession of arms, was at first unknown and for many generations deeply resented by our forefathers. Yet but slight acquaintance with the history of our land will, I make bold to say, establish this fundamental fact, that so far from the English race having relied, when the foundations of our greatness were so securely laid, either upon bodies of men specially trained to the use of arms, or upon the doubtful aid of hired mercenaries, the truth is that by the ancient polity of our realm the State has always asserted a primary claim upon the manhood of all its sons, and those sons, from peer to peasant, have conceived their first and chiefest duty to be to the country that gave them birth. We shall find, too, that that duty has been cheerfully and voluntarily rendered; that conscription has been dispensed with because the spirit and devotion of our people have ever responded to the nation's call nor been ever heedless of the nation's needs Long before the iron heel of the Norman Conqueror pressed upon the Saxon shore it was well understood by thane and ceorl alike that each must arm at his country's call. Upon the crimsoned field of Sanguelac the Saxon earl confronted the mailed chivalry of Northern France, surrounded by his yardlings and his cottiers no less than by his theowes and his serfs. The farmer of twenty acres, the husbandman with his five acres, the hind who tended swine under the spreading oak, flocked from many a distant "tûn" or smiling "ham," under the banner of their own thane, their friend, their neighbour and their lord, to oppose their naked breasts to the awful charge of knights and barons clad in complete armour and to sustain on foot the onsets of the steeds of war. We search in vain in our earliest records for enactment of Witan or decree of king fastening this obligation of national defence upon the Saxon race. The obligation was so well known, so well understood and so inherent in the very nature of citizenship of a free state, that the craft of lawyers was not needed to define it, the force of law not needed to exact it. It is indeed difficult to conceive how the national life of England could have been preserved in those days of our country's making, had not every able-bodied man not only had some tincture of the science of war, but also been ready to spring to arms at the first echo of the invader's tread. True, the channel on the South and the German Ocean on the East were to us as nature's bulwarks against Frank and Teuton foe; but on the Northern and Western borders there was seldom rest from the gaunt and martial Scot or the restless and fiery Cymry. At any moment the beacon might blaze upon the peaks, hill calling unto hill, and the towering crags signalling afar; and at the summons the dalesman of Northumbria must leave the plough, the peasant of the Western Marshes cast aside his flail, and donning morion and leathern jerkin, seize his trusty pike and stand for his home, his hearth and the altars of his God. There was then no earl so proud but answered to the call, no churl so base as shirk the war's alarm.

Circa; 1066. The introduction or development of the Feudal system under the Norman dynasty did not, rightly viewed, alter the essential character of the military service that had prevailed before. That service had been based upon the recognition of the obligations imposed by citizenship or by honour to fight, and if need be to die, in the country's cause. It is true that the Norman system chrystalised, defined and systematised what had been duties vaguely understood and variously interpreted. It is true also that the tenure of land became more avowedly based upon military service. A holding of six hundred acres was deemed to constitute a knight's fee. The knight paid to the Crown whence he derived the title to his fee, a rent or *redditum* of specified service in the field in lieu of money. Clearly such rent or *redditum*, computed in service instead of in pounds sterling, cannot be likened to the compulsory service of the conscript, for it was at a man's choice to hold land or be landless. Beneath the knight or tenant *in capite* were the *villani* and other subtenants who took the place of the yardlings and the cottiers of Saxon times. Their attendance upon their superior in the field was but their rent in kind. The middle ages present to us the picture of an armed force composed of small bodies of men, each body recruited from the same estate, its units knit together by ties of blood, or the oft more binding ties of friendship, serving under a knightly leader who in times of peace dwelt in their midst, often joined in their sports, knelt at the same altar, confessed to and was shrived by the same priest, and whose lady's heart, when the fate of the campaign was still at issue, knew the same fears, the same fond hopes, as stirred the good wives of the vassals in the ranks. When Norman knight and Saxon bowman fought on the same field, under the same banner, against the same foe, braved the same danger, endured the same defeat and exulted in the same victory, what wonder is it that racial hatreds died away and that the bitterness of Hastings was forgotten in the pride of Agincourt! Mutual esteem begot mutual toleration and the perils of the stricken field taught a common brotherhood and made a common nationality more shrewdly than the laboured pleadings of the Church or the crabbed enactments of the law.

An arrangement that only provided for an army composed of smaller armies, each drilled and each equipped according to the capacity or the mood of its manorial lord, could not for ever satisfy the growing needs of a nation that more and more was emerging from the isolation of its storm-swept shores, and was more and more making its being felt in the councils of kings and the destinies of mankind. It was essential that the men who for three parts of the year were well content to bide at home and know its joys, to dig the fields or guide the plough, to strew the golden corn and reap the gleaming harvest, but who at blaze of beacon or word of messenger riding in hot haste, must don the steel harness and seize the trusty weapon and haste against the Scot upon the border, or cross the waters and confront the chivalry of France—it was essential, I say, that such men should be welded into cohesion, and that some uniformity of equipment, some instruction in the art of common and concerted action, should be provided. It is doubtless to a perception of this truth that we owe the first statutes of Assize at Arms. They show that the armed forces of the land were to be, in future, not the mere retainers of powerful lords but the forces of the Crown, the defenders of the nation, the soldiers not of duke or baron, but the soldiers of their country and their king.

Statutes of Assize at Arms, 1181.

Thus the Assize of Arms of 1181 provided that every military tenant, that is every tenant holding by service, then deemed the most honourable tenure, if not the only one that conferred honour, dignity and esteem, should be armed, not, as theretofore, just as completely, or as slenderly, as his caprice, his pride, or his parsimony inclined him, but should be furnished with a coat of mail, a shield, (on which, be sure, his coat of arms was picked with all points of heraldry), and a lance, and that the followers he led in his train, should be clad in habergeon,* an iron skull cap, and bear a lance.

Judges thereof.

Itinerant judges of the Assize at Arms visited each manor and saw to it that each freeman had been mindful to equip himself in conformity with his rank and means; a system of visitation which may serve to remind us that the volunteers in the first days of what is distinctively termed the Volunteer Movement, had ancestors, many centuries ago, who suffered the same grievances and no doubt made the same complaints as they.

Stat. Philip and Mary, 1584.

A similar enactment of Philip and Mary required every man, according to his position, to keep a sufficiency of arms; the household armoury was to be equipped with the weapons then in use, and penalties were imposed upon those who absented themselves from the musters of the Sovereign or his Lieutenant.

The Lord Lieut.

This mention of the Lord Lieutenant of the County, who once bore so prominent a part in connection with our modern Volunteers, points to the supersession in matters military of the Sheriff, who in

Posse Comitatus.

former days had been responsible for the levy of the *posse comitatus* or levy of the County.†

But changes of great magnitude and moment, little noticed perhaps in their course, and whose full significance and import was only to be realised by historical retrospect, had, long ere this period, been gradually transforming the whole social and economic life, and

---

*A sort of steel or iron waistcoat protecting breast and back.

†By the Army Regulations Act 1871 (34 and 35 Vict. cap. 86) the jurisdiction of the Lord Lieutenant over the Militia and Auxiliary Forces was revested in the Crown to be exercised through the Secretary of State for War.

with it the manners, customs and needs of our country. The Wars of the Roses had decimated the baronage of England. Great estates, that were almost principalities, had been broken up or confiscated, the resources of the great nobles had been exhausted, their pride humbled, and they ceased to vie with each other in the strength and splendour of their establishments. The civil law gained strength in proportion as the feudal power declined and the general people (who once had trusted to the favor of their territorial lord) learned to lean for justice and protection for life and property upon the King's Courts. The more settled state of the country favored commercial arts; and men began to seek wealth in the mart, rather than in pillage, and reputation in the senate instead of in the field.

Rise of Commerce and the Towns.

Cedant arma togae, concedat laurea laudi.

Thriving and busy towns began to take the place of drowsy hamlets, the population to desert the fields and seek the walled cities, where life was easier, property safer and gains quicker. But the lusty lads who forsook the plough for the loom and the meadow for the counting house took with them the martial spirit of their sires. No student of history can have failed to observe how frequent and how important a part the train-bands of the cities played in the conflicts of former days. It is to them we must look for the true prototype of our modern Volunteer, and the brief and imperfect sketch I have given of life in feudal days may help us to understand how readily, how naturally, the draper's apprentices, the grocer's assistants and the lawyer's clerks of the Middle Ages formed themselves into military companies and underwent their drill; and how readily, too, the grave merchant of the Exchange put himself at their head and led them to the contested field. In the reign of the third Edward the citizens of London had established their companies of archers and these companies, in the reign of the eighth Henry, were incorporated by Royal Charter under the style of "The Fraternity or Guylde of St. George, maisters and rulers of the City Science of Artillery as aforesaid rehearsed for Longbows, Crossbows and Hand gorms." This Guylde of St. George dinted its mark deep in the stormy days of Charles I, and it was the knowledge that behind them stood the City Companies that emboldened the Parliaments of that hapless monarch to resist the unconstitutional encroachments of the Royal Prerogative. But of this more anon.

Archers' Companies, temp. Edward III.

Guylde of St. George.

It may be noted, in passing, that refugees from the City of London who at that period fled their country in despair of their

Hon. Artillery Company of London.

country's freedom, transplanted to the free soil of New England
1638. an offshoot of this Ancient and Honourable Company of Artillery of London. In 1638 was established at Boston U.S.A. a Volunteer Corps bearing the name of the "Ancient and Honourable Company of Massachussets," and this company, we may be sure, was not idle, when, a century and a half later, the citizens of Boston rose against the tax on tea, and gave the signal for the revolt of a continent.

Of Massachussets.

In the conflict between Charles and Parliament, the King relied mainly upon the noblemen and country gentry, and these doubtless strained to the utmost, not only their own treasures, but also every power the feudal system gave them over the tenants of their estates. The Parliament, whose strength lay in the towns, had to create an army. They had, or assumed, the power of taxation, and called upon the towns to furnish the equipment and maintenance of their forces. When the monarchy was restored and the peers of the realm returned to the House from which they had been ejected, and the Cavaliers to the estates from which they had fled, they were perhaps not sorry to borrow at least one lesson from the parliament of Roundheads. The counsellors of the King had been quick to perceive how much more expeditious and effective was a tax upon the general wealth than the cumbrous system of armed levy devised in feudal times. Military tenures were abolished, and thenceforth a standing army of regular forces and a professional class of trained soldiery became a necessity, though a necessity but sullenly acquiesced in, and long viewed with a suspicion and resentment which the armed domination and insolent dictation of Cromwell's regiments may well explain and justify. From that time increasingly as the years went by and reign succeeded reign, the social life of the people underwent a marked change and the great masses of the nation turned individual attention to their private affairs and the pursuit of wealth, leaving to the military forces and our fleet the defence of our shores, the vindication of our honour and the prosecution of our wars abroad.

Abolition of Military tenures, 1660.

The Irish Volunteers, 1779.

How readily, however, the people of these realms learned the lessons that had become, by the usage of centuries, a very part and parcel of the national being, history furnishes us with more than one instance. Even Ireland did not disdain to copy the example of the "predominant partner" and the action of that country in 1779 may be referred to as not only furnishing an illustration of the merits, but also as suggesting the possible dangers, of the Volunteer Movement. In that year England was menaced by foes on every hand and the wildest apprehensions prevailed of a descent by the French upon the Irish coast. The loyal and Protestant nobility and gentry and the substantial tradesmen of Ireland obtained permission from the Government to establish a Volunteer Force, and the Irish readily availed themselves of an opportunity that at once gratified their martial spirit and ardour and enabled them to attest their devotion to the Crown. But the Volunteer Army of the Duke of Leinster was not merely an army of soldiers: it proved to be also a body of politicians. It demanded the repeal of Poyning's Statute and the practical independence of the ancient parliament of Ireland, which Poyning's measure had reduced to a mere Office of Record. The English Minister was in no mood to yield to a demand the consequences of which none more clearly saw, but demands backed by an armed force may not lightly be gainsaid, and Pitt reluctantly yielded, only, a few years later, to devote the supremest faculties of his great mind to devising and carrying the Act of Union.

In our country, too, the constant dread of Napoleon's sinister designs, from which this nation knew no respite till the despot of Europe fled from the field of Waterloo, led to the formation of Volunteer Corps in every county and almost in every village in the land. Revival of Volunteer Corps in England

Two outward and visible signs remain after the lapse of a century to remind us of the fears that then agitated every English breast: the Martello Towers and the Volunteers. The Martello Towers that still linger upon our coasts as the storehouses of a decrepid body of Coastguards move our mirth; but the days are long past when the cynic jester might speak lightly of the Volunteers.

The Volunteer movement between the years 1794 and 1804 led 1794-1804.
to the enrolment of no less than 429,165 men. Of the corps thus formed fuller mention will be made hereafter.

On October 26, 1803, George III. reviewed in Hyde Park no less than 12,401 London Volunteers, and two days later a further muster of 14,676. It may be cited as an example of the attachment of some of the men who have donned the Volunteer's uniform that when, in 1860, Her late revered Majesty reviewed in Hyde Park 18,450 Volunteers, there marched as a Private in the ranks, though bearing the weight of no less than four score years, Mr. Tower of Wealdhall in Essex, who, fifty years previously, had passed in review before that monarch's royal grandsire.

On January 1, 1804, the Official returns shewed the stupendous total of 341,600 Volunteers in England alone; a fact which a comparison of the population of the beginning of the last and the present century renders more significant.

After the fall of Napoleon these men, the object of their enlistment accomplished, stacked their arms and their battalions were disbanded, save only those corps of Volunteer Cavalry whom we know as Yeomanry, some of which we have with us to this day, and some few corps of Volunteers, whom the unsettled state of the manufacturing districts induced to continue a precarious existence.

The Voluntary enrolments which were made at the troubled times of the French Revolution were succeeded by quick disbanding after the fear of invasion had passed away. The impulse of that day may be styled volunteering by panic. More than half a century was to pass before we reached the era of Volunteering by fixed principle and from the deliberate and final conviction of the people that a permanent and formidable auxiliary to the regular forces was not only desirable but was also attainable without resort to the cruel conscription of France or the cast iron system of the German Landwehr.

That volunteering by panic was likely to be a remedy almost worse than the disease little reflection will persuade us to admit. At a grave juncture, men of all ages, sizes and conditions offer their services. Their patriotism is beyond question. It were cruel to throw cold water on so excellent a spirit. They are formed into Corps, into Battalions, into Brigades. They are ignorant of drill, unlearned in the use of arms, unused to military discipline, and unaccustomed to the very real hardships even of a summer campaign. And their officers have little more of necessary and practical knowledge than the troops they command. One can no more become a soldier by a *Coup d'oeil* than he can "learn Greek before breakfast."

The manner in which the Volunteers of the beginning and even the middle of the last century were regarded by men who may be allowed to be competent critics, is well expressed by the words which the author of the *brochure*, "The Battle of Dorking," written at the time of the Franco-German War,* puts in the mouth of an officer of the regular forces as his eye travels over a mob of Volunteers gathered to repel an imaginary German invasion: '"You are Volunteers I suppose,?' he said quickly, his eye flashing

*Blackwood's Edinburgh Magazine, May, 1871

the while. ‘Well, now, look here. Mind I don't want to hurt your feelings, or to say anything unpleasant, but I'll tell you what; if all you gentlemen were just to go back, and leave us to fight it out alone, it would be a devilish good thing. We could do it a precious deal better without you, I assure you. We don't want your help I can tell you. We would much rather be left alone, I assure you. Mind I don't want to say anything rude—but that's a fact.”’

These vigorous expressions possibly well reflect the views once entertained by the Regular Forces of their lightly considered civil Auxiliaries. That such sentiments no longer find a place in the mind even of the most self-sufficient and arrogant of the officers of the King is due to the permanent character which, in the middle of the last century, the Volunteer movement began to assume, never to again discard.

That vital and pregnant change, which has added incalculably to our national security, first manifested itself after the events of 1859. With the Volunteer Movement of that period I purpose to deal fully in a subsequent part of this work. It is however first desirable, if not indeed essential, to a full comprehension of the Voluntary services of the citizens of our country at different periods and various crises to undertake a general survey of such services from the earliest times and to this task I now address myself.

PART I.

SECTION II.

The Evolution of the Volunteer Force.

Before engaging in a consideration of those Corps of Volunteers which for purposes of distinction I may term "Statutory Volunteers," it is desirable, as I have said, to devote some little space to a brief examination of those earlier Volunteer Associations from which the Statutory Volunteers may be said to have been gradually evolved in the course of successive generations. No supposition could be more fallacious than that at a fixed and definite period of our history some ingenious and sagacious Minister of War conceived the idea of the Volunteer Corps as they now exist, embodied his idea in a Bill, won the assent of Parliament to his scheme and triumphantly grafted the offspring of his individual genius upon the existing institutions of our land. The exact contrary is the case. Like everything else in this country of slow growth and abiding progress the Volunteers have been evolved rather than created, and it is an enquiry both instructive and interesting to discover from what archaic germs and by what slow process of gestation we have at length obtained the admirable force of civilian soldiers who are the proper subject of this treatise.

Early Volunteer Associations.

It will I think be found on a careful examination of the genesis and character of all earlier Volunteer Associations of a Military nature that they will fall under one or other of the following heads:—

(1) Volunteer Associations originating by Royal Charter.

(2) Independent Associations.

(3) Those existing partly through the exercise of the Royal Prerogative and partly by Parliamentary sanction and herein of the Militia, Local and General, and of Armed Associations.

Although the constitution of the Militia may at first sight appear little germane to an inquiry into the history of the Volunteers the reader will, I apprehend, if he peruse this volume to its close, arrive with me at the conclusion that no clear perception and comprehension of the origin of the Statutory Volunteers can be attained without some such course of historical investigation as I have here outlined.

Nor is it at all possible to understand those earlier Volunteer Associations that owed their being to the Royal pleasure without some comprehension of the Royal Prerogative. It is far from my design to embark upon a disquisition on constitutional law or tell again the thrice told story of the disputes that have raged between King and subjects upon that thorny theme—the Prerogative: an elusive term the attempt to define which cost one monarch his head and another his throne.. Nor is an investigation into the extent or limitations of the powers implied in that elastic and mysterious term so imperative now as in former days, for even the Royal Prerogative is now admittedly exercised only on the advice of responsible Ministers of State, acting as the servants of a Parliamentary majority and liable to all the ills that await the Statesman so crass or so daring as to affront the sovereign people. But our enquiry carries us back to less happy days when the mutual rights and privileges of King and people were not so rigidly defined and clearly understood as now, and that enquiry will be the easier when we comprehend how vast were the powers that were by all conceded to be vested in the Crown and comprehend too how vaster still were those powers the inordinate folly of the Stuarts impelled them to attach to the Prerogative.

The Prerogative.

That our Sovereigns down to a period comparatively recent arrogated the sole power of declaring war and making peace is a commonplace of history, though it is obvious that since the time of the third Edward that power must have been materially tempered by the necessity of appealing to the Commons to furnish forth the sinews of war. In feudal times that restriction was probably not so harassing as at first view it presents itself; for by the very nature and essence of feudal tenures the King could, at his Royal pleasure, call upon his military tenants to place at his disposition the covenanted supplement of mailed warriors and equipped men-at-arms. But even in those days current coin of the realm must have been needed, and though the Royal Exchequer was enriched by the rentals of the enormous tracts of Crown lands and swollen by the iniquitous system of forced loans and benevolences, the student of history is well aware how constantly our proudest monarchs were constrained to make a virtue of necessity and humble themselves before their not always very obsequious Commons. It was reserved to the hapless Charles I to endeavour to push the doctrine of the Divine Right of Kings to its most intolerable limits and the bitter differences on the subject of the Prerogative were at length submitted to the arbitrament and pronouncement of the Law

Hampden's Case.

Courts in the celebrated case of Ship-money—a case to which I only refer in order that one may comprehend the more clearly how boundless in its extent was the power claimed for the Crown to establish armies and fleets and to levy upon the goods of the subjects for their provision, equipment and permanent maintenance. Thus broadly was the Royal Prerogative defined by Sir George Croke in Hampden's case, and I quote the words of that judge because he was one of the judges who pronounced against the claims of the Crown to levy ship-money. "The law," he declared, "provideth a remedy in case of necessity and danger for then the King may command his subjects, without Parliament, to defend the Kingdom. How? By all men of arms whatsoever for the land and by all ships whatsoever for the sea, which he may take from all parts of the kingdom and join them with his own navy, which hath been the practice of all former Kings in their necessity."

Croke's Judgment.

Hatton's Judgment.

Sir Richard Hatton, another of the judges, was much more emphatic than Croke in his definition of the Prerogative. "I confess," he said, "there are some inseparable Prerogatives belonging to the Crown such as the Parliament cannot sever from it, and I will prove to you out of the books, cases and Statutes, that the King cannot release his tenant *in capite*. It was endeavoured that a law should be made that the Court of Wards should be shut up; it was resolved that it had been a void law. Such is the care for the defence of the kingdom which belongeth inseparably to the Crown, as head and supreme protector of the kingdom. So that, if an Act of Parliament should enact that he should not defend the kingdom or that the King should have no aid from his subjects to defend the kingdom, those acts would not bind because they would be against natural reason. I do agree in the time of war when there is an enemy in the field, the King may take goods from the subject, such a danger and such a necessity ought to be in this case as in the case of a fire like to consume all without speedy help, such a danger as tends to the over-throw of the kingdom." Upon one point the judges agreed; that "when the good and safety of the kingdom in general is concerned and the whole kingdom in danger, His Majesty might by Writ under the Great Seal command all his subjects at their charge to provide and furnish such number of ships with men, munition and victuals, and for such a time as he should think fit, for the defence and safeguard of the kingdom; and that by law he might compel the doing thereof in case of refusal or refractoriness and that he was the sole judge both of the danger and when and how the same was to be prevented and avoided."

It is little to my purpose to add to these extracts what every student of the history of those troublous times is familiar with; that the King himself was (16 Car. 1, 14) constrained to assent to a Statute declaring the decision upholding ship-money to be against the law; and to pronounce the sealing words "*Le Roy le veut*" to an enactment (16 Car. 1, 8) declaring that "it hath been the ancient right of the subjects of this realm that no subsidy, custom, import or other charge whatsoever, might or may be laid or imposed upon any merchandise exported or imported by subjects, denizens or aliens, without common consent of Parliament"—a salutary and requisite repudiation of the King's claim to levy customs at his royal pleasure. Enough has been said to indicate to the general reader how extensive were the powers of raising the materials of war that even those most jealous of the Prerogative conceded to be vested in the Crown.

16 Car. 1, c. 8.

It will not be necessary, after this preamble, to enquire to what authority such an association as the Artillery Company, or "The Fraternity of St. George," owed its being. The answer is obvious: the Prerogative. That voluntary Associations for the practice of the long-bow were of earlier date than chartered Associations there can be no question. Had the parish records of our country been preserved with the scrupulous care their interest and importance alike demanded, but sought in vain, I make no doubt that it would be found that in every hamlet, village and borough its youth and manhood were united in some rude corps for perfectioning in the mastery of what was then the national arm of offence and defence—the long bow. How formidable was that arm the battles of Agincourt and Poitiers and many another stricken field bore bloody witness. But I do not find any earlier instance of incorporation by Charter than the one I have mentioned. The citizens of London had been enrolled in companies of Archers as early as the reign of Edward III, but it was not till that of bluff King Hal that I find record of incorporation. The preamble to the Statute of that King (3 Henry VIII, c. 3) throws so pleasing a light upon the customs of our forefathers that the reader will, I hope, condone more than a passing allusion to it. The preamble sets forth that "The Kyng our Sovereign Lord, callyng to his most noble and generous remembrance how by the feate and exercise of the subjecttes of this his realme in shotying in long bowes, there hath contynually growen and been within the same grete nombre and multitude of good archers which hath not only defended this realme and the subjecttes thereof against the cruell

Companies of Archers.

3 Henry VIII 3.

malice and danger of their owteward enemys in tyme heretofore passed, but also with litell nombre and puyssance in regarde have done many notable actes and discomfetures of warre against the infidelis and other, and furthermore subdued and reduced dyverse and many regyons and countrees to their due obeysaunce, to the grete honour, fame, and suertie of this realme, and to the terrible drede and fere of all strange nacions any thyng to attempte or do to the hurte or damage of theyme or any of them." The Statute proceeds to enact that any man "not lame, decreperte, or maymed, beyng withyn the age of LX yeres" shall have a "bowe and arrowes redy contynually in his house to use himself and do use himself in shotying"; he was also to "teche and bring upp" his children and servants "in the knowledge of the same shotying." "Buttes" were to be made "in every citie, towne and place" and maintained at the common charge.

The Fraternity of St. George.

In view of this Statute the formation of such an association as the Guild of St. George is easily understood. The Charter or Patent of that Fraternity was issued August 25th, 1537, and directed to Sir Christopher Morris and others. It licensed these gentlemen to be "Overseers of the science of Artillery, viz:—for long bows, cross bows, and hand guns—the said Sir Christopher Morris and others as aforesaid and their successors to be Masters and Rulers of the said science of artillery with authority to establish a perpetual fraternity or guild and to admit all honest persons whatsoever, as well strangers as others, into a body corporate having perpetual succession by the name of "Masters and Commonalty of the Fraternity or Guild of Artillery of Long Bows, Cross Bows and Hand Guns." The Charter conferred the usual powers of acquiring and holding land with the use of a Common Seal. The Fraternity were authorised to exercise themselves in shooting with long bows, cross bows and hand guns at all manner of marks and butts,* and at the game of popinjay—in the Charter called "popymaye"—and other games, as at the fowles in the City of London and suburbs, and in all places within the realms of England, Ireland, Calais and the Marches of Wales and elsewhere within the King's Dominions—his forests, chases and parks, without his especial warrant, reserved and excepted: as also game of heron and pheasant within two miles of the Royal Manors, Castles, and other places where the King should fortune to be or lie for the time only. No other Fraternity of like kind was

*Anyone familiar with rural England must often have been struck by the recurrence of the term "The Butts" as a name of topography.

to be permitted without the licence of the Masters and Rulers of St. George. The patent further granted to the members of this ancient guild the use of any sort of embroidery or any cognizance of silver they should think proper on their gowns and jackets, coats or doublets, and to use in them any kind of silk or velvet satin or damask (the colors of purple and scarlet excepted) and also to have on their gowns or other garments all sorts of furs not above that of Martyns without incurring the penalty of any Act or proclamation respecting apparel—a necessary provision in view of the existing sumptuary law, and one moreover that would seem to indicate that these brethren of St. George were men of substance and position, a fact further emphasized by their exemption by their patent from service on common inquests.

Train Bands.

From this Guild or formed on its pattern were the historic Train Bands, the great majority of which, indeed all save those of the City of London and their Auxiliaries, were disbanded after the Restoration (14 Car. II), an act of reprisals which might have been forgiven to an even more magnanimous monarch than Charles II, for the historical student does not need to be reminded of the zeal with which the Train Bands supported the Parliamentary cause. That the Train Bands of London were exempt was doubtless due to the Royal anxiety to conciliate the City.

The Hon. Artillery Co.

The Fraternity of St. George with the Train Bands of the City of London were, as I have said, exempted from the terms of this Statute, for we find the Fraternity of St. George united with, though not entirely absorbed into, the Honourable Artillery Company. How closely allied were these two forces may be gathered from the fact that in 1719 His Majesty (Geo. I) ordered that all the Commission and Staff Officers of the City Trained Bands should become members of the Artillery Company and exercise with them at all convenient times in order to qualify themselves the better for their respective stations, and no Commission was to be granted in the Trained Bands from the Court of Lieutenancy unless a certificate that the applicant was a member of the Artillery Company was produced.

Whilst on the subject of the Artillery Company it may be convenient to mention that Mr. Clode in his admirable work, "The Military Forces of the Crown," claims for this Company that it is the oldest corps in the realm either of the Volunteer or regular forces, being established under an Act passed in the reign of Henry VIII (3 Hen. VIII, 3), its military organization resembling that of the Trained Bands of the City of London and many other corporate towns before the Restoration. These Bands were formed under the sanction of the civic authorities; their officers, subject to the approval of those authorities, were chosen by the suffrage of all ranks, and the rules and regulations governing the Bands appear also to have been devised and enforced by the like authority. However this may be it is certain that in the case of the Artillery Company Parliament exercised over it no control. It was self-supporting, received no pay or aid from Parliamentary or other public funds and was governed by Royal Warrants granted by successive Monarchs from the time of Henry VIII. Major Raikes in his history of the Company finds some pardonable difficulty in classifying it, regarding it as a kind of hybrid, "belonging neither to the Militia, Yeomanry nor Volunteers, nor yet to the more ancient Trained Bands," whilst some authorities have described it as forming part of the "Militia or City Guard of London," others as a form of "Volunteer Military Association." It may, perhaps, however, be submitted, with some show of reason, that the members of the Company, at least, knew the nature of their Association and the authority under which it existed, and the difficulty experienced by Major Raikes appears to be minimized by a perusal of the records embodied in his own valuable work. One of these commemorates the fact that at a Court of Assistants of the Company held 11th November, 1795, an address was presented by the Company to the King (Geo. III) congratulating him upon his providential escape from assassination; and the address described the Company as "*A Volunteer Corps*" "existing from ancient times under the authority of your Royal Prerogative and formed by your Majesty's Royal Warrants," and expresses the hope "that the Company has always been found ready in aid of the civil power for the preservation of the peace of the Metropolis and the defence of the property of our fellow subjects." Major Raikes also reproduces a petition of the Court of Assistants to the King, of the year 1797, in which the Company adverts to the fact that it possesses ground for military purposes "such as no other *Volunteer Corps** in any other part of the country enjoys." To these conclusive documents it is scarcely necessary to add that under the Volunteer Act of 1804 the members of the Company were called upon to complete their eight days drill in order to qualify for the certificate of exemption from service and that in the same and subsequent years Courts Martial of the Company were held for the

Address of Hon. Artillery Co. to the Crown.

Petition of the Hon. Artillery Co.

*The italics are mine. R. P. B.

purpose of trying sundry military offences, courts professedly held under the authority of the Volunteer Act of 1804. These Courts Martial were serious affairs. In 1804 a drummer, for absence from duty, was sentenced to fifty lashes with the cat. In 1806 another drummer received only, in consequence of previous good behaviour, the mitigated punishment of twenty lashes. The drummer of those days, it is perhaps desirable to add, did the duties of the bugler of to-day.

Courts Martial of the Hon. Artillery Co.

It must not be assumed that our national records furnish us with no other examples of voluntary Military Associations than those identified with the City of London. At all times of imminent national danger the peaceful citizen of this country has ever displayed an amazing facility in discarding the pruning hook for the spear or abandoning the pen for the sword. One or two instances of this will not be out of place here. Fuller particulars may be found in Froude's history of the period. In the reign of Elizabeth, in preparation for the Invincible Armada, Volunteer Military Schools were established throughout the country. Nor were tutors for such seminaries far to seek or few in number. France, Flanders and Ireland had been the schools in which hundreds of Englishmen had learned the art of war, and in the Military Schools of Elizabeth gentlemen who had served abroad drilled the sons of the knights and squires of the shires. In the City of London no less than 300 merchants were to be found who had had some taste of actual service and possessed at least such tincture of military science as enabled them to drill their companies. For eight years before the proud galleons of Spain spread their sails for England's shores, the people of our Island had been assiduously perfecting themselves in the art of arms, and when at length the Duke of Parma embarked, one hundred thousand men were officered and appointed, ready at a day's notice to fall into their companies and move wherever required, waiting to oppose his landing on English soil. In the uncertainty as to where and when that landing might be effected, these Volunteers, for Volunteers they clearly and truly were, were left at their homes, but their line of action was accurately prescribed for them. The musters of the Midlands, 30,000 strong, were to form a separate army for the defence of the Queen's person; the rest were to gather to the point of danger; the coast companies had orders to fall back wherever the enemy landed, removing cattle and avoiding battle till the forces of the neighbouring counties joined them. If the landing should be effected in Suffolk, Essex or Kent, thirty to forty

Volunteers temp. Elizabeth.

thousand men could be thrown in their way before they could reach London, whilst twenty thousand still remained to encounter the Duke of Guise if he attempted an attack on Hampshire or Dorsetshire. The English array, exclusive of the City Trained Bands, consisted of 130,000 men, one part disposed to guard the Southern coast, another stationed at Tilbury for the defence of the capital, and the remainder at other parts of the coast where a landing might be apprehended. Froude in his history presents us with a not unpleasing picture of Elizabeth herself, on a Neapolitan charger, exercising every day with the Train Bands in St. James's Park, a fact on which De Quadra makes admiring if slightly sarcastic comment, in his letter to his court.

Order in Council temp. Elizabeth re Volunteers.

In this same reign of the Virgin Queen we find specific mention of Volunteers, for there is preserved an Order in Council issued "for the encouragement of Harquebuse and Matchlock Volunteers," and a body of some 4,000 strong was raised in the maritime towns armed with these weapons. In 1586, again, the City of London framed regulations for registering all citizens capable of bearing arms and dividing them into companies, divisions and sections with appointed places of rendezvous.

Colchester Volunteers temp. James I.

The example set by the city in the formation of the Fraternity of St. George and the Artillery Company was not lost upon the country at large. In the reign of James I (June 16th, 1621), a petition was presented to the Privy Council by the Bailiffs and Aldermen of Colchester stating that by the most worthy example of London in the "Artillery yard" they wished for permission to establish a similar organization to enable them to render service to the country by training in military science under some worthy captain to be approved by the Council. The prayer of the petition was granted subject to the members of the Association being approved by the Aldermen of the Borough. Again, on October 25th, 1628, a similar petition from the Aldermen of Bury St. Edmunds was conceded by the Council

The Bury St. Edmunds.

Allusion has more than once been made in these pages to the part played by the Train Bands in the Civil War. The subject of those Bands is so closely allied to the history of the Volunteers that no apology is needed for fuller reference to them. There is every reason to suppose that Train Bands were intended to serve not merely as a defence against aggressions from without but also in the repression of internal disorder. One has only to think of Dogberry to realize in some measure the absurd inadequacy of the city watch or municipal police. The Train Bands were, in times of internal peace, somewhat in the nature of a special constabulary, and in some cases they appear to have been known also as Volunteer Corps. Thus I find in Mr. E. T. Evans' "Records of the 3rd Middlesex Rifles" that, prior to the civil wars, Parliament ordered the persons charged with the collection of taxes in the counties of Kent, Sussex and Hants, if they experienced difficulty or resistance in the discharge of their duty, to call upon the Train Bands or Volunteer Corps to assist them. Mr. Evans adds that these Volunteers were on a very small scale and in most cases engaged only to serve in their own parishes or districts and are presumed to have been formed, in the inland towns at least, for the purpose of assisting the civil authorities in the suppression of disorder, which at that time was rife. Many of them were actually employed for that purpose, and in the absence of an efficient police their services were doubtless of great value. A time was at hand when the Train Bands, more especially those of the Metropolis, were to assume a position in the state that made them the arbiters of war and peace.

Train Bands, 1492, temp. Henry VII.

As early as the reign of Henry VII, I find mention of municipal Train Bands—a more searching inquiry might discover earlier mention; but the consideration of the history and nature of those associations is only incidental to the proper subject of these pages. Mr. Montague Burrows in his "Historic Towns—Cinque Ports," records that in 1492 Henry VII used the Cinque Ports' Navy, like his predecessor, to transport his army to France. He had no reason to complain of Sandwich's (one of the Cinque Ports) loyalty in defence of his Crown. When the King's enemies, under one known in England as Perkin Warbeck (his real name being Peter Osbeck), appeared in the Downs, it is recorded that the *Train Bands* of the town (enticing them on shore at Deal) fell upon them so heartily that those who landed were all killed or taken prisoners, a service for which Henry gave them "grete thankes," as well he might. From the same authority I glean that Tenterden, a corporate member of Rye, another of the Cinque Ports Confederation, was, in 1559, reputed to be able to provide a good average of trained men, and did actually contribute 24 men and four horses to the muster of Elizabeth's troops; whilst for practical purposes of coast defence the following non-corporate members of the Cinque Ports Confederacy, annexed to Dover in the Middle Ages, to wit St. John's, St. Peter's and Birchington, were, in 1572, reputed capable of supporting 204 men for the "general" and 170 for the "special" Band.

Sandwich.

Tenterden. 1559.

Other towns, 1572.

Train Bands, temp. Eliz. 1572.

In that same year of 1572, the Civil War then raging in the Netherlands, Elizabeth, anxious to assist the Flemings in their struggle for civil and religious liberty and displeased at the erection of the power of Spain so near to her own dominions, commanded the citizens of London (March 25th-26th) to assemble at their several halls. "The Masters collected and chose out the most likely and active persons of their companies, to the number of 3,000, whom they appointed to be pikemen or men-at-arms. To these were appointed divers valiant captains who, to train them up in warlike feats, mustered them thrice every week, sometimes in the Artillery Yard, at other times at the Mile End and in St. George's Fields. On the 1st of May they mustered at Greenwich before the Queen's Majesty when they showed many warlike feats."*

Eodem temp. Gentlemen Volunteers.

The same national emergency prompted Captain Thomas Morgan, an officer of distinguished merit, who was countenanced by several noblemen and others favourable to the Flemish cause, and assisted by a deputation from Flushing, to raise a company of 300 men, amongst whom were upwards of 100 gentlemen of property inspired with a noble enthusiasm for the cause of religious liberty. This company was the nucleus of a numerous body of British troops which, after the peace of Munster, were recalled to England and in 1648 united in one regiment. On its recall to England in 1645 it was known as the Holland Regiment, but it is now better known as the 3rd Regiment of Foot or the Buffs.†

This Regiment, as also the Marines, Royal London Militia, and the 3rd Grenadier Guards, all of which are deemed to owe their origin to the Train Bands of London, have the singular privilege of marching through the city with fixed bayonets, colors flying and drums beating.‡

Other Gentlemen Volunteers, 1660.

We read of other gentlemen Volunteers at a later period. On the dissolution of the army at the Restoration, Volunteer Corps were formed in all directions under the leading men of the counties, and trained Bands assisted in the duties then lately discharged by the Royal Forces. In Yorkshire, Sir Francis Boynton, one of the Deputy Lieutenants for the East Riding, under Lord John Bellasis, the Lord Lieutenant, raised not only a Regiment of Foot,

*Holinshed's Chronicles, pp. 1807-8.

†Cannon's "Historical Records of the British Army" compiled by command of His Majesty William IV.

‡James's "Military Dictionary" (published 1816): Cooper King's "Story of the British Army."

but a gallant troop of *Gentlemen Volunteers* who rode their own horses and mustered them at Kilham. The loyal gentlemen of Northumberland mustered at Bockenfield Moor 126 gentlemen Volunteers, besides their servants, "all bravely armed and horsed."*

Train Bands reverted to.

Reverting once more to the Train Bands, after a digression only to be pardoned from a desire to observe some measure of chronological sequence, we learn from Whitelocke that those of the City of London consisted principally of apprentices whose members had been compelled by ordinances of Parliament to reckon their military service as part of their apprenticeship: "That all apprentices who will list in their army shall have their time of that service in for their freedom."†

James, in his "Military Dictionary," already quoted, expresses the opinion that these Bands were more nearly allied to the Militia than to the Volunteer forces of the country. Be that as it may, we find that in 1614 the Lords of the Council wrote to the Lord Mayor requesting him to cause "a general view" to be taken of the City's forces and an enrolment made "of such trayned members as in her late Majesty's time were put into companies by the name of the Trayned Bands." A tax of a fifteenth was voted by the Common Council to meet the necessary expenses of arming 6,000 men of the Train Bands, and tenders were invited for the supply of the necessary weapons. Dr. Sharpe, in his "London and the Kingdom," has reproduced from the City Journals some of those tenders, which are interesting as shewing the nature and cost of the equipments of the citizen soldier of those days. "Jerome Heydon, an iremonger at the lower end of Cheepside," was ready to sell corselets comprising "brest, backe, gorgett, taces‡ and head-pieces" at 15/-; pikes with steel heads at 2/6; swords, being Turkey blades at 7/-; "bastard" muskets at 14/-; great muskets with rests at 16/-; a headpiece, lined and stringed, at 2/6; and a bandaleer for 1/6."

That the Train Bands consisted of sober, God-fearing citizens of substance and repute, and of their apprentices is abundantly clear—a class far removed from the somewhat profane, reckless swashbucklers who formed so large a part of the forces of the King

*Scott's "British Army," quoting "Mercurius Publicus" from December 31 to January, 1660-1, and "Kingdom's Intelligence" from February 11 to 18, 1660-1.

†Whitelocke 64.

‡Armour for the thighs.

in the Civil War. Who does not recall the lines of Cowper, writing truly at a later period, but still of the same force:—

"John Gilpin was a citizen
Of credit and renown,
A Trained Band Captain eke was he,
Of famous London town."

Roundway Down, 1643.

That the Train Bands rendered yeoman service in the troublous times of the first Charles is known even to Macaulay's schoolboy. The authorities are unanimous on the point. At the battle of Roundway Down (July 13th, 1643), so Mr. C. R. B. Barrett in his "Battles and Battlefields in England" informs us, the London Train Bands, comprising part of the Parliamentarian Force and 1,800 in number, "worthily supported their traditions till overwhelmed." Mr. James Grant, in his "British Battles on Land and Sea," tells us the pikemen of the London Train Bands "opposed both the Cornish Musketeers and their pikemen, the entire Royalist Cavalry and Waller's guns, so that if they gave way it was not without good reason."

Gloucester, 1643.

In the same year the commander of the City resolved to raise the siege of Gloucester. Every shop in the City, we are told by Dr. Sharpe in his "London and the Kingdom," was ordered to be closed and also business suspended till Gloucester should be relieved. The regiments to be sent were chosen by lot, and were under Lord Essex. These were two troops of Trained Bands, two of the Auxiliaries and a Regiment of Horse. On the march from Hounslow Heath to the beleagured city the troops suffered great privations. "Such straits and hardships," wrote a sergeant of one of the London regiments, "our citizens formerly knew not; yet the Lord that calleth us to do the work enabled us to undergo such hardships as He brought us to." The relief of Gloucester, affirms Mr. Green in his "History of the English People," "proved to be the turning point in the war." Gloucester was the Ladysmith of the Civil War. Not less distinction awaited the Londoners at

Newbury, 1643.

Newbury, a fortnight after the raising of the siege of Gloucester. "Again and again," writes Dr. Sharpe, "did Rupert's Horse dash down upon the serried pikes of the London Trained Bands, but never once did it succeed in breaking their ranks, whilst many a Royalist's saddle was emptied by the City Musketeers, whose training in the Artillery Garden and Finsbury Fields now served them in good stead." Whilst the enemy's cannon was committing fearful havoc in the ranks of the Londoners, they still stood their ground "like so many stakes." "They behaved themselves to wonder," wrote Lord Clarendon in his "History of the Civil War," "and were in truth the preservation of that army that day." Ten days later two regiments of the City Trained Bands, chosen by lot, and those of Southwark and Westminster took part in the recapture of Reading. Orders were issued that if any member of the appointed regiments failed to appear on parade, his shop should be closed and he himself expelled beyond the line of fortification.*

Reading, 1643.

At Marston Moor we have the curious spectacle of the Train Bands of one city fighting under the banner of the King against Train Bands engaged on the other side, a spectacle perhaps often to be observed in those days of divided households. When Prince Rupert and the Earl of Newcastle sallied forth from the city of York, to fall upon the Parliamentary forces supposed to be in retreat, the York City Regiment, under Sir Henry Slingsby, was left to guard the city; whilst upon the field itself Sir Thomas Melham, Captain of the *Yorkshire Gentlemen Volunteers*, was left among the slain.† At Naseby, too, the Trained Bands made their dint, for Mr. Grant, in the work already quoted, tells us that "General Skippon, a rough blunt veteran of the Low Country, showed great tact and skill in disciplining the Trained Bands of London." At this battle poor Skippon was wounded, "shot under the arme six inches into the flesh." The pain of having his wound dressed caused him to groan: "Though I groan I grumble not," he said, and sent for the chaplain to pray with him.

Marston Moor, 1644.

Naseby, 1645

To that reader whose conceptions of our national life and the military enterprises of our country are largely formed upon what he observes with his own eyes to-day it must be a matter of ever increasing wonder that a few thousands of citizen soldiers should have been, as they undoubtedly were, the arbiters of war, and decide for all time the destinies of what was fated to become an Empire greater and prouder far than Rome when the Imperial City was the mistress of the known world. But it must be remembered that the England of Charles I was a vastly different country from the England of what may still be called the Victorian Era. The only considerable ports were London, Bristol and Newcastle. Lord Macaulay, in his "History of England," presents us with a vivid picture of urban England about this period. Next to the capital, but next at an immense distance, stood Bristol. Its population numbered nigh thirty thousand souls, a population nearly equalled by that of Norwich.

England in 1640.

*Gardiner's "History Great Civil War," cited by Sharpe.

†Leadman's "Battles fought in Yorkshire."

The inhabitants of York, the capital of the North, were but ten thousand; Worcester, the Queen of the cider land, had but eight thousand; Shrewsbury, the seat of the Court of the Marches of Wales, but eight thousand; Nottingham, probably as many; Gloucester, renowned for the stubborn defence so disastrous to Charles I, between four and five thousand; Exeter, the capital of the West, but ten thousand; Manchester, where the cotton manufacture was yet in its infancy, was then "a mean and ill-built market town," containing under six thousand people; Leeds about the same number; the industry of Sheffield, famed even in Chaucer's day for its ware, was carried on in a market town, sprung up near the castle of the proprietor, described in the reign of James I as a "singularly miserable place, containing about two thousand inhabitants, of whom a third were half-starved and half-naked beggars"; Birmingham did not return a single member to Parliament, though it boasted that its hardware was known as far as Ireland. Its population in 1685 did not amount to four thousand; the population of Liverpool could scarce have exceeded the like number, its shipping was about fourteen hundred tons, the whole number of seamen belonging to the port less than two hundred.

It may then be well understood that the manhood of such a city as London, accustomed to the quickening arts of commerce, their minds more acute, their faculties more keen than those of the peasant, accustomed too to united action, learned, from their apprenticing, in the discipline of drill and the use of the rude arms of the period, might and did prove themselves a body of men against which the Cavalry of Rupert and the gallant but undisciplined squires and nobles of England were hurled in vain.

The London Apprentices.

Another factor too must not be overlooked. People are apt to form their notions of the city apprentices of that period from their observations of the city counter-jumpers of to-day. Nothing could be more misleading. Readers of Sir Walter Besant's "Life of Sir Richard Whittington," thrice Lord Mayor of London, will not need to be reminded that the city apprentice was often, perhaps more often than not, a youth of gentle nurture and honourable descent. For the younger sons of the gentry of that day there was not the range in the selection of a calling the more favoured of our times enjoy. For the eldest son there was, of course, the entailed estate. An eldest son was an eldest son then and no question. For the second, if he could bring himself to it, there was the family living or domestic chaplaincy, and the country rector or domestic chaplain was a mere hanger-on of the thrice favoured first-born; another might eat his way to the Bar; but for still another there was but the choice of trailing a pike in the Netherlands as a soldier of fortune, the sport of chance, to-day with a purse fat with doubloons, to-morrow stranded in a ditch; or he might engage himself, as the founders of many of our now proudest houses did, in some one or other of the great emporiums of trade that lined the shores of the Thames or displayed their wares in Cheapside or Cornhill. Thus it chanced, I doubt not, that in many a tough encounter of the Civil Wars, when an elder son, baronet of broad acres, gallant in plume and velvet and embroidered scarf, charged at the head of horse, bred and mounted from his own estate, his love locks floating in the breeze, he was met by the pike of a younger brother, crop haired, set of visage, psalm chanting, but sad at heart to lift his hand against one who had lisped his early prayers at the knees of a common mother.

It has been objected to the Volunteer movement by those who regard it with disfavor, or at least with very lukewarm approval, that it tends to create in the masses a military and bellicose, shall one say a Jingo, spirit and unfits for the prosaic duties of civil life—the daily task, the common round. This is necessarily an *à priori* assumption and, unfortunately for those who entertain it, is contradicted by the stubborn facts of history. Mr. S. Pepys in his quite incomparable diary, writes of the disbanded soldiers of Cromwell, and inclusively also of the train bands, in these terms—and Pepys was a courtier tho' a courtier with eyes: "They generally are the most substantial sort of people and the soberest; and he (Mr. Surgeon Pierce) did desire me to observe it to my Lord Sandwich, among other things, that of all the old army you cannot see a man begging about the streets; but what? You shall have this captain turned a shoemaker; this lieutenant, a baker; this a brewer; that a haberdasher; this common soldier, a porter; and every man in his apron and frock, &c., as if they had never done anything else; whereas the others go with their belts and swords, swearing and cursing and stealing, running into people's houses, by force oftentimes, to carry away something."

It may perhaps be objected that the levies of Essex and other Parliamentary leaders were not strictly levies of Volunteers, *i.e.*, of men drilling and serving without fee or reward, but rather part of an army as much entitled to be styled a regular army as the forces arrayed under the Royal Banner. No such criticism, however, can be urged against a later muster, for though its privates and non-commissioned officers, who doubtless were absolutely dependent on their daily toil for their daily bread, received pay, the officers gave their services gratuitously, and the paymaster's chest was probably furnished, not by the State, but by private subscription. I refer to the formation, on the initiative of the venerable Archbishop of York, of the "Yorkshire Blues" in 1745. For some time prior to the landing of the Young Pretender the country had been agitated by repeated rumours of a Jacobite descent upon our shores. Men still in their prime remembered the incursion of the Chevalier St. George or the Old Pretender in 1715, when the rebels marched so far south as Preston. It was certain that the young Prince would essay a landing and a rising in Scotland where the strength of his following lay. The men of the northern shires of England had lurid visions of kilted, half-savage Highlanders sacking their houses, their shops and their shrines. They were far removed from the central seat of Government and of the military Executive. News travelled slowly; the roads were bad, and troops, even mounted troops, moved perforce but tardily. It was possible for York to be laid in ruins many days before tidings of its investment could reach the Metropolis. Little wonder therefore that, as we read, eight hundred of the principal nobility, clergy and gentry of the County of York should assemble in York Castle (September 23, 1745), to take measures for the protection of the North. The County contributed the sum of £31,420, the City £2,420, and the Ainsty of the City and Shire of York £220. With these sums four companies of Infantry, each seventy strong, exclusive of sergeants, corporals and drummers, were raised and styled "The Yorkshire Blues." They remained under arms four months. The citizens of York likewise raised another body for the special protection of their ancient city. These Volunteers, called "Independents," provided their own uniforms and accoutrements. They remained embodied for a period of ten months.

The "Yorkshire Blues."

In 1798 the Corporation and inhabitants of the City of Liverpool shewed themselves not less forward than those of York in the display of patriotic virtue. In that year they petitioned the House of Commons for leave to arm themselves for defence of that port at their own expense. The petition was prompted by apprehension of the danger that menaced the docks and shipping of that port in case the enemy (France) should direct his attempts in that quarter. They also craved leave to erect batteries, fit out gun boats, and to prepare any other means of defence at an expense one half of which was to be paid by the Corporation and the other half to be levied by rate on the inhabitants. Mr. Pitt, in commenting on the petition, which was granted, said he could scarcely consider it as a private petition. It offered, he said, a most useful suggestion and might be made the ground work of a most excellent general defence.

The Volunteers of Ireland.

I cannot conclude this section of my work without narrating with, I hope, pardonable detail, the gallant part played by the loyal sons of Ireland in the darkest hour of Britain's chequered story—a task to which I am not less allured by the Celtic strain which flows in my veins than constrained by the interest and importance of the topic itself.

In the year 1760, we being then at war with France, that country attempted a distraction by a descent upon Ireland. In that year Thurot and a small following of Frenchmen effected a landing at Carrickfergus, where, more than a century before, Cromwell had first set foot on Irish soil. Thurot seized that town and moved towards Belfast, but the stout Protestants of the "black North" opposed an obstacle he could neither elude nor surmount. Lord Charlemont thus describes this rude but effective line of defence: "The appearance of the peasantry who had thronged to its defence, many of whom were my own tenants, was singular and formidable. They were drawn up in regular bodies, each with its own chosen officers, and formed in martial array—some few with firelocks, but the greater part armed with what is called in Scotland the Lockaber axe, a scythe fixed longitudinally to the end of a long pole—a desperate weapon and which they would have made desperate use of. Thousands were assembled in a small circuit, but these thousands were so impressed with the necessity of regularity, that the town was perfectly undisturbed by tumult, by riot or even by drunkenness." Thurot was fain to re-embark his force, some of his officers and men being left, wounded and prisoners, in the hands of the spirited peasants and townsmen who had risen to oppose this audacious inroad.

Eighteen years later (1778) there was every reason to anticipate another and more formidable descent by the French upon the Irish coast. The people of Belfast appealed for protection to the Executive at Dublin Castle. The reply must have brought them small comfort. The Lord Lieutenant of the County had written to the Castle that "he had received information of a possible attempt by three or four privateers in company in a few days on the Northern coasts." The Secretary, Sir Richard Heron, replied that "the greatest part of the troops being encamped near

Clonmel and Kinsale his Excellency can at present send no further military aid to Belfast than a troop or two of Horse or part of a Company of Invalids." Sixty troopers for the defence of the rich and loyal province of Ulster at a time when the cruisers of the enemy swept the channel and the southern and western parts of the Island were seething with sedition!

It behoved the loyal inhabitants of the North to look to themselves. Armagh led the way, forming a Voluntary Armed Association on December 1, 1778. Lord Charlemont, the Lord Lieutenant of the County, assumed the command. The 36th Regiment of Foot chancing to be quartered at Armagh about this time, facilities for drill instruction were forthcoming. In April, 1782, was raised a Troop of Volunteer Horse, to which Catholics were admitted, and of this, too, Lord Charlemont accepted the command. In July, 1778, Limerick had embodied a force of Volunteers, an example followed, in May, 1779, by the town of Galway. In the same year Belfast's sons swelled the patriot train. In September of that year the Volunteers of the County of Down, Antrim and the neighbourhood of Coleraine mustered 3,925 strong, and still the movement spread till, by the end of 1779, all Ireland, from North to South and from East to West, bristled with the arms of unbought valour. And this despite the little encouragement received from the Government. In June, 1779, the Lord Lieutenant wrote to Lord Weymouth that he had refused and would refuse arms "for the use of these self-created troops and companies in this kingdom." A few weeks later, July 23rd, the Castle made ignominious surrender, the Lord Lieutenant announcing that by the advice of the Privy Council he had supplied the Volunteers with part of the arms intended for the Militia. In October, 1779, the Volunteer forces of Ireland, now mustering 20,000 strong, and under the command of the Duke of Leinster, received the unanimous thanks of the Irish Parliament for their patriotism and spirit in coming forward and defending their country. It cannot be denied that some sentiment other and nearer than attachment to the Crown animated the recruits of this formidable association of armed patriots. There is no need here to recapitulate the undoubted wrongs under which Ireland then groaned, wrongs that pressed alike on peer and peasant, on Protestants and Romanists. It was doubtless the sense of these iniquities that proved a more effective recruiting sergeant than the dread of the French or devotion to the Crown. The Irish of all classes resented the impotence of the emasculated Irish Parliament and cried aloud for the unfettering of their trade from the artificial shackles an imbecile fiscal policy had forged. Only this fact accounts for the presence at the head of the Irish Volunteers of such men as the Earl of Charlemont, Commander-in-Chief, and, as Generals, the Duke of Leinster, the Earl of Tyrone, the Earl of Aldborough, Lord de Vesci, Sir B. Denny, Rt. Hon. Geo. Ogle, Sir James Tynte, the Earl of Clanricarde, the Earl of Muskerry, Sir Wm. Parsons, the Hon. J. Butler, the Rt. Hon. Henry King.

Their Chief Officers.

By the year 1782 the Irish Volunteers constituted not an auxiliary force but an army, an army able to defy and dictate to the Ministers in Downing Street. How formidable a force was now gathered the following statistics will show :—

Their Levies.

PROVINCE OF ULSTER.

Infantry	33,440
Eight Corps of Cavalry	292
Eight Corps of Artillery	420
Total of Ulster	34,152

ARTILLERY.

Six-pounders	16
Three-pounders	10
Howitzers	6
Total pieces of Artillery	32

PROVINCE OF CONNAUGHT.

Infantry	12,678
Eight Corps of Cavalry	421
Artillery	250
	13,349
Added afterwards—Infantry and Cavalry	987
Total	14,336

Artillery pieces—10 Six-pounders and 10 Three-pounders.

PROVINCE OF MUNSTER.

Infantry	17,031
Cavalry	804
Artillery	221
Total	18,056

Artillery pieces—14 Six-pounders and 14 Three-pounders and 4 Howitzers.

PROVINCE OF LEINSTER.

Infantry	21,381
Cavalry	580
Artillery	382
Total	22,343

Artillery pieces—2 Nine-pounders, 16 Six-pounders, 14 Three-pounders and 6 Howitzers.

TOTAL NUMBERS.

Ulster	34,152
Munster	18,056
Connaught	14,336
Leinster	22,343
Total	88,887
22 Corps who made no returns estimated at	12,000
Total strength of all arms ..	100,887

Artillery, 130 pieces.

In his history MacNevin states that he found no more difficult branch than that of uniforms connected with the Volunteers. He said there were supposed to be manuscripts in some private libraries in Dublin, but from want of catalogues and classified arrangements it was impossible to reach them, and that the newspapers and books of the day were singularly deficient in details on this, or, it may be added, on any subject connected with the Volunteer Organization. Mine has been a similar experience.

I glean from this same historian a few interesting particulars of the Irish uniform:—that of the Lawyers' corps was scarlet, faced blue, gold lace—their motto, "*pro aris et focis*"; the Attorneys' Regiment of Volunteers was scarlet and Pomona green; a corps called the Irish Brigade and composed principally of Catholics (after the increasing liberality of the day had permitted them to become Volunteers) wore scarlet and white.

The first Volunteers of Ireland (1st July, 1766) had scarlet faced with blue. The colonel of this corps was Sir Vesey Colclough, Bart. The uniforms were mostly scarlet faced either with blue, black, white, green, pea green, lemon green, or deep green. Some few corps wore blue faced with blue. Some regiments of Irish Brigades wore scarlet faced with green, having for their motto, "*Vox populi, suprema lex est.*"* Others had silver epaulettes and silver lace—the Burros-in-Ossory Rangers (August, 1779) wore silver epaulettes—the Castledurrow Volunteers (July 1, 1779) had a green uniform, edged white and silver lace—the English Rangers (August 24, 1779), commanded by Major Thomas Berry, had silver epaulettes—so also had the Roxborough Volunteers (1777). A number of corps had gold lace or gold epaulettes, viz.: "The

*A frank confession of political design.—R. P. B.

Lieut. Coll. Northend Nichols.

Goldsmith's Corps," commanded by the Duke of Leinster, wore blue faced with scarlet, and a professional profusion of gold lace; the Ballyleek Rangers (1779), Glin Royal Artillery Volunteers (April, 1776) blue, faced blue, scarlet cuffs and capes—the Kilkenny Volunteers (June 10, 1779) blue, faced scarlet—the Merchants' Corps (June 9, 1779) scarlet, faced blue—the Roscrea Blues (July 21, 1779) blue, faced blue—the Royal Regiment (County Antrim) scarlet, faced blue; and the Tralee Royal Volunteers (January 7, 1779) scarlet, faced blue; all these had gold lace. The Drogheda Association (1777) had scarlet, faced Pomona green, with gold laced hats; and the Eyrecourt Buffs (June 1, 1779) scarlet, faced buff, with gold epaulettes.

There were numerous corps of Volunteer Cavalry and Infantry in the Province of Munster. I describe the uniforms of some of them, as this subject may prove, I hope, interesting to many.

CAVALRY.

True Blue of Cork (1745) blue, laced silver epaulettes, white buttons—Colonel, Richard, Earl Shannon—Mitchelstown Light Dragoons (July, 1774) scarlet, faced black, silver epaulettes, yellow helmet, white buttons, Colonel, Viscount Kingsborough—Blackpool Horse (1776) green laced, gold ditto epaulettes, buff waistcoat and breeches—Bandon Cavalry (May 6, 1778) dark olive green jacket, half lapelled, crimson velvet cuffs and collar, silver epaulettes—Muskerry Blue Light Dragoons (June 1, 1778) blue, lapelled, edged white, silver epaulettes, white jackets, edged blue—Imokilly Horse (Sept. 1, 1778) scarlet, faced black, yellow buttons, gold epaulettes, yellow helmets, white jackets edged red—Kilworthy Light Dragoons (July, 1779) scarlet, faced green, gold epaulettes, yellow buttons and helmets—Colonel, Stephen, Earl Mount-Cashel—Doneraile Rangers Light Dragoons (July 12, 1779) scarlet, faced green, edged white, gold epaulettes, yellow buttons and helmets—Colonel, St. Leger, Lord Doneraile—Cork Cavalry, scarlet, faced blue, silver lace, silver epaulettes, white buttons—Great Island Cavalry (June 24, 1782) scarlet, faced green, gold epaulettes, yellow buttons, white jackets edged red—County Clare Horse (July 24, 1779) scarlet, faced dark green, silver epaulettes and buttons, white jackets, green cape—County Limerick Horse (June 8, 1779) scarlet, faced black, yellow buttons, buff waistcoat and breeches, yellow helmets—Riddlestown Hussars, scarlet, faced blue, silver epaulettes, white buttons, white jackets faced blue—Clanwilliam Union, (July 17, 1779) scarlet, faced blue, laced silver, silver epaulettes, white buttons, white jackets faced blue—Colonel, John, Earl Clanwilliam—Lora Rangers (1779) scarlet, faced green, yellow buttons, gold epaulettes—Munster Cavalry Corps, scarlet, faced blue, gold lace, gold epaulettes, buff waistcoat and breeches, yellow buttons, buff jackets—Clogheen Union (Jan. 6, 1781) scarlet, faced light blue, edged silver lace, white buttons, silver epaulettes, white jackets edged red—Newport Cavalry, scarlet, green collar and cuffs, yellow buttons, gold epaulettes, Colonel, Lord Jocelyn—Curraghmore Rangers (Nov. 1, 1779) scarlet, faced white, silver epaulettes, white buttons, white jackets, faced red, half lapelled—Colonel, George, Earl Tyrone.

Infantry.

Cork Boyne (1776), blue, faced blue, yellow buttons, gold epaulettes and lace—Mallow Boyne (1776) blue, edged buff, buff waistcoat and breeches, yellow buttons, Colonel, Sir James Lawrence Cotter, Bart:—Bandon Boyne (1776) same as uniform of Mallow Boyne with the addition of gold epaulettes—Culloden Volunteers of Cork (March 23, 1778) blue, faced scarlet, yellow buttons, officers gold epaulettes—Bandon Independents (March 29, 1778) scarlet, faced black, gold epaulettes, yellow buttons, green jacket faced black—Youghall Rangers (April 19, 1778) grass green, faced scarlet, gold lace and yellow buttons—Hawke Union of Cove (May 9, 1778) blue edged and lined buff, yellow buttons, buff waistcoat and breeches—Doneraile Rangers (July 12, 1779) scarlet, faced green, yellow buttons, gold epaulettes, Colonel, St. Leger, Lord Doneraile—Inchiquin Fusiliers (County Clare) (February 12, 1779) scarlet, faced light blue, silver buttons, braided wings on shoulder straps, hat cocked one side, with large plume of black feathers—Colonel, Murrough, Earl of Inchiquin—Royal Tralee Volunteers (January 4, 1779) scarlet, faced deep blue, edged white, yellow buttons, gold lace epaulettes and wings—Colonel, Sir Barry Denny, Bart:—Royal Glin Artillery Volunteers (County Limerick) (June, 1779) blue, laced gold, gold epaulettes, scarlet cuffs and collar, yellow buttons, gold laced hats—Castle Connel Rangers (July 8, 1778) scarlet, faced black, laced wings, Colonel, Sir Cornelius Maude, Bart:—Ormond Independents (March 23, 1779) scarlet, faced black, silver epaulettes and wings—Killcooly True Blues (1779) blue, edged buff, yellow buttons, buff waistcoat and breeches—Colonel, Sir William Barker, Bart:—Waterford Independents (Nos. 1 and 6 March, 1778) scarlet, faced black, white buttons, silver laced hats—Dungarvan Volunteers (Nov. 1, 1779) scarlet, faced black, silver laced wings, white buttons—Colonel, Right

Honourable John Beresford—Taken altogether there was very little affectation of nationality either in their mottos or uniforms.

Many of the Irish Corps were embodied in 1777 and 1778, but these were for the most part only incorporated for a local or occasional purpose without any view to general organization. All these corps afterwards adopted the principles of the National Army of Volunteers and became part of its strength—the bulk of the corps being formed in 1779.

No appointment could have been more popular than that of James Caulfield, Earl of Charlemont, who, in 1780, was appointed Commander in Chief of the United Army of Irish Volunteers. His reply to the address of a meeting of the Dublin Volunteers, held at the Eagle Tavern in Eustace Street, and over which the Duke of Leinster presided, gives so clearly (as MacNevin records it) the position occupied by the Irish Volunteers, the services they had rendered and the spirit which animated them, that I present it in full as a perfect vindication, as Curran said, of "that illustrious, adored, and abused body of men."

The Earl of Charlemont.

1780, July 15.

"Gentlemen,

You have conferred upon me an honour of a very new and distinguished nature, to be appointed without any solicitation on my part, the reviewing general of an independent army, *raised by no other call than that of public virtue;* an army which costs nothing to the state and has produced every thing to the nation, is what no other country has it in her power to bestow. Honoured by such a delegation I obeyed it with cheerfulness. The inducement was irresistible; I felt it the duty of every subject to forget impediments which would have stood in the way of a similar attempt in any other cause.

His Manifesto.

I see with unspeakable pleasure the progress of your discipline, and the increase of your Associations; the indefatigable, steady, and extraordinary exertions, to which I have been a witness, afford a sufficient proof that in the formation of an army, public spirit, a shame of being outdone, and the ambition to excel, *will supply the place of reward and punishment—can levy an army and bring it to perfection.* The pleasure I feel is increased when I reflect that your Associations are not the fashion of a day, but the settled purpose and durable principle of the people, from whence I forsee that the advantages lately acquired will be ascertained and established, and that solid and permanent strength will be added to the Empire.

I entirely agree in the sentiment you express with regard to the exclusive authority of the legislature of this kingdom. I agree also in the expediency of making the assertion, it is no more than the law will warrant and the real friends of both nations subscribe.

I have the honor to be,

Gentlemen,

Your most obliged, faithful, and obedient humble servant,

CHARLEMONT."

Reviews.

Reviews through all Ireland by the commanding officers in each district followed Lord Charlemont's appointment as Commander-in-Chief. He himself visited Belfast to review the Ulster regiments, and was there attended by Sir Annesley Stewart and Grattan as his Aides-de-Camp. Some 2,788 men in two Brigades were reviewed on this occasion.* The other reviews were by the Earl of Belvidere of the Volunteer troops at Westmeath, by Lord Kingsborough of the Limerick and Clare and Wicklow Volunteers, by Lord Erne of the Londonderry Volunteers, by Lord Shannon of the Volunteers of the south, and by Lord Carysfort of the Associated Corps of the County and City of Dublin. In February of 1785 a motion was submitted in the Irish Parliament House for a grant of clothing for and the establishment of a Militia. This was treated by a portion of the House as a vote of censure on the Volunteers and looked upon as an intentionally fatal blow at their existence. The force gradually fell off, and although the Volunteers lingered for some years after, holding annual reviews and passing addresses and resolutions, their proceedings were ineffective, the old leaders fell away, men of wealth threw up their commissions and new men succeeded to the control. Nevertheless, between the years 1798 and 1804 there were 70,000 Irish Volunteers.

Their disbandment.

At length the Volunteers came into direct collision with the regular army. Government issued an order that every assemblage of the body should be dispersed by force. In defiance of this decree a few country corps fixed on holding a review in the county of Antrim, the Regulars marched to the spot to disperse them, but the Volunteers abandoned the design, and thus the Irish National Army of Volunteers passed away from the scene for ever.

---

*NacNevin, "Belfast Politics—History of Belfast and Local Papers."

PART I.

SECTION III.

The abolition of military tenures at the Restoration left the Crown dependent for its armed forces entirely upon such powers as might be deemed to be vested in the King by virtue of the Royal Prerogative, or as might be construed to be reposed by ancient statutes. By 13 Edward I, for instance, every freeman between the ages of 15 and 60 years was obliged to be provided with armour to preserve the peace; but he was under no obligation to leave his county or shire "save upon the coming of strange enemies into the realm." The 4th Philip and Mary c. 2 imposed upon the owners of land, according to their estates, an obligation of finding, keeping and sustaining within the realm of England, horses and armour for its defence. The Statute 3 and 4 Edward VI c 5 first mentions Lords Lieutenant of counties and decrees that the inhabitants of the county, on request made, shall be bound to give attendance upon the same lieutenants to suppress any commotion, rebellion or unlawful assembly. In the disputes between Charles I and Parliament the latter had claimed, without any show of constitutional title, the right to control the levying and officering of the national militia. One of the first acts of Charles II was to secure a declaration that the "sole supreme government, command and disposition of the Militia within all His Majesty's realms and dominions, and of all forces by sea and land, and of all forts and places of strength is, and ever was, the undoubted right of His Majesty and his royal predecessors, Kings and Queens of England, and that both or either House of Parliament cannot nor ought to pretend to the same, nor can nor lawfully may raise or levy any war, offensive or defensive, against His Majesty, his heirs or lawful successors." A standing army was the inevitable outcome of the abolition of military tenures, and on the Restoration attempts were also made to more accurately define the relation of the Crown to the Militia and to place that body on a more settled and satisfactory basis.

The Restoration.

13 Edwd. I, c. 6. (Statute of Winchester.)

4 Philip and Mary, c. 2.

3 & 4 Edwd. VI., c. 5.

The King's Military Prerogative re-asserted.

The Militia.

This was partially effected by the Statute 14 Car. II. cap. 3, which empowered the Lords Lieutenant of counties to call together such persons, at such times, and to arm and array them in such manner, as therein declared, and to form them into companies,

14 Car. II. c. 3.

troops and regiments, and in case of insurrections, rebellion, or invasion, to lead, conduct and employ them, either in their own counties or in others, as they should be directed by His Majesty. By the Militia Act, 1882, which is a Voluntary Enlistment Act and consolidated and amended the previous Acts, the service of the Militia is also restricted to the United Kingdom. By the statute of Charles the Militia Force was to consist of horse and foot soldiers, provided by or at the expense of owners of property, not of land exclusively, in the proportions set out in the Act. Its numbers, as dependent upon the wealth of the inhabitants, were undefined.*

Militia Act, 1882 (45 & 46 Vict. c. 49).

It is not necessary that I should, in a work devoted to the Volunteers, enter fully into the constitution and nature of the Militia, a term which took its present significance in the controversies of the Civil wars. "I do heartily wish," said Whitlock, addressing the Commons on 1st March, 1641, "that this great word, this new word,—the Militia,—this harsh word, might never have come within these walls." But without some reference to this body the genesis of the Volunteers would be incomprehensible to the ordinary reader, for the earlier Volunteers were but a graft upon the Militia.

In the century that elapsed between the Militia Act of Charles II. and the Act to which I must now refer, the Militia had, largely probably from lack of occasion for their services, fallen into a lax and disorganised condition. We learn from Grose's "Military Antiquities" † that "tho' the Militia occasionally mustered and exercised, yet, being found expensive and troublesome to the country, it was by degrees neglected, insomuch that, the City of London excepted, the name of a Militia muster was almost forgotten; but about the year 1756, the nation being so much alarmed by the apprehension of an invasion that a levy of Hanoverians and Hessians were called in for its defence, many leading persons resumed the idea of a well disciplined Militia."

In the year 1757, therefore, an Act of considerable moment was placed upon the Statute Book. It recited that a "well ordered and well disciplined Militia is essentially necessary to the safety, peace and prosperity of the Kingdom; and the laws now in being for the regulation of the Militia are defective and ineffectual." The Act authorised the Crown to "issue forth Commissions of Lieutenancy for the several counties and ridings of

*Clode I., 34.

† Grose: "Military Antiquities," I. 33.

the Kingdom; and such lieutenants were to have full power and authority to call together all such persons, and to arm and array them at such times and in such manner as therein expressed." The Lieutenant of every county and riding was "to have the Chief Command of the Militia thereof." The 16th Section specified the number of "private men" to be raised under the Act in each county and riding. For the West Riding of the County of York, the number was One thousand two hundred and forty. On the first Tuesday of June in each year, His Majesty's Lieutenants, together with two or more Deputy Lieutenants, were to meet in some "city or principal place" in their county or riding. There they were to "issue their Orders" to the Chief Constables of the several parishes "to return to them, upon a day and at a place then to be mentioned, fair and true lists of all men then settled in their respective districts between the ages of 18 and 50 years." Peers of the realm, Members of Parliament, University men, Clergymen and other Ministers, Constables and other Peace or Parish Officers, Articled Clerks, Apprentices and Seamen, were not to be included in the lists. The lists were to specify which of the persons therein included "laboured under any infirmities incapacitating them from serving as Militia men." On the Sunday morning before the return was made the lists were to be affixed to the Church door or otherwise publicly displayed. The Lieutenant and Deputies, the lists received, were to meet and appoint what number of persons in each district should serve in the said Militia towards raising the statutory number prescribed for each county. It was a simple sum in proportion. The Deputy Lieutenants were to hear and determine any appeal by anyone objecting to his inclusion in the lists. They were then "to appoint what number of men in each respective parish, &c., should serve in the said Militia, in proportion to the whole number contained in the lists." This would constitute the quota of a parish. The quota was then "immediately to be chosen by lot out of the whole number of men liable to serve for each respective parish, &c." This was the Militia ballot so often referred to in the military records and general history of those times. The persons upon whom the lot fell were then enrolled "to serve in the Militia of such county, riding or place, as private Militia men, for the space of three years, or provide fit and approved substitutes." When the Militia men had been secured in the manner above set forth the Lieutenant and Deputy Lieutenant were to form the Militia into regiments, consisting of not more than 12 and not less than 7 Companies of forty men each at the least, "of persons living as near to each other as conveniently could be," and were to post to each Company proper commissioned and non-commissioned officers. These Militia men had not to endure any very exacting course of drill. They were to be "trained and exercised" in half Companies on the first Monday in the months of March, April, May, June, July, August, September and October, and in Companies on the third Monday of the same months. They were also to be trained and exercised in regiments or by battalions on the Tuesday, Wednesday, Thursday and Friday in Whitsun week. In other words the Militiaman's duty was discharged by two days' drill in each of the spring, summer and autumn months, and by four days' drill in Whitsun week—twenty days' drill in all. The rendezvous for each man for Company or half Company drill was to be within 6 miles of his residence.

The Militia were to be embodied "in case of actual invasion, or upon imminent danger thereof, or in case of rebellion," and might be led to any part of the Kingdom, and when so embodied Militia men were to be entitled to like pay as the King's forces, and to the benefit of Chelsea Hospital.

31 Geo. II., c. 26. The Act last recited was followed by an explanatory, amending and enforcing Act, from the preamble to which it may be gathered that the Lords Lieutenant and other officials had not been very diligent to carry the earlier statute into effect. It will only be
Sec. 17. necessary to advert to the 17th and the 36th sections of this Statute. The former of these sections provided that "if the Churchwardens or Overseers of any Parish should produce to the Deputy Lieutenants any number of *Volunteers* not being seamen or sea-faring men, and such Volunteers should be approved by the Deputy Lieutenants," such Volunteers should be accepted *pro tantis* in substitution of an equivalent number of the Parish quota. For each Volunteer who failed to put in an appearance to be sworn in and enrolled the Parish was to pay £10 out of the Poor Rate. The
Sec. 36. thirty-sixth section must be quoted in full: "Whenever the Militia shall be ordered out into actual service, it shall and may be lawful for the Captain of any Company of Militia men to augment his Company, by incorporating, with the consent of His Majesty's Lieutenant, any number of persons who shall offer themselves as Volunteers, and who shall appear to him to be sufficiently trained and disciplined, and provided with proper cloaths, arms, and accoutrements, and who shall take the Oath appointed to be taken by this Act, and sign their consent to serve for the Militia for the

time of such actual service, and to submit to the same Rules and Articles of War as Militia men are liable to during the time of their continuing on actual service."

This proviso is, I believe, the first recognition by Parliament of the levy from which the modern Volunteer may fairly claim to have a lineal descent.

The next Statute, the Militia Act of 1762, (as amended by that of 1764), contained a similar proviso, and it is unnecessary to repeat the clause enabling the Captain of a Company to augment its numbers by Volunteers.

2 Geo. III., c. 20, s. 120.

4 Geo. III., c. 17.

It will be observed that this and the preceding statute confided the power of accepting the services of Volunteers to the *Captain* of a Company, and that the power was only to be exercised during periods of active service. We are brought a step nearer to the Volunteer of to-day by an Act of 1778 (18 Geo. III. c. 59), which may be said to be the first parliamentary provision for the existence, but still in connection with the Militia, of a *distinct company* of Volunteers. The eighth section of this Statute enacts "that it shall and may be lawful for the Commanding Officer, with the consent of His Majesty's Lieutenant, or, in the absence of His Majesty's Lieutenant, with the consent of any two or more of the Deputy Lieutenants, to accept a number of Volunteers to serve in the said Militia, either to be incorporated into the other companies *or to be formed into a distinct company, in which latter case commissions may be granted by His Majesty's Lieutenant to Officers legally qualified to command the same.*" The ninth section provided that the number of Volunteers in a battalion should never be suffered to be in excess of the Militiamen proper, and that they should, during actual service, be entitled to the same pay and accoutrements as the regular Militia.

Militia Act, 1778. (18 Geo. III., c. 59.)

How eagerly the people availed themselves of the opportunity alike of displaying their patriotism and gratifying their martial instincts, may be judged from a statement of Mr. Grose that some Militia Regiments had as many as 14 of these Volunteer Companies. When, as often occurred in the Welsh counties, there were to be found but two companies, the senior Captain ranked as Major.

A still further recognition of voluntary service was made by a Statute of 1779 (19 Geo. III., c 76) which (sec. 1) provided that "if any person or persons properly qualified according to the law then in force should offer to His Majesty's Lieutenant of any County to raise one or more company or companies *to be added to*

Militia Act, 1779. (19 Geo. III., c. 76.)

Independent Companies.

the Regiment or Battalion of any county or riding, it should be lawful for His Majesty's Lieutenant to accept such services and appoint such Officers accordingly," and on due certificate such company or companies were to be entitled to the same allowance of bounty, subsistence money, arms and clothing, as the rest of His Majesty's Militia Forces in the Kingdom. The second section contained the proviso that "when any such *companies of Volunteers* should be added to any regiment, such addition should not make it necessary to separate such regiment into two Battalions, but such regiment should remain and continue one regiment." The third section subjected the Volunteer Companies to "all the rules, regulations, forfeitures, clauses, matters, and things" then in force relating to the Militia. The fourth section provided for the dissolution of the Volunteer companies on the disembodiment of the Militia or at His Majesty's earlier pleasure—a clause that seems to point to the fact that even at this late period the volunteer forces were only regarded as a temporary provision against imminent danger, to be discarded like a cast-off glove the moment the peril was overpast.

Anent the Companies of Volunteers raised under this Statute it will be convenient here to quote the remarks of Mr. Grose.* "About this time (1779)," writes Mr. Grose, "many new regiments were raised, several of whose Colonels, Field Officers and Captains, having never served before, or having no military rank, it was stipulated by the Secretary of War with them that they should not be entitled to either rank or half-pay after the reduction of their corps, but the Ensigns of those Officers who came from the half-pay or out of established regiments and gained only one step were permitted to retain their acquired rank, with the half-pay belonging to it." In a foot note Grose adds "Divers independent Companies were also raised towards the close of this war† and that of 1762,§ some of which were afterwards regimented. These were mostly raised by subalterns, who undertook to complete them against a fixed time, and at their own expense, on condition of being appointed to the command of them. The best idea of these companies may be gathered from the definition of them by a private soldier at Belleisle, during the siege of Palais. A number of these Independent Companies, being regimented, were sent out to that place. One night, in the trenches, an officer over-heard

* "Military Antiquities," Vol. 1, 173.

†War of American Independence. §The year 1762 witnessed the close of the Ten Years' War.

several of the men in high dispute concerning the meaning of the term *independent*, in which they could by no means agree, till one of them, an old grenadier, raising his voice, called his comrades a pack of stupid fellows for puzzling at so obvious a term: "You see what stuff they are," (said he), "now it is plain they are called independent, because they are not to be depended on."

It cannot have escaped the careful reader that the statutes I have cited regarded Volunteer Companies merely as a tag to the Militia. That was an association not lightly to be borne. The Volunteer private was generally a man who esteemed himself entitled to higher comradeship than that of the Militiaman. The Volunteer officers were gentlemen of position, influence and fortune, highly esteemed in their own districts, and who had made considerable sacrifices of time, effort and money, in the discharge of what they conceived to be a patriotic movement. They brooked it ill to find themselves regarded merely as a tolerated appanage to an inferior branch of the national service. The time was at hand when Parliament or the War Office was constrained to concede to the Volunteers a position alike of more independence and of enhanced dignity. The conclusion of the war of American Independence found this country sorely shaken in power, reputation and resources. The grant of independence won at the point of the sword seemed to our exultant enemies abroad the beginning of the end, the handwriting on the wall. The Act of 22 Geo. III. c 79, passed in 1782, was styled "an Act for encouraging and disciplining of such corps and companies of men as should *voluntarily* enrol themselves for defence of their town or coast, or for the general defence of the Kingdom during the present war." It declared in the gravest of terms that "the utmost exertions are now requisite for increasing the Military Force in this Kingdom." The first section provided

Volunteer Act, 1782.

> "That any Corps or Companies of Volunteers who are now or shall hereafter be formed in any towns or elsewhere in Great Britain during the continuance of the present war under officers having commissions from His Majesty or from the Lieutenants of counties or others who may be specially authorised by His Majesty for that purpose, and who shall at any time in case of actual invasion or rebellion march out of their respective towns or counties for the purpose of acting against any rebels or invaders of this kingdom shall in that case be entitled to receive pay in such manner and at such rate as the officers and soldiers of His Majesty's Regular Forces do now receive, and shall, during the time of their so receiving pay as above, be subject to military discipline as the rest of His Majesty's Regular and Militia Troops."

The second section declares that

> "No officer or soldier of any Volunteer Corps shall be liable to be tried or punished by any Court Martial at any time unless such Court Martial be composed entirely of officers serving in the Volunteers Corps, if a sufficient number can be obtained to constitute such Court Martial."

And the third section

> "That all commissioned officers of the said Corps who shall be disabled by the enemy in actual service shall be entitled to half-pay, and all non-commissioned officers and soldiers so disabled to the benefit of Chelsea Hospital, and the widows of commissioned officers killed in the service to be pensioned for life."

Many Volunteer Corps were formed under this statute, but by its terms were disbanded on the conclusion of the war of American Independence. Many of the officers and men, however, again offered their services when, twelve years later, there again arose the necessity of appealing to the patriotism of the people.

Militia Act, 1794.

At the time of the French Revolution, the War Office, with that fatuity that seems at times to beset our public Departments, once more reverted to the thrice discredited experiment of grafting the Volunteers upon the Militia. The Act, 34 Geo. III., c. 16, entitled "an Act for augmenting the Militia," after reciting that "in the present situation of public affairs it is highly necessary and expedient that the number of the Militia Forces should be augmented," provided that

> "If any person or persons properly qualified according to the Laws now in force shall offer to His Majesty's Lieutenant of any county or riding to raise one or more Companies to be added to the regiment or battalion of any county or a riding it shall and may be lawful for His Majesty's Lieutenants to accept such offers and to appoint such officers accordingly."

This is practically the same provision as and a re-enactment of Section 1. of the previously expired Act of 19 Geo. III., c. 76. The Section (1.) then proceeds with the following additional provision,

> "and that it shall likewise be lawful for His Majesty's Lieutenant to accept and cause to be enrolled any number as His Majesty may from time to time during the continuance of this Act think proper to authorise, to be added as privates to the establishment of such regiment or battalion as aforesaid, and to give to such officers raising Companies or privates as aforesaid such temporary rank not above the rank of Lieutenant Colonel as His Majesty shall direct; and on the certificate of His Majesty's Lieutenant or of the Commanding Officer of the regiment or battalion to which such Company or Companies shall be annexed, that such Company or Companies are actually raised, such Company or Companies shall be entitled to the same allowance of bounty, subsistence-money, arms and clothing, as the rest of His Majesty's Militia Forces in this kingdom."

Section 2 provided,

"That all persons who shall engage to serve either in Companies or as Volunteers to be added as privates as aforesaid, in pursuance of this Act, shall be entitled to serve till such time as the Militia shall be disembodied or till such earlier period at which His Majesty shall think fit to reduce the said Volunteer Companies or to discharge the said privates."

Section 3,

"That when any such Companies or Volunteers to be added as privates shall be added to any regiment, such addition shall not make it necessary to separate such regiment into two battalions, but such regiment shall remain and continue one regiment."

Section 5,

"That the Churchwardens and Overseers shall and they are hereby empowered, with such consent as aforesaid, to give to any Volunteer or Volunteers, enrolled by virtue of the said Act, any sum or sums of money not exceeding £10 each."

Section 6,

"That all the Rules, Regulations, Penalties, Forfeitures, Claims, Matters and things contained in the Act of the 26th year of His present Majesty or in any other Act that shall be passed in this Session of Parliament relating to the raising, training, paying, clothing, embodying and calling out of the Militia shall be applied, practised and put into execution with respect to the additional Volunteer Company or Volunteers added as privates as aforesaid by this Act directed to be raised."

And by the last clause (Section 7) this Act was to continue in force until the 1st January, 1795, and from thence to the end of the then next session of Parliament.

So far as the West Riding was concerned this statute, doubtless from the indisposition of the gentry and the better part of the operative classes to associate with the Militia, was practically a dead letter, and I find on the authority of Raikes, in his "History of the 1st Regiment of Militia," that no Volunteer Companies or men were raised in the West Riding under the 34, Geo. III., c 16.

Almost simultaneously with the last Act (34, Geo. III., c. 16), then passed so recently as the 28th March, 1794, for augmenting the Militia and raising Volunteer Companies and additional Volunteer privates, another Act appeared on the Statute Book, namely, on the 12th April, as 34, Geo. III., c. 31, intituled, "An Act for encouraging and disciplining such corps or companies of men, as shall voluntarily enrol themselves for the defence of their Counties, Towns, or Coasts, or for the general defence of the Kingdom during the present war." It will thus be seen that there were two statutes in force concurrently on the same subject, one

Volunteer Act, 1794. (34 Geo. III., c. 31.)

having reference to Volunteer Companies in augmentation of the Militia, and the other to Volunteers on entirely independent establishments. The latter of these statutes was the first to recognise the Volunteers as an organic entity.

Each county, therefore, had a choice, and from what we shall see of the levies actually raised under these two Acts, that choice fell emphatically upon Volunteering under the latter of these two statutes, which I proceed to give at length, offering no apology in so doing, considering that, in addition to its brevity, it also formed at the time the only existing statutory authority for the raising of the volunteer infantry in England independently of the Militia.

After declaring by the preamble of the Act "that the utmost exertions were then requisite for increasing the Military (be it observed, not Militia) Forces in this Kingdom," it enacted, by Section 1,

> "That any Corps or Companies of *Volunteers* who now are or shall hereafter be formed, in any counties or towns in Great Britain, during the continuance of the present war, under officers having commissions from His Majesty, or from the Lieutenants of counties or others who may be specially authorised by His Majesty for the purpose, and who shall at any time, on being called upon by special direction of His Majesty in case of actual invasion or appearance of invasion, voluntarily march out of their respective counties or towns, or shall voluntarily assemble within the same, to repel such invasion, or who shall voluntarily march on being called upon, in pursuance of an Order from His Majesty, or from the Lord Lieutenant or Sheriff of the county, to act within the county or the adjacent counties for the suppression of riots or tumults, shall in such cases be entitled to receive pay in such manner, and at such rates, as the officers and soldiers of His Majesty's Regular Forces do now receive, and shall, during the time of their being continued in such service and so receiving pay as above, be subject to military discipline as the rest of His Majesty's Regular and Militia Troops. Provided always that no officer or soldier of any Volunteer corps shall be liable to be tried or punished by any Court Martial at any time, unless such Court Martial be composed entirely of officers serving in Volunteer corps, formed as aforesaid, such Court Martial to be assembled by Warrant under His Majesty's sign manual, or by Warrant from some general or other officer duly authorised to hold Courts Martial."

By Section 2,

> "That it shall be lawful for all mayors, bailiffs, constables, tithingmen, headboroughs and other chief magistrates and officers of cities, towns, parishes, tithings and places, and (in their absence) for any one Justice of the Peace inhabiting within or near any such city, town, parish, tithing or place (but for no others), and they or he are or is hereby required to quarter and billet the sergeants, corporals and

drummers of such corps or companies as aforesaid, and their horses, in inns, livery stables, alehouses, victualling houses, and all houses of persons selling brandy, strong waters, cyder, wine or metheglin, by retail, upon application made to any such mayors, bailiffs, constables, tithing-men, head-boroughs, or other chief magistrates, or officers by His Majesty's Lieutenants, or other the officer commanding the said corps or companies."

By Section 3,

"That if the officer commanding any such corps or company as aforesaid shall discharge from such corps or company any person who shall have been enlisted or enrolled as aforesaid, and if such person shall refuse or neglect, on being required by such commanding officer, to deliver up any arms, accoutrements, or clothing, which shall have been entrusted to his custody, every person so refusing or neglecting shall, on being convicted thereof before any Justice of the Peace of the county within which such corps or company shall have been formed, forfeit and pay the sum of Ten Pounds to be levied by distress and sale of the offender's goods and chattels by warrant under the hand and seal of such Justice, rendering the over-plus (if any) on demand, after deducting the charges of such distress and sale, to the person whose goods and chattels shall have been so distrained and sold; and for want of sufficient distress, such Justice is hereby required to commit such offender to the common gaol of the county, riding or place where the offence shall have been committed, for any time not exceeding one month; and the moneys arising by such penalties shall be paid to the treasurer of the county, riding or place where such offence shall have been committed, to be applied as part of the stock of such county, riding or place."

By Section 4,

"That all commissioned officers of the said Corps, who shall be disabled in actual service, shall be entitled to half-pay; and all non-commissioned officers and soldiers so disabled, to the benefit of Chelsea Hospital; and the widows of commissioned officers killed in the service, to a pension for life."

By Section 5,

Exemption of Volunteers from Militia service.

"That no person who shall be enlisted or enrolled in any corps or company of Volunteers as aforesaid, shall, during the time that he is serving in the said corps or company, be liable to serve personally or provide a substitute to serve in the Militia, provided he shall produce to the Deputy Lieutenants, assembled at the sub-division meetings holden in the several counties for the purpose of hearing appeals against the Militia List returned from each parish, an affidavit of his having been enrolled as aforesaid, and a certificate signed by the commanding officer of the said corps or company, that he has, for the space of six weeks immediately preceding such sub-division meeting, punctually attended at all such times and places as may have been agreed upon for the exercise of such corps or company."

And by Section 6 it was provided

"That this Act shall continue in force during the present war only."

It has for many centuries been a well recognised and established constitutional rule that it is unlawful for the Crown to keep in its pay armed forces, except with the previously expressed sanction of Parliament. Instances have occurred when this rule has been disregarded by Ministers, one notable occasion being when a circular, dated 14th March, 1794, Mr. Pitt then being at the head of affairs, was addressed to Lords Lieutenant of counties for raising Volunteers without previous Parliamentary sanction. Clode, in his "Military Forces of the Crown," states that this was the final attempt recorded, in breach of the above rule, to raise supplies for the defence of the Kingdom without Parliamentary consent.

Mr. Pitt's Circular.

This unauthorised circular, with the plan and scheme for providing for the safety of the country against any attempts on the part of the enemy and for the augmentation of the forces for internal defence, affords such interesting and instructive reading, that I produce it in full :—

Whitehall,

14th March, 1794.

It is naturally to be supposed that gentlemen of weight or property, in different parts of the kingdom, will separately stand forward, in order to carry into execution the several parts of the plan for the secürity of the country ; but it seems also desirable that a general subscription should be opened, to be under the direction of committees, for the purpose of assisting in carrying into execution all or any of the measures therein suggested, as circumstances shall appear to require.

In order to provide more completely for the security of the country against any attempts which may be made on the part of the enemy, it may be expedient to adopt some or all of the following measures :—

1— To augment the Militia by Volunteer Companies *as was practised in the last war*,* or by an additional number of Volunteers, to be added as privates to each Company.

2—To form Volunteer Companies in particular towns, especially in those situated on or near the sea coast, for the purpose of the local defence of the particular place where they may be raised according to the accompanying plan ; or such other as may, on application for that purpose, be approved of as best adapted to the circumstances of any particular towns.

3—To raise Volunteer troops of fencible cavalry, consisting of not less than fifty nor more than eighty per troop, who will be to serve only during the war and within the Kingdom. The officers will have temporary rank only, and will not be entitled to half-pay. The arms, accoutrements and clothing will be furnished by the Government, but the levy money for the men to be furnished by the persons who undertake to raise such troops ; and the horses to be found by them but to be paid for at a reasonable price by the Government.

---

*That of American Independence.

A person raising two troops to have the temporary rank of major; four troops, that of lieutenant-colonel; and six troops, that of colonel.

4—To form other bodies of cavalry within particular counties and districts, to consist of gentlemen and yeomanry, or such persons as they shall bring forward, according to the plans to be approved of by the King, or by the Lords Lieutenant, under the authority of His Majesty, and the officers to receive temporary commissions from His Majesty; and the muster rolls also to be approved by His Majesty or by the Lords Lieutenant at periods to be fixed. No levy money to be given; and the horses to be furnished by the gentry or yeomanry who compose the corps, but the arms and accoutrements to be supplied at the expense of the public. Such corps to be exercised only at such times as shall be fixed by warrant from His Majesty, or by application of the Lords Lieutenant; to be liable to be embodied or called out of their counties by special direction from His Majesty, in case of actual appearance of invasion; and to be liable to be called upon by order of His Majesty, or by the Lord Lieutenant or Sheriff of the county, to act within the county or the adjacent counties, for the suppression of riots or tumults. In either case, while actually in service, they shall receive pay as cavalry, and be liable to the provisions of the Mutiny Bill.

5—To enrol and appoint places of rendezvous for a sufficient number of persons in different parishes and districts, particularly in places near the sea coast, to serve as pioneers, or to assist the regular forces in any manner that may be necessary on the shortest notice in case of emergency.

17th March, 1794.

"PLAN OF AUGMENTATION OF THE FORCES FOR INTERNAL DEFENCE.

Companies of Infantry for manning batteries on the coast: each to consist of—

1 captain; 2 lieutenants; 3 sergeants; 2 corporals; 2 drummers; 60 private men at least; one-third to be armed with firelocks, the others to have pikes 8 feet long.

The officers to be recommended by the Lords Lieutenant of Counties, but to have commissions from the King.

To assemble two days in each week to practise.

The officers to be allowed pay, and the non-commissioned officers and private men each one shilling a day for the days they are at exercise. To have clothing given by Government that they may all be uniform. Not to be removed more than 5 miles from home, unless ordered by His Majesty on the appearance of invasion, when they are to be called out and paid like other militia, but not to be removed out of their county.

To be under military law when embodied and under the command of a general officer.

Officers on half-pay will be accepted, if recommended."

Although, as I have said, this circular was totally alien to the spirit of our constitution and subversive of the salutary principle that makes the armed forces of the Crown dependent on a vote in Committee of supply—a principle without which every form of Government, whatever its name, is in effect an absolute tyranny—it appears to have excited little adverse comment at the time, and was probably condoned even by those disposed to carp at it by the maxim that necessity knows no law. And what were England's necessities then and for 20 years thereafter we can form little conception to-day. The Lords Lieutenant and the Magistracy throughout the length and breadth of the land bestirred themselves to give it effect and Volunteer Forces were formed under the 34, George III., c. 31 ; but the treaty of Amiens and their consequent disbandment effected that these corps have left few traces to perpetuate their memory.

Before embarking upon a consideration of the many enactments which, from the year 1797 till the next century was well advanced, followed each other in rapid and bewildering succession, it is convenient to pause and consider what was the plight of England that necessitated provision after provision, suggested scheme after scheme and placed one day upon the Statute Book a measure only to be amended, abrogated and displaced by some new device the next. Verily the condition of our national fortunes was enough to try the stoutest nerves and to flutter the staunchest heart. Ireland was honeycombed with sedition. The French expedition of 38 ships under Hoche was only prevented from landing by a hurricane that swept Bantry Bay. As in the days of the Armada, so then, the very elements raged to defend our shores. The North of Ireland seemed almost of a mind with the Southern and Western Provinces, where English statesmen have been taught to regard treason as a natural product of the soil. General Lake, dispatched to stamp out the smouldering fires of rebellion, discovered 50,000 muskets, 72 cannon, and 70,000 pikes—a large provision in such times and in so poor a country. The spies of the Government, subtle and ubiquitous, informed by their peculiar arts alike of the plans of the Irish conspirators and of the allurements held out to them by the French, left the British Ministers no room for doubt that the attempt of Hoche would be renewed, and one cannot hope every day for a blighting storm. As a matter of fact the attempt was renewed in the following year by General Humbert who landed at Killala.

But it was from France the real danger was to be feared, and Napoleon used Ireland merely as a pawn in the game, and no man could predict the hour when the artillery of war forging across the

Straits of Dover might be hurled against our shores. The designs of Napoleon were almost as well known in this country as at the Tuilleries, and what was not known was magnified by the fears excited by a career that had scarce known the name of failure.

It will hardly be credited that so universal was the sense of imminent danger that even the clergy contemplated taking up arms, but their ardour was damped by the hierarchy. At a meeting of the two Archbishops and eleven Bishops, held April 28th, 1798, the following resolutions were passed unanimously. Resolved, "that it would not conduce, in any considerable degree, to the defence and safety of the country, and would interfere with the proper duties of the profession, if the clergy were to accept commissions in the army, be enrolled in any military corps, or be trained to the use of arms." Resolved further, "that in the case of actual invasion or dangerous insurrection, it will be the duty of every clergyman to give his assistance in repelling both, in any way that the urgency of the case may require."

It was at this juncture that Ministers devised those Armed Associations whose constitution is so generally neglected by the ordinary historian, but which are interesting alike as shewing to what extremities our country was reduced, how curious the measures resorted to, and how undauntedly the people responded to the call of their country voiced by Parliament.

Armed Associations. (38 Geo. III., c. 27.)

These Associations appear to have been formed under the Statute passed in April, 1798. The preamble recited that it is desirable to make provision "for applying in the most expeditious manner, and with the greatest effect, the voluntary services of the King's loyal subjects for the defence of the Kingdom." The Lord Lieutenant of each County is directed to procure returns of the numbers of men residing within the several counties, ridings, stewartries, cities and places, who shall be of the age of 15 years and under the age of 60 years; distinguishing which of them are, by reason of infirmity, incapable of active service, and which of them are engaged in any Volunteer Corps, and what corps, and which of them are willing to engage themselves to be armed, arrayed, trained and exercised for the defence of the Kingdom, and upon what terms; and which of them are willing to engage in cases of emergency, either gratuitously or for hire, as boatmen, or as drivers of carriages or horses, or drivers of waggons, carts, or cattle, or as pioneers, or other labourers for any works or labour which may be necessary for the public service. Aliens and

Quakers were to be classed apart. Enquiries were to be instituted as to what stores of hay, &c., existed, that might be useful to an enemy, and that it might be necessary to remove or destroy; also as to the best means of removing to a place of security the sick and infirm. Officers were to be appointed to "array, train and exercise" such men as might volunteer. It is obvious that Ministers could only be justified in taking such precautions by the most pressing apprehensions of the imminent landing of a foreign foe, and of the possibility of his not only landing but over-running the country. The immature age, too, at which the youth of the country were to be permitted to serve points to a severe dearth of able bodied men. The act was limited to the continuance of the war with France. Novel as were its provisions it had a smooth passage through Parliament. Mr. Tierney said, "the only way to render the Bill perfectly satisfactory to the country, was to give every person an opportunity of undertaking a voluntary service." "He gave the measure," he added, "his hearty approval, and should continue to do so as long as the service on the part of the people was not compulsory. It would, indeed, be extremely invidious, and be productive of much animosity, if the names of those who, from the nature of their occupations, could not serve, were to be exhibited at the Church door of their parish and be stigmatised as disaffected to the Government, when, in the hour of real danger, no persons could be more sincere and zealous in their endeavour to repel the enemy."

Mr. Secretary Dundas in reply said that he "was happy to find the House on consideration was convinced of the necessity of the measure and the general good consequences that must be derived from its being carried into effect. He had, at the opening, said that the service was totally to be left to the patriotic ardour and voluntary zeal of the people. There was nothing like a requisition intended, but unless a regular return was made it was impossible to know where the Lords Lieutenant were to apply for the succour and aid intended. Some counties, he said, had done a great deal to meet the Bill. From the return which had been made by several hundreds to the Lords Lieutenant of many counties, those who wished to aid at the present conjunction desired to know how they should arm or whether they should assist as waggoners or with carts, pitchforks, &c." The House, he added, "would see the necessity of arming the people before the hour of danger, and to ascertain the number who were willing to be arrayed." He concluded by declaring "that it was not intended to act invidiously by publishing the names of those who would not serve or exhibiting their names on the church door.

The committee then went through all the clauses, and the report thereon was ordered to be received on the following day. On the 31st March, on the Bill being brought up, Mr. Dundas said "that he had received several letters from farmers and others in the county of Kent expressing their zeal to contribute to the public service, and also their apprehensions of being liable to be carried away under the direction of the Lord or Deputy Lieutenant upon every rumour or danger on the coast that might result from French menaces. They therefore wished to restrict their services to such occasions as the Commanding Officer should deem necessary. That feeling the propriety of these suggestions it was his intention to bring in a clause to that effect on the third reading of the Bill on Monday."

On the 20th April, 1798, Mr. Secretary Dundas delivered to the House a message from His Majesty, and on its being read, he moved the thanks of the House and its ready concurrence with His Majesty in every measure for the defence and safety of the realm. MR. SHERIDAN then rose, and in a speech of peculiar brilliancy and erudition, in very energetic language pointed out the necessity for the House supporting the Government. He then entered into the several excuses different persons made for not coming forward, excuses which he ridiculed, and proved the necessity of every man undertaking the duty of preparing and arming himself for the safety of the country. He thought the system of arming might be adopted with great propriety by certain classes of persons for the defence of the Metropolis. He instanced likewise the propriety of certain people who were often seen attendant upon persons of property being made serviceable to the state. It was common, he said, for persons in fashionable life to have one or two hulking fellows stuck behind their carriages. *An Armed Association** of these would be highly beneficial. He mentioned likewise, in a strain of irony, a class of gentlemen who ought to come forward on the present occasion—these were young gentlemen of fashion and spirit who were often seen entering into fruit shops or lounging up and down Bond Street. Though no rigid censor, he must say their time, he thought, might be much better employed in training themselves to defend their country. The address was then voted *nem. con.*

*Can it be that Sheridan was the first to apply this term to the forces raised under this Act? It is not used in the Act itself.—R. P. B.

These Armed Associations are clearly distinguished from the ordinary Volunteer Corps. They were a sort of emergency corps, and their duties were expected to be purely local. They were intended, apparently, rather to harass the enemy in his march through the country than to confront him in battle. They were to be a sort of guerilla, and at the same time they were to assist the military authorities in matters of forage, and in alleviating for the aged and infirm the horrors attendant upon the presence of an armed force in the heart of the country. The officers' commissions strictly define the limitations of their service:

"George R.

George III. by the Grace of God of the United Kingdom and Ireland, King, Defender of the Faith, &c.

To our trusted and well beloved .

Greeting.

We do by these presents constitute and appoint you to be, during our pleasure, captain of a Company of the Association of the inhabitants of the parish of in the county of associated to serve, without pay, for the protection thereof in case of any emergency, at the requisition of the civil power, but not to take rank in our army nor the said Association to be subject to military discipline or to serve out of the said parish, except of their own accord.

Given at our Court at St. James' the on the year of our reign.

By His Majesty's command,

PORTLAND."

To Esq., Captain
in the Association of the
parish of

To facilitate the working of the statute, Mr. Secretary Dundas addressed a circular letter of instruction to the Lords Lieutenant of Counties, and suggested plans or schemes of procedure accompanied the circular. It directs the Lords Lieutenant immediately to determine on the place or depôt to which the live and dead stock were to be removed; the manner in which they were to be taken care of at such depôts, the routes which they were to take and those which they were to avoid, in order not to interfere with the movements of the military; the allotment of yeomanry or other escorts for their protection, or for enforcing the regulations established respecting them; the necessary arrangements for removing infirm persons, women and children, and next to them such articles of property as were most valuable; the precautions to be taken for destroying the remainder, and for obtaining, by previous estimate agreeably to the provisions of the Act, some grounds by which the amount of compensation to be made to owners of property so destroyed might be ascertained; the separate place of rendezvous to which every description of persons, whether connected with the armed force or otherwise, should repair, on the signals of alarm being made, the arrangement of those signals, &c.

No Volunteer was to be admitted into the Armed Associations whose habitual occupation and place of residence were not within the division of the county to which the Association might extend. Those who preferred cavalry might be received into the nearest troop, or formed into separate troops, of not less than 40 nor more than 80 men. The officers were to be recommended by the Lords Lieutenant, and entitled to yeomanry cavalry allowance and assistance. To be trained for six hours, once a week, and in case of invasion serve within the military district to which they belonged.

The armed Infantry was to consist of companies, from 60 to 120 men, armed as volunteer corps of towns, or a certain proportion with pikes, with uniform clothing or a fair allowance for the same, and to be commanded by proper officers, resident, and having not less than £50 income in land within the county, or renting land in the same to the amount of £1,000. The sons of persons so qualified, or persons having previously held some military commission, rendering themselves eligible for such a situation, were exempted from these restrictions.

Persons accustomed to military service, on half-pay or not, were to be preferred and allowed full pay. To be trained six hours once a week, and serve within the limits above.

Every man of the Volunteer Corps, who thought proper to claim it, was to be entitled to 1/- per week, paid by the Government. A depôt for the arms to be provided at a safe place within each county. None but known and respectable housekeepers, or persons who could bring at least two such housekeepers to answer for their good conduct, were to be admitted. The circular concluded by strongly recommending to every description of persons, to lay aside all untimely and misplaced jealousy respecting the military power, with which every arrangement must be concerted.

Schedule number 1 contained columns for the total of men between the ages of 15 and 60, infirm or incapable of active service, serving in Volunteer corps or Armed Associations, aliens, quakers, persons, who, from age, infancy or other cause, might probably be incapable of removing themselves.

Schedule number 2 contained columns of the oxen, cows, young cattle and colts, sheep and goats, pigs, horses, waggons, carts, corn mills. Quantity of corn that could be ground in a week. Ovens. The amount of bread the same could bake in 24 hours. Quarters of wheat, oats, barley, beans and peas. Loads of hay and straw. Sacks of potatoes, flour, or other meal. Quarters of malt.

Schedule number 3 referred to the returns to be made of the number of persons between the ages of 15 and 60, willing to serve, and in what capacity, whether on horseback or on foot. The Cavalry was to be armed with swords and pistols, the Infantry with firelocks and pikes. The number of persons between the ages of 15 and 60 willing to act as pioneers and labourers, the implements they could bring; such as felling axes, pick axes, spades, shovels, bill-hooks, saws. The number of persons between the ages of 15 and 60 willing to act as servants with cattle. The number of persons between the ages of 15 and 60 willing to act as servants with teams. The number of persons between the ages of 15 and 60 willing to act as guides.

I extract from the *Annual Register* the plan sent to all the parishes of Great Britain, May, 1797. It is as follows:—

"PLAN of the General Association of the inhabitants of the parish of to serve without pay for the protection thereof, in case of any emergency, at the requisition of the civil power, to be submitted to the confirmation of the vestry to be called for that purpose.

1—A General Association shall be formed, which Association shall be composed of householders and such other inmates as shall be recommended by two householders at the least, being themselves members of the Association, and approved, if judged necessary, by a committee of the Association to be chosen at a general meeting.

2—That the members of the Association shall put down their names and places of abode in a book, to be provided and kept in the vestry for that purpose.

3—The parish to be divided into districts; the inhabitants of each district, who enrol themselves, to be divided into classes of 50 each, to be commanded by an inhabitant of that district, who shall be considered as captain of the class, and act as such, under a commission from His Majesty. This officer to be recommended by a committee of the Association to the Lord Lieutenant. Each class shall carry a flag to distinguish it, and the person who is to carry it shall be nominated by the captain of each class.

4—The majority in any class shall be empowered to reject from that class any individual, whether householder or inmate, who shall appear to them to be an unfit member thereof.

5—In case of alarm and at the requisition of the civil power, the class to be assembled at a rendezvous, which shall be previously appointed by the captain.

6—Places of general rendezvous for all classes shall be appointed by the committee of the Association.

7—All persons enrolling themselves to furnish their own arms; which arms shall be either firelocks and bayonets, pikes, or any other arms which shall be approved of by the committee.

8—A list of the members in each class to be made, and a copy lodged with each member in that class, together with a copy of such instructions, signed by the captain of the class, as may be found necessary for their more speedily collecting together, in case of alarm, and for regulating the proper quantity of ammunition which each member furnished with a firelock shall constantly be provided with.

9—No member of the Association to be required to meet to exercise, but each class may be mustered with their arms, by its captain, at such convenient and stated times as shall be agreed upon; those who furnish themselves with firelocks will, at their request, be allowed a sergeant or corporal by Government, to teach them the use of firearms, in order that they may more conveniently act together, either in separate classes or jointly with others in the same class, as shall be agreed upon by the members of the association. This was to be determined by each parish to suit the convenience of members.

10—A hat and feathers, or some other mark of distinction, to be adopted; or those provided with firelocks, if formed into classes by themselves, to have a uniform if they chuse it.

11—Not to go out of the parish except of their own accord.

12—No person who is engaged in any military corps, or other Association, to be appointed as captain; but such persons may enrol themselves and only engage to join this Association when not called away by other duties.

N.B.—The above plan is only suggested as a general outline, which may be varied and modified in such a manner as may best suit the local situations and conveniences of the inhabitants of such parishes as shall think proper to associate for the mutual security and protection of themselves and their property, upon the principle here laid down.

As some small expense must necessarily be incurred for the purchase of flags for the different classes, paying for the stamps of the commissions (His Majesty being graciously pleased to grant them free of every other expense), and some other trifling incidental charges, a subscription to be opened where every householder who approves of this plan, and will give it support, may subscribe any small sum he pleases, not exceeding the sum of shillings, to defray the same. Such female householders as are willing to signify their approbation of this plan, and give their support to it, to be requested to authorise some householder in the parish who is himself a member of the Association, to sign their names, and to attest that it is by their authority; and in that case such female householder may, in concurrence with another householder, being a

member of the Association, recommend any householder or inmate, being proper persons, to join in the Association, and the person so recommended shall be enrolled in like manner as the other members of the Association.

The method adopted in various localities for complying with the statute and establishing an Armed Association was somewhat after this wise. Individual inhabitants were first approached and sounded. The co-operation of a number of the leading citizens assured, a town's meeting was convened and a chairman selected. In corporate towns doubtless the Mayor presided, in others the Constable. The resolutions submitted pledged the meeting to contribute every assistance, collectively and individually, to the support of the constitutions of the country, the due execution of the laws, the maintenance of civil order and government, and the immediate suppression of all riots or tumults. Then followed a resolution to establish an Association consisting of householders or such other inhabitants of the neighbourhood as might be recommended individually by two householders, the right being reserved to a committee to reject an undesirable candidate. This committee supervised the funds of the Association, but had no military authority. It was responsible to a quarterly meeting of the Association. The subaltern officers were selected by ballot of the members of the Association, and recommended to the commanding officer, who laid the recommendation before the King.

The members of the Association provided their uniforms at their own cost. They drilled together twice weekly, and were, on occasions, as that of a fire for instance, summoned by beat of drum.

The armed companies were formed into divisions, one of which was assigned to each subaltern officer, who, having the address of every gentleman in his division, had to forward all orders for his attendance at the general rendezvous, which orders, in cases of emergency, were to be secret. No gentleman of the corps was to go out of his district without informing the commanding officer by letter of the time he intended to be absent and of his return, and leaving directions by which letters might reach him as early as possible.

Artificers.

The arms and accoutrements were usually found by Government. To many of the Armed Associations were attached auxiliary corps of artificers. These were intended for the assistance of the armed portion of the force, or any other service which the exigencies of the moment might require, and particularly to convey and work the engines in case of fire.

The services of the corps were limited to its own parish from which it was not bound to move on any service unless by general consent. Their military ardour proved so strong that as often as not the members of the Association offered to extend their services in case of emergency anywhere within their military district.

Those householders to whom it would have been an inconvenience to have borne arms were sworn to act as special constables and, as forming part of or connected with the Association, they had assigned to them their different duties.

Most elaborate and detailed plans and schemes were formulated for expeditiously assembling the members of the Association, particularly the artificers and special constables attached to the Corps, in the event of fire. In fact, officers, non-commissioned officers and men in their various departments and grades were told off to some exact duty and each one assigned a place.

With such particularity was the scheme prepared in some cases that each member of the Corps was directed to keep his regimentals, firelocks, &c., in his bedroom, so as to be able to dress the moment he got up, also to provide himself with a dark lantern, to be lighted at the nearest watch-box.

Voluntary subscriptions for the support of the Associations were freely made. In 1798 no less than two and a half million pounds was subscribed to this fund. Sir Robert Peel, of Bury, alone contributed £10,000; the Bank of England, £200,000; the King and Queen, out of their private purse, £20,000 and £5,000 respectively. Nor did the nobility and gentry of the country content themselves with pecuniary assistance. The most considerable of the Associations and the one charged, perhaps, with the most responsible duties was that of Pimlico. The royal palace stood within its district. Its committee included men so eminent as the Right Honourable William Windham, M.P., His Majesty's Secretary at War, other Secretaries of State, the Duke of Hamilton, the Earls of Carlisle, Egremont and Ossory, Viscount Belgrave, Viscount Morpeth, Lord Malmesbury, K.B., members of the Indian Board and the chief members of the Treasury and Admiralty Boards.

The Bloomsbury and Inns of Court Associations admitted tradesmen and other householders and also "clerks of gentlemen in the profession of the law." But great discrimination was exercised in the admission of candidates to so truly select a corps.

1798. April 19th. Nor was the city behind the more aristocratic quarters of London in forming Armed Associations. At the Court of Common Council it was reported that the Duke of York had written to enquire what steps were contemplated by the city fathers. It transpired that only one, the Cornhill Association, had been formed. It was resolved to take steps for spreading the movement to every ward of the city. The Phœnix Fire Office offered the services of the firemen, to be trained as artillerymen at the expense of the Office. The directors of the Bank of England resolved to form a regiment for the defence of the Bank. On April 26th each alderman was desired to repair to his ward and call the inhabitants together for the purpose of forming associations for learning the use of arms.

39 Geo. III, 35. The members of these Armed Associations enjoyed in common with the Volunteers two privileges. Opinions may differ as to the relative value of these privileges: the one was, under certain
39 Geo. III, 32. conditions, exemption from the Militia ballot. The other, which required an Act of King, Lords and Commons to secure it, was exemption from the duty on hair powder.

Uniforms. The mention of powder suggests the cognate topic of uniforms which, in the corps of Volunteers existing at this period, varied with the taste of the officers and commanders. The costumes most in vogue were blue or scarlet, with facings of different colors. Some corps adopted coats and hats, others jackets and caps with the appointments of Fusileer regiments. Prior to 1796 a three-cornered hat was worn which, in that year, gave place to the hat vulgarly styled a 'stove-pipe.' It surmounted powdered hair worn *en queue*, or, as we say, pig-tail, a fashion not extinct till 1808.

Pay. As to the pay, if pay it might be called, of those who were members of Volunteer corps, or, apparently, of Armed Associations, it is scarcely necessary to say it was characterised by the niggardliness ever displayed by the War Office in its dealings with the voluntary forces of the country. An officer of a company, if entitled to the half-pay of a subaltern, was to be allowed the difference between his half-pay and the full pay of the rank by virtue of which he held his half-pay. One subaltern officer in a company, who should have been theretofore engaged in a military line, but did not enjoy half-pay, was to be entitled to a daily allowance equivalent to the half-pay of whatever subaltern commission he might hold in the company. There was to be no pay for chaplains or surgeons except on actual service. The non-commissioned officers and privates, *should they think proper to claim it*,—a proviso eminently calculated to raise invidious distinctions—were to be allowed 1/- per day, for every day of exercise, not exceeding one day a week. Three hours' exercise constituted a day of service. Where a sergeant, properly qualified to drill a company, was employed, he was to be entitled to full pay.

The rates of pay were adjusted in accordance with the following table:—

For each day of exercise:—

	£	s.	d.
Colonel	1	2	6
Lieutenant-Colonel		15	11
Major		14	1
Captain		9	5
Lieutenant or Quarter-Master ..		4	4
Ensign		3	5
Adjutant		3	9
Sergeant		1	0
Corporal		1	0
Drummer		1	0
Private		1	0
For each day in cases where constant pay was allowed:			
Captain on half-pay as such (being precluded by law from receiving his half-pay)..		9	5
Lieutenant on half-pay as such (being still to receive his half-pay as formerly)..		2	2
Ensign on half-pay as Ensign (being still to receive his half-pay as formerly)..		1	8
One Sergeant per Company ..		1	6¼

The verbiage in this schedule is that of the War Office of 1798, not that of the author. One is uncertain which most to admire: the elegance of the English or the skill by which the rates of pay are so arranged as to give the greatest possible amount of trouble to a bookkeeper.

A quaint document, entitled the "Original conditions of enrolment of Loyal Lincolnshire Volunteer Villagers,"—an Armed Association—and dated May 9th, 1798, is interesting reading. The members agreed to enrol themselves in order to form one or two companies of Infantry, of not less than sixty nor more than one hundred and twenty men each, upon the following terms, namely:—To be trained at least once a week, at least for three hours, and to fix a second time for training in the week, as often as their engagements in country business would admit of it; but the training once a week was to be on a Sunday, and the attendance on Divine Service was to be a part of their duty when they met for the purpose. To be armed with firelocks. To have a fair allowance to provide uniform and clothing, at the expense of the Government; and such of the Company as might think proper to claim it, to have the one shilling per week graciously offered by His Majesty, upon its appearing that such persons had attended the muster and training above mentioned, by the return properly signed. It was agreed to obey the officers upon all occasions, when under their command, in the same manner as if the Association were called into actual service. The members desire to be styled "The Loyal Lincolnshire Volunteer Villagers," and they expected to receive the usual pay of infantry when on actual service. By certain additional conditions of enrolment, the Loyal Lincolnshire Volunteer Villagers engaged to subject themselves to the following forfeitures, in the cases under-mentioned, namely:—

1—For being absent without leave of their commanding officer, two shillings; each non-commissioned officer, one shilling; each private, sixpence.

2—For withdrawing from the field of exercise, without leave of commanding officer, before the expiration of the time of exercise, each non-commissioned officer, one shilling; each private, sixpence.

3—For withdrawing wholly from the Association, without consent of commanding officer, each commissioned officer, twenty-one shillings; each non-commissioned officer, ten shillings and sixpence, together with his complete uniform; each private, five shillings, together with his complete uniform.

4—For being in a state of intoxication at the roll-calling or during the exercise, each commissioned officer, ten shillings and sixpence; each non-commissioned officer, two shillings; each private, one shilling.

5—For appearing at the roll-calling not properly dressed in uniform (except when it happened that the weather of the day of exercise was rainy or snowy), and with all the accoutrements and arms clean and in perfect order, of whatever rank the defaulter might be, the forfeit of one shilling, the like forfeit for refusing to obey the command of the commanding officer.

6—It was a duty expected of the sergeants to visit in their respective districts to examine the arms, and if they reported the arms or accoutrements of anyone unclean, such person to forfeit one shilling, and if the arms were not forthcoming for his inspection, the person to whom such arms were allotted to forfeit two shillings and sixpence.

7—Every Volunteer of the Association to be accountable for the uniform, arms and accoutrements, and to deliver them up in perfect condition whenever required; but in case of refusal or their being damaged or misused, to forfeit the original price of them.

8—Silence during the exercise being essentially requisite, every Volunteer who should then talk or speak after the word "attention" was given, should first be called to by name by the officer or sergeant giving the word of command, and for the second default of that kind, and so for every other the like default during the exercise, should forfeit sixpence.

9—The several forfeits were to be weekly collected by the sergeants in rotation, and paid into the hands of the captain of the company, to increase a fund for due demonstration of joy upon the next anniversary of His Majesty's birthday.

N.B.—Certain of the signatories further agreed and consented to give up from their pay 17/8 to provide better clothing than could be procured from the 20/- allowed for that purpose by the Government. (This regiment, it may be added, is now the 2nd Loyal North Lancaster Regiment, formerly the 81st Foot).

It is estimated by Mr. Clode that between the years 1794 and 1804 the Volunteer forces of the country numbered not less than 410,000 men, inclusive of 70,000 Irish Volunteers. These forces received from Parliament the most gratifying recognition of their patriotism in offering their services in the hour of their country's need. I do not hesitate to set forth the votes of thanks of both Houses and also those of the Common Council of the City of London, which latter, of course, had special reference to the metropolitan levies. Before doing so one may conveniently at this point describe those reviews of the London Volunteers in the years 1799 and 1801 which were doubtless intended as a Royal recognition of the Volunteer forces throughout the country, and also those ceremonies subsequent to the conclusion of the Treaty of Amiens which were fondly believed by the country to voice the *Nunc dimittis* of the Volunteers.

The King having expressed his intention of reviewing the 1799.
London Volunteers on his birthday, the 4th June, in Hyde Park, the Honourable Artillery Company paraded at head-quarters at 4 o'clock in the morning, and at half-past five marched off to Hyde Park, where they were amongst the first to arrive, and took up their post on the right of the line. At nine o'clock a signal gun was fired announcing the approach of His Majesty, when the guns of the Company fired a royal salute of 21 guns. The King passed down the ranks and afterwards the whole force marched past, headed by the Company; and "general officers of the greatest reputation were heard to say that they never saw anything better done." Sixty-five corps, containing 8,000 officers and men, were present under arms on this occasion. The King was attended by the Prince of Wales, the Dukes of York, Kent, Cumberland,

and Gloucester, and a numerous staff. A large number of spectators were present, not less, it was said, than 100,000. The evolutions were considerably impeded by a high wind and much rain.

The following General Order was issued :—

"GENERAL ORDERS."

"His Royal Highness, the Commander-in-Chief, has His Majesty's particular commands to communicate to the several corps of Volunteers assembled this morning in Hyde Park, the great satisfaction with which His Majesty witnessed their regularity and military appearance, and the striking manifestation of their cordial and affectionate attachment to His Majesty. It is particularly pleasing to His Majesty to observe the effects of the unwearied diligence and attention of the officers, and of the zeal and alacrity of the Volunteers composing this truly respectable force, which entitle them to the strongest expressions of His Majesty's approbation, and which gratify the just sentiments of national pride, in the same proportion in which they add to the public security. His Majesty cannot express the satisfaction He has received on this occasion without the pleasing recollection of the principles of attachment to the constitution under which those corps have been formed, and without considering their appearance and conduct on this day as a proof of their firm determination to support His Majesty in transmitting it, with its blessings, unimpaired, to their posterity. His Royal Highness has peculiar pleasure in making known His Majesty's gracious sentiments on an occasion so acceptable to his feelings; and he requests the respective commanding officers to take the earliest opportunity of communicating them to the several corps seen by His Majesty this morning.

FREDERICK, F. M.

"Horse Guards, June 4th, 1799."

On the Saturday following the 4th June, a grand dinner was given by the commanders and field officers of the Volunteer corps who were inspected in Hyde Park. Amongst those present were His Royal Highness the Duke of York, Commander-in-Chief, in the chair; the Prince of Wales, the Duke of Gloucester, the Stadholder of Holland, Cabinet Ministers, General Officers of the London District, Lord Mayor and Sheriffs, Earl of Leicester and many other public characters,—the health of His Royal Highness being drunk as Captain-General of the Honourable Artillery Company.

Whilst on the subject of dinners, one not less alluring to the civilian than the military mind, it may amuse to refer to the Gargantuan repast enjoyed by some 5,000 Volunteers of Kent, on August 1, 1799. The King, accompanied by the Queen and Princesses Augusta and Elizabeth, had reviewed these troops at Lord Romney's seat, Moat Park, Maidstone. The men were regaled by Lord Romney and accounted for the following substantial bill of fare, from which it might fairly be augured that if their prowess with the bayonet equalled that with the knife and fork they would be no mean foe.

3 score lambs in quarters.
200 dishes of roast beef.
700 fowls, 3 on a dish
220 meat pies.
300 hams.
320 tongues.
220 fruit pies.
220 dishes of boiled beef.
220 joints of roast veal.
7 pipes of port wine, bottled off, and
16 butts of ale, and as much
small beer was also placed in vessels to supply
the company.*

Another review in Hyde Park was ordered for Wednesday, the 22nd of July, 1801, when 4,734 men were present. On this occasion the following letter was issued from the Horse Guards:—

"Horse Guards, July 22nd, 1801.

Sir,

Their Royal Highnesses the Prince of Wales and the Commander-in-Chief desire that their warmest acknowledgements may be communicated to the several Corps of Volunteers which assembled this morning in Hyde Park, for the order, regularity and discipline which they displayed on the occasion. The Commander-in-Chief will endeavour, in his representation to His Majesty, to do justice to the attention of the commanding officers, which was evinced in the most satisfactory manner by the soldier-like appearance of their respective Corps, and likewise to the assiduity with which the officers and private men have discharged those honorable duties which an affection for His Majesty's person, and a just regard for the best and dearest interests of their country, originally induced them to undertake, and in which they are prompted by the same considerations to persevere with unabated zeal.

This day has afforded a subject of peculiar gratification with reference to the circumstance of the present moment, when the enemy again threaten an attempt on our coast. While the exertions of His Majesty's Forces by sea and land are thus assisted and seconded by the co-operation and support of the armed Volunteers of the country, the utmost confidence may be justly entertained that, under Divine Providence, we may bid defiance to the efforts of our enemies.

By order of His Royal Highness the Commander-in-Chief,

HARRY CALVERT, Adjutant General."

The preliminaries of the Peace of Amiens were signed on the 1st of October, 1801, and on the 10th, General Lauriston, first aide-de-camp to Bonaparte, arrived in London with the ratification, on which occasion the following circular letter was addressed to the

*Annual Register, XLI.

Lord Mayor, and by him communicated to the Volunteer Corps of the City of London:—

"Downing Street,
October 10th, 1801.

My Lord and Gentlemen,

I have received the King's commands to signify to you that in consequence of the happy event of the ratification of preliminary Articles of Peace between His Majesty and the French Government, it is become unnecessary to proceed further in the execution of the measures directed to be taken for carrying into effect the provisions of the Act of the 38th of the King, in the event of any attempt being made by the enemy to effect a landing in Great Britain.

His Majesty has directed me to add, that it is impossible for him on this occasion not to repeat, in the strongest terms, the deep and lasting sense which he entertains of that steady attachment to our established constitution, and that loyalty, spirit and perseverance, which has been manifested by the several Corps of Yeomanry and Volunteers in every part of this Kingdom. It is therefore His Majesty's pleasure that you should forthwith communicate this letter to the commanding officers of each Corps of Volunteers within the City of London, and direct them to read the same to their respective Corps, when next assembled, and to return them thanks, in His Majesty's name, for a conduct which has contributed so essentially towards maintaining the public security, and enabling His Majesty to bring the contest in which he has been engaged to an honourable and advantageous conclusion.

His Majesty has, at the same time, commanded me to state that there is every reason to hope that a continuance of the same disposition which has produced the signature and ratification of preliminaries of peace, will speedily lead to a definite treaty, but that, until that period arrives, it is indispensably necessary that there should be no relaxation in the preparations which have been made for the general defence. I have it, therefore, in command from His Majesty, to express his firm reliance, that the several Corps of Volunteers will continue to hold themselves in readiness for immediate service, and to be regularly trained and exercised as often as their circumstances will respectively admit.

I have the honour to be,
My Lord and Gentlemen,
Your obedient humble servant,
HOBART.

To the Lord Mayor and Court of Lieutenancy
of the City of London."

On Thursday, the 29th of April, 1802, the City Volunteers paraded and marched to St. Paul's Churchyard, the Honourable Artillery Company taking up their post on the right of the line of the City Volunteers, who extended down the south side of Fleet Street to St. Dunstan's Church, where the East India Volunteers formed the left of the line. The Lord Mayor received the King's Warrant and proclaimed the peace at the end of Chancery Lane, and then proceeded, accompanied by the Heralds, Life Guards, &c., to Wood Street and the Royal Exchange, where the proclamation was again read. Each Corps remained at the "shoulder" as the Lord Mayor passed, then wheeled into column, and when he arrived at the end of the line, the whole, headed by the Honourable Artillery Company, followed his lordship to the Mansion House. The Lord Mayor presented to each commanding officer a copy of the following vote of thanks from the House of Commons to the officers and non-commissioned officers and men, a letter of thanks from the King, after which the several Corps marched off to their respective quarters.

Martis, 6 Die Aprilis, 1802.

Resolved, *Nemine Contradicente*—

"That the thanks of this House be given to the officers of the several corps of Yeomanry and Volunteer Cavalry and Infantry, and of the Sea Fencibles which have been formed in Great Britain and Ireland during the course of the war, for the seasonable and eminent service they have rendered to their King and country."

Resolved, *Nemine Contradicente*—

"That this House doth highly approve of, and acknowledge the services of the non-commissioned officers and men of the several corps of Yeomanry and Volunteer Cavalry and Infantry, and of the Sea Fencibles, which have been formed in Great Britain and Ireland, during the course of the war, and that the same be communicated to them by the colonels and other commanding officers of the several corps, who are desired to thank them for their meritorious conduct."

Ordered—

"That Mr. Speaker do signify the said resolutions by letter to His Majesty's Lieutenant of each county, riding, and place in Great Britain, and to His Excellency the Lord Lieutenant of that part of the United Kingdom called Ireland.

J. LEY, Cl. D. Dom. Com."*

The following votes of thanks were resolved upon by the House of Lords and communicated by the Lord Chancellor to the Lords Lieutenant of Counties throughout Great Britain: —

Die Martis, 6 Aprilis, 1802.

Resolved, *Nemine Dissentiente*, by the Lords Spiritual and Temporal, in Parliament assembled,

"That the thanks of this House be given to the officers of the several corps of Yeomanry and Volunteer Cavalry and Infantry, and of the Sea Fencibles, which have been formed in Great Britain and Ireland during the course of the war, for the seasonable and eminent services they have rendered to their King and country."

---

*Commons' Journals, vol. lvii., pp. 303, 304; and Hansard's Parliamentary History, xxxvi., p. 463.

Die Martis, 6 Aprilis, 1802.

Resolved, *Nemine Dissentiente*, by the Lords Spiritual and Temporal in Parliament assembled,

> "That this House doth highly approve of, and acknowledge the services of the non-commissioned officers and men of the Corps of Yeomanry and Volunteer Cavalry and Infantry, and of the Sea Fencibles, which have been formed in Great Britain and Ireland during the course of the war, and that the same be communicated to them by the colonels and other commanding officers of the several Corps, who are desired to thank them for their meritorious conduct."

City of London.

At a Court of Common Council, held at the Guildhall, on Tuesday, the 15th of June, it was*

Resolved unanimously,

> "That the thanks of this Court be given to the commanders, and rest of the officers and gentlemen, of the several loyal Volunteer Military Associations for their readiness in coming forward in defence of their country, and fellow-citizens at a moment of great national difficulty and danger. For their spirited conduct in support of the civil power, and for opposing and suppressing, with temper and firmness, a lawless and misguided multitude, threatening to destroy not only the public peace, but the property of the city and metropolis. For their vigilance and generous exertions in preserving the property of their neighbours from the calamities of fire. For their persevering zeal and patriotism, in sacrificing their own personal convenience to their constitutional endeavours to protect the religion, laws, and liberties of their country from the machinations of foreign and domestic enemies."

WOODTHORPE.

On the 1st of June 1802 being appointed for a general Thanksgiving for peace, the City Volunteers attended divine service at St. Paul's.

Peace of Amiens, March 28th, 1802.

On the conclusion of the Treaty of Amiens, or shortly thereafter, the Volunteers and Armed Associations were for the most part disbanded, a few remained. It is interesting also to observe that some of these Corps or Associations appear to have become so imbued with the martial spirit that their members abandoned civil life and joined *en masse* those regiments more intimately connected with their own localities. Thus, the Staffordshire Volunteers became absorbed in the 80th Regiment (now the 2nd South Staffordshire), raised by Lord Paget for the third time in the year 1793. Also the Loyal Lincoln Volunteers (Villagers) became merged in the 81st Regiment (now 2nd Loyal North Lancaster), raised and embodied at Lincoln in 1794. The Prince of Wales Volunteers became part of the 82nd Regiment (now 2nd Prince

*Journals, vol. lxxx, fol. 276.

of Wales Volunteers, South Lancaster), embodied in 1793, and chiefly recruited in the counties of York, Lancaster, Lincoln, Stafford and Worcester. The Bucks. Volunteers became part of the 85th Regiment (now 2nd, the King's, Shropshire Light Infantry) which was raised at Buckingham in the latter part of 1793; and the Perthshire Volunteers became absorbed in the 90th, the third occasion of its being raised, in 1794 (and now 2nd Cameronians, Scottish Rifles); and each of these regiments now bears the name of the respective bodies of Volunteer Associations which it absorbed.

Notwithstanding the exuberance of the joy with which the Treaty of Amiens was hailed in this country it was soon evident to all thinking men that the Peace could be of no long continuance. Napoleon frankly avowed that a "renewal of war was necessary for his existence, as the memory of old victories was likely speedily to pass away," a cynic declaration enough of itself to condemn his memory to eternal infamy. He began insidiously to so outrage the sensitive pride of this country as to make inevitable a renewal of hostilities. In August of the year that witnessed the ratification of the Treaty he annexed the Isle of Elba, in September the whole of Piedmont, in October Parma and Placentia. He occupied Switzerland with a force of 30,000 men under Marshal Ney, and assumed the title of Mediator of the Swiss Republic. He not only refused a commercial treaty with England but obliged all the countries dependent on him to do likewise, and thus closed half Europe to English trade.* He aimed at constituting himself censor of the press of England and demanded the suppression of any journal so audacious as to adversely criticise his actions. His emissaries, under the guise of commercial agents, swarmed in Ireland, where they fomented the abortive rising led by Robert Emmett. In brief, neither in letter nor in spirit, was Napoleon faithful to the solemn treaty he had concluded in March, 1802. He was encouraged in this course of action by the pusillanimity of the first Minister, Addington, and by the mistaken belief that a nation of shopkeepers, as we were contemptuously dubbed on the continent, would submit to any indignity, if only its trading and money making were not seriously jeopardised. It was patent to the meanest understanding that Napoleon was only biding his time, and, if war were to come, it was well that it should come at our time rather than his. On May 18, 1803, the declaration of war was published. "It was," says Dr. Bright, "a war of a distinctively

May 18th, 1803. Declaration of War.

*Dr. Bright's "History of England."

different character from that which preceded it The one had been undertaken in the interests of aristocracy and of property, in a panic of fear of the growth of the liberty of the people. There were many in this country who sympathised with the principles of the French Revolution. But now the whole nation was driven to defend itself, and while defending itself, Europe also, from the aggressions of a gigantic and all absorbing ambition."

The statutes under which were enrolled the Volunteers with whom we have heretofore been concerned had expired with the Peace of Amiens.

The preliminaries of peace were signed October 1, 1801, but the definite treaty of Amiens was not signed, as has been said, till 28th March, 1802. It was a treaty that contained in itself the seeds of discord. The English disliked it because it ceded too much to France, Napoleon disliked it because it did not cede enough. Both parties probably regarded it as but affording a breathing space. Accordingly two short months after the signature of the treaty, June 22nd, 1802, we find the British Parliament declaring in the preamble to the statute, 42 Geo. III, c. 66, that it was expedient to enable His Majesty to avail himself of the offers of certain Yeomanry and Volunteer Corps to continue their services and that "it would tend to encourage the continuance of such Corps of Yeomanry and Volunteers if persons enrolled and serving therein were to be exempted from serving personally or providing substitutes for the Militia." The second section of the Act provided that "every person enrolled or to be enrolled in any Corps of Yeomanry or Volunteers in Great Britain which should thereafter be continued or formed in Great Britain, who should have attended the exercise of his Corps a certain number of days of muster and exercise, and should be returned on the muster roll and certified to have attended the respective number of days therein mentioned, should be exempt from being liable to save personally or to provide a substitute in the Militia of Great Britain."

1802. June 22nd. 42 Geo. III., c. 66.

43 Geo. III., c. 121.

This statute was supplemented by an Act of 1803, regulating the returns and musters of the Corps raised under that of 1802, and providing in relation to such Corps that no persons enrolled therein should be entitled to or have any exemptions from being balloted to serve in any additional military force, raised or to be raised for the defence of the United Kingdom, unless they should appear to be and were returned under the now reciting Act as effective. The condition of efficiency for infantry, was, by section 2, declared to be attendance, properly armed, accoutred and equipped at the muster or exercise of the Corps, unless excused for certified sickness, and being returned not only as having attended such muster and exercise, but being, in consequence thereof, effective and fit for service.

Under the Act of 1802, the Secretary for War addressed to the Lords Lieutenant of counties a letter in the following terms:—

"Downing Street,
March 31st, 1803.

My Lord,

The frequent references lately made to me from some of His Majesty's Lieutentants of counties in consequence of the anxiety expressed by a large proportion of the Volunteer Corps to renew their engagements having induced the King's confidential servants to consider upon what footing it would be possible to place these establishments, and to determine the extent of the aid to be afforded by Government to those whose services His Majesty may be pleased to accept, I convey to your Lordship in the accompanying paper, a general outline of the plan it is intended to act upon for the purpose of your being enabled to satisfy any enquiries which may be made to you with regard to the sentiments of Government in this respect.

It may be right however that I should intimate to your Lordship that, altho' the actual state of affairs has rendered it advisable that I should make this communication at this time, the plan must rather be considered with a reference to a permanent system than a situation of emergency; the application of it in point of extent to depend upon and be regulated by circumstances.

With this view I must request of your Lordship to receive and to communicate to me for His Majesty's information any offers of service that may be made to you in the County of
in order that such a selection may be made as may be best calculated to give the most useful effect to that loyalty and public spirit by which the Volunteer institution has uniformly been distinguished.

I have the honor to be,
My Lord,
Your Lordship's most obedient humble servant,
HOBART."

His Majesty's Lieutenant of the
county of

The following is the plan or scheme accompanying the Secretary's letter:—

PROPOSED CONDITIONS OF SERVICE FOR CORPS OF VOLUNTEER INFANTRY.

Every Corps receiving pay to engage to serve in the military district in which it is situated. Every officer, non-commissioned officer and private to take an oath of allegiance and fidelity to His Majesty.

The Companies not to be less than two sergeants, two corporals, one drummer and fifty privates, each with one captain, one lieutenant, one ensign, two lieutenants to the flank Companies, and to such as consist of eighty men; no Company to have more than one hundred privates.

Field officers in proportion to the whole number of private men in the Corps to be the same as in the British Militia; an adjutant and sergeant-major to be allowed a Corps of 300 private men and upwards; one officer in each Company, if taken from the half-pay list, to have constant pay of his Volunteer commission not higher than that of captain; if not on half-pay but formerly a commissioned officer in the Military service, to have constant pay equal to the half-pay of his Volunteer rank not higher than that of a captain; the other officers not to receive any pay, the adjutants excepted.

When not called out on actual service the adjutants, sergeant-majors and one sergeant per Company to be allowed constant pay as in the disembodied Militia; pay (as disembodied Militia) for the rest of the sergeants, and for the corporals, drummers and privates to be allowed for two days in the week from Lady-day to Michaelmas, and for one day of muster in each one month; but for effectives only, present under arms.

Per diem.		Per diem.	
Adjutants	6/-	Sergeant	1/6
Sergeant-Major ..	1/6	Corporal	1/2
and 2/6 per week in addition		Drummer	1/-
		Private	1/-

To be allowed for clothing :—

£3 3 9 for each Sergeant.
£1 11 3 for each Corporal.
£2 3 6 for each Drummer.
£1 10 0 for each Private.

and to be repeated at the end of three years.

An annual allowance to be made to each Company in lieu of all contingencies (exclusive of agency; for each business a general agent will be appointed by Government) viz:—£25 per Companies of 50 private men with an additional allowance of £5 for every 10 men beyond that number. The whole to be clothed in red with the sole exception of the Companies of Artillery which are to have blue clothing.

Field officers and adjutants to be allowed a tax for one horse each; the whole officers and men to be exempted from the hair powder duty and from being balloted for the Militia during their service in the Volunteers.

"When called out in case of actual invasion to be paid and disciplined in all respects as the regular Infantry; Artillery Companies to be paid as Artillery when on actual service."

Renewal of hostilities, May 18th, 1803.

Defence Act, 11th June, 1803.

43 Geo. III., c. 55.

Hostilities were renewed, we have seen, on May 18, 1803, and Parliament, on June 11, *i.e.*, within a month, passed the Defence Act of 1803. That statute recited that it was expedient that His Majesty should be enabled, for preventing and repelling an invasion of the United Kingdom of Great Britain and Ireland, to accept the voluntary services of His Majesty's loyal subjects for the defence of the United Kingdom. The first clause provided for a return of able-bodied males between 15 and 60 years of age, specifying which of them were engaged in any and what Volunteer Corps or troops or companies of Yeomanry, and which of them were willing to engage themselves to be armed, arrayed, trained and exercised for the defence of the United Kingdom. The second clause provided for the appointment of proper officers "to be ready for arraying, training and exercising as aforesaid" such men as should be enrolled. The Act was to expire with the close of the hostilities with France.

I find only the following record of any circular from the War Office in which reference is made to that statute, and it will be observed that the circular and accompanying forms are intended to meet the case of those citizens who had not been enrolled under the Defence Act, but whose services nevertheless might be otherwise utilized.

"Whitehall, Nov. 8th.

My Lord,

As in the first event of the French making an attempt to invade this kingdom it will be of great importance to provide for the internal good order and tranquility of the country, it is His Majesty's pleasure that I should desire your Lordship earnestly to recommend to the Magistrates of the County of York (West Riding) to enquire in their several districts what trusty householders or others, who are not enrolled in any Volunteer Corps, or liable to military service from being included in the first and second classes under the General Defence Act, will, in the event above mentioned, engage to come forward and act as special constables for the purposes above mentioned within their respective parishes and districts, and to take a list of such names, with their places of residence. I should recommend that the special constables so to be sworn in should be formed into small divisions with persons selected from each division and placed at the head thereof as superintendents by the resident magistrates.

I enclose for the further information of the magistrates printed copy of the paper specifying the mode in which this measure has been executed by the magistrates in several districts of the metropolis.

I have the honour to be,

My Lord,

Your most obedient servant,

C. YORKE."

SPECIAL CONSTABLES.

THE Magistrates of

request that all householders (who are not enrolled in any Volunteer Corps, or liable to military service from being included in the first and second classes under the General Defence Act) of the Parishes of

who are willing to act as special constables in case of an attempt by the enemy to invade this country will immediately call at signify their assent and register their names, place of residence and profession.

By order of the Magistrates.

WE whose names are hereunto subscribed, being householders of the Parish of   in the County of   , do hereby agree to become special constables in case of attempt by the enemy to invade this country and to be subjected in all respects to the drill and direction of the civil magistrates.

Name   residence   No. of house
profession

Certificate of Magistrates at the

WE whose names are hereunto subscribed, being three of His Majesty's Justices of the Peace at and for the County of   , do hereby certify that we have nominated and appointed each and every of the foregoing householders of the Parish of   to execute the office of special constable within the said county, and that they and each of them have been duly sworn before us to that effect in manner and form following, that is to say:—

"I, A.B., do sincerely promise and agree that in the event of the enemy of this country putting to sea for the purpose of invading it, or of actual invasion, I will execute the office of special constable for the County of   and that I will aid and assist the civil power therein to the best of my skill and knowledge.

So help me God."

As witness our hands.

The General Defence Act was speedily followed, tho' not superseded, by the Levy *en masse* Act, passed July 27th, 1803.

44 Geo. III., c. 90
Levy *en masse* Act, July 27th, 1803.

The Levy *en masse* Act menaced conscription but gave the alternative of volunteering. The French Republican was taunted with saying *Sois mon ami ou je te tuerai*: the Levy *en masse* Act said, in effect, "Become a Volunteer or you shall be made a conscript." It is desirable to set out its provisions with some detail. It recites that "it is expedient to enable His Majesty more effectually and speedily to exercise his ancient and undoubted Prerogative of requiring the military service of all his liege subjects in case of an invasion of the realm by the foreign enemy." The male inhabitants of the country between 17 and 55 years of age were separated into 4 classes.

First Class.—Men from 17 to 30 years of age, unmarried and having no child or children living, under the age of 10 years.

Second Class.—Men between 30 and 50 and having no children as aforesaid.

Third Class.—Men between 17 and 30 who were or had been married and who had not more than two children living, under the age aforesaid.

Fourth Class.—All men not included in the former classes.

The lists were to specify which of the men classified suffered from any bodily infirmity disqualifying from military service.

Clergymen, Licensed Dissenting Ministers, Quakers, Medical Practitioners, Peace Officers and the Judges of the Supreme Court were exempt from classification. The lists when completed were to be exhibited for inspection on the Parish Church doors.

By Section 25 His Majesty was empowered to order that every parish in Great Britain be provided and supplied with such necessary arms and accoutrements, in order to the instruction of the men enrolled for military service under the Act, as His Majesty should think fit. These arms were to be safe-guarded in some proper and convenient place, and Parliament suggested as such a place "the church or chancel of every such parish." The church-wardens, elders, constables and schoolmasters were to be the custodians of these weapons, and were empowered to levy a rate for keeping them clean and in proper order and condition The King was empowered to order the men of the first, second and third classes to be exercised for two hours on the Sunday of each week, and on such additional days as might be found least to interfere with the general occupations of the men. Power was also given during the then emergency to drill the men for any 3 or more successive days in the course of different weeks, but the total drilling not to exceed 20 days. The Lord Lieutenant was to appoint fit and proper persons to be officers to "train and discipline" the men, in the proportion of one captain, two lieutenants and one ensign to every 120 men. The captain of each company had the appointment of three sergeants, three corporals and one drummer to every 120 men. The officers were to rank with "officers of the Militia of the youngest of their rank."

The muster roll was to be called on each exercise day, and absentees or defaulters were liable to fine. If His Majesty should think fit to order extraordinary training during the ordinary hours of labour 1/- per attendance was to be paid to any one who should earn his living by daily labour only, such pay to be paid out of the Poor Rate. In all cases of actual invasion, or on the appearance of the enemy in force upon the coast, the Lords Lieutenant were to draw out, assemble and embody all the men enrolled for military service under that Act. They were to be attached to any regiment of regular Militia or Fencibles and might be led to any part of the kingdom, but on no pretence whatsoever were they to serve out of Great Britain. The 53rd Section of the Act is however most important in its bearing on the Volunteer movement.

It provided

"That in all cases in which any Volunteer Corps shall have been or shall be formed, or in which any persons between the ages of 17 and 55 years shall engage themselves as volunteers, whose effective members respectively shall amount to such proportion of the number of men enrolled for military service as shall appear satisfactory to His Majesty, not being less than three-fourths of men enrolled for service of the first class, and such Volunteer Corps or Volunteers shall have agreed or shall agree to march to any part of Great Britain for the defence thereof, in case of actual invasion or the appearance of any enemy in force upon the coast, and for the suppression of any rebellion or insurrection arising or existing at the time of such invasion,"

then and in such case it was competent for the Crown to suspend the operation in the districts of such Volunteer Corps of the Act under consideration. The 54th Section provides that such Volunteers should be liable for service in any part of Great Britain for the defence thereof or upon the appearance in force of any enemy upon the coast or to suppress any rebellion or insurrection arising or existing during such rebellion. The same section contained the salient proviso that "no person enrolled or serving in any Volunteer Corps, so long as the services of such corps should be continued by His Majesty, and as such person should remain an effective member thereof, should be placed in any Regiment, Battalion or Corps of Regulars, Militia or Fencibles. The Volunteers were, however, to be subject to the terrors of the Mutiny Act.

It is possible that the clause exempting Volunteers from attachment to the Regulars, Militia or Fencibles co-operated to no small extent with that patriotic ardour which has never been lacking in this country to stimulate the Volunteer movement of this period. Mr. Clode states that out of 500,000 persons liable to serve under the Act 420,000 offered voluntary service. The return of Volunteers up to December 9, 1803,* amounted to

380,060 for Great Britain
82,941 for Ireland.

463,001

The following extracts from the official circular letters sent by His Majesty's Ministers to the Lords Lieutenant of the various counties, dealing with the force to be raised under the Levy *en masse* Act are surely worthy of preservation in permanent form :

"That Volunteer Corps, consisting of 6 troops or companies and upwards, will be allowed a lieutenant-colonel commandant, a lieutenant-colonel and

* 59 Com. Journal, p. 502.

major: if of 5 troops or companies, a lieutenant-colonel and major; if of 4 troops or companies, a lieutenant-colonel; if of 2 or 3 troops or companies, a major; and that a distinct captain be allowed to each troop or company.

That Volunteer Corps of Infantry established in conformity to the provisions of the 43 George III. chap. 96 (the Levy *en masse* Act) be at liberty to draw for the following allowances, namely: 20/- per man for clothing once in every 3 years and a shilling per day for 20 days' exercise within the year, provided such allowance be not drawn for any exercise on a Sunday, nor for any man exercising on a week-day who shall not also have been trained and exercised on the preceding Sunday, unless prevented by illness or such other cause as shall be deemed satisfactory by the Commanding Officer of the Corps, and certified accordingly. In addition to these allowances every person belonging to the respective Corps raised under the said Act was to be entitled, if called out into actual service, to the several sums specified in the 59th and 60th clauses thereof. These sums are, two guineas to provide necessaries upon being ordered out into actual service, and one guinea on being permitted to return home after the defeat and expulsion of the enemy, or the suppression of any rebellion or insurrection.

That the allowances above specified have been settled upon after the most mature consideration, and that no circumstance is likely to induce any alteration thereof, unless it could be so arranged as not to be productive of an increased expense to the public, it being the object of the Act for general enrolment for military service (under the authority of which Act the Volunteer Corps are to be established), to obtain such a force, in addition to that which has already been provided, as may enable His Majesty to avert or frustrate the attack with which this country is threatened, and, by combining economy with vigour, to continue the contest so long as it may be necessary for the honour and security of the British Empire."

The unanimity with which His Majesty's subjects flocked to enrol themselves as Volunteers, evidenced by the numbers I have cited, made the Levy *en masse* Act superfluous; but the following letter from the War Secretary to the Lords Lieutenant shews a determination on the part of the authorities to preserve, if possible, the machinery the Act provided for enumerating and classifying the people with a view to military necessities.

"Downing Street, August 18th, 1803.

My Lord,

The zeal, loyalty and public spirit which continue to be manifested in every part of the Kingdom having had the effect of producing Volunteer forces of services to so considerable amount as to render it unnecessary for His Majesty to order and direct the Lieutenant or Deputy Lieutenants of the County of to cause the persons comprised in the first, second, and third classes of persons enrolled for military service in conformity to the provisions of the Act of 43 Geo. III. chap. 96, or any or either of them to be trained or exercised in the use of arms; I am to inform your Lordship that it is His Majesty's pleasure to suspend for the present such provisions of the Act as require the men enrolled for military service to be trained and exercised, subject nevertheless (conformably to the 53rd clause of the said Act), to such conditions as to the number of effective men to be constantly existing in the Volunteer Corps in the County, and to such other rules and regulations as to exercise and musters, or inspection by the General or other officers, as to His Majesty shall seem necessary.

In order, however, to enable His Majesty, if He shall judge it advisable, at a future period to resort to the clauses respecting the training and exercise, your Lordship must be aware of the absolute necessity of carrying into execution those provisions of the Act which relate to enrolment in the several districts and parishes, and to the returns which are to be made to the Secretary of State.

I am further to acquaint your Lordship that the inconvenience which must unavoidably arise from carrying the Volunteer service to an unlimited extent has determined His Majesty not to authorise at the present any additional Volunteer Corps to be raised in any County where the number of effective members of those corps, including the yeomanry, shall exceed the amount of six times the Militia, inclusive of the supplementary quota, making in the County of , men, and in providing that number your Lordship will avail yourself of your own knowledge and experience with a view of such a selection as may be best suited to local considerations.

That, in the event of the effective members of the Corps already recommended by your Lordship having arrived at , you will postpone the communication of any further offers until His Majesty should be pleased to signify His intention to increase the Volunteer force in the County under your Lordship's charge.

I have the honour to be, &c.,

(Signed) HOBART."

The following circulars are interesting mainly from the light they throw upon the favour which the Government of the day seemed disposed to extend to the Volunteer Corps.

" Downing Street, August 19th, 1803.

My Lord,

I have had the honour to receive your Lordship's letter of the 17th instant, and I lose no time in acquainting you that the printed regulations for Volunteer Infantry, issued in June last, are not to be considered in any respect applicable to Corps accepted by His Majesty since the date of my circular letter (the 3rd of August), restricting the allowances before given to Volunteer Corps of Infantry to the allowances of 20/- for clothing and a shilling per day for 20 days' exercise.

With respect to arms I have to request your Lordship will inform me what quota will be necessary (in addition to those with which the several Corps can provide themselves, and of those already in the possession of the Yeomanry and Volunteers), to complete the number required for the several Corps already authorized by His Majesty.

Your Lordship will understand it to be the intention of Government that the whole number of Volunteers now proposed to be armed should not exceed six times the amount of the Militia, inclusive of the supplementary quota.

Upon the receipt of your Lordship's answer to this letter, instructions will be given to the Board of Ordnance to send the arms, as soon as they can be prepared, to such places within the Riding as you may point out, that they may be distributed under your Lordship's directions to the several Corps according to your Lordship's discretion.

The discrimination which it will become your Lordship's duty to make in the distribution of the proportion of arms you will receive should be guided by a reference to the local situation of the Corps requiring them.

I have the honour to be, my Lord,

Your Lordship's most obedient humble servant,

HOBART."

To His Majesty's Lieutenant of
the County of

" Whitehall,

January 14th, 1804.

My Lord,

His Majesty's confidential servants have thought it to be their duty, on further considering the importance of which the Volunteer system is capable, to extend to it every useful aid and assistance which it can receive consistent with a due attention to that principle of economy on which the whole system is founded, and have resolved to allow all Adjutants and Sergeant-Majors on permanent pay to Corps of the different descriptions, a force consisting of the following numbers without any other conditions or restrictions than such as may be applicable to the whole Volunteer establishment :—

Cavalry. x x x x x x

Infantry : to every Corps of Infantry (including Artillery), consisting of not less than 500 effective rank and file, one adjutant and one sergeant-major on permanent pay will be allowed (pay when not called out into actual service, 6/- per day).

Ditto of sergeant-major, ditto, 1/6 per day, and 2/6 per week extra.

To every Corps of Infantry consisting of not less than 300 effective rank and file, one adjutant, but no sergeant-major will be allowed on permanent pay (pay, 6/- per day as above).

To a Corps of Infantry under 300 effective rank and file, but consisting of not less than three companies of sixty privates each, one sergeant-major will be allowed on permanent pay (pay as above 1/6 per day, and 2/6 per week extra).

When the Corps to which the adjutants and sergeant-majors are appointed shall be called out on actual service by competent authority these staff officers will receive the pay of their respective ranks as in the line.

The adjutants are to be recommended by the Lords Lieutenant, have His Majesty's approbation in the usual manner, but no recommendation of an adjutant can be attended to unless the person recommended has served at least 4 years as a commissioned officer or as a sergeant-major in the Regulars or embodied Militia, Fencibles or East India Company's Service, and the recommendation must likewise distinctly express the actual period of the service of the person recommended and specify the present corps in which that service was performed.

Sergeant-majors may be appointed by the Commandant of the Corps from among persons who have served at least 3 years as non-commissioned officers in His Majesty's Regulars, embodied Militia or Fencible forces, and the period of such service and the number of the Corps in which it was performed are to be distinctly specified in the first pay list which shall be transmitted to the War Office after the appointment takes place.

All adjutants and sergeant-majors who are placed on permanent pay are to consider themselves as at all times at the disposal of and under the commanding officers of the Corps for the time being, and are expected to give their attendance whenever required for the drill, good order and management of the Corps.

It is not intended by this arrangement to make any alteration as to the appointment of adjutants or sergeant-majors *without pay*. They will still be allowed a Corps of sufficient strength as directed by the Militia laws, and, as before pointed out, by the War Office Regulations of the 28th September, 1803.

To His Majesty's Lieutenant of the

The following authoritative statement, which I find set out in the *Leeds Mercury* of October 8th of that year, also bears on the subjects touched in the circular.

"If a Corps or part thereof be called upon to act in cases of riot or disturbance a charge may be made for such services for all the effective officers and men employed in such duty at the undermentioned rates, the same being supported by a certificate from His Majesty's Lieutenant or the Sheriff of the County, but if called out in case of actual invasion the Corps is to be paid and disciplined in all respects as the regular Infantry.

Field Officers or Captain of a Company	9/5
Lieutenant	5/8
Second Lieutenant or Ensign	4/8
Adjutant	8/-
Quarter-Master	5/8
Surgeon..	10/-
Sergeant-Major	1/6
and 2/6 per week in addition	
Sergeant	1/6
Corporal	1/2
Drummer	1/-
Private	1/-

Pay at the rate of 1/- per man per day for 20 days' exercise within the year to the effective non-commissioned officers, not being drill sergeants paid by the parish, drummers and privates of the Corps agreeably to their terms of service. No pay to be allowed for any man who shall not have attended for the complete period of 20 days. Such Corps as have offered to serve free of expense and have been accepted on these terms can claim no allowance under those heads of service.

All effective members of Volunteer Corps and Companies accepted by His Majesty are entitled to exemption from ballot allowed by 42 Geo. III., cap. 66, and 43 Geo. III. cap. 121, provided that such persons are regularly returned in the muster rolls to be sent to the lieutenant or clerk of the general meetings of his Company at the times, in the manner and certified upon honour by the commandant in form prescribed.

It is proposed that the following number of inspecting field officers for the Yeomanry and Volunteer Corps shall be immediately appointed and attached to districts :— Inspecting Field Officers

North East ..	2		North West ..	2
Yorkshire ..	3		South Inland ..	1
Eastern	2		North Inland ..	1
Southern	3		London	1
South West ..	1		Home	1
Western	2		North Britain ..	4
Severn	1			

These officers are to be continually employed in visiting and superintending the drill and field exercises of the several Corps of Yeomanry and Volunteers in their respective districts, during those periods of the year which are appointed for that purpose. It will be the duty of these officers to muster within every two months each Corps under their superintendence, when they are to make a report of the number under arms, on the state of the clothing, horses, arms and accoutrements, and adding any observations which may occur as necessary for the information of the commanding general.

The following Circular Letters from the War Secretary to the Lords Lieutenant reveal, better perhaps than the historic page, the constant, ever pressing apprehension of a hostile landing that possessed our forefathers. To them a French descent was a real and living menace, an abiding threat, a danger any day might see realized.

"Whitehall, February 16, 1804.

My Lord,

Referring your Lordship to the directions contained in my circular letter to you of the 31st October last, for the removal in cases of emergency or rendering useless, if need be, such horses, draught cattle and carriages as shall not be wanted for the purpose therein mentioned, I am to desire that your Lordship will consider, in every respect, as included in those directions, all such vessels, boats or crafts as shall not be wanted for the like purpose or shall not be armed and equipped for the annoyance of the enemy. War Office Circular, Feb. 16th, 1804.

As I am informed by His Royal Highness, the Commander-in-Chief, that only one light cart per company can, on such emergency, be allowed to Volunteer Corps for carrying their camp kettles and necessaries on their march, I beg leave to recommend it to your Lordship to give directions that one such cart be allowed to each company of Volunteers, and that one such cart be always kept marked and numbered as the carriage intended for the use of that particular company.

In consequence, also, of the late suggestion from His Royal Highness, the Commander-in-Ohief, I have strongly to recommend it to your Lordship, in communication with the General Commanding the District in which the county of   is included, to give directions for allotting and marking a sufficient number of waggons for moving the Volunteer Force where it is not placed in the vicinity of the coast ; and it would be found extremely useful if boards, such as are used for seats in market carts, could be provided and kept in readiness at the places or place of general assembly, ready to be hung upon the waggons, to which place of assembly these waggons should be held bound to repair upon the signal of alarm being given.

I have the honour, &c."

Circular transmitted to the Lords Lieutenant of Counties.

"Whitehall, March 10, 1804.

War Office Circular, March 10th, 1804.

My Lord,

Referring your Lordship to my Circular Letter of the 16th ulto., I have now the honour of acquainting you that, in order to prevent any delay which may arise in the execution of the measures therein recommended, His Royal Highness, the Commander-in-Chief, has authorised the generals commanding districts to defray the expenses of numbering the waggons and providing the seats to be slung upon them in case of emergency. As the expense also of such carriages as may be thought necessary for the use of the Volunteer force will be defrayed by the public, it is presumed that the lieutenancy will find no difficulty in allotting such as are most fit for the purpose, especially as it is not intended, when the allotment shall have been made, that the several carts or waggons should be diverted from their reach or until the exigency of affairs shall require it.

In order to more effectually secure the regular attendance of the members of Volunteer Corps at Inspections, I am to inform your Lordship that His Majesty's pleasure has been signified to the Secretary of War that to all such Corps of Volunteer Infantry as do not receive any greater allowance than those granted on the 3rd August, 1803, there shall be paid one day's* pay at the same rate with the Militia when at annual exercise, to each non-commissioned officer, drummer and private who shall be present on the day of inspection of his Corps by any General or Inspecting Field Officer over and above the 20/- per annum for training and exercise already allowed, provided that such Inspection shall not happen oftener than once in two months, and that such issue shall be made on a return of the effective members present under arms, signed by the commanding officers and certified by the General or Inspecting Field Officer by whom the Inspection shall be made.

I have the honour to be, &c.,

C. YORKE."

Another Circular, of the 19th March, 1804, from the War Office to the Lords Lieutenant is instructive, as shewing how sedulously the Government of the day encouraged the Voluntary service, only, as we shall see, to disparage it when the imminence of the danger had passed.

War Office Circular, 19th March, 1804.

It appearing that the instruction and discipline of such of the Corps of Yeomanry and Volunteers of the maritime counties as have been placed on permanent pay and duty by His Majesty's order on the existing appearance of invasion have been essentially promoted by that measure, and there being reason to believe that many remaining Volunteer Corps, in different parts of Great Britain, are ready and willing to assemble under the authority of His Majesty for this purpose, I have therefore received instructions from His

*Sergeant 1/6, corporal 1/2, drummers and privates 1/-.

Majesty's hands to request a confidential communication of your opinion whether any, and which, of the Yeomanry or Volunteer Corps, being already properly armed and equipped, are likely, upon His Majesty's invitation, to assemble on permanent pay and duty, for a period not exceeding a month nor less than 10 days. I beg leave to remind you that His Majesty is empowered by 42 Geo. III. c. 66 (1 to 10) to invite any military or Volunteer Corps voluntarily to assemble, and that all such Corps as shall voluntarily assemble as expressed in the clause are entitled to pay and quarters and subject to military discipline during the time they shall continue to so assemble.

I have reason to believe that His Royal Highness, the Commander-in-Chief, has written to the Commanding General in the district on the subject, and I hope that you will have the goodness to communicate with the General commanding the district confidentially on the occasion.

I hope to be favoured with your Lordship's sentiments at your earliest convenience, accompanied with a list of such of the Corps as are most ready and prepared to step forward on the present juncture.

Your Lordship will be pleased at all times to observe that previous to the actual assembling of any Corps or detachment of a Volunteer Corps on permanent pay and duty, the proposal for their so assembling is to be made, in the first instance, by the Commandant of the Corps through the Inspecting Field Officer to the Lord Lieutenant of the County, transmitting a duplicate, at the same time, to the General Commanding the District. These proposals are, in each case, to be accompanied by an exact return of the effective members and rank of the Officers who are to be assembled, and by the statement of the time and place proposed for their assembling, and of the period for which it is intended they should remain on duty.

If, upon communication between His Majesty's Lieutenant and the Commanding General, the proposal be approved, it is to be transmitted by the Lord Lieutenant, with as little delay as possible, to the Secretary of State for the Home Department, in order that His Majesty's special directions may be given thereupon and signified by such Secretary of State to the Lord Lieutenant before any corps or detachment shall be actually placed on duty, and that the requisite authority may be given for the issue of their pay and allowances.

During the period of any Volunteers being so assembled they are to be under the command of the General Officer Commanding in the District, or, if in garrison, under the Governor or Commander thereof for the time being, and they are in all respects diligently to conform to the rules, regulations and conditions of His Majesty's military service; and the Commanding Officer of the Corps or detachment is to follow such directions as shall be communicated to him through His Majesty's Secretary at War, with respect to the payment, subsistence and economy of the men assembled.

It is intended to advance to each non-commissioned officer, drummer and private so called out, in proportion to the length of time for which they may agree to assemble, a sum not exceeding one guinea for the purpose of assisting in providing necessaries, and the captains of companies may draw for the same upon the Receiver General of the county, in the same manner as the captains of Militia regiments are allowed to do; and may also lay out the same in the manner which they shall think most advantageous for the men, for whom it is, amongst other things, particularly desirable that great coats should be provided where they are wanted; and such captains or commanding officers shall, on or before the 24th day of the month next ensuing that in which they shall have received such money as aforesaid, account to such Volunteers how the said sum has been applied and disposed of, and shall, at the time of settling such account, pay the remainder, if any, to the said Volunteers. It is thought desirable to avoid, as much as possible, the calling out, on permanent pay and duty, any men having families who are likely to become chargeable, and it is to be observed that the wives and families of the men so called out are not entitled to any allowance, unless such men shall actually leave their families, and then only when such families are unable to support themselves.

The commanding officer is to cause the Articles of War to be read to his Corps as soon after it has first assembled as may be practicable, and to repeat the same from time to time in the manner practised in the Regular and Militia forces.

"Whitehall, September 24th, 1804.

My Lord,

Referring your Lordship to Mr. Yorke's circular letter of the 12th April, in which your Lordship was apprised that there would be no objection to allow ten days' additional pay at the rate of 1/- per man per day to each non-commissioned officer, drummer and private of such corps of Volunteer Infantry accepted subsequent to the 3rd August, 1803, if recommended by your Lordship, as may be willing to perform so many additional days' exercise in the course of the two then ensuing months without leaving their homes, I have to acquaint your Lordship that all such corps as have not before availed themselves of this permission will be allowed pay in the manner and under the other restrictions contained in the above circular letter for ten days within the ensuing six months."

Aug. 8th, 1805, Circular by General Commanding to Volunteer Officers.

The following circular by the General Commanding the London District to the Commanders of the Volunteer corps of his county, is still another proof, if proof were needed, that the Volunteers of that period were counted upon when danger threatened.

"Sir,

In consequence of intelligence received by Government of the embarkation of large bodies of troops in Holland, of a fleet of men-of-war being ready to sail from thence, and of the increased preparations of the French at Boulogne, I have received from His Royal Highness, the Commander-in-Chief, instructions to direct the general officers and inspecting field officers attached to the Volunteer corps to give notice to those corps of the possibility of their being speedily called upon for service and also to suspend all furloughs for working during the harvest until further orders.

I have the honour to be,

Your most obedient and humble servant,

HARRINGTON.

General Commanding the London District."

It was at this time, the reader will remember, that Nelson, Collingwood and Sir Robert Calder were engaged in watching the movements of the French Fleet. Fourteen months later the Battle of Trafalgar was to shatter the French navy and minimize, if not dispel, any real dread on our part of a French invasion of our shores—a result which we shall see affected not a little the attitude of Ministers to the Volunteers. Before, however, adverting to the noticeable change in the Government policy manifested in 1806, it will be well to record the many manifestations of Royal and Parliamentary approval, by which, from 1802 to 1805, the voluntary movement was recognized and stimulated.

In August, 1803, for instance, the House of Commons voted its thanks to the Volunteers and Yeomanry Corps of the United Kingdom "for the promptitude and zeal with which, at a crisis the most momentous to their country, they had associated for its defence."*

The letter of the Speaker to the Lords Lieutenant may be here preserved.

"House of Commons, August 10th, 1803.

My Lord,

By the command of the House of Commons I have the honour to transmit to you their unanimous vote of thanks to the several Volunteer and Yeomanry Corps in the Kingdom, for the promptitude and zeal with which, at a crisis the most momentous to their country, they have associated for its defence; accompanied with an order that a return be prepared, to be laid before the House in the next session of Parliament, of all Volunteer and Yeomanry Corps whose services shall have been accepted by His Majesty, describing each Corps, in order that such return may be entered on the Journals of the House, and the patriotic example of such Volunteer exertions transmitted to posterity. In communicating this resolution and order I have the greatest satisfaction at the same time in bearing testimony to the confidence with which the House is impressed, that the same spirit and exemplary zeal will be exercised throughout the present contest until, with the blessing of Providence, it shall be brought to a glorious issue.

I have the honour to be,

My Lord,

Your Lordship's most obedient humble servant,

CHAS. ABBOTT,

Speaker, &c., &c., &c."

To the Right Hon. Lord

September 19th of the same year was appointed for a General Fast. The Volunteer Corps of the United Kingdom attended their Parish Churches, at which appropriate and patriotic sermons were delivered. The occasion was also utilised for the administration of the Oath of allegiance. In October of the same year over 27,000

General Fast.

* 59 Com. Journal, p. 502.

Volunteers of the Metropolis and its vicinity passed in review before the King in Hyde Park. On this occasion the Commander-in-Chief issued the following letter:—

"Horse Guards,
October 29th, 1803.

His Royal Highness the Commander-in-Chief has received the King's command to convey to the several *Volunteer and Associated Corps* which were reviewed in Hyde Park on the 26th and 28th instant His Majesty's highest approbation of their appearance, which has equalled His Majesty's utmost expectations. His Majesty perceives with heartfelt satisfaction that the spirit of loyalty and patriotism on which the system of the Armed Volunteers throughout the kingdom was originally founded has risen with the exigencies of the times, and at this moment forms such a bulwark to the constitution and liberties of the country as will enable us, under the protection of Providence, to bid defiance to the unprovoked malice of our enemies, and to hurl back, with becoming indignation, the threats which they have presumed to vent against our independence and even our existence as a nation. His Majesty has observed with peculiar pleasure that amongst the unprecedented exertions which the present circumstances of the country have called forth, those of the capital of the United Kingdom have been eminently conspicuous. The appearance of its numerous and well regulated Volunteer Corps which were reviewed on the 26th and 28th instant indicates a degree of attention and emulation, both in officers and men, which can proceed only from a deep sense of the important objects for which they have enrolled themselves, a just estimation of the blessings we have so long enjoyed, and a firm and manly determination to defend them like Britons and transmit them unimpaired to our posterity. The Commander-in-Chief has the highest satisfaction in discharging his duty by communicating these, His Majesty's most gracious sentiments, and requests that the commanding officers will have recourse to the readiest means of making the same known to their respective Corps.

FREDERICK,
Commander-in-Chief."

It is quite impossible to over-rate the more than zeal, one might almost say the frenzy, with which the men of our country flocked to enrol themselves in the several corps of Volunteers. Not to wear a uniform of some sort was at that time a reproach no youth of spirit could brook. The swain who did not don the livery of Mars at least once a week sighed in vain at his lady's feet. Incentives were not needed to stimulate the general people to the extremity of bellicose passion, but incentives none the less were forthcoming. Napoleon was universally vilipended. Nurses awed their infant charges to silence, if not to sleep, by the whisper of his awesome name. He was, the clergy affirmed, a Mahommedan. Now it is quite true that in his Egyptian Expedition Napoleon, to whom one creed was probably much the same as another, coquetted with the Moslem faith. It was alleged by his detractors in

England, and probably piously believed, that he had poisoned his prisoners and sick at Jaffa. This was not true, tho' Napoleon had been known to defend the legitimacy and even the humanity of such an act on occasions. It was asserted that he had "incited his hell-hounds to execute his vengeance on England, by promising to permit anything," that he had "engaged to enrich his soldiers with our property, to glut their lust with our wives and daughters." The clergy declaimed from their pulpits. Church and chapel for once agreed. The poets wrote inflammatory ballads. General fast days were solemnly kept and used by the Volunteers for drill. Every male householder rated at £8 per year or over was to be sworn in as a Constable, unless a Volunteer or physically disqualified. Job-masters offered their horses, Pickford and other large firms their waggons, for transport. H. R. H. the Duke of Clarence became a private in the Teddington Regiment.* Pitt, as Lord Warden, headed 3,000 Volunteers, and announced his intention of taking the field in person. It was to this Peter Pindar referred in the verse:

> "Come the Consul whenever he will—
> And he means it when Neptune is calmer—
> Pitt will send them a d——d bitter pill
> From his fortress, the Castle of Walmer."

Wilberforce wrote, "my spirit will lead me to be foremost in the battle." The old King vowed to place himself at the head of his army. It was arranged that, in the event of the French effecting a landing, the Queen and Princesses should find sanctuary with the Bishop of Worcester.† The treasure of the Bank of England was to be conveyed to that historic City of the West in 30 waggons, escorted by Volunteers, and hid in the crypt of the Cathedral. The Artillery and stores at Woolwich were to be transported to the Midlands by the Great Junction Canal. An elaborate system of signalling by beacon fires was devised. These beacons were

---

*Woodburne: "The Story of our Volunteers" (Newman & Co., 1881).

†The King wrote to the Bishop of Worcester:—"We are here in daily expectation that Bonaparte will attempt his threatened invasion, but the chances against his success seem so many that it is wonderful he persists in it. I own I place that thorough dependence upon the protection of Divine Providence that I cannot help thinking that the usurper is encouraged to make the trial, that his ill-success may put an end to his wicked purposes. Should his troops effect a landing, I shall certainly put myself at the head of mine and my other armed subjects to repel them; but as it is impossible to foresee the event of such a conflict, I shall think it right the Queen and my daughters, should the enemy approach too near Windsor, should cross the Severn, and shall send them to your episcopal palace at Worcester."

erected along the coast and all through the country, to give the signal for everyone to repair to the post assigned to him, and all men fit to serve held themselves in readiness to act on the shortest notice. Everywhere was a strained, nervous anxiety that left its trace upon every brow. But if some of the military precautions of the day provoke a smile, the crisis had the effect of unifying the nation, of stifling party strife and rancours, and of causing each citizen to act as if the very life and being of the nation depended upon himself alone. Sir Walter Scott, in his "Antiquary," pictures vividly the condition of the nation at that vital crisis: "Those who witnessed the state of Great Britain, and of Scotland in particular, from the period that succeeded the war, which commenced in 1803, to the Battle of Trafalgar, must recollect those times with feelings which he can hardly hope to make the rising generation comprehend. Almost every individual was enrolled, either in a military or civil capacity, for the purpose of contributing to resist the long suspended threats of invasion which were echoed from every quarter." He puts into the mouth of Mr. Jonathan Oldbuck, the Laird of Monkbairns, the following humorous plaint: "I called to consult my lawyer; he was clothed in a dragoon's dress, belted and casqued, and about to mount a charger which his writing-clerk (habited as a sharpshooter) walked to and fro before his door. I went to scold my agent for having sent me to advise with a madman; he had stuck into his head a plume which, in his more sober days, he wielded between his fingers, and figured as an artillery officer. My mercer had his spontoon* in his hand as if he measured his cloth by that instrument instead of a legitimate yard. The banker's clerk who was directed to sum my cash account blundered it three times, being disordered by the recollection of his military tellings-off at his morning's drill—I was ill, and sent for a surgeon: he came:—

> But valour so had fired his eye,
> And such a falchion glittered on his thigh,
> That, by the Gods, with such a load of steel,
> I thought he came to murder—not to heal!

I had recourse to a physician, but he also was practising a more wholesale mode of slaughter than that which his profession has been at all times supposed to open to him. I hate a gun like a hurt wild duck, and detest a drum like a Quaker; and they thunder and rattle out yonder upon the town's common, so that every volley and

---

*A spontoon was a weapon like a halberd and was formerly used by the Officers of Foot instead of a half-pike. When the spontoon was planted on the ground the regiment halted; when it was pointed to the front the regiment advanced; when to the rear, retired. R. P. B.

roll goes to my very heart." Oldbuck's diatribe was deprived of much of its force by the comments of the ladies of his household, as indeed is common in other households than those of Scotland. "Dear brother," exclaimed his sister Griselda, "dinna speak that gate o' the gentlemen Volunteers. I assure you they have a most becoming uniform." But the sharpest shaft of all was discharged by his niece, Miss McIntyre, "I am sure," she said, "that my Uncle sent twenty guineas to help out their equipments."

Nor did Sir Walter Scott confine his allusions to the Volunteers to prose. He composed the "Song of the Edinburgh Light Horse Volunteers."

If ever breath of British gale
Shall fan the tricolour,
Or footsteps of invader rude
With rapine foul and red with blood,
Pollute our happy shore,
Then farewell home! and farewell friends!
Adieu each tender tie!
Resolved we mingled in the tide
Where charging squadrons furious ride,
To conquer or to die.
To horse! to horse! the sabres gleam,
High sounds our bugle call;
Combined by honour's sacred tie,
Our word is *Laws and Liberty*,
March forward one and all.

Having said so much anent the circumstances that called the Volunteers of 1803 into being it is now perhaps permissible to place on record such matter as I have been able to gather concerning the nature of their drill and kindred subjects. I have in my possession a small volume of some 40 pages or so, bound in stiff cardboard and covered with green paper. It was published in 1803 and issued from the Horse Guards, and was known as the "Green Book." The proper title was "A manual for Volunteer Corps of Infantry." The prefatory remarks of the Manual direct attention to the fact that in a country like Britain, much intersected with enclosures and covered in many parts with woods, it was necessary that all Infantry corps should become acquainted with the mode of warfare generally practised by light troops, and the hope is expressed that the instructions in the Manual may merit, under the circumstances of the contest in which Great Britain was engaged, the particular attention of those who had voluntarily come forward for the defence of their country. Tho', to the general reader, these instructions may prove but tedious reading, I venture to think the Volunteers of to-day will peruse with interest the instructions issued for the guidance of their forerunners of a century ago.

The manual exercises, with the words of command, are explained in simple language. In regard to the motions for securing, grounding and troiling (trailing), as well as piling arms, &c., the Green Book suggests that it would be sufficient for the soldiers to be taught to perform them in the most convenient and quickest methods. One shudders at the thought of the ingenuity which would be displayed by some citizen soldiers if left to adopt at discretion the most expeditious way of performing these movements.

The Platoon Exercises.

The directions in the exercises were simple and short. The words of command for loading and firing motions were no less than nine in number, as follows:—(1) handle cartridge, (2) prime, (3) load, (4) draw ramrods, (5) ram down cartridge, (6) return ram rods, (7) make ready, (8) present, (9) fire. These orders seem in these times very primitive and cumbrous, and must have occupied a considerable time. How long the process took with well-trained soldiers is not disclosed, but some minutes at least!

Then followed a concise "Explanation of the position of each rank in the Firings," viz.:—for the front rank, kneeling, centre rank, rear rank and firing by platoons.

The second part of the Manual is on "Manœuvres and general attentions for Light Infantry." The instructions are, shortly, as to distances of files when in line by battalion, the space for open order, manner of extending from left, right or centre, of firing on the spot, in advancing and retreating, with instructions as to movements being in quick time, that no running unless ordered, confusion to be avoided, posting of officers, that cover be taken advantage of, and how arms to be carried.

Then follow instructions to "Companies formed in Battalions." These are in the nature of rules as to what should be done under certain conditions, and close with the instructions that signals are to be made by the drum, for instance:—to advance, "Grenadiers' March"; to halt, "Troop"; to cease firing, "General"; to assemble, or call in all parties, "To Arms." These signals were always to be considered as fixed and determined ones, and never to be changed. All of those signals made from the line or column were to convey the intention of the commanding officers of the line to the officers commanding the battalion, who would either communicate them to the several companies or detachments by word or signal.

The work continues with general tactical observations to the effect that the nature of the service of Infantry in a close country would form an addition to the foregoing instructions which would not be misplaced. After premising that vigilance, activity and intelligence were particularly requisite, it laid down that the first duty of troops was to guard against surprise, to be alert and watchful, and that when they could with certainty discover the approach of the enemy at a distance they might rest and refresh themselves at their ease; that rapidity of movement was the chief characteristic of light infantry, and therefore limitation in baggage essential; that intelligent advantage of cover should be taken and that practise requisite to this end: that opportunities should be watched; that light infantry ought to be aware that they had little to apprehend in any situation from artillery, and that in a close country they were greatly an over-match for cavalry; that light troops should be expert marksmen; the necessity for a due proportion of reserves, who should be concealed; that skirmishers in retiring should keep up a good countenance and avoid hurry; that no body of troops should at any time march without an advance guard; directions as to the business of patrols, rear guards, outposts and piquets; and concluding with the expression of the hope that every officer would bestow the most scrupulous attention on whatever might tend to secure him against the disgrace of being surprised upon his post.

The Manual then proceeds to explain that the foregoing pages contained a few useful hints in the training of Volunteer Corps which might enable commanding officers to diversify their instructions with advantage, and, after calling attention to the requisites necessary to confirm men in the practice of duties which they were called upon to perform in the field with the greatest readiness, reference is made to the persevering and laudable endeavours of those who voluntarily stood forward during the then last war for the defence of their country brought the knowledge of the military profession amongst them to very great perfection, and that when a more trying situation of affairs had induced them to step forth, the same steady and unremitting zeal would cause them to prepare themselves with patience and industry to maintain honourably the independence of their country, and defend to the utmost those blessings which were exclusively enjoyed under the happy constitution of Britain. These tactical rules are very similar to those in use at the present day.

The second part of the Manual is an abstract from the regulations for the formation, exercise, &c. of His Majesty's forces, from the formation and exercises of a battalion in all its formations and movements up to and inclusive of its inspection and review.

The concluding chapter of the Manual contains useful hints as to how small corps in certain situations can obstruct the enemy's approach or cover themselves without the aid of an engineer, and particularly directing attention to the various objects of defence with which the country everywhere abounds, with plates illustrating the instructions given. I am indebted to Mr. S. J. Chadwick, Solicitor, of Dewsbury, for the loan of this Manual.

1804, 44 Geo. III., c. 54.

The Acts relating to the Militia and Volunteers already cited were shorn of all but historical importance by the passing (June 5th, 1804) of the statute 44 Geo. III. c. 54, entitled "An Act to consolidate and amend the provisions of the several Acts relating to Corps of Yeomanry and Volunteers in Great Britain, and to make further regulations relating thereto." The number of Volunteers in Great Britain, according to the Estimates 1803-4, was 379,343; and it was certainly desirable that the law relating to so large a body of armed men should not require to be sought in the disconnected clauses of scattered statutes. It was this consideration, no doubt, and the necessity for some amendment of existing regulations that led to the Consolidation Act of 1804, which, though repealed by 26 and 27 Vic., c. 65, s. 51, so far as relates to the Volunteers of Great Britain, may still lay claim to the careful attention of the historical student, as being the statute upon which General Peel, in 1859, based the circular authorising the Volunteer levies of that year, a historic document which may be said to mark the "new birth" of the Volunteer movement.

26 & 27 Vict., c. 55, s. 51.

The third section provided that

"It should be lawful for His Majesty to continue the service of all Corps of Yeomanry or Volunteers accepted before the passing of that Act, and also to accept the services of any Corps of Yeomanry or Volunteers that might be formed after the passing thereof, such Corps respectively being formed under officers having or who should have commissions either from His Majesty or any Lieutenant of a county or any other person or persons who might be specially authorised by His Majesty for that purpose, as to His Majesty might seem proper, upon such terms and conditions, and under and according to such rules and regulations as had been approved by His Majesty in regard to such Corps whose services had been accepted before the passing of that Act, and upon such terms and conditions, and under and according to such rules and regulations with regard to such Corps whose services should be accepted after the passing thereof, as to His Majesty might thereafter seem fit and proper, and to disband or discontinue the services of any Corps of Yeomanry or Volunteers then formed or thereafter to be formed respectively, or of any parts of such Corps, whenever it might seem expedient to His Majesty to do so."

No limitation was placed on the number of Volunteers whose services might be accepted under this Act. The voluntary nature of the service induced Parliament to waive the usual restrictions.

The 4th section enacted that

"Every person enrolled or to be enrolled and serving as an effective member of any Corps of Yeomanry or Volunteers in Great Britain, and who should be duly returned or certified as such under the Act, should be exempt from being liable to serve personally or to provide a substitute in the Militia of Great Britain or in any additional force raised or to be raised for the defence of the realm and more vigorous prosecution of the war under any Act or Acts of the last Session of Parliament, or under any Act or Acts of the present or future Session of Parliament* and should remain exempt so long as he should continue to be and be returned or certified an effective member, in manner by that Act required, and no longer."

Conditions of efficiency.

The conditions of efficiency as defined in the 5th section were, for a member of the Infantry,

"To have duly attended, properly armed and accoutred, at the muster or exercise of the Corps to which he belonged, eight days at the least in the course of the four months next preceding each return made under the Act, unless absent with leave or from sickness duly certified."

The ninth section provided for three returns yearly, viz.:—on April 1, August 1, December 1, of each year. Section 5, then, really imposed attendance on 24 days yearly.

If arms and accoutrements had not been issued to a Volunteer at the expense of His Majesty in time to permit of his appearing at muster and exercise properly armed and accoutred, an attendance unarmed and unaccoutred was to count towards efficiency.

Inspection.

No members of any Corps of Yeomanry or Volunteers were to be entitled to any exemption under that Act, unless the Commanding Officer thereof should, at the times of transmitting the

*See 43 Geo. III. c. 121. The exemption from the Militia is from serving or finding a substitute therein after being balloted and drawn—that from the additional force was from being balloted for at all. R. P. B.

muster roll in manner directed by that Act, certify that such Corps had been inspected at least once in the space of the preceding four months by some General or Field Officer of His Majesty's Regular forces, or, if such Inspection had not taken place, that such Corps had been ready and willing to be so inspected at its usual place or places and times of meeting.

This appears to be the first statutory provision for the inspection of Volunteers as a condition of efficiency.

Volunteers to be deducted from the Militia quota.

By the 16th section the Lieutenant or Deputy Lieutenants of every county, when they fixed, at any General Meeting, the proportion of men to serve in the Militia or any such additional force for the several hundreds or other divisions, should deduct the number of Yeomanry and Volunteers exempted as aforesaid from the number of persons liable to the ballot and apportion the quota for the several divisions accordingly.

Volunteers when liable for service.

By the 22nd section,

"In all cases of actual invasion or appearance of any enemy in force on the coast of Great Britain, or of rebellion or insurrection arising or existing within the same, on the appearance of any enemy in force on the coast, or during any invasion, all Corps of Yeomanry and Volunteers should, whenever they should be summoned by the Lieutenants of the counties in which they should be respectively formed, or their vice-Lieutenants or Deputy-Lieutenants, or upon the making of any general signals of alarm, forthwith assemble within their respective districts, and should be liable to march according to the terms and conditions of their respective services, whether the same should extend to Great Britain, or be limited to any district, county, city, town, or place therein."

Persons not responding to the summons were to be deemed deserters and liable to punishment as such.

Volunteer Officers to lead their own Corps.

Whenever (section 24) any Corps of Volunteers assembled for active service they might be put under such General Officer as His Majesty might think fit to appoint, or as should be commanding in the district. "Provided always that such Corps should be led by their respective officers under such command as aforesaid."

Courts Martial.

By section 25 no officer serving in any of His Majesty's other forces was to sit on any Courts Martial upon the trial of any officer, non-commissioned officer, drummer, trumpeter, or private man in any Corps of Yeomanry or Volunteers.

Rank of Volunteer Officers.

By section 26 all officers in Corps of Yeomanry or Volunteers, having commissions from His Majesty or Lieutenants of Counties, or others who might be specially authorised by His Majesty for that purpose, should rank with the officers of His Majesty's Regular and Militia forces as the youngest of their respective ranks.

By section 27 the commanding officer of any Corps of Yeomanry or Volunteers, when not summoned or assembled upon actual service, was empowered to discharge any member of the Corps under his command, not being a commissioned officer, for any disobedience of orders or breach of discipline while under arms, and also for any neglect of attendance or duty, or misconduct, or improper behaviour as a member of his Corps, or for other sufficient cause, the existence and sufficiency of such several causes respectively being to be judged by such commanding officer, and immediately to strike such person out of the muster roll of the Corps to which he should belong.

Commanding Officer's power of dismissal.

A further section (the 29th) empowered the commanding officer in certain cases to order an offender into custody.

The 30th and 31st sections empowered a Volunteer, on giving up his arms, accoutrements, clothing and appointments (if furnished at the public expense, or by any other person or by public subscription), in good order and condition (reasonable wear and tear excepted) and paying up his subscriptions, dues and penalties, to quit the Corps on giving fourteen days' notice in writing.

Power of Volunteer to quit.

By the 36th section Volunteers assembled on the summons of the Lord Lieutenant or upon a general signal of alarm were to be entitled to a bounty of two guineas, and during such service to receive pay and be billeted as the other forces; and their families, if unable to support themselves, were to be relieved at the public charge during the absence of their head in the discharge of his duty.

Pay.

After the defeat or expulsion of the enemy from Great Britain, and suppression of any such rebellion or insurrection (the Legislature, by the way, seems never to have contemplated the defeat of the Volunteers), the men were to be returned to their respective counties, and any Volunteer willing to receive the same was to have a bounty of one guinea.

Commissioned officers disabled on active service were to be entitled to half-pay according to their ranks; non-commissioned officers, drummers and private men to the benefit of Chelsea Hospital; the widows of officers killed on service to such pensions for life as were given to the widows of officers in His Majesty's Regular forces.

Pensions.

Armoury.

The 42nd section provided for the selection of a proper place in the parish or place in which the Corps should be formed, or in each of the different parishes or places, if more companies than one were formed in different parishes and united in one Corps, for the depositing and safe keeping of the arms and accoutrements of the Corps, and also for the appointment of proper persons to repair and keep such arms in good state and condition; and for the annual viewing of such arms and accoutrements by any two or more Deputy-Lieutenants.

Rules to be approved by principal Secretary of State.

By the 56th section all rules and regulations were to be submitted by the commanding officer to His Majesty's principal Secretary of State, and unless and until approved by him were to be inoperative.

Number and cost of Volunteers. 1804-8.

The number of Volunteers during the years which ensued between the passing of the Volunteer and Yeomanry Act of 1804 and the establishment of the Local Militia in 1808, and their annual cost to the country during part of that period appear clearly from the following table:—

January men.	July men.	Cost.
1804—380,195	369,503	£1,282,818 12 7
1805—360,814	354,683	1,159,485 1 4
1806—351,508	349,226	1,171,011 0 4 (to April 25, 1806)
1807—334,910	333,761	
1808—336,404	no returns.	

The number of men deficient on the original establishment up to May 2nd, 1808, was 58,655.

By the returns of December 1st, 1806, the Volunteer force numbered:—

Cavalry	29,886
Infantry	294,503
Artillery	11,803
Total in Great Britain	336,192

It appears that the War Office strongly favoured the adoption of scarlet in the uniform of Volunteers of this period, as Lord Hobart, in announcing the acceptance by His Majesty of an offer to raise 500 privates in the city of Edinburgh, on the footing of the late first regiment of Royal Edinburgh Volunteers, strongly recommended that an exception be not urged in what related to the clothing of the regiment, as it had been judged expedient that the clothes of the Volunteers, as well as the Regular Infantry, should be scarlet.

The great drain upon the national treasury implied in the above figures could only be justified by the necessity of levying so large a body of men, and by a conviction that the levies were really worth the cost they entailed. The Secretary for War, Mr. Windham, was apparently not satisfied upon the latter of these points, and he introduced a measure, subsequently carried into law as the General Training Act of 1806, and which has the peculiar distinction of never having been acted on and never repealed until the year 1875.*

General Training Act, 1806. 46 Geo. III., c. 90.

Mr. Windham, on introducing the Bill, I quote from the report in the *Leeds Mercury* of April 13, 1806, after dealing with the outline of his plan relative to the regular army, said: "He should proceed to a subject which he considered of equal importance, and that was the Volunteers. They all knew that corps of this description had been formed upon false conceptions. The Government said, 'the country is in danger, every man must arm.' The Volunteers armed, and then they said, 'let us look and manœuvre like soldiers,' and in this the Government had acquiesced. To this he attributed all the difficulty which had since arisen. He differed entirely from those who accepted the service of many of these Corps. The Volunteers were nevertheless of some service; but they now cost Government about £5,000,000 a year, and as the Volunteer subscriptions for their support were in a great measure exhausted, their continuance to the end of this year would incur a charge of £10,000,000, a sum which was completely lost to the defence of the country in any other way. He should therefore propose great reductions in this force as at present constituted, and instead of trying to perfect their discipline he would admit of considerable relaxation in that respect. This would be attended with no disadvantage, but he should not wish to reduce them altogether until another species of service grew after them."

The right honourable gentleman also mentioned various items of expense attending Volunteer Corps, inspecting officers, permanent duty, drill sergeants &c., amounting to £817,000, of which it was his intention to propose the immediate discontinuance. Those who in future entered into the Volunteers' Corps were to be considered as serving at their own expense. Those who discontinued their services would be liable to the levy *en masse* but in consideration of their previous training they would be entitled to some indulgences. In case of an actual necessity for employing any part of the levy *en masse* it was intended to select that portion by lot according to their

*Milita (Voluntary Enlistment) Act, 1875, 38 and 39 Vic, c. 69, sec. 98.

various classes, distinguished by the ages of 16, 24, 34 and 40 years. The Act containing these regulations would be annual. The number of Volunteers in the respective districts would be deducted from the amount of the force required previous to the ballot. The days of training within the year he should propose to be 26, for each of which the individuals under training would receive a shilling. The officers and men appointed to instruct them would be drawn from the Militia and the 57 second battalions of the regiments of the line, the officers of which had been all appointed before a single man was got and who were now gaping like oysters when the ebb was leaving them. He would now turn them to grass in this new pasture, and if they could put any flesh on their bones it would be a very desirable object. The government would defray the expense of Volunteer clothing for this year but no longer. He then concluded with moving for leave to bring in a bill to repeal the Act 44 of his then present Majesty known by the title of the Additional Force Act.

The *Leeds Mercury* of April 9th set forth a summary of Windham's Training Bill, as it was called, and it is of interest to preserve not only this, but the contemporary comments on the proposal, as illustrating a phase of Volunteer development.

"The Defence Bill," said the *Mercury*, "it is proposed to repeal, because though it has for some weeks past been more productive than for any similar period since it was enacted in 1804 numberless objections, independent of its inefficiency, which we urged against it at that time, continue unremoved and undiminished. The principal are, its partial operation, being confined to those counties which contain large and populous towns such as Lancashire, Cheshire, Yorkshire, Warwickshire, &c., whereas counties not possessing such advantages have no alternative but to pay the fine of £20 a man.

LEVY EN MASSE.

This measure to be partially carried into effect. The persons liable to it to be divided into three classes from the age of 16 to 24, 24 to 32, and from 32 to 40, none above the latter age.

The number to be drilled not to exceed 200,000 in one year. The drills to be in their own parishes and for 26 days. The battalions which were appointed to receive the men under the Defence Bill, and the Militia, to supply the drill sergeants. The portion to be drilled to be drawn by lot, when each man to be paid a shilling each time. No clothing allowed. Thus the whole population of the country will, by rotation, learn the use of arms, and in case of invasion the casualties in our Regulars may be supplied, *ad infinitum*, by draft from the different counties and parishes of men so far advanced in military discipline, or they may be formed into separate irregular Corps to harass the enemy under the command of experienced officers. Such persons as wish to avoid the Levy *en masse* Bill will be required to enrol themselves as Volunteers or to pay the fine.

VOLUNTEERS.

No reduction whatever to take place. The whole to be put on the same footing namely, those raised in June to be put on the same allowances as those raised in August. That as the former, instead of being required to attend 85 drills and paid for the same, are now only required to attend 26 drills, including inspections, for these attendances the whole are to be paid as before. The permanent duty is to be dispensed with, it being conceived to be no longer necessary. The pay of drill sergeants to be reduced and the expense of inspecting field officers saved. £1 per man to be allowed at the expiration of the 3 years for clothing. All persons who become Volunteers from this time, in order to avoid the levy *en masse* bill, to be supplied with arms, but to put the country to no expense. The Lords Lieutenant of Counties to appoint some of their deputies to inspect the Volunteer Corps. Corps of Yeomanry Cavalry to be allowed for contingent expenses £2 per man instead of £120 per troop. The annual expense of Volunteer Corps estimated at nearly £1,500,000. The proposed saving to the country as follows:—

Change from June to August allowances ..	£210,000
Pay of drill sergeants	54,700
Permanent duty given up	300,000
Marching guineas	198,000
Inspections	35,000
Sundry articles of saving	80,300
Total ..	£878,000

In case of the Volunteers being called out, no Volunteer officer (who had not had rank in the regulars) to command regular officers except under the rank of Captain.

The *Mercury's* leader of April 26th on Mr. Windham's proposals, and the speeches in the House anent those proposals are also instructive. The leader was as follows:—

"We trust that the unpleasant sensations excited in the minds of the Volunteers by the first opening of the new military plan of Mr. Windham will be in a great measure removed by the softened explanation he has given of those parts of his speech which had given the most offence. Immediately after this explanation was a motion made by Mr. Percival in the House of Commons for the production of papers relative to the Volunteer establishment, and in which he commented with great severity upon that part of the plan which went to substitute the Levy *en masse* instead of the present system. Upon this occasion Mr. Windham in reply said it never entered into his mind to propose the disbandment or even the reduction of this force, for that the whole of his alteration in the Volunteer system consisted of a few measures of economy. They went merely to put the Volunteers on the original voluntary service, and in fact the general tendency of his plan was rather to increase than diminish their numbers. The Bill only went to put those into the mass who were unwilling to serve at their own expense, and to take out of the mass those who wished to serve at their own expense. Mr. Windham further said that he had been charged with saying that the army was degraded by the Volunteers wearing the same colour. All that he had said to merit this imputation was that, as the army everywhere existed as a distinct body, and its character depending in a great measure on this distinction, a part of its discipline and character was lost when this distinction was multiplied. He further stated that what he meant by relaxing the discipline of the Volunteers was simply that they should attend a similar number of days and that there should be no permanent duty. With respect to their attendance at drills on the other days or their being subject at proper times to military law no alteration was made.

It appears that the Volunteers on the August establishment (comprising about five-sixths of the whole number) will, in case the proposed arrangement be carried into effect, be placed in point of allowances in a better situation than that in which they now stand under the Act of Parliament by which they were constituted, and under which they are legally entitled to only 20 days' pay."

The following extract of the effective strength of the Volunteers in Great Britain, distinguishing Infantry, Cavalry and Artillery, according to the returns dated 1st December, 1806, shews to what magnitude the auxiliary force had at this time attained :—

INFANTRY.

Field Officers	1,258
Captains	3,854
Subalterns	7,456
Staff Officers	1,786
Sergeants	13,826
Trumpeters and Drummers ...	6,762
Rank and File	259,501
Total	294,443

Mr. Windham was succeeded at the War Office by Lord Castlereagh, and it is to the latter statesman we owe that Local Militia Act, which, in my humble judgment, contains that principle of "universal service," which authorities of infinitely more experience and weight than I pretend to, do not hesitate to advocate as the only satisfactory solution of the military problems that are, more and more insistently, forcing themselves upon the thoughtful minds of our country. Lord Castlereagh's measure was, it may be observed, called by hostile critics, a Conscription Bill; but to employ terms of abuse when arguments are lacking is a species of strategy to which a lawyer at all events is too accustomed to be misled by it.

Lord Castlereagh's Memo., March, 1807.

Lord Castlereagh appears to have been profoundly impressed by the urgent necessity of constituting some national reserve that should be alike sufficient, efficient and economical. He submitted a memorandum to the Cabinet in March, 1807, which embodied his views as to the principles that should guide the legislature in the constitution of the auxiliary reserve.

The arguments he adduced are as applicable to the present time as to the date when they were conceived and I therefore extract the principal terms of the memorandum.

The following principles are suggested as the proposed system of training:—

"That learning the use of arms should be imposed as a *positive duty* upon all individuals within certain ages—say between the ages of 20 and 30—to be enforced by fine."

"That the State shall furnish the means and pay the expense of instruction, but not allow pay to those to be trained for attendance on drill musters, &c."

"In order to put individuals to the least possible inconvenience, instead of compelling them to assemble at times and places that may be extremely inconvenient to them, to be drilled, they should be relieved from all such attendance, and should be required, however, in lieu thereof, to have themselves trained at their own times and places, in the manual and platoon exercises."

"In order to facilitate instruction, Government to employ and distribute in each county such a number of drill sergeants as might be adequate generally to instruct all the individuals within the military ages. They might consist of the permanent sergeants and corporals of the Sedentary Militia, of sergeants of Volunteer Corps choosing to undertake the duty, or of any other individuals who might be approved as competent by the inspecting field officers and adjutants of the Sedentary Militia, to whom the control and superintendance of the whole system might be given.

Men not certified as trained to be mustered once in six months in their respective parishes; and if found not drilled, to be fined 10/-, the fine to be increased 10/- every succeeding half-yearly muster till a certificate is obtained, the fine to be double on persons worth the sum of £   or £   per year.

Local Militia Act, 1808. 48 Geo. III., c. 3.

The cardinal principle of "universal service," which so evidently possessed the mind of Lord Castlereagh, did not fail to impress itself upon the statute promoted by him and known as the Local Militia Act of 1808.

Lord Hawksbury in supporting the introduction of the Bill explained that the new force intended to be constituted under its provisions was designed to supersede the Volunteers, a feat, by the way, it very nearly accomplished. He did not, continued the noble lord, object to the Volunteer system so far as it went, but it could not be altogether relied on, as its efficiency rested upon a spirit which might dwindle and evaporate. The Local Militia, being more permanent and compulsory, would remedy this defect. It was intended to raise 213,609 men between the ages of 16 and 30. The age of 16 was, in the Act, raised to 18.

It may be thought that the terms and operations of this statute, avowedly a Militia Act, do not fall within the scope of this work; but it will be found, on examination, that most of the Volunteers of the country availed themselves of the permissive clauses of the statute, and the local militiamen were in fact, *mutato nomine*, Volunteers. The very preamble establishes a distinction between them and the Regular Militia forces. It set forth, that "it is expedient in the present circumstances of Europe that a Local Militia force shall be established, trained and permanently maintained, under certain restrictions, in England, to be called forth and employed, in case of invasion, in aid of His Majesty's Regular and Militia forces for the defence of the realm. The statute then enacts that "a permanent Local Militia force shall be balloted and enrolled in England." The number to be raised, together with the Yeomanry and effective Volunteers, to be equal to six times the quotas contemplated under 42 Geo. III. c. 90. The men to be raised were to be balloted out of and from the persons between the ages of 18 and 30 returned in the lists then existing or thereafter to be compiled. No person balloted to serve in the Local Militia was to be allowed to find or provide any substitute to serve in his stead or be entitled to any bounty or half bounty. Many persons exempted in the Regular Militia were not to be so exempt from the Local, *e.g.*, articled clerks, apprentices, poor men with less than three children, persons under the height of 5 feet 4 inches but reaching 5 feet 2 inches. Every Local Militiaman was enrolled for service for 4 years, at the end of which time he was to be free from the chances of the Regular Militia ballot for 2 years. Tho' substitution of service was prohibited, exemption might be purchased, a man of over £200 yearly income escaping by paying a penalty of £30, one of less than £200, but over £100, £20, and a person of less than £100 yearly income, £10. If a man could produce a certificate that he was an effective member of a Volunteer or Yeomanry Corps and would engage to serve therein at his own expense without pay or allowance, half of the above fines were to be remitted. It is evident that this measure exposed the poorest private in a Volunteer Corps to a fine of £5 at a time when £5 notes were even less plentiful than now. It is no matter of wonder then that the Volunteers throughout the kingdom promptly transfigured themselves into Local Militiamen. To prevent the expense of a ballot the statute provided that every person who should voluntarily enrol himself in the Local Militia should be entitled to and receive the sum of 2 guineas, to be paid upon his enrolment, over and above any sum to which he might be entitled for necessaries. In addition, every person enrolled under the Act was, upon being called up for training and exercise, to be entitled to the sum of one guinea for the first year of his service, and half a guinea for each succeeding year of service. The men were to be formed into regiments, battalions and companies, and have such proportion of officers, sergeants, corporals and drummers as were allowed to the Regular Militia when embodied, and these officers and non-commissioned officers were to take precedence as the youngest of the same grade of the Regular Militia. No higher rank than that of lieutenant-colonel could be enjoyed by any officer of the Local Militia as such. Every officer of any corps of Volunteers transferring himself with his corps into the Local Militia was to be eligible to the same rank in the Local Militia. The Local Militia were liable to be called out for training and exercise for 28 days, not necessarily consecutive, exclusive of the days spent in going to and from the rendezvous. Regard was to be had to the local circumstances of each county, and to the seasons most important to the course of industry and cultivation within the same. In cases of invasion or the appearance of an enemy upon the coast or of any rebellion or insurrection arising out of such invasion, the Local Militiamen could be marched to any part of the United Kingdon. They were also to be at the disposal of the Lord Lieutenant for the suppression of any riots or tumults in their own or an adjacent county. When embodied for service they were to be entitled to the same pay as the Militia when embodied, and when not embodied to the same pay as the Regular Militia when not embodied.

Parliamentary Returns of Local Militia.

The experiment—for such it was—initiated by the Act of 1808, whose provisions I have so fully recapitulated, was entirely successful. In the first year, says Mr. Clode, 250 regiments were raised; 184 regiments with 139,440 men for England, and 66 regiments with 45,721 for Scotland, so that the government was able to reduce the bounty from £2 to £1 1s. 0d. In the year 1812 the Returns laid before Parliament shew that 214,418 men out of an establishment of 240,388 men were serving in the Local Militia, and that 68,643 men out of an establishment of 99,368 men were serving in the Volunteer corps.

It was the custom for the officers of the Volunteers to read to their men the provisions of the Local Militia Act, and to exhort them to join the Local Militia. The officers themselves set the example, and it was largely followed though not universally. The historic Cinque Port Volunteers, for instance, were disbanded, being absorbed in the Local Militia.*

That the executive by every means in its power encouraged the Volunteers to transfer their services to the Local Militia, and that a very considerable proportion, though by no means all, of the Volunteers did so transfer their services, proofs are abundant. The following circular from the War Office to commandants of Volunteer corps betrays the anxiety of the Department to foster the movement:

"War Office, August 5th, 1808.

Sir,

As a considerable proportion of the Volunteer corps which have already offered to transfer their services into the Local Militia have been assembled on permanent duty in the course of the present year, and it is understood that it would be particularly inconvenient to many other corps desirous of transferring their services into the Local Militia to be assembled and called out for exercise during the ensuing Autumn unless in case of absolute necessity, I have received directions to acquaint you that it is not His Majesty's intention to call upon any corps of Volunteers transferring their services into the Local Militia to assemble for exercise until the Spring of the next year.

I have the honour to be, &c.,

JAS. PULTENEY."

As another instance of official favour to the Local Militia, I may mention that orders were given by the Commander-in-Chief that no regiment of the line or of the Regular Militia should recruit in any town in which any Corps of Local Militia was assembled for exercise; nor enlist any man serving in any such corps until the period of his training was complete.†

Even the adjutants reaped advantage from the unwonted beneficent spirit pervading the War Office, and even the *Leeds Mercury*, from whose issue of 27th August, 1808, I extract the following, was constrained to admit the justice of the Government's action:—

"We are informed that an additional allowance of 2/- a day is to be given to Volunteer adjutants, a measure we highly approve, as most of them have been long in the service, and at the present they have no lodging money, and but in few instances, forage for a

---

*Leeds Mercury, June 24th, 1809.

†Leeds Mercury, June 3rd, 1809.

horse which the individual is compelled to keep for the public service. This reduces his pay to about 15/- per week. It is to be hoped that the grant will be retrospective to the date of their commissions as a partial indemnification for the expense they have already been at."

The same organ, which readers who have not the privilege of being Yorkshiremen may need to be told was, in the early years of the century, the undaunted champion of Whiggery in the North of England, and which I therefore quote without apology as a fair exponent of the Opposition views, thus writes of the success of the Local Militia Act (September 24, 1808) :—

"The Volunteer force on which so many eulogiums have been spoken and written seems doomed to fail. My Lord Castlereagh has certainly some claim to skill in this business. Mr. Windham while in office spoke of the inefficiency of this force with much freedom, and the then Opposition extolled the Volunteers to the skies. So soon, however, as the present Secretary of War came into office, he was led to overturn the system, but he proceeded more warily about the business. He effected by sap what his predecessor, a sort of upright and downright man, attempted by storm, and in order to put the finishing touches to the business it is now said that the pay and exemptions of the remaining Volunteer Corps are to be withdrawn, and the Local Militia raised to at least 200,000 men."

In that part of its leading article which was based upon the supposition that pay was to be withheld from the Volunteers the *Mercury* was at fault. The Volunteers, such as remained of them, continued to be entitled to and receive the pay and to enjoy the exemptions secured to them under the terms of their engagement.

1810. 50 Geo. III., c. 25.

By section 3 of an Act passed in 1810 the number of days' attendance at exercise and training sufficient to exempt Volunteers from liability to enrolment in the Local or General Militia was reduced from the twenty four days fixed by the statute of 1804 to a period not exceeding eighteen days.

Local Militia Act, 1812. 52 Geo. III., c. 38.

The men enrolled under the Act of 1808 were so enrolled for a term of 4 years, and it was apparent that the greater part of the Local Militia would fall to be disbanded in 1812. The force had, however, been too popular, and, presumably, too useful, to be suffered to cease to exist. In 1812 the Local Militia Acts were consolidated. There was, however, some alteration in principle which formed the subject of parliamentary animadversion. The idea on which the Act of 1808 was based was that the whole of the adult male population, within certain prescribed ages, should be trained to military service. The Act of 1812 proposed to allow, and did allow, those who had already served for four years to continue their services, under certain conditions, thus constituting, as it were, a species of professional local militiamen. It was to this deviation from the original conception sanctioned by Parliament that Mr. Whitehead referred when he said "The noble lord originally proposed that measure (the Act of 1808) as one by which the whole male population of the country might be gradually trained. The greater part of the Local Militia now embodied had already served three years, and would therefore fall to be disbanded in the course of the following year, the men not being capable, by the present law, of continuing embodied more than four years. The present bill, however, proposed that, on an understanding taking place between the commandant and the men, a certain portion of the present Local Militia might be continued. Thus, then, was the plan of proceeding in a series and of training the whole population of the country by degrees to be abandoned." Mr. Secretary Ryder in defending the scheme of the bill did not deny that "the acceptance of the voluntary services of such corps of the Local Militia as chose to offer themselves was a deviation from the original conception of 1808, which had rested upon the ballot. But he defended the innovation on the grounds, first, it would produce a much more efficient force; secondly, it would relieve the country from a great inconvenience and burden, by preventing the necessity of calling persons away from their avocations in husbandry, &c., during the harvest; and lastly, it would cause a saving of not less than £100,000 a year."*

By the terms of the Act of 1812 no enrolments were to be made when the number of men serving in any county, including effective but excluding supernumerary Yeomanry and Volunteers, amounted to six times the original quota of the Militia fixed for such county under the General Militia Acts. This provision, then, fixed a numerical limit to the numbers of the Local Militia. Infantry Volunteers might, under the direction of the Lord Lieutenant, transfer themselves into the Local Militia of the same district, and, if they had served on and from the 12th May, 1809, were to be

*21 H. D. (O. S.) p. 868; quoted by Clode, "Military Forces of the Crown," vol. 1., cap. XIV., para. 146, 147.

entitled to a bounty of two guineas and an allowance for necessaries from the secretary at war.

With the consent of the inhabitants, Volunteers belonging to the same or some adjoining place might be enrolled and a rate established, to the payment of which persons in the Local or Regular Militia were not liable, for paying bounties not exceeding two guineas each. Sec. 36. Rate-aided Volunteers.

If a sufficient number of persons between 18 and 35, not under 5 feet 2 inches, fit for military service, having not more than two children under 14, voluntarily enrolled themselves, no ballot was to take place in that parish. Sec. 37.

The Local Militia might be called out yearly to be trained, for not more than 28 days in each year. It was not to be marched out of the county, unless into an adjoining one for convenience of training. On actual service it might be marched to any part of Great Britain, but on no account to be ordered to go out of Great Britain. It was not to be kept embodied for more than six weeks after the enemy had withdrawn from the coast, or the rebellion or insurrection necessitating its services been suppressed. Training limited to 28 days.

In 1813, however, the Crown was authorized to accept from the Local Militia voluntary offers of service out of their counties for a period not exceeding forty days in the whole year, and limited by the duration of the Act to the 25th March, 1815. 54 Geo. III., c. 19, extended by 56 Geo. III., c. 76.

The Battle of Waterloo, which effected so many other things, gave the death-blow to the Local Militia. It destroyed, as was thought, the necessity for such a force. Accordingly, on May 21st, 1816, an Act of one clause received the Royal assent. It recited that it was expedient that His Majesty should be empowered to suspend any ballot or enrolment for the Local Militia, and His Majesty was empowered to direct, by an Order in Council, that no such ballot or enrolment should take place; but that such ballot and enrolment should remain and continue suspended for the period specified in any such Order of Council, and from time to time, by any like Order or Orders in Council, to continue such suspension so long as His Majesty should deem the same expedient. 56 Geo. III., c. 38.

A suspensory order was accordingly issued on the 27th of June, 1816, and so on annually till the year 1836, when the issue ceased.

On June 24th, 1817, the office of Agent-General for Local Militia and Volunteers was abolished, and his duties transferred to the Paymaster-General and Secretary at War. June, 1817. Office of Agent Genl. of Local Militia and Volunteers abolished.

PART I.

SECTION IV.

The Battle of Waterloo gave England peace for many long and tranquil years. That battle, indeed the whole of the prolonged contest with Napoleon, a contest in which most of the thrones of Europe were supported by British arms and British gold, had so firmly established the prestige of the United Kingdom that for forty years we were free from European complications. The Indian Mutiny, the Chinese War, necessitated no call upon the voluntary services of the people. Even the Crimean War, waged at a distance so remote from our shores and with an enemy so weak in the means of transport, excited in no breast the slighest apprehension of a descent upon our coast. The Volunteer levies had been almost entirely disbanded. They had served their turn and it was fondly hoped that never again would occasion arise for their services. The Duke of Wellington, almost alone among the statesmen of his day, did not share the general confidence. In his 77th year he addressed to Sir John Burgoyne a pathetic letter that revealed the misgivings that beset a mind that to the last was full of anxious thought for the country he had served so well. "You will see," he wrote in 1847, "from what I have written that I have contemplated the danger. I have done so for years. I have drawn to it the attention of different administrations at different times. You will see likewise that I have considered of the measures of prospective security and of the mode and cost of their attainment. I have done more. I have looked at and considered those localities in quiet detail and have made up my mind upon the details of their defence. Those are questions to which my mind has not been unaccustomed. I have considered and provided for the defence—the successful defence—of the frontiers of many countries. I am especially sensible of the certainty of failure if we do not, at an early moment, attend to the measures necessary for our defence and of the disgrace, the indelible disgrace, of such failure. x x x x. I am bordering upon 77 years of age, passed in honor. I hope that the Almighty may protect me from being the witness of the tragedy which I cannot persuade my contemporaries to take measures to avert."

Disbandment of Volunteers after Waterloo.

The Duke of Wellington on the national defences (1847).

It chanced that in the general disbandment, in addition to the Honourable Artillery Company, one regiment of those raised in 1803 had escaped entire extinction. It had been originally known as "The Duke of Cumberland's Sharp Shooters." It had been remodelled under another name, "The Royal Victoria Rifle Regiment." It was entirely self-supporting, regularly organised, possessed a staff of officers, a good rifle range, an armoury, orderly room and drill ground. But its tenure of life was frail and precarious. It had existed as a rifle club for a quarter of a century and it was only in 1853 that it was allowed to assemble Volunteers for regular drill. In 1858 it mustered but 57 effective men. In this diminutive force Captain Hans Busk held a commission. He was a barrister-at-law and High Sheriff of Radnorshire. He appears to have taken to heart the solemn warnings of the great Duke, or perhaps his own reflections and observations had led him to like conclusions. He infused new life and vigour into the Royal Victoria Rifle Regiment. By the middle of 1859 the force, which a year before had dwindled to 57 effectives, mustered no less than 800 strong. He spread broadcast copies of the Duke of Wellington's letter from which I have quoted. He wrote and published a Rifleman's Manual. He lectured wherever he could get a hearing, he interviewed ministers, but without success; and if not the author of the Volunteer movement of modern times, as to which I offer no opinion, none can question his devotion to the cause.

The Royal Victoria Rifles.

Captain Hans Busk.

It would not, indeed, serve any useful purpose to burden these pages with a discussion as to who was the originator of the 1859 movement. There were other aspirants than Captain Hans Busk for the honour, and much was written and said at the time in support of those who claimed the distinction of first advocating so important an organization. Its rise had been by some ascribed to *The Times* newspaper, and to that spirited production of the Poet Laureate which will find a fitting place in a subsequent page. This "*Form, Riflemen, Form*," provoked Captain J. E. Acklom, late of the 28th Regiment, and Barrack Master at Jersey, one of those who claimed the distinction I have referred to, to exclaim, "As well say that Sebastopol fell because 'Cheer, Boys, Cheer,' was versified." Captain Acklom himself wrote a spirited brochure full of "thoughts that breathe and words that burn," under the title of "Ready, or England for ever safe from the Invader," presentation copies of which were distributed to all leading members of Parliament, military men, the Clubs, the Horse Guards, Lords Lieutenant of counties, high Government officials, and a copy was sent also to

Captain Acklom.

His Royal Highness the Prince Consort, to whom the pamphlet was dedicated. Captain Kinloch also laid equal claim to be the originator of the movement, and, to quote from the *United Service Gazette* of 30th April, 1859, he too was "amongst the most earnest and intelligent of the authors of an improved system of Home Defence." Captain Kinloch expressed the hope that General Peel (the Secretary for War) would see the matter in its true light, and gain some additional credit from his country by countenancing the plan.

The Long Acre Meeting. April, 1859.

The leaven worked. In April, 1859, a mass meeting, known as the Long Acre Indignation meeting, was held in St. Martin's Hall, protesting against the insufficiency of the National Defences.

Exeter Volunteers.

Already, however, in Exeter, a Volunteer Corps had been established. Sir John Bucknell and his friends Dr. Pycroft and Mr. George Haydon had, in 1852, discussed the initiation of what was afterwards the 1st Rifle Volunteer Corps. In January of that year they had approached the then Earl Fortescue, suggesting a Corps of Volunteer Riflemen, and the Earl had communicated with Sir George Grey, the Secretary of State, who had replied intimating the readiness of his Government to advise the acceptance, in certain cases, of the services of Volunteer Corps. On March 26th, the new Secretary of State, Mr. Walpole, announced that the Queen had been pleased to accept the offers of the riflemen of Essex. In due course officers were appointed. The earliest commission in what may be termed the new or resuscitated Volunteer service was given to Captain Denis Moore, the Town Clerk of Exeter. In 1852 also, Mr. Nathaniel Bousfield, of Liverpool, had gathered around him nearly a hundred gentlemen with uniform and arms, who, in 1855, formed the Liverpool Drill Club, but the application of the club for enrolment as a corps was not received with favour. When, two years later, the formation of corps was of daily occurrence, Sir Duncan MacDougal wrote "I consider Captain Bousfield and his Corps of Lancashire Rifles to have been the immediate cause of the late Government having issued the circular authorizing the formation of Volunteer Corps." On 11th June, 1859, Mr. Bousfield received the first commission granted to a Volunteer under the great revival.*

Thus examples and prototypes were not wanting when the events passing in France in 1859 added weight to the arguments of those who viewed our national unpreparedness with gravest

*Woodburne's "The Story of our Volunteers."

concern. The third Napoleon had destroyed the Republic and assumed the Imperial crown. Rightly or wrongly he was credited in this country, despite his solemn protestations, with sinister designs. The victories of Magenta and Solferino and the wild language of the French press and the French mob stirred the public mind on this side the Channel to its profoundest depths.

Tennyson's appeal to the Nation.

Mr. Tennyson voiced the national attitude in words which are more valuable as a political fragment than as a triumph of his poetic genius :—

*There is a sound of thunder afar
  Storm in the South that darkens the day
Storm of battle and thunder of war!
  Well, if it do not roll away,
Storm, storm, riflemen form!
  Ready, be ready, against the storm!
Riflemen, riflemen, riflemen, form!

Be not deaf to the sound that warns,
  Be not gull'd by a despôt's plea!
Are figs of thistles? or grapes of thorns?
  How can a despot feel with the free?
Form, form, riflemen, form!
  Ready, be ready, to meet the storm!
Riflemen, riflemen, riflemen, form!

Let your reforms for a moment go!
  Look to your butts and take good aims!
Better a rotten borough or so,
  Than a rotten flesh and a city in flames!
Storm, storm, riflemen, form!
  Ready, be ready, against the storm!
Riflemen, riflemen, riflemen, form!

Form, be ready to do or die!
  Form in freedom's name and the Queen's!
True we have got *such* a faithful ally
  That only the devil can tell what he means.
Form, form, riflemen, form!
  Ready, be ready, to meet the storm!
Riflemen, riflemen, riflemen, form!

The following story, preserved by Lieutenant-Colonel J. G. Hicks in his "Records of the Percy Artillery" aptly illustrates the popular mood :—

"The late Lord Elgin on his way to India was dining at the Tuileries alone with the Emperor, Louis Napoleon. (They were old friends). It was after the outburst against England of the

*First published in "The Times," 9th May, 1859.

French colonels and the attempt to bully our Parliament into passing a special Act in connection with the attempt on the Emperor's life which led to the Volunteer movement of 1859. The Emperor recounted with some pride all the successes of his life, all he had been able to achieve and attain to in his career. When the Emperor finished, Lord Elgin said quietly, 'O but your Majesty has omitted the greatest achievement of all.' 'What was that?' said the Emperor with a puzzled look., 'Your Majesty has made the British a *Military* nation!' "

The War Office was roused from its accustomed torpor, and cast about for some vent for the national fervour. The machinery that lay to its hands was antiquated, if not obsolete, rusty and cumbersome. The Government may possibly have drawn inspiration from what had passed in India, two short years before, in the agony of the Indian Mutiny. In that awful ordeal the Volunteer Corps of the European and Eurasian communities had rendered services to whose value Havelock and other generals bore generous testimony. After 1859 the Volunteer forces of India were re-organised on the model of the British, and have more than once rallied to the assistance of the Civil power.* But not only precedent, authority, was needed for the action of the Government.

Yeomanry and Volunteer Act, 1804. (44 Geo. III., c. 54.)

In an unrepealed statute, cumbered with the dust of more than half a century, designed for other times and other conditions, the Executive found the semblance of a warrant for its action. It was the Yeomanry and Volunteer Consolidation Act of 1804, the essential provisions of which I have already set out. The 3rd section of that Act provided, it will be remembered, that it should be lawful for the Crown to continue the services of all Corps of Volunteers accepted before the Act and to accept the services of all Corps of Volunteers formed after the passing thereof: such Corps to be under the command of officers having commissions from the Crown or Lords Lieutenant, and to serve under such terms and conditions as to the Crown should seem meet. Those terms are recapitulated in the Circular next set forth. A Volunteer constituting himself an "Effective" under the Act was exempt from the Militia ballot, or rather from being liable to service if he should draw "an unlucky number" in such ballot.

Gen. Peel's Circular, May 12th, 1859.

It was under the provisions of this statute that General Peel, then Secretary for War, addressed to the Lords Lieutenant of

*The Army Book of the British Empire, p. 457.

counties his memorable, if somewhat jejune, circular of May 12th, 1859. It states that Her Majesty's Government having had under consideration the propriety of permitting the formation of Volunteer Rifle Corps, under the provisions of the statute of 44 Geo. III. c. 54, as well as of Artillery Corps and Companies in maritime towns, in which there might be forts and batteries, the Secretary would be glad to receive through the Lords Lieutenant, and to consider, any proposal with that object which might emanate from the counties under their charge. The circular then summarizes the provisions of the Act as follows:—

"That the Corps be formed under officers bearing the commission of the Lieutenant of the county."

"That its members must take the oath of allegiance before a Deputy Lieutenant or Justice of the Peace or a Commissioned Officer of the Corps."

"That it should be liable to be called out in case of actual invasion or appearance of an enemy in force on the coast, or in case of a rebellion arising out of either of those emergencies."

"That while thus under arms, its members be subject to military law and entitled to be billeted and to receive pay in like manner as the regular army."

"That all commissioned officers disabled in actual service be entitled to half-pay, and non-commissioned officers and privates to the benefit of the Chelsea Hospital, and widows of commissioned officers, killed in service, to such pensions for life as were given to widows of officers of Her Majesty's Regular forces."

"That members should not quit the Corps when on actual service, but might do so at any other time by giving 14 days' notice."

"That members who had attended 8 days in each 4 months, or a total of 24 days' drill or exercise in the year, be entitled to be returned as effective."*

"That members be exempt from Militia ballot or from being called upon to serve in any other levy."

NOTE.—The Circular appears to misstate the effect of the Act, the 17th section of which exempts from service, but expressly and in terms, *not* from ballot.

"That all property of the Corps be legally vested in the commanding officer and subscriptions and fines under the rules and regulations be recoverable by him before a magistrate."

---

*By 56 Geo. III., c. 39, sec. 1 this was reduced to 2 days in each month or 5 consecutive days.

The conditions on which any proposal would be accepted were stated to be :—

"That the promotion of the Corps be subject to the provisions of the Act."

Members to provide own arms, &c.

"That its members undertake to provide their own arms and equipments and to defray all expenses attending the Corps except in the event of its being assembled for actual service."

"That the rules and regulations which might be thought necessary be submitted to the Secretary for War in accordance with the 54th section of the Act."

"The uniform and equipments of the Corps might be settled by the members, subject to the approval of the Lord Lieutenant, but the arms, tho' provided at the expense of the members, must be furnished under the superintendence and according to the regulations of the War Office, in order to secure uniformity of guage."

Establishment.

"The establishment of officers and non-commissioned officers was to be fixed by the Secretary for War and recorded in the books of the War Office, and in order that he might be enabled to determine the proportions the Lords Lieutenant were requested to specify the precise number of private men which they would recommend and into how many companies they proposed to divide them."

The Circular concluded by reminding the Lords Lieutenant that the Secretary trusted to them to nominate proper persons to be appointed officers, subject to the Queen's approval.

I imagine that the records of this or any other country would be ransacked in vain to find a parallel to this Circular, which, whilst inviting the artisans and peasantry, whose earnings only in exceptional cases were more than sufficient for their daily needs, to volunteer for the defence of their country, cast upon rank and file alike the expense of finding their arms, accoutrements and uniforms. This ill-timed parsimony appears the less excusable when it is borne in mind that the Act on which the Circular is avowedly based provided for the supply of arms to the men at the cost of the Government (section 6) and, moreover, that, by section 16, the Militia quotas for each district were to be reduced by the number of effective Volunteers in that district, thus effecting a considerable saving to the country, but saving at the expense of the Volunteers. Again, by the 42nd section of the same Act, Magazines for the storage of arms were to be provided at the cost of the county, which also was to bear the expense of keeping the arms and accoutrements in proper order and condition. No such assistance was to be forthcoming for the Volunteers invited by General Peel's Circular, and one may be permitted to question whether it was competent for the Secretary for War to pick and choose such sections of the statute as his fancy dictated.

The Circular of the 12th May was supplemented by another of the 25th of the same month. It will be evident from its perusal that the original idea of the Government was the formation of companies rather than battalions. The conception of an united and considerable body of Volunteers, capable of being welded together into battalions, regiments and brigades, had not yet dawned upon the official mind, which probably was influenced by the Duke of Wellington, whose views as to the Volunteer force may be gathered from his remarks at Woolwich, in October, 1859, that "a Volunteer Corps should not, under any circumstances, comprise more than 100 men," and that the Corps which he himself commanded (the Royal Victoria Rifles) was "too numerous."

The supplementary Circular of May 25th was as follows. I reproduce it *in extenso* as a copy is not easily procurable:—

"War Office, Pall Mall,
25th May, 1859.

With reference to the Circular of May 12th sanctioning, under certain conditions, the enrolment of Volunteers, it seems essential, in order that the patriotic exertions of those who come forward may contribute most effectively to that which they have at heart—namely:—the defence and security of their country—that they should not be left in ignorance of the nature and character of the service to which they are thus binding themselves; but that the objects which such bodies of Volunteers should have in view should be clearly explained to them, as well as the peculiar duties expected from them, together with the best means of qualifying themselves for their effective discharge.

Genl. Peel's 2nd Circular, May 25th, 1859.

Premising that the Volunteers may be of two classes, one comprising those who may be instructed to act as riflemen or sharpshooters in the field; the other, those whose services may be rendered most valuable in our seaports and other coast towns, in manning the batteries constructed for their defence, it must be borne in mind that:—

1—The first essential, without which no body of Volunteers, however composed or organised, can hope to render available or really useful service, is that it should be amenable, when called upon to act, either in garrison or in the field, to military discipline; for without such discipline no general or other officer under whom they may have to act will be able to place much dependence on their assistance or co-operation in the hour of need.

2—In the second place, the conditions of service should be such as, while securing and enforcing the above necessary discipline, to induce those classes to come forward for service as Volunteers who do not, under our present system, enter either into the Regular Army or the Militia.

3—In the above view, the system of drill and instruction for bodies of Volunteers should not be such as to render the service unnecessarily irksome or to make demands upon the time of the members that would interfere injuriously with their ordinary avocations; thus either indisposing to the service, in the first instance, those who might otherwise have gladly joined it, or driving them again out of it, after a short experience of the inconveniences to which they have been exposed.

4—It should not be attempted, therefore, as regards Rifle Volunteers, to drill or organise them as soldiers expected to take their place in line, which would require time for instruction that could ill be spared; but it should be rather sought to give each individual Volunteer a thorough knowledge of the use of his weapon, and so to qualify the force to act efficiently as an auxiliary to the Regular Army and Militia, the only character to which it should aspire.

Establishment.

5—It is evident that this object will be best attained by the enrolment of Volunteers in small bodies, in companies consisting of an establishment of one captain, one lieutenant, one ensign and 100 men of all ranks, as a maximum, or in subdivisions, and even sections of companies, with the due proportion of officers, and composed of individuals having a knowledge of and thorough dependence upon each other personally; and it should rarely, if ever, be sought to form them into larger corps entailing the necessity of a lengthened and complicated system of drill instruction.

6—The nature of our country, with its numerous inclosures and other impediments to the operations of troops in line, gives peculiar importance to the service of Volunteer Riflemen, in which bodies each man, deriving confidence from his own skill in the use of his arm and from his reliance on the support of his comrades—men whom he has known, and with whom he has lived from his youth up—intimately acquainted, besides, with the country in which he would be called upon to act, would hang with the most telling effect upon the flanks and communications of a hostile army.

7—The instruction, therefore, that is most requisite, is practise in the use and handling of the rifle; and, with a view to this, sites for firing at a target should be established, if possible, in every locality in which companies or bodies of Volunteer Riflemen are formed, and every encouragement given to the men to avail themselves of them, leaving it to themselves to select their own hours for practise, or for such further instruction, as sharp-shooters, as it may appear desirable to give them, namely:—how to extend and avail themselves of cover, to fire advancing or retiring, to protect themselves from cavalry, or other simple movements, which, while leaving every man his independent action, would enable them to act together with more effect. Interested as the more wealthy classes throughout the country will be in the efficiency of such bodies of Volunteers formed in their own neighbourhood, they will doubtless co-operate heartily with the Lords Lieutenant of counties in endeavouring to find such sites for practise, and in whatever else may tend to further the object in view.

Issue of Targets and Ammunition.

8—Her Majesty's Government will authorise the issue, from the public magazines at the cost price, of targets and of the regulated annual allowance of practise and exercise ammunition for each trained Volunteer, viz:—ninety rounds of ball and sixty of blank cartridge, and 165 percussion caps; and for the training of each recruit 110 ball and 20 blank cartridges, 143 percussion caps and 20 ditto for snapping practise. Requisitions for the same to be made to the Secretary of State for War upon forms which will be supplied on demand from this office.

With a view to the supply of ammunition from the Government stores for the use of Volunteers, it is a primary and indispensable condition of their formation that the rifles with which they are armed should be perfectly uniform in guage with those in use by the Regular Army, and that there should be a similar uniformity in the size of the nipple, in order to suit the Government percussion cap.

9—The apparatus for testing the guage consists of two plugs, one of ·577 inch, and another of ·580 inch. Each rifle to be serviceable must admit the former and exclude the latter.

All the barrel makers in Birmingham, and the "setters up" in that town, as well as in London, are provided with similar plugs to those which are used in the "view rooms" at those places, and as the arms of each corps will be subject to an examination by competent viewers from the Government Small Arms Department, under the direction of Lieutenant-Colonel Dixon, R.A., Superintendent of the Royal Small Arms Factory, (for which purpose application must be made to the War Office), Commanding Officers of Corps and all who purchase arms, should hold the manufacturers responsible for the correctness of the guage of the barrels and the nipples.

10—It may further be a question whether it would not be found advantageous, with a view to the better preservation of the arms and accoutrements of the company, to provide, if possible, in the neighbourhood of the practice-range or parade ground of each company, a dry and airy building or room, as a store, where they could be deposited and properly cleaned and attended to, at the expiration of each day's drill. Store-room.

11—It is also desirable that the uniform adopted should be as simple as possible, and that the different companies serving in each county should be assimilated, and, though this point is left to the decision of the Volunteers subject to the approval of the Lords Lieutenant, it is considered that a recommendation on the subject would be of advantage." Uniform.

Although the subsequent sections of the circular are not concerned with Volunteer Rifles, it is not desirable to omit them in view of the difficulty that exists in procuring a copy of this document.

12—"As regards Artillery Volunteers, their primary object will be to aid, in the most efficient manner, in the manning of the batteries erected for the protection of our coast towns, so that the Royal Artillery and Militia may be, to as great extent as possible, disposable for other services.

13—These Volunteers may consist of a different class from that which will come forward for the more active duties of riflemen in the field. Married men, resident on the spot, and such as either could not absent themselves even for a day from their usual business, or might be physically unfit for field duties, might yet find ample time for learning how to work a great gun mounted in their immediate neighbourhood, and might be fully adequate to whatever exertion its exercise might require. The interest they would have in thus contributing to the security of their property and families, which would at once be endangered by any hostile attack, would be even stronger than that which would lead Volunteer Riflemen to the field.

14—The same principle which is recommended for the organisation of riflemen should be adopted for the Artillery Volunteers, except that the latter should be divided into still smaller bodies. For instance, the most effective system would be that which would associate ten or twelve men, all neighbours intimately acquainted with each other, in the charge and working of a particular gun mounted, so to speak, at their very door.

15--One of their number should be appointed to act as captain of the gun, to the charge and working of which their duties should be strictly limited. They might arrange their own time for drill and practice, an artillery man being charged with the duty of imparting the former, and all that would be required of them would be that they should be able to prove, on a half-yearly inspection, that they had duly profited by the instruction so given and had qualified themselves for the important trust reposed in them.

16—Always working and practising with the same gun, they could not but become well acquainted with its range and the points to which it would have chiefly to be directed.

17—In the same manner, associations may be formed in many of our commercial ports and open rivers for manning or working boats or ship's launches, armed with single guns in the bow, and which might, on occasion, be even more serviceable than the stationary shore batteries. Considering the vast amount of property in vessels, docks, timber yards, &c. exposed in most of these rivers to sudden attack from privateers, ship-owners and others would probably be well disposed, and think it indeed only a wise precaution on their part, to place any spare boats in their possession, which are adapted for the above named purposes, at the disposal of such Associations and even themselves to promote their organisation."

Mr. Secretary Herbert's Circular, July 13th, 1859. See Appendix for Text.

On July 13th of the same year, Mr. Secretary Sidney Herbert issued still another Circular to the Lords Lieutenant. It had possibly been realised that something more was needed than addressing hortatory counsels to the members of the Volunteer Corps. The Government now expressed its sense of the public spirit displayed by large numbers of Her Majesty's subjects who had offered to form Volunteer Artillery or Rifle Corps under the Act 44 Geo. III. c. 54. Though engaged, the Circular acknowledged, in important and often lucrative occupations, they had expressed their willingness, at their own cost and at a considerable sacrifice of time, to instruct themselves in drill and in the use of the arm, whether rifle or great gun, which they proposed to adopt, with a view to fit themselves to act as auxiliaries to Her Majesty's Regular forces in case of public danger. "But though," continued the Circular, "the very essence of a Volunteer force consists in their undertaking to bear, without any cost to the country, the whole cost of their training and service previous to being called out for actual service, Her Majesty's Government are of opinion that it will be but fair to the Volunteers, as a just acknowledgment of the spirit in which their services are rendered, to relieve them, in some degree, of the expense which their first outfit will entail upon them, and of which the purchase of arms is necessarily the heaviest item." Clearly, there was nothing left to be desired in the verbal expression of the nation's gratitude, but the more substantial recognition fell far short of the glowing professions with which the Circular opened. Volunteers are reminded that a Musketry Instructor cannot drill more than ten men at once. Government therefore proposed to issue to each Corps a number of Enfield Rifles equal to one quarter the number of the Corps! Any member, however, might provide himself with a breech-loader at his own expense, but if it was not of the regulation gauge in barrel and nipple, he could not be supplied with Government ammunition for practice. In case of the active service of Volunteers being required each Corps must be exclusively armed with the rifle common to all regular forces of Her Majesty, such arms to be provided by the Government. The Secretary of State was to be satisfied, as a condition precedent to the issue of this grudging 25%, that "a sufficient and safe practice range could be obtained within a reasonable distance of the head quarters."

Limited issue of Enfield Rifles by Government.

The Corps must also provide, to the satisfaction of the Lords Lieutenant but at the expense of the members, a secure place of custody for their arms and a competent person to take charge of them, and the Corps was, very properly, to be subject to inspection by a military officer deputed for that purpose.

Arsenal.

Another clause of this circular is conceived in a more rational spirit. It states that the Commander-in-Chief, with a view to afford every facility for the instruction of the Volunteer force, had sanctioned the reception of two officers or members of each Company, at their own expense or that of the Corps *bien entendu*, at the School of Musketry at Hythe.

School of Musketry at Hythe.

Captain King, of the Cheshire Rifles, was among the Volunteer officers who availed themselves of the valuable facility thus afforded, and in a lecture about this period he described minutely the course of instruction. "There were," he said, "forty-two of us altogether, of all classes, two peers, three country gentlemen, barristers, university men, merchants and tradesmen of all classes. The daily work was instruction in the cleaning of the rifle," every part of which was explained to these tyro soldiers, though presumably the country gentlemen would not require much instruction in this branch. They were taught how to dismount and remount the lock, and the names of every part of it; the propelling power which drove the bullet was explained, the nature of an ellipse, and the necessity for aiming above the mark at a distant object. They learned to shoot, lying, at distances of 150 to 900 yards, their rifles supported on a sand-bag resting on

The nature of the instruction at Hythe.

a tripod; they were led out to the beach and taught to guage distances, and over and above all they were drilled in the rapid, easy, but effective use of the weapon that gave the Volunteer Corps the distinctive title "Rifles." Many of these students were in the barrack-yard at 6-30 a.m., they assembled at 9-30 and worked till 1 p.m., and again from 2-30 to 4-30 p.m. In the evenings they were examined in the lessons of the day. Clearly a gentleman who, at his own no trifling cost, underwent this discipline, meant honestly to qualify himself to discharge the duties he had undertaken.

It may be added that Volunteers attending the school of musketry were, by a Circular of 26th October, desired by the Inspector-General of Musketry to take with them the rifles used by them in their corps, so that the rifles might be carefully sighted, during instruction, to the required distance. Volunteers were also cautioned against the dangerous practice of altering the locks of the rifles.

There would appear to have been, in some of the corps of this period, a disposition to leave the selection of officers to the vote of the privates. The Circular of July 13th, 1859, curtly states that while the Secretary for War will not be disposed to question the grounds upon which a Lord Lieutenant may recommend any person for a commission for Her Majesty's approval, he could not recognise the principle of the election of their officers by any body possessing, in any sense, a military organisation.

Memorandum, July 13th, 1859.

The Circular of the 13th July was accompanied by a memorandum, which, whilst reiterating some of the terms of the Circular, contained new and interesting matter. The 4th section provided for the drafting of rules and regulations for the government of the force, to be submitted to and approved by the Secretary for War.

Uniform.

The memorandum stipulated that the uniform and equipments of all the corps must be approved by the Lord Lieutenant, and should be, as far as possible, similar for Corps of Artillery and Rifles respectively, within the same county, in order to enable the Government at any time to form the corps into battalions. The formation of sub-divisions and sections of Artillery and sub-divisions of Rifle companies, with a proportionate number of officers, was sanctioned. The following were to be the establishments of the Rifles.

Establishment: Rifles.

A Company to consist of not less than 60 nor more than 100 Effectives,
with 1 Captain,
1 Lieutenant,
1 Ensign.

A sub-division of not less than 30 Effectives,
with 1 Lieutenant,
1 Ensign.

The Secretary expressed his assent to the formation, on the recommendation of the Lord Lieutenant, of a battalion, provided that a sufficient number of companies and of men were raised to justify such an organization. When, therefore, as many as eight companies, or a force not less than 500 strong, tho' with fewer companies, were raised, the Government would sanction the appointment of a lieutenant-colonel, a major, and an adjutant to be paid by the corps.

Eight companies to form a Battalion.

Adjutant to be paid by Corps.

In the rural districts of a county in which, from the remoteness from each other of the several companies, it might be inconvenient to unite them in battalions, the Lord Lieutenant might recommend to Her Majesty the appointment of a field officer of the rank suited to the amount of the force in each district, to superintend the whole of the several companies and sub-divisions not forming a part of any battalion.

Field Officer in rural districts.

The Act of 44 Geo. III. c. 54, section 9, had made a casual allusion to supernumeraries and non-effectives and the existence of such a body of men was distinctly contemplated by the Schedule to that Act. The 12th and 13th Clauses of the Memorandum provided that the sanction of the Secretary for War must be obtained for the enrolment of any supernumeraries beyond the establishment, whether as effective members for general service or of individuals who, desirous to contribute by their influence and means to the formation of Volunteer Corps, might be unequal to greater physical exertion than the mere attendance at the stipulated drills and the performance of local duties. The admission of honorary members, or non-effectives, willing to contribute towards the expenses of the corps, might also be sanctioned by the Secretary.

Supernumeraries.

Hon-Members.

On the delicate question of precedence the Memorandum was explicit. Artillery Corps, as in the regular service, were to rank before the Rifle Corps. The whole Volunteer force of a county was to take precedence, throughout Great Britain, according to the date of the first company of their respective arms in a county—a provision well calculated to stimulate to a race for precedence. The several companies were to rank, as Artillery and Rifles respectively, within their own counties, in the order of their formation. The whole county force and the several companies and sub-divisions were to be entered in the Army List. Officers were to take precedence according to the dates of their commissions. Those of similar commissions of the same date were to rank according to the precedence of their respective counties, or, if

Precedence.

belonging to separate companies in the same county, according to the precedence of their respective companies, and if belonging to the same corps according to the order in which their names appeared in the Army List.

Accoutrements, &c.

The Artillery Corps were not required to have small arms. Each Volunteer was to provide himself with a waist-belt of black or brown leather, for the reception of small arms. Gold lace was not to be worn, that being a special distinction for officers of the Regulars. Accoutrements, to be provided at the expense of the members, were to consist of waist-belt of black or brown leather, sliding frog for bayonet, ball bag containing cap-pocket and twenty-round pouch. Supplies of ammunition were to be issued to the Artillery Volunteers free of cost. The Rifles were to have no special allowance for training recruits, but duly qualified effectives were to be entitled to the following annual issues at cost price:—

100 Rounds Ball per man.
60 ,, Blank ,,
176 Percussion Caps.
20 ,, ,, for snapping practice.

Manuals of Instruction.

Manuals of Instruction for Rifle Volunteers were to be issued, and the men enjoined to mark, learn and inwardly digest the same.

Report of Committee on Volunteer Rules and Regulations, August, 1859.

In August of the same year were published the proceedings of a Committee appointed by the War Secretary, for the purpose of drafting model rules and regulations for the government of Volunteer Corps when not on actual service and subject to military discipline. The following noblemen and gentlemen constituted the Committee:—

The members of the Committee.

President:—Viscount Ranelagh, South Middlesex Rifles.
Earl Spencer, Althorp Rifles.
Major Clifford, Victoria Rifles.
Mr. J. H. Orde, Yarmouth Rifles.
Mr. Wilbraham Taylor, South Middlesex and Barnet Rifles.
Captain Denis Moore, Exeter and South Devon Rifles.
Mr. R. Blackburne, Edinburgh Rifles.
Mr. A Gladstone, 5th Lancashire Rifles.
Mr. W. H. Hyett, Gloucestershire and Stroud Rifles.
Captain Hicks, London Rifle Brigade.
Mr. Templer, Bridport Rifles.
Mr. Wm. Laird, Birkenhead Rifles.

The skeleton rules and regulations recommended by the Committee were adopted generally throughout the country, and amongst other Corps by the 6th West York Rifle Volunteers; and the reproduction of the rules of that body, as set out in the

Appendix, will obviate the necessity for that of the skeleton or model rules recommended by the Committee.

Contemporaneously with the Committee on Rules sat also a Committee on Military Organisation. From the evidence of the Duke of Cambridge before this Committee it would seem he had no very exalted opinion of the Volunteer levies. He said he should not like to rely too much on any Volunteer Corps, and expressed the opinion that they were a very dangerous means of meeting an enemy. General Sir John Burgoyne stated his belief that the Volunteers would not be of great service, as they would be what he called a mob; but if they were organised as soldiers and learned a little exercise and subordination and drill, and moved about as soldiers, then he should have a very different opinion of them. He should prefer clubs, and would have it as in old days. He did not consider the arrangements under which the Volunteers were enrolled as satisfactory; still he wanted to see the whole population skilled in rifle practice. He considered discipline and exercise essential to effectiveness. He thought the present Rifle Corps were a set of gentlemen who could afford to provide for themselves, and give up their time and get no remuneration for it.

Committee on Military organisation.

Evidence of H.R.H. the Duke of Cambridge.

Of General Sir John Burgoyne.

But however mean may have been the opinion of the Volunteers held and avowed by the Regulars, the Volunteers took themselves very seriously. Colonel Cooper-King, in his "Story of the British Army," writes of the auxiliary forces that sprang up in 1859. "For the third time the civilian laid aside his mufti and clutched the uniform and rifle. By the middle of 1859 there were 60,000 men armed and willing to fight. It is not necessary here to enter into the controversy of the merits or demerits of this force. It began one way, it has finished in another. It began helped by a fulsome praise that can only be called hysteric; for the first idea it had was to reduce or abolish the army for the sake of a force not soldiers, but merely men with arms, and which was for a time the laughing stock of Europe! Anything more ludicrous and, from a military point of view, contemptible, than the early days of these willing and patriotic enthusiasts cannot be imagined. They played at soldiers in the most absolute way, and though much improved they are very far from being perfect now. At first they were regarded merely as local corps of varying strength, and were to have merely a company organisation. A separate manual, called "The Drill and Rifle Instruction for Corps of Rifle Volunteers," was compiled with the specific purpose of minimizing the instruction to

Col. Cooper-King on the Volunteers, 1859

be given. This could, it was considered, be imparted in six lessons, and Sir Charles Napier, in his 'Letter on the Defence of England,' strongly advised the new soldiery not to let any one persuade them to serve more. Of course, all this has long since changed, and now the Volunteer undergoes the same training as the soldier or the militiaman; but without that continuity that alone can make it of first value. Discipline and drill, if not synonymous terms, run hand in hand. The former naturally follows on the latter, if it be continuous and sustained."

Perhaps the somewhat puerile, or should one say feminine, concern displayed by Volunteer officers on the questions of uniform and military etiquette, may account for not a little of the disposition that undoubtedly existed at this period, to poke fun at the movement generally. The War Office had no little difficulty in restraining the extravagances of the officers of some corps; *taste* the following out of many documents bearing on the matter:—

THE SILK SASH.

"War Office, Feb. 15th, 1860.

The wearing of Sashes.

My Lord,

My attention having been recently directed to the practice adopted by some of the Volunteer corps, in which a silk sash is worn over the uniform by honorary members, and even in some cases by enrolled members, when not upon parade, I have to request that, as the practice in question would be open to considerable objection, you will signify to officers commanding the Artillery and Rifle Volunteer corps, within the limits of your jurisdiction, that the custom of wearing the sash should be discontinued in those instances in which it may now prevail, and should not be introduced for the future.

I may observe that this article, when worn in the regular army, is the distinguishing mark of an officer, but that it forms no part of the dress of either Artillery or Rifle Corps in Her Majesty's regular forces.

I have the honour to be, my Lord, your Lordship's obedient servant,

(Signed) SIDNEY HERBERT."

Her Majesty's Lieutenant for

Gold lace, too, and swords appear to have had a peculiar though unhallowed fascination for some officers and other Volunteers, and the indulgence of this taste had to be sternly checked, as appears by the following Circulars:—

"War Office, 24th April, 1860.

The wearing of Swords.

My Lord,

It having been represented to me that swords are sometimes worn by members of Volunteer corps when off duty who are not entitled by their rank to do so, I have the honour to request that you will have the goodness to intimate to the several corps serving in your county that this privilege is limited to the commissioned officers, and to direct that arms should not be worn by non-commissioned officers or privates of Volunteer corps, except when proceeding to or returning from duty; and that on these occasions the authorised weapons only should be carried by them.

I have the honour to be, my Lord, your obedient servant,

S. HERBERT."

Her Majesty's Lord Lieutenant for the County of

"War Office, 30th April, 1860.

My Lord,

It having been represented to me that the officers of several Volunteer corps wear indiscriminately upon their uniforms the forms and patterns of lace and appointments which in the Regular service and Militia denote the rank of the wearer, I have the honour to request that, in order to prevent the confusion and error which must arise from such proceeding, your Lordship will have the goodness to require that the distinctions of rank which are prescribed in the dress regulations for the army should also be observed strictly by the officers of the Volunteers of various grades serving in your county, so far as they are applicable to Volunteer corps. It is also to be borne in mind that Volunteer officers are not permitted to wear gold lace, and that silver lace must be substituted for gold wherever gold is authorised in the accompanying extracts from the dress regulations for the regular army. The wearing of Gold Lace. V. Genl. No. 801.

I may take this opportunity to observe, with reference to a recent Circular from this Department relative to sashes, that although this article of dress is not worn by Rifle Regiments in general, I do not propose to insist upon its discontinuance by the officers of such corps as have your Lordship's sanction to wear it, but the sash cannot be worn by any other class of members of Volunteer corps whatever.

I have the honour to be, my Lord, your Lordship's obedient servant,

SIDNEY HERBERT."

To His Majesty's Lord Lieutenant for the County of

The Dress Regulations referred to by Mr. Secretary Herbert are as follow:— Dress Regulations.

RIFLE REGIMENTS.

Distinctions of Rank.

Colonel—Crown and Star Lieutenant-Colonel—Crown Major—Star	Collar, laced all round with black lace, figured braiding within the lace. Sleeve ornament: lace and figured braiding, eleven inches deep.
Captain—Crown and Star	Collar, laced round the top with black lace, with figured braiding below the lace. Sleeve ornament: knot of square cord with figured braiding, eight inches deep.
Lieutenant—Crown Ensign—Star	Collar, laced round the top with black lace, and plain edging of braid. Sleeve ornament: knot of square cord and braid, seven inches deep.

The collar badges in silk embroidery.

The adjutant to wear the uniform of his rank.

The paymaster, quartermaster, surgeon and assistant-surgeon to wear a plain shako; no tuft. The medical officers, instead of the regimental pouch and belt, to wear a black shoulder belt, with a small case of instruments, according to pattern.

HORSE FURNITURE.

The saddle cloth of a field officer to be trimmed with one row of half-inch regimental lace, the same as worn on his coat, edged with a small Vandyke of scarlet cloth and the badge of his rank, according to the Infantry regulations, embroidered in silver in the corners. The adjutant's saddle cloth to be trimmed only with a gold cord edged with a small Vandyke of scarlet cloth.

For mounted officers a Shabraque of black lamb-skin, three feet four inches long, twenty-one inches deep in front, and twelve inches behind, with rounded corners in front and rear.

Bridle of black leather but cavalry pattern, with green front and roses and bronze bosies: breast plate and crupper of black leather. Chains:—steel chain reins.

Salutes.

A concession was however made in the same year upon a matter that appears not a little to have occupied the attention of Volunteer officers about this period. I refer to the question of salutes, a fruitful source of difference between the Regulars and the Volunteers till the issue was finally settled by the following memorandum:—

"16th August, 1860.

All officers of Volunteers holding commissions are entitled, when in uniform, to the same salute as officers of Her Majesty's Guards and Line and Militia, according to their rank. All Guards are to pay the same honour to Volunteers under arms as are laid down in paragraph 24 of Her Majesty's regulations.

By command,

JAMES YORKE SCARLETT,

Adjutant-General."

The popularity of the Volunteer movement on its revival in 1859.

It is refreshing to turn from these comparatively minor matters and from the somewhat dreary recital of official circulars to note the spirit and temper with which the people received the invitation to form themselves into auxiliary levies. It was as if by magic that an armed force sprang up. All sorts and conditions of men, from peer to peasant, men of all professions, trades and callings, combined to enrol themselves, gave freely of their time to this self-imposed duty, submitted willingly to discipline and gave, too, cheerfully and liberally of their substance to secure the success of an organisation whose need the general people seem to have realized even more vividly than did the authorities of the War Office.

The members increased so rapidly that the original idea of the Government was entirely overpassed, and instead of counting the force by companies, sections or sub-divisions of companies only, in the year 1860 no less than 119,000, and in May, 1861, no less than 170,000 Volunteers had been enrolled in Great Britain. It was estimated that men had been enrolled as Volunteers at the rate of 7,000 in each of the twenty-four months that had elapsed from the issue of General Peel's circular.

At the end of January, 1860, Her late Majesty, in the speech from the throne, graciously adverted to the magnitude and spontaneity of the country's response to the official circular:—"I have accepted with gratification and pride the extensive offers of service which I have received from my subjects. This manifestation of public spirit has added an important element to our system of national defence." In the House of Lords, Lord de Grey and Ripon declared that the "Volunteer Corps had been constituted in such manner as to give the Government the strongest hope that they would be a valuable addition to the defensive forces of the country."

It may almost be said that the country forced the hand of the War Office, for, in December, 1859, we find that Department disposed to deal more generously with the Volunteer forces, and then and thenceforward more concerned for its practical efficiency, and apparently awakening to a perception of the truth that the Volunteer forces must once for all be recognised as a very significant factor in our military resources.

Circular of Mr. Secretary Herbert, 20th Dec., 1859.

These signs of a change of mood on the part of the Executive were many. Among them may be cited the following circular of Mr. Secretary Herbert to the Lords Lieutenant, dated 20th December, 1859:—

"My Lord,

Issue of Enfield Rifles.

I have the honour to inform you that Her Majesty's Government have determined to issue to Volunteer Rifle Corps, after the 1st of January next, an additional supply of long Enfield Rifles (pattern 1853), to the extent of 50 per cent. on the effective strength of the corps. This supply will raise the aggregate issue to 100 per cent. on the effective strength of the force: and I have to request that you will be good enough to communicate this decision of the Government to the commanding officers of the various Corps in your county, who should at once forward the prescribed requisitions to this office for such portion of the supply as they may be entitled to under the regulations.

I hope to be in a position, in the course of next year, to exchange those rifles gradually for the short Enfield, in the case of any corps which may desire it, and on the understanding that the long rifles must be returned in good condition, fair wear and tear excepted, or that the corps must pay for any damage they may have received."

From this date till the codification of the "Regulations for the Volunteer Force" on January 19th, 1861, Circulars and Memoranda, all designed to improve the organisation and increase the efficiency of the arm of the reserves with which we are concerned, were issued from the War Office in quick succession. It is important that these should be preserved and recorded in due order of sequence, because they throw interesting light on the development of the official mind and prove incontestably that the Volunteer forces were not a departmental creation but that they sprang into being in consequence of and owed their genesis to the spirit and determination of the people, a people whose most intimate convictions, or perhaps one might more properly say, instincts, cannot be better expressed than in the words of the Right Hon. W. Windham speaking in 1806: "A state of war is in itself a state of evil. We wish not for it; we would fain avoid it; we would be at peace—could we be so with honour and security to ourselves. But whether at war or in the most profound peace let us never neglect to encourage and maintain a military aptitude and spirit in the people. History tells us that in all nations and times, the extinction of this spirit has been rapidly followed by the loss of every other national virtue."

Feb. 18th, 1860, Circular Memorandum *re* Drill Instructors.

On February 18th, 1860, then, in consequence doubtless of the new leaven working in the mind of the Executive, we have a circular memorandum from Adjutant-General G. A. Wetherall stating that the Commander-in-Chief had approved of non-commissioned officers of Infantry being attached as drill instructors to corps of Rifle Volunteers. These instructors were to be returned "on duty" for the period of three months, should their services be so long required, and receive the pay of two shillings and sixpence a day and lodgings, to be paid by the corps.

This provision of an instructor for three months, *if he should be so long required*, was quite in keeping with the idea then very general and which, as I have said, Sir Charles Napier had very emphatically endorsed, that six lessons would amply suffice to teach all that it was necessary or desirable that a Volunteer should know of military exercises. It was doubtless, too, upon this conception, that the Green Book, "Drill and Rifle Instruction for Volunteer Rifle Corps," published in 1859, on the authority of the Secretary for War, was based. It will interest the Volunteers of to-day to learn what, at that period, was deemed to constitute the complete Volunteer education.

The Green Book, 1859.

First Lesson.

The first lesson was confined to instruction in the falling-in and telling-off of a squad; opening for squad drill; the position or attitude of the Volunteers, which was to be "perfectly easy and natural, without any stiffness or constraint," a posture more easily enjoined than attained, say by a tailor accustomed to the goose-board; standing at ease, facing, closing the squad, dressing and dismissing a squad.

The second lesson was addressed to marching; stepping out; stopping short or marking time; the diagonal march; breaking off and re-assembling; the double march and wheeling. Second Lesson.

The third lesson to the manual exercise and method of piling arms. The Third Lesson.

The fourth lesson to platoon exercise by numbers, coming to the ready; to shoulder and order from the capping position; to firing and re-loading; kneeling and platoon exercise in slow and quick time. Fourth Lesson.

The fifth lesson to the formation of a squad in two ranks; telling off; firings; skirmishing; extending from the halt; closing on the halt; extending and closing on the march; advancing and retiring in skirmishing order; inclining to a flank; changing front or direction whilst skirmishing; firing in skirmishing order; rallying a square or resisting cavalry. Fifth Lesson.

The sixth and concluding lesson dealt with the formation of the Corps or Company, the posts of officers, dispersing and assembling, advancing and retiring and wheeling, wheeling into columns of sub-divisions or sections, company square, skirmishing, skirmishers closing on the support, relieving skirmishers, and bugle calls. Sixth Lesson.

The Green Book gives the gratifying assurance that these six lessons contain "all the drill Volunteers need know," but adds that "if, when they become thoroughly drilled, they have spare time, they may learn to form four deep in the manner prescribed by the Manual." There is added musketry instruction on the meaning of the different parts of the rifle, dismounting and remounting the lock. The "trajectory," as distinguished from the "line of fire," is carefully explained, the Volunteer is instructed how to aim and adjust the back-sight of his rifle; in position drill and snapping caps ("until the tendency to wink at the explosion is overcome,") blank firing, judging distances, target practice, file firing and volley firing, and firing in skirmishing order. After all, a useful little manual, easy to be understood, and doubtless adequate for the ends then desired and deemed attainable.

From the 18th February to the 17th of March, 1860, is no great length of time, but the circular quoted below plainly points to the universality with which, throughout the kingdom, sufficient companies had been formed to constitute battalions, and the consequent necessity arising for battalion organisation and drill. Battalions become general throughout the country.

We find, accordingly, the War Office Circular subjoined, providing for the appointment of an adjutant:—

War Office Memorandum, Feb., 1860. Appointment of Adjutant to be recommended by Lord Lieutenant.

"War Office, February, 1860.

My Lord,

Having had under my consideration the expediency of the appointment of an Adjutant, commissioned by Her Majesty, to every brigade of Artillery and battalion of Rifle Volunteers, I have the honour to inform you that I shall be prepared to submit for the Queen's approval the names of such officers as you may recommend for the several corps serving in your county, subject to the following qualifications and conditions of service:—

Qualifications of Adjutant.

1—That the candidate should have served at least four years, either in the line or in the army of the late East India Company, or in Her Majesty's Indian forces or in the embodied Militia.

2—That his application should be accompanied by testimonials as to conduct from his former Commanding Officer.

3—That the candidate shall be subject to an examination at the nearest garrison as to his fitness to hold the office of Adjutant under such regulations as His Royal Highness the General Commanding in Chief may, with the concurrence of the Secretary of State for War, be pleased to direct; and that he shall also have passed through a course of instruction in musketry at Hythe or be prepared to do so when called upon.

His rank.

4—The rank of an Adjutant is properly that of a subaltern; but if appointed out of Her Majesty's Regular forces or Indian army or Militia, he may retain the rank which he held in either of these services; but no Adjutant shall be entitled, by virtue of his superior rank, to take command of any Company of Volunteers, any officer of the company being present, except for the purpose of instruction drill.

Declaration by Adjutant.

5—Every officer appointed an Adjutant of Volunteers will be required, before receiving his commission, to transmit to the Secretary of State for War the following declaration:—

"I do hereby declare, upon my honour as an officer and a gentleman, that, in order to obtain the appointment of an Adjutant in the Volunteers, I have not given, paid, received or promised, and that I do not believe that anyone for me has given, paid, received or promised, directly or indirectly, any recompense, reward or gratuity to any person or persons whatever.

"Witness (C. D.) Signed (A. B.)"

His Pay.

6—The pay of an Adjutant of Volunteers shall be 8/- a day and 2/- to cover the forage of a horse or for travelling expenses, providing the Commanding Officer has exempted him for the time being from the liability to keep a horse. Any other incidental expenses must be borne by the corps.

To devote whole time to his office as Adjutant.

7—As the public services of an Adjutant are to be made fully available at all times, it is necessary that it should be perfectly understood beforehand by candidates that the Secretary of State will not allow them, if appointed, to follow any other profession or hold any other appointment, public or private.

I have the honour to be, my Lord, your Lordship's obedient servant,

SIDNEY HERBERT."

Previous to 1863, the adjutant, though recommended by the Lord Lieutenant, was practically appointed and paid for by the commanding officer. "In that year, however, under the Volunteer Act, the adjutants having been awarded pay, the War Office had to be satisfied of their qualifications before appointment," says Mr. David Howe, in his prize essay on *The Volunteer Question.** "Those thus qualifying were allowed to remain with their Corps till they died or voluntarily retired; but a subsequent order enjoined all officers appointed prior to 21st February, 1877, to retire at the age of sixty; and all appointments after that date to hold office only for five years. Since 1878, all adjutants have come direct from the army, and have returned to their own regiments on the expiry of their five years' service. This arrangement has done much to smooth matters between the two forces. Five years are generally quite enough to enable an adjutant to understand the Volunteers, and to carry back with him to the regiments a very different conception than he had on joining it. He is also able to clear away the cobwebs from the minds of his brother officers, and there is not the slightest doubt that in bringing the two forces more together it has enabled each more thoroughly to understand the other, and thus break down the wall of partition that divided them."

War Office Circular, March 24th, 1860. Consolidated and Administrative Battalions.

Another circular, that of 24th March, 1860, signed by Mr. Secretary S. Herbert, followed hard upon the one last set forth. I quote it *in extenso* as it contains the principles to be observed in the new experiment of welding isolated companies into consolidated or administrative battalions. The circular is addressed to the Lords Lieutenant of counties.

It may be explained that the term "consolidated" applies to a battalion whose constituent companies are drawn from the same town or city, where such town or city is populous enough to furnish the requisite number of companies; the term "administrative" to a battalion whose constituent companies are drawn from areas geographically contiguous but not connected by any ties of local government.

"War Office, Pall Mall, March, 1860.

My Lord,

Having had under consideration the expediency of forming the various scattered bodies constituting Volunteer Rifle Corps into battalions, in order to facilitate the administration of the Volunteer force generally, as well as to

---

*See "The Volunteer Question" (T. & A. Constable, Edinburgh University Press), p. 307.

increase its efficiency, I have the honour to inform your Lordship that, with a view to carrying out this organisation, it is proposed to adopt the following principles:—

1—That a battalion of Volunteers may be formed either as a consolidated body, composed of various companies in densely populated districts acting together as one corps, in the meaning of the Act of Parliament, 44 Geo. III., chap. 54, or,

2—It may be a consolidated body for drill and administrative purposes only, being composed of various companies forming in themselves distinct and (financially considered) independent corps, in the meaning of the Act; or,

3—A battalion may be formed, for administrative purposes only, from the various corps scattered over a rural or thinly populated district.

It appears to me, therefore, that in order to meet these several forms of battalion organisation, it is desirable to lay down the following rules:—

For a consolidated battalion formed on either of the two first principles:—

1 Major 1 Adjutant	will be allowed to 4 companies of minimum strength.
1 Lieut.-Colonel 1 Adjutant	will be allowed to 6 ,, ,,
1 Lieut.-Colonel 1 Major 1 Adjutant	will be allowed to 8 ,, ,,
1 Lieut.-Colonel 2 Majors 1 Adjutant	will be allowed to 12 ,, ,,

When the companies exceed twelve, the corps will constitute a regiment, and be formed into two battalions, each with field officers and adjutants in the above proportion, the whole to be commanded by the senior lieutenant-colonel.

Although I am prepared to sanction the formation of a battalion of 4 companies, it is intended to provide only for cases in which no more than that number of companies can be formed in a town, and where it is not considered advisable to bring in any rural companies, and it should be understood that no two battalions of this strength can be formed in one place.

With regard to the third principle of formation, which is applicable to rural districts, where the companies, &c. are greatly scattered, I have to explain to your Lordship that it is not intended that this formation into battalions should render the separate companies liable to be removed from their own neighbourhood or brought together at any time when not called out for actual service, except with their own consent; or that the independent existence of the several corps should be in any degree affected; my object is to accomplish a unity of system in correspondence, drill, inspection and returns throughout the entire force.

The following staff will therefore be allowed for rural battalions:— *Establishment of Rural Battalions.*

1 Major, 1 Adjutant } to 4 or 5 companies of minimum strength.

1 Lieut.-Colonel, 1 Adjutant } to 6, 7, 8 or 9 companies of ,, ,,

1 Lieut.-Colonel, 1 Major, 1 Adjutant } to 10, 11 or 12 companies of ,, ,,

I have further to state to your Lordship:—

1—That in effecting the formation of these battalions, the concentration of companies should be considered with reference to locality and not to their numerical standing in the Army List.

2—That each company may continue to have its own rendezvous and drills, but that there should also be a battalion rendezvous established, and, where the local distribution and convenience of the different companies will admit of it, certain days set apart for battalion drills. *Battalion rendezvous and drills.*

3—That although I have not thought it desirable to insist upon a rigid adherence to that uniformity in the clothing and equipment of corps serving in the same county, which was recommended in Article 6 of the Memorandum of the 13th July, 1859, I trust that in future renewal of the clothing the propriety of adopting a uniform colour for companies belonging to the same battalion will be duly considered. *Uniform.*

I beg therefore to acquaint your Lordship that I am desirous to see the different companies of Volunteers throughout the country united, as far as possible, into battalions under the foregoing rules, and I shall be glad to be favoured with your Lordship's views as to the best means of carrying out the proposed organisation among the companies formed in the county under your charge."

On 4th September, 1860, the Secretary for War, Earl de Grey and Ripon, issued an Official Memorandum of considerable importance, defining the principles to be observed in the formation of Administrative Battalions, the object being two-fold: to secure cohesion and uniformity, or what we should now probably term co-ordination, and yet retain the individuality and independence of the constituent companies. This memorandum is as follows:—

"The object of the formation of an Administrative Battalion is to unite the different corps composing it under one common head, to secure uniformity of drill among them, and to afford them the advantage of the instruction and assistance of an adjutant; but it is not intended to interfere with the financial arrangements of the separate corps, or with the operation of the respective rules, or to compel them to meet together for battalion drill in ordinary times, except with their own consent, *1860, Sep. 4th. Memorandum of Earl de Grey as to Administrative Battalions.*

In order to secure this amount of independence to the various corps composing an Administrative Battalion, it is necessary that each should remain a distinct corps in the meaning of the Volunteer Acts, for if this were not the case the funds of all the corps would at once become vested in the Field Officer commanding the battalion, under 44 Geo. III. cap. 54, sec. 50, and the powers specially conferred by those Acts on Commanding Officers will therefore remain vested in the officer commanding each separate corps.

The chief of these powers are as follows :—

1—Commanding Officers may grant leave of absence (section 7) to Volunteers.

2—They are required to grant Certificates (section 10) to effective Volunteers resident, or liable to be balloted for the Militia, (section 27), in any other county.

3—They may discharge Volunteers (section 28) for disobedience of orders, or any other sufficient cause, when not on actual service ; and in case of misconduct not provided for by the rules of the Corps, may disallow the day as a day of attendance, or direct the forfeiture of a day's pay if otherwise due.

4—They may order Volunteers (section 29) disobeying orders during exercise into custody.

5—They may appoint places (section 42) for depositing arms and accoutrements, and persons to take care of them.

6—All monies subscribed for the use of any corps (section 50) and all articles not being the property of Her Majesty's Government or of any particular individual, belonging to or used by the corps, are vested in the Commanding Officer.

As the rules of each corps must also, in accordance with the Acts of Parliament, remain in full force, any powers which those rules may confer on the commanding officer of the particular corps will continue to be possessed by him after his corps has become part of an Administrative Battalion as much as before. These rules can of course at any time be modified, as the corps may wish, provided the alterations obtain the sanction of the Lord Lieutenant and the approval of Her Majesty, in the usual way ; but until so modified, they will remain in force and legal operation. An Administrative Battalion cannot have rules having legal force under the Act 44. George III., chap. 54, distinct from those of the separate corps of which it is composed, and no authority except that of Her Majesty can over-ride the rules of any corps until they have been altered in manner above alluded to.

Field Officer Commanding.—The position of the Field Officer Commanding an Administrative Battalion is, under the circumstances, very similar to that of a Colonel of a brigade of Royal Artillery. Subject to the limitations imposed by the law, as above indicated, he will have the general charge of the drill and discipline of the several corps composing his battalion ; he will inspect them from time to time, and will be responsible that the provisions of the law are obeyed and the orders of the Secretary of State for War relating to the use of arms, the regulations about clothing, distinctive marks of rank, &c., are adhered to, and that uniformity in drill, and, as far as can be attained, consistency with the rules of the separate corps in interior economy also is preserved. When present at the drill or parade of any corps he will invariably take the command. If two or more corps in the battalion should wish to meet together for united drill, or if any corps should desire to attend the field-day of another battalion or of any corps out of its own battalion, the permission of the Field Officer Commanding must first be obtained, and the drill, movements &c., as far as the corps under his command are concerned, will be arranged by him.

The Field Officer Commanding the battalion will also be the channel of communication between the officers commanding corps and the Secretary of State for War or Lord Lieutenant.

When there are two Field Officers to an Administrative Battalion the junior will discharge such portion of the above duties as the Field Officer Commanding the battalion may from time to time assign to him, and, in the absence of the commanding officer, he will take the command of the battalion.

Adjutant.—The Adjutant is under the orders of the Field Officer Commanding the battalion; but he is bound to conform to all instructions which he may receive from the War Office through the Inspector of Volunteers; such instructions will be transmitted to him through his commanding officer. He will also comply with the requisitions of the Assistant Inspector of his district, and will attend him on his inspections, if required. Besides the ordinary duties of an Adjutant with which it is ascertained by examination that every officer appointed to that post in a Volunteer battalion is acquainted, it will be his duty to visit the different corps composing his battalion as often as may be practicable consistently with their local distribution, and in accordance with the orders of his Commanding Officer. He should have a copy of the muster roll of each corps and should keep them correctly filled up to the end of each month with all the alterations entered from the originals in the possession of the Commanding Officer of the corps. He will conduct the correspondence of the battalion under the direction of the Field Officer Commanding, and he will be required to keep a diary according to a form to be issued shortly, open at all times to examination by the Inspector or Assistant Inspector of Volunteers. He will prepare and furnish all such returns as may from time to time be called for by the Secretary of State for War.

Correspondence and Returns.—The Commanding Officers of corps forming part of an Administrative Battalion will correspond with the War Office or with the Lord Lieutenant through the Field Officer Commanding their battalion, and all letters addressed to them from the War Office or Lord Lieutenant should be transmitted through the same channel. All returns required by Act of Parliament to be furnished by commanding officers of Volunteer Corps should be sent in in a similar manner, except that ordered by the 44 Geo. III. chap. 54, sec. 11, to be delivered to the District Surveyor of Taxes, which should be sent direct to him by the Commanding Officer of each corps. The responsibility imposed by section 15 of the same Act rests with the Commanding Officer of each corps, and not with the Field Officer Commanding the battalion. All returns other than those required by law which may be ordered by the Secretary of State will be furnished, as above directed, by the adjutant.

ARMS AND STORES.—The Commanding Officer of each separate corps will be held responsible for all arms and other stores issued by the Government for the use of his corps, and for all payments which may become due on account of such stores, but the correspondence relating to these matters will, like all other correspondence, be transmitted through the Field Officer Commanding the battalion.

4th September, 1860. DE GREY AND RIPON."

In conjunction with this Memorandum may be conveniently arranged the Royal Warrant of 19th June, 1860, relating to Adjutants. These officers, it may be premised, had to pass an examination in the interior economy, drill and instruction of a regiment of infantry, together with the provisions of the Mutiny Act and Articles of War and the general duties of an Adjutant of a regiment of infantry. The pay of the Adjutant is fixed by the Warrant referred to, which is in these terms:—

Royal Warrant, June 19th, 1860.

" Victoria R.

Whereas we have judged it expedient to grant Commissions under our Sign Manual to Officers who may be appointed Adjutants in the Artillery and Volunteer forces raised under the Act 44 George III, chap. 54, and to make provisions for the grant of retired pay to such officers; our will and pleasure is that this our Royal Warrant, to be administered and interpreted by our Secretary of State for War, shall be the sole authority for the issue of such retired pay, which shall be governed by the following rules and regulations:—

1—Retired pay shall be granted to Adjutants of Artillery and Rifle Volunteer Corps after they shall have completed the undermentioned periods of service in our Regular or Indian forces, our Marines, embodied Militia, or the Army of the East India Company, and in a Volunteer Corps, viz.—15 years, 5 years of which as Adjutant of Volunteers, 3/- per diem; 20 years, 7 years of which as Adjutant of Volunteers, 4/- per diem; 25 years, 10 years of which as Adjutant of Volunteers, 5/- per diem; 30 years, 15 years of which as Adjutant of Volunteers, 6/. per diem.

2—Such pay shall be granted to those Adjutants who may, through age or infirmity, become unfit for the performance of the duties of their Commissions, or whose services may cease to be required by reason of the reduction of their Corps by Our order; but no Adjutant of a Volunteer Corps whose Corps may dissolve of its own accord or otherwise fall below the establishment entitling it to an officer of that description shall have any title to retired pay.

3—And no Adjutant on the retired list who shall accept any military office or employment of profit under Government, shall be entitled for the period during which he holds such office to claim any portion of the said retired pay.

4—Every Adjutant who shall claim the retired pay to which he may become entitled under the provisions of this our Warrant, shall, previous to receiving the same, produce to the paymaster-general of our forces a declaration taken and subscribed before a justice of the peace or some other person authorised by law to administer such declaration, in the words or to the effect following :—

"I, A. B. do solemnly and sincerely declare that I was serving as Adjutant in Volunteer Corps from the to the and that I now claim to receive retired pay at the rate of a day, from the to the during which period I did not hold or enjoy any office or employment of profit, civil or military, under the Crown, or any other Government, besides the retired pay of a day now claimed, except my half-pay as ."

Given at our Court at St. James's this 19th day of June, 1860, in the 23rd year of our reign.

S. HERBERT.

The position and emoluments of Adjutants were further defined by official memoranda dated respectively the 8th and 25th September, 1860, which I subjoin:

Official Memos., Sept. 8th and 25th, 1860, as to Adjutant's pay and position.

"War Office, 8th September, 1860.

With reference to the circular letter from this office of the 29th February, last (V. Gen. No. 740) relative to the appointment and pay of Adjutants of Volunteer Corps, I have now the honour to state that it has been decided that, in addition to the pay and allowance as laid down in that communication, an allowance at the rate of £4 per company per annum will be made to all Adjutants of Volunteers from the dates of their respective commissions, to cover contingent expenses incurred in connection with correspondence, &c., with this Department. I have further to state that an additional allowance of two shillings per diem in lieu of travelling expenses will be made to the Adjutants of every Administrative Battalion in which the head-quarters of any of the corps composing the battalion may be situate at a distance of more than five miles from the head-quarters of the Battalion.

I have the honour to be,
Your most obedient humble servant,
SIDNEY HERBERT."

Her Majesty's Lieutenant for the County of

The Memorandum published 15th September as to the duties of the Adjutant is merely a repetition of such parts of the War Secretary's memo. of September 4th as refer to Adjutants and need not therefore be again transcribed.

Sept. 15th, 1860, Memo. as to duties of Adjutant.

The importance of periodical reviews of the Volunteers began about this period to be recognised by the War Office, and the following letter was addressed by the Secretary for War to the Commander-in-Chief:—

7th July, 1860, Letter of Secretary for War to Commanding Officers as to Reviews.

"War Office, 7th July, 1860.

Sir,—It appears to me that it would tend greatly to promote the efficiency of the Volunteer force, and to insure its permanence, if opportunities were afforded to the various corps in different parts of the country to be occasionally brought together for the purpose of being reviewed by some officer of high rank and position.

In ordinary times the law gives the Government no power to compel the attendance of Volunteer Corps at a distance from their local head-quarters, nor would it be desirable to do so; but I have every reason to believe that reviews of this kind, appointed after consultation with the various corps concerned and at a time convenient to them, would be largely attended and would be highly acceptable to the Volunteers.

I have therefore to request that if your Royal Highness concurs with me in the opinion above expressed, you will be pleased to give such directions as may be necessary to enable the general officers commanding districts to undertake the duty of reviewing occasionally such Volunteer Corps within their respective districts as may be willing to assemble for the purpose.

It would in each case be necessary to ascertain first, through the Lords Lieutenant of counties, what time for holding the review would best suit the convenience of the Volunteers residing within reasonable distance of the place selected for the purpose, and the necessary arrangements would then be made by the General Officer of the district, assisted by the Assistant Inspectors, within his command.

By these means much encouragement would, in my opinion, be given to the Volunteer movement, the General Officers would be enabled to make themselves acquainted with the different corps within their district, and an opportunity (which it might otherwise in many parts of the country be difficult to obtain), would be afforded to the Volunteers for meeting together in considerable bodies and taking part in combined movements; and I have therefore to request your Royal Highness' co-operation in carrying this plan into effect.

I have, &c.,

(Signed) S. HERBERT."

A copy of the letter was, on July 20th, 1860, forwarded by the Horse Guards to the General District Commanding Officer of the regular forces of the country, who were directed by the Commander-in-Chief to place themselves in communication with Lords Lieutenant of counties and with the local Assistant Inspectors of Volunteers, with a view to occasional assembly of the Volunteers in convenient localities, for review, either in battalion or brigade, and to their working, on such occasions and whenever practicable, with the regular troops under their command.

Assistant Inspectors.

It was also announced that three Majors of depôt battalions about to be reduced would probably be selected assistant inspectors for the following districts:—

North Western, head-quarters, Liverpool; Welsh, Swansea; South Scottish, Glasgow.

The officers appointed were to be stationed as follows:

Major Nelson, London; Lieutenant-Colonel Luard, Guildford; Major Hume, Exeter; Lieutenant-Colonel Ibbetson, Cambridge; Major Dick, Birmingham; Major Harman, York; Major Jones, Edinburgh.

That these inspections were intended to be of a searching and thorough nature and no mere gala parade, is clear from the kind of information the Inspector had to report to the War Office.

The following form speaks for itself:—

"Report of the annual Inspection of Volunteer Corps. Reports of Inspectors.

1—What is the name of the Commanding Officer? (N.B.—Should the Commanding Officer not be present, his absence is to be accounted for, and the second in command reported upon as a Commanding Officer).

2—Is he well acquainted with, and does he pay proper attention to the interior economy of his Corps, and is he competent for the command of it in the various situations of the service?

3—Does he discharge his duties in general with zeal?

4—Do they (the officers) according to their several situations afford the officer in command that support he is entitled to require from them?

5—Have any of them served in the Regular or other services? If so, state their names.

7—Do unanimity and good understanding prevail in the Corps?

8—Is any officer non-effective, and from what cause?

9—Do they appear to be well selected, properly instructed, active and intelligent and well acquainted with their respective duties?

10—Are they respectful to their officers, and do they support their own authority in a becoming manner?

11—What number of members have passed through the School of Musketry, and through what course of instruction?

12—Are they well drilled and disciplined?

13—Do the Trumpeters and Buglers appear perfect in the different soundings, and otherwise fit for their situations?

14—Are they well drilled, attentive and steady under arms, and obedient and respectful to their officers?

15—Do the numbers on parade correspond exactly with the parade state?

16—Are the drills, field exercises and movements performed according to regulation, with correctness and a proper degree of celerity?

17—Is the ammunition securely stored and in good order?

18—What number of rounds can be carried by each member on service, and how distributed in the pouches?

19—Are the arms and accoutrements in a serviceable state, clean and properly marked?

20—Where are the arms kept?

21—What is the uniform?

22—Are the Volunteers provided with great-coats or cloaks?

23—Have they valises, saddle-bags, or knapsacks for service?

24—Are the companies told off into squads under the subaltern officer?

25—Where is the rifle range, and how far is it from the head-quarters of the Corps?

26—What is its extent?

27—How many members have fired in the first, second and third periods of target practice respectively?"

The rest applies to Artillery and is omitted.

If the issue of circulars could have insured the efficiency of the Volunteers, they must, in the sixties, have been the most efficient body of armed men in the world. I have now to invite the attention of the reader to a Circular Memorandum addressed to Infantry, which may perhaps be more conveniently introduced at this stage than in its strictly chronological order.

"Horse Guards, S. W.,
1st May, 1860.

The general principles of Light Infantry movements, as well as the movements of a company or battalion, when acting as Light Infantry, are laid down in the "Field Exercises," and the right application of these movements in the field may be studied with advantage in various works by authors of much practical experience, but, in addition to these important points, His Royal Highness the General Commanding-in-Chief deems it essential that the attention of commanding officers should be directed to the necessity of constantly exercising the individual intelligence and judgment of the men under their command, when acting as Light Infantry.

The improved range and accuracy of fire of the arms now in general use render it doubly important that every soldier should, when skirmishing, be prepared to take such advantage of ground and cover as will enable him, with the least exposure of his own person, to inflict the greatest amount of injury on his opponents.

With this view commanding officers are enjoined to lose no opportunity of profiting by all suitable ground in the vicinity of their quarters for the instruction of young soldiers in this important part of their duty, and they should bear in mind that the character of a regiment, as to its proficiency in Light Infantry movements, depends mainly on the individual intelligence, skill and activity displayed by the men themselves.

It would be found advantageous, where the ground admits, to detach one or more companies, with their supports, to a distance of about 1000 yards in front of, and facing, the battalion drawn up in line, when they will extend and advance in skirmishing order towards the battalion, being occasionally halted, in order that the officers, by examining the back sight of the rifles, may ascertain that they have been adjusted for the proper distances.

The officers of the companies in line will point out to the men of their companies any error that may be committed by the skirmishers in their advance and the advantages to be derived from such cover as the ground may present, from running rapidly from point to point, &c.; the line being in the position of the enemy, the men will soon learn what errors, as regards unnecessary exposure, should be avoided.

Each company, in its turn, should be exercised as skirmishers and be occasionally relieved, advancing and retreating, and the advantage of the new line of skirmishers being completely concealed in the latter movement should be pointed out.

Officers in command of supports—bearing in mind the improved range and accuracy of firearms—should also be careful in the selection of their ground, as the fire of the enemy's skirmishers is sure to be directed on any exposed solid body. Supports and reserves, if not under cover, should always lie down when halted.

The attention of the skirmishers should be especially called to the following points:—

Skirmishers, when under fire, must take advantage of all cover. The men of a file should always work together; both men should never be unloaded at the same time; they should always, when practicable, load under cover—before moving to the front, when advancing, and after falling back, when retiring.

Young soldiers (particularly when first opening fire) are apt to waste their ammunition; its value, therefore, cannot be too carefully impressed on their minds, and they should be made to understand that the principal advantage of their rifle, viz :—accuracy of fire, is lost, if, in moving from spot to spot, they do not consider well the distance they are from the object they are about to fire at, and are not careful to adjust the back-sight accordingly.

The files must be careful not to get in front of each other. When small objects, such as trees or rocks, afford cover for a few files only, the men must not crowd behind them in numbers, as they will be safer in the open, where they should load and fire lying, and move rapidly when the advance or retreat renders a change of position necessary, throwing themselves at once on the ground.

Bugle sounds should be avoided as much as possible, the men should be practised at "passing the word," and made to understand signals.

The men should be taught that good cover may be obtained from the slightest rise or fall of ground, more especially when engaged at long ranges; a slight furrow, a few stones or small bushes will often afford cover in the absence of trees, rocks, walls, banks &c.

Skirmishers should be taught to judge rapidly for themselves of the nature of the ground on which they are acting, and of the best mode of occupying it. In defending a line of heights, the edge of a wood, or any ditches, walls &c., they should follow the windings of the cover instead of remaining in line, taking care to leave no considerable gaps and not to collect in groups.

A line of skirmishers may be exercised with advantage in passing obstacles, such as ponds, farm buildings, &c., the men opposing these obstacles doubling in rear of the files on the right and left, but running out to their proper places as soon as the obstacles are passed.

Before quitting one position, each file should decide on the next they intend to occupy, which they should make for in double time. When at close quarters one man of a file should cover the advance or retreat of his comrade while running from point to point, the men protecting each other in turn while exposed.

The fire of skirmishers may often be better employed against the enemy's files on their right and left than against those in their immediate front, who are most likely to be completely covered.

It is impossible for the officers to place each file of their companies; the men must be made to understand that they are responsible for the cover each file may select.

They should keep in sight the files on their right and left, and, when the ground permits, should resume the general line of dressing and their proper distances, making use of their own intelligence, without waiting for special directions.

The dressing of a line of skirmishers is a matter of no importance, as long as the connexion between the files is kept up; in advancing or retiring those files having cover should remain in their position until those on their right and left have passed them by fifteen or twenty paces; in advancing, files should run on to cover when the general line is within fifty paces of it, holding it as above. The file of one protected skirmisher is of more value than that of five when exposed.

Whenever opportunities offer, Commanding Officers should instruct their men in the mode of making rifle-pits and placing sand-bags, sods &c. on a wall or parapet to fire through; also in the duties of covering parties in sieges, how to keep down the fire of batteries, the advantages of the different modes of firing, kneeling, lying &c.; in short, no pains should be spared to make each man a thorough and efficient Light Infantry soldier.

Another important point to which the General Commanding-in-Chief would take the opportunity of directing attention of Commanding Officers, both of regiments and brigades, is the practice of time marches:—i. e., they should direct companies or wings or battalions to occupy a distant position to which several roads lead, some of greater length and easier to march over than others. The heads of these columns should arrive simultaneously in position, and the time of departure be regulated accordingly.

Small bodies of troops may accomplish longer marches, even over bad roads, than deeper columns can accomplish over better roads. Practice will soon enable officers to ascertain these points and to calculate almost to a certainty the time required under every circumstance.

By command,

(Signed) JAMES YORKE SCARLETT,

Adjutant General."

The Regulations of January 19th, 1861.

The year 1861 which, as will be seen, witnessed the authorisation of Camps at Aldershot and Shorncliffe, was further made memorable to the Volunteer by the issue from the War Office of the Volunteer Regulations of that year—assuredly not the least of the many signal services rendered to his country by the Earl de Grey and Ripon. Indeed that issue must have been hailed with gratitude by all connected with the force—the Lords Lieutenant, the Commanding and other officers and even such privates as attempted to understand the rules of the service in which they had engaged. I reproduce these Regulations in the appendix *verbatim*, partly because they form the basis of all subsequent regulations and partly, also, because of the difficulty experienced in obtaining a copy of them. They are not deposited in the British Museum; they are not to be found in the admirable library of the Royal United Service Institution, nor, so far as I am aware, in any public library; no copy is to be obtained from the King's printers, and they are only preserved, by what I must consider a happy chance or commendable prescience, in the files of the *Volunteer Service Gazette.*

Altho', as I have said, the text of these Regulations is to be found in the appendix, I must, to preserve some continuity of narrative, indicate briefly the various matters covered by this important document.

Summary of Regulations of 1861.

The Regulations were published by the authority of the Secretary of State for War and superseded all circulars and orders theretofore issued relative to the Volunteer force, and were to be strictly observed until altered by proper authority. Necessary alterations were to be notified to all Commanding Officers by a Circular Memorandum embodying the new regulation and referring to the part of the Regulations of 1861 modified or cancelled thereby.

It should of course be remembered that this set of regulations, as also subsequent periodical regulations, were not, on the date of their issue, strictly original documents, then for the first time to be observed, but rather the embodiment or codification in systematized form of Orders in Council, General Orders, Memoranda, Circulars and other official communications which, as occasion arose, were issued to the service.

Classification of Volunteers c. 3.

Clause 1 of the Regulations stated the statute 44 George III. c. 54, as the Act under which the Volunteer Corps were raised. The 2nd clause cites from that statute the circumstances in which the Volunteers might be embodied for active service. By clause 3 members are classified as either enrolled or honorary, and subsequent clauses define these members. Clause 6 provides that "the Volunteer Force is composed of the following arms—Light Horse Volunteers, Artillery ditto, Engineer ditto, Mounted Rifle ditto and Rifle ditto." Clause 7 states the "general object of the force, when on actual service," to be "to supplement the Regular, Militia, and other forces in the country." The 8th clause determines the establishments of Rifle Volunteers for sub-divisions, for companies, for battalions of four, of six, of eight and of twelve companies. Rifle corps of over twelve companies were to be divided into two battalions with separate establishments. A company and a subdivision, or two or more companies of Rifles, might be formed into one corps, under the command of a captain-commandant.

Composition of force, c. 6.

Their general object, c. 7.

Their Establishments.

Formation of Corps.

Clauses 9 to 21 inclusive set forth the steps necessary to be taken to form a corps, and the various matters on which the Lord Lieutenant must be satisfied before offering its services to Her Majesty.

Precedence of the Force and its Officers.

Numerical and special Designations.

Appointment of commissioned Officers.

By clause 22 the Volunteer Force "in which general term the Yeomanry are included, takes precedence immediately after the Militia." Other clauses relate to the relative precedence of different corps and of the officers of the Volunteer Force. Clauses 29 and 30 deal with the numerical and special designations of corps. By clause 32 the commissioned officers, except the Adjutants, are to be appointed by the Lord Lieutenant, but (33) "all proposed appointments and promotions of commissioned officers, except adjutants, are submitted for the Queen's approval by the Lord Lieutenant through the Secretary of State." (36) Commissions could only be vacated by "promotion, resignation, deprivation or death"; and (38) appointments, promotions and resignations were to be gazetted.

Double Commissions, c. 40.

By clause 40 "an officer cannot ordinarily hold two substantive commissions at once in the Volunteer Force."

Raising Corps for rank, c. 41.

By clause 41, "when two corps are raised by the influence of one person, this person may, if the Lord Lieutenant considers it necessary, be appointed Commanding Officer of both the corps, but when the force is called out for actual service, he will be required to resign the command of one of them."

By section 42, "when a corps consists of more than one x x x x company and is not under the command of a Field Officer, the senior captain is allowed, on the recommendation of the Lord Lieutenant, to bear the designation of 'Captain Commandant.' This title does not require a separate commission, or confer any additional rank."

Quarter-master, c. 43.

By section 43, Quartermasters and Paymasters disallowed when the force is not on actual service, but two supernumerary Lieutenants might be sanctioned to every Corps under the command of a Field Officer.

Musketry Instructor, Hon. Colonels, Chaplains, Assistant Surgeons, cc. 44-50.

Clauses 44 and 45 refer to the appointment of Musketry Instructors; clauses 46 to 48 to the appointment of Honorary Colonels and other honorary officers. By clause 50, "no officer holding an honorary commission can, in virtue of it, take precedence of any officer holding a substantive commission of the same rank."

Substantive Officers to be effective members, c. 51.

Clause 51 contains the very emphatic declaration that substantive officers should be effective members of their corps; though, in particular cases and for special reasons, a relaxation of this salutary rule might be permitted by the Secretary of State on the representation of the Lord Lieutenant.

Enrolled Members, cc. 55 & 59. Conditions of Efficiency, c. 60.

The 55th and following clauses deal with enrolled members, who are classified as either effectives or non-effectives. Clause 60 defines the conditions of efficiency.

Rules, c. 64.

By clause 64, the Commanding Officer of every Corps is required to transmit to the Lord Lieutenant, for submission to Her Majesty, the rules proposed for the government and discipline for the corps when not on actual service. Model rules drawn up by a committee of Volunteer officers, assembled at the War Office on August 10th, 1859, were to be furnished for the guidance of the Volunteers.

Clause 66 is devoted to Courts of Enquiry which, though not judicial bodies and having no power to administer oaths, are to "assist the Lord Lieutenant or any officer in command in arriving at a correct conclusion on any subject on which it may be expedient for him to be thoroughly informed." Such Courts, if having reference to a commissioned officer, could "only be convened under the authority of the Lord Lieutenant, to whom it would report, and must be composed of officers of Volunteer establishments within the county." Courts of Enquiry, c. 66.

Clauses 67-83 inclusive, after reciting that it is desirable that the small corps of . . . . Rifle Volunteers in the several counties, should, when of sufficient numbers, be united in Administrative Battalions, if it is not practicable to form them into a corps having a more compact organization, declare that the Administrative Organization, 67-83.

"object of this administrative organization is to unite separate corps under a common head, to secure uniformity of drill among them and to afford them the advantage of the instruction and assistance of an Adjutant; but it is not intended to interfere with their constitution or financial arrangements, with the operation of their respective rules, or with the powers specially conferred on their Commanding Officers by the 44 Geo. III, c. 54, or to require them to meet together for united drill in ordinary times, except with their own consent."

Clause 71 allows the following administrative staff:— Administrative Staff, c. 71.

For 4 companies, 1 Major and 1 Adjutant; for not less than 6 companies, 1 Lieutenant-Colonel and 1 Adjutant; for not less than 8 companies, 1 Lieutenant-Colonel, 1 Major and 1 Adjutant; for not less than 12 companies, 1 Lieutenant-Colonel, 2 Majors and 1 Adjutant.

By clause 77, "Subject to the powers conferred by the law upon the Commanding Officer of each Corps, the Field Officer commanding an Administrative Regiment, Brigade or Battalion, was to have the general charge of the drill and discipline of the several corps composing it. He would inspect them from time to time and take notice of and, if necessary, report any infraction of the provisions of the law or of the Orders of the Secretary of State for War, relating to the use of arms, the regulations about clothing, distinctive marks of rank &c. He was also to be responsible that uniformity in drill was preserved throughout the force under his command. When present at the drill or parade of any of the corps, he would invariably be in command, and if two or three of them should wish to meet together for united drill, his permission must first be obtained, and the movements &c. would be subject to his approval. If any of the corps should desire to attend the field day of any corps not under his command, his permission must also be obtained in the first instance." Duties of Field Officer Commanding, c. 77.

Clauses 87 to 94 lay down the rules for united drills, for reviews and rifle shooting matches. Of these clauses, the 92nd provides that "Reviews of large bodies of Volunteers may be held from time to time by the General Officers Commanding Districts, or other officers of high rank and position in the Army." It was, however, to be distinctly understood that no Volunteer Corps could be compelled to attend any such review in time of peace. Drills, Reviews &c., cc. 87-94.

Clauses 95 to 101 are concerned with the uniforms and accoutrements. Though (95) every Volunteer Corps was allowed to choose its own uniform and accoutrements, subject to the approval of the Lord Lieutenant, and provided no gold lace were introduced, it was (96) stated to be desirable that a uniform colour should be chosen for the clothing of corps of each arm within the same county. Uniform &c., cc. 95-101. Kit, c. 96.

Clause 98, premising that the force should at all times be prepared for actual service, prescribes the Volunteer's Kit.

Stores, cc. 102-123. Arms gratuitously, c. 102.

The 102nd clause declares that "every Volunteer Corps is supplied gratuitously with arms from the Government Stores, to the full number of its enrolled members if required."

The arms, however, were not to be issued till the Lord Lieutenant was satisfied that provision had been made for their custody and charge at the expense of the Volunteers. There were elaborate regulations for the marking of the rifles, cleaning, alteration of locks &c.

Ammunition, c. 113.

Clause 113 prescribed the proportion of ammunition to be allowed to Volunteer corps, viz:—"For every enrolled member, for his first year of service, gratis, 110 rounds ball, 20 rounds blank, 163 caps; allowed to be purchased, 110 rounds ball (including 20 rounds for prize shooting), 100 rounds blank, 231 caps; total 220 rounds ball, 120 rounds blank, 394 caps; after his first year of service, gratis, 90 rounds ball, 60 rounds blank, 165 caps; allowed to be purchased, 130 rounds ball (inclusive as aforesaid), 60 rounds blank, 209 caps; total 220 rounds ball, 120 rounds blank, 374 caps."

Adjutants, cc. 127-146.

Clauses 127-146 are devoted to the appointment, qualifications, examination, pay and general allowances, rank and duties of the Adjutant.

By section 141, "except for the purposes of instruction no Adjutant is entitled, by virtue of his superior rank, to take the command of any force of Volunteers, when any officer of the corps to which he belongs is present."

Drill Instructors. Regulations, Aug. 22nd, 1861, cc. 147-167.

The Regulations of 19th January, 1861 (clauses 147-167) referred to the appointment and duties of drill instructors. These clauses, however, were superseded by Articles 147-167 of a War Office Memorandum of August 22, 1861, which will be found in the appendix as part of the Regulations of January, 1861.

Sergeant-Major, c. 149.

C. 167.

By Article 147 sergeant-instructors were to be provided at the public expense to Volunteer corps in the proportion of 1 to each corps of from 1 to 3 companies, 2 to each corps of from 4 to 7 companies, 3 to each corps of from 8 to 12 companies or upwards. One of the sergeant-instructors in each battalion might be appointed sergeant-major. The appointment, which was to be considered temporary, rested with the Commanding Officer of the corps, who, for any sufficient reason, might deprive a sergeant of it. The qualifications of sergeant-instructors, their appointment, their pay, their supersession are fully dealt with. The "principal duty of a sergeant-instructor (Art. 167) is to attend to the drill and instruction of the corps to which he is attached; but the Commanding Officer of the corps may employ him to take charge of the arms of the corps or to discharge other similar duties of a military character, provided they do not interfere with his special functions. He will not be permitted to engage in any trade or business."

Instruction in Musketry, cc. 171-180.

Clauses 171-180 are devoted to the instruction of Volunteers in Schools of Musketry classes which were to be periodically formed, the course of instruction to extend over fourteen days, students to bear their own expenses or be subsidized by their corps. They were not to be required to pay any fee, and ammunition was to be issued to them gratuitously. A Volunteer could not attend such a class unless "thoroughly acquainted with the manual and platoon exercises." He must remain at the School till the termination of the course of instruction, unless specially absolved, and must bind himself "to impart instruction in the authorised system of musketry on his return to his corps."

Volunteers desiring to qualify to act as Sergeant-Instructors of their corps, were permitted an extension of instruction of 6 or 8 days after the termination of the course, and were then to be examined as to their ability to impart instruction. C. 173.

Proficiency Badges, c. 177.

By clause 177 those Volunteers who had attained the proficiency defined in part V. of the Regulations for conducting the musketry instruction of the army, were to be permitted to wear the cross-muskets upon the sleeve of the tunic. But as this badge denoted a degree of proficiency rarely to be attained by Volunteers, in consequence of the limited ranges for shooting, and as it was, nevertheless, desirable to establish some marks of distinction for proficiency in shooting, the following badges were permitted :--

(*a*) Range of 300 yards: best marksman, a rifle embroidered horizontally.

(*b*) Range of 350 to 600 yards: best marksman, a rifle embroidered horizontally, with a star immediately above it.

(*c*) Range of 900 yards: every Volunteer obtaining seven points and upwards in the 1st class, a rifle embroidered horizontally, with two stars immediately above it.

(*d*) Range between 650 and 900 yards: the Volunteer obtaining the greatest number of points above seven in the 1st class: a rifle embroidered horizontally, with three stars immediately above it.

Badge of Volunteer Sergeant-Instructor, c. 178.

By clause 178, a Volunteer obtaining a certificate that he was capable of imparting instruction in musketry might wear a cross-musket and crown.

No badges were to be worked in gold.

Details of practice, cc. 180-181.

The 180th clause sets out in copious detail the practice for the various ranges. Clause 181 indicates the books of instruction to be used, and in reference to this clause, a Volunteer Circular (number 20), dated 17th March, 1862, was issued, which provides that Volunteers, though armed with the long Enfield rifle, were to be instructed in the manual and platoon exercises prescribed for the short Enfield rifle, except as regards the modes of fixing and unfixing bayonets, in which instances the directions laid down for the long rifle were to be followed; and all orders in the "Field Exercise" for the guidance of troops carrying the short rifle were to be considered as applicable to Volunteers, although armed with the long rifle. To a similar provision in March, 1862 (W. O. C., 17th March, 1862), I have already had occasion to allude. V Genl. No. 1883.

Attachment of Officers for Instruction, c. 182.

By clause 182, any Commissioned Officer of Volunteers might be temporarily attached, for the purpose of receiving instruction, to Infantry Regiments of the Regular Army, or to Infantry Regiments of the Militia, for any period not exceeding one month.

Districts for Military Inspection, c. 196

Assistant Inspectors, c. 197.

The 196th clause divided Great Britain into districts for military inspection. Every division is placed under an Assistant-Inspector, whose duties are defined, and who particularly "after every inspection of a corps, is to furnish a confidential report to the Secretary of State."

An important departure in the various attempts to promote the efficiency of the Volunteers was made also in the year 1861. A camp of Volunteers was, in September of that year, attempted at Newton, but the result was not encouraging. Another, of the Berkshire Rifles, at Uppington, was more successful. About this period, too, some of the Liverpool and Chester corps formed camps, their members drilling early and late and engaging during the day in their ordinary avocations. On October 8th the Secretary for War issued a circular stating the conditions under which Volunteers would be brigaded with regular troops in the camps at Aldershot and Shorncliffe. The following is a copy of this circular, which I set forth almost in full as the first relating to this subject.

Brigading in Camp.

"War Office,
8th October, 1861.

Sir,

The Secretary of State for War, being anxious to facilitate and encourage the instruction of the Volunteers by brigading them with the regular troops at the camps at Aldershot and Shorncliffe, has, with the concurrence of His Royal Highness the General Commanding-in-Chief, determined upon the following regulations which are to be observed by all Volunteer Corps who may be desirous to avail themselves of this mode of instruction.

1—The instruction of Volunteers in camp and the issue of camp equipage for their use will be confined for the present to the camps of Aldershot and Shorncliffe, and the number of Volunteers to be admitted to the respective camps at one time cannot exceed:—

At Aldershot	1,500
At Shorncliffe	500

2—The application from any corps for permission to be stationed at either of the above camps is to be made to the Secretary of State for War (upon the Form A) not less than a fortnight before the date proposed for the assembly of the corps at the camp. It is to contain an exact state of the officers, non-commissioned officers, men and horses of which the force will be composed, and should also specify the period that the Volunteers propose to remain in camp and in what manner they desire to be subsisted.

3—If the Secretary of State should, after communication with the General Commanding-in-Chief, approve the application, the Quartermaster General will, under the orders of His Royal Highness, make the necessary arrangements for the issue of camp equipage to the Volunteers, unless the necessities of the service should render it desirable to place them in barracks or huts. A form of requisition (B) will be furnished to the commanding officer of the corps upon which he will demand such of the articles of camp equipment enumerated therein as may be required by the Volunteers under his command while in camp.

4—It is desirable that, on the day previous to a Volunteer corps going into camp, an officer to act as the Quartermaster of the corps, accompanied by a non-commissioned officer and two men per company, should proceed to the camp for the purpose of taking over the camp equipment and making the necessary arrangements for the reception of the corps on the following day. On arrival, this officer will report himself to the Assistant-Quartermaster General from whom he will receive his instructions. The General Commanding the Division will cause the camp to be pitched for the Volunteers by a fatigue party in the ground allotted for the purpose, and the straw laid in the tents, and he will also attach to the corps an intelligent and trustworthy non-commissioned officer of the line to act as Quarter-Sergeant, who will receive an extra allowance of 6d. a day while so acting, to be paid by the corps.

5—On the arrival of a corps in camp the Commanding Officer will transmit to the Quartermaster General a report of his arrival, accompanied by a state of the corps for the information of the Lieutenant-General Commanding.

6—When the Volunteers leave their encampment the Commanding Officer will report their departure in the same manner as he did their arrival, and the officer acting as Quartermaster, with the same detail which accompanied him in arrival, will remain until the following day, when a Board of Officers will be assembled (of which the Superintendent of Stores and the officer acting as Quartermaster to the Volunteer Corps shall be members) for the purpose of assessing any damage done to the camp equipment beyond fair wear and tear, and in the case of barracks or huts the Barrack master will be a member of the board.

7—If the Volunteers desire to receive rations from the Commissariat they will be delivered to the Corps at stated hours. But if they are desirous of providing provisions at the contract prices special arrangements will be necessary to obtain them at the hours suitable to the Volunteers. In both cases payment will be made according to the existing contract rates.

The daily rations in camp consist of the articles mentioned in the annexed statement (C).

Volunteers, although they may not be called out for service, must, when encamped with Regular troops, conform to all the ordinary regulations of a military camp not only for the purposes of efficient instruction, but in order to ensure regularity in carrying out the arrangements which are essential to their health and comfort as well as the protection of their property while in tents.

On the arrival of a Volunteer Corps in camp, the quarter and rear guards are to mount immediately.

These guards should furnish two sentries each, posted on the front, rear and both flanks.

Care is to be taken that the compliments due to the respective ranks of officers or to armed parties approaching their posts are duly paid by guards and sentries.

Every corps constituting a battalion should have a captain and a subaltern on duty for the day.

These officers should never quit the camp during their tour of duty.

The captain of the day will have the general charge of the camp and will see that the regulations for the cooking and cleanliness of the camp have been duly carried out,

He will be present at guard-mounting and he will visit the guards once in the day, and also in the night.

The subaltern of the day will assist the captain of the day in his various duties.

If the corps receive rations or provisions at the contract price, he will be present at and, with the Acting Quartermaster, superintend their issue, and satisfy himself as to their quality and quantity.

He will visit the meals of the Volunteers and receive any complaints, which he will duly enter in his report to the captain for the consideration of the Commanding Officer.

He will inspect the kitchens an hour after the dinners and see that they are clean and well regulated.

He will visit the guards day and night at different hours from the captain.

At night he will also visit the sentries, accompanied by the corporal of the guard.

At tattoo he will collect the reports and ascertain that all lights and fires are put out except those that are authorised.

The report of the Subaltern of the day will be made to the Captain, who will transmit it with his own to the orderly tent by 10 a.m. on the day succeeding that on which he was on duty.

When a battalion in camp is composed of more than one corps there will be a Battalion Captain of the day, but each corps will have its own Orderly Subaltern of the day for the purposes of its own interior economy.

The duties of the Acting Quartermaster in camp are very important, and require to be zealously and energetically performed.

The camp equipment issued for the use of his corps is in his charge.

He is responsible for the general arrangements and cleanliness of the camp.

For this purpose the pioneers of the corps are to be placed under his orders, whose duty it will be to remove all rubbish and dirt from the vicinity of the tents.

Proper kitchens are to be constructed and no other cooking places to be allowed in camp.

He will attend the delivery of rations or provisions, carefully inspecting them before they are issued, and he will superintend the equalization of the messes, rectifying any just complaint.

An Orderly Sergeant and Orderly Corporal should be told off for daily duty, the first to accompany the Captain of the day and the second the Orderly Subaltern and assist them in their duties.

They will not quit the camp at any time during their duty, and will be observant of all strangers in the camp, particularly when the corps is out at drill.

For general purposes the Volunteers will find it convenient to arrange that one of their number in each tent should be the Orderly of the day for the purpose of bringing the meals from the kitchens and looking after the general management of the tent throughout the day.

Officers Commanding Corps are recommended to obtain, through the Assistant-Quartermaster General, the sanction of the General Commanding to instruction being afforded to the Volunteers in pitching and striking camps.

I am, sir, your obedient servant,

DE GREY AND RIPON

(FORM C).

SCALE OF RATIONS FOR FIELD SERVICE.

Bread	1¼-lbs.	per man, per day.
Fresh Meat*	1-lb.	,, ,,
Coffee	⅓-oz.	,, ,,
Tea	⅙-oz.	,, ,,
Sugar	2-oz.	,, ,,
Salt	½-oz.	,, ,,
Pepper	1/36 oz.	,, ,,

FUEL.

3-lbs. firewood per man per day.
1-lb. coals, with 1-lb. kindling wood to every 36-lbs. of coals.
Straw for bedding or paillasses.
1 truss of 36-lbs. per two men with paillasses.
2 trusses of 36-lbs. per five men without paillasses.

With paillasses the straw should last 16 days, and should then be refreshed with half a truss per paillasse, at the end of 32 days the whole to be removed and fresh bedding issued.

Without paillasses the straw should be refreshed at the end of eight days with one truss per five men, and the same quantity at the end of the succeeding eight days; at the end of 24 days fresh bedding should be issued. In wet weather the straw should be more frequently changed.

FORAGE.

10 lbs. of oats, 12 lbs. of hay, and 8 lbs. of straw per horse per day,
8 lbs. of oats, 10 lbs. of hay, and 8 lbs. of straw per battalion horse per day.
2 lbs. of oats extra to horses picketed in the open air.

Local Camps

It was apparently soon found that it was necessary to make provision for instruction in Camp life and duties of those Volunteers whose ordinary duties precluded them from proceeding either to Aldershot or Shorncliffe. Accordingly, in March, 1862, the following Circular was issued providing for the authorizing of Local Camps, the issue thereto of camp equipage and stores, and the attendance thereat of an Officer of the regular army, who was to assume command of the Camp and impart military instruction in camp duties. The Circular was as follows:—

"War Office,
14th March, 1862.

Circular, March, 1862, re Local Camps.
V Genl. No., 1819.

Sir,

With a view to extending the means which have already been afforded to Volunteers of deriving instruction in camp duties by brigading with the Regular troops at the Camps of Aldershot and Shorncliffe, the Secretary of State for War has approved of the issue of the following additional regulations for the guidance

*The field ration of meat in England was, in 1861, ¾-lb., to be probably increased to 1-lb. on active service.

L

of such corps as desire to have instruction in camp duties, but are not able to proceed to either of the above-mentioned camps.

1—When it is proposed to form a camp of Volunteers for the above-mentioned purpose, an application for permission to do so, stating the place, date of formation, duration and probable number of Volunteers, must, in the first instance, be sent to the Lord Lieutenant of the county in which the camp is to be situated, who, if he approves of the proposal, will forward it to the Secretary of State for his sanction. If this sanction be given, each corps wishing to join the camp will then apply through its own Lord Lieutenant for permission to do so. In the case of a corps belonging to an Administrative regiment, brigade or battalion, the application must be sent through the Field Officer Commanding.

2—The second paragraph relates to the issue of camp equipage to the Volunteers from the nearest military stores; the cost of transport to be defrayed by the corps.

3—The Secretary of State for War will request the General Commanding-in-Chief to appoint an officer of the Regular Army to command in the camp and impart instruction to the Volunteers in camp duties.

This officer will be assisted by a non-commissioned officer of the Regular forces, who will act as staff sergeant.

The Volunteers must provide their own supplies; but it is desirable that this should be done in such a manner as to afford instruction in the distribution and cooking of rations as in the field; and it will be the care of the officer appointed to the charge of the camp to avail himself of all circumstances that are capable of affording instruction of this nature to the Volunteers.

4—This paragraph details the steps to be taken for the selection and marking out of the ground and for insuring the comfort and cleanliness of the troops.

(Signed) DE GREY AND RIPON."

Other clauses of the circular do not appear to call for notice.

23 Vict., c. 13, as to interest in Friendly Societies, &c.

The Regulations of 1861 were succeeded by the statute of 1863, but it will be convenient, before considering that enactment, to refer to three statutes that are not more important from their provisions than from the evidence they afford that Parliament was, by this time, if not fully alive, at least rapidly awaking to the importance of the Volunteers as an arm of defence. The first, passed in 1860, provides that no person, by reason of his enrolment or service in any corps of Volunteers, shall lose or forfeit any interest he may possess at the time of his being enrolled or serving, in any Friendly or Benefit Society, any rules of such society to the contrary notwithstanding. The second statute, passed also in 1860, "The Rifle Volunteer Grounds Act," authorised Volunteer corps, with the consent of the Secretary of State for War, to purchase land for rifle practice, but such land was to be previously inspected by a Government Inspector and reported on as capable of being so used, "with due regard to the safety and convenience of the public." Power

23 & 24 Vict., c. 140. Acquisition of land for Rifle Practice.

was also given to tenants in tail and life tenants, with the consent of the next in succession, to grant to Volunteers a practice ground of not more than 4 acres or to grant the use of not more than 20 acres for such purposes. The Commissioners of Public Works, of Woods and Forests, the Chancellor and Council of the Duchy of Lancaster, were empowered to grant licenses to use land within their respective jurisdictions for terms of 21 years.

Corporations, ecclesiastical or lay, aggregate or sole, were conceded the like powers, subject to the consent and conditions set forth in the Act. The very necessary process of diverting ancient footpaths was also provided for. The next statute, passed in 1861, exempted from dues, duties, pontage or toll, Volunteers, if in uniform, on march or going to and from inspections &c., also their horses, waggons and other vehicles.

24 & 25 Vict., c. 126, Exemptions from Tolls &c.

The time was at hand when Parliament was to be invited to undertake legislation of a most important and comprehensive character affecting the Volunteers. On the 28th March, 1862, a deputation had waited upon Sir George Lewis at the War Office, for the purpose of representing the advantages of a Royal Commission to enquire into the state of the Volunteer Force. The deputation was the result of a resolution unanimously agreed to at a meeting of members of both Houses of Parliament, and consisted of the following:—The Duke of Marlborough, the Earl of Shaftesbury, the Earl of Chichester, the Earl Ducie, Lord Overstone, Lord Eversley, Lord Henneker, M.P., Mr. A. Black, M.P., Mr. A. Mills, M.P., Mr. G. W. Hope, M.P., Mr. Phillips, M.P., the Hon. A. Kinnaird, M.P., Mr. Gregson, M.P., Mr. Bass, M.P., Mr. A. W. Kinglake, M.P., Mr. Deedes, M.P. Accordingly in May, 1862, a Royal Commission was appointed to enquire into the character and condition of the Volunteer Force and to report upon every matter connected with its organisation, with the view of placing it on a better and more substantial footing. The following noblemen and gentlemen constituted the Commission: Viscount Eversley, the Earl of Ducie, Viscount Hardinge, Lord Overstone, Lord Elcho, M.P., (the founder of the Elcho shield), Lieutenant-Colonel Bartelott, M.P., the Right Honourable E. P. Bouverie, M.P., Major-General Eyre, Lieutenant-General Sir George Wetherall, Lieutenant-Colonel Sir Archibald Campbell, Lieutenant-Colonel Gladstone, Major Vernon Harcourt and Colonel McMurdo.

May, 1862, Royal Commission on Volunteer Force.

The Members of the Commission

The report of this commission was published on October 29th, 1862. The commission recommended that for every man who attended nine drills a year, six of which were to be battalion

Oct. 29th, 1862, Report of the Commission.

£1 Capitation Grant for efficiency.

parades, in the case of a consolidated, and three in the case of an administrative battalion, a sum of £1 should be paid to his commanding officer, in the nature of a capitation grant, for the subsidy of the corps. A further grant of 10/- was recommended for every man who fired 60 rounds in class firing and passed out of the third class. A grant of 30/- was recommended for every efficient in the Artillery. Every efficient was to be entitled, at the end of the year, to a certificate of proficiency and entitled to wear a chevron on his arm.

10/- Grant for class firing.

Strength of Volunteers of all arms in 1862.

The strength of the force at this time was 162,681, made up of:—

662	Light Horse
24,363	Artillery
2,904	Engineers
656	Mounted Rifles
134,096	Rifle Volunteers
162,681	

Of the Rifle Volunteers, 48,796 were organized in 86 consolidated battalions, and 75,535 in 134 administrative battalions. The report stated the condition of the force to be, generally speaking, satisfactory, and the committee believed that by steady perseverance in the course thitherto pursued, and by due discipline, it would be a valuable auxiliary to the British Army as a means of national defence.

26 & 27 Vict., c. 65. Volunteer Act, 1863.

It was upon the report of this commission that the Volunteer Act of 1863 (21st July, 1863) was based. It is not necessary that I should recapitulate all the clauses of a statute so easily accessible but I may be permitted to advert to some of its most important provisions, more especially as it is to this day the controlling statute of the Volunteer force, taking the place of the originating Act of 44 Geo. III. c. 54. The Act empowered Her Majesty to constitute for any Volunteer Corps a permanent staff, consisting of an adjutant bearing Her Majesty's commission, and of as many sergeant-instructors as might seem fit. With the exception of the permanent staff the Volunteers were to be officered by gentlemen appointed with Her Majesty's approval, but bearing the commission of the Lord Lieutenant. These officers were to rank with those of the Regular and Militia forces as youngest of their rank; but with officers of the Yeomanry according to the dates of their respective commissions in their respective forces.

The following oath was to be taken by officers and men alike:—

The Oath of Volunteers.

"I do sincerely promise and swear that I will be faithful and bear true allegiance to Her Majesty Queen Victoria, and that I will faithfully serve Her Majesty in Great Britain for the defence of the same against all Her enemies and opposers whatsoever according to the conditions of my service."

Terms on which a Volunteer might resign.

A Volunteer, except when on actual military service, might quit his corps on giving fourteen days' notice, delivering up his arms and uniform in good order, and paying arrears of monies due from him under the rules of the corps. Volunteers on actual service or undergoing an inspection might be put under the command of General or Field Officers of the Army, superior in rank to every officer of the Volunteer force; but so that they should still be led by their own officers under such command. An annual inspection of every Volunteer corps was to be held by a General or Field Officer of the Army.

On active service Volunteers to be under Field Officer.

But led by their own Officers.

The important, the all-important, question of efficiency, was dealt with thus: the Act provided (section 11) that Her Majesty in Council might from time to time declare what was requisite to entitle a Volunteer to be deemed an efficient Volunteer, by an Order in Council defining, for that purpose, the extent of attendance at drill to be given by the Volunteer and the course of instruction to be gone through by him and the degree of proficiency in drill and instruction to be attained by him and his corps, such proficiency to be judged of by the Inspecting Officer at the annual Inspection of the corps, or otherwise, as by Order in Council might from time to time be determined. The draft of any scheme was to lie for a specified period on the table of both Houses before final adoption by the Council.

Order in Council, July 23rd, 1863, as to what constitutes an effective.

Accordingly on July 27th, 1863, an Order in Council was issued declaring that a Volunteer should be deemed to be an effective if he obtained a certificate that he had fulfilled the requirements and possessed the qualifications stated in such one of the thereunto annexed forms of certificate as might be applicable to his case and not otherwise. The forms of certificate are applicable to the Artillery Volunteer Corps, Engineer Volunteer Corps, Mounted Rifle Volunteer Corps and Rifle Volunteer Corps, both those having and those not having the establishment of a battalion. It is not necessary that I should subjoin other forms of certificate than those to be used by the Rifle Volunteers:—

Form of Certificate of Efficiency.

"We hereby certify

1—That A. B., No. , was enrolled in the Rifle Volunteer Corps on , 18 .

2—That he attended during the (for recruits, 18; for others, 12) months ending the 30th November, drills ordered by the Commanding Officer (for recruits, 30 squad, company or battalion drills, or instruction in musketry; for others, in the case of Corps having the establishment of a battalion, six battalion and three company drills, in the case of Corps having an establishment less than that of a battalion, three battalion and six company drills).

3—That he possesses a competent knowledge of squad and company drill, including the manual and platoon exercises and skirmishing as a company, as laid down in the Field Exercises of Infantry.

4—That he possesses a competent knowledge of the preliminary musketry drill laid down in the Musketry Regulations of the Army.

5—That he was present at the last Annual Inspection of the Corps (or absent with leave, or from sickness duly certified).

Commanding Officer,
Adjutant."

Embodiment of the Volunteers, Sec. 17.

Section 17 authorises Her Majesty, in case of actual or apprehended invasion of any part of the United Kingdom, to direct the Lieutenant of counties throughout Great Britain to call out the Volunteer Corps of their respective counties or any of them, for actual military service. Any officer or private not responding to the call and not incapable by infirmity for military service, was to be dealt with as a deserter.

It will be noticed that the occasion justifying the mobilization of the Volunteers under the Act of 1863 is not quite the same as that defined in the Act 44 Geo. III. c. 54. The latter statute was more comprehensive. It provided for the case of:—

1—Actual invasion.

2—The appearance of any enemy in force on the coast of Great Britain.

3—Rebellion or insurrection arising or existing within the same, on the appearance of such enemy in force on the coast, or during an invasion.

The terms of the statute of 1863, "actual or apprehended invasion," may be taken to cover cases 1 and 2, contemplated by the statute of Geo. III.; but they clearly do not cover the contingency of internal dissensions.

63 & 64 Vict., c. 39. Volunteer Act, 1900.

This omission of the Act of 1863, whether intentional or accidental, was not repeated, it will be seen, in the Act of 1900: the terms there used, "imminent national danger and great emergency," being elastic enough to provide against any possible contingency.

Reverting, however, to the Volunteer Act of 1863, it was provided that every officer and Volunteer and non-commissioned officer of the Permanent Staff (except such as waived their claim) was to be entitled, on being called out for actual military service, to two guineas for necessaries, and to receive pay and be billeted and quartered and have relief for their wives and families (being unable to support themselves) in like manner as officers, non-commissioned officers and men of the Militia.

Part 5 of the Act of 1863 substantially repealed all previous existing Volunteer Acts, as also the provisions I have already extracted from earlier statutes relating to the acquisition or leasing of land, the exemption from tolls and as to benefit societies

Every officer of the Volunteer Force and every efficient Volunteer and every non-commissioned officer of the Permanent Staff was by this statute exempted from serving personally or providing a substitute in the Militia. **Exemption from Militia service.**

Although this Act of 1863 may be regarded as the controlling statute of the Volunteer forces of the country, exception may be taken to some of its provisions and criticism directed to its omissions. **Some objectionable features of the Act** The 21st section, for instance, empowered the Commanding Officer of a Volunteer Corps to discharge therefrom any Volunteer and strike him from the muster roll, either for disobedience of orders, neglect of duty, misconduct as a member of the corps, or for other sufficient causes, the existence and sufficiency of such causes respectively to be judged of by the Commanding Officer. It is true there was a rider to this drastic provision enabling Her Majesty to signify her pleasure in such manner, and give such directions, with reference to such cases of discharge, as to Her Majesty might appear just and proper; but one may be allowed some scepticism as to the chances of a private appealing to the War Office against a commanding officer. The clause evoked considerable discussion and protest in Parliament. An instance was quoted of a commanding officer dismissing 4 sergeants at once, simply for asking that a general meeting of members might be called and the statutory balance sheet exhibited. The objections to the clause did not proceed from civilians alone. Lieutenant-Colonel Luard, Assistant Inspector of Volunteers, declared the power "to be greater than is awarded to any officer in the army and one not to be in the hands of the commanding officer of any Volunteer Corps." A deputation of Volunteer officers and men waited on Earl de Grey and protested against the clause. But the Government was obdurate and the provision was retained. One other serious blemish is to be observed in the Act. I refer to the clause which practically constitutes attendance at nine drills the qualification for a certificate of efficiency. The utter inadequacy of such a provision should surely need no demonstration. I cannot better express the objections to which the clause is open than in the words of an able writer on the Volunteer question, Mr. David Capern, who, in his "Principal events of the Volunteer Force 1859-1871," penned the following pregnant criticism. After stating the total number of Volunteers, at the time of his monograph, to be 170,671, he proceeds:—"It would be worth knowing how many of these men possess an ordinary knowledge of their duties and how many do not. A very active experience of nearly twelve years has convinced me that the standard of efficiency is a myth. The country is called upon to contribute one pound every year for any man who attends six battalion and three company drills, and the same sum is paid for the man who attends 100 drills, passes through class firing and becomes a marksman. This is an anomaly and one that should be speedily removed. The men comprising the Volunteer force may be divided into four classes:—

1—Those who do make themselves acquainted with the duties of a soldier.

2—Those who care nothing about the force or the country either, and merely attend the nine drills because they are hunted up to the head-quarters of their regiments by indefatigable non-commissioned officers.

3—The 'paper' men, who perhaps attend one or two drills in a year, in the majority of cases none at all, and who are consequently always returned as non-efficient; and

4—What are called the shooting men, who care little about efficiency in drill, since they in most instances only comply with the requirements of the Act of Parliament.

Many men of the latter class simply make the Volunteer force a source of profit to themselves, for we find them going from meeting to meeting and winning 'All-comers' prizes with the greatest ease; but of what use would they be with their crack shooting on active service, when, from their own ignorance of the drill, they would obstruct and impede those of their comrades who were efficient? The Duke of Cambridge, at a meeting of Volunteer officers in St. James's Hall, said, 'To make a good soldier a man must know his drill. If he does not know his drill, shooting, in my opinion, is merely thrown away.' '

"In order," continues Mr. Capern, "to ensure the Volunteer force being placed in a proper state of efficiency, some radical alterations must be made. The number of drills a man should perform in a year ought not to be one less than 30 for old members and 50 for recruits, and these should be classified, viz.:—so many battalion, company, skirmishing, position, aiming, and judging distance drills. An alteration of this kind would bring the force to its level. Numbers of men would, of course, not perform these drills, and would either withdraw altogether or become 'paper men,' but the country would be far better without them, because the Government would have men upon whom they could rely, should their active services ever be required. The firing through the annual course, at any rate passing into the 2nd class, should be made a *sine qua non*. No officer should be allowed to hold a commission unless properly qualified and holding a certificate to that effect, and if increased efficiency were guaranteed there is no doubt the Government would entertain the question of increasing the capitation grants for the rank and file."

The Regulations of Sept. 18th, 1863.

I must now direct attention to the Regulations of 1863.

These Regulations are now out of print, but a copy in my possession enables me to institute a comparison between them and those of 1861, an enquiry useful not only as shewing the conditions under which the Volunteer force existed forty years ago, but also as shewing the changes two brief years witnessed in the governing laws of a body that might still, in 1863, be regarded as in a state of flux, probably no one having very definite ideas either of the form it was ultimately to assume or of the form it was desirable it should assume.

The Volunteer corps of 1861 and previous years were, by the Regulations of that year, stated to be "raised under the Act 44, Geo. III, c. 54." That statute was repealed by the Volunteer Act of 1863, so far as the Act related to Volunteers in Great Britain. The Volunteer corps of 1863 and subsequent years were stated to be "raised under the Volunteer Act of 1863."

As I have already pointed out the liability to active service of the Volunteers under the later Act differed from that of the earlier levies and I have sufficiently indicated the points of difference.

In the Regulations of 1863 the establishment of Rifle Volunteers is set out in tabular form. I reproduce the table and for the purpose of comparison I include in it the establishment of 1861, distinguishing the two. In the table two numbers divided by a line signify the maximum and minimum strengths.

ESTABLISHMENTS OF 1861 AND 1863.

Description of Corps.	Lieut-Colonels.	Majors.	Captains.	Lieutenants.	Ensigns.	Adjutants.	Surgeons.	Assistant-Surgeons.	Staff Sergeants. Sergeant-Majors.	Staff Sergeants. Quarter-Master Sergeant.	Staff Sergeants. Armourer.	Staff Sergeants. Orderly Room Clerk.	Staff Sergeants. Bugle-Major.	Colour-Sergts.	Sergeants.	Corporals.	Buglers.	Privates.	Total Enrolled Members.	Notes
Sub-division .. 1861				1	1					1					3/2	3/2	1	49/22	59/30	No change.
Sub-division .. 1863				1	1					1					3/2	3/2	1	49/22	59/30	
Company 1861			1	1	1					1				1	4/2	5/3	2	84/48	100/60	No change.
*Company 1863			1	1	1					1				1	4/2	5/3	2	84/48	100/60	
Battalion of 4 Comps. 1861		1	4	4	4	1	1		1	1	1	1	1	4	16/8	20/12	8	332/188	400/240	
†Battalion of 4 Comps. 1863																				
Battalion of 6 Comps. 1861	1		6	6	6	1	1	1	1	1	1	1	1	6	24/12	30/18	12	501/285	600/360	A Major allowed by the establishment of 1863; not by that of 1861. The total is equalized by the reduction of the privates of 1863 by 1.
Battalion of 6 Comps. 1863	1	1	6	6	6	1	1	1	1	1	1	1	1	6	24/12	30/18	12	500/284	600/360	
Battalion of 8 Comps. 1861	1	1	8	8	8	1	1	2	1	1	1	1	1	8	32/16	40/24	16	669/381	800/480	Two Majors in 1863; only 1 in 1861.
Battalion of 8 Comps. 1863	1	2	8	8	8	1	1	2	1	1	1	1	1	8	32/16	40/24	16	668/380	800/480	
Battalion of 12 Comps. 1861	1	2	12	12	12	1	1	2	1	1	1	1	1	12	48/24	60/36	24	1008/576	1200/720	Two Lieutenant-Colonels in 1863; only 1 in 1861.
Battalion of 12 Comps. 1863	2	2	12	12	12	1	1	2	1	1	1	1	1	12	48/24	60/36	24	1007/575	1200/720	

* A company and a subdivision, or two or more companies, may be formed into one corps, under the command of a Captain-Commandant, in accordance with Article 42 (Regulations, 1861) and Article 46 (Regulations, 1863), and such a corps will be entitled to an assistant surgeon, in addition to the establishment due to the number of companies, &c., of which it is composed.

† By the regulations of 1863, in cases in which special circumstances may render it impracticable to form a battalion of 6 companies, the formation of a battalion of 4 or 5 companies, under the command of a major, will, if recommended by the Lord Lieutenant, be authorised. In all cases a corps of 4 companies is entitled to a major, subject to the conditions prescribed in Articles 92 and 93.

N B.—When a corps is below its maximum establishment, sergeants should only be appointed in the proportion of one to every twenty enrolled members.

On the subject of corps formation, the Regulations of 1863 contain an article not to be found in those of 1861. It is as follows:— Formation of Corps. Art. 9.

Article 9, "The Secretary of State, in considering offers of the services of new corps, will have regard to the number and description of corps already existing in the same district, to the circumstances of the locality and to the limits imposed by the amount of the sums placed at his disposal by Parliament in the Volunteer Vote. It is therefore advisable that Lords Lieutenant, in forwarding such offers of service, should, in addition to the information asked for in Articles 11 and 16, state any special local circumstances which render it advisable, in their opinion, to sanction the formation of the proposed corps."

It is possible that the avidity with which the country generally had thrown itself into the Volunteer movement between 1859 and the issue of these Regulations had somewhat appalled the War Office, and suggested the exercise of more discrimination in the sanction of corps formation.

By Article 12 (b) of the Regulations of 1863, the extent of range afforded, as a condition precedent to the sanction of corps formation, was fixed at not less than 300 yards. By the Regulations of 1861 the limit was not less than 200 yards. Extent of Range. Art. 12.

By Article 19 of the Regulations of 1863, the formation of a new corps, below the establishment of a regiment, brigade or battalion, was not to be sanctioned unless it was to form part of an administrative regiment. No similar proviso is contained in the Regulations of 1861. New Corps below Establishment of Battalion not to be sanctioned. Art. 19.

By the Regulations of 1861, the Volunteer corps were bracketed with the Yeomanry as taking precedence immediately after the Militia. Precedence. Art. 27.

By Article 22 of the Regulations of 1863, the Volunteers were subordinated in precedence to the Yeomanry.

By Article 27 of the Regulations of 1863: "Officers of the Volunteer force rank with officers of Her Majesty's Regular and Militia forces as the youngest of their respective ranks, and rank with officers of the Yeomanry force according to the rank and date of their respective commissions in the respective forces." This article is not contained in the Regulations of 1861.

By Article 31, "the relative precedence of medical officers in the Volunteer force is regulated by the same rule as that prescribed for medical officers of the army." This also is new. Medical Officers. Art. 31.

By Article 5[illegible] of the Regulations of 1863: "the appointment of an honorary Quartermaster and that of an honorary Assistant-Quartermaster, are to be allowed on the recommendation of the Lord Lieutenant to an Administrative Regiment or Corps having the establishment of a regiment, brigade or battalion; the duties of these officers being, in addition to those generally performed by Quartermasters, a superintendence of the disbursement of the private funds of the corps or regiment, but they are not to interfere in any way with the financial duties assigned in these Regulations to the Adjutant as Acting-Paymaster." There is no corresponding provision in the Regulations of 1861.

The Regulations of 1861 contained the somewhat bald provision that "substantive officers should be effective members of their corps, unless by special permission in a special case the rule were relaxed." Article 56 of the Regulations of 1863 is much more stringent. The day of the drawing-room officer of Volunteers was evidently passed. "Every officer is required to possess a competent knowledge of his duties, and to give a proper attendance at the drills of his corps. Any officer who does not attend the number of drills prescribed for the enrolled Volunteers of his corps to qualify him for certificates of efficiency, will not be allowed to retain his commission, unless it should be represented by the Lord Lieutenant to the Secretary of State that there are special reasons for a relaxation of this regulation."

Article 54 of the Regulations of 1861 enabled a commanding officer to reduce a non-commissioned officer for any sufficient cause, *after the circumstances had been duly investigated and recorded by a Court of Enquiry*. In Article 59 of the Regulations of 1863 the clause in italics is omitted and the power confined to the commanding officer, independently of any Court of Enquiry.

By Article 55 of the Regulations of 1861 no person below the age of 17 years was to be enrolled in a Volunteer corps. By the 60th Article of those of 1863 boys of fourteen years and upwards might, with the sanction of the Secretary of State, be enrolled for the purpose of being trained as buglers or trumpeters.

As in 1861, so in 1863, enrolled members were to be classed as efficients and non-efficients. Efficients were, by Article 67 of the Regulations of 1863, to have fulfilled the conditions prescribed in the Order in Council dated 27th July, 1863, the form of Certificate respecting which I have already set out.

The Regulations of 1863 are a little more explicit on the subject of Courts of Enquiry than those of 1861. A Commanding Officer of an Administrative Regiment is authorised to assemble a Court to investigate any matter with which he himself has the power of dealing—presumably to lighten the burden of responsibility. A Court could only be convened by the Lord Lieutenant if the conduct of an officer were the subject of an investigation, and must be composed of Volunteer officers of the county. The Court might be directed by the convener either to collect and arrange evidence merely, or, in addition, to express an opinion on the facts; it was to have no power to pronounce judgment on the issue. The proceedings might be directed to be open or close and, when concluded, a report signed by the president and members, was to be forwarded to the convening authority.

Courts of Enquiry. Art. 74.

The objects of administrative organisation are, in the Regulations of 1861, stated to be

Administrative organisation. Art. 79.

1—Union of separate corps under common head,

2—The securing of uniformity of drill among them,

3—Affording advantage of assistance and instruction of an Adjutant.

To these desired consummations the Regulations of 1863 added,

4—To enable them to receive, through the Adjutant as the Government accountant, their share of the sums voted by Parliament for their aid.

The autonomy of each corps is safeguarded in 1863 as in 1861 in all financial matters "unconnected with public money."

The administrative staff established by the Regulations of 1863 will be gathered from the Table already set out.

Administrative staff. Art. 82.

By Article 88 the Field Officer Commanding an administrative regiment, in addition to the duties imposed upon him by Article 77 of the Regulations of 1861, was charged with the transmission to the Secretary of State for War of the annual return from the several corps under his command.

Duties of Field Officer Commanding.

The Regulations of 1861 (Article 84) provided for the temporary attachment, under special circumstances, of small corps to other corps for the purposes of drill. The provision was permissive. The 95th Article of the Regulations of 1863 is peremptory, and directs that corps of Volunteers not of sufficient strength to constitute by themselves a regiment, brigade or battalion, and not

Attachment of Corps. Art. 95-96.

so circumstanced as to admit of their forming an administrative regiment with other corps of the same arm *are to be* attached to another corps of the same arm or administrative regiment of a different arm; the objects being not only to enable corps thus attached to have the assistance of an Adjutant, but also to receive through him, as a Public Accountant, their share of the sums voted by Parliament for their aid. Attached corps became connected with the Administrative regiment or corps to which they were attached for drill purposes only.

Assemblies of Volunteer Corps. Art. 97.

The 97th Article of the Regulations of 1863 prohibited Volunteer corps from quitting, as a military body, their own county, unless with the sanction, special or general, of the county proposed to be entered.

Articles 99 and 104 substitute a force of "2000" men and upwards wishing to assemble together for drill for that of a "brigade" as provided by Articles 87 and 101 of the Regulations of 1861.

Inspection in Camp Duties.

The 110th and following section of the Regulations of 1863 state fully the conditions under which Volunteer corps desirous of obtaining instruction in Camp duties were to be allowed to assemble for the purpose of forming a Camp of Volunteers, or to proceed to one of the Military Camps in Great Britain, with a view to being brigaded with the regular troops there stationed. These do not vary materially from the regulations of 1861.

Uniform, Clothing and Accoutrements. Arts. 124-135.

By Article 124 every Volunteer corps was to be allowed, subject to the Lord Lieutenant's approval, to choose its own uniform and accoutrements, but the colour of the cloth was to accord with one of the sealed patterns deposited at the Royal Army Clothing Depôt at Pimlico, unless, on the representation of the Lord Lieutenant, a special colour was sanctioned by the Secretary of State. Volunteers were, however, reminded that it was desirable that a uniform colour should be chosen for the clothing of each arm within the same county. Under all circumstances corps of the same Administrative Regiment were to be clothed alike; but where the rule entailed a change in the uniform of a corps two years' grace was to be permitted.

Gold lace, of course, was again inhibited.

Supply at cost price. Art. 128.

The following materials were to be obtained at cost price from the public stores: blue or green shakos, scarlet, white, blue (No. 2), green and grey (cloth or tweed) tunics; blue (No. 2), green and grey (cloth or tweed) trousers; red, blue, and green serge frocks;

rifle green tartan trousers; artillery blue and grey great-coats. They were to be had cut out and basted, but not made up, and without badges; the braid or trimmings to be of the army pattern.

Article 131 recognized the feasibility of the uniform being made up by local tradesmen, but the following table was given as a guide to the cost of trimmings and tailoring.

Cost of making-up.

	s.	d.
For Sergeants' Tunics...	10	1
Privates' do.	8	7
Sergeants' Trousers	2	2
Privates' do.	1	10

The quantity of cloth issued for the above being:

For a single Tunic	$1\frac{15}{36}$ yds.
For 25 Tunics	$35\frac{15}{36}$ yds.
For pair of Trousers	$1\frac{11}{36}$ yds.
For 25 pairs of Trousers ...	$32\frac{23}{36}$ yds.

or in other words 32 yards 23 inches. The reflection seems obvious that not only uniformity of colour was desired in the service but also uniformity of stature.

The provisions as to the Volunteers' Kit are identical with those of 1861. Kit.

The note to Article 101 of Regulations, 1861, requiring Volunteers in mourning to wear a piece of black crape, 3ins. wide, round the left arm above the elbow, is omitted from the Regulations of 1863. Mourning.

Articles 136-173 inclusive, are devoted to stores, a term comprising arms and ammunition. Article 136 lays upon the Commanding Officer of a Volunteer Corps responsibility to the Secretary of State for all the stores supplied by the Government for the use of his corps. Other articles under this heading are much the same as those of the Regulations of 1861, but Articles 148-159 as to the repair and browning of arms are new. The first of these Articles authorises Volunteer corps to send any Government arms in their possession requiring repair to the Government Small Arms Establishment at Pimlico. Stores. Arts. 136-173. Repair, Browning &c., of arms. Arts. 148-159.

The cost of carriage was to be borne by the corps, and the arms were to be sent in monthly or quarterly. The bore of a barrel would be tested if required. The cost of the repair was to be notified to the Commanding Officer, and on receipt of a cheque or post-office order the arms would be returned, a canny stipulation suggesting that the War Office was not forgetful of the comfortable legal doctrine of lien. Arms would be re-browned and the band blued at the public expense every two years on the certificate of the Adjutant that they had been in use for the proper period since last browned, and that they actually required the process.

Adjutants' Pay. Art 192

Articles 181-201 are devoted to the Adjutant, who is more generously dealt with in the matter of pay, &c., in the Regulations of 1863 than in their predecessors. His pay is increased from 8/- to 10/- per day, and he is allowed 1/- a day in lieu of servant, and 2/3 a day for lodging.

Adjutant at School of Musketry. Art. 194.

An Adjutant not possessing a certificate of qualification as Officer-Instructor in Musketry, was, by Article 194, required to attend a course of instruction at the School of Musketry at Hythe or Fleetwood; and if he failed to obtain a certificate, was required to attend a second course; and if he again failed he was to forfeit his appointment.

Instructors. Arts. 202-226.

By Article 202 the number of Sergeant-Instructors paid by the public and allowed to Corps of Volunteers are stated as follows:—

From	1 to 3 companies,	1	Sergeant-Instructor.
,,	4 to 7 ,,	2	,,
,,	8 to 11 ,,	3	,,
,,	12 to 15 ,,	4	,,
,,	16 and upwards	5	,,

The allowance of 4 and 5 Sergeant-Instructors is new.

By Article 167 of the Regulations of 1861 the Sergeant-Instructor was not to be permitted to engage in any trade or business. By clause 205 of the Regulations of 1863 Sergeant-Instructors might be permitted by their Commanding Officers, with the approval of the Secretary of State, to work at a trade or follow some occupation, on the express understanding that they were at all times available for the public service, and that the trade or occupation was not to interfere in any way with the duties which they were required to perform under Article 224 of those Regulations.

By Article 153 of the Regulations of 1861 Sergeant-Instructors who had not previously gone through a course of instruction at a School of Musketry must be prepared to do so if required. This provision is not contained in the Regulations of 1863.

Attestation of Sergeant-Instructor. Art. 208.

By Article 208, on receipt of the Secretary of State's approval of the appointment, the Commanding Officer was to cause the man to be attested for five years' service as a Sergeant-Instructor, unless in any particular case the Commanding Officer recommended the appointment for a shorter period

By Article 217 a Sergeant-Instructor was accorded, from the date of his appointment or transfer from the regular forces, consolidated pay at the following rates :— Pay.

If in receipt of pension, 2/4 a day, if not in receipt of pension, 2/7; if he had received from the School of Musketry at Hythe or Fleetwood a certificate of qualification as Sergeant Instructor in Musketry, an additional allowance of 2d. per day. If he was appointed Sergeant Major a further allowance of 6d. per day.

By Article 224 a Sergeant-Instructor was not to be employed in receiving or disbursing the funds of the corps.

Capitation Allowances Arts. 259-262.

By Article 260 an annual allowance of £1 is for the first time granted to every Officer, Sergeant-Instructor (when belonging to the permanent staff), and efficient Volunteer.

An additional allowance of 10/- is granted to every such Officer, Sergeant-Instructor and efficient Volunteer fulfilling the requirements contained in the following certificate :—

Certificate for Extra Grant.

"We further certify that A. B. fired in the course of the preceding twelve months twenty rounds in the first, twenty rounds in the second, and twenty rounds in the third period, in accordance with the Musketry Regulations for the army, and that he, in one of the three periods, passed into the second class.

Commanding Officer,

Adjutant,

Headquarters,

1st Dec., 18 ."

For Administrative Regiments.

By Article 261 an annual allowance of 4/- was granted to an Administrative regiment for every Officer, Sergeant-Instructor (when belonging to the permanent staff), and efficient Volunteer of every corps of which the headquarters were at a greater distance than 5 miles from the headquarters of the regiment, to cover the expense of attendance at united drill. The Commanding Officer of the Administrative regiment was to use his discretion respecting the distribution of this allowance to the several corps composing the regiment under his command, having regard to the expenses necessarily incurred by such corps respectively in attendance at united drill.

In the case of a corps of the strength of a battalion and not forming part of an Administrative regiment, which had one or more companies of which the regular places of assembly for drill were at a greater distance than 5 miles from the headquarters of the corps, the Secretary of State would, on the recommendation of the Lord Lieutenant, sanction the issue to the corps of the allowance specified above on account of the companies thus situated.

Finance. Arts. 263-278.

As I have said the Adjutant, in his capacity of Acting Paymaster, was entrusted with the receipt and disbursement on authorised services of the annual capitation allowances. For this reason probably he was (Article 263) required to give security for the due performance of his financial duties in one of the following modes:—

Security by Adjutant.

(*a*) Five hundred and thirty pounds deposited in the public funds, in the joint names of himself and the Secretary of State for War, the dividends being receivable by himself; or,

(*b*) A policy of the European Assurance Society for £500; or,

(*c*) Two bonds from sureties, for £500 each; or,

(*d*) The bond of one surety for £500, and a policy of the European Assurance Society for £250.

His personal bond for £500, in addition to his other securities, was also in every case required.

Capitation Allowances, how to be applied. Art. 267.

By Article 267 the capitation allowances were to be applied, at the discretion of the Commanding Officer, either to past or current expenditure; but the payments were to be made by the Adjutants and to be strictly confined to the following heads of expenditure, viz:—

HEADQUARTERS { Orderly Room, Drill Shed or Drill Ground. Magazine or Armoury.

Care and repair of arms, ranges, clothing and accoutrements; cost of conveyance to and from battalion drill, field days or reviews, and rifle practice; cost of all supplies received from the War Office on repayment.

Cadet Corps. Arts. 279-286.

Article 279 sanctioned the formation, in connection with a Volunteer corps or Administrative regiment, of Cadet Corps formed of youths of 12 years of age and upwards. These corps were to be officered by gentlemen holding only honorary commissions; they were, unless by special sanction, to wear a like uniform to the corps &c., to which they were attached; to those of sufficient age to carry on rifle practice, arms were to be issued in the proportion of 10%, but cadets were not to fire in military formation unless they had been inspected and pronounced qualified to do so by the Adjutant.

And with the cadets one may close an abstract of the Regulations of 1863 which has been drawn out to a length only to be excused on the ground that many readers will not be able readily to obtain a print of the Regulations themselves, and the further reason that they shew the successive steps taken by the Volunteer force in its development from a comparatively rude beginning to a highly organised body of men.

The Regulations appear at first to have elicited unqualified approval from not only the Auxiliaries, but from such of the general public as interested themselves in and understood the scope and potentialities of the Volunteer movement.

Volunteer Returns, 1863 to 1889.

This satisfaction made itself manifest in the enrolment of the Volunteers, which may be said, from 1863 to 1869, to have kept pace with, if not abreast of, the increase in the population, and that despite the fact that, during these years, neither at home nor abroad, neither in our domestic nor our foreign affairs, was there ought to excite misgivings for the national safety or honour.

The following are the figures :—

	Strength.	Increase.	Decrease.
1863	131,850	...	...
1864	134,866	3,016	...
1865	140,383	5,517	...
1866	141,301	918	...
1867	145,752	4,451	...
1868	153,530	7,778	...

The year 1869, however, shewed a most startling and, to me, inexplicable change in the tendency of the Volunteer statistics.

The barometer, if one may so express it, had been going steadily up. In 1869 and 1870 it fell very markedly. The fall was arrested in 1871 when it was but 230, and this may be accounted for by the unsettled state of affairs on the Continent, then in the throes of the Franco-German War. But 1872 and 1873 witnessed a very marked shrinkage in the returns, to be followed, in 1874, by a quite unaccountable but most welcome revival. The figures are :—

	Strength.	Increase.	Decrease.
1869	149,985	...	3,545
1870	146,836	...	3,149
1871	146,606	...	230
1872	135,885	...	10,721
1873	130,665	...	5,220
1874	133,694	2,658	

From 1874 to 1886 there was an almost unbroken record of increased Volunteer enrolments.

	Strength.	Increase.	Decrease.
1875	137,429	4,106	...
1876	141,177	3,748	...
1877	147,296	6,119	...
1878	154,770	7,474	...
1879	157,474	2,704	...
1880	159,109	1,635	...
1881	160,346	1,237	...
1882	159,867	...	479
1883	161,468	1,601	...
1884	165,687	4,219	...
1885	173,047	7,360	...
1886	174,271	1,224	...

In 1887 the numbers began to decrease.

	Strength.	Increase.	Decrease.
1887	173,695	...	576
1888	170,473	...	3,222
1889	168,150	...	2,423

An explanation of this decrease may probably be found in the increased stringency of the Regulations and it is certainly matter for congratulation rather than regret that the feather-bed Volunteer was scared away from a service to which personal vanity rather than patriotism had attracted him.

Proportion of Volunteers to population.

The proportion of Volunteers to the population was :—

			In 1861.		In 1871.
England	...	...	·629	...	·655
Wales		...	·655	...	·620
Scotland	...	...	1·119	...	1·316

A comparative analysis of the Volunteer Returns of the three countries discloses the fact that Volunteering is more popular in rural and sparsely inhabited districts than in the more densely thronged centres of industry. As Mr. T. H. Fry observed in a note to his very useful and carefully compiled statistics :—" It is chiefly the more thinly populated parts which have done well, while Warwick, Surrey, Kent, York, Leicester, Derby, Stafford and Notts., with their teeming populations, have raised only about one-third the rate of the Scotch counties. Birmingham is the only one of the large towns which has a low percentage ; but Sheffield and Bradford are much behind the others." Rutlandshire has never raised any Volunteers under the 1859 Movement.

As I have said I have no theory which I can confidently put forward to account for the fluctuations in the Volunteer returns above set forth; but it is possible that an explanation may be found for the diminutions (1869 to 1873) in the spirit of the times. The years embraced in the tables were years of unexampled commercial prosperity, years indeed in some of which England was monopolizing industries in which France and Germany had largely shared. They were years of fat budgets and overflowing treasuries, and the people seemed intent solely on the pursuit of gain. The party in power professed loudly the gospel of peace on earth and goodwill towards men, and evinced a very proper readiness when smitten on the one cheek to present the other. It is not under such influences that the ideas that stimulate Volunteering fructify and flourish. There is much, too, in the suggestion of Captain Cartaret W. Carey, (Highland Light Infantry, and Adjutant Lanarkshire Rifle Volunteers), expressed in his prize essay on "The present and future organisation of the Volunteer Force," in which he discusses the causes of the fluctuations in the returns: "To the increase in the number of athletic clubs, during the past few years, for lawn tennis, cycling, football, &c., we may probably look for a cause of the decrease of numbers. In almost every town and village these institutions now are numerous, and there can be no doubt that many young fellows, with the facilities given, prefer to devote their leisure hours to sportive recreation rather than to the drilling and musketry requirements for Volunteers."

Suggested reasons for decrease in enrolments.

It might be added that the increase of professional football, with its inevitably attendant gambling, is steadily lowering the *morale* of the classes from which Volunteers are mainly recruited. Whilst hesitating to adopt the pungent terms in which Mr. Rudyard Kipling refers to the "muddied oaf," I cannot blink the fact that thousands and tens of thousands of the youth of the country flock to see a cup match who regard with sublime indifference the Volunteer evolutions that are at once more useful in their object, more healthful and more gentlemanly.

The War Office, after the issue of the Regulations of 1863, was not disposed to adopt the counsel of Lord John Russell on another occasion to "rest and be thankful." Indeed it may be said that the rule of Earl de Grey and Ripon marked the advent of a new era in the movement. The War Office had apparently at length arrived at the conclusion that the auxiliary forces were capable of being made a really valuable, effective and reliable arm of defence, and though the actions of the Department betray those signs of red-tape of which the public is so generally impatient, and though its policy was necessarily hampered by the restraints of the Exchequer, yet it must be frankly admitted that from this time forward the attitude of the Office has been constantly favourable to the development and encouragement of the Volunteer movement. One, however, comes across some curious instances of the shifts to which the Department was reduced in the attempt to combine efficiency with encouragement. Take for example the Circular of July 22nd, 1867, which had reference to Article 245 of the Volunteer Regulations of 1863 :—

1867, July 22. War Office Circular, Enfield Rifles.

V. Gen. No. 3582

1.—"Volunteers, although armed with the long Enfield Rifle, are to be instructed in the manual exercise prescribed for the short Enfield Rifle, except as regards the modes of fixing and unfixing bayonets, in which instances the directions laid down for the long rifle are to be followed; also all orders contained in the field exercise for the guidance of troops carrying the short rifle are to be considered as applicable to Volunteers, although armed with the long rifle.

2.—Volunteers being armed with muzzle-loading rifles their instruction in the platoon exercise will continue to be carried on in the mode laid down for the short rifle in the edition of the Field Exercise dated January, 1862."

It is refreshing to turn from the dreary iteration of Circulars and Regulations to matters if not so important certainly more enlivening.

1866, Oct. Visit of Volunteers to Brussels.

In the month of October, 1866, some 1,400 Volunteers went to Brussels to attend the *Tir Nationale* and participate in the hospitality of the King of the Belgians. The English Volunteers were reviewed by His Majesty, and afterwards entertained with more than regal grandeur at a banquet. The place selected for holding it was the *Pavillon du Rivage*, and 1,200 guests sat down, the largest number for which the King was able to obtain accommodation in any of the buildings in Brussels. The cost per man was 40 francs, or 40,000 francs for the whole, of course exclusive of the enormous expense incurred for fittings and decorations, and there were 200 servants in attendance upon the guests.

1867, July. Visit of Belgian Volunteers to England.

The British Volunteers were not to be outdone in hospitality. They perhaps felt that either in the field or at the table they were prepared to meet any continental soldier and beat him too.

In July the Belgian Volunteers visited this country for the purpose of fraternizing with their English brothers-in-arms and taking part in the rifle contest at Wimbledon. The English riflemen had been so hospitably treated at Brussels in the previous year that a committee was formed to arrange for the visit of our Belgian friends, and to raise a fund for defraying the expenses. Special prizes were to be given for them to shoot for, and they were to be taken to nearly every public place of interest. It was also arranged that they should take part in the forthcoming review. On the 12th, they were entertained at a banquet in the Guildhall, under the presidency of the Lord Mayor, when 3000 guests sat down to dinner. On the 13th, they assembled at Wimbledon, when a silver medal was presented to every man by the Prince of Wales. On the following day (Sunday) many of them visited the camp, when divine service was held in the large bell-tent, the Rev. Charles Kingsley officiating. On the 16th, they were entertained by the Queen at Windsor Castle. On the 18th, they were entertained at a ball held in the Agricultural Hall, on a scale never before attempted in this country, for 9,000 persons were present and 7,000 sat down to supper. The Prince of Wales, Prince Teck, Prince and Princess Louis of Hesse, and the Duke of Cambridge were present. On the 19th, they were entertained at a banquet by Miss Burdett-Coutts in the grounds of her mansion at Highgate, and in the evening were present at a special concert in the Agricultural Hall, when nearly all the great vocalists of the day were engaged.

Volunteer Committee on capitation grant, 1867.

In February, 1867, a committee of Volunteer officers was formed to consider chiefly the adequacy of the capitation grant. A resolution was moved by Lord Elcho, seconded by Lord Truro and unanimously adopted, declaring the desirability of urging upon the War Office the general sense of the force that, as the necessary expenses of Volunteer corps were not covered by the Parliamentary grant, which had to be largely supplemented by subscriptions of officers and men, those who freely and without pay gave their services to the State should be relieved from the necessity of such personal expenditure. The committee had taken steps by communicating with the Volunteer officers throughout the Kingdom to ascertain the views of the force upon this point. The conclusions of the committee were embodied in a memorandum to the War Office, on March 16th, 1867. The following quotation from the memorandum contains its gist :—"The experience of eight years has conclusively shown the insufficiency of the grant, and the consequent heavy personal expenditure entailed on the Volunteers. One captain, in a private letter to the chairman, states that his company has cost him £500, and it is confidently believed that

There are very many instances of similar and indeed much larger sums being expended by officers in support of their corps. The expenditure that is generally entailed upon officers renders it difficult to find men willing to accept such commissions. The choice is thus limited, and unless an additional grant is made, there is in many cases immediate danger of a collapse of a portion of the force. Assuming, then, the facts as stated to be true, the question is, what should be the amount of the additional grant?

It appears to the committee that an additional sum of £1 for efficients, retaining the present 10/- for extra efficiency, would suffice; and they would venture to urge that such increased grant should, if possible, be proposed in the current year."

It is, however, one thing to propose and quite another to dispose; and as the adage teaches, proposition and disposition are confided to entirely different authorities.

On the 19th April, 1870, Lord Northbrook, then at the head of the War Office, issued a circular rearranging the various military districts of Great Britain as follows:—

District.	Counties, Lieutenancies, &c., included in:—
1—Home. (Head-quarters, Gun House, St. James's Park, London).	Bedfordshire, Berkshire, Buckinghamshire, Hertfordshire, City of London, Middlesex, Oxfordshire, Surrey, Tower Hamlets.
2—South Eastern. (Head-quarters, Dover).	Cinque Ports, Kent (except Woolwich), Sussex (except Chichester and Littlehampton, so far as regards the Regular forces), Tilbury Fort.
3—Southern. (Head-quarters, Portsmouth).	Chichester (so far as regards the Regular forces). Dorsetshire, Hampshire, (except Aldershot), Isle of Wight, Littlehampton (so far as regards the Regular forces). Wiltshire.
4—Western. (Head-quarters, Devonport). 1st Western Sub-District (Devonport). and ditto. (Bristol).	Cornwall, Devonshire, Somersetshire. Brecknockshire, Cardiganshire, Carmarthenshire, Glamorganshire, Gloucestershire, Haverfordwest, Herefordshire, Monmouthshire, Pembrokeshire, Radnorshire.
5—Eastern. (Head-quarters, Colchester).	Cambridgeshire, Essex (except Tilbury Fort and Purfleet), Huntingdonshire, Lincolnshire, Norfolk and Suffolk.

DISTRICTS (continued).	COUNTIES, LIEUTENANCIES, &c., included in :—
6—Northern. (Head-quarters, Manchester). 1st Northern Sub-District (Liverpool).	Anglesea, Carnarvonshire, Cheshire, Derbyshire, Flintshire, Isle of Man, Lancashire, Merionethshire, Montgomeryshire.
2nd ditto (Birmingham).	Derbyshire, Leicestershire, Northamptonshire, Nottinghamshire, Rutlandshire, Shropshire, Staffordshire, Warwickshire, Worcestershire.
3rd ditto (York).	Cumberland, Durham, Newcastle-on-Tyne, Northumberland, Westmoreland; Yorkshire, East Riding; Yorkshire, North Riding; Yorkshire, West Riding.
7—Woolwich.	
8—Aldershot.	
9—North Britain. (Head-quarters, Edinburgh). 1st North British Sub-District (Edinburgh).	Berwickshire, Berwick-on-Tweed, Clackmannanshire, City of Edinburgh, Fifeshire, Forfarshire, Haddingtonshire, Kincardinshire, Kinrosshire, Linlithgowshire, Mid-lothian, Peebleshire, Perthshire, Roxburghshire, Selkirkshire, Stirlingshire.
2nd ditto (Glasgow).	Argyleshire, Ayrshire, Buteshire, Dumbartonshire, Dumfrieshire, Kirkcudbrightshire, Lanarkshire, Renfrewshire, Wigtonshire.
3rd ditto (Inverness).	Aberdeenshire, Banffshire, Caithness-shire, Cromarty, Elginshire, Inverness-shire, Nairnshire, Orkney and Shetland, Ross-shire, Sutherlandshire.

By Sections 4 and 5 of the Circular of Lord Northbrook all Volunteers who, during the year 1870, should undergo inspection or be voluntarily doing any military duty were placed under the command of the General Officers of the Regular forces Commanding in the Districts within which such Volunteers should be undergoing inspection or doing military duty, during such duty or inspection; but so that such command should be so exercised that such Volunteers should be led by their own respective officers, and that officers appointed to inspect or to command such forces, whether alone or joined with the Regular forces, should be senior in rank to every officer of the force commanded or inspected. Sects. 4 and 5.

The Circular contained regulations as to drill, marching out and inspection, and as to camps, arms and clothing, but it is unnecessary to set these forth as the whole Circular, with the exception of the rearrangement of the military districts as above exhibited, was cancelled by the Auxiliary and Reserve Forces Circular of 1872.

War Office Circular, Aug. 29th, 1870.

On August 29th Lord Northbrook issued an important Circular dealing, (*inter alia*), with the Schools of Instruction for Officers of the Reserve forces. As this circular was practically superseded by later ones of November 1st, 1870, and of 28th May, 1872, it will suffice to state in their proper places the provisions of the latter documents.

War Office Circular, Aug. 30th, 1870.

Special capitation grant of £2 10 0 to proficient officers.

Then followed a Circular of August 30th, 1870, which "with a view to give encouragement to Officers and Sergeants of Volunteers in acquiring a thorough knowledge of their duties," offered a special capitation allowance of £2 10 0 to each combatant Officer or Sergeant of Volunteers, not including the permanent staff, who should obtain a certificate of proficiency as thereinafter prescribed. This certificate was, in effect, to be obtained by attending the Schools of Instruction for Reserve forces mentioned in the Circular of the 29th August and the subject can be dealt with in connection with later circulars which, as I have said, practically superseded those of August 29th and 30th of 1870. This introduction into the Volunteer scheme was the outcome of the deliberations of a Departmental Committee which sat in 1869-70.

War Office Circular, Aug. 31st, 1870.

Another Circular of the date in the margin dealt with the subject of Volunteer Camps and to this, too, and to some others which were subsequently incorporated in the "Auxiliary and Reserve Forces Circular" of 1872, I only refer that the reader may form some notion of the painful and tedious processes by which at length some sort of form and consistency was attained in the rules and regulations affecting their instruction, drill, efficiency, allowances and other important matters so nearly touching the Volunteers.

War Office Circular, Sept. 1st, 1870.

Issue of Snider Rifles.

Their storage or custody.

It is, however, desirable to refer with more particularity to one Circular, that of September 1st, 1870, in which the Secretary of State announced his decision to commence the issue of Snider Rifles to the Rifle Volunteer force. The first issues were to be made to the battalions which had the highest percentage of efficients in proportion to the enrolled strength in the Annual Returns of December 1st, 1869—an ingenious method of recognising the efforts that various corps might have made towards the attainment of proficiency. The arms were to be deposited after drill in the Armouries of the corps, except those of such members as received the written permission of the commanding officer to retain their arms at home. Commanding officers giving such permission were enjoined to warn their men that the Snider arm, a more delicate weapon than the Enfield, would quickly deteriorate if not properly cared for and that any neglect in that respect might also be attended with danger to themselves. Provisions were made for the appointment of certified armourers and Government viewers of arms and it was also required, as a condition precedent to the issue of Snider arms to a battalion or an administrative regiment, that the requisite number of sergeant-instructors should have gone through a ten days' course of instruction at the Royal Small Arms Establishment, Birmingham

Certified armourers and viewers.

Anyone curious in tracing organic developments may refer to these Circulars, but I apprehend the general reader will be quite content with the comprehensive codification of successive Circulars which was issued 28th May, 1872, and to which it is necessary to refer with some particularity.

Reserve Forces Circulars, Nov. 1st, 1870, Dec. 9th, 1870, Jan. 1st, 1871.

It is desirable to premise that in the year preceding this Circular a most important change had been made in the administration of the Volunteers by their transfer from the jurisdiction of the Lord Lieutenant to that of the War Secretary, and, as a necessary consequence, the grant of Commissions by the Sovereign direct instead of through the Lord Lieutenant. There can be no question that a system which had culminated at length in constituting the Lord Lieutenant a mere channel of communication between the War Office and the Volunteer corps or Battalions led to much friction, waste of time and expense, and though the historical sense shrinks from the contemplation of a *Custos Rotulorum* and head of the *posse comitatus* shorn of powers that had been appurtenant to his office for centuries a utilitarian age consoles itself for what it loses in the picturesque by what it gains in efficiency and economy.

The Jurisdiction of the Lord Lieutenant revested in the Crown.

The Act that accomplished this reform was the Regulation of the Forces Act, 1871. Part II, section 6, provides that after a day to be named by Order in Council*

34 and 35 Vic. c. 86.

> "All jurisdiction, powers, duties, command and privileges over, of, or in relation to the Militia, Yeomanry, and Volunteers of England, Scotland and Ireland, vested in or exercised by the Lieutenants of counties, or by the Lord Lieutenant of Ireland, either of his own motion or with the advice of the Privy Council of Ireland, shall revert to Her Majesty and shall be exercisable by Her Majesty, through the Secretary of State, or any officers to whom Her Majesty may, by and with the advice of the said Secretary of State, delegate such jurisdiction, powers, duties, command and privileges; saving nevertheless to the Lieutenants of counties and to the Lords Lieutenant of Ireland their powers and privileges as to the appointment of Deputy Lieutenants, and as to Lieutenants of counties their powers, duties and privileges in relation to the Militia battalion.

*The Order in Council was issued 5th February, 1872.

By the same section

"All Officers in the Militia, Yeomanry, and Volunteers, of England, Scotland or Ireland were to hold Commissions from Her Majesty, and such Commissions should be prepared, authenticated and issued in the manner in which Commissions of Officers in Her Majesty's land forces were prepared, authenticated and issued according to the law or custom for the time being in force."

Lords Lieutenant, however, were still to have power to recommend for Commissions on first appointments to the rank of Cornet, Ensign, or Lieutenant in any regiments or Corps of Militia, Yeomanry or Volunteers—a clause possibly intended as a solatium to Lords Lieutenant.

25 and 26 Vic. c. 4. Commissions how to be signed.

These Commisions, it may be well to state, are not issued under the Royal Sign Manual, an Act of 1862 having empowered Her Majesty to direct that any Commissions for Officers might be issued without Her Royal Sign Manual but have thereon the signature of the Commander in Chief and one of Her principal Secretaries of State in the case of the land forces.

Volunteers training with Regulars to be under Mutiny Acts.

The Regulation of the Forces Act of 1871 contained one other most important provision. Section 9 of that enactment brought the Auxiliaries one step nearer to the Regulars. It provided that when any part of the Volunteer force was assembled for the purpose of being trained or exercised with the Militia or Regular Forces they should be subject to the Mutiny Act and Articles of War in the same manner as the Act of 1863 had subjected them when on actual service.

Auxiliary and Reserve Forces Circular, May 28th, 1872.

We are now in a position to address attention, undistracted by antecedent minor Circulars, to the somewhat lengthy but all important Regulations and Instructions promulgated by the direction of the Secretary of State for War on May 28th, 1872, the details of which however were to be liable to modification on the establishment of Brigade Depôts.

By these Regulations the term "Auxiliary forces," as applied to the Volunteers, first received official sanction. Her Majesty placed all Volunteers, when assembled for drill or inspection, or voluntarily doing any other military duty, under the command of the officer Commanding in Chief and of the General Officers of the Regular Forces Commanding in the districts within which such Volunteers might be undergoing inspection or doing military duty. The permanent staff of all administrative regiments and corps were at all times to be under such Military command, but the command of Volunteers was to be so exercised that the men should be led by their own respective officers.

Guards of Honour or Escort might, as a matter of course, be provided for members of the Royal Family or the Lord Lieutenant of a county on arrival in the neighbourhood of the head-quarters of a regiment or corps; but in no other case, without the special authority of the General Officer Commanding the district, was a body of auxiliary forces to take part in any public procession or ceremony or form a Guard of Honour. Guards of Honour.

At a review or brigade field day of only Militia and Volunteer forces of any county, the Lord Lieutenant of the county, if present in uniform, was to be entitled to the salute on coming on to the ground, as well as at the marching past; but the military command was to be exclusively in the hands of the officer in command, who would give the order for salute and march past at the head of the troops. Lord Lieutenant to be saluted at Reviews &c. Clause 8.

In the case of reviews or brigade field days of auxiliary forces of different counties, or of regular, auxiliary and reserve forces combined, the senior officer present was to take the salute.

The only decorations to be worn on the left breast were to be those given by the Queen, or, with the permission of the Queen, received from a foreign Sovereign. Decorations. Clause 8, Section 3.

The Lord Lieutenant was to recommend for the consideration of the Secretary of State, for submission to Her Majesty, the names of candidates for first appointment as subalterns. Candidates for first appointments as subalterns so recommended must not be less than 17 years of age. Candidates for first appointments

If the Lord Lieutenant did not exercise his limited right of recommendation within 30 days of a vacancy arising, his power lapsed and was vested in the Commanding Officer. Clause 9.

In all cases of promotion and appointment to higher than subaltern ranks, the recommendation was to be submitted by the Commanding Officer through the general officer commanding the district, or, in the case of an administrative regiment, through the field officer commanding the regiment, who was to forward it to the Adjutant-General. Sections 8-10.

Her Majesty's approval of appointments and promotions was to be notified in the Gazette. Appointments to be Gazetted, Clause 9, Section 13.

Commissions of Volunteer officers were to be prepared, authenticated and issued in the same manner as the commissions of officers in the Regular forces, and the commissions of those officers already in the auxiliary forces to be thenceforth deemed to have been issued by Her Majesty. Section 14.

Section 15. Officers above 60 years of though an extension of 5 circumstances.

Examination of Officers, Section 43. Every officer on first app captain or field officer, or on pr not served and passed his exa in the case of a captain or su field officer, in a similar arm within one year of his appoint officer, to be examined for a c to which he had been appoin (with the exception of Lieuten on by the Inspector), not in po obtain their certificates befor failing to obtain their certific called upon to resign. It was

Lieutenant-Colonels and Captains Commandant. Clause 9, Section 52. When the establishment o entitled it to two Lieutenant- title of "Lieutenant-Colonel consisted of more than one com mand of a field officer, the senio of "Captain Commandant." additional rank nor were sepa account of them.

Section 53. A field officer on the staff o have a commission as command corps composing it.

Section 58. It was recognised that pron not always be conducted accord as it was desirable that local reg be commanded by "gentlemen had "not served in the lower r enjoined to be discreet in sub persons.

Section 59. Any officer who did not atte for the enrolled Volunteers of hi cates of efficiency was not to be unless it should be represented t were special reasons for relaxati

; doubtless felt that many officers would be unable to bear ... of attending Schools of Instruction or of attachment ... the Regulars or the Militia. It was accordingly provided ... of all arms might, if they preferred it, receive the ... instruction from the Adjutant and Sergeant-Instructors ... rps, brigade or battalion, whose duty is was to afford such ... n. Examination of Officers instructed by Permanent Staff. Clause 31. Section 1.

...ule such officers, if below the rank of Field Officer, were ... mined either on the day of inspection or on the day ... or following it, at the discretion of the Inspecting Officer. ...nation was to be conducted by a Board consisting of the ... Officer, the Adjutant of the corps, brigade or battalion, ... nearest available Captain of Regulars or Adjutant of ... Auxiliary Forces of the same arm. When a quarter... s examined a quartermaster of the Army or Militia ... substituted for the captain or last-mentioned Adjutant. Section 2.

...al Officers were to be examined by a Board consist... principal Medical Officer of the district and two other ...cal Officers. Section 5.

...rtificate of a Medical Officer was in the following form:— Certificate of Medical Officer.

...ertify that of (who holds two diplomas or ... to practise medicine and the other surgery in Great Britain and ... is registered under the Medical Act of 1858), is well acquainted ...ure and intended application of the various articles composing the ... Army Hospitals in the Field, and with the authorized means for ... of sick and wounded soldiers, and the proper modes of employing

... certify that he has competent knowledge of the treatment of the ... injuries to which troops are liable in the field, particularly with ... special circumstances of campaigning, and that he is acquainted ...es to be performed by Army Medical Officers in camp and bivouacs ... marches, as named in Section 21, Sanitary Regulations for Field ...82, &c., of the Official Code of Army Hospital Regulations.

...re of Board of Examining Officers.

Station.

Date.

...ort of the names of Officers who had obtained certificates ... made and the letter "P" placed after their names in the Section 10.

...nteer sergeants were obliged to obtain a certificate of ... within one year after their appointment. They were to ...ed by the adjutant of the corps, brigade or battalion to ... belonged and their certificates of proficiency signed by Clause 32, Secs. 1-2-3. Sergeants' Certificates.

Section 15. Officers above 60 years of age were to resign their commissions, though an extension of 5 years might be conceded in special circumstances.

Examination of Officers, Section 43. Every officer on first appointment to a commission as subaltern, captain or field officer, or on promotion to be a field officer, who had not served and passed his examination for the rank of lieutenant, in the case of a captain or subaltern, and of captain in that of a field officer, in a similar arm of the Regular forces, was required, within one year of his appointment or of his promotion to be field officer, to be examined for a certificate of proficiency for the rank to which he had been appointed or promoted. Existing officers, (with the exception of Lieutenant-colonels, if favourably reported on by the Inspector), not in possession of such certificates, were to obtain their certificates before Inspection day in 1874. Officers failing to obtain their certificates after two attempts were to be called upon to resign. It was a case of *aut disce, aut discede.*

Lieutenant-Colonels and Captains Commandant. Clause 9, Section 52. When the establishment of an administrative regiment or corps entitled it to two Lieutenant-colonels, the senior was to bear the title of "Lieutenant-Colonel Commandant," and when a corps consisted of more than one company and was not under the command of a field officer, the senior captain was to bear the designation of "Captain Commandant." These titles did not confer any additional rank nor were separate commissions to be issued on account of them.

Section 53. A field officer on the staff of an administrative regiment might have a commission as commanding or field officer in any one of the corps composing it.

Section 58. It was recognised that promotions in the Volunteer force could not always be conducted according to a regimental system, inasmuch as it was desirable that local regiments, corps or companies should be commanded by "gentlemen who had local influence," but who had "not served in the lower ranks." Commanding officers were enjoined to be discreet in submitting the names of fit and proper persons.

Section 59. Any officer who did not attend the number of drills prescribed for the enrolled Volunteers of his corps to qualify them for certificates of efficiency was not to be allowed to retain his commission, unless it should be represented to the Secretary of State that there were special reasons for relaxation of the regulation.

At Aldershot, Glasgow, London, Manchester and Dublin, Schools of Instruction were opened for officers of the Volunteer Infantry, who were expected to remain under instruction for one calendar month. Schools of Instruction, Clause 10, Sections 1 and 2.

Twenty-five was to be the maximum and ten the minimum number of officers in a class. Officers were to join in uniform, those at Aldershot taking full as well as undress uniform. Sections 3 and 4.

They were to receive 5s. a day for a month. They might remain another month at their own expense. Quarters, with fuel and light, were to be assigned to these officers, or an allowance of 2s. 3d. a day in lieu thereof, if they secured their certificates. They were also to be recouped their travelling expenses. Daily subsidy of 5/- whilst at School of Instruction, Sections 7-8-9.

Captains who had obtained certificates of proficiency might qualify for certificates as field officers, but at their own expense. Section 13.

Candidates for commissions in the auxiliary forces might, at their own expense, be attached to schools of instruction. Section 15.

At the conclusion of the course of instruction, each officer or candidate who had passed a satisfactory examination was to be granted a certificate, and the letters "P. S." were to be placed after his name in the Army list. The certificates of field officers, captains and subalterns of Rifle Volunteers ran as follows:— Certificates of Proficiency.

Of a Field Officer.

"I certify that of the has passed through this School of Instruction, and is conversant with the drill of a company and of a battalion, and able to give instruction in the same. Of Field Officer who had attended a School of Instruction.

That he can command a battalion in brigade.

That he is competent to superintend instruction in aiming and position drill, and to superintend blank firing and ball practice.

That he is acquainted with the proper mode of route marching, and the duties of guards.

Also that he can ride."

The Certificate was also to state if the Officer had been shewn the mode of posting picquets and their sentries, and the duties of Orderly Officer, and whether he had attended lectures and on what subjects.

To be signed by the Officer Commanding the School of Instruction.

The Certificate of a Captain and Subaltern

was expressed as follows:— Of Captains and Subalterns attending as above.

"I certify that of the has passed through the School of Instruction and is conversant with the drill of a company, in close and extended order, and able to give instruction in the same.

That he can command a company in battalion.

That he is competent to instruct a squad in aiming and position drill, and to superintend blank firing and ball practice.

That he can command a guard, and is acquainted with the mode of marching reliefs and posting sentries.

Also that in his written answers to questions he has expressed himself with (clearness or tolerable clearness)."

The certificate was also to state whether the officer had been shewn the mode of posting picquets and their sentries, and the duties of orderly officer, and whether he had attended lectures, and if so, on what subjects, and to be signed by the officer commanding School.

Clause 11. Section 1. Examination of Adjutants.

On and after 22nd February, 1871, Adjutants were to hold their appointments for a term of 5 years only. They were to be selected from Captains of Infantry of the Army, serving with their regiments or on half-pay. Previous to appointment candidates were to be examined (unless they had held commissions as Adjutants of their regiments for not less than 12 months) by a Board of Officers as to their qualifications for the duties of Adjutant, including a knowledge of the duties of Brigade-Major. They must also have or secure a certificate that they could ride. An Adjutant not possessing a qualifying certificate as Officer-Instructor in musketry must attend a school of musketry at Hythe. If he did not on a second essay secure his certificate he could not retain his appointment as Adjutant.

Pay of Adjutants, Section 14.

As the public services of an Adjutant were to be available at all times he was debarred from following any profession or holding any other appointment, public or private.

The pay and allowances of an Adjutant were the same as allowed by the Regulations of 1863.

Medical Attendance, Section 15, Clause 43, Section 1.

The Adjutant was entitled to medical attendance for himself and family at the public expense. It is amusing to read in clause 43 that the surgeon of a corps or administrative regiment attending an Adjutant and his family professionally was to receive an allowance of 2d. a week for each person, to be paid by the Adjutant and charged in his accounts.

The earlier Volunteer levies contrasted with those of 1872.

We may with advantage depart for a moment from the consideration of this memorable Circular to contrast the Volunteer of 1872 with his prototype of the Napoleonic period and even of the year 1859, but thirteen short years before. I have laboured in vain if the reader has failed to form a tolerably accurate conception of the levies of those periods. It might almost be said that the auxiliaries of 1872 had nothing in common with their predecessors but attachment to their native land and the patriotic resolve to defend it against armed aggression. Patriotism is a noble virtue, but patriotism alone does not make a soldier, still less does it make an army. It is doubtless the motive power of the machine, and whilst it is true that a machine without steam is useless, it is even more true that steam without mechanical organisation is not merely useless, it is dangerous. Now the levies of the closing years of the 18th and the early years of the 19th centuries were animated by a spirit beyond all praise, but when they met for drill it may be assumed with confidence that if there was one man on parade who knew less what was expected of him than the private, that man was the officer commanding him. Privates and officers alike were for the most part as ignorant of drill, of tactics, of the use of arms, as they were of the interior economy of the planet Mars. To be able to sit a horse well and look effective (in a lady's eye) is not the Alpha and Omega of an officer's duty; but that was all most officers professed to be able to do. Moreover drill instructors were scarce. Old veterans with one leg and one arm were disinterred from the Workhouses and once more found life worth living as the well paid and eagerly courted instructors of the Guardians and their relations. And the confusion that reigned in the country was reflected at the War Office. It is only necessary to read the Orders in Council, the Circulars and the Memoranda that tripped each on the heels of its predecessors to see that the Government had no clear, no settled plan of dealing with the ardent bodies of men they had by a breath called into being. They had evoked the Volunteer and they did not, for a while, know what to do with him. They made their plans as they built and the wonder is that out of chaos, they, in so comparatively short a period, fashioned a force which, whatever its imperfections, was, in 1872, admittedly a force capable of indefinite possibilities under judicious guidance. But to return to the Circular of 1872, after, I hope, a pardonable digression.

The Circular of 1872, continued

Clause 12 of the Circular treats of the steps to be taken by the General Officer commanding a district for the brigading of the auxiliary forces for exercise or reviews.

Brigading Volunteers for Reviews &c. Clause 12. Section 2.

When the proposed review or brigade drill would entail any expense on the public for the movement of regiments of the line or Militia, or for allowances to Volunteers under clause 35 of the Circular, the General Officer commanding the district was to apply to the Adjutant-general for the sanction of the Secretary of State, stating approximately the number of men proposed to be assembled and the cost of the arrangements. If it were desired to include in

N

Section 4. the review or brigade-drill corps of a district other than that in which the review or drill was to be held, the Secretary of State's permission was to be obtained.

Section 6. When Officers commanding regiments or corps wished to initiate a review or brigade-drill, the senior Commanding Officer was to notify their wish to the General Officer commanding the district, who, if he approved, would proceed as above directed.

Section 8. The General Officer commanding a district was to appoint commanding officers and staff at reviews, in the following proportions:—

For a force not exceeding 3,000, a colonel or lieutenant colonel with an aide-de-camp.

For a force exceeding 3,000, a general officer with an assistant adjutant-general and two aides-de-camp.

In every case also a brigade-major would be appointed to each brigade.

Section 9. When a brigade was to be composed partly of regular and partly of auxiliary forces, the General Officer commanding the district was to appoint an officer of the regular army to command. When it was to be composed of auxiliary forces only, he was to use his discretion as to appointing an officer of the regular forces or the senior Commanding Officer in the brigade as brigadier. The General Officer would select an officer of the regular forces or a staff officer of pensioners or an Adjutant of Militia, Yeomanry or Volunteers in his district, whose corps would not be present, to act as Brigade-Major. The officer's travelling expenses to be borne by
Section 10. the public. Militia or Volunteer Brigadiers were to be at liberty to appoint their own aides-de-camp, but no travelling expenses were to be charged on their account to the public.

Reports. Clause 16, Section 2. As soon as the annual inspections were concluded, the General Officers Commanding were to forward a report upon each branch of the auxiliary forces, accompanied by any suggestions which they might wish to make. A list was also to be furnished of all brigade field days and encampments that had taken place in the district, with the number present on each occasion.

Section 3. General Officers Commanding were also to compile from the quarterly returns and adjutants' diaries of the various corps and administrative regiments of Volunteers in their respective districts a return showing the duties performed by the several adjutants of Volunteers in the districts during the preceding financial year.

With a view to giving encouragement to officers and sergeants of Volunteers in acquiring a thorough knowledge of their duties a special capitation allowance of £2 10 0 was to be granted on account of each officer or efficient sergeant of Volunteers, not including the permanent staff, who obtained a certificate of proficiency in the manner prescribed in clauses 10, 30 or 31 of the Circular. Special capitation allowance. Clause 29, Section 1.

This allowance was in addition to the £1 or £1 10, as the case might be, which an officer or sergeant might have earned under articles 259 or 260 of the Volunteer Regulations 1863. Section 2.

An officer of Volunteers holding a commission in the Militia was not to be allowed to earn the special capitation allowance of £2 10 0. Section 5.

After an officer or sergeant had received his certificate of proficiency he was to be allowed to earn the special capitation allowance of £2 10 0 on the commanding officer certifying in the annual returns and nominal roll that he continued to possess a competent knowledge of the subjects mentioned in the certificate. In the case of a sergeant it was to be shown that the Adjutant had, during the year, seen him drill and act as instructor to a company and had been satisfied with his proficiency. Section 6.

The 30th clause contains an important provision—that commissioned officers of Rifle Volunteers might be temporarily attached, for the purpose of receiving instruction, to Infantry regiments of the regular army for any period not exceeding one month or to regiments of Militia for the annual training period. During the period of attachment the officer was required to attend regularly the drills prescribed and in other respects to conform to the arrangements made for his instruction, he paying the usual fee of £1 to the sergeant-major or sergeant detailed to instruct him. At the conclusion of the course of instruction the officer was to be examined by a Board consisting, in the case of a Field Officer, of two Field Officers (one of whom must be senior in rank to the officer under examination), assisted by the Adjutant; in other cases the Board was to consist of a Field Officer, a Captain and the Adjutant. When a quartermaster was examined a quartermaster of the Army or Militia was to be substituted for the captain. If the officer was found qualified he was to be granted a certificate in one of the following forms;— Clause 30. Attachment of Commissioned Officers of Volunteers to Regulars or Militia for Training. Examination by Board of Officers. Section 5.

Certificate of Proficiency by Board of Examiners. Section 5.

For Field Officers Not Having Attended a School of Instruction.

"We certify that of the is conversant with the drill of a company and of a battalion, and able to give instruction in the same.

That he can command a battalion in brigade. That he is competent to superintend instruction in aiming and position drill, and to superintend blank firing and ball practice.

That he is acquainted with the proper mode of route marching and the duties of guards.

Also that he can ride.

Signatures of Board of Examining Officers appointed by General Officers Commanding District, or formed in Line or Militia Regiment to which the Officer may have been attached.

Station,
Date,

For Captains and Subalterns Not Having Attended School of Instruction and for Sergeants.

"We certify that of the is conversant with the drill of a company, in close and extended order, and able to give instruction in the same.

That he can command a company in battalion.

That he is competent to instruct a squad in aiming and position drill and to superintend blank firing and ball practice.

That he can command a guard and is acquainted with the mode of marching relief and posting sentries.

Also that in his written answers to questions he has expressed himself with (clearness or tolerable clearness).

Signatures of Board of Examining Officers as above.
In the case of a Sergeant, signature of Adjutant, countersigned by Officer Commanding Volunteer Battalion.

Station,
Date,

Certificate of Proficiency for Quartermasters and Quartermaster Sergeants.

"We certify that of the is conversant with the mode of drawing and issuing ammunition, arms, forage, fuel, and rations.

That he understands the system of packing and loading baggage, so as to facilitate its issue at the end of a march.

That he is acquainted with the mode of drawing and issuing camp equipments.

Also that he is competent to make out returns and keep the books relative to the above.

Signatures of Board,

Station,
Date,

It was doubtless felt that many officers would be unable to bear the expense of attending Schools of Instruction or of attachment either to the Regulars or the Militia. It was accordingly provided that officers of all arms might, if they preferred it, receive the necessary instruction from the Adjutant and Sergeant-Instructors of their corps, brigade or battalion, whose duty is was to afford such instruction. Examination of Officers instructed by Permanent Staff. Clause 31. Section 1.

As a rule such officers, if below the rank of Field Officer, were to be examined either on the day of inspection or on the day preceding or following it, at the discretion of the Inspecting Officer. The examination was to be conducted by a Board consisting of the Inspecting Officer, the Adjutant of the corps, brigade or battalion, and of the nearest available Captain of Regulars or Adjutant of Regulars or Auxiliary Forces of the same arm. When a quartermaster was examined a quartermaster of the Army or Militia might be substituted for the captain or last-mentioned Adjutant. Section 2.

Medical Officers were to be examined by a Board consisting of the principal Medical Officer of the district and two other army Medical Officers. Section 5.

The certificate of a Medical Officer was in the following form:— Certificate of Medical Officer.

"We certify that of (who holds two diplomas or licenses, one to practise medicine and the other surgery in Great Britain and Ireland, and is registered under the Medical Act of 1858), is well acquainted with the nature and intended application of the various articles composing the equipment of Army Hospitals in the Field, and with the authorized means for the transport of sick and wounded soldiers, and the proper modes of employing them.

We also certify that he has competent knowledge of the treatment of the wounds and injuries to which troops are liable in the field, particularly with regard to the special circumstances of campaigning, and that he is acquainted with the duties to be performed by Army Medical Officers in camp and bivouacs and during marches, as named in Section 21, Sanitary Regulations for Field Service, pp. 82, &c., of the Official Code of Army Hospital Regulations.

Signature of Board of Examining Officers.

Station,

Date,

A report of the names of Officers who had obtained certificates was to be made and the letter "P" placed after their names in the Army List. Section 10.

Volunteer sergeants were obliged to obtain a certificate of proficiency within one year after their appointment. They were to be examined by the adjutant of the corps, brigade or battalion to which they belonged and their certificates of proficiency signed by Clause 32, Secs. 1-2-3. Sergeants' Certificates.

such adjutant, countersigned by the commanding officer of their battalion.

Sergeants holding such certificates were to wear a star embroidered on the sleeve above the chevrons, and their names were to be published in regimental orders.

Company and Battalion Drill. Clause 34. Secs. 2-3-4-6.

Clause 34 is devoted to company and battalion drill and marching out. Commanding Officers (Sect. 2) were to determine what drill was to take place and who was to drill at certain parades. If the Commanding Officer was not present, the officer in temporary command was to carry out his arrangements. The Commanding Officer was authorised to direct any officer to assume the command for the purpose of manoeuvring the battalion, despite the presence of other officers senior to him.

Section 3 Muster-roll.

At a company drill the adjutant was to have with him a copy of the company's muster-roll which was to be called over in his presence and be checked by him

He was to be furnished with the roll of recruits and examine those tyros in squad drill, rifle exercise and company drill. The rolls were to be submitted to the inspecting officer at the annual inspection.

Section 4. Certificate of Efficiency.

The adjutant was to note the names of the Volunteers present found qualified in drill &c. for certificates of efficiency. A Volunteer not to receive his certificate till he had so satisfied the adjutant at that or a later visit and the adjutant was not to sign the certificate of any Volunteer whom he had not, during the year, seen at drill and considered qualified.

Drill by Adjutant. Clause 34, Section 5.

The 5th section of clause 34 directed the Adjutant to personally drill a company in the capacity of drill-instructor during a portion of the period of the drill. Even the officer commanding the company was desired to fall in for instruction: the subaltern officers were to do so as a matter of course. As officers and sergeants should have an opportunity of drilling in his presence, the Adjutant was directed, during part of the time, to hand over the company to one or more of them, he being present as instructor.

Instruction in Brigade Drill. Clause 35, Section 1.

Volunteers must attend, once during the year, a special drill for brigade instruction when called upon by the General Officer commanding the district.

Section 2.

On such occasion the force was to consist of one brigade only, or if more than one, each brigade must be drilled separately.

The General Officer commanding the district or an officer of the Regulars appointed by him was to command.

The instructional drill was to be of not less than two hours' duration.

Not less than half the enrolled number of each corps was to be present.

There was a conditional capitation allowance of 1/- for travelling expenses.

Field Officers of administrative regiments or corps were to attend unless specially exempted. Section 4.

Section 6 of this clause is short but awe inspiring. If a corps failed to attend brigade drill when required, or if less than half of its enrolled numbers were present, it was to forfeit its claim to the whole or portion of the capitation allowances for the ensuing financial year. Section 6 Capitation Grant to be forfeited in certain cases.

By clause 36 a portion of the Volunteer Force was, in each year, to be assisted out of the public funds to form Regimental Camps of Exercise. The annual Inspection was to be made in camp when a corps of Volunteers formed its own Regimental Camp, but when encamped in conjunction with the Regulars or Militia, the inspection was not to be in camp. The camp was to last for 3 clear days. Clause 36. Camps.

The travelling expenses of Volunteers to and from camp were to be borne by the State; a sum of 10s. was to be allowed to corps for each Volunteer (all ranks) remaining 8 days, of which 6 clear days were in camp. A sum of £1 was earned by 13 clear days in camp. Capitation Grants for Camp attendances. Secs. 15-17.

Officers were to receive, in addition, the army field camp allowance for the number of days they were in camp; a Field Officer 2s. 6d., a Captain 1s. 6d., and Subalterns 1s. a day. Great coats and straps were to be lent to the Volunteers during their stay under canvas, but they had to take with them their own mess-tins, haversacks, knapsacks, valises or canvas bags duly stocked with combs, brushes, sponges, housewife *et hoc genus omne*. Army Field Allowance to Officers in Camp. Section 19. Great Coats. Secs. 28-29.

The Volunteers in camp had to perform the camp duties of fatigue, cooking, &c. Section 34.

Attendance at the annual inspection, unless for good cause shewn, was to be an indispensable condition of efficiency. Corps in administrative regiments were to be separately inspected at their own head quarters every third year. Clause 38, Section 3. Attendance at Annual Inspection. Section 10.

Clause 39. Section 1. Efficiency Badges, Section 2.

Capitation grants were not to be granted for Officers unless they had attended the number of drills prescribed for efficients. A badge of efficiency was to be worn by men duly qualified, a ring of silver lace round the sleeve of the right arm above the cuff. Men returned 5 times as efficients in the annual returns of their corps might wear one star: those so returned ten times, two stars above the ring.

Clause 40. Indignation Meetings forbidden in Camp.

Meetings in camp for the purpose of expressing an opinion upon the acts of a Commanding Officer, or of recommending him to take a particular course of action and memorials to the same effect were strictly prohibited. The remedy of a Volunteer thinking himself aggrieved was by representation to the captain, with right of appeal to the Commanding Officer, and from him to the General Officer commanding a district.

Salutes. Section 6

Volunteers in uniform were to salute all officers of the Regulars and Auxiliaries in uniform.

Clause 41 Uniform.

No alteration in uniform to be made without the previous authority of the Secretary of State.

Clause 44. Regulations as to Sergeant Instructors.

There are regulations as to the appointment, age and pay of Sergeant Instructors, but I think, with no more than the mere statement of the fact, and a reference of the reader to clause 44 for fuller details, we may now conclude the synopsis of this voluminous circular.

15th October, 1872. Order in Council as to Efficiency.

I have already set out the conditions of efficiency, a purely technical term, as prescribed in 1863. It is now necessary to state the modifications introduced by the Order in Council of the 15th October, 1872, which provided that, in order that the efficiency of the Volunteers might be increased, the certificate should, in addition to or in substitution for the requirements prescribed by the former Order in Council, contain the particulars in the now reciting Order enumerated.

Certificate of Efficiency.

The form of the Certificate for efficiency sufficiently declares the conditions of efficiency and I therefore extract it fully :—

"We hereby certify

1—That A. B., No. , was duly enrolled in the Muster Roll of the Rifle Volunteer Corps on the , and is actually a member of the Corps on this date.

2—That he does not belong to the Regular, Militia, Yeomanry, or Army Reserves (including enrolled Pensioner forces); and that he is not enrolled in any other Volunteer Corps.

3—That he attended during the twelve months ending the 31st October, drills of this Corps, ordered by the Commanding Officer; each of such drills being of not less than one hour's duration.

These drills were, for Recruits, if present at Inspection 30 squad, Company or Battalion drills (including the inspection), or instruction in musketry. If absent from Inspection 32 such drills.

For other than Recruits: if present at Inspection, nine Company and Battalion drills (including the Inspection) of which three at least should have been Battalion drills. If absent from Inspection, 11 Company and Battalion drills, of which at least three should have been Battalion drills.

To constitute a Battalion drill reckoning towards efficiency, 100 at least of all ranks (exclusive of Permanent Staff and Band), must be present, of whom not less than 16 must be Officers and Sergeants. Attendance at Brigade drill might be counted as a Battalion drill; but attendance at a Review must not be so reckoned.

To constitute a Company drill reckoning towards efficiency, 20 at least of all ranks (exclusive of Permanent Staff and Band), must be present, of whom not less than three must be Officers and Sergeants.

The Certificate was also to state:—

4—That the Volunteer fired five rounds of blank ammunition in volley firing, and five rounds in independent firing, during the year, in a squad of not less than five files.

5—That he fired rounds of ball cartridge in class firing during the year, and passed into the 2nd class. The figures, 20, 30, 40 or 60, rounds were to be inserted. If a Volunteer remained in the 3rd class, of course it was not stated that he had passed into the 2nd class.

In view of the last clause, the Certificate might state, if the facts warranted it, that on the day of , the Volunteer completed the three periods of class firing, under the special superintendence of the Adjutant or other officer appointed under the Secretary of State's authority to act as such, and obtained the number of points to qualify him (so far as target-practice was concerned), as a marksman under the Musketry Regulations of the Army.

The Certificate was to add:—

6—That the Volunteer possessed a competent knowledge of squad and Company drill, including the manual and firing exercises and skirmishing as a Company, and as laid down in the Field Exercises of Infantry.

7—That he possessed a competent knowledge of the preliminary Musketry drill laid down in the Musketry Regulations for the Army.

8—That he was present at (or absent from, owing to certified sickness or by leave of the Commanding Officer), the last Annual Inspection of the Corps.

Head-quarters, Commanding Officer.

1st November Adjutant.'

Certificates might be withheld for untidiness.

The Order in Council to which the above form of certificate was an appendix contained the very salutary provision that the Inspecting Officer at the annual inspection might direct the withholding of a certificate for or in respect of any Volunteer whose sword, carbine or rifle might in his opinion be in bad order and condition. Further, all certificates might be withheld by the Secretary of State from all efficients belonging to a Volunteer corps not inspected during the year by reason of its own default.

Auxiliary and Reserve Forces Circular, April 21st, 1873.

An entirely new feature was introduced into Volunteer organisation by the Auxiliary and Reserve Forces Circular of 1873, and the accompanying general regulations and instructions in connection with the localization of the forces. A moment's consideration of these documents will lead to the conclusion that they are based upon the principle of assimilating the auxiliary to the regular forces as far as can possibly be done consistently with the preservation of the voluntary nature of their service. The Order of 8th April, 1873, directs that thenceforth the several corps of Rifle Volunteers should be attached to and form part of the army in the United Kingdom and be attached to one or other of the 70 brigades or corps of the army mentioned in the schedule, subject nevertheless to the important condition that no Volunteer should be required to serve in any other manner than that in which he might have been required to serve, or should be liable to any greater punishment than that to which he might be subject, if this Order had not been made.

Clause 22, Volunteer Corps attached to Brigade or Army Corps.

Clause 23, Military Districts, Section 2.

The military districts of Great Britain and Ireland are divided into 66 Infantry sub-districts, each designated by the number of the brigade belonging thereto, as set forth in the said schedule. The Auxiliary and Reserve forces portion of each sub-district brigade was to consist of the Infantry Militia and Rifle Volunteer Corps detailed in the said schedule together with the Infantry Reserve located in the sub-district. The line portion of the brigade was to have a local connection with the sub-district by means of the brigade depôt which had been or would be formed therein.

Brigade Depôt, Section 3

Officer Commanding Brigade Depôt, Section 4.

The Officer commanding the brigade depôt was invested with the command of the whole of the Infantry forces within his sub-district, battalions of the line excepted.

Clause 25, Adjutants not to be elected to municipal office.

Adjutants of Auxiliaries were to forfeit their Adjutancies on election to any municipal office, the duties of the two offices being considered by the Secretary to be incompatible. They were also now first required to wear the uniform of the regiments of Auxiliary forces to which they were appointed: a provision more relished by the Volunteers than by the Adjutants. All officers of the Infantry Auxiliaries wearing the waistbelt over the tunic were to keep their swords hooked up at Levées and Drawing Rooms. Dress of Adjutants and other Officers.

The General Regulations and Instructions issued July 24th, 1873, to be read with clause 23 of the foregoing circular, provided that to each Infantry Sub-district would be assigned 2 battalions, (one Sub-district in England was to have 3), of Infantry of the Line to be linked together for the purposes of enlistment and service. In each Infantry Sub-district the Brigade Depôt was to be under the command of a Lieutenant-Colonel. It was to be composed of two companies from each of the Line Battalions assigned to the Sub-district. These Line Battalions, the Militia Battalions, the Brigade Depôt, the Rifle Volunteer Corps and the Infantry of Army Reserve, were to constitute the Infantry Sub-district Brigade Depôt, the whole to be under the command, with the exception of the Line Battalions, of the Officer commanding the Brigade Depôt. General Regulations, July, 1873. Assignation of Battalions to Sub-districts.

This Officer Commanding was charged with the immediate command of the Depôt, the command, training and inspection of all the Infantry of the Auxiliary and Reserve forces within the Sub-district. He was to be assisted by a Major from the Home battalions and by the following officers and non-commissioned officers belonging to the four companies composing the Brigade Depôt, viz:— Other Officers of Brigade Depôts.

From each of the Line Battalions of the Brigade—two Captains and two Lieutenants or Sub-Lieutenants, two Colour-Sergeants, four Sergeants, two drummers and five Corporals.

The Majors of the Home Line Battalions were to serve alternately with the Brigade Depôt, not, as a rule, for a longer period than two years.

The Regulations recommend that the yearly drills of Volunteer corps should be performed, whenever possible, continuously, whether in camp or otherwise. The officer commanding a brigade depôt was to encourage such a practice by every means in his power and he was also to be responsible for the efficient training of the Volunteer corps thereto belonging, whether the yearly drills were continuous or intermittent. He was desired to attend such drills either in person or by his Major and so satisfy himself as to the efficiency of all ranks Yearly drill, ss. 50 and 52.

Army and Reserve Forces Circular, 1873. Sections 1-2.

Abolition of 2nd Lieutenant, Cornet and Ensign. Section 3.

With the publication on July 24th, 1873, by the War Office of the Regulations and Instructions of that date disappear from the auxiliary service the familiar titles, 2nd lieutenant, cornet, and ensign; and officers serving in these ranks on 31st May, 1873, were to be styled "Lieutenants," and subaltern officers appointed after that date were to bear the rank of sub-lieutenant, and on appointment receive probationary commissions, holding the grade of sub-lieutenant for 2 years.* If in that period they passed the qualifying examination they would at its expiration and on the recommendation of the Commanding Officers of their regiments be promoted to be lieutenants and their commissions as such be ante-dated to the time of their original appointments to the service. A star on the collar was to be worn by sub-lieutenants as a badge of rank.

Higher ranks, Section 5.

Officers appointed after 31st May, 1873, to higher ranks without the usual length of service in the lower ranks would hold probationary commissions until they passed the prescribed examination, after which they would receive permanent commissions which would be issued to all substantive officers appointed between 31st March, 1872 and 1st June, 1873.

As Volunteer corps do not carry colours, the office of ensign may appear anomalous. This notwithstanding, one cannot avoid a passing qualm at the disappearance from the force of a rank and title intimately associated with the most cherished traditions and legends of the army.

The ensign of the Roman legion bore its insignium or standard, hence the title. Who does not recall the words of the ensign of Cæsar's tenth legion on his first landing in Britain: how he flung his standard into the waves and leaping after it exclaimed, "*Desilite, commilitiones, nisi vultis aquilam hostibus prodere; ego certe meum rei publicae atque imperatori officium praestitero.*"

The honourable distinction of Ensigns.

The Ensigns of the British have been not less devoted than this gallant Roman. Ward, in his "Animadversions of Warre," published in 1639, says, "an Ensigne, as being the foundation of the Company, ought to be endued with valour and wisdome, and to equal his superior Officers in skill, if it were possible." "I have

---

*In 1854 by W. O. C. dated Whitehall, Nov. 9th, the rank of 2nd Lieutenant was abolished in the army, officers thenceforth being appointed Ensign.

read," he adds, "in history, of Ensignes that, rather than they would undergo the dishonour of losing their colours, being so dangerously charged by the enemy that either they must yield them up or be slaine, have chosen rather to wrappe them about their bodyes and have leapt into the mercilesse waters, where they have perisht with their colours most honourably to their immortal fames.* Soldiers know that the virtue of the Ensigne setteth forth the virtue and valour of the Captaine and his whole band." Captain Thomas Venn, in his "Military Observations," published in 1672, is in the same strain: "The dignity and estimation of Ensigns in all ages hath been held most venerable and worthy; they have been esteemed the glory of the Captaine and his company; and indeed they are no less, for where they perish with disgrace there the Captain's honour faileth and the soldier is in hazard of ruine, for if the loss proceed either from their cowardice or misgovernment it hath been death by the law of arms to all that survive, and the best mercy that can be expected is that every soldier shall draw a lot for his life (file by file) so that one out of every file perisheth for it."

The Ensign was accorded many marks of honor. "Whenever he entered into a city, town or garrison he was to be first lodged before any other Officer and not in any mesne place and his quarters were to be secure from danger. Though wholly at the Captaine's command, yet, in justice, no Captaine or other Officer can command the Ensign from his colours; for they are as man and wife and ought not to endure a separation."

But alas! we live in a utilitarian age. A generation that could substitute the Griffin for Temple Bar was not likely to respect an Ensign.

Letter of General Wolfe.

I am loth to dismiss this subject without inserting a copy of a letter written by the heroic but ill-fated general whose monument on the Heights of Abraham stirs so deeply the English colonist when first his feet fall on Canada's distant shore. This letter, or rather a fragment of it, is reproduced by Mr. Charles Dalton, editor of the English Army Lists and Commission Registers, (1661 to 1714), in No. 298, December, 1902, of the *Journal of the Royal United Service Institution*. The letter was originally addressed by General Wolfe to Ensign Hugh Lord of the 2nd Battalion of Lord Charles Hay's Regiment, 33rd Foot.† Hugh Lord was gazetted Ensign,

---

* Ensign Epps in Flanders.

† It is a curious coincidence that the Huddersfield Corps to which the second part of this work is devoted is linked with this regiment. R.P.B.

15th September, 1756, promoted Lieutenant 1758, his battalion in the same month becoming the 72nd Foot, under the young Duke of Richmond. He was at the siege and capture of Havana, 1762. In 1763 he became, by purchase, captain in the 72nd, and on its disbandment in the autumn of that year was placed on half pay. In May, 1778, he obtained the majority of the 75th, (Prince of Wales's), Regiment of Foot, having as a brother officer Captain Thomas Picton of the "Fighting Third," who fell at Waterloo. In 1783 Hugh Lord, his regiment being disbanded, was again on half pay, but in 1801 was consoled by the command of one of the 11 companies of Invalids in Jersey. In 1808 he retired on full pay of Major and died in 1829 at the ripe age of 88. The letter of General Wolfe was, so far as preserved, as follows:—

"Dear Hughy,

By a letter from my mother I find you are now an Officer in Lord Charles Hay's Regiment, which I heartily give you joy of, and, as I sincerely wish you success in life, you will give me leave to give you a few hints which may be of use to you in it. The field you are going into is quite new to you, but may be trod very safely and soon made known to you, if you only get into it by the proper entrance.

I make no doubt but you have entirely laid aside the boy and all boyish amusements, and have considered yourself as a young man going into a manly profession, where you must be answerable for your own conduct; your character in life must be that of a soldier and a gentleman; the first is to be acquired by application and attendance on your duty, the second by adhering most strictly to the dictates of honour and the rules of good breeding. To be more particular in each of these points, when you join your Regiment, if there are any Officers' guards mounted, be sure constantly to attend the parade, observe carefully the manner of the Officers taking their posts, the exercise of their espontoon,* &c.; when the guard is marched off from the parade, attend it to the place of relief, and observe the manner and form of relieving, and when you return to your chamber (which should be as soon as you could, lest what you saw slip out of your memory), consult Bland's Military Discipline† on that head; this will be the readiest method of learning this part of your duty, which is what you will be the soonest called on to perform.

When off duty get a Sergeant or Corporal, whom the Adjutant will recommend to you, to teach you the exercise of the firelock, which I beg of you to make yourself as much master of as if you were a simple soldier. The exact and nice knowledge of this will readily bring you to understand all other parts of your duty, make you a proper judge of the performance of men, and qualify you for the post of an Adjutant, and in time many other employments of credit.

---

* A sort of half-pike.

† A treatise on Military discipline by Humphrey Bland, Esq., Brigadier General of His Majesty's Forces, London, 1743.

When you are posted to your company, take care that the Sergeants or Corporals constantly bring you the orders; treat those Officers with kindness, but keep them at a distance, so will you be beloved and respected by them. Read your orders with attention, and if anything in particular concerns yourself, put it down in your memorandum book, which I would have you (keep) constantly in your pocket ready for any remarks. Be sure to attend constantly, morning and evening, the roll-calling of the company; watch carefully the absentees, and enquire into the reasons for their being so; and particularly be watchful they do not endeavour to impose on you sham excuses, which they are apt to do with young Officers, but will be deterred from it by a proper severity in detecting them." (*Desunt Caetera*).

Other officers than Ensigns might with profit lay to heart the counsels of this friendly letter and therefore, and not alone for its historic interest, I have deemed it well to include it in these pages.

Auxiliary and Reserve Forces Circular, April 1st, 1874.

On April 1st, 1874, the War Office issued further Regulations and Instructions.

Promotion from the ranks, Section 5.

The 5th section of clause 22 introduces that principle of promotion by merit which has, in the regular army, raised more than one soldier from the ranks to proudest eminence. The pity is that with merit do not always exist the means to support the status of an officer. That "eternal want of pence that vexes public men" and which the late Laureate so feelingly deplored is not confined to public men and has prevented many a meritorious non-commissioned officer assuming the rank his abilities and services would adorn. By that section "a Sergeant of the Volunteer force who had held a certificate of efficiency for two years in that rank might, if recommended for the rank of Officer, be appointed to the probationary rank of Sub-Lieutenant, until reported on at the next Inspection. If the Inspecting Officer informed the Commanding Officer and stated in his Inspection Report that the Officer was qualified for promotion, he would be promoted to the rank of Lieutenant without further examination on being recommended by the Commanding Officer of his regiment."

Examinations of Officers of Volunteers, Clause 23, Section 34.

Every Officer appointed to a Commission as Subaltern, Captain or Field Officer, or promoted to be a Field Officer in that Force, unless he should have served in a similar arm of the Regular forces and have passed his examination therein for the rank of Lieutenant, in the case of a Captain or Subaltern, and of a Captain in the case of a Field Officer, was required, at or before the second inspection of his corps after he had obtained such appointment or promotion, to pass an examination as under. An Officer failing to obtain his certificate on his first examination might try again six months later and if he then failed he must resign.

Nature and subjects of examination for Subalterns and Captains.

The examination was to be a practical one.

FOR SUBALTERNS AND CAPTAINS.

(a)—In drilling a Company in close and extended order.

(b)—The command of a Company in Battalion.*

(c)—Duties of Commander of a Guard, and mode of marching reliefs and posting sentries.

(d)—Practical knowledge of the Rifle exercise, manual and firing, aiming and position drill and blank firing.

(e)—Knowledge of and competency to superintend target practice †

A Subaltern obtaining a certificate of proficiency in the foregoing subjects was excused from further examination on becoming a Captain.

For Field Officer.

FOR FIELD OFFICERS.

(a)—Drilling a Company and a Battalion.

(b)—Movements of a Battalion in Brigade.

(c)—Proper mode of route marching and the duties of guards.

(d)—Riding.

Clause 23. Section 40. Retirement of Officers unfavourably reported on.

Officers appointed previous to the 1st April, 1872, to commissions which they were holding in 1874 would, if they were not in possession of certificates of proficiency, be specially reported on at the annual inspection of 1874. If they were favourably reported on as having a practical knowledge of drill and of the duties and command of a company or battalion (including, for Field Officers, the duty of Mounted Officer in the field), according to their rank, the Inspecting Officer might give certificates to that effect, and such officers would be entitled to the letter "P." If an officer was unfavourably reported on, he must be again reported on at the next inspection, when, if the report were still unfavourable, he would be required to resign his commission.

Clause 38. Uniform.

As all Administrative Battalions and Corps of Rifle Volunteers now formed part of the Brigades of the Infantry Sub-District in which they were located, any applications from such battalions or corps for permission to change the colour of their uniform to that of either of the Line Battalions of the Brigade was promised favourable consideration. No corps would, however, be compelled to adopt a uniform of a different colour from that then worn, except

---

* Not compulsory for Subalterns, but if the Officer did not pass in them he must do so, after promotion to the rank of Captain.

† Officer having Certificate as Captain or Subaltern excused from examination in Company drill or the duties of Guards.

in the case of those Administrative Regiments in which the several corps were not clothed alike.

Only one subaltern officer was, in future, to be borne on the establishment of a Company or Sub-Division of Rifle Volunteers. The appointment of a supernumerary subaltern allowed on recommendation of Lord Lieutenant. Establishment, Clause 40.

Fifteen years after the issue of the Regulations of 1863 the War Office issued, as a sort of Volunteer *Corpus Juris*, the Regulations of 1878. Between those years there had been, as the reader has seen, many Circulars and Memoranda dealing with such subjects as the Special Capitation Grant to Proficient Officers, Issue of Snider Rifles, Establishment of Brigade Depôts, Localization of Forces, Schools of Instruction, Attachment of Commissioned Officers of Volunteers to the Regulars and Militia for training, Volunteer Camps, Military Districts and their command, the Examination of Officers, &c. The operative parts of these Circulars, intermediate between 1863 and 1878, are mostly incorporated in the Regulations of 1878, and they might therefore have been ignored altogether and their effect stated in an abstract of the provisions of the Regulations of 1878. That course would, perhaps, have been proper to be pursued had I been engaged upon a mere statement of what may be termed the law of Volunteers; but I conceived that in a history of the Volunteer Movement the more appropriate course was to notice the intervening changes and developments in the order of their occurrence, contenting myself, in the consideration of the Regulations of 1878, merely with such modifications or innovations as they may have introduced. Volunteer Regulations, 1878.

The Table on the following page shews the Volunteer Establishment as authorized.

It will be noticed that the second lieutenant, the shuttle-cock of the War Office, abolished in 1873, was reinstated in 1878. He disappeared in 1884, reappears in 1887 and is apparently perpetuated in 1901. Second Lieutenant.

Although by the Regulations of 1878 a second lieutenant was borne on the establishment of corps consisting of only one company or sub-division, in corps of larger establishment one second lieutenant only was allowed for every two lieutenants, except where there was an uneven number of the latter, when an additional second lieutenant was allowed. 1878, Paragraph 23.

o

Description of Corps.	Lieut-Colonels.	Majors.	Captains.	Lieutenants.	Second Lieuts.	Quartermaster.	Surgeon.	Staff Sergeants. Quarter-master Sergeant.	Staff Sergeants. Armourer.	Staff Sergeants. Orderly Room Clerk.	Staff Sergeants. Bugle Major.	Colour-Sergts.	Sergeants.	Corporals.	Buglers.	Privates.	Total Enrolled Members exclusive of Perma. Staff.	Permanent Staff. Adjutant.	Permanent Staff. Sergeant-Instructors, including acting Sergeant Major.
Sub-division				1	1			1					3/2	3/3	1	49/23	59/30		Permanent instructors paid by the public are allowed for corps as follows:— From 1 to 3 corps one instructor 4 to 7 " two " 8 to 11 " three " 12 to 15 " four " 16 to 19 " five " The number allowed on the staff of administrative regiments in each case by the Secretary of State.
Company			1	1	1			1				1	4/2	5/3	2	84/48	100/60		
Battalion of 6 Companies	1	1	6	6	3	1	1	1	1	1	1	6	24/12	30/18	12	505/289	600/360	1	
Battalion of 8 Companies	1	2	8	8	4	1	1	1	1	1	1	8	32/16	40/24	16	675/387	800/480	1	
Battalion of 12 Companies	2	2	12	12	6	1	1	1	1	1	1	12	48/36	60/36	24	1,016/584	1,200/750	1	

N.B.—When a corps is below its maximum establishment 1 sergeant and 1 corporal should only be appointed for every 20 enrolled members.

Para. 30, sect. 2.—The establishment of a corps will be reduced if the enrolled strength at any time falls below the minimum establishment assigned to it, unless the Secretary of State sanctions its continuance.

In addition to the number of second lieutenants borne on the establishment, a sufficient number of supernumerary second lieutenants to complete the number of officers of that rank to one for each unit was to be allowed for each corps the establishment of which exceeded that of a company. Paragraph 24. Supernumerary Second Lieutenants.

The names of candidates recommended as supernumerary second lieutenants would in all cases be submitted through the Lord Lieutenant. Paragraph 285.

Officers appointed to the rank of sub-lieutenant under previous regulations might be recommended for promotion to be lieutenants as soon as they had passed the prescribed examination—their commissions as lieutenants bearing date as of the date of their first appointment to the Volunteer force. Sub-lieutenants were to take precedence of all second lieutenants. Paragraph 286.

Acting surgeons were to rank as lieutenants, irrespective of their length of service, except those anterior to 1st October, 1877, who were to continue to act as majors. Paragraph 57, Acting Surgeons.

The relative rank of an Acting Chaplain was to be captain; that of quartermaster, lieutenant. Paragraph 58, Chaplain.

By paragraph 317, section 9, the Secretary of State signified his readiness, on the recommendation of Commanding Officers of Administrative Regiments and Corps of Volunteers, to recommend to Her Majesty the names of officers of Volunteers retiring after 15 years' service as commissioned officers in Her Majesty's forces, of which not less than 10 should have been with the Volunteers, with a view to their being permitted to retain their rank and wear the uniform of the regiment or corps of Volunteers to which they belonged, provided that the last 3 years of such service should have been in the rank they held on retirement. If otherwise, to retire with rank previously held. Paragraph 317, Honorary rank.

Lance-sergeants and lance-corporals, not exceeding one sergeant and two corporals for each company, might be appointed by the Commanding Officer when the duties of the corps required it. Section 10, Paragraph 380, Lance-Sergeants and Corporals.

No person less than 5 feet 3 inches in height or measuring less than 32 inches round the chest was to be enrolled as a Rifle Volunteer. Section 11, Paragraph 389, Height and chest measurement of recruits.

The civil magistrates might call upon all the subjects of the Crown, Volunteers not excepted, to quell riots, but Volunteers on such occasions must not appear in uniform. Section 15, Paragraph 430-34.

The Civil Authority was not in any case entitled to call upon or order Volunteers to act as a military body in the preservation of peace.

Volunteers acting as special constables must be armed only with the constable's staff.

Volunteers at disposal of Magistracy in certain cases.

In case of serious riots and disturbances, the Civil Authority might require all subjects to arm themselves to meet the occasion. Then the Volunteers, apparently, might use the arms of their services

They might also repel with arms an attack on their storehouse or armouries.

Section 16, Paragraph 440, Medals and Decorations.

Medals and decorations given by the Queen or foreign sovereign, (the acceptance having been sanctioned by Her Majesty), were to be worn on the left breast; medals awarded by the Royal Humane Society for bravery in saving human life, on the right breast. No other medals or decorations were to be worn by Volunteers in uniform. This regulation was not, however, intended to apply to authorised prize shooting badges to be worn on the arm.

Section 20, Uniforms.

The 20th section is purely sartorial. It deals with the dress and undress uniforms of officers, their mess jackets, and the tunics &c. of the men.

Paragraph 608.

When a difference existed in the clothing or appointments of corps composing Administrative Regiments all the corps were to conform to the approved patterns before April 1st, 1879, in the case of Administrative Regiments existing in 1874, and in cases of Administrative union of corps since that date, within 5 years from the date of such union.

Paragraph 609.

With the exception of the changes last referred to, no alteration of the colour of the uniform of a Volunteer corps was to be permitted, except for the purpose of assimilation to one of the Line Regiments of its Sub-district Brigade.

Paragraph 610.

When a corps or Administrative Regiment of Rifle Volunteers was permitted to adopt a scarlet tunic or patrol jacket, the authorised facings would be those of the Infantry Militia Regiment of the county. Should there be more than one such Militia Regiment with different facings, the Secretary of State was to decide which of the facings the regiment or corps of Volunteers concerned was to adopt.

Paragraph 612.

To distinguish Volunteers from the Regulars, all regiments were to wear on the sleeve an Austrian knot: those clothed in green a light green knot, those in blue a scarlet knot, those in scarlet a knot of the colour of their facings, unless the facings should be scarlet, in which case a dark blue or black knot was prescribed.

It being desirable that all regiments clothed in green should adopt green facings of the same shade as their uniform, or as that of the Austrian knot aforesaid, no change to be permitted save with that object. Paragraph 613.

A corps might, with permission, wear the patrol jacket instead of the tunic. Paragraph 614.

In Rifle Volunteer corps wearing the busby the feathers or horsehair on the lower part of the plume was to be of light green, when the corps was clothed in green, and of the colour of the facings when clothed in scarlet or grey. Paragraph 615.

Prescribes the dimensions of the badge worn on the Glengarry bonnet by corps wearing it. Paragraph 616.

Volunteers were to wear on their shoulder-straps the initials of their county (Y.W. for instance, to denote the West Riding), and the number of their corps in the county and if they belonged to a corps in an Administrative Regiment, the number also of their brigade or battalion. Paragraph 617.

When a corps belonged to an Administrative Regiment of a different county, the shoulder-strap was to show the county of the regiment as well as of the corps. Paragraph 618.

This regulation to be carried out before April 1st, 1879. But in the case of reorganization five years from the date of such reorganization would be allowed. The letters and numbers would be of the same colour as the Austrian knot in the case of corps clothed in green, blue or scarlet; in the case of corps clothed in grey, of the same colour as the facings, or as the braidings or piping, if the facings were grey. It was recommended that the shoulder-straps should have an edging of the same colour as the letters and numbers.

A badge of efficiency was to be worn by efficients, consisting of a ring half an inch wide, either of silver lace or cloth or braid, to be worn round the sleeve of the right arm above the cuff, passing under any other lace or embroidery belonging to the uniform. Efficiency Badge, Paragraph 619-20.

Men returned as efficient five times in the Annual Returns might wear above the ring a star made of silver, silk or worsted. The silver star was only to be adopted when the ring was of silver lace. A further star might be worn for every quinquennium of efficient service. Efficiency Star, Paragraph 621-22.

Paragraph 623. A Volunteer entitled to wear an efficiency star or stars, but returned as non-efficient in an annual return of his corps, might continue to wear the star or stars, though not the efficiency ring, during the ensuing Volunteer year.

Paragraph 626, Gold lace &c. To the prohibition of gold lace was now added that of gilt or brass ornaments.

Paragraph 627, Undress. No corps was to adopt any undress without due authority and, when authorised, it must be of the same colour as the full dress. An Austrian knot, as in full dress, was to be worn on the sleeve.

Paragraph 642, Belts and Pouches. Corps clothed in blue or scarlet were to wear white belts and black pouches; corps clothed in green, black belts and pouches; those in grey, black or brown belts and pouches.

Paragraph 644, Officers' cord and braid. Officers of regiments clothed in scarlet or blue were to wear silver cord and braid, the cord and braid being edged with scarlet in the case of regiments clothed in blue. Officers of regiments clothed in grey were to wear cord and braid of silver or other material, as might have been authorised, and officers clothed in green were to wear black cord and braid with light green edging.

Paragraph 645. The cord and braid of Rifle Volunteer officers clothed in grey or green were to be of the same pattern and applied in the same form as those on the sleeve of rifle regiments of the regular forces.

Paragraph 646. Officers of Rifle Volunteers clothed in scarlet were to follow, as regards full dress uniform, the patterns of the Infantry Militia, except that they were to wear white belts and pouches instead of sashes, and, instead of flat lace, silver cord, with a silver braid edging on each side, worn on the sleeve.

Paragraph 648. Officers of Volunteers were to wear gold in the badges of rank on the collar where silver was worn by officers of the Regulars.

Paragraphs 649-50. Officers were to wear cross-belts and pouches, both in full dress and undress. No officer to wear silver belts or silver stripes on the trousers on any parade.

Paragraph 652. Officers of Rifle Volunteers clothed in scarlet or grey, might, if they wished, wear silver pouch and sword belt, silver sword knots and silver stripes on the trousers, at balls or on state occasions, subject to the following regulations:—

(*a*)—Lace was to be of the same pattern as for Infantry of the line.

(*b*)—The sword-belt to be 1¼ inches wide, with slings ¾ inch wide, and be lined with crimson morocco leather.

(*c*)—The pouch belt was to be 2 inches wide and lined with crimson morocco leather; the pouch of morocco leather of the same colour as the ordinary pouch and edged with ¾ inch silver lace.

(*d*)—The stripe in the trousers for Rifle Volunteers to be 1⅛ inches wide, with a crimson silk stripe, ⅛-inch wide, in the centre.

The provision of the silver belts and other articles referred to in paragraphs 651 and 652 to be purely optional with each officer, and ordinary belts and pouches might be worn in full dress on all occasions. Paragraph 653.

All mounted officers of Volunteers must wear steel spurs, those of the Rifle Volunteers might wear high boots like mounted officers of Regular Infantry. Such officers were also to wear brown scabbards with steel mountings; other mounted officers steel scabbards. Paragraphs 654-5-6.

Officers of Rifle Volunteers clothed in scarlet to wear a blue forage cap of the pattern worn in the Infantry of the regular forces; the band to be of black oak-leaf lace with an edging of the colour of the facings, the buttons to be of the colour of the facings. The patrol jackets to be of the Infantry pattern, the Austrian Knot on the sleeve having an edging of the same colour. Undress for Officers.

Officers of Rifle Volunteer corps clothed in green to wear a green forage cap (without peak), having a black braid band with light green edging and light green button, and a green patrol jacket of the pattern worn by the 60th Rifles, the black braid on the sleeve being edged with light green.

Officers of Volunteer corps clothed in grey to wear a grey forage cap (without peak), with band and button of silver, black, grey, or the colour of the facings, and patrol jackets of the pattern worn by the 60th Rifles. The braid on the sleeve to be of black or grey, with an edging the colour of the facings.

Mess-jackets and waistcoats were permitted, but their use was optional. **Paragraph 659. Mess-jackets**

The mess-jackets and waistcoats of Mounted Rifles and Rifle Volunteers clothed in scarlet to be in accordance with the patterns worn in the Infantry arms of the Regular forces, substituting silver for gold. The outer edge of the Austrian or other knot on the sleeve to have a tracing of braid of the colour of the facings. Mess jackets of officers of Volunteers clothed in green or grey to be of the **Paragraph 660.**

same colour as the full dress uniform and of the pattern worn in the 60th Rifles, subject to the regulations as to braid in par. 658 (c) but in the case of corps clothed in grey the waistcoat might, if the Commanding Officer preferred it, be of the colour of the facings.

Paragraph 662, The Sash.

The Infantry sash was not to be worn by officers or sergeants.

Paragraph 663, Distinctions of rank.

The distinctions in uniform appointed in the Regular forces and Militia to denote the rank of the wearer were to be strictly observed by Volunteers of the various grades, as far as they were applicable to the Volunteer force. In that respect the Dress Regulations for the Army were to be the guide.

Paragraph 664, Acting Chaplain.

Acting Chaplains of Volunteers were authorised, but not compelled, to wear the same uniform as Chaplains to the forces of the 4th class, with the following additions:—

(*a*)—The top of the cuff to have an edging of grey braid terminating in an Austrian knot of the same size as that worn on the sleeve of the tunic of officers of Infantry of the line.

(*b*)—The button on the forage cap to be grey instead of black, and the band to have a grey edging.

Paragraph 665, Sergeants' Chevrons.

Sergeants of regiments clothed in scarlet or blue were to wear silver chevrons, edged with scarlet in the case of regiments clothed in blue; sergeants of regiments clothed in grey, chevrons of silver or other material, as might have been authorised; those of regiments clothed in green, light green chevrons.

Paragraph 666, Sergeants' Proficiency Stars.

The stars of proficient sergeants were to be of the same material as their chevrons and similar to those worn on the badges for good shooting, but of 1½ inches instead of ¾ inch in diameter. These were to be worn above the chevrons and any other badge of rank authorised to be worn by non-commissioned officers.

Paragraph 668, Sergeant Instructors.

Sergeant Instructors were to wear three chevrons on each arm, above the elbow, surmounted by a crown.

Paragraph 670, Crossed Muskets.

Crossed muskets were only to be worn by those non-commissioned officers who held certificates from the School of Musketry at Hythe.

Paragraph 671, Horse Furniture.

The horse furniture of Mounted Officers of Rifle Volunteers, clothed in grey or green, was to be similar to that of Rifle Regiments of the Regular forces, except that in the cases of corps having brown belts the bridles and breast-plates would be of brown leather. In the throat ornament the outer part of the horsehair to be of the colour of the facings, and the inner part of the colour of the uniform ; but in the case of corps clothed in green the throat ornament to be light green over dark green, whether the facings were light green or not. The horse furniture of Mounted Officers of Rifle Volunteers clothed in scarlet, to be similar to that of Mounted Officers of Infantry Militia.

Neither standards nor colours to be carried by Volunteer corps. Paragraph 672, Standards and Colours.

Officers and men of the Volunteer force were to be permitted, under certain restrictions, the use of the military gymnasia, a permission, strangely enough, of which few Volunteers avail themselves. Section 27, Paragraph 808.

In February, 1878, Mr. Secretary Hardy appointed a Committee on the financial state and internal organization of the Volunteer force in Great Britain. The original members of the Committee were the Right Honourable the Viscount Bury, K.C.M.G., Parliamentary Under Secretary of State, Lieutenant-Colonel Lloyd-Lindsay, V.C., M.P., Financial Secretary, Lieutenant-General F. C. A. Stephenson, C.B., Commanding Home District, Major-General E. G. Bulmer, C.B., Assistant Adjutant General for Auxiliary forces, Brevet-Colonel R. Biddulph, C.B., R.A., Assistant Adjutant General for Auxiliary forces, Mr. George D. Ramsay, Director of Clothing, Mr. H. T. de la Bère, and Sir Bruce M Seton, Bart., to act as Secretary. During the sitting of the Committee Colonel Biddulph being ordered to Cyprus on duty was replaced by Colonel Fitzhugh, R.A. Committee of 1878 and its Report.

The Committee was directed to inquire—

1—What were the necessary requirements of the Volunteer force to be covered by the capitation grant.

2—Whether the then grant was sufficient for its purpose.

3—If not, in what form any increased assistance should be given.

4—Whether any alteration in the organization of the force was necessary.

5—Whether any increase of efficiency of the force was desirable and, if so, in what direction and to what extent.

6—Whether the then mode of issuing the capitation grant was one that tended to the economical administration of public money.

7—Whether any change was desirable in the conditions of appointment and retirement of Adjutants.

The report of the Committee was presented in January, 1879, and its members felt themselves called upon, before reporting upon the specific points submitted to them, to bear testimony to the generally sound and healthy condition in which they found the Volunteer force. It had, they observed, increased from year to year in numbers, and it had cheerfully answered every call upon it for increased efficiency and, regard being had to its numbers and conditions, it was probably as inexpensive a force to the State as any that could be desired, and it contained within itself the means of indefinite expansion. For these reasons the Committee had not thought it right to propose any material change in the constitution of the force, their object being to bring the Volunteer force completely under the operation of the general scheme for the localization of the Army, whilst interfering as little as possible with its existing constitution, and they had confined themselves to the suggestion of certain improvements framed in accordance with the recognized principle of calling for increased efficiency in return for increased assistance.

Recapitulating, in the words of the Report, the most important of the changes proposed by the Committee, they were found to rest partly with the force itself; for others Government interference would be required. Without proposing to interfere with the statutory right of the Volunteer to resign at 14 days' notice, the Committee suggested that an engagement, capable of being enforced in the civil Courts, should be entered into between the recruit and his corps, by which he should engage to serve for not less than four years, so that the first expense of his uniform and equipment should be repaid to the corps out of the capitation grant earned by the Volunteer, an agreed sum being repaid to the corps if the Volunteer should exercise the statutory right within the period covered by the agreement. In other words the Committee proposed to constitute retirement under penalties. A further suggestion was that Volunteer corps should form an integral part of the Territorial Brigade in each Sub-district. This, it was hoped, besides bringing military influence to bear more directly on the force and therefore increasing efficiency, would have the effect of adding to the social value of a Volunteer officer's commission, by associating that officer more directly with the Regular and Militia forces. With a view of seeing the utmost possible economy in the administration of the capitation grant, it was recommended that the force should gradually be consolidated into a smaller number of battalions, each consisting of a larger number of men than had thitherto been the case.

A uniform pattern of clothing and equipment, in which the Volunteers should conform to the Regular Army, was suggested, such clothing and equipment to be issued by Government on payment, such payment to be on an improved and more economical system than that existing. An increase in the capitation grant was not deemed desirable, but more generous allowance was suggested to corps for men attending regimental camp, and for travelling expenses. The appointment was recommended of a regular officer, holding Field Officer's rank, in lieu of an additional Adjutant, to large regiments of two or more battalions when consolidated.

Abstract of Volunteer Returns in 1863 & 1878.

The report of the Committee concludes with an abstract of the Annual Returns of Volunteer Corps, from which it appeared that the maximum authorised establishment of the force amounted in 1863 to 226,156 of all ranks, of which establishment 113,511 were efficient, out of 162,935 enrolled members; in 1878, the establishment had been raised to 244,263 of all ranks, of whom 194,191 were efficient, out of 203,213 enrolled members. Thus the percentage of efficients to enrolled members had steadily increased from 69·66 in 1863 to 95·55 in 1878, a fact which proved the progressive development of the force both in numbers and efficiency.

The Committee added an expression of opinion which could not fail to gratify the *amour propre* of the Volunteer. "The movement had played, and would yet play, a most important part. It represented a great reserve power in the country, and was the channel through which men who did not enter the Army or Militia were able to enrol themselves and give their services in the defence of the country."

Volunteer Regulations 1881.

On April 1st, 1881, the War Office repealed the Regulations of 1878 and all circulars and orders relative to the Volunteer force issued up to that date and substituted in their stead the Regulations of 1881. Alterations in future were to be notified by monthly circulars. The main alteration is that whilst the thirteen paragraphs of section 5 of the Regulations of 1878 were devoted to Administrative Regiments those of 1881 are silent on that point and substitute the brief proviso, (sec. 5), "Corps of Volunteers which, in the Secretary of State's opinion, are not of sufficient strength to entitle them to the services of a separate Adjutant, are attached to another corps of the same or a different arm." By par. 66 a corps thus attached does not become part of the corps to which it is attached and has no connection with it, except when drilling, or when receiving instruction from the Adjutant. The object of such

Section 5, paragraph 64. Attachment of Corps.

Paragraph 66.

Paragraph 65. Object of such arrangement.

arrangement was that sergeant-instructors of a corps attached to another corps of a different arm might receive, through the Adjutant as a public accountant, their pay and allowances, and, in the case of a corps attached to another of the same arm, such corps would also have the advantage of the instruction of an Adjutant and of the services of that officer for the purpose of assisting in gaining the certificates of efficiency prescribed by Order in Council.

It is from 1881 that we must date the disappearance of the Administrative regiments as such.

Establishment.

The authorised establishment was the same as that in the 1878 Regulations.

Efficiency.

The conditions of efficiency were modified by the Regulations of 1881 pursuant to Order in Council of 31st July, 1881. They were to be as follows:—

For Recruits: if present at Inspection 30 squad, company, battalion (including the Inspection) or musketry drills. If absent from Inspection with leave of the Commanding Officer or through sickness duly certified, 32 such drills.

Second year: if present at inspection, 30 squad, company, battalion (including the Inspection) or musketry instruction drills, or such number not less than nine of company and battalion drills (including the Inspection), three of which should have been battalion drills, as would, with the number performed in the previous year, amount to 60.

If absent from Inspection with leave of the Commanding Officer, or through sickness duly certified, 32 such drills, or such number not less than 11 of company and battalion drills (including the Inspection), three of which should have been battalion drills, as would, with the number performed in the previous year, amount to 62.

Third and fourth and subsequent years: if present at Inspection nine company and battalion drills (including the Inspection), of which three at least should have been battalion drills. If absent from Inspection with leave of the Commanding Officer, or through sickness duly certified, 11 company and battalion drills, of which three at least should have been battalion drills.

Volunteers when they had completed the 60 or 62 drills, as the case might be, during their first two years of service, and had been returned four times as efficient, qualified for their certificates of proficiency, if present at Inspection, by seven company and battalion drills (including the Inspection), of which at least three were to be battalion drills. If absent from such Inspection, with leave or through certified sickness, by nine company and battalion drills, three to be battalion drills.

Squad drills, at which not less than four rank and file were present, might be reckoned, when necessary, to complete the number of company drills, but would only be counted in proportion of three squad drills in lieu of one company drill.

To constitute a battalion drill reckoning towards efficiency, 80 at least of all ranks (exclusive of Band) were to be present, of whom not less than 16 of all ranks were to be officers and sergeants. Similarly to constitute a company drill, 16 at least of all ranks (exclusive of Band) were to be present, of whom not less than two were to be officers and sergeants, or officers or sergeants.

Attendance at a brigade drill or review to count as a battalion drill.

In addition, all ordinary Volunteers were also to pass the requisite quota of volley firing, and qualify in rifle practice and class firing.

The Regulations of 1881 also enjoin certain modifications in uniform to which it is desirable to direct attention.

Applications for permission to change the colour of the uniform of Rifle Volunteer Corps were promised favourable consideration, provided the change were to scarlet. It may be assumed that this preference for scarlet was another indication of the desire of the authorities to so constitute and regulate the Volunteers that they might, if and when occasion arose, be, if not incorporated, at least intimately allied with regiments of the line for purposes of actual service. Section 20, paragraph 681.

When a corps was allowed to adopt scarlet tunics or frocks (patrol jackets), the authorised facings would be similar to those worn by the senior regiment of the Regular forces belonging to the sub-district brigade. Paragraph 682. Facings of Scarlet Tunic.

To distinguish Volunteer regiments from the Regulars, the former were to wear on the sleeve an Austrian knot. Those clothed in green, a light green knot, those clothed in blue, a scarlet knot, those clothed in scarlet, a black knot—not as in the Regulations of 1878 a knot of the colour of their facings. Paragraph 684. Distinctive marks of Volunteer Uniform.

There is a slight alteration introduced in the provision as to officers' undress, braid being substituted for cord. Paragraph 698. Undress.

Instead of the white belts and black pouches prescribed in 1878, a corps clothed in blue or scarlet was to adopt buff belts and buff pouches. Paragraph 720. Belts and Pouches.

The Regulations of 1878 required *all* Mounted Officers of Volunteers to wear steel spurs. In 1881 their Field Officers were required to wear brass spurs. Paragraph 732. Spurs.

Medical Officers of Volunteer Corps were to wear the uniform of their respective corps, but with cocked hats similar to those worn by surgeons of the Regular forces. Silver was to be substituted for gold on the cocked hat when silver lace was worn on the uniform, in other cases the loop and button at the side were to be of bronze, and the bullion tassel at each corner black. The Paragraph 743. Head Dress of Medical Officer.

plume was to be of blackcock's tail feathers, 5 inches long, without feathered stem. Medical Officers appointed to the rank of surgeon before 1st October, 1877, were to wear a plume 6 inches, instead of 5 inches, in length.

Paragraph 752. Uniform or purely civilian dress to be worn.

The 752nd paragraph conveyed a hint which presumably was not uncalled for:—"Volunteers will be careful on all occasions to appear either in the authorised uniform of their corps, or in purely civilian dress. The unsoldier-like appearance of Volunteers dressed partly in uniform, partly in civilian costume, brings discredit not only on themselves, but on the force to which they belong."

Regulations of the Forces Act, 1881. 44 & 45 Vict., c 57. Consolidated Corps

The year 1881 witnessed also the passing of the Regulation of the Forces Act, dealing (*inter alia*) with Consolidated Corps. The 9th section, sub-section 1, provided that every Volunteer Corps formed under the authority of the Secretary of State, whether formed before or after the passing of the Act, by the consolidation of two or more Volunteer Corps, should, as from the date of consolidation, be deemed to have been a corps formed under the Act of 1863, and the Officers and Volunteers of the Consolidated Corps should be deemed to have been duly appointed and enrolled as Officers and Volunteers of the Consolidated Corps; and the Commanding Officer of the Consolidated Corps was to become the Commanding Officer of every part thereof, and the corps property thereof vested in a Commanding Officer of a constituent corps was, by that section, vested in the Commanding Officer of the Consolidated Corps.

Territorialization.

It is now essential that I should advert to a process of organization that affected materially, and for the better, though indirectly, the status of the Volunteer corps of the country. I refer to the principle which, for want of a better term, I may call the principle of Territorialization. This principle was explained by Mr. Cardwell, so far back as 22nd February, 1872,* as meaning the connection of two line battalions with each territorial district for *recruiting* purposes—emphasis should be placed on the word "recruiting."

It was not intended to *locate* battalions in a district, their localization affected recruiting, not quartering. With the two line battalions were to be associated two militia battalions and the Volunteers of the locality; the whole to rest on a brigade depôt or

* On February 16th, 1872, there had been laid on the table of the House a memorandum in which H.R.H. the Field Marshal Commanding in Chief laid down the plan on which the organization of the land forces should be effected.

centre which could be converted into a third battalion. One of the line battalions was to be abroad and the other at home. The Militia, Volunteers and depôt of the district were to be under a colonel; the Militia were to train, as a rule, at the headquarters of the territorial district and be inspected by the Colonel, who would act as "Brigadier and Commander in Chief" of the whole. It would thus, it was conceived, be possible to give the auxiliary forces the benefit of a superior training, all forces would be effective, we should be at last working on a system, and a system was what we never yet had.*

In 1876 a Committee under the presidency of Colonel Stanley (Lord Stanley of Preston) stated its opinion that territorial regiments ought to be formed. In 1881 it was decided to proceed actively with the formation of territorial regiments as recommended in 1876. With infinite pains a scheme for constituting and naming the territorial regiments and for renumbering the regimental districts was drawn up by a Committee† under the Adjutant-General, Sir G. Ellice, and is now in force. The names of the regiments, in some cases long, were determined on with great deference to, and as far as possible in compliance with, regimental feelings and wishes, and a plan of numbering adopted which, though not consecutive, has the merit of preserving the number of the senior of the two old units which go to compose the modern territorial regiment. The old facings of regiments were suppressed and a uniform, white for English, yellow for Scottish, green for Irish and blue for Royal regiments, was adopted.

Lord Stanley's Committee in 1876.

The battalions of Volunteer Infantry of each regimental district belong to the territorial regiment but are numbered *inter se* separately and consecutively, beginning with 1, and are not numbered in the same sequence as battalions of Regulars and Militia.

All the battalions of Militia and Volunteers, of the regiment, as well as the regimental depôt, are under the immediate orders of the Commander of the regimental district, who is Colonel, discharging functions that in the main are administrative.

There are 215 Volunteer battalions, being 1 corps of 3 battalions, (The Queen's Rifle Volunteers, Royal Scots,) and 212 unattached battalions.

---

*Army Book of the British Empire, p. 63.

† "Committee on the formation of territorial regiments as proposed by Colonel Stanley's Committee" February, 1881.

These battalions vary in strength, depending on local circumstances and on the population, as follows:—

1 Battalion has 23 companies (3rd Volunteer Battalion, Welsh Regiment).				
2	Battalions each	16	companies.	
1	Battalion has	15	companies.	
6	Battalions each	13	companies.	
29	"	12	"	
13	"	11	"	
44	"	10	"	
19	"	9	"	
65	"	8	"	
11	"	7	"	
18	"	6	"	
3	"	4	"	(Eton College, Inns of Court, 9th Middlesex).
1	Battalion has	3	"	(Corps of Cyclists).
1	"	2	"	(Isle of Man).
1	"	1	"	(Bank of England).

Battalions of less than six companies have no Adjutant of their own, but are attached to other battalions.

The Territorialization scheme by which the old regiments disappeared was effected by a General Order issued in May, 1881, under the head of "Army Organization," and was to take effect, unless otherwise stated, on 1st July, 1881. By this scheme it is provided (by paragraph 2 of the Order), that "the Infantry of the Line and Militia will, in future, be organized in Territorial Regiments, each of four battalions for England, Scotland and Ireland; the first and second battalions of these being Line Battalions, and the remainder Militia; these regiments to bear a Territorial Designation corresponding to the locality with which they are connected, and the words 'Regimental District' will, in future, be used to take the place of 'Sub-district' hitherto employed.

"Paragraph 8, Honours and Distinctions: all distinctions, mottoes, badges and devices appearing hitherto in the Army List, or on the colours of the Line Battalion of a Territorial Regiment, will, in future, be borne by both battalions. Battalions which have not hitherto borne a special device will adopt a national badge.

English Regiment	... ...	A Rose.
Scotch "	... ...	A Thistle.
Irish "	... ...	A Shamrock.
Welsh "	... ...	A Dragon.

Paragraph 9, Uniform: with the exception noted in paragraph 13 (which applied to Militia), the uniform of all the battalions was to be the same. The title of the regiment was to be shown on the shoulder-straps.

Paragraph 10: The facings and the officers' lace of the Territorial Regiments were to be the same for all regiments belonging to the same county (Royal and Rifle Regiments excepted), and were to be as follows, viz.:—

		Facings.		Lace.
English and Welsh	...	White	...	Rose.
Scotch	...	Yellow	...	Thistle.
Irish	...	Green	...	Shamrock.

Paragraph 16: changes of facings and alterations in badges to come into effect both for Line and Militia on 1st July, 1881."

Although, as will be observed, the above General Order promulgating territorial designations &c of units dealt only with Regulars and Militia, yet the Volunteers were also affected by the scheme and their battalions soon became those of territorial regiments. The Volunteers generally were dealt with by W. O. C. as individual cases arose and required to be dealt with. In the case, for instance, of the 1st, 2nd and 3rd Somersetshire Rifle Volunteer Corps, which was the first corps to become Volunteer battalions under the scheme, a General Order was promulgated in the following form: "G. O. 261. Army Organization—Her Majesty the Queen has been graciously pleased to approve of the designation of the 1st, 2nd and 3rd Somersetshire Rifle Volunteer Corps being, in future, respectively the 1st, 2nd and 3rd battalions of the Prince Albert Somersetshire Light Infantry, the order of precedence within the county already assigned under the Volunteer Regulations being still maintained." Captain F. A. Adams, in his Prize Essay "On the present condition and future organization of the Volunteer Force" thus comments on the change effected by the introduction of the territorial system:—

"Whatever its results may have been as affecting the Regular Army, it has certainly been productive of benefit to the Volunteer service. It has made Volunteer Battalions integral parts of their territorial regiments, and has associated them more directly with the line. Volunteer Battalions now wear the distinguishing badges of line battalions—badges which tell of hard fought fields and British endurance in action—and are more directly affiliated to the line than they formerly were. This is as it should be, and it is evidently the desire of the War Office authorities to foster such a tendency. Adjutants or Sergeant-Instructors are now appointed to Volunteer Corps preferably from the line battalions, and they bring with them to the Volunteers many little regimental ways and customs the due recognition of which tends to bind more closely together the various units of the territorial organization." *

Volunteer Regulations, 1884.

There had been Regulations in 1878, 1881, and again, in 1884, we find another issue—the Volunteers, if not enjoying the doubtful boon of triennial Parliaments, being favoured with triennial Regulations. The Regulations of 1884 bear marks of the changes consequent on territorialization.

Section 2. Supernumerary Lieutenants.

Section 2, paragraph 23: First appointments to the rank of subaltern officers were to be made to that of lieutenant. Paragraph 24: In addition to the establishment of lieutenants, supernumerary lieutenants to complete the number of officers of that rank to two for each unit were to be allowed for each corps. Paragraph 27: Supernumeraries would not be enrolled without authority from the Secretary of State and no authority would be given for increase of establishment unless the enrolled strength of a corps was equal to its existing maximum establishment and 80 per cent. of the establishment had been returned as efficient in the preceding annual return. Paragraph 29: When supernumeraries were authorised one sergeant and one corporal might be appointed for every 20 members. Paragraph 30: The establishment was to be reduced if the enrolled strength of the corps should at any time fall below the minimum establishment assigned to it, unless the Secretary of State, on representation of the General Officer commanding the district, considered that an exception should be made on the ground of there being reasonable expectation of the corps speedily returning to proper strength. The authorised establishment was consequently slightly altered owing to the disappearance of the second lieutenants from the table of establishment and the substitution of supernumerary lieutenants, which latter did not appear as necessarily forming the requisite quota of officers.

Establishment in 1884.

The following table shews the authorised establishment in 1884:—

---

* The Volunteer Question, p. 103, 1891, London, E. Stanford, Cockburn St., Charing Cross, S. W.

ESTABLISHMENT, 1884.

Description of Corps.	Lieut-Colonels.	Majors.	Captains.	Lieutenants.	Super. Lieuts.	Quartermaster.	Surgeon.	Staff Sergeants: Quarter-Master Sergeant.	Staff Sergeants: Armourer.	Staff Sergeants: Orderly Room Clerk.	Staff Sergeants: Bugle-Major.	Colour-Sergts.	Sergeants.	Corporals.	Buglers.	Privates.	Total Enrolled Members, exclusive of Perml. Staff.	Permanent Staff: Adjutants.	Permanent Staff: Sergeant-Instructors (including acting Sergeant Major).
Sub-division				1				1					3/2	3/2	1	42/25	50/30		Same as in 1878.
Company			1	1				1				1	4/3	5/3	2	84/48	100/60		
Corps of 6 Companies ..	1	1	6	6		1	1	1	1	1	1	6	24/18	30/18	12	505/385	600/360	1	
Corps of 8 Companies ..	1	2	8	8		1	1	1	1	1	1	8	32/24	40/24	16	675/387	800/480	1	
Corps of 12 Companies ..	2	2	12	12		1	1	1	1	1	1	12	48/36	60/36	24	1,016/654	1,200/720	1	

Section 6, paragraph 93. Adjutant's pay and allowances.

By the Regulations of 1881 the rate of lodging allowance of an Adjutant in lieu of quarters &c. was fixed at that for a regimental captain in the regular forces. The Regulations of 1884 vary this as follows :—

Regimental Majors	Regimental Majors' rates.
Captain and Majors on the half-pay list	Regimental Captains' rates
Lieutenants	Regimental Lieutenants' rates.

Paragraphs 207-8-9-11. Schooling of Children of Permanent Staff.

The Regulations of 1881 had contained the bald proviso that the children of the Permanent Staff of the Volunteer force were entitled to the privilege of being admitted gratuitously to the army schools. This was much amplified in 1884. When the children between the ages of 3 and 14 years of non-commissioned officers and others of the Permanent Staff of the Volunteer force serving under their army engagements attended a certified efficient or inspected school, in consequence of the families not residing near an army school, the ordinary school fees, at Board School rate or that of the certified or efficient school where no Board School, as also the cost of books and other school materials, were to be borne by the public.

Examination in tactics. Section 7, paragraph 402.

By paragraph 402 Subalterns, Captains and Field Officers of Auxiliary forces might present themselves for examination in tactics before the Board assembled at headquarters of military districts in January and July of each year.

Paragraph 403.

The examination for Captains and Field Officers was to be held on the basis laid down for promotion to the rank of Major, and for Lieutenants on the basis laid down for promotion to the rank of Captain (on this subject) by Appendix II of the Queen's Regulations and Orders for the Army 1883.

Paragraph 404.

Captains and Field Officers would, however, still be allowed to attend the examination laid down for lieutenants in the army.

Paragraph 409.

Officers gaining certificates were entitled to have the nature of their certificates inserted after their names in the Monthly Army List, according to the following distinguishing letters, viz :—

Subalterns, Captains and Field officers passing the examination for Lieutenants of the army	*t*
Subalterns, Captains and Field officers passing the examination and obtaining special mention	T
Captains and Field Officers passing the examination for Captains of the army	(T)

More than 1000 officers have obtained certificates in tactics, many with distinction.

The affiliation of the Volunteer forces to territorial regiments necessitated some changes in the provisions as to uniform &c. Applications for permission to change the colour of the uniform of Rifle Volunteer Corps were to be favourably considered, provided the change were to that worn by the territorial regiment to which the corps was affiliated. Volunteer battalions of territorial regiments might wear the uniform of the regiment, with the distinctions undermentioned and with certain restrictions as regarded badges. Uniform, Accoutrements and Horse Furniture. Section 19, paragraph 691.

When a corps was allowed to wear scarlet tunics or frocks (patrol jackets) the facings were to be of the same colour as those worn in the territorial regiments. Paragraph 692. Facings.

Volunteer battalions of a territorial regiment were to wear on the shoulder-strap the title as approved for the territorial regiment, with the addition of the letter V and the numeral. Distinctive marks of Volunteer Uniform. Paragraph 700.

The shoulder-straps of Volunteer battalions of territorial regiments were to have no edging. Paragraph 702.

Badges of rank were no longer to be worn on collars, except in the case of chaplains. Officers were to wear shoulder-straps, as below, on tunics, stabling jackets and shell jackets:— Officers' badges of rank, Paragraph 740.

Rifle Volunteer Corps, clothed in scarlet	Universal pattern, in silver.
Do. in grey, with silver cord on sleeves	Ditto ditto.
Do. in grey, with cord on sleeves of other material than silver.	Universal pattern, colour and material of the cord on sleeves.
Do. clothed in green.	Black chain gimp.

Shoulder-straps of the same material as the garment were to be worn by all officers, except chaplains, on frock coats, patrol jackets, cloaks and great-coats. In corps clothed in scarlet, blue, or green, the straps for patrol jackets and frock coats were to be edged with half-inch black mohair braid, except at the base, but without braid edging on cloaks and great-coats. Black netted button at the top in all cases. Similarly, grey shoulder-straps, edged with grey braid, or braid of the colour of that on the garment, were to be worn with grey patrol jackets. Netted button at the top, of the colour of the braid. Paragraph 741.

Paragraph 742.

Badge of rank to be worn as follows:—

Colonel	... Crown and two stars below.
Lieutenant-Colonel	... Crown and one star below.
Major	... Crown.
Captain	... Two stars.
Lieutenant ...	... One star.
Supernumerary Lieutenant	... No badge.

These were to be in gold on the shoulder-straps of tunics, stable jackets and shell jackets; and in silver on the shoulder-straps of frock coats, patrol jackets, cloaks and great-coats.

The new distinctions of rank were to be worn on saddle-cloths, in gold, by Field Officers.

Chaplains were to adopt the new distinctions of rank and wear them on collars as theretofore.

Uniform of aides-de-camp to the Queen, Paragraph 746.

The uniform of Volunteer officers appointed aides-de-camp to the Queen was either to be their regimental uniform with silver aiguillettes, or that laid down by the Dress Regulations for the army for aides-de-camp to Her Majesty appointed from the regular forces, with the exception that silver was to be substituted for gold in the aiguillettes, embroidery, lace, buttons, cocked-hat, sword-knot, sword-belt and slings and waist plate. The sash was to be of gold and crimson silk net, with plaited runner and fringe tassels of gold and crimson silk.

Paragraph 753.

The following regulation was perhaps designed as a check upon any officer who might be vain enough to desire to display himself before the uninformed eyes of our continental neighbours in costume designed to secure for him an adventitious importance:— "Officers while abroad are not permitted to wear uniform, except at court, or when employed on duty, or on the occasion of state ceremonies to which they have been invited."

Paragraph 761, Uniform of Medical Officers.

Some alteration was made in the uniform of Medical Officers. They were to wear the uniform of their respective corps, with the following exceptions:—

Cocked-hat and plume Sword-belt Pouch-belt Field-pouch	As for Officers of the Army Medical Department of corresponding rank, silver being substituted for gold, and gold for silver, in the lace and ornaments on belts and pouches.

In corps in which the officers wore silver lace, the lace, button and the bullion of the tassels of the cocked-hat to be in silver; in other corps the loop and button to be bronze, with bullion tassels in black. The buttons to be of regimental pattern.

The badge on the field-pouch to be as on the dress-pouch, and the waist-plate or clasp of regimental pattern.

1886, 1887. Lord Harris' Committee and Report.

In 1886, Lord Harris, Parliamentary Under-Secretary for War, presided over a Committee appointed to enquire: (1) What were the necessary requirements of the Volunteer forces to be covered by the Capitation Grant; (2) Whether the present grant was sufficient for its purpose; (3) If not, in what form any increased assistance should be given. The other members of the Committee were the Right Honourable W. St. John Brodrick, M.P., Financial Secretary to the War Office; Major-General the Honourable J. C. Dormer, C.B., Deputy Adjutant-General, Auxiliary forces; Mr. R. H. Knox, C.B., Accountant-General of the Army; Colonel Henry Eyre, M.P., 2nd Notts. Rifle Volunteers; Colonel R. W. Routledge, 2nd Volunteer Battalion the Royal Fusiliers; Mr. H. D. de la Bère (War Office), Secretary. The report of the Committee is dated 11th January, 1887, and the following excerpts from it will indicate the general tenor of its recommendations so far as they affected the Volunteer Infantry:—"Taking as a model a regiment with eight companies of 80 men each, and forming our estimate on the basis explained above, we consider that the necessary charges, for which no special allowances are made, and which have therefore to be defrayed from the Capitation Grant, will amount to about £1,108. The total efficiency grant which such a corps could earn would only be £960. Whatever might be earned for proficiency and tactics may be regarded as a set-off against loss by non-efficients and various unascertained expenses. A deficiency of £148 per corps, or 4/7 per head, may therefore be assumed to exist at present, and we consider that on the whole there are good grounds for an addition of 5/- to the present efficiency grant. In making this recommendation we desire to express very strongly our opinion that the time has now arrived when efficiency with the rifle should be an indispensable condition for the earning of any capitation whatever, and that the higher rate of capitation we propose should only be granted for those who pass out of the 3rd class. It is therefore recommended that the 30/- grant should still be made on account of men who become efficient according to present rules, provided that they hit the target at least twelve times during their musketry course; and that 35/- should only be granted for men who pass into the 2nd class. Those who fail to pass out of the 3rd class during the course of any three consecutive years of their service should cease to draw any grant whatever."

The Committee also recommended an annual allowance of 4/- for each man earning capitation to corps whose head-quarters were more than five miles distant from the range; the increase of the Tactics grant to 30/-; and a grant of 30/- to officers obtaining signalling certificates.

The Report points out that it would be possible for an officer who took an interest in his work to earn over £7 for his corps every year.

Volunteer Regulations, 1887.

In 1887, new Regulations for the Volunteer force were issued. The second lieutenant, still the sport of Fate seated at the War Office, re-appears. There is provision also for supernumerary lieutenants in the cases of corps of six and more companies, but they were not to be counted in the total strength of a company.

The Establishment.

The authorised table of Establishment is shown on following page.

Section 2, paragraph 71. 2nd Lieutenants.

Section 2 paragraph 71 provided that first appointments to the rank of subaltern officer should be made to that of second lieutenant and on completion of 3 years' service as such, a second lieutenant might be recommended for promotion to the rank of lieutenant, provided that the total establishment of lieutenants were not thereby exceeded. In special cases appointments might be made direct to the rank of lieutenant.

In addition to the establishment of subaltern officers, supernumerary second lieutenants, to complete the number of officers of that rank to two for each company, should be allowed for each corps. When vacancies existed in the rank of lieutenant, owing to no second lieutenant having qualified for promotion, extra supernumerary second lieutenants might be appointed, provided that the total establishment of subaltern officers were not exceeded.

Section 2, paragraphs 83-86-87, Steps of rank, and of Honorary rank.

If recommended to the Military Secretary by Commanding Officers through General and other officers commanding districts, steps of rank might be granted while serving to every lieutenant-colonel or major who had served 20 years as a commissioned officer in the Auxiliary forces and to every captain and surgeon who had served 15 years. Steps of honorary rank, with permission to wear the uniform of his regiment, might, after such period of service as aforesaid, be granted to those officers on retiring. Quartermasters of 15 years' service, whether serving or retiring, might be granted the honorary rank of captain.

TABLE OF ESTABLISHMENT FOR RIFLE VOLUNTEERS (1887).

Description of Corps.	Lieut-Colonels.	Majors.	Captains.	Lieutenants.	Second Lieuts.	Supernumerary and Lieutenants.	Quartermaster.	Surgeon.	Staff Sergeants. Quarter-master Sergeant.	Armourer.	Orderly Room Clerk.	Bugle Major.	Colour-Sergts.	Sergeants.	Corporals.	Buglers.	Privates.	Total Enrolled Members exclusive of Permt. Staff.	Permanent Staff. Adjutant.	Sergeant-Instructors, including Acting Sergeant Major.
Sub-division				1	1	*			1					3/2	3/2	1	49/22	59/30		In accordance with the rule laid down in section 3.†
Company			1	1	1				1				1	4/2	5/3	2	84/48	100/60		
Corps of 6 Companies ..	1	1	6	6	3	3	1	1	1	1	1	1	6	24/12	30/18	12	505/289	600/360	1	
Corps of 8 Companies ..	1	2	8	8	4	4	1	1	1	1	1	1	8	32/16	40/24	16	675/387	800/480	1	
Corps of 12 Companies ..	2	2	12	12	6	6	1	1	1	1	1	1	12	48/24	60/36	24	1,016/584	1,200/720	1	

N.B.—When a corps was below its maximum establishment, 1 sergeant and 1 corporal should only be appointed for every 20 enrolled members.

* The numbers shown in this column not included in the totals.

† This rule as to the numbers of Sergeant-Instructors is the same as under the preceding Regulations.

These battalions vary in strength, depending on local circumstances and on the population, as follows:—

[illegible] companies, [illegible] Volunteer Battalion, Welsh [illegible]

[illegible]

Paragraph 9. [illegible] 13 (which applied [illegible] Militia [illegible] to be the same. The [illegible] shoulder-straps

Paragraph 10: The [illegible] Territorial Regiments [illegible] belonging to the same [illegible] and were to be as follows [illegible] —

	[illegible]	[illegible]
English and Welsh ..	[illegible]	[illegible]
Scotch	[illegible] ..	[illegible]
Irish	[illegible]	[illegible]

Paragraph [illegible] changes [illegible] to come into effect [illegible]

Although, as will be observed, [illegible] gating territorial designations [illegible] and Militia, yet the Volunteers [illegible] and their battalions [illegible] The Volunteers generally [illegible] cases arose and [illegible] of the 1st, 2nd and 3rd Somersetshire Rifle Volunteer [illegible] was the first corps to become [illegible] scheme, a General Order was promulgated [illegible] "G. O. [illegible] Army [illegible] graciously pleased to approve of the [illegible] and 3rd Somersetshire Rifle Volunteer [illegible] respectively the 1st, 2nd and 3rd [illegible] Somersetshire Light Infantry [illegible] county already assigned under the Volunteer [illegible] still maintained." Captain F. [illegible] the present condition and future organization [illegible] Force" thus comments on the change effected by the [illegible] of the territorial system :—

"Whatever its results may have been in affecting the Regular Army, it has certainly been productive of benefit to the Volunteer service. It has made Volunteer Battalions integral parts of their territorial regiments, and has associated them more [illegible] with the line. Volunteer Battalions now wear the distinguishing badges of line battalions—badges which tell of hard fought fields and British endurance in action—and are more directly affiliated to the

Paragraph 88.

Commissioned officers, duly recommended, retiring after 15 years' service, might be permitted to retain the rank and wear the uniform of their regiments.

Paragraph 151, Retirement for age.

Officers above 60 years of age were required to resign their commissions. Power was, however, given to extend in special cases the age limit to 67 years.

Volunteer Medical Staff Corps, paragraph 220.

Volunteer Medical Staff Corps were first authorised by the Regulations, (of 1887), now under consideration. Sergeants of these corps within one year from appointment were to obtain certificates of proficiency.

The following chart shews the establishment for Volunteer Medical Staff Corps:—

TABLE OF ESTABLISHMENT FOR VOLUNTEER MEDICAL STAFF CORPS.

Description of Corps.	Surgeon-Commandant.	Surgeons.	Quartermasters.	Staff Sergeants, 1st Class.	Staff Sergeants, 2nd Class.	Sergeants.	Buglers.	Corporals.	Privates.	Total, exclusive of Permanent Staff.	Permanent Staff.	
											Adjutant.	Sergeant Instructors, including Acting Sergeant Major.
Company		3	1	1	2	4	2	8	79	100		1
Division of 4 Companies	1	12	5	4	8*	18	8	34	314	400	1	4

* Includes 1 Sergeant Bugler.

Examination of Medical Officers. Paragraph 144.

Medical Officers who had not served as such in the Regular Army or in the Royal Navy would, in order to obtain certificates of proficiency qualifying for the special capitation allowance of £2 10s. 0d., be required to pass an examination on the organization of field hospital and bearer companies, in the rendering of first aid to the wounded, and the sanitary and other duties generally of a Medical Officer in camp and on the line of march. The examination was to be by a Board convened by the principal Medical Officer of the district and passed within one year of the grant of the commission.

Sergeants of the Volunteer Medical Staff Corps must obtain certificates of proficiency within one year of their appointment. They were required to pass:— Paragraph 220.

1—A practical examination in drilling a bearer company in the prescribed evolutions.

2—An examination as to the duties of a commander of a Guard and the mode of marching reliefs and posting sentries.

3—A written and oral examination in the subjects enumerated in paragraph 268 (1) (d) of the Regulations for the Army Medical Department, 1885.

A member of the Volunteer Medical Staff Corps, in order to be reckoned as an efficient, must obtain a certificate that he had fulfilled the requirements and possessed the qualifications stated in the following form of certificate. Paragraph 245. Certificate of efficiency in Medical Staff Corps.

We hereby certify:

1—That   No.   was duly enrolled on the muster-roll of the Volunteer Medical Staff Corps on the   18   and is actually a member of the corps at this date.

2—That he does not belong to the Regular, Militia, Yeomanry, or Army Reserve (including Enrolled Pensioners) forces; and that he is not enrolled in any other Volunteer corps.

3—That he attended during the 12 months ended 31st Oct., 18   the following drills of this corps ordered by the Commanding Officer, each of not less than one hour's duration. For recruits: If present at inspection, 16 ambulance and 20 other drills (including the inspection). If absent from inspection with leave of the Commanding Officer, or through sickness duly certified, 16 ambulance and 22 other drills. For 2nd year men: If present at the inspection, 16 ambulance and 20 other drills (including the inspection), or such number, not less than 8 ambulance and 9 other drills (including inspection), as will, with the number performed in the previous year, amount to 32 ambulance and 40 other drills. If absent from inspection as aforesaid, 16 ambulance and 22 other drills, or such number not less than 8 ambulance and 9 other drills, as will, with the number performed in the previous year, amount to 32 ambulance and 40 other drills. 3rd, 4th and subsequent years: If present at inspection 8 ambulance and 9 other drills (including inspection); if absent from inspection, 8 ambulance and 10 other drills. (Extra drills, about 6, would be required for instruction with pack equipment).

4—That he possesses a competent knowledge of Squad, Company and Bearer Column Drill,* as laid down in the Field Exercises of Infantry and Instruction for Medical Staff Corps.

5—That he was present at the last annual inspection or absent with leave or from duly certified illness.

No more than two drills in any one day would be allowed to reckon towards efficiency. Paragraph 261.

---

* To constitute a Bearer Column Drill reckoning towards efficiency, 50 at least of all ranks must be present, of whom not less than 12 must be Officers and Sergeants.

Paragraph 269, Sergeants to retain rank and uniform on retirement.

A graceful compliment was, by the Regulations of this year, paid to the non-commissioned officers. Sergeants retiring after 10 years' service in that rank were, on the special recommendation of their commanding officer, and under the authority of General Officers commanding districts, to be suffered to retain their rank and to wear the sergeant's uniform of their battalion or corps, with such distinguishing mark on the sleeve as might be sanctioned by the Commanding Officer.

Paragraph 343, Hythe Courses.

At each of the classes for the regular course of Musketry instruction, formed at the School of Musketry and extending over about 60 days, vacancies were to be reserved for 5 officers and 10 sergeant-instructors of Volunteers.

Requirements for Capitation grant: section 4, paragraph 352. The higher grant.

The trained Rifle Volunteer was to be entitled to the "higher grant," as afterwards defined, by firing 20, 40, or 60 rounds, as the case might be, of ball ammunition in the course of target practice for the trained Volunteer, and passing into the second class.

The lower grant.

Failing to pass into the second class, he would, (for two years only), earn the "lower grant," as afterwards defined, if he had fired 60 rounds and had struck the target at least 12 times, exclusive of ricochet hits; and after the expiration of that period he would not earn any grant whatever unless he passed into the second class.

Recruits.

The recruit was to be entitled to the "higher grant" by firing 60 rounds of ball ammunition in the course of target practice for the recruit and striking the target at least 12 times, exclusive of ricochet hits.

Failing to strike the target 12 times, as above, he would earn the "lower grant" if he had fired 60 rounds in his course of target practice.

Targets.

The distances, targets, positions, and points to be obtained in classes are set out in the Appendix to the Regulations, pp. 310-320, q.v.

Figures of merit. Part 2, section 2, paragraph 671.

Paragraph 353 set forth the method of calculating the "figure of merit" of a company, battalion, or party of recruits and for this too, I must refer the reader to the Regulations themselves.

Ordinary Capitation grant.

An annual allowance of £1 15s. 0d, denominated the "higher grant," was to be granted to Volunteer Corps:—For every combatant officer, except Field Officers who had attended the drills prescribed for efficients (not being recruits) of his arm of the service or who had been duly exempted from such drills.

For every Field Officer and for every non-combatant officer (not being an honorary officer), except quartermasters, who had attended the number of drills prescribed for efficients (not being recruits) of his arm of the service.

For every trumpeter or bugler (except boys), borne on the authorised establishment of the corps and having attended the prescribed number of drills.

For every boy (to the extent of two for each company) serving as a trumpeter, bugler or musician, duly qualified as such and having attended the drills prescribed for efficients.

An annual allowance of 10/-, denominated "the lower grant," was to be granted to efficients of Rifle Volunteer Corps.

Paragraph 672, the lower grant.

Volunteers of Rifle Volunteer Corps enlisting in the Regular Army, Royal Navy or Royal Marines, who had completed the number of drills constituting them efficients for the year, to be so reckoned in the year preceding the year of enlistment. Also efficients of 1st class Army Reserves attached to a corps of Rifle Volunteers, provided they had fulfilled the conditions for obtaining the "lower grant" above set forth.

A special additional capitation allowance of £2 10s. 0d. was to be granted on account of each officer or sergeant of Volunteers holding a certificate of proficiency, whether an enrolled member of the corps, or (in the case of a sergeant), attached as a supernumerary from the 1st class Army Reserve, for every year in which he should earn the ordinary capitation allowance.

Special Capitation allowance, part 2, section 2, paragraph 676.

A special capitation allowance of £1 10s. 0d. was to be granted for each officer of Volunteers possessing a certificate in tactics for every year in which he should earn the ordinary capitation allowance.

Paragraph 677, Tactics.

A special capitation allowance of £1 10s. 0d. was to be granted for each officer of Volunteers possessing a certificate in signalling for every year in which he should earn the ordinary capitation grant.

Signalling, paragraph 678.

The examination for this grant consisted in

(*a*)—Correctly reading from and sending with the large flag at the rate of 8 words a minute.

(*b*)—Correctly reading from and sending with the small flag at the rate of 12 words a minute, and the bull's eye lamp at the rate of 9 words a minute.

(*c*)—Shewing a fair knowledge of the heliograph and limelight.

(*d*)—Thoroughly understanding the Manual of instructions in army signalling.

Part 1, section 5, paragraph 471, Signalling Examination.

Great Coats, paragraph 680.

A special capitation allowance of 2/- was to be granted on account of each efficient Volunteer, exclusive of officers, certified by the Adjutant to have been, on 1st September, 1887, in possession of a great-coat of approved pattern.

Badges. Part 1, section 4, paragraphs 363-67.

One must not dismiss these Regulations of 1887 without reference to the introduction of badges for good shooting.

The best "marksman" in a battalion was to be entitled to wear a badge of crossed rifles and crown in silver, or, for corps clothed in green, silk of the colour of the Austrian knot on the sleeve of the tunic.

The best "marksman" in a company was to wear a badge of crossed rifles, worked in silver or silk as above.

"Marksmen" were to wear a badge of crossed rifles, worked in worsted of the colour of the Austrian knot on the sleeve of the tunic.

The sergeants of the best shooting company were to wear the badge as for the best "marksmen" in the battalion.

No other marks of distinction for class firing were to be worn by Volunteers in uniform.

The sergeants aforesaid were to wear the badge on the right forearm. Others were to wear them on the left forearm.

Badges for good shooting were to be worn only during the Volunteer year following that in which they were earned.

Commissioned officers must not wear these badges.

Paragraph 693, Travelling to and from ranges.

An annual allowance of 4/- in aid of the expense of travelling to and from the range was authorised on account of each efficient Volunteer the head-quarters of whose company were distant more than five miles from the ordinary rifle-range.

Paragraph 951, Uniform.

The Regulations of this year do not change to any appreciable extent those already established as to uniforms.

Volunteer Regulations, March, 1890, section 4, Camp allowances.

The Volunteer Regulations of March 1890 were issued with the Army Orders of date 1st March, 1890, "as alterations and additions made in the Volunteer Regulations of 1887." The most important clauses are contained in Section 4 respecting Camps and Marching Columns. They provide for an allowance of 2/- a day (representing ordinary pay, subsistence &c.) for each day of continuous attendance for not more than 6 days annually, together with a sum of 4/- to cover the time consumed in joining and quitting the camp for each officer, non-commissioned officer or private attending a brigade camp for not less than 3 continuous days.

An allowance of 16s. (i. e., 2s. per day and 4s. for time spent in travelling) was allowed for every officer, non-commissioned officer and private attending a camp with the Regulars for 6 continuous days. Paragraph 645.

Volunteers extending their stay in camp with the Regulars to a period of 13 days might be allowed 30s. (i. e., 2s. a day and 4s. for time spent to and fro). Paragraph 646.

A like allowance of 2s. a day was to be made to rank and file of the Volunteers attending a regimental camp for not less than 3 continuous days. Paragraph 648.

Those attending brigade camps or with the Regular forces under the provisions aforesaid were to be allowed a *viaticum* of 1d. per mile up to a maximum limit of 8s. per head. A like concession was made on account of the expense of proceeding to annual inspections, battalion drills and rifle ranges, if held at or situate at places more than 5 miles from the head-quarters of a company. Travelling allowance, paragraph 660.

By the Regulations promulgated to the army by H.R.H. the Commander-in-Chief with the approval of the Secretary of State for War, it was provided :— Army Order, 1890, Nov. 17.

1—From 1st November, 1890, the capitation allowance was only to be issued to those Volunteer Infantry non-commissioned officers and men who, in addition to fulfilling the conditions of efficiency, possessed the following articles of equipment :—waist-belt, water-bottle with straps and carriages, frogs (except for men equipped with sword-belts with carriages), haversack, mess-tin with straps and cover, great-coat with straps, braces, ammunition pouches or bandoliers, to carry 70 rounds of ammunition (for men equipped with rifles or carbines.)

To provide these articles (other than the great-coat) all Infantry Volunteers enrolled on 31st October, 1890, and not belonging to a corps on the list of the "Patriotic Volunteer Fund," were to be allowed the sum of 12/-. The allowance to a Medical Staff Volunteer was 5/. Each year a "repair" allowance of 1/- was sanctioned. Great-coats were to be issued in kind from the army clothing department to all Volunteers enrolled on October 31st, 1890, whose corps was not on the said list or, in special cases, an allowance made of 12/- where the great-coats had been obtained elsewhere.

On increase of establishment after 31st March, 1891, an allowance was authorised of 30/- in case of each additional Infantry Volunteer, and 23/- of each Medical Staff Volunteer, to cover the cost of the equipment required by section 1.

It may be observed in passing that from this period forward Regulations began to be issued annually, to the great lightening of the mental labours of Commanding and other officers. This departure had long been urged upon the War Office by that vigilant guardian of the interests of the force, the *Volunteer Service Gazette.*

Volunteer Regulations, 1891. The Establishment.

The Regulations of this year fix the establishment of subaltern officers as one lieutenant for each company, and one second lieutenant and one supernumerary second lieutenant for every two companies, *e.g.*, a battalion of six companies was entitled to six lieutenants, three second lieutenants and three supernumerary second lieutenants, making in all 12 subalterns or two per company.

Paragraph 12, Special reasons for new Corps.

In considering offers of the services of new corps regard would be had to its mobilization requirements.

Formation of Brigades, Paragraph 25.

The Infantry Volunteer force having been organized into brigades, composed of the Volunteer battalions detailed in the Army List, an officer was to be appointed to the command of each brigade, assisted by the following Staff:—

Staff.

1 Brigade Major.

1 Aide-de-Camp.

1 Staff Officer for administrative Supply and Transport duties.

1 Brigade Surgeon, ranking as Lieutenant-Colonel.

Paragraph 27.

For the purpose of executive supply duties a Supply Detachment would be formed in each brigade, composed as follows:—

Supply, &c., detachment.

1 Captain as Supply Officer.

1 Non-commissioned officer as Assistant.

4 Non-commissioned officers as Clerks and Issuers.

1 Non-commissioned officer, } as Butchers, and for general
3 Privates. } purposes.

The members of these detachments, except the captains, were to remain on the establishment of their own battalions.

Paragraph 29, Signalling Company.

A signalling company was to be formed in each brigade. Each battalion to have two certificated non-commissioned officer assistant-instructors and 6 signallers holding badges, these to form a section of the brigade signalling company. Two officers with signalling certificates to be selected to command the signalling company.

For each brigade a bearer company was authorised with the following establishments :— Bearer Company, paragraph 30.

1 Surgeon Major or Surgeon,
2 Surgeons or Acting Surgeons,
7 Staff-Sergeants or Sergeants (the senior to act as Warrant Officer),
1 Bugler,
53 rank and file.

Total 64 all ranks.

Officers appointed aides-de-camp to Her Majesty the Queen were to retain their appointments for 10 years only. Paragraph 56, Queen's aides-de-camp.

Corps entitled to a medical officer of substantive rank, if consisting of less than 12 companies, to be allowed 2 surgeons; if of more than 12 companies, 3, in addition to the surgeon borne on the establishment. Paragraph 63, Medical Officers.

Acting Surgeons and honorary Assistant Surgeons obtaining certificates of proficiency would, on the recommendation of their Commanding Officer, be gazetted and commissioned to the rank of Surgeon. Paragraph 65.

After 15 years' service as Medical Officers for the Auxiliaries, Surgeons might be granted the substantive rank of Surgeon-Major. Paragraph 66, Surgeon-Major.

A Quartermaster of the Volunteer Medical Staff Corps was required to be examined not only in the usual duties of a quartermaster but in Paragraph 93. Quartermaster of Medical Staff Corps.

(*a*)—Duties in Field Hospitals and in connection with bearer companies.

(*b*)—Knowledge of medical and surgical equipment used on field service.

(*c*)—Mode of packing and loading Field Hospital and bearer company equipment.

(*d*)—The preparation of returns and the mode of accounting for the medical and surgical equipment used in the field.

Except under special circumstances of a special nature approved by the Secretary of State for War a battalion with a strength of less than 300 (all ranks) was not permitted to attend a brigade camp; and no brigade camp was to be formed unless at least 3 battalions of not less than a strength of 1,050 (all ranks) were present. Brigade Camps, paragraph 283.

Marching columns are stated to be intended to afford instruction in the details of military movements on the line of march, and should be composed, where practicable, of various arms Paragraph 293, Marching Columns.

of the service. They were to be organized under the direction of the General Officer commanding the district and be under the command of specially selected officers.

The strength of a marching column must not be less than 300 of all ranks.

Paragraph 334, Schools of Musketry.

The vacancies to be reserved at the classes of these Schools are now fixed at 20 for officers and 40 for sergeant-instructors of Volunteers.

Paragraph 346.

There were to be classes at Aldershot for instruction in supply duties.

Paragraph 356, Examination in Tactics, Military Law, &c.

Officers of Volunteers were to be entitled to present themselves for examination in tactics, military law, field fortification and military topography at the same time as officers of the Regular forces in the manner laid down in the Queen's Regulations. Distinguishing marks were granted only for success in the examination in tactics.

Regulations, 1901, paragraph 358.

By the Regulations of 1901, however, when an officer had passed in all the subjects (tactics, field fortification, military topography and organization and equipment, and, except Chaplains only, in military law), within five years, the fact was to be shown in the Army list by the letter (Q) if a Chaplain or Field Officer when he passed, and by the letter (*q*) if a subaltern.

Paragraph 366, Classes for signalling and examination.

Classes at convenient centres were appointed in signalling, each class to consist of not less than 8 or more than 20 officers and non-commissioned officers, and was to last for 91 days at least. Applicants for instruction must engage to attend not less than three times a week.

Paragraph 372.

The examination was to be as follows:—

(*a*)—Correctly reading from and sending with the large flag at the rate of 9 words a minute.

(*b*)—Correctly reading from and sending with the small flag at the rate of 12 words a minute, and the bull's eye lamp at the rate of 10 words a minute.

(*c*) and (*d*)—As before.

Certificates were to be granted to successful examinees.

Paragraph 515, Allowances to Officers attending Schools of Instruction.

The table set out in this paragraph contains the allowance to officers attending Schools of Instruction. It is 5/- daily for officers of all ranks for one month at Aldershot or London; the same sum for half a month to Field Officers, after having obtained a Captain's certificate.

An allowance, not exceeding £100 a year, to be granted to the Brigade-Majors of such Volunteer brigades as the Secretary of State might deem to require it. Paragraph 524, Allowance to Brigade-Major.

A special capitation allowance was granted to each officer of Volunteers possessing certificates in tactics. (Par. 565.)

Medical Officers were to take with them to camp their own professional instruments. (Par. 838.)

Badges, to be provided at the cost and be the property of the corps, of crossed flags for proficiency in Army signalling, might be worn by assistant Instructors and signallers of Volunteer Corps under specified conditions. Paragraph 879, Badges for Signallers.

Officers commanding Volunteer Infantry Brigades were to wear the uniform of a Brigadier-General, except officers commanding regiments or regimental districts who were *ex officio* Brigadiers of Volunteer brigades, who would wear their regimental uniforms. Paragraph 918, Uniform.

Articles 914, 915 regulate the full dress and mess dress of Brigade Majors, Supply Officers, administrative aides-de-camp to Officers Commanding Infantry Volunteer Brigades and Brigade-Surgeons.

In the horse furniture of Mounted Officers of Rifle Volunteers clothed in scarlet, silver or white metal was substituted for gold or brass. Paragraph 920, Horse Furniture.

The modifications introduced by the Regulations of 1892 must not pass unnoticed. Volunteer Regulations, 1892.

In the establishment the term Surgeon is discontinued for that of Medical Officer, and in corps of 6 and 8 companies 3 Medical Officers, and in corps of 12 companies, 4 Medical Officers allowed.

By section 1, paragraph 26, a Brigade-Surgeon-Lieutenant-Colonel is added to the staff of the officer commanding a brigade.

Paragraph 37 allots to Medical Officers the following substantive ranks :— Paragraph 37.

Brigade-Surgeon-Lieutenant-Colonel,
Surgeon-Lieutenant-Colonel,
Surgeon-Major,
Surgeon-Captain,
Surgeon-Lieutenant.

The appointment of a Brigade-Surgeon-Lieutenant-Colonel was to be made on the recommendation of the Brigadier after consultation with the principal Medical Officer of the district. Paragraph 58.

Section 11, paragraph 60, Appointment and promotion of Medical Officers. First appointments of Medical Officers were, in all cases, to be to the rank of Surgeon-Lieutenant, who was to be allowed to every corps not entitled to a Medical Officer on the establishment, his appointment ceasing whenever the corps should be called out on active service.

Paragraph 62. Corps entitled to a Medical Officer of substantive rank were to be entitled, if having twelve or more companies, to four Medical Officers, if having less than twelve companies, to three.

Paragraph 64. The promotion of all Medical Officers was to be submitted to the Military Secretary and be made on the recommendation of the Commanding Officer who was to support his recommendation by a certificate of service. If so duly recommended Surgeon-Lieutenants would be promoted to the rank of Surgeon-Captain on completion of three years' service and on obtaining the necessary certificate of proficiency. Surgeon-Captains, similarly recommended, to be promoted Surgeon-Major after 15 years' service, and Surgeon-Majors promoted Surgeon-Lieutenant-Colonel after 20 years' service.

Paragraph 69, Supplementary Acting Chaplains. The allowance of one Acting Chaplain to each corps, might, to meet the local requirements of scattered corps, be supplemented by the appointment of additional Acting Chaplains, with the approval in each case of the Secretary of State.

Paragraph 258a, Firing of subalterns. Subalterns were required to fire the individual practices of the annual course, their performances to be included in the figures of merit of the company to which they belonged.

Paragraph 365a, Officers at School of Signalling. Volunteer officers attached to the corps of army signallers were to be permitted to attend a course of instruction at the School of Army Signalling, Aldershot, for a period not exceeding three months.

Paragraph 458a. Volunteer Officers having 20 years' commissioned service, not necessarily consecutive, might be granted a decoration designated "The Volunteer Officers' Decoration." Honorary colonels of corps with the necessary qualifying service to be eligible for this decoration. Half the time served in the ranks to count towards qualifying service.

This decoration was to be granted "for good and long service."

Paragraph 460a, Finance Committee. A finance committee of a corps was to be appointed, consisting of not less than 3 members beside the Commanding Officer, "to aid that officer in the management of the finances of the corps." The committee was to be responsible for limiting the expenditure of the grants made from public funds to purposes sanctioned by the regulations, for presenting annually to the corps a correct statement of the receipts and expenditure of such funds, and for advising the Commanding Officer from time to time as to the financial condition of the corps. Orders to tradesmen and other contracts were to be given and made by the Commanding Officer, and the committee were warned against entering into personal responsibility by giving orders or making contracts.

Officers of Volunteers authorised to perform the duty of an Adjutant during his absence on sick or excess leave, or on duty, were to be granted, instead of the Adjutant, lodging, fuel and light, servants' allowance and forage and stable allowance (if keeping a horse) at army rates. Paragraph 491, Acting Adjutants.

The allowance for signalling was to be granted to one officer and one non-commissioned officer per unit, who should be in possession of the signalling certificate, if an establishment of one regimental instructor, one regimental assistant-instructor and six signallers (two non-commissioned officers and four men) were maintained, and if the signallers annually passed the requisite test for badges. Paragraph 566, Special Capitation allowance, Signalling.

The test was defined by paragraph 879 as follows:— The Test.

Units, to qualify for badges, must obtain a figure of merit of 325 in the following subjects:—

(*a*)—Sending with and reading the large flag

(*b*)—Reading the small flag.

(*c*)—Reading the lamp.

(*d*)—Sending a service message on the small flag through a transmitting station.

The minimum rate of reading correctly from and sending a test message with the different instruments is laid down.

The Staff of Volunteer Brigades were to have the same allowances as Volunteers for attendance at and travelling to and from a brigade camp. Paragraph 579a, Corps allowances, Staff Brigade.

Non-commissioned officers or men admitted to a military hospital on account of injuries received in the performance of military duty were to be free of charge. Hospital provision.

In Volunteer Rifle Corps wearing the old pattern busby, the feathers or horsehair on the lower part of the plume to be of light green, when the corps was clothed in green, and of the colour of the facings when the corps was clothed in scarlet or grey. Paragraph 857, Uniform.

Patrol jackets Paragraph 895a. The serge patrol jacket, of the pattern approved for officers of the Regular Army, silver being substituted for gold and an Austrian knot on the sleeves might be adopted for full dress and undress, but all officers belonging to the same corps must be dressed alike. The tunic was obligatory for all officers attending at Court, levées, or at public ceremonies apart from the men.

Paragraph 928a, Cadet Corps. Cadet Corps, if on parade with the Volunteer Corps to which they were attached, were to take precedence with that corps; if with other corps, in the absence of their own, to take precedence after those corps; if on parade with Cadet Corps only, each corps to take the precedence of the corps to which it belonged.

Cadet Battalions, paragraph 947. Officers serving in the Militia might be recommended for appointments as Honorary Major in Command, Honorary Captain, Honorary Subaltern or acting Adjutant; but Volunteer Officers, while serving, might not hold any appointments in Cadet Battalions.

1893, Jan. 7, 'Army Order.' Number to be present at Brigade Camp. The Army Order of January, 1893,—the issue of Army Orders instead of Regulations or Circulars, from this date, in connection with the Volunteers, is significant—contained a very important and beneficial change in the regulations as to brigade camps. According to paragraph 283 of the Volunteer Regulations of 1892 no brigade camp could be formed unless there was a total strength present of 1,050 of all ranks. Under the new Order a brigade camp must consist of not less than three battalions, and any battalion not 300 strong at least was only to receive the allowance for a regimental camp. The minimum number for a brigade camp was thus reduced from 1,050 to 900.

Volunteer Regulations, 1893, paragraph 24a, Cyclist Sections. The Regulations of 1893 introduced a new and valuable auxiliary to the Volunteer service. I refer to the cyclist. Cyclist sections were authorised in a Volunteer Infantry battalion and were to consist of 1 officer, 2 non-commissioned officers, 12 to 20 privates and 1 bugler.

The section might be formed as soon as an officer or a non-commissioned officer and any privates were accepted by the Commanding Officer as eligible, and would be included in the authorised establishment of the battalion. In the case of a battalion having its companies scattered, the section might consist of sub-sections belonging to each or any of the local companies. The section commander was desired to assemble all or some of the sub-sections under his own command as often as possible.

The approval of the General Officer commanding the district was necessary to the formation of a section of more than 12 privates. In appendix XII. to the Regulations will be found very carefully drafted instructions concerning the formation of these companies and for the guidance of officers commanding the sections. An officer was to be specially qualified for the post, possess energy, sagacity and self-resource, and a fair knowledge of tactics and military duties in the field. The men must be good riders, pronounced medically fit and with good eyesight. A knowledge of military sketching and army signalling was to be desired. The officer and non-commissioned officers ought to possess riding powers at least equal, if not superior, to those of the average rank and file.

Appendix xii.

Selection of Officer.

Of the Men.

The officer to be armed with a revolver and also carry a field glass. The sword, when carried, was to be attached to the machine. The non-commissioned officers and men were to be armed with rifles and bayonets and the former were to carry whistles. Every member should possess a good general knowledge of the construction of cycles and be able to make adjustments and execute simple repairs. A competent cycle repairer should, if possible, be included in the ranks of each section.

Arms, &c.

Cycle repairs.

The uniform was to consist of:—

Patrol jacket, knickerbocker breeches, spats, active service cap, hose tops, great-coats, accoutrements.

When on the march the officer was to take up such a position as would best enable him to superintend the movements; the bugler to accompany him; a leader was to be detailed to regulate the pace according to the directions of the commander; the section was to march on as large a front as the width of the road and the traffic would admit. The officer was to acquaint himself with the rules concerning giving, transmitting and delivering messages in the field and train his men therein.

Cycling drills ordered by the Commanding Officer and of not less than one hour's duration might be counted towards the number of drills required for efficiency.

Appendix v, Drills for Cyclists.

In the case of actual mobilization for service, or whenever the various battalions of a brigade were assembled as a brigade, they were to be under the command of the officer commanding the brigade. At all other times the dispositions as regards inspections, discipline and other administrative work were to be carried on by officers commanding battalions, through officers commanding regimental districts and the general officer commanding the

Paragraph 26a, Formation of Brigade, Command.

district. These latter, however, were enjoined to consult the officer commanding a brigade on all matters of importance affecting the battalions of the brigade generally.

Supply Detachment, Section 27. The Captain of the Supply Detachment instituted in 1891 might, under the Regulations of 1893, be made supernumerary in his Volunteer Battalion if recommended by his Commanding Officer and the General Officer commanding the district.

Paragraph 875a. A badge was prescribed for this Detachment. It was to be worked in silver thread on cloth of Brunswick-green colour, the crown in centre being raised, and was to be worn on the left arm immediately above the elbow.

Paragraph 53. First appointment and promotion of Captains and Field Officer. Recommendations for first appointment to the rank of Captain or Field Officer were to be submitted to the Military Secretary through General Officers commanding districts. If the appointment involved the supersession of any other officer reasons for such supersession were to accompany the recommendation. Promotions to the ranks of Captain and Field Officer, with reasons for supersession, were to be made in like manner.

Appointment of Staff Officers of Brigades, paragraph 58. Brigadiers were to submit their recommendations of officers for appointment to the Brigade Staff through the General Officer commanding the district.

Paragraph 58a. Brigade-Majors were, if possible, to be selected from among retired Officers of the Regular Forces, but Aides-de-camp might be chosen from among either retired officers or officers of the Militia, the Yeomanry or Volunteers.

Paragraph 58b. The Brigade Supply and Transport Officer was, if possible, to belong to one of the battalions of the Brigade—he would be seconded in his Volunteer Battalion, if recommended, but in that case capitation allowances would not be drawn on his account by the battalion.

Paragraph 58c. The Brigade - Surgeon - Lieutenant - Colonel was to be recommended by the Brigadier, after consultation with the principal Medical Officer of the district.

Paragraph 58d. There was to be no fixed limit to the tenure of the appointments dealt with in paragraphs 58, 58d, except in the case of the Brigade Major, who would hold appointment for five years and be eligible for periodical extensions of two years if strongly recommended and not over the age of 55.

Paragraph 58e. Officers serving in the Regular forces not to be eligible for appointment to the brigade staff.

The ranks of Medical Officers were fixed as follows:— Brigade-Surgeon-Lieutenant-Colonel (on staff only), Surgeon-Lieutenant-Colonel (after twenty years' service as Medical Officer), Surgeon-Major (after 15 years' service as Medical Officer), Surgeon-Captain (after 3 years' service as Medical Officer, if qualified, and a vacancy existed), Surgeon-Lieutenant (on first appointment). Promotion to the rank of Brigade-Surgeon-Lieutenant-Colonel was to be made by selection as vacancies occurred in the several Volunteer Infantry brigades.

Paragraph 60, Appointment and promotion of Medical Officer.

The 99th paragraph contained the novel provision that Members of Parliament should not be seconded as officers of Volunteers.

Paragraph 99, Members of Parliament.

A brigade camp was, in future, to consist of not less than three battalions. The General Officer commanding the district in which a brigade camp was held was, after his inspection of the camp, to make a special report on it to the Adjutant General, enclosing a report in detail from the brigadier.

Brigade Camps, paragraphs 283 and 279.

Classes for officers of the Medical Staff Corps and for Medical Officers were to be formed at Aldershot; for Infantry Officers at Aldershot and London. Officers of the Medical Staff Corps were to be allowed to attend an Infantry School of instruction provided they received no allowances and the vacancies were not required for the Militia or Volunteer Infantry.

Schools of Instruction, paragraphs 5, 294, et seq.

Candidates for commissions in the Volunteer force might be attached to Schools of Instruction if they desired it, but they were not to be entitled to allowances. An officer wishing to join a class was to apply through his Commanding officer. No Infantry officer could join the classes till he had obtained a certificate signed by his Adjutant and Commanding Officer that he had been properly instructed in the manual and firing exercises and in parts I. and II., Infantry drill, if the officer wished to obtain a Captain's or Subaltern's certificate, parts I. II. and III. if he required a Field Officer's certificate. An officer of the Volunteer Medical Staff Corps and a Volunteer Medical Officer, before receiving a certificate from the School of Instruction, must prove his knowledge by being specially tested in the elementary drill required, unless he already possessed a certificate of proficiency.

Paragraph 296.

Officers and non-commissioned officers of Infantry brigades might join classes at Aldershot for a fortnight's course and on passing through the course in a satisfactory manner would receive a certificate to that effect from the officer commanding Army Service corps, Aldershot.

Classes of instruction for the Supply Detachment, paragraph 346.

Examination in foreign languages, paragraph 360a.

Officers were to be allowed to present themselves for examination in Russian, Turkish, Arabic, Persian and German, at the same time and under the same conditions as officers of the Regular forces. They were not, however, to be eligible for the rewards offered by Army Order 248 of 1890.

Paragraph 374a, Discipline.

This paragraph reminds Volunteers that they become subject to military law—

1—When they join a camp with the Regular forces.

2—Assemble for training or exercise with any portion of the Regular forces; or

3—With any portion of the Militia when subject to Military law.

Army Act, 1881.

It will be useful, perhaps, here to set out the section of the Army Act of 1881 dealing with the same subject.

By the 8th sub-section of section 176 it is provided that it shall be the duty of the Commanding Officer of any part of the Volunteer force not in actual military service, when he knows that any non-commissioned officers or men belonging to that force are about to enter upon any service which will render them subject to military law, to provide for their being informed that they will become so subject, and for their having an opportunity of abstaining from entering on that service.

Military Lands Act, 1892, paragraph 466.

Sub-section 7 of section 6 of the Regulations of 1893 is concerned with the purchase of land by Volunteer Corps, under the provisions of the Military Lands Act 1892, which enabled Volunteer corps, with the consent of the Secretary of State, themselves to purchase land under that Act for military purposes. The Secretary's consent was not to be given till he was satisfied, by the report of an Inspector, that the land was capable of being used for such purposes "with due regard to the safety and convenience of the public."

County or Borough Council might acquire land for Volunteers.

The Council of a county or borough might, at the request of one or more Volunteer Corps, purchase under that Act and hold land on behalf of the Volunteer Corps for military purposes.

With certain exceptions the compulsory purchase clauses of the Lands Clauses Acts were incorporated with the Military Lands Act.

Section 5.

Power was given to Volunteer Corps, with the consent of the Secretary of State, to borrow from the Public Works Loan Commissioners the purchase money on the security of the land itself and of any grant to the corps out of money provided by Parliament. Borough Councils were also empowered to borrow the money needed for any such purchase by them. There are the usual provisions for repayment within a period not exceeding 50 years.

We have already seen that Volunteer Sergeants retiring after ten years' service might be permitted to retain their rank and wear the uniform of their corps. By the Regulations of 1894 a like privilege was extended to Sergeant-Instructors. By section 152 the services of a Sergeant-Instructor might be retained, with his consent, for a period not exceeding two years beyond the age fixed for his discharge.

Volunteer Regulations, 1894, part 1.

Paragraph 131. Sergeant-Instructors.

The requirements for efficiency as contained in the forms in the appendix to these Regulations shew some variation on former issues :—

Efficiency, paragraph 187.

FORM OF CERTIFICATE.

1—That A.B., No. , was duly enrolled in the muster roll of the Volunteer Rifle Corps, on the day of , and is actually a member of the corps on this date.

2—That he does not belong to the Regular, Militia, Yeomanry, or Army Reserve (including Enrolled Pensioners), forces; and that he is not enrolled in any other Volunteer Corps.

3—That he attended during the twelve months ending the 31st October, 18 , drills of this corps ordered by the Commanding Officer; each of such drills being of not less than one hour's duration.

4 (a)—For the 35/- Grant for the Trained Volunteer: That he fired (21, 42 or 63) rounds of ball ammunition in class firing during the year and passed into the 2nd class.

(b)—For the 10/- Grant for the Trained Volunteer: That he fired three times in the 3rd class during the year, firing each time 21 rounds of ball ammunition, and that in one of those trials he made 20 points.

5—In the case of a recruit: That he attended the lessons and drills referred to in Table A, Appendix viii., Volunteer Regulations.

6 (a)—For the 35/- Grant for the recruit: That he fired 42 rounds of ball ammunition in class firing during the year and passed into the 2nd class.

(b)—For the 10/- Grant for the recruit: That he fired 42 rounds of ball ammunition in class firing during the year and made 30 points.

7—That he possessed a competent knowledge of the drill and manœuvring of a company, as laid down in Infantry drill, and the manual exercises.

8—That he was present at the last annual inspection of the corps (or absent with leave or from certified sickness).

The drills referred to in paragraph 3 of the certificate are: for recruits, if present at inspection, 30 squad, company, battalion (including the inspection), or musketry instruction drills. If absent (with leave or from certified sickness), 32 such drills.

For the 2nd year: if present at inspection, 30 squad, company, battalion (including the inspection), or musketry drills or such number, not less than nine of company or battalion drills (including inspection), three of which should have been battalion drills, as would, with the number of the previous year, amount to 60.

If absent from inspection with leave or from certified sickness the total drills must be brought up to 62.

For 3rd and 4th and subsequent years also, for Volunteers enrolled before November 1st, 1879: If present at inspection 9 company and battalion drills (including inspection), of which 3 at least battalion drills, 11 such drills if absent as aforesaid.

In cases where a Volunteer belonged to an organized cyclist section, cycling drills ordered by Commanding Officer, and of not less than one hour's duration, to be counted toward the total number of efficiency drills.

(a)—For recruits and 2nd year Volunteers: 10 cycling drills of any kind.

Cyclist Corps

(b)—For Volunteers in 3rd and subsequent years: 3 cycling battalion or 3 cycling company drills.

Medical Staff Corps Certificate.

Medical Staff Corps Certificate.

1—That A. No. was duly enrolled on the muster roll of the company Volunteer Medical Staff Corps on the 18 , and is actually a member of the corps on this date.

2—That he does not belong to the Regular, Militia, Yeomanry or Army Reserve (including Enrolled Pensioner) forces; and that he is not enrolled in any other Volunteer Corps.

3—That he attended during the twelve months ended the 31st October, 18 drills of this corps, ordered by the Commanding Officer; each of such drills being of not less than one hour's duration.

4—That he possesses a competent knowledge of squad, company and bearer company drill, as laid down in the Infantry drill and Manual for the Medical Staff Corps.

5—That he was present (or absent as aforesaid), from the last annual inspection of the corps.

The drills referred to in paragraph 3 of the certificate are:—

For recruits: If present at inspection, 16 bearer company and 20 other drills (including inspection). If absent from inspection as aforesaid 16 bearer company and 22 other drills.

In 2nd year: If present at inspection, 16 bearer company and 20 other drills (including inspection), or such number not less than 8 bearer company and 9 other drills (including inspection), as would, with the number of the previous year, amount to 32 bearer company and 40 other drills.

If absent from inspection as aforesaid, 16 bearer company and 22 other drills, or such number not less than 8 bearer company and 11 other drills as would, with the number of the previous year, amount to 32 bearer company and 42 other drills.

For 3rd and subsequent years: If present at inspection, 8 bearer company and 9 other drills (including inspection). If absent from inspection as aforesaid, 8 bearer company and 10 other drills.

BRIGADE BEARER COMPANIES.

The certificate in this case is identical with the last foregoing, except that the Adjutant of the corps testifies to the particulars in clauses 1 and 2 of the certificate and the Commanding Officer of the bearer company to particulars in clauses 3, 4 and 5 of the certificate.

Paragraph 284a, Infantry Brigade camp. Paragraph 288a.

Paragraph 284a of the Regulations required that of every three attendances by a battalion in camp, one at least should be in a brigade camp. A battalion belonging to an Infantry brigade would not be allowed to attend a regimental camp more than twice out of every three attendances in camp, save under very exceptional circumstances.

Examination in tactics, &c., part 1, section 5, paragraph 356.

Officers of Volunteers, except Medical Officers, Veterinary Officers and Chaplains, might present themselves for examination in Tactics, Field Fortification and Military Topography and, except Chaplains only, in Military Law, at the same time as officers of the Regular forces in the manner laid down in the Queen's Regulations.

District Classes, paragraph 366.

Classes for instruction in Signalling of Volunteer Officers, except Medical and Veterinary Officers and Chaplains, and of non-commissioned officers, except those of the Medical Staff Corps, were to be formed in each district whenever a sufficient number of candidates was forthcoming.

Paragraph 449a, Leave of absence.

Officers who contemplated being absent from the drills of their corps for periods of not less than three months were to notify their intention in writing to their Commanding Officer, assigning reasons.

Paragraph 458f, Long Service Medal.

Volunteers, including those who had retired after completing 20 years' service, and officers who had served in the ranks but had not qualified for the Volunteer Officers' Decoration, would, on completion of 20 year's service in the Volunteer force, be granted a medal designated "The Volunteer Long Service Medal," provided that they were recommended by their present or former Commanding Officer in manner prescribed. Names of recipients to be promulgated in Army Orders.

Camp allowances, paragraph 573.

The following allowances were to be granted for each person whose attendance at camp reckoned towards qualifying him for the efficiency capitation grant.

Brigade camps, camps with Regular forces, 2/- daily allowance, (representing ordinary pay, subsistence &c. for a period not less than 3 nor exceeding 6 days); 4/- for time occupied in travelling; and 1d. a mile *viaticum* up to 8/-. In Regimental Camps, Infantry Medical Staff Corps as above, except that there was no allowance for time occupied in reaching or leaving camp and the *viaticum* is restricted to 4/-

Section 3, paragraph 875, Badges.

Stretcher bearers of Volunteer Corps were to wear on parading as such an armlet of special pattern, similar to that worn in the regular army, viz., a white web band with the letters S. B. in red upon it.

Paragraph 909c, Uniform.

Officers of Volunteer Corps which had adopted the territorial uniform of a Light Infantry regiment (and consequently wore green helmets), were to wear green forage caps.

Paragraph 934a, Cadet Corps.

Cadet corps and cadet battalions were to be allowed camp equipment on the same scales and conditions as other corps.

Cadet battalions were to be provided with unserviceable or "D. P." arms, and part worn slings, for drill purposes only, to the full extent of their enrolled strength, if required; those arms not to be used for firing ball cartridge.

Volunteer Regulations, 1895.

The Volunteer Regulations of 1895 call for little comment.

Medical Staff Corps, paragraph 169.

Paragraph 169 defined the subjects for examination for the certificate of proficiency in the case of sergeants of the Volunteer Medical Staff Corps and brigade bearer companies.

1—Practical examination in bearer company drill.

2—An examination as to the duties of a commander of a guard and the mode of marching reliefs and posting sentries.

3—A written and oral examination in the subjects laid down in the Manual for the Medical Staff Corps for promotion to the rank of corporal in that corps.

Instruction, subalterns, paragraph 258a.

The provision in previous Regulations requiring subalterns to fire the individual practices of the annual course is varied by the addendum that they are not to be required to do so in order to earn the capitation grant. Their performances were to be included in the figure of merit of the company to which they belonged.

Paragraph 261a, Best marksman defined.

The best marksman in a company was defined to be that marksman who, not having had to fire a second trial in the 1st class, made the highest aggregate number of points in his class firing.

Camps, paragraph 276a.

There were to be no regimental hospitals, but circular single linen tents in due proportion were allowed for battalions in camp. Those men, however, who were likely to require prolonged treatment were to be removed either to the nearest military hospital or to their homes.

Instruction by permanent Staff, paragraph 353.

The examining board for a Field Officer was now determined to be a Field Officer of the Regular forces (who must be senior to the officer under examination), assisted by two senior captains of the Regular forces, or one senior captain of the Regular forces and an Adjutant of Militia, Yeomanry, or Volunteers.

Forfeiture of Medal, paragraph 458m.

How jealous was the War Office of the dignity of the force, a jealousy of which the force should be the last to complain, is shewn by the provision that when the conduct of an officer or a Volunteer, after he had been awarded the long service medal, had been such as to disqualify him from wearing it, he might be deprived of it by the Secretary of State, by whom also it might be subsequently restored.

Cadet Corps establishment, paragraph 927.

An establishment was to be allotted to every cadet corps on its formation in accordance with the establishments of Volunteers of the arm of the service to which the cadet corps was attached.

Disbandment, paragraph 942.

A cadet corps whose enrolled strength had fallen below 40 was to be disbanded unless there was established, to the satisfaction of the Secretary of State, reasonable expectation of the number of members being increased.

Volunteer Regulations, 1896.

One at least of the alterations introduced by the Regulations of 1896 was of no slight importance. Volunteer Officers will have no difficulty in determining to which one I refer.

Commanding Officers' tenure, paragraph 55a.

All appointments made to the command of a Volunteer Corps were, subject to the age limit, of which hereafter, to be held for a period of four years, and any extensions of tenure to be for a like period, and then only granted on the recommendation of General Officers commanding districts.

Retirement by age, paragraph 111.

All officers, (including quartermasters, medical officers, veterinary officers and chaplains), were to be liable to retirement on attaining the age of 60, unless duly granted an extension of service, and retirement was to be compulsory in all cases at the age of 67, without exception.

Resignation of Commandant, paragraph 114.

When the establishment of a corps entitled it to two Lieutenant-Colonels, the senior was to bear the title of "Commandant"; which term, however, was to be a designation, not a rank.

Physical Examination, paragraph 156.

Every person offering himself for enrolment as a Volunteer was now, for the first time, required to pass a physical exmination by the Medical Officer of the corps. Previous Regulations had merely defined the height and chest measurements. Paragraph 156 of the Regulations of 1895 required the Medical Officer to satisfy himself:—

(*a*)—That the candidate's vision was sufficiently good to enable him to see clearly with either eye at the required distance as laid down in Army Form I., 1,220.

(*b*)—That his hearing was good.

(*c*)—That his chest was capacious and well-formed, and that his heart and lungs were sound.

The standards of height and chest measurement for the Rifle and Medical Staff Corps (except for boys enrolled for the purpose of being trained as trumpeters, buglers, or bandsmen), were:—

Height—5 feet 3 inches; and upwards.

Chest measurement—under 5 feet 6 inches, 32 inches; 5 feet 6 inches and under 5 feet 10 inches, 33 inches; 5 feet 10 inches and over, 34 inches.

Instruction, Brigade Majors, paragraph 345a.

Brigade-Majors of Volunteers were granted permission to be attached for instruction to Infantry brigades at Aldershot for a period of one month.

Paragraph 349.

Encouragement was given to officers to avail themselves of the permission to attend Schools of Instruction or be attached to the regular forces by withholding from those who received their instruction from the Adjutant or Sergeant Instructor the outfit allowance to which I shall presently refer.

When an officer had passed in tactics, field fortification, military topography, organization, equipment, Russian, Turkish, Arabic, Persian and German, the letter (Q) was to be affixed to his name in the monthly army lists.

Distinguishing letters for examinations, paragraph 358.

A subaltern officer, or a captain appointed direct to that rank, gazetted on or after 13th March, 1896, on being first granted a commission in the Volunteer service, either as a subaltern or captain, was to be granted the sum of £20 in aid of his outfit, payable as follows:—

Outfit allowance, paragraph 514a.

(*a*)—£10 on appointment,

(*b*)—£10 after undergoing a month's course of instruction at a School or with the regular forces, and on obtaining the required certificate for the arm to which he belonged.

The allowance was also to be granted on the same conditions for a subaltern or captain re-appointed after the 13th March, 1896, provided he had left the Volunteer service before that date.

In the case of an officer who, from any cause except ill-health or death, failed to serve three years as efficient, or failed to qualify for the second half of the allowance within that time, the whole of the amount paid to him in aid of his outfit was to be refunded, and if not repaid by him personally, the funds of his corps were to be liable for the refund. Paragraph 514b.

The capitation allowance of 17/6 was to be granted for each efficient in excess of the number for whom an extra half capitation grant was issued under Army Order 76 of 1896. Capitation on increase of efficients, paragraph 567a.

The "higher grant" of £1 15s. od. was to be granted subject to the conditions as to possession of equipment &c. for Paragraph 558, Higher Grant.

(*a*)—Every Field Officer, Veterinary Officer and Acting Chaplain, who had attended, with his unit, the drills prescribed for efficients of his arm of the service in the 3rd and 4th years. The presence of the Acting Chaplain with his corps in camp was to suffice to entitle the corps to the allowance on his account.

(*b*)—For every quartermaster certified by his Commanding Officer to have satisfactorily performed his duties.

(*c*)—For every captain and subaltern who had attended with his unit the drills prescribed for efficients of his arm of the service in their third and fourth years, or been exempted therefrom by reason of being attached to the regular army for duty, under the authority of the Secretary of State.

(*d*)—For every Medical Officer who had attended with his unit at six drills (including inspection), or at eight if absent from inspection with leave or from certified illness.

(*e*)—For every trumpeter or bugler (except boys), borne on the authorised establishment, duly qualified as such, and who had attended the number of drills prescribed for efficients in his arm of the service in their third and fourth years.

(*f*)—For every boy serving as trumpeter, bugler or bandsman (to the number of two for each company), duly qualified as such and who had been officially present during the number of drills prescribed for efficients in their third and fourth years.

The chevrons on great coats were to correspond in all respects with those worn by the Regular forces. Badges were to be in gold on shoulder-straps of silver gimp or cord, and in silver on cloth shoulder-straps. Mounted Officers were to wear steel spurs and they might also wear high boots as authorised for officers of the Uniform. Paragraph 671. Badges of Officers' rank Paragraph 905.

Paragraph 907. Swords and scabbards.

Regulars. Officers of Medical Staff Corps and Rifles, clothed in scarlet, to wear brass spurs at court, at levées, and in the evening. All officers under the rank of General Officer to wear steel scabbards.

On retirement after completing not less than 5 years' service in this appointment, officers commanding Volunteer Infantry Brigades were permitted to wear the uniform of a Brigadier-General on the retired list.

Volunteer Regulations, 1897.

There are innovations in the Regulations of 1897 calling for special notice.

Establishments, paragraph 4.

The maximum authorised establishment of a corps included all ranks except secondary and honorary officers and supernumerary second lieutenants.

Second Lieutenant, paragraph 51.

A second lieutenant might be recommended for promotion to the rank of lieutenant, provided he was qualified and that the establishment of lieutenants was not thereby exceeded.

Gazetting of appointments paragraph 115.

Unless otherwise stated in the *Gazette*, appointments, promotions and resignations were to take date following that of the *Gazette*. No ante-date would be given after the publication in the *Gazette*.

Attendance at Inspection, paragraph 215.

A provision eminently calculated to secure attendance at inspections was that of paragraph 215, to the effect that unless at least two-thirds of a corps (exclusive of members of the brigade bearer company) were on parade, the inspection would not take place.

Expenditure, paragraph 613, A.B.

Some alteration was made in the services upon which the capitation and other allowances might be expended. The providing and maintenance of head-quarters, drill grounds, ranges etc., were made a first charge. The following expenditure was only to be allowed if, after the above charges had been provided for, such expenditure would not lead to the income for the year being exceeded:—payments to men in camp, band expenses (not to exceed 7½% of the efficiency and proficiency grants), prizes (not to exceed 5% of such grants).

The ordinary expenditure of a corps was not to exceed its income for the year, unless the deficiency could be immediately met from private funds. When extraordinary expenditure was contemplated the sanction of the Secretary of State must first be obtained. All buildings, corps property, must be kept fully insured against fire. The letter R was directed to be worn with their uniform on the shoulder-straps by officers retiring with honorary rank, retiring sergeant-instructors, sergeants and honorary

Uniform, paragraphs 863a, 103, 131. 174, 185.

members. For officers and non-commissioned officers, not below the rank of sergeant, it was to be in silver or silver embroidery. For other ranks, in bronze or white metal.

Badges, Signallers. Paragraph 879 (2).

To qualify for badges signallers must attain the standard of proficiency laid down in the signalling instructions.

Military Lands Act, 1897.

In this year a further Military Lands Act, cited as that of 1897, was passed and is so easily accessible that it is unnecessary to set forth its provisions.

Volunteer Regulations, 1898. Retirement by age.

The changes effected by the Regulations of 1898 were of no great moment. By paragraph 111 Chaplains were excepted from the rule retiring officers at the age of sixty.

Course for Sergeant-Instructors, paragraph 347.

Previous Regulations had provided for one sergeant-instructor from every corps being sent for one month's instruction to the regimental depôt. Paragraph 347 of the Regulations of 1898 required that *all* the sergeant-instructors of every Volunteer Rifle Corps should be so sent for one week and the course was to include instruction in recruiting duties. A privilege of possibly much value was now accorded to them. The Regulations of the preceding year had permitted sergeant-instructors to impart instruction in drill in local schools, and I doubt not many a civilian reader of these pages can recall the "Drill-master" of his school days. The Regulations of 1898 were more elastic. They debarred members of the permanent staff from engaging in any kind of trade, but, with the consent of the General Officer commanding the district, they might accept such employment as did not interfere with the performance of their military duties.

Trade or civil occupation, paragraph 431.

Outfit allowance, paragraph 514a.

The allowance of £20 was extended to quartermasters, payable as to first instalment on grant of commission and as to second instalment on obtaining certificate of Commanding Officer as to efficiency. Also to surgeon-lieutenants and surgeon-captains appointed direct to that rank, the first instalment to be paid on appointment to the establishment and the second on obtaining the Medical Officer's certificate after passing through a course of instruction at Training School.

Cadet Corps companies and battalions Paragraph 925, et seq.

There were new Regulations as to the composition, formation, establishment, designation and procedure of Cadet Corps.

Uniform, paragraph 914.

Brigade Majors, Supply Officers, (administrative), and Aides-de-camp, if not in possession of the uniform of a Volunteer unit, were allowed to wear the uniform of their rank, with the addition of the distinctions worn by officers holding similar appointments in the Regular forces, but with silver substituted for gold for those distinctions.

Volunteer Regulations, 1899.

The Regulations of 1899 contain sundry provisions to which attention should be called.

Examination for promotion.

By clause 168, a Rifle Volunteer was ineligible for promotion to the rank of Sergeant unless he had passed the Captain's examination in the following subjects:—

(*a*)—Practical examination in the drill and manœuvring of a company.

(*b*)—The command of a company in battalion.

(*c*)—Duties of commander of a guard and mode of marching reliefs and posting sentries.

(*d*)—Practical knowledge of the manual and firing exercises, aiming, drill and blank firing.

(*e*)—Knowledge of and competency to superintend target practice.

Before promotion to the rank of quartermaster-sergeant a Volunteer must pass in the same subjects as a quartermaster.

Trained Rifle Volunteers, paragraph 260.

In order to earn the "higher grant" of 35/- the trained Volunteer (under the rank of lance-sergeant) must have fired 28 rounds of ball ammunition in the compulsory individual practices of the annual course during the year, have passed into the 2nd class and have then fired 14 rounds in the compulsory collective practices.

The trained Volunteer who was a colour-sergeant, sergeant or lance-sergeant, in order to earn the 35/- grant, must have fired 28 rounds of ball ammunition in the individual practices of the compulsory annual course during the year, and have passed into the 2nd class and must also have commanded a section, of the minimum strength of 4 rank and file, during the compulsory collective practices.

In order to pass into the 2nd class he must, in order to earn the "lower grant" of 10/-, have made at least 27 points in one of his trials in the compulsory individual practices of the annual course during the year.

Recruits.

For the recruit to earn the "higher grant" he must have not only attended the preliminary drills but have completed the recruits' course of 49 rounds of ball ammunition during the year, and passed into the 2nd class; or, failing to pass into the 2nd class, he must, in order to earn the "lower grant" of 10/-, have completed the recruits' course of 49 rounds of ball ammunition during the year and have made 35 points, in addition to having attended the preliminary drill.

The best marksman in a company or battalion was defined to be that efficient Volunteer who, not having had to fire a second trial, made the highest aggregate number of points in the individual practices of the annual course. Best Marksman, paragraph 261a.

A limited number of non-commissioned officers to be permitted to attend the course of instruction at the School of Musketry at Hythe. They must be colour-sergeants, sergeants or lance-sergeants, holding the position of half-company or section commanders intending to remain active members of their corps for at least four years. N.C.O.'s at Hythe, paragraph 348a.

Volunteer officers having 20 years' service, which need not be continuous, might be granted a decoration designated "The Volunteer Officers' Decoration." The following would be allowed to reckon towards the 20 years:— Volunteer Officers' Decoration, paragraph 458a.

(*a*)—All commissioned service in the Volunteer force, including service as honorary-colonel;

(*b*)—Half the time served in the ranks of a Volunteer Corps;

(*c*)—All service qualifying for the Colonial Auxiliary forces Officers' Decoration, provided that at least 10 years' qualifying service had been spent in a Volunteer force of Great Britain.

Volunteers might be granted a medal designated "The Volunteer Long Service Medal," after 20 years' service (which need not be continuous) in the Volunteer force. The medal might also be granted to Volunteers who had retired after completing 20 years' service, and to officers who had served in the ranks but had not qualified for the Volunteer Officers' Decoration. Volunteer long service medal, paragraph 458g.

An allowance of £20 in aid of outfit was to be granted to the undermentioned officers on first appointment to the Volunteer force, if gazetted on or after March 13, 1896; or on re-appointment, if the officer had left the Volunteer service before that date:— Outfit allowance, paragraph 514a.

To Field or Company Officer.	On obtaining the appropriate certificate after a month's instruction (or in the case of Field Officers of the Rifles, a half-month) at a School, or with the Regular forces.
Quartermaster.	On obtaining the certificate of his Commanding Officer that he was proficient.
Medical Officer appointed to the establishment of his unit.	On obtaining his certificate of proficiency.

Efficiency allowance, paragraph 582d.

The "higher grant" of £1 15s. 0d., the efficiency grant, was to be claimed for :—

Every officer of the Volunteer Medical Staff Corps who had attended with the corps, or of an Infantry brigade bearer company who had attended with his bearer company, at six drills (including inspection), or at eight drills if absent from inspection with leave or through certified sickness. Such drills might, with the sanction of the Commanding Officer, consist of any of the drills prescribed for efficients of the Volunteer Medical Staff Corps or bearer company respectively.

Allowance to Transport section of the Medical Staff Corps, paragraph 595c.

Companies of the Volunteer Medical Staff Corps selected to furnish bearer companies and field hospitals to the Field Army were to be granted, under specified conditions, an allowance of £40 per annum to meet the expenses incidental to procuring the necessary horses.

Prize-shooting Badges, paragraph 880.

Authorised prize shooting badges, including the Queen's Prize and repository badges given by the National Rifle and the National Artillery Associations, were authorised to be worn by Volunteers in uniform on the arm.

Regulations, 1901. Cyclist companies, paragraph 24a.

Previous Regulations had sanctioned Cyclists' *Sections*. We now, (1901), have Cyclist companies, which, with the Secretary of State's permission, might be allowed in all Rifle Volunteer Corps having a total establishment of at least 600. The minimum establishment of a Cyclist company was to be 75. Sections might, as before, be formed in the absence of Cyclist companies.

Precedence of Cadet Officers paragraph 37.

Cadet Corps officers now first to be granted substantive commissions—An officer holding a commission in a cadet corps or cadet battalion would, except in such corps or battalion, rank junior to all other commissioned officers of the Volunteer force.

Hon-Colonels of Medical Staff Corps, paragraph 57.

For Volunteer Medical Staff Corps commanded by a Surgeon-Major, an Honorary-Surgeon-Lieutenant-Colonel Commandant, or, in the case of five or more companies, an honorary-commandant with the rank of Honorary-Surgeon-Colonel might be recommended.

Paragraph 60, Rank of Medical Officers

Promotion of the following Medical Officers was altered as follows:—Surgeon-Lieutenant-Colonel, after 20 years' service as Medical Officer, or on appointment to command a division of 5 companies; Surgeon-Major, after 15 years' service as Medical Officer, or on appointment to command a corps of 2 to 4 companies, or as second in command of a division of 5 companies.

Sergeants of the transport sections in the Volunteer Medical Staff Corps desirous of instruction in transport duties might be attached to the Army Service Corps in the district for such a course as might be considered necessary by the Officer Commanding Army Service Corps. On completion of the course they were to be examined by an Army Service Corps Officer, and, if successful, granted a certificate of efficiency. Sergeants of Transport section, instruction, paragraph 348a.

French is added to the list of languages for examination. French, paragraph 360a.

The allowance for cyclists was to be granted for each efficient member of the cyclist company of an Infantry corps who was able at the annual inspection to satisfy the Inspecting Officer that he was in possession of a suitable cycle and the required equipment. The allowance was to be withheld unless the corps had a cyclist company consisting of at least 75 members and would only extend to the maximum authorised strength of the company. Cyclist allowance, paragraph 366b.

Officers appointed to the staff of a General Officer commanding were to wear regimental uniform with the addition of the staff distinctions detailed in the Dress Regulations, silver being substituted for gold in all cases. Uniform, paragraph 913a.

In 1901, commissioned officers in the proportion of one captain and one lieutenant per company were to be allowed, and they were to be granted commissions, as in ordinary Volunteer corps. They were to be nominated by the officer commanding the Volunteer Corps to which they were affiliated. An officer of the corps might hold either of the above appointments. When the enrolled strength of a cadet corps was not less than 50 boys, under 17 years of age, an additional subaltern might be recommended as second lieutenant. No allowance of any kind, except that of ordinary pay and allowance for an officer of similar rank and arm of the service undergoing an authorised course of instruction, would be admissible for officers of cadet corps or companies as such. Cadet Corps. Commissioned Officers, paragraph 930.

Cadet corps and companies might, with due permission, adopt a special uniform of the following description:—A Norfolk jacket of woollen material of a neutral tint, with roll collar and shoulder-straps, but without facings. Cadet Uniform, paragraph 940.

Trousers of same material as jacket. The designations of the Volunteer Corps to which the Cadet Corps belonged to be worn on the shoulder-straps. Slouch hat of fur or woollen felt of same colour as the jacket and trousers.

Officers, paragraph 947.

Commissioned officers were allowed to each Cadet battalion as follows :—

1 Lieutenant-Colonel (for 6 or more companies),
I Major (for 4 or more companies),
1 Captain per company,
1 Lieutenant ,,
1 Second-Lieutenant ,,
1 Quartermaster,
1 Medical Officer.

These officers, who must be over 17 years of age, were to be recommended by officers commanding Cadet battalions.

An Acting Chaplain and Adjutant would be allowed to each Cadet battalion.

Officers serving in the Militia or Volunteers might be allowed to serve with Cadet battalions, but would not be granted commissions therein, though their names would be shown in the army list as attached thereto for duty.

Officers of Cadet battalions, as such, would only be allowed the ordinary pay and allowance for officers of similar rank and arm of the service undergoing an authorised course of instruction.

Special Army Order, April 22, 1902.

On this date Field Marshal Lord Roberts, Commander-in-Chief, issued in a convenient form certain Volunteer Regulations as to the conditions of efficiency. Such of them as affect the Rifle Volunteers are as follows :—

I.

Conditions of efficiency under this Order.

In order to be reckoned as an efficient and to qualify for the efficiency grant of 35/-, an officer must comply with the following conditions according to his rank or appointment :—

(*a*) Field Officer.

For Field Officer.

Attend (1) the annual inspection and (2) camp or the number of regimental or battalion parades prescribed for a trained Volunteer of his arm of service.

(*b*) Acting Chaplain, Regimental Medical Officer, Veterinary Officer, Quartermaster.

Obtain a certificate from his Commanding Officer that he is competent to execute and has satisfactorily performed all the duties of his appointment during the year.

(c) Battery or Company Officer.

Fulfil with his unit the conditions prescribed for a Volunteer, recruit or trained man, as the case may be, of his arm of the service. For Company Officer.

A Volunteer, in order to be reckoned as efficient and to qualify for the efficiency grant of 35/-, must, unless exempted, attend camp and comply with the conditions prescribed for his arm of the service. For Private.

The Training to be as follows:—

Infantry.

Recruits' training will consist of at least 40 attendances of not less than one hour each, at which, if possible, not less than 4 rank and file are present. At least 20 of these attendances must be made before camp. Recruits' training.

It will include a progressive course of instruction as follows:—

30 attendances in squad and company drill, rifle exercises, care of arms, skirmishing, and 10 attendances in aiming, judging distance, firing exercises, and, where possible, miniature range or target practice.

Company training for trained officers and Volunteers will consist of at least 10 attendances of not less than one hour each, at which not less than one officer, 4 non-commissioned officers and 20 rank and file, exclusive of bandsmen, buglers, pioneers and boys are present. Company training.

It will, as far as possible, include instructions in skirmishing, scouting, outposts, attack and defence and other Field duties.

The instruction should be given bv the Company Commander or, in his absence, (for which sufficient reason must be furnished to the Commanding Officer), by the senior officer assisted by the other officers and non-commissioned officers present.

Camps.—Regimental camps will only be held when specially authorised by the Commander-in-Chief. They will not be sanctioned unless the two previous attendances have been at Brigade camps or camps with Regular forces.—

III.

No corps, (except 1st Orkney, R.G.A. Volunteers, 7th Isle of Man V.B, Liverpool Regiment, and the 7th Volunteer Battalion, Gordon Highlanders) will be exempted by the Commander-in-Chief from attending camp, except for very special reasons, and under no circumstances in two consecutive years.

Officers and Volunteers of corps so exempted will be required to give 6 additional attendances at recruit, company, or battery drill, or, for infantry, battalion drill.

Infantry Corps will be required to hold three parades of the battalion or half battalion (not less than four companies), attendances at which will count towards the six extra attendances.

To constitute a battalion or half battalion parade, not less than one half of the competent officers and 25% of the enrolled strength of the companies present, exclusive of bandsmen, drummers, buglers, pipers, pioneers and boys, must attend. Such parade to last not less than one hour.

Each company must be represented on three occasions, unless specially exempted.

TRAINING AND CAMPS.

1—The training of Volunteer corps in peace will be governed by what they are required to do in war.

2—Owing to limited time and opportunities, it is difficult for Volunteers to obtain thorough instruction in all the duties of a soldier. It is, therefore, important that the annual training of all ranks should be strictly confined to learning and practising only the essentials for war.

* * * * * *

6—The annual training of corps will, as far as possible, be based on a systematic and progressive course of instruction, beginning with the training of recruits and culminating in camp.

7—RECRUITS' TRAINING. The first few months of the Volunteer year should be principally devoted to the instruction of recruit officers and men. No recruit will reckon an attendance at company training, who, in the opinion of the Adjutant, is not sufficiently advanced to take his place in the ranks.

Company training should be completed before the commencement of regimental and battalion training or camp.

* * * * * *

10—The training in camp will invariably be progressive, commencing in the Infantry, for example, with the instruction of the section and company, each under the respective leaders, and ending during the last day or two in camp in the exercise of the battalion or brigade, a working day of an average of six hours being taken as a minimum.

Theoretical instruction by means of lectures, schemes worked out on a map &c. should be imparted on wet days.

All exercises in the field should be preceded by a clear explanation of the work about to be undertaken.

11—The instruction of the Infantry should proceed upon the following lines:—

Scouting and reconnaissance,

Skirmishing,

Attack and defence,

Outpost by day and night,

Advanced and rear guard,

Escorts for guns or convoys,

Minor tactical schemes of company-*v*-company,

Battalion-*v*-battalion,

Blank ammunition and distinguishing marks by opposing forces should invariably be used.

All exercises should conclude with a conference at which officers and non-commissioned officers should be encouraged to explain any action they may have taken. Commanding Officers should seldom interfere with the course of a tactical exercise executed under their supervision. Even if subordinate leaders are making mistakes, unless the mistake is of a character to render the instruction abortive, the exercise should proceed and the mistake be pointed out at the subsequent conference.

Special attention must be devoted to training officers and non-commissioned officers to act on their own initiative and accept responsibility. They should frequently be placed in positions requiring prompt action and ready resource. Such situations, *e. g.*, the sudden introduction into the fight of a superior force, the laying of an ambush or other surprise, a counter attack &c., should be improvised.

This Order in Council, which I produce *verbatim*, substituted a new "Scheme relative to Certificates of Efficiency" in place of the corresponding scheme and certificates then in force:— Order in Council, 11 August, 1902.

1—A Volunteer who is a member of a corps on the 1st November in any year shall be entitled to be deemed an efficient Volunteer during the ensuing 12 months if, subject to the conditions hereinafter prescribed, he has, during the preceding year, fulfilled the requirements stated in the schedule hereto in accordance with regulations made by one of our Principal Secretaries of State.

2—Where the situation and circumstances of any Volunteer Corps in any particular year are such as, in the opinion of the Secretary of State, to create serious obstacles to the fulfilment by any of the Volunteers belonging to that corps of the requirements for efficiency, the Secretary of State shall have power to relax or dispense with one or more of the requirements from any of the Volunteers belonging to such corps in such year, or to substitute equivalent conditions of efficiency.

3—Where any corps shall have been precluded by an epidemic from complying with the requirements herein prescribed, or shall in the first year of its service have encountered exceptional difficulties in the completion of its organization and efficiency of its members, it shall be competent to the Secretary of State to modify or dispense with, so far as applies to such year of service, the stipulated conditions of efficiency of any members of such corps.

4—No corps, except as specified hereunder, will be exempted by the Commander-in-Chief from attending camp, unless for very special reasons, and exemption for two consecutive years will never be granted unless exceptional reasons justify the Secretary of State in specially exercising his power under Articles 2 and 3 hereof.

The following corps are not obliged to attend camp, but are liable to the extra attendances in lieu:—

1st Orkney R.G.A. Volunteers.

7th (Isle of Man) Volunteer Battalion, Liverpool Regiment.

7th Volunteer Battalion, Gordon Highlanders.

5—No Volunteer who is absent from the annual inspection of his corps, except in case of sickness duly certified, or by leave granted in writing for special cause by the Commanding Officer, shall be entitled to be deemed efficient.

6—Where a corps is, by its own default, not inspected during the year, or where the officer inspecting a Volunteer Corps at the annual inspection in any year reports that the corps is not efficient in training and instruction to his satisfaction, or that irregularities have occurred in its training and administration, then, notwithstanding anything hereinbefore provided, the Secretary of State shall have power to direct that none of the Volunteers belonging to the corps shall be deemed efficient.

7—The Commanding Officer, or the inspecting officer, shall have power to direct that a Volunteer shall be deemed non-efficient, if he considers it proper to do so, on account of the want of efficiency of that Volunteer, or on account of his arms or equipments being in bad order and condition.

8—Terms used in this Order, or in the schedule hereto, have the same meanings as they have when used in the Volunteer Act, 1863.

The term "recruit" used in the schedule shall not include a Volunteer who has served for two months in the Royal Navy, Regular Army, Army Reserve, Royal Marines, or Royal Irish Constabulary, or has attended the preliminary drill, or drill on enlistment, or annual training of a Militia unit, or has performed one year's efficient service in the Imperial Yeomanry, the Volunteers, or the permanent forces of a colony, or in the year immediately preceding his enrolment has attended as a member of a cadet corps or cadet battalion, sanctioned by the Secretary of State, the number of drills prescribed for the arm of the service which he has joined.

Recruits who join too late in any year to become efficient therein, may be allowed to reckon attendances made before the 1st November towards the number required for efficiency in the following year.

9—The provisions herein contained shall take effect from the 1st November, 1901.

SCHEDULE V.—VOLUNTEER RIFLE CORPS.

Year of service.	1. Recruits' training.	2. Company training.	3. Musketry.	4. Camp or attachment to the Regular Forces for not less than 6 clear and consecutive days, during which inspection in field duties will take place.	5. Annual inspection.
During 1st year ..	40 attendances (6 additional if the unit is exempted from camp).	.. .. ..	Under the rules and with the exemptions laid down in the Musketry Regulations, but not to exceed the requirements from a soldier of the same arm of the Regular Forces.	Obligatory, unless the corps is exempted by special authority, or in individual cases of sickness duly certified, or of leave granted, under regulations issued by the Secretary of State.	Obligatory, except in case of sickness duly certified, or of leave granted for special cause by the Commanding Officer.
During each subsequent year (also 1st year for men not classed as recruits).	.. .. ..	10 attendances (6 additional if the unit is exempted from camp).			

Note.—1. Staff sergeants, bandsmen, drummers, pipers, fifers, buglers and pioneers will be reckoned as efficient provided they attend the annual inspection and the annual camp or such number of battalion parades as may be prescribed in lieu.

2. Regimental or Brigade Army Service Corps transport. Conditions of efficiency—(1) A competent knowledge of transport duties. (2) Attendance of not less than 3 days with transport in camp (if one is held), and at the annual inspection of transport.

VI.—ROYAL ARMY MEDICAL CORPS (VOLUNTEER) AND BRIGADE BEARER COMPANIES.

	1.	2.	3.	4.
Year of service.	Recruits' training.	Company training.	Camp or attachment to the Regular Forces, for not less than 6 clear and consecutive days, during which inspection in field duties will take place.	Annual inspection.
During 1st year	45 attendances (6 additional if the unit is exempted from camp).	.. ..	Obligatory, unless the unit is exempted by special authority, or in individual cases, of sickness duly certified, or of leave granted, under regulations issued by the Secretary of State.	Obligatory, except in case of sickness duly certified, or of leave granted for special cause by the Commanding Officer.
During each subsequent year (also 1st year for men not classed as recruits).	.. ..	15 attendances (6 additional if the unit is exempted from camp).		

NOTE.—Transport Section, Bearer Companies and Field Hospitals:—The conditions as to efficiency will be the same as regards the number of recruit and company attendances and camp, but attendances may include all exercises and instruction bearing upon Transport duties.

VII.—UNIVERSITY AND PUBLIC SCHOOLS' CORPS.

Members of the 1st (Oxford University) Volunteer Battalion, Oxfordshire Light Infantry, the 4th (Cambridge University) Volunteer Battalion, Suffolk Regiment, the 2nd Bucks (Eton College) Volunteer Rifle Corps, and the 27th Middlesex (Harrow School) Volunteer Rifle Corps, and members of an authorised cadet corps or company belonging to a public school who are enrolled Volunteers, will be required to perform half the number of attendances laid down for their arm of the service. They will be allowed to substitute for six days' attendance in camp a minimum period of 87 consecutive hours, exclusive of Sundays, provided that they attend during the year three days of tactical exercises under local arrangements.

It would be unjust to conclude the review of the various Regulations and the changes they affected without some notice of that excellent feature of the service, the Engineer and the "Royal Transport Corps," formed by the patriotic exertions of the late Mr. Charles Manby, C.E. and a Lieutenant-Colonel in the corps. This corps may be said to be auxiliary to the auxiliaries, though indeed every arm of the service is auxiliary to every other. The Engineer and Royal Transport Corps present a Council of Volunteers formed by (1) eminent civil engineers, (2) general managers of the main railway lines, (3) the chief employers of labour. These officers have the rank of lieutenant-colonel. The functions of the corps include, (*a*) the arrangement and carrying into effect of any sudden and general concentration of troops to oppose invasion; and (*b*) the rapid execution of works upon the railway and lines of defence by the means at the disposal of the great contractors, directed by the Civil Engineers. The ready labour power of this useful corps is estimated at from 12,000 to 20,000 navvies, with tools, barrows and commisariat complete. It has already performed important services in tabulating and printing at great private cost complete timetables and special reports for six general concentrations against possible invasion. A special Return was also prepared by the corps, (the first of its kind), of the entire rolling-stock of all railways in Great Britain. This important work, which is published annually, shows where the requisite number of carriages can be obtained for the composition of Troop trains.* The authors of the "Army Book for the British Empire," published in 1890, writing of this corps, consisting of officers only, state their number at 32; but "as these 32 are men accustomed to the organization and management of the traffic on our great lines of railway, and to other great engineering operations in connection with railways; and as they have in their daily work the most highly trained staffs it is possible to conceive, this *Cadre* in reality represents a probably unequalled organisation for moving troops. Even Volunteers do not usually realize that the railway manager whose name he sees at the top of a page in "Bradshaw" is probably a Volunteer Lieutenant-Colonel, and that all the problems of concentration suggested by the War Office have been worked out in detail by the Railway Volunteer Staff Corps."

The Arms of various periods.

The rifle, it is scarcely necessary to say, has been the distinctive weapon of the Infantry Volunteer since 1859. In that year and down to September, 1870, the use of both the long and short

* Encyclo. Britannica.

Enfield Rifles was sanctioned. In 1870, B. L. Snider Rifles were issued in the manner already explained and were in use to 1884. In 1887 the Regulations then operative sanctioned the Martini-Henry Rifle, which alone continued to be used up to 1896, when, in addition to that rifle, the Magazine Lee-Metford was also authorised and continued in use till 1898 when the Magazine Lee-Enfield Rifle was also authorised in lieu of the Martini-Henry and the Magazine Lee-Metford and the Magazine Lee-Enfield are the authorised arms to this day.

Not half a century has elapsed since the institution of the modern Volunteer Force. During that period scarce a year but has witnessed some important attempt to increase its efficiency, to make of it a really valuable and reliable arm of the national defences. I have, in the preceding pages, detailed at great length the successive steps by which the Volunteer corps have progressed from their small beginnings to whatsoever state of perfection they may be deemed to have attained. We have seen them commenced without uniform save what each individual officer and man might provide for himself, or be indebted for to a generous public; without arms save those furnished in like manner to the uniform; without instructors save such as each company might retain; without drill sheds and armouries; without grant or allowance from the State for any purpose whatsoever; with officers for whose military education there was no provision; without facilities for instruction in the commonest duties of a camp; without the means of transport and without members trained to supervise that essential department; without trained medical officers to tend their health in camp, to bind their wounds upon the field—in brief, a mere body of men with rifles. The various statutes, the successive Regulations, Orders in Council and Army Orders have produced a body of men uniformed and armed like Regular soldiers at the expense of the State; with every facility for attaining proficiency in the duties of a soldier; with officers whose own fault it is if they are not fully acquainted with the duties of their rank. We found the Volunteer corps isolated units; we leave them arranged into companies, battalions and regiments, each with its full complement of officers, with all the advantages of Adjutants and sergeant-instructors; with all the incentives to excellence that badges, decorations and distinctions can offer, united in close bonds with their territorial regiments whose camps they may share; their needs, alike in times of peace and in the possible chances of war, provided for with anxious care. They possess their medical staff, their stretcher-bearers, their ambulance; they have cyclists at their beck and call, signallers, transport corps, railway corps. What human ingenuity could devise, it appears to me human ingenuity has done to make the Volunteer force an effective one and its service an attractive one, as it is assuredly an honourable one. That a large measure of success has rewarded the efforts of the War Office and the devotion alike of officers and men cannot be gainsaid. It is doubtless true that the movement now is not so much in evidence as in former years. Men no longer rush to be enrolled by their thousands and their tens of thousands. But given the menace of a foreign invasion, and not merely the menace but the real and vivid apprehension of it, I make no doubt the citizen of to-day would be as eager to volunteer as was his father fifty years ago. Does it follow from all this that the Volunteer force is such an organization as we can safely confide in, if our Navy be defeated, dispersed or evaded; if disaster befell our Regular army and if to the Volunteers and to the Volunteers alone we must turn for the defence of our hearths and homes? That is the question I purpose to consider in the following and concluding Section of this part of this work.

PART I.

SECTION V.

On the 14th February, 1902, Mr. George Shee read before the members of the Royal United Service Institution a paper on "The advantages of compulsory service for home defence, together with a consideration of some of the objections which may be urged against it." Major the Right Honourable Lord Newton, Lancashire Hussars (Imperial Yeomanry), presided on that occasion, and at the adjourned meetings necessitated by the discussion to which the paper gave rise. In that discussion officers of the Regular Army, of the Navy, of the Auxiliary forces, civilians, laymen and one bishop took part, and it is only necessary to set forth the names of those noblemen and gentlemen to show how difficult it would be to convene a body of experts more competent to discuss the question under consideration in its military, social, economical and political aspects. They were:—The Right Honourable the Chairman, Sir Robert Giffen, K.C.B., LL.D., F.R.S.; Mr. Clinton E. Dawkins, C.B. (late Financial Member, Council of Governor-General of India); Colonel A. M. Brookfield, M.P. (1st Cinque Ports R. V. Corps); Colonel T. S. Cave (1st Volunteer Battalion, Hampshire Regiment); Major-General C. E. Webber, C.B., p. s.c. (late R. E.); Major-General J. B. Sterling (late Coldstream Guards); Admiral Sir N. Bowden-Smith K.C B.; the Right Reverend F. J. Jayne, D.D. (Bishop of Chester); Colonel the Earl of Wemyss, A.D.C. (late London Scottish Rifle Volunteers); Colonel Sir C. E. Howard Vincent, K.C.M.G., A.C.B., A.D.C., M.P. (Queen's Westminster V.R.C.); Sir John Colomb, K.C.M.G., M.P. (late Captain Royal Marine Artillery); Lieutenant-Colonel O. T. Duke (late 5th Battalion Rifle Brigade); Colonel R. Pilkington, M.P. (2nd V. B. Prince of Wales Volunteers, South Lancashire Regiment); Colonel Viscount Hardinge (7th Battalion Rifle Brigade); Colonel W. T. Dooner, p s.c. (A.A.G., Thames District); Admiral the Honourable Sir E. R. Freemantle, G.C.B., C.M.G. (Rear Admiral of the United Kingdom); Major-General T. Bland Strange (late R.A.); Major J. E. B. Seely, D.S.O., M.P. (Hants Carbineers Imperial Yeomanry); Lieutenant Colonel W. C. Underwood (late 4th Hussars); Colonel E. Pryce

Jones, M.P. (5th V. B. South Wales Borderers); T. Miller-Maguire, Esq, LL.D., Captain Stewart L. Murray (Gordon Highlanders); Mr. Edward P. Warren; Colonel F. Graves (late commanding 83rd Regimental District); Lieutenant-Colonel T. H. Baylis, K.C. (late 18th Middlesex V.R.C.); Sir Ralph H. Knox, K.C.B. (late permanent Under Secretary of State for War); Major W. H. S. Heron-Maxwell (late Royal Fusiliers); Lieutenant-Colonel R. M. Holden, 4th Battalion, the Cameronians (Scottish Rifles); Colonel F. H. Mountsteven (3rd Battalion Devonshire Regiment, late Captain R.M.L.I.; Commander the Hon. Henry N. Shore (R.N. retired); First Engineer George Quick (R.N.); Major A. C. Yate (29th Duke of Connaught's Own Baluck Infantry); and Lieutenant-Colonel E. Gunter, p.s.c. (late East Lancashire Regiment).

A report of this important debate will be found in Volume xlvi. (May 1902) of the Journal of the Royal United Service Institution. I have perused and again perused that report. I have culled, without further acknowledgment being, I trust, deemed necessary, from the speeches of those who engaged in the debate, facts, arguments and suggestions for the purposes of this, the concluding section of the first part of this work; and I confidently recommend a careful consideration of each and all those speeches to those interested in the subject to which I purpose to devote this section: the future of the Volunteers, or more accurately speaking, the future of the Auxiliary forces of the Crown for Home Defence. **Report of the Debate.**

A preliminary question suggests itself. It is not merely an important question; it is *the* important question, upon the answer to which must depend all our conclusions as to our auxiliary forces. It is this: do we in very sooth require a military force for Home Defence at all?

I cannot help thinking that there is a sort of undefined feeling, almost amounting to a conviction, in the minds of great numbers of my fellow countrymen, that we are in no real need of any such force. It is that sentiment which lies at the root of the somewhat contemptuous toleration which, and which only, many intelligent citizens of these isles extend to the Volunteers; a sort of nebulous but none the less baneful persuasion that the Volunteers will never be needed and that if, by some utterly unlikely and incalculable fortuitous concatenation of circumstances, they should be needed, they would be to all intents and purposes useless. I fear there is too much truth in the judgment passed upon the national character by the Persian traveller, Mirza Abu Taleb Khan, who visited this **Do we require an Auxiliary for Home Defence?**

[illegible]

[illegible]

[illegible]

[illegible]

[illegible]

[illegible]

---

any imminent danger of invasion since the Armada, and who think that because 'Britannia Rules the Waves' it is quite unnecessary to have a strong, well-disciplined, well-drilled land force. We cannot expect that storms will always be in our favour. In 1798 Buonaparte would never have got safely as far as Malta, had not a storm blown Nelson to the little island of S. Pietro, near Sardinia. If these elusions occurred in the days of Nelson, what right have we to assume that we shall have better luck in these days of ours ?"

Oh ! but that is a hundred years ago and the conditions are altogether altered. So they are ; but are they altered for the better from Britain's point of view. ?

The reader will observe the name of Dr. Maguire amongst the speakers in the debate at the Royal United Service Institution. Dr. Maguire is a barrister, and, as such, accustomed to the Socratic method of debate. "Will the gallant Admiral deny—and I should like an answer if I can get one—that the British Navy in the years 1803 and 1804 was, relative to the other navies, in as good a position as it is now.?

Admiral Freemantle—"Better."

Dr. Maguire—The gallant Admiral admits that 100 years ago our navy, was, relative to other navies, in as good (he says better) a position as our navy is in now. I see Captain Stuart Murray there—Will he assert that in the years of 1801 to 1805, from the point of view of corn supply and food supply generally, the United Kingdom was not in as good a position, having regard to the chances of war, as it is now. ?

Captain Murray—"Better."

Opinion of Major-General Strange.

Supplement these very unhesitating expressions of opinion by the remarks of Major General Strange in the same debate.

"Are there many people in this room who seriously think that the day is far off when Holland will become part of Germany ? If that happened will not Belgium go to France ? If so you will have a hostile coast from the Baltic to the Bay of Biscay. Look at the map, and mark the tortuous channels about those islands at the mouth of the Maas, Schedlt &c. Why did we spill our blood for a century and rack our armies with fever till 'they swore terribly in Flanders,'* if it was not to hold all those little islets that would cover any number of transport fleets to invade England ? A number of penny Thames steamers would suffice in these days. It

* My Uncle Toby.

is three hours' steam across. I ask our gallant Admirals honestly—Do they propose to blockade the coast of Europe? Nelson could blockade Toulon for two years, and even then Napoleon gave him the slip with 30,000 men; but now-a-days we must coal. I will not say a word about submarines, about which everybody, except Admirals, is thinking. But would it be possible to blockade the coast of Europe in the presence of the ever increasing ordinary torpedo boats of which France alone possesses more than ourselves? We know the enormous task our navy has to perform all over the seas—those seven seas where, as Kipling says, 'our Empire flag is unfurled.' Just think and try to calculate what mark the greatest number of ships you could obtain would make upon the enormous area of those seas? I know that the navy is our first line of defence. All I say is, for goodness sake do not rest the Empire on a one legged stool. The most important leg, we all know, is the navy. But do not say we want no National Army for Home Defence because our navy is to be everywhere."

Now such observations as those I have just given cannot be disposed of by patriotic declamation and by the singing of Music-hall songs. They give food for thought to anyone who has got brains to think. But they are not more grave than those of

Of Captain S. L. Murray.

Captain Stewart L. Murray in the same debate: "If we look at the amount of transport which our enemies* would have available, we must agree with what Sir John Colomb said in this Theatre, that if once our Navy is defeated we shall have to face an invasion before which our little army and auxiliary forces would be helpless. That is to say that if the possibility on which our present military system is avowedly based† were ever to happen that military system would be found utterly inadequate to perform the duty for which it nominally exists. Most people in this country are utterly unaware of the vast troop carrying capacity of the great mercantile

The strength of Germany in transports.

marine which has sprung up on the shores of Europe during the last 30 years. It has come by degrees and therefore it has been ignored. But it sums up to a tremendous total. Germany has now a steam mercantile marine of 1,500,000 tons, nearly all in great ocean Liners. France has a mercantile marine of 1,000,000 tons, Russia of 600,000. Now we are accustomed to think only of

---

*Captain Murray of course would be understood to say "our possible enemies."

† The defeat or break down of our Navy. R.P.B.

ocean transport for a long voyage, allowing five tons per man. But for a short voyage you only require one ton per man, and five tons per horse. For such a voyage it is calculated that only 120,000 tons are required for an army corps complete Of course the men would be crowded like sardines, but for a short voyage that would not matter. Now apply this to the available transport. I will take as an instance Germany. The Hamburg-American Line and the North German Lloyd have each a steam tonnage of 600,000 tons in ocean liners In 1910, when the new German Navy will hold the balance of Naval Power, and when we may expect trouble to begin, each of those Lines will have 800,000 steam tons. Even at the present moment there are at Hamburg and Bremen always nearly 400,000 tons lying alongside the wharves, and in a fortnight that number would be doubled. In 1910 we must consider that there will be always from 500,000 to 600,000 lying there, and 1,000,000 or 1,200,000 available with a fortnight's warning—for an invasion of this country all the available mercantile marine would of course be commandeered, for a small war that would not be done, but for a great war of course it would. Divide 120,000 tons into these figures, and we get the number of army corps which Germany could transport to our shores. We see that she has at present transport enough, if commandeered, to transport three army corps, and in 1910 will have enough always available to transport four army corps across the North Sea. Now as regards their facilities for embarkation. The growth of this new mercantile marine has been accompanied by a corresponding growth of harbour and wharfage accomodation. Along the ports on the Weser alone there are now no less than ten miles of wharves suitable to great liners, all with railway access, all with great cranes for loading &c , all with deep water alongside ; along these wharves nearly 200 liners could load up simultaneously if required. It is unnecessary to go into further figures. It is plain if our navy is ever defeated Germany alone will be able at present to throw three army corps on to our shores, and in 1910 will be able to throw four army corps. But that is not all. Those three army corps would entrench themselves, while the liners went back at full speed to Germany ; in a week another three army corps would arrive to reinforce the first three, and the liners returning to Germany would bring over three more in another week, so that we should have to face at the end of a fortnight from six to nine army corps, grouped in two or three armies, and our task would be to overwhelm these before they received further reinforcements. Suppose eight army corps, or, roughly 300,000 men, were thus thrown upon our shores. To make certain of victory we should require to be two to one, that is to say, we should require 600,000 men. All these 600,000 would have to be troops sufficiently well trained and sufficiently disciplined to be able to accomplish successfully that hardest of all tasks, namely, to attack trained European troops occupying fortified positions. We should be obliged to attack, for the industrial and financial conditions of this country would necessitate a short and decisive offensive campaign, for a defensive campaign would produce utter ruin commercially. But how are such numbers of trained troops to be obtained? There is only one way, and that is by a system of universal service. If the possibility of a naval defeat is the basis of our military system, as it admittedly is, then there is no escape from the logical conclusion that universal service for home defence is absolutely necessary. No other system will give us any security from overwhelming invasion and conquest." I earnestly beg of the non-military reader to remember that these are not the words of irresponsible men, half informed. They express the convictions of men whose whole lives have conduced to qualify them to speak with authority. They were uttered, too, before an audience all or nearly all of whom were well able to expose any misstatement of fact or to detect any fallacy of reasoning. They cannot be lightly dismissed. What these speakers say is either so or not so, either fact or the hallucinations of hare-brained alarmists. Shall their warnings, like those of the unhappy Cassandra, fall upon ears which the inordinate pride that the Persian traveller imputed to us has closed to all save the words of honeyed flattery and beguiling adulation?

"Universal Service" advocated.

French opinion as to the feasibility of invading England

If we are blind or wilfully close our eyes to our vulnerability we must not suppose our neighbours are not fully alive to the situation. The *Revue des Deux Mondes* * asks pathetically:— "*L'étincelant cuirasse de l'empire britannique est-elle sans défaut? Et nous est-il interdit d'espérer sur quelque théâtre d' operations bien choisi un succés momentané de nos vaisseaux qui permette à notre armée d'intervenir dans la lutte? . . . être maître de la Manche pendant quelques jours!*"

German opinion.

Baron Edelsheim's scheme for the invasion of England by Germany is based upon the opinion of the military authorities of that country that such an invasion is a quite feasible undertaking

* xclv. p. 795, quoted by Captain Spencer Wilkinson in *The Volunteer Question*, p. 42.

if they could only obtain temporary command of the North Sea, and one which would certainly be attempted, if it were desired to bring this country to its knees.*

And it is not merely with questions of transports that we have to make our account. We have also to forecast, so far as human foresight will enable us, the probable conditions under which, if ever, the Volunteers may be called upon for the defence of our hearths and homes, the expedition with which our possible antagonist can mobilize its force, and our own preparedness for resisting an attack with the means which, under the circumstances, we are likely to have at our disposal. Of course, to a man obstinately and doggedly persuaded that no such attack can ever be made, these pages can have no possible interest. Indeed, to him, the Volunteer force must present itself as a huge absurdity, the living embodiment of an ineffable imbecility. If our fleet is at all times, under all conditions and against all combinations, to be an impregnable barrier which the fury of the elements or the guns of opposing armaments neither can nor shall at any time weaken or break down, then, indeed, we need no Home Defence save the waves that break upon our shores. *Cessat quaestio*; there is no more to be said, and our Volunteers may pile their arms and doff their uniforms once and for all, and bewail, at their leisure, the time and labour they have thrown away, under the delusion they were fitting themselves to do good and needed service in the hour of trial. But, frankly, I consider the man who holds this extravagant notion of England's invulnerability beyond arguing with, if not beyond praying for, and it is not to him these pages are addressed. In what follows it is assumed to be conceded that the invasion of Britain, and its successful invasion, is a contingency whose possibility cannot be reasonably denied. As it is pithily expressed by Commandant du Genie A. Marga, in his *Géographie Militaire* †:—"The power of Great Britain is vulnerable in her vast colonial possessions, in particular in India, but a decisive struggle with a great European Power will not end without an attempt to land an army upon the English coast."

And in such a struggle it must not be supposed our opponent will consult our convenience as to the day and hour at which the

* Captain A. T. Moore, R.E., Journal R.U.S.I., volume xlvii, No. 299, p. 57.

† Quoted by Captain Spencer Wilkinson in his Essay on "*The Volunteer Question*," since re-published separately as a brochure, "*The Volunteers and the National Defence*" (Westminster, A. Constable & Co.).

attempt shall be made. We may rely on it that the moment will be chosen most embarrassing for us. Let us suppose a case, and a case no one will deny to be not merely possible but more than probable: the case of an invasion of India by Russia from the north. Such an invasion is said by authorities and owned by strategists* to be designed by Russia. Suppose, too, a by no means unforced supposition, that such an invasion were accompanied by one of those mutinies of the native races which, to our infinite credit be it said, every day of British rule in India makes more improbable, but which we cannot yet afford to dismiss as a negligable factor in the event of a Russian attempt. At such a conjuncture, would not much of our regular army be required for the defence of our Indian Empire? England has not yet echoed the late Mr. Henry Fawcett's cry, "perish India," and until beaten to its very knees will never relinquish the land won by the genius of Hastings and of Clive and consecrated by the martyrdoms of the Indian Mutiny. But not only would such a war of defence put a great strain upon our army, it would make a heavy call upon our navy. The experiences of the South African War are fresh in our memory. Even that was an anxious time. But we were fighting against an enemy that possessed absolutely no navy, not even a fleet upon paper. But Russia has a fleet. It would be necessary, therefore, to employ our own navy to convoy our troop transports, and what would be of infinitely more difficulty, to protect our exports and imports. It is not probable that the United States, which possesses now a fleet to make its wishes respected in the councils of Europe, would consent to food stuffs being considered contraband of war; but food stuffs do not constitute the whole of our imports and food stuffs are not even an item in our exports. We are a nation of traders, and traders cannot carry on business without stock. How much of the raw material of our innumerable industries is imported and how much we depend on being able to send to foreign markets the finished product few people realize. But unless the highway of the sea were preserved inviolate Britain in a brief space would suffer losses besides which the losses of many adverse campaigns would be as naught, and to preserve inviolate the trackless seas would draw from the environment of our shores no mean portion of the King's navy. Conceive, then, such a position of affairs: a large portion of the army and possibly of the Militia engaged abroad and a large portion of our navy occupied in conveying transports,

The circumstances that would favour such invasion.

* Lieutenant Duncan Watson in "*The Volunteer Question*," Essay IV, page 152.

protecting our mercantile fleet and in blockading the ports or watching the navy of our antagonist. It is not an inconceivable position and it is assuredly not one to be lightly contemplated. To express the situation in the most moderate terms we should be, if not naked, at least in a state of unenviable exposure. It is just such a crisis as would offer to a continental nation inclined to pick a quarrel with us an opportunity not to be disregarded. I protest that I am entirely innocent of Gallophobia, but it is confessed on all hands that we are not much loved by either France or Germany; and neither country is at much pains to dissemble its dislike. Perhaps we have ourselves to thank for this, and I admit that John Bull is not always seen in an amiable light when making the Grand Tour. But causes do not alter facts and the fact remains that if Russia were engaged in war with us and courted a French alliance her overtures would probably be addressed to very willing ears. Of course we might be able to set off a German alliance, but on the other hand we might not. Germany would have to see some very material advantages before it consented to pull our chestnuts out of the fire and of such advantages we do not happen to have any to offer. So that England, one hand, nay more than one hand, already tied behind its back, from its operations in India, would be left thus maimed and crippled to await a French descent upon its coasts. Captain Wilkinson in the admirable Essay to which I have more than once expressed my indebtedness quotes from Baron P. E. Maurice,* writing in 1851, the estimate that France, maintaining at that time an army of 540,000 men, could land in England, in case the opportunity of crossing the channel unmolested offered itself, an army of 150,000 men. Commandant Marga in the *Géographie Militaire* gives 200,000 as a reasonable estimate of the force required. He lays down as a condition of the enterprise that, as only a limited number of troops should be landed, the invader should aim at a surprise, and should chose for his landing a point as near as possible to his objective, i.e. to London. These data, comments Captain Wilkinson. "have an important bearing on the quality of the troops that would be employed and on the nature of the attack. A force of 200,000 is less than half of that which is at all times with the colours either in France or in Germany. It could therefore be prepared and moved off without any previous calling out of reserves. In that case it would be in every sense a picked

Baron Maurice on the force necessary for such invasion.

Captain Wilkinson on the same subject.

The German and French facilities for mobilization.

* *De la Défense Nationale en Angleterre.* Paris, 1851, pp. 40, 81.

force; its battalions would be smaller* and handier than those usually employed in Continental war, and it could be mobolized without the loss of time involved in the assembling and equipment of numerous reservists. This implies the entire suppression of the four, five or six days now assigned to the process of mobilization, for the troops without reservists can be entrained at any time at a few hours' notice. It also involves a further consequence of special interest to our enquiry. In the absence of the movement among the civil population caused by the calling in of the reserves, the whole of the preparations, until the troops march from the barracks to the railway station, can be kept secret. Even the march to the train, effected by small units in many places at the same time, would excite no immediate attention. A delay of the diplomatic rupture until the troops were actually entrained would, therefore, give the attacking power an advance in the preparations which might even be equivalent to the arrival of the invading troops at their ports of embarkation at the time when in England the order for mobilization was issued."

What forces could we oppose?

Now in the absence of the Regulars and the Militia or of a considerable portion of them what force would our country possess to oppose the trained levies of the invader? The Volunteers and the Volunteers only. To put in the field the ordinary citizen, undrilled, unaccustomed to discipline and concerted action, unfamiliar with arms, would be not war, but murder. The days of the pike and scythe, when a stout arm and a brave heart were more than half the battle, are gone and gone for ever. We should have to turn as our last resource to the Volunteers. And the question is, should we or should we not be forced to lean upon a broken reed? I confess I cannot endorse the eulogium of Mr. Chamberlain when (June 16th, 1890), speaking at Birmingham, he said of the Volunteers:—"The Volunteer force now consisted of an army of a quarter of a million well trained marksmen." In the same speech Mr. Chamberlain, whilst expressing the opinion that so long as we maintained "our inviolate sea" we might feel assured that no large invasion of this country would ever take place, admitted that "there might be many contingencies under which a considerable and well equipped force might be landed on these shores. This could be done with greater facilities than in former times, owing to the great development of steam. If from

Rt. Hon. J. Chamberlain, M.P. on the Volunteers as marksmen.

* The Battalion on a war footing in France is 1,000 strong; in peace, 550 officers and men. Wilkinson (u.s.)

any cause, such as a stress of weather, or accident to the fleet, we were to lose command of the Channel, even for a few hours, there was nothing to prevent such a landing being effected, and as our principal cities were left defenceless, an invader might, by way of ransom and other methods, inflict upon our resources an irretrievable injury." But Mr. Chamberlain, as we have seen, took comfort from the existence of a "quarter of a million well trained marksmen." The actual numbers of the Volunteers it may be here stated are now more than a quarter of a million. On January 1st, 1902, they were, including the staff, 277,396. But I imagine no one acquainted with the facts will say we have anything like that number of "well trained marksmen." Lord Wolseley, then Adjutant General, speaking in the same year as Mr. Chamberlain, quoted (only to express his concurrence in it), a remark of a line officer that "there was not a battalion of Volunteers in England that could shoot against any battalion which could be selected from the Regular army."

Volunteer strength, 1902.

Lord Wolseley on the shooting of the Volunteers.

It is misleading to judge, as the general public may perhaps be excused in doing, the general attainments of a Volunteer Corps by the result of rifle-shooting competitions. The "pot hunter" is often a danger, sometimes a discredit, to the corps to which he belongs. Too often Volunteering means to him only prize cups and prize money. He cares nothing for drill, he has no *esprit de corps* and must laugh in his sleeve consumedly at the idiotcy of a government that provides him gratuitously with the means of practising a costly art that he has not the remotest idea of ever displaying except for his own benefit. General Mackay, speaking at the United Service Institute, is credited with the following anecdote: "When possible I always expressed a desire to see some men shoot. On one occasion at ——— there was a man who had shot for the Queen's Prize at Wimbledon, in the squad shooting. He shot very well, also a non-commissioned officer with him. There was, however, a young fellow who was not initiated into the mysteries of the shooting art, who was missing the target shot after shot. The young fellow said to his comrade, as the wind was blowing briskly across the range, 'Are you aiming on the target'? 'Oh yes' was the reply. I went to the man afterwards and said 'Did you aim on the target'? 'Yes' he said. 'But you did not aim through your back sight.' 'No sir.' 'Then,' I said, 'Why did you not tell that young man what to do, why did you not instruct him how to aim'? 'Oh sir,' he said, 'It is part of my game; I go to Wimbledon, and if I was to

Shooting competitions a misleading test of general efficiency.

General Mackay on prize shooting.

tell him exactly what to do he would possibly take the wind out of my sails the next time." It is a very slight reform to suggest that no man, however excellent at the target, should be allowed to compete in Volunteer matches unless he could first produce a certificate of drill efficiency.

But even the possession of such a certificate is no guarantee of any but nominal or what may be termed official efficiency. I do not ask the reader to accept my judgment on this point. I quote from the Essay of Lieutenant Duncan Watson;* "There are great numbers of the Volunteers who are highly efficient. They have a good knowledge of drill as it is taught, and are expert at executing the commands. They are enthusiastic and intelligent, both qualities of the highest order in the modern soldier. They are healthy, strong and athletic, and have consequently good powers of marching and endurance—qualities also which are absolutely necessary to the private soldier. But look at the *per contra*. There are as many inefficient as efficient Volunteers. Every officer must be conscious in his heart that at least half the men in his command are not soldiers in any sense of the term. With the exceptions of a few crack corps, who are really good, not more than 50% of the Volunteers are fit for active service in the field. All who earn the grant and pass the inspecting officer are nominally, and according to Regulations, efficient. But many who are numbered as efficients in the returns are not so, if tried by any real test. If rightly considered, these men are not only inefficient in themselves, but are the cause of inefficiency in their regiments. Inefficiency in any man, more especially in a good number of men, tends to deteriorate the body as a whole. It erects a standard of inefficiency in a company or a regiment. A competition is raised, like that of a donkey race, where the last who reaches the post gains the advantage. Members regulate their attendance at drill by the minimum standard.

This is not an exaggerated statement, as many officers must know who have experienced the difficulty of making members attend drill. The willing men grumble because the careless and indifferent do not drill with equal regularity to themselves; and it very often happens, through this influence, that in the end the enthusiastic member becomes indifferent himself.

Therefore, I say, the merely nominally effective man is a real drawback to the Volunteer force, and the nation and the service would be better without him. If we descend to particulars in this

* The "*Volunteer Question*," Essay, 10, p. 163.

line of enquiry, what do we find? Many Volunteers are much too old for private soldiers—old members who will not attend drills, and who are so easy-minded that they will not even take the trouble of resigning. Many are 'fat and scant of breath'—irrevocably out of condition. Many, especially in towns, though strong in the chest and arms, are quite exhausted by a march of three or four miles at a march out. If they were required to march one day's march in real warfare, many would drop in their tracks, not from want of spirit, but through sheer fatigue. Many cannot drill and cannot shoot. Taken altogether, the Volunteers at present are not to be depended on as a well-trained body of men, leaving out of the question the infinitely superior organization of an effective army." It was not without good cause that Lieutenant Watson adopted as his *nom de plume* the motto "*Esse quam videri.*"

Lieut.-Col. Mayhew on Volunteer Officers

Nor has the lash of criticism been reserved entirely for the back of the Volunteer private. Volunteer officers have been divided by Lieutenant-Colonel C. G. A. Mayhew, Brigade-Major, North Midland Brigade,* into (1) those who join the force from patriotic motives and look upon soldiering in the light of a serious profession (2) those who do so for amusement, or for the sake of wearing the uniform, and take little or no interest in their duties. "That the first named class" observed Lieutenant-Colonel Mayhew, "increases annually can be proved by the number of officers who qualify at the School of Instruction and present themselves for examination in the extra subjects open to them, but even now it is a small portion of the force. The majority of the officers know something of drill, for which they are obliged to pass a qualifying examination for the rank they hold. Except at Schools of Instruction the examination is not very strict, and unless great ignorance of the subjects is shown the Board of Examination is remarkably lenient. Little or nothing is known, however, about discipline, administration, interior economy, or any of the higher subjects, by the great mass of the commissioned ranks. Much credit is due to those officers who, in spite of many disadvantages, and with limited time at their disposal, use their utmost endeavours to make themselves efficient in the true sense of the word."

The German system of Universal service

Let us turn a moment from the not too gratifying contemplation of the admitted defects of the British Volunteer to the study of the soldier, against whom, in, I fear, an evil hour for him, he may find

* See "*The Volunteer Question,*" Essay v, p. 194.

himself pitted by the remorseless chances of war. I mean the possible invader from the Fatherland. "In Germany," I quote from "The Army Book of the British Empire,"* "the service is universal—that is to say, that as soon as a man arrives at 20 years of age he has to present himself to be medically examined for the army. Motives of economy determine the exact number of those who shall be taken each year. But no exemptions on the ground of personal favour and no substitutes are permitted. There are no unlucky numbers. The physically strongest are taken—those who are actually physically unfit for service in the army are rejected on that ground. Those who are not completely developed are put back for a time. Those who are not required to make up the necessary number are noted for forming what is known as the *Ersatz* reserve, and are liable to be called up at any moment to fill up any vacancies caused by waste. "Most of them undergo a certain amount of training. The only exemptions permitted are such as the State in its own interest allows. Those who go to the Cadet schools to be trained as officers naturally pass through a different curriculum. Students at the University and others who are able to show that they can qualify themselves for service more rapidly than the ordinary recruit, are permitted to serve as one year Volunteers, living out of barracks but doing their ordinary drills, paying for themselves certain expenses which do not fall upon the recruit, but subject to rigid tests as to their actual efficiency as soldiers by the time that they have completed their course. Those who wish to remain in the army as non-commissioned officers have considerable inducement to extend their service from the fact that all the many offices of the State, on the Government railways, telegraphs and in the bureaux are reserved for men who have thus served.

The moral distinction between this system and at least the later stages of the conscription, as it existed in France, is of a very marked character. *Not to have served under the Universal Service system denotes a certain at least physical inferiority.*† The effect of this on the general view of any army service, in the ranks and among the population at large, is one that grows as time ripens the system. Now-a-days it is common to hear, in a railway carriage, a man who has not, for some reason or other, served, addressed with a kind of pitying condolence, by his more fortunate

* By Lieutenant-Colonel W. H. Goodenough, R.A., C.B., and Lieutenant-Colonel J. C. Dalton, (H.P.) R.A, (Eyre & Spottiswoode, 1893.)

† The italics are mine.—R P. B.

brethren who have passed through the ranks. 'Ah, you have not served?' in a tone that seems to imply 'Poor fellow, what was it then that was the matter with you?' As it was recently graphically expressed by a distinguished Englishman: In this country we think consumption a terrible misfortune for anyone, because of the danger to life which it implies; in Germany the first thought is, 'He is consumptive! He will not be able to serve.' On the whole, it were well that these distinctions between 'conscription' and 'universal service' were better understood by English writers for the press, who not unfrequently talk as if conscription were the form of service which now exists on the Continent and attribute to it all those conditions of 'unlucky numbers' and the like which belonged to a far distant past."

In Germany, then, many German soldiers serve for three years with the colours before being transferred to the reserves and all must serve for at least one year. During this year of service the German recruit is carefully and systematically instructed in his work by very experienced and highly trained officers for some six or seven hours a day.

The British Volunteer usually signs an agreement to serve for three years. During the first and second year of his service he is obliged to attend altogether sixty drills, and during the third year nine drills, making a total of sixty-nine drills during his three years' service, each drill being of one hour's duration. His zeal will probably lead him to exceed this minimum, and he may be expected to have been under instruction at the utmost for perhaps 90 hours altogether by the expiration of his period of service, when, if a reserve existed, he would be eligible for transfer to it. If the hours occupied in class firing be also taken into consideration, it may be estimated that during his three years of service, a zealous Volunteer will usually have given as much time to gaining a military knowledge as a German recruit will be compelled to devote in one month to the same object."*

It will be conceded that the one question with which the nation is concerned in the matter of the Volunteers is: how would they stand the strain of actual war? The average citizen does not care a bawbee about the Volunteer's uniform, his drills, his salutes, his honorary distinctions &c. All he knows is that he is paying a round million or so annually for what he is asked to believe is a

* Major C. E. D. Telfer, in *The Volunteer Question*, Essay vii., 263. (This, of course, must be taken subject to any improvements effected since the essay, which was printed in 1890. (R.P.B.)

very economic form of national assurance. The ordinary ratepayer will not begrudge his quota if he is getting value received ; but if he is only getting tinsel for gold the ordinary ratepayer will be quite justified in buttoning his pockets and demanding his *quid pro quo* for the future. Now consider what a call upon the Volunteers an invasion of this country would necessarily involve. Captain Spencer Wilkinson in the very admirable essay to which I must once more refer (p. 50 *et seq.*), sets forth at large the rapid succession of events from the declaration of war till the opposing forces confront each other on English soil :—the calling out of the Volunteers, the medical inspection, the elimination of the sick, the issue to each man passed for service of his kit and ammunition, the collection, loading and horsing of the regimental transport ; its entraining and detraining ; the march, of which, under ordinary conditions, the Volunteers have actually no experience ; the quartering of the troops at the end of each day's march, the steps to be taken on march for the security of the column by advanced guard, flank guard and rear guard, and by outposts during a halt ; the exploration of the line of route by patrol and reconnaissances ; and, finally, the battle, the reconnaissance of the enemy, the commander's disposition of his forces, the artillery duel, the infantry combat, the pursuit or retreat. I must refer the reader to the vivid pages of Captain Wilkinson for the full description of these quick succeeding changes in the lurid drama. And as he reads those graphic lines I fear the impression will be graven deep upon his mind that the Volunteer Force must either be revolutionized or supplanted if we are to have a really effective auxiliary for home defence.

What actual warfare would mean to the Volunteer.

Is he prepared for the strain?

Captain Wilkinson concludes his enquiry into what an effective force should be and what our Volunteer Force is, and is not, by an answer in the concrete. He quotes an account from the local newspaper of the then most recent inspection of a well known Volunteer battalion which was admittedly one of the best in the country.

A test case.

" The sham fight consisted of an attack by eight companies over the open ground at the south end of the park and was well seen by the spectators. Three or four companies were placed in the wood at the north end of this open space to represent the enemy. The remainder of the battalion was moved to the south end about 900 yards from the position which they proceeded to attack. The eight companies were told-off, four to form firing line, supports and reserves, two for the second line, and two for the third line. A ninth company was moved to the wood on the west side of the open ground, and from here fired obliquely on the defenders. The movement was carried out according to the method laid down in the *Field Exercise* of 1889, and conformed very fairly with the rules there given. The men were evidently well trained and were, for Volunteers, fairly in hand. Here and there the men in the firing line were a little crowded, owing, no doubt, to the want of a sufficiently clear instruction about the direction, and throughout the movement, the distances between the several successive groups were too short. With the representation of a charge by the second line the movement and the day's work ended. The inspection showed that the corps had lost none of its old excellence, the average training of the men being up to the present high-water of Volunteering."

This is smooth reading so far; evidently a battalion of more than average efficiency engaged in a not very complex affair of attack and defence. And yet there are nine companies being ordered like lambs to the slaughter by, no doubt, a very well meaning and self-satisfied Commanding Officer. Read the sequel from the same report:—

"The test of fitness for war is not the execution of formal movements, which is a preliminary, but their application. This can be illustrated from Saturday's work. If the 'attack' had been a drill it would have been carried out on a parade ground, without blank cartridges, as a test of form. In that case great accuracy would have been required. The neglect of distances and the crowding in the firing line would have been indications that the training was imperfect; in other words, that the companies had not had enough exercise by themselves to be fit to work together as a battalion. But the choice of varied ground, the use of blank cartridge and the detachment of a strong enemy, mark the practice as a manœuvre, as something distinct from drill. The object is to accustom all ranks as nearly as may be to the actual conditions of battle. The supposition was that an isolated battalion of eight or nine companies was to attack the three companies in the wood. It would also be assumed, though this was not mentioned, that the attackers had the assistance of artillery, which would have prepared for their advance. Upon these suppositions the attack, as it was carried out, *would have resulted in the destruction of the battalion as a fighting force.** The ground for 700 yards in front of the position is without cover, while the defenders had the best

*The italics are mine.—R. P. B.

possible cover. "Under these conditions a frontal attack is almost hopeless, however well conducted, and its chance is not mended by detaching a handful of men to a point obliquely in front of the enemy. But a frontal attack might be attempted, if combined with a flank attack, provided the attacker used a largely superior force. The attacker on Saturday had two companies to fire at the defenders' three. After reinforcing he had four companies (minus the casualties) actually firing. The whole affair lasted only a few minutes, so that the attackers hardly fired at all. Thus, the men were taught that they can advance across open ground against a well posted enemy and, without firing more bullets than are fired against them, can in a few minutes march right up to the position and charge. Yet this is 20 years after the disasters of the Prussian Guards at St. Privat, and of the 38th Brigade at Mars la Tour, which have written in letters of blood in every Continental drill book that no infantry position can be approached until its defenders have been crushed under a hail of bullets."

The vital defect of the Voluntary principle.

Now I do not propose to myself the entirely uncongenial and thankless task of carping at the Volunteers, of whom I am proud to have been both a private and a commissioned officer. The defects of the Volunteer system are either inherent or remediable. I believe myself they are inherent and incapable of remedy. I will give my reasons, nay, one reason will suffice. It goes to the root of the whole matter.

A Volunteer can resign by giving fourteen days' notice and handing in his clothes and arms. That is to say, he not only elects to become a Volunteer, but he practically elects to remain a Volunteer *de die in diem*. Volunteers may resign by individuals, by companies, by battalions and by regiments, saying neither with your leave nor by your leave. Every drill-instructor, every Adjutant, every captain and every Commanding Officer knows this. He has the fear of a strike ever before his eyes. He issues his orders standing on a mine that may explode beneath him at any moment. Instead of a captain having his company in the hollow of his hand, the company has him and he knows it. And what is worse the company knows it too. True, a Volunteer must obey orders under penalties. But his revenge is to resign and persuade as many of his comrades as possible to do the same. Imagine a school in which every schoolboy knows that if the head-master or any of the other masters offend him he may pack up and go, practically at his convenience. And this is just what a company of Volunteers is, but we expect discipline and efficiency under such conditions, which, as Euclid would have said, is absurd.

Now holding very strongly the conviction that in the fact I have stated lies an all-sufficient reason why such a force—call it what you like—can never be and will never be a really reliable auxiliary, it is useless to dwell upon the many suggestions that have been made for increasing the efficiency of the force, *e. g.*, the increase of capitation grant, the greater stringency of drills, and the right of commissioned officers to be introduced at court! **Inadequacy of certain suggested remedies.**

I have proposals more drastic to submit. I claim for them no originality and my one excuse for embodying them in this work is that they may serve for consideration and discussion among those who know how surely the question of an efficient auxiliary will have to be faced by the nation at large. The sooner that question is recognised as one to be explained to, and sooner or later decided upon by, the electorate, the sooner will those responsible for the machinery that is to produce that efficient auxiliary be able to address to their task their intelligence and their experience.

My proposal briefly is that the male population of Great Britain, between certain ages, should be actually and not merely theoretically, regarded and classified as liable to military training and if need be to military service. As we have seen, the law has always recognised the implication in the mere fact of citizenship of liability to such service; but it does not now insist upon what should be a logical corollary, the obligation to military training. I will endeavour to state the broad outlines of my suggestions with sufficient precision to make clear what I propose and what I do not propose. In the first place I emphatically do not countenance any scheme for compulsory service in the regular army. Such compulsion is unnecessary. There always has been and always will be in our country a sufficiently large number of youths for whom the colours have an irresistible attraction. Whether the inducements to enlist, in the shape of increased actual or deferred pay and more substantial pension pay on retirement or disablement, should or should not be offered by the recruiting sergeant, is an enquiry into which it is no part of my present duty to enter. I am not now concerned with the regular army. My labours are necessarily restricted to an enquiry into the best means to be adopted for procuring and maintaining what we admittedly do not now possess, a sufficient and an efficient body of auxiliaries for Home defence.

The revival of the Local Militia suggested.

Service in the Regular army not affected by proposal.

The population available for Local Militia. Census, 1891.

Now let us consider the material from which such a body must be drawn. I take my statistics for this purpose from the Report of the Registrar General upon the Census Returns of the year 1891. Those of 1901 are not available in form convenient for my enquiry and for all the purposes for which I use them in this work the returns of 1891 are substantially as valuable as those of ten years later.

No. of males of the Recruiting ages.

According to these returns the number of males in England and Wales of what the Report calls the Recruiting ages, *i.e.*, from 18 to 25 years, is 1,828,694.

And of the Military ages.

The number of men of what the Report calls Military ages, *i.e.*, from 18 to 45, is, in the same countries, 5,538,694.

In each million of the population of twenty nine millions in England and Wales there were, in the Urban districts, 74,525 males between the ages of 20 and 25, in the Rural districts, 65,608.

I purpose to confine my attention to the males between 20 and 25 years, and of these we may assume that there are in England and Wales at the present time, in round numbers, some two millions.

The population roughly classified by occupations.

It is desirable to form some approximate notion of how these two millions are distributed among the various industries of the country. Now, the report shews that of every 100,000 agricultural labourers, 31,562 are between the ages of 20 and 25 years, say, one third of the whole. Of course I do not assert that this proportion of one third to two thirds will in all occupations represent the number of males between the ages of 20 and 25 years; but I do think it may furnish a fair working basis for the purpose of rude approximation, beyond which it is quite unnecessary to go.

Now apply this test to the various classes from which an auxiliary force might and should be recruited. I need not exhaust the long list of professions, trades and occupations, but what I subjoin will suffice to give an adequate idea of the *personnel* of such a body :—

			No. of those that may be taken as between 20 and 25, and males.
Professional class.	Barristers, Solicitors, and Clerks ..	47,518	15,000
	Schoolmasters and Teachers ..	51,000	17,000
	Civil and Mining Engineers ..	9,600	3,000
	Architects	7,842	2,000
	Artists	12,282	4,000
		Carried forward ..	41,000

Brought forward		.. ..	41,000
Musicians (including Organ Grinders) of whom perhaps 50% were females	38,606	.. ..	6,000
Photographers, of whom an equal percentage were possibly females ..	10,571	.. ..	2,000
Male Domestic Servants	58,528	.. ..	20,000
Those engaged in Commercial transactions	416,000	.. ..	100,000
Those engaged in Transport	983,000	.. ..	300,000
Farmers, practically all males ..	223,610	.. ..	70,000
Agricultural labourers, mostly males,	756,557	.. ..	280,000
Gardeners, males	179,336	.. ..	60,000
Woodmen	9,448	.. ..	3,000
Corn Millers	22,759	.. ..	7,000
Corn Dealers	11,647	.. ..	4,000
			893,000

Domestic class.

Commercial class.

Agricultural.

Industrial classes.

This class includes all such persons with specified occupations as were not, in the report, referred to the professional, domestic, commercial or agricultural classes, and by itself largely outnumbers all these classes put together. In 1891, it comprised 7,336, 344. These seven million three hundred thousand souls were distributed over a vast variety of industries: paper manufacturers, steel and pencil makers, printers, bookbinders, engine, machine and tool makers, carvers, makers of clocks and scientific instruments, the building trades, (builders, bricklayers, masons, slaters and tilers, carpenters and joiners, plasterers, whitewashers, paperhangers and plumbers, an aggregate of 680,000), china and earthenware manufacturers, glass manufacturers, ship builders and coach makers, the textile industries, 1,060,492. The mining industry (coal, iron, copper, tin, lead and other minerals) occupies 555,000, metal workers, 480,000.

The shopkeepers (chemists, booksellers, grocers, butchers, coal dealers &c.) account for 632,000. The dock labourers for 55,000, general labourers 596,000.

In some of these industries as many women as men are engaged; in some two women to one man, in others (glove making *e.g.*) three women to one man. In others, mining, *e.g.* the industry is almost confined to males. But if of the 7,336,344, referred to the industrial classes we say one third, *i.e.* 2,700,000 were males, and that of these males, one third, *i.e.* 900,000 were between 20 and 25 years of age, we shall err, if at all, on the right side.

Summary.

We have thus some 900,000 males between 20 and 25 years of age, furnished by the industrial classes, and a like number by the professional, commercial, domestic and agricultural classes, making in all that 1,800,000 males of the recruiting ages (18-25) which the report of the Registrar General speaks of.

We have, then, in England and Wales alone, roughly speaking, over 1,800,000 youths in the first flush of manhood, when, if ever, the body is capable of benefiting by physical training, when the mind is apt at seizing and appropriating instruction, and when the heart is full of courage and enthusiasm. Now to this vast body of youths let the severest medical tests be applied; eliminate those who are below the military standard of height; who are halt or deformed; who suffer from defect of vision or hearing; who are disposed to diseases of the chest, heart or lungs. Is it an extravagant estimate that there will still remain a select residue of 300,000 fit to go anywhere and do anything, only requiring military discipline and technical training to mould them into an Army of National Defence that would enable us to contemplate the dispersion or elusion of our navy, not, certainly, with indifference, but without panic or dismay?

48 Geo. 3, c. 3.

The reader will not, I trust, have forgotten the terms of the Local Militia Act of 1808. That Act provided for the balloting for the Local Militia, without the benefit of substitution, of males between the ages of 18 and 30. That Militia might be used for the suppression of riots &c. and might be embodied for service in any part of Great Britain in case of actual or apprehended invasion. The 38th section provides that the Local Militia, in such proportions and under such regulations as might be directed, should be called up for the purpose of being trained and exercised, regard being had "to the local circumstances of each county, and to the seasons most important to the course of industry and cultivation within the same." No Local Militiamen were to be trained or exercised more than 28 entire days in each year, exclusive of the days of going to and from the barracks. During the period of drill and when embodied for service the Local Militiaman was to be entitled to the same pay, clothing &c. &c., as the Regular Militiaman, and in case of death or disablement on service there were the usual provisions for pension, &c.

How its service would operate.

Now, *mutatis mutandis*, why should not the Local Militia of 1808 be revived and substituted for the Volunteers? The ages for service might be, instead of as in 1808, from 20 to 25 years. We should have, as we have seen, 300,000 men each year eligible for training. Four year's training of 28 days of 6 hours per day would produce, given the right material to work upon, a force equal to any test and to any emergency. There are many reasons that commend such an experiment. Who will dispute that regular physical drill for 28 continuous days, conducted on scientific principles, accompanied by the ample rations of the barrack mess and enlivened by the recreations of a soldier's life, would benefit any youth, no matter his birth, no matter his station and no matter his occupation? Frame for frame I incline to think the inhabitants of England, I will not include Wales, are a bigger, a more sinewy and muscular race than the Germans. Yet who has not felt a pang when he has contrasted the slouching hind of our English fields and the bowed and emaciated "hands" of our English manufacturing centres, with their Teuton fellows, compact of frame, well knit, elastic and alert.

Nor would the physique only of our manhood be improved. Discipline has a beneficial moral effect. *Quis nescit obedire nescit imperare.* The habits of cleanliness, neatness, or should one say, spruceness, of regularity and punctuality, and of prompt and unquestioning obedience, once deeply rooted in the nature of a man, become virtues and virtues that would have an appreciable value in civil and industrial life. Drill does not brutalize, it quickens the intelligence, increases the mental receptiveness of a man. Ear, eye, touch and thought become the instant servants of the complete soldier, and the qualities acquired in the drill yard would not be lost in the counting-house or the factory.

The number of men recruited annually under a system of local militia.

But it will be objected that to withdraw each year 300,000 men from the labour market would be to ruin the industries that are vital to our existence. Well, I do not suggest the withdrawal of any such annual number. It would be necessary to determine the exact number or establishment of the force which is to be substituted for the Volunteers. Assume for illustration's sake that 300,000 is the number determined upon. It exceeds by 20,000 our present Volunteer force. Well, to secure this 300,000, the Government might call up

In the first year	...	75,000,
,, second year	...	75,000 more,
,, third year	...	75,000 more,
,, fourth year	...	75,000 more,
		300,000

In the fifth year the 75,000 men of the first year would not again be called up; they would become fused with the civil population; they would form a reserve; if you like, an unacknowledged and non-official but still an effective reserve, of men, who, at a crisis, could be counted on to swell our battalions. Their places would be taken by 75,000 new recruits and so each year after the first four there would be a constant influx of raw levies and efflux of trained men

The selection of but 75,000 men yearly for training, out of an available 300,000, would, in all probability, dispense with any necessity for the ballot. There would be required but one in eight of those actually on the lists. I err strongly in my estimate of my fellow country-men of all classes, if, of the picked youth of our land, at least twelve per cent. would not scorn to await the casting of lots, and cheerfully proclaim their readiness to undergo 28 days' drill per annum for four consecutive years.

Consider the nature of the occupations of the men who constitute the eighteen hundred thousand who are within the recruiting ages. There are the professional classes, lawyers, architects, clerks, &c. I know something of the members of the legal profession. I affirm with confidence their quota would ever be ready. I have no reason to suppose the possession of the legal mind either exalts to a higher plane of patriotism or incites to martial ardour in a higher degree than is to be observed in other professions. Take the agricultural classes: will anyone dispute that there are hundreds of young farmers, who, apart altogether from patriotic motives, would hail as a welcome change from the wholesome but somewhat monotonous pursuits of their daily life the stir, the bustle, the colour, and the martial strains of a month in camp. And these young farmers with, belike, their own ground landlord as their commanding officer, would make splendid subalterns. And whence could they better recruit their companies than from the peasants who till the soil the landlord owns, and the farmer farms? Service under the same flag would teach, though I do not know the lesson is needed, mutual respect between landlord and farmer and labourer. What is more to our present purpose it would draw for the country's needs, from the dales of Westmoreland and Cumberland, from the moors of Yorkshire, from the fens of Lincolnshire and Cambridgeshire, from the downs of Sussex and from the crags of Wales a body of Local Militia against which the best regiments of either France or Germany would be hurled in vain. And if to officer troops so worthy of our isle the young squires and farmers would proudly volunteer, may we not say, too, the peasants themselves would court, not shirk, the issue of the ballot, or forestall it by voluntary engagement? There are none too many distractions in the yokel's life to make him averse to a month's encampment if it put no strain upon a purse always slender. There are many months of enforced idleness or partial idleness in any year for the husbandman. These months are to him not merely a weariness of the flesh; they are a costly holiday he cannot afford and would fain dispense with.

Nor would the Local Militia appeal merely to those who ride to the markets of our country towns or tread with leaden feet in the wake of the gleaming ploughshare. The miner who delves in the gloomy caverns beneath the fair surface of the earth, would, I am persuaded, relish the month's yearly respite from his grim and grimy labours. The miner is well paid—I do not say he is too well paid. He earns money rapidly and he spends it often neither well nor wisely. He is too prone to diversify his arduous and dangerous toil by outbursts of rude debauch. It is absurd to say, if he can afford to do this, he cannot afford to undergo, in those years when he is little likely to be oppressed by family claims, but when his wages often scale the highest, one month's yearly training that would not merely enure to his country's good but would be to him a most wholesome exchange for the muddy dissipation of the tap-room. What I have said of the miner may be said, though with perhaps less cogency, of the millhand and the factory operative. How entirely beneficial it would be for the young man to escape from the heated, stuffy atmosphere of the mill or factory to the breezy stretch of the camp, to expand in manual exercise the chest too long bent over the slowly growing warp, to swell the muscles that in a mill almost forget their natural use—what need to dwell on all this? It is an argument that each reader may apply for himself to the industries with which his own experience has familiarised him.

Some objections.

But a pseudo-political economy here claims to speak. To withdraw each year 75,000 of the very pith and sinew of our nation from the labour market would be to artificially enhance the price of labour. Well, for the matter of that, every emigrant ship that leaves our shores tends to enhance the price of labour. But I think even capitalists are beginning to discriminate between the quantity and the quality of labour. There has been, I believe, a short sighted race of employers who believed that early marriages, large families and improvident, not to say dissolute, habits among the industrial classes were not unmixed evils. True they spelled the workhouse and the gaol. But they meant, too, a labour market in which there were always three dogs for two bones and so wages were kept down. But "a heretic blast has blawn fra the wast" and now even the most conservative of employers (I do not use the word in a political sense), recognise that it is well, not merely for the men but also for the master, that he who earns his living by the sweat of his brow, should be hale and hearty in body, sober of habit and of trained and acute intelligence. Surely, too, it is better that the congestion of our labour market should be relieved by a month's withdrawal from labour to the not unpleasant duties of the barracks and the camp than by either the suicidal lock-out or strike or by that half employment that neither suffices to keep a man well alive nor compels him resignedly to die.

There is one other aspect from which a system of Local Militia may be regarded. We have seen that for a German youth to be medically pronounced unfit for service secures for him truly the pity of the fair, but not, probably, precisely that pity which is said to be akin to love. I imagine, and I think with good grounds, that in England, too, a day is not far distant when a youth will count it as a slur upon his manhood not to be deemed fit to draw sword or shoulder gun *pro focis et pro aris*, when for the wild scrimmage of the football field with its championship cups, its professionalism and its betting we shall see substituted a rational pride in our army of defence and a just emulation to excel in martial carriage and that manly bearing bespeaking the healthy form and the well braced muscles which delight the eye of the wise man and happily delight, too, the eye of lovely woman.

The cost of a Local Militia.

And now, to conclude alike this section and the first part of this work, one word as to the possible cost of such a scheme of Local Militia as I have ventured, I would rather say to suggest than to contend for. The present cost of the Volunteers is to the nation over one million pounds a year; what that cost is to private benevolence and the officers of the force no man can pretend to say. Now under the plan I have sketched in broad outline it may be supposed the Volunteers would be rather absorbed, as in 1808, than abolished. They would die a natural or at least an easy death, the force being as it were bled to euthanasia by drafts into the Local Militia. Assuming that each year, for the first four years, but 75,000 men would be taken to complete the Local Militia establishment of 300,000, it is reasonable to suppose many of the recruits would be from the Volunteers. Indeed it would be hazardous to dispense with the Volunteers until the full complement of the Local Militia were attained and then truly the Volunteer would disappear but disappear neither "unwept, unhonored nor unsung." He would be reincarnated in the Local Militiaman and the transformation would not be a costly one. In the debate in the Theatre of the Royal United Service Institution it was stated by the late Permanent Under Secretary of State for War that "the total cost of an infantry private soldier per annum may be taken at £48 10s. 0d., say £4 per month, indeed £3 14s. 7d. for the lunar month of twenty-eight days." The cost of 300,000 Local Militia would at this rate not very greatly exceed what is now spent upon our Volunteers, and even if that cost were far exceeded I do not think the British taxpayer would grumble beyond his usual wont if he were persuaded, as by stubborn facts persuaded he would be, that he had value for his money, of which he is now, so far from being persuaded, somewhat cynically doubtful.

END OF PART I.

PART II.

SECTION I.

(A.D. 1794-1802.)

I purpose, as I have already indicated, to devote the second part of this work to an account of such levies in the town and district of Huddersfield as may fairly be included in a history of the Volunteer Movement, confining my enquiries to the period commencing in the year 1794 and ending in 1874. The contents of Part II. constitute, as it were, a living commentary upon those of Part I. In chronicling the steps that were taken in successive epochs and at various crises it will not be necessary to tell again the story of the national emergencies that called for the voluntary arming of the people nor to set forth again the clauses of the statutes giving sanction and validity to the several levies. That has been done, I trust, with at least sufficient amplitude and particularity, in the first part of this enquiry. In addressing myself to this record of a necessarily limited range I am oppressed by the feeling that to the reader to whom Huddersfield is but a name upon the map many details I must perforce preserve will be of no, or little, interest. And yet I would fain persuade myself that even to such a reader these annals of an industrial community, these often quaint and curious records of a people for the most part engaged in the mill or the mart will so patently reveal that touch of patriotism and of valour common to all the sons of our native land that they may find acceptance even with those who have never heard the clack of a loom nor watched the shuttle's swift track athwart the warp. To those, however, who dwell in Huddersfield or in the valleys or on the hills that lie on its every side these records of a century ago must possess an even pathetic interest. As one turns the yellow, worn pages of the Books of companies and corps of gallant men gone hence, their little part in life's drama played, the drop-scene fallen, the lights extinguished and the audience departed, names start to meet the eye that the mind had long forgot. There are the names of men who obviously, in their day, acted no mean part on the local stage. Yet of them one seeks in vain some appropriate memento, some cold "*Hic jacet*" on the storied urn or monumental statuary, some brief obituary of a vanished life. Other names there are of men whom a century ago our forefathers delighted to honour—one seeks their descendants and pity stays the search. Still other names there are that gladden the heart and kindle the eye; for they are the names of men who laid broad and deep the foundations of that industry which has enriched our town and all the district round, men whose public services are enshrined in our local annals and traditions and whose noble benefactions many a godly institution and many a towering spire still enduringly attest.

34 Geo. 3, c. 31.

The first local levy, therefore, to which I shall invite attention was that of 1794, raised under the statute of that year authorising the Crown to accept offers to raise companies of Volunteers in augmentation of the Militia. The Secretary of State for War having directed the attention of the Lord Lieutenant of the various counties to the provisions of this enactment the magistrates of the West Riding in session at Pontefract, April 30th, 1794, under the presidency of Mr. Bacon Frank, deliberated as to the steps necessary or desirable to be taken in the grave circumstances of the time to secure the national safety. They arrived at the following resolutions:—

Meeting at Pontefract, April 30, 1794.

Resolutions.

"That it is our unanimous opinion that in the present critical situation of this Kingdom it is highly expedient that the greatest exertions should be made in every part of it, and particularly in this populous part of the West Riding of Yorkshire to increase, under the sanction of Parliament, the means of internal defence and security against invasion and intestine commotion."

"That for the purpose of carrying the above Resolution into effect the Nobility, Gentry, Clergy and Freeholders of the West Riding of Yorkshire be desired to meet at the Moot Hall in Pontefract, at 12 o'clock on Wednesday, the 21st day of May next, to consider what will be the proper measure to be adopted for the purpose of obtaining such defence and security."

The names of twenty-one magistrates are subscribed to this resolution, but I observe that only one name is connected with this district, that of Sir George Armytage, Baronet, of Kirklees Park. A meeting in pursuance of this resolution was held May

24th, 1794, in the Moot Hall at Pontefract, under the presidency of the Lord Lieutenant, and the nobility, gentry, clergy and freeholders of the Riding attended in great numbers. Earl Fitzwilliam was a prominent figure. He subscribed £1,000, and enrolled himself as a Volunteer, being doubtless mindful of the truth that example is better than precept. A further £6,000 was subscribed before the close of the meeting, which unanimously resolved, "that the larger towns within the Riding be invited to raise bodies of Cavalry, and other parts of the Riding do unite in raising such corps." By the end of another week £30,000 was raised in the Riding, and the county magnates, returning from Sessions to their own homes, bestirred themselves to give effect to the resolutions adopted at Pontefract. A meeting was held at the George Inn, Huddersfield, on June 28th, 1794, and I set out the result of its deliberations *in extenso*, as the gathering may be regarded as the first step taken in this district towards the initiation of the Volunteer movement. Sir George Armytage, Baronet, presided, and it is the merest tribute of justice to his memory to say that from that day till the sword was sheathed after the decisive victory of Waterloo, Sir George Armytage gave, without stint, his time, his personal assistance and his money, to this great and patriotic undertaking. The resolutions were as follow:—

Further Meeting, May 24, 1794.

Meeting at Huddersfield, June 28, 1794.

Resolutions.

"That it is the opinion of this Meeting that a Volunteer Corps of Infantry be raised for the protection and defence of the West Riding of the County of York."

"That such Corps shall consist of not more than two hundred men."*

"That a subscription be entered into for carrying the above resolution into speedy effect."

"That a Treasurer shall be appointed who shall call for the subscriptions by such instalments as the Committee shall direct."

"That the thanks of this meeting be given to Sir George Armytage, Bart., and Richard Henry Beaumont, Esquire, for their liberal exertions in promoting the public good and the interests of this town and neighbourhood."

The response to the appeal for contributions was prompt and liberal. I reproduce the list of subscribers, for I imagine that many will like to see again the names of those who, at the close of the eighteenth and the beginning of the nineteenth centuries, were distinguished citizens of our town or intimately connected with it.

* This number was speedily exceeded.

List of Subscriptions.

List of Subscriptions in Huddersfield.

Name	£	s.	d.
The Right Hon. the Earl of Dartmouth ..	105	0	0
Sir George Armytage, Bart.	100	0	0
Sir John Lister Kaye, Bart.	105	0	0
R. H. Beaumont, Whitley Hall	100	0	0
Thomas Holroyd	50	0	0
John Whitacre	50	0	0
Joseph, Thomas, and Law Atkinson	100	0	0
Robert Scott	50	0	0
Thos. Allen	30	0	0
John Horsfall	30	0	0
John Battye	21	0	0
H. and W. W. Stables ..	31	0	0
John Houghton	20	0	0
Joseph Brook	20	0	0
John Dobson	10	0	0
Sarah Nichols	50	0	0
Joseph Taylor	10	10	0
James Crosland	10	10	0
Benjamin Walker.. ..	31	10	0
Joseph Blackburn ..	10	10	0
T. Haigh and Son ..	50	0	0
Northend Nichols.. ..	25	0	0
Benjamin North	50	0	0
J. Haigh	30	0	0
William Horsfall	20	0	0
George Woodhead ..	25	0	0
Joseph Stringer	15	0	0
Joshua Clegg	10	10	0
Samuel Walker	21	0	0
James Dyson	10	10	0
A. Horsfall and Son ..	30	0	0
John Dyson	10	10	0
Richard Atkinson.. ..	5	5	0
Allen Edwards	1	1	0
William Walker	2	2	0
S. Stocks	10	10	0
William Bradley	5	5	0
R. Peel	1	1	0
James Thompson.. ..	5	5	0
William Horsfall	3	3	0
Joseph Dransfield ..	3	3	0
William Holt	2	2	0
Francis Downing.. ..	5	5	0
John Edwards	2	2	0
Joseph Bradley	1	1	0
William Atkin	1	1	0
William Walker	10	10	0
John Parkes	5	5	0
Daniel Crosland	5	5	0
James Medwood	10	10	0
Thomas Marshall.. ..	5	5	0
David Hepworth	2	2	0
John Oxley		1	0
John Booth	5		0
John Townsend	5	5	0
B. and S. Dyson	10	10	0
William Armitage ..	10	10	0
Rowland Houghton ..	15	15	0
Mrs. Butman	10	10	0
Eli Laurence	5	5	0
M. Mason, Jun.	20	0	0
Richard Wood (Slaithwaite)	5	5	0
Samuel Wood	5	5	0
George Hirst	3	3	0
John Brook	10	10	0
Benjamin Clay	10	10	0
W. Prince	1	1	0
Thomas Depledge ..	1	1	0
R. Thewlis..	2	2	0

The measures taken for carrying into effect the resolutions adopted at the meeting of June 28th appear to have been prompt and vigorous, the promoters being doubtless stimulated no less by the generous response to their appeal for financial assistance than by their sense of the exigence of the national needs. A corps of Infantry was established having for its official title the name, "*The Huddersfield Corps of Fusilier Volunteers.*" On December 6th, 1794, the "London Gazette" contained a notice announcing the first appointment of officers as follows :—

To be Major Commandant:	Sir George Armytage, Bart.	First Officers.
To be Captains,	Richard H. Beaumont and Northend Nichols, Esquires.	
To be Captain-Lieutenant and Captain	Joseph Haigh, Gentleman.	
To be First Lieutenants	Joseph Scott and William Horsfall, Gentlemen.	
To be Second Lieutenants	Walter Stables, Bramel Dyson, John Hudson, Gentlemen.	
The Agent of the corps was:	Mr. Croasdaile, Pulteney Street, London.	

The commissions of the above officers bore date November 18th, 1794, and the same names appear in the Army List in 1796.

The agent of a company was properly the Colonel's clerk.

The rank of Captain Lieutenant

Of the rank and title of Captain-Lieutenant, now extinct, some further notice may be welcome That officer was the commanding officer of the colonel's company whenever the colonel himself was absent or surrendered the command to him. Though he had in fact only the military status of a lieutenant and received only a lieutenant's pay he commanded as junior captain. His position was, indeed, in more than one respect anomalous; for though he received only a lieutenant's pay, yet, according to the rates of pensions to officers' widows to take effect as from Christmas, 1798, a captain-lieutenant's widow was to be entitled to the same pension as a captain's, viz.: £30 per annum, the ordinary lieutenant's being only £26 the year. The price of a captain-lieutenant's commission in the Foot Guards was, according to Grose's Military Antiquities,* £2600; that of an ordinary lieutenant but £1500. The rank was abolished in the British army in July, 1802, Field Officers being no longer allowed companies, although the custom of colonels and Field Officers retaining their companies continued until 1803. Captain-Lieutenants were to rank as lieutenants, and all supernumerary lieutenants were to be commissioned as ensigns. The rank of captain-lieutenant was abolished in the Militia on 26th June, 1802, by statute, 42 George III., c. 90, section 68, providing "that no Colonel or Field Officer in the Militia shall be a Captain of a company." Previous to this enactment the colonel or Field Officers

* The first edition of this work was in 1796, the second was published in 1801 and brought down to 1800, so that the latest regulations as to the price of commissions were of date anterior to that year.

were (nominally) captains of companies and received pay as such, the senior subaltern of the colonel's company being a captain-lieutenant, or senior subaltern of the regiment. On March 26th, 1778, a Royal Warrant conferred on the captain-lieutenant the rank of captain.

Personal Notices of some Officers.

Something more than the bare mention of their names and ranks seems due to the memories of the first gallant officers of the parent corps of the Huddersfield Volunteers. Of Sir George Armytage and Mr. R. H. Beaumont of Whitley-Beaumont I can add nothing that is not already familiar to the student of our local annals. Captain, afterwards Lieutenant-Colonel, Nichols—he held the higher rank in the "Upper Agbrigg Volunteers"—was a Justice of the Peace and Deputy Lieutenant of the West Riding. His family had been long settled in the neighbourhood of Elland. His grandfather was Jonathan Nichols of Wellhead, Greetland. His father, Isaac Nichols, married Miss Northend of Longshaw in Northowram. Northend Nichols served as captain-lieutenant in the 54th Regiment of Foot, whence, in 1781 he exchanged into the 37th Foot, in which regiment he distinguished himself during the long and arduous campaign in North America, as well as in other parts of the globe.* On his retirement from the army in 1791 he held the commission of captain. As we have seen he did not rest upon his laurels and when, in 1794, he joined the Huddersfield Volunteers his long and varied military experiences were doubtless justly valued. He spent his declining years at Elland. His great-grand-niece, Miss Lucy Hamerton, of Elland, is the authoress of an interesting monograph, "Reminisences of Olde Eland." There is there preserved a story of Captain Nichols that seems to throw some light upon his character. In the Elland Parish Church was aforetime an ancient pew on the door of which were the name, Nichols, and the date, 1690, doubtless the pew in which many generations of that ancient and honourable family had worshipped. When the Church was renovated, it was proposed to remove this pew but the gallant captain is said to have stood before its door with drawn sword threatening to be the death of any who should lay sacrilegious hands upon his cherished seat. It was suffered to remain until after his death at Elland, July 27th, 1818, at the ripe old age of four score years and one. I had recently the honour of visiting Miss Hamerton when she shewed me a miniature on

Lieut. Col. Nichols.

---

* "Account of monuments in Elland Church," by John William Clay, J.P., reprinted from the *Yorkshire Archæological Journal.*

ivory of the captain. I reproduce it in a coloured plate. He is portrayed in the uniform of a captain of the 37th Regiment which, at this time, (*circa* 1790), had yellow facings and silver buttons. Only two regiments at that period had yellow facings with silver lace loops in pairs.

For information respecting some of the other officers of the Huddersfield Volunteer Fusiliers I am largely indebted to a little book entitled, *Some of the Founders of the Huddersfield Subscription Library*, published in 1875 by my esteemed and deeply lamented friend, the late George William Tomlinson.

Captain (afterwards Lieut. Col.) Joseph Haigh

Captain Joseph Haigh was the son of John Haigh, of Golcar Hill. His mother, a Manchester lady, was an intimate friend of that Reverend Hammond Robertson whom Charlotte Brontë has immortalised in "Jane Eyre." Joseph himself was born in 1765, so that at the time we are now concerned with he was in the prime of manhood. He was engaged in the business of a clothier with his cousin Benjamin, under the style of "J. & T. Haigh," residing at Golcar Hill, presumably in the parental home. He married the daughter of William Fenton, Esquire, of Spring Grove, Huddersfield, and sister of Captain Lewis Fenton, first member for the borough. He amassed in business a large fortune. His Golcar property sold after his death for more than £100,000. He purchased an estate at Whitwell, near York, for more than twice that sum. His daughter married Sir Edward Lechmere, of Rhyd Court, Worcestershire, Bart.

According to Mr. Tomlinson, Haigh was a very handsome man, inheriting his mother's good looks and dignified carriage, and was highly respected in the town, being looked up to "more like a little king than an ordinary individual." He built Springwood Hall, and lived there until he went to Whitwell. He died in 1835, nigh half a century after the days when he was a dashing young captain of the Huddersfield Fusiliers.

First Lieut. Joseph Scott.

Mr. Joseph Scott was born at Woodsome in 1774, so that when he received his commission he was a youth of twenty or so. His father was a merchant, who occupied Woodsome Hall in the absence of the Earl of Dartmouth, receiving that nobleman as a guest when he visited his estates in this district. Perhaps he will be best remembered from the fact that in 1812, after the Luddite riots, he screened many a poor dupe from the consequences of his folly. The Luddites went to Woodsome to be "untwisted," as they called it, *i.e.*, relieved of the oaths they had taken to King Lud. Scott, in later life, removed to Badsworth, where he died

First Lieut. William Horsfall.

I imagine this was the Horsfall who was shot on Crosland Moor in 1812 by the Luddites.

Second Lieut. W. Stables.

This gentleman resided at Crosland Hall, near Meltham, and carried on business as a merchant in partnership with his nephew, the firm being W. W. and H. Stables. Their warehouse was the building in Chapel Hill now converted into the Model Lodging House. Mr. Stables was a zealous Churchman, and active in municipal affairs. He died in 1847, and is buried in the crypt of the Parish Church.

Of Second Lieutenant Hudson I can give no particulars. Second Lieutenant Bramel Dyson was a merchant, and resided at Birkby.

Shortly before the disbanding of the corps in 1802 I find the names of other officers in the *Gazette*, which notified the appointment of Captain-Lieutenant Joseph Scott to be captain of an additional company; Lieutenant Stables to be captain, *vice* Scott; John Woolley, gentleman, to be first lieutenant, *vice* Stables; Jarvis Charles Seaton, gentleman, to be second lieutenant; Thomas Atkinson and Joseph Crosland, gentlemen, also to be second lieutenants.

Second Lieut. T. Atkinson

Mr. T. Atkinson was a woollen manufacturer at Colne Bridge. He was very active against the Luddites, and was said to have been the next man after Horsfall marked by them for destruction. He married a lady of the Battye family, having a brace of pistols in his pockets as he stood at the altar.

Captain Seaton.

Mr. Gervais Charles Seaton was a member of a banking firm, Perfect, Seaton, Brook & Co., of this town and at Pontefract, and in March, 1797, was a lieutenant and captain-lieutenant and paymaster of the 1st West York Supplementary Militia or 3rd West York Militia.

First Lieut. Woolley.

Mr. Woolley was a manufacturer residing at Thorpe in the house till comparatively recently occupied by Mrs. Dougill. This house is now known as Finthorpe and is the residence of Edwin Walter Last, Esquire, General Manager of the West Riding Union Banking Company, Limited. Mr. Woolley was very active against the Luddites, who threatened to burn his house down.

The Chaplain.

The Chaplain of the corps was the Reverend John Lowe, M.A., Vicar of Brotherton. On New Year's Day, 1795, he preached before the Huddersfield Royal Fusiliers, presumably in the Parish Church, a sermon on the duties of a Christian Soldier.

[illegible] 1801

As I have said, Sir George Armytage was the Commanding Officer of this corps. His commission was dated 18th November, 1794, under the hand of the Lord-Lieutenant of the county. He was, as we have seen, assisted by two captains, one captain-lieutenant commanding the Commanding Officer's company, and two first and two second lieutenants.

Uniform

The uniform of the corps was the cocked hat of the period, worn across the head, coats of red cut away at the hips and faced with blue, white breeches buttoned down the length of the leg and presenting a gaiter-like appearance (see Plate). The men powdered their hair and I came across, in the *Leeds Mercury* for April, 1795, a curious calculation that the men then under arms in the United Kingdom, estimated at 250,000, allowing a pound of flour a week per head, wasted 5,500 tons of flour per year, enough to bake 359,333 quartern loaves of bread, or breadstuff for 50,000 people for 12 months.

The Colours.

One must not omit mention of the colours of the corps. Colours are now, alas! a forbidden glory. Those of the Huddersfield Fusiliers were presented to them, in the name of the ladies of Huddersfield and district, by Lady Armytage, wife of the Commanding Officer.

The Colours themselves are strictly in accordance with the Royal Warrant of 1743, wherein it is ordered that "The first colour of every marching regiment of foot is to be the great Union, the second colour is to be of the colour of the facing of the regiment, with the Union in the upper canton. In the centre of each colour is to be painted, in gold Roman figures, the number of the regiment within a wreath of roses and thistles on one stalk, except those regiments which are allowed to wear royal devices or ancient badges."

The first or King's Colour displays the red cross of St. George fimbriated white, and the white saltire cross of St. Andrew upon a blue ground. This, in fact, had been the national flag of England since the union with Scotland in 1707. The centre of the red cross is ornamented with the Royal arms of England, as they were then displayed, namely England and Scotland impaled, France, the Hanoverian arms, and lastly, those of Ireland.

The regimental colour is of blue silk, the facings of the regiment, with the Union (as in the King's Colour) in the upper corner near the spear head. In the centre, upon the blue silk, is displayed an allegorical design representing Britannia holding a shield bearing the words, "For Our King and Country"; below, upon two labels, appears the title of the corps, *Huddersfield Volunteers.* The whole within a wreath of laurels.

These colours now hang, honoured relics, in the great hall at Kirklees Park, the former in a fairly good state of preservation, the latter tattered and faded, their pristine blue converted to a sombre green. (See plate). In addition to the colours there remain in Kirklees Hall two other treasured mementoes of these anxious times. One is a silver flagon cup with lid, two-handled, elegantly chased and designed. On the one side there is the device of the regimental colours, on the other the inscription :—

Presentation Cups.

"*As a token of respect and gratitude, presented by the Non-commissioned Officers and Privates of the Royal Huddersfield Fusiliers to Sir George Armytage, Baronet, their Commander, on the 24th October, 1796.*"

See plates.

This flagon or cup is supplemented by a smaller cup also presented to Sir George Armytage It is a two-handled, covered cup of gold, inscribed on the one side with the arms of the Commanding Officer of the battalion, on a heater-shaped shield. The arms of the Armytage family occupy the centre of the shield impaled with or supported on either side by the arms of Harbord and Bowles. Sir George Armytage was twice married,—his first wife being daughter of Sir Harbord Harbord, afterwards Lord Suffield; his second wife, daughter of Oldfield Bowles, Esquire, of North Aston, Oxon, and the display of the shield is a noticeable variant of the usual heraldic arrangement of the arms of the husband or baron on the dexter side of the shield and the wife or *femme* on the sinister. This handsome cup bears the legend :—

"*The principal inhabitants of the town and neighbourhood of Huddersfield, impressed with a high sense of the services of the loyal Volunteers and as a particular testimony of gratitude and respect for their Commander, Sir George Armytage, Bart., presented him this day, June, 1802.*"

Lieutenant-Colonel Nichols also was the recipient of a two-handled, silver-covered cup, similar in size and shape to that presented to Sir George Armytage, and inscribed as follows :—

"*The principal inhabitants of the town and neighbourhood of Huddersfield present this Cup to Northend Nichols, Esquire, late Major in the Huddersfield Volunteer Corps, as a testimony of gratitude and respect for his services, June, 1802.*"

This cup is now in the possession of his great-great-great-nephew, the Reverend Laurence Collingwood Hamerton, now residing at Normanhurst, Basingstoke, Hampshire.

I have described the uniform of the corps raised in 1794. I have described its colours, and the testimonials by which the people of the district evinced their sense of the services of its Commanding Officer and major, and presumably of the corps itself. There is one other matter which perhaps even a patriot Volunteer might be excused from deeming of at least equal importance, the subject of pay.

According to the War Office Regulations of 1798 the pay and allowances to Volunteer local corps was according to the following rates or scale:— Pay.

"The officers are allowed pay at the rates specified in the annexed Tables for the days of exercise only, except that constant pay is allowed to one officer of each company if taken from the half-pay list, not exceeding the pay of a captain.

No pay is allowed to chaplains, nor for surgeons, unless on actual service.

The non-commissioned officers and private men are allowed one shilling per day each for every day of exercise, or number of hours in different days equivalent thereto, not exceeding two days in the week. Six hours are reckoned equal to a day's exercise.

One sergeant in each company receives constant full pay."

Table of rates of pay for Volunteer Infantry, when not on actual service, for each day of exercise :—

	£	s.	d
Colonel	1	2	6
Lieutenant-Colonel		15	11
Major		14	1
Captain		9	4
Lieutenant		4	4
Ensign		3	5
Adjutant		3	9
Sergeant		1	0
Corporal		1	0
Drummer		1	0
Private		1	0

For each day where constant pay is allowed.

Captain on half-pay, as such being precluded by law from receiving his half-pay.

Lieutenant on half-pay, as such being still to receive his half-pay as aforesaid.

Ensign on half-pay, as such being still to receive his half-pay as formerly.

One Sergeant per company.

Clothing allowance.

I find the allowance for "clothing" consisted of a coat, waistcoat, breeches, round hat and cockade, and the cost:

	£	s.	d.
For a Sergeant	3	3	0
Drummers	2	3	6
Corporals	1	11	6
Private men	1	9	0

The accoutrements consisted of a belt, pouch and sling and were allowed for each man furnished with a fire lock. (These articles were either supplied from the Ordnance Department or an equivalent, according to the following rates, was given in money by that department, at the option of the commandants): —

	£	s.	d.
For a Musket, Bayonet and Scabbard ..	1	16	11
For a Halbert	0	9	6
For a Drum and Stick	0	19	0
For a Cartridge Box	0	2	6
For a Tanned Leather Sling	0	1	4

The anxiety at the War Office that the Volunteers should be not merely numerous but effective is abundantly shewn by the frequency of inspections or reviews. There was a Military Festival, as it was styled, at Leeds, on May 26th, 1795; a review of the Leeds, Bradford, Halifax, Huddersfield, and Wakefield Volunteers, by General Cameron, on Chapel Town Moor, on June 27th, of the same year. There was another review on the 4th August, 1796, of the Volunteers of Huddersfield, Halifax, Leeds, Wakefield and Bradford, by General Scott, on Heath Common. A coloured plate of the latter function is in the possession of Sir George Armytage, and the Leeds Thoresby Society possess another copy, presented by Mr. Arthur Middleton, of Leeds. On each of these occasions, Sir George Armytage commanded the Huddersfield force. A full account of the Military Festival appeared in the newspapers of the day and appears to be of sufficient interest to justify reproduction here. My extract is from the *Leeds Mercury*:—

Military Festival, May 26, 1795.

"On Tuesday, the 26th May, 1795, the Military Festival commenced at 3 o'clock, the Halifax Corps of Volunteers, commanded by Colonel Hamer, arriving at the Head-quarters, the old King's Arms, attended with two brass Field pieces, one in front, the other in the rear, each piece drawn by two grey horses. The greatest concourse of people ever known on any former occasion assembled to welcome them as they entered the town, and the streets through which they were to pass were crowded many hours before they arrived.

At half past six the Bradford Corps, commanded by Colonel Busfield, arrived at their headquarters, Crosland's Hotel. The concourse of people was then so great as nearly to prevent their marching up Boar Lane into Briggate. They had also two Field pieces, one in front and the other in the rear, each drawn by two grey horses.

At half past seven the Wakefield Corps, commanded by Major Tottenham, arrived at their headquarters, old King's Arms. At 8 o'clock, the Huddersfield Corps, commanded by Major Sir George Armytage, arrived at their headquarters, Crosland's Hotel.

On Wednesday morning, at half past eight, the different corps assembled near the Mixt Cloth Hall, and marched from thence to Chapeltown Moor, where they had a Field Day and went through their different evolutions and firing with the greatest exactness. They returned to town again about 4 o'clock in the afternoon. In the evening there was a concert at the Music Hall, in Albion Street, by desire of Colonel Lloyd.

The concert was numerously attended and the Theatre was also uncommonly crowded.

On Thursday (the Grand Review Day), the different corps assembled near the Mixt Cloth Hall, and at half past ten o'clock marched up Boar Lane, Briggate, and by the Market Place to Chapeltown Moor in the following order:

FRONT.

Trumpeters,
Yorkshire West Riding Yeomanry Cavalry,
Bradford Artillery,
Two Field Pieces.

Colonel Lloyd,
Leeds Volunteers.

Colonel Busfield,
Bradford Volunteers.

Major Sir George Armytage, Bart.,
Huddersfield Volunteers.

Major Tottenham,
Wakefield Volunteers.

Colonel Hamer,
Halifax Volunteers.

Halifax Artillery,
Two Brass Field Pieces.

REAR.

At half-past twelve the whole took the field in the following stations, the ground being previously marked out and corded round.

	Yorkshire West Riding Yeomanry Cavalry.					
Bradford Artillery.	Leeds. Colonel Lloyd.	Bradford. Colonel Busfield.	Huddersfield. Major Sir George Armytage, Bart.	Wakefield Major Tottenham.	Halifax. Colonel Hamer.	Halifax Artillery.
	Red with blue.	Red with blue.	Red with blue.	Red with blue.	Red with black.	
	Yorkshire West Riding Yeomanry Cavalry.					

Note —Bradford uniform: For "Red with blue" read "Red with buff." R.P.B.

Having grounded their arms for about 20 minutes they went through the following manœuvres in a soldierlike manner equal to the most experienced troops of the line:—

1—General salute and marched round in slow and quick time.

2—The manual exercise.

3—Primed and loaded with cartridge.

4—Fired one round by companies from flanks to centre; began at the right.

5—Advanced in line and fired one round by companies from flanks to centre; began at the left.

6—Advanced in line and fired one round by companies from centre to flanks.

7—Formed a new line in the rear.

8—Formed a close column in the rear of the right division.

9—The column advanced in ordinary time.

10—The right division formed the line and fired one round by companies from right to left of the line.

11—Formed a close column in the rear of the left division.

12—The column advanced in ordinary time.

13—The left division formed the line and fired one round by companies from left to right of the line.

14—Formed a new line in the rear.

15—Advanced by wings from the left and fired one round from left to right.

16—The right wings advanced into a line.

17—Formed a new line in the rear.

18—Fired by regiments one round from flanks to centre; began at left.

19—Advanced in line.

20—Fired by regiments one round from flanks to centre; began at the left.

21—Advanced in line.

22—Fired by regiments one round from centre to flanks.

23—Retired in line.

24—The right line advanced, at the same time opening ranks.

25—The line halted and gave the grand salute, the colors dropping.

After which the whole corps left the Field in the same order as they took it, and arrived in Briggate about four o'clock in the afternoon.

The great concourse of people and number of horses and carriages assembled in Chapeltown Moor exceeded all conception.

The forenoon was uncommonly fine, but about 1 o'clock a little rain came on, when the spectators began to disperse in all directions.

On Thursday evening there was the most brilliant assembly ever known in this town. Yesterday the different corps of Volunteers returned to their respective homes, much satisfied with the civility they received.

Notwithstanding the mass of people assembled in Leeds, on Chapeltown Moor and in all the roads leading from Chapeltown, on the Wednesday and Thursday, it is recorded that not even the most trivial accident occurred."

As, at the festival above described and doubtless at other reviews, the Leeds, Bradford, Wakefield and Halifax corps were associated and acted with the Huddersfield Volunteers, it will be of interest to some at least of my readers to learn the names of the officers, who, in 1795-6, were thus brought into such close and friendly co-operation with the Volunteers of this district:—

Leeds Officers.

LEEDS.

RANK.	NAME.	DATE OF COMMISSION.
Lieutenant-Colonel Commanding	Thomas Lloyd,	26 May, 1794.
Major	George Beaumont,	26 Dec., 1794.
Captains	Joseph Wilkinson,	26 May, 1794.
	Thomas Cookson,	,, ,,
	Christopher Smith,	26 Dec., ,,
	Atherton Rawstorne,	,, ,,
Captain-Lieutenant and Captain	Thomas Close,	26 Dec., ,,
	Richard Pullan,	26 May, ,,
1st Lieutenants	Thomas Ikin,	26 May, ,,
	John Bischoff,	26 Dec., ,,
	Jonathan Wilks,	,, ,,
2nd Lieutenants	Francis Ridsdale,	26 Dec., ,,
	John George Child,	,, ,,
	Henry Dunderdale,	,, ,,
	Thomas Edward Upton,	,, ,,
	John Hill,	,, ,,
	Harry Wormald,	,, ,,
Adjutant	Thomas Close,	,, ,,

Bradford Officers.

BRADFORD.

RANK.	NAME.	DATE OF COMMISSION.
Lieutenant-Colonel Commanding	Johnson A. Busfield,	1 July, 1795.
Major	Joseph Stephen Pratt,	,, ,,
Captains	John Sturges,	21 June, 1794.
	John Hardy,	1 July, 1795.
	John Barcroft,	,, ,,
Captain-Lieutenant and Captain	William Sharp,	,, ,,
Lieutenants	Francis Atkinson,	21 June, 1794.
	William Bolland,	23 March, 1795.
	John Robert Ogden,	,, ,,
	John Green Paley,	,, ,,
	Samuel Hailstone,	1 July, 1795
	William Henry Dates,	,, ,,
Ensigns	Richard Grice,	23 March, 1795.
	Greenwood Bentley,	1 July, ,,
Chaplain	Rev. Wm. Atkinson,	23 March, ,,
Adjutant	William Sharp,	1 July, 1795.
Agent	Mr. Mackay, Fludyer St., London.	

WAKEFIELD.

Wakefield Officers.

Lieutenant-Colonel Commanding	John Tottenham	1 July, 1795.
Captains	Jeremiah Naylor,	31 May, 1794.
	Benjamin Kennet,	" "
	Henry Andrews.	" "
Lieutenants	Edward Brooke,	" "
	William Charnock,	" "
	George Oxley,	" "
	Robert Allott,	" "
	Joshua Haigh,	5 July, "
Ensigns	Francis Ingram,	31 May, 1794.
	William Smyth,	1 July. 1795.
Chaplain	Rev. Wm. Bawdwen,	" "
Surgeon	William Mitchell,	" "
Agent	Mr. Donaldson, Whitehall.	

HALIFAX.

Halifax Loyal Officers.

Lieutenant-Colonel Commanding	Joshua Hamer,	24 Nov., 1794.
Major	Thos. Horton,	8 Dec., 1794.
Captains	Charles Hudson,	" "
	Lewis Alexander,	" "
	Thomas Priestley,	" "
	George Greenup,	24 Aug., 1795.
Lieutenants	John Waterhouse,	2 Aug., 1794.
	Thomas Lord,	" "
	John Richardson,	" "
	Thomas Ramsden,	8 Dec., "
	Chas. David Faber,	" "
	John Wilkinson,	" "
	William Wilcock,	24 Aug., 1795.
Ensigns	William Norris,	8 Dec., 1794.
	Edward Wainwright,	24 Aug., 1795.
Adjutant	Thomas Priestley,	28 May, 1794.
Agent	Mr. Mackay, Fludyer Street, London.	

Loyal Addresses, Sept., 1796.

The Huddersfield corps seems to have been, at this early period of its existence, aflame with enthusiasm for the task they had undertaken. In September, 1796, they unanimously agreed "to address the King and to offer their services, in case the common enemy should make an attempt to invade us, to march to any part of the kingdom where their services might be required." At this time, too, the three original companies were supplemented by an additional company and a battalion was thus constituted, with Sir

George Armytage as lieutenant-colonel and Mr. Northend Nichols as major. Their commissions bear date January 11th, 1797. Nor were the Volunteers alone in their manifestations of loyalty and devotion to the Crown. I may perhaps be pardoned if I incorporate in this record the following address presented to the King by the inhabitants of Huddersfield in 1798, for though it can scarcely be said to be a Volunteer document it bears eloquent testimony to that state of the country without a knowledge of which it is not easy to understand the formation of the corps of that period:—

"To the King's Most Excellent Majesty,

Most Gracious Sovereign,

We, your Majesty's dutiful and loyal subjects, the inhabitants of the town and neighbourhood of Huddersfield, beg leave to approach your Majesty with our hearty prayers that the blessings of God may rest upon your Royal person, and to assure your Majesty of our determination to support, to the utmost of our ability, your Majesty's person and government against all your enemies.

Struck with horror at the manifest inveteracy of your insulting enemies and their ambition in prosecuting such plans as have an eminent tendency to subjugate Europe to their uncontrolled dominion, we, as a commercial district, feel ourselves by such proceedings particularly called upon to step forward to oppose the meditated ruin of our navy and our commerce, which, under Divine Providence, are the bulwark and support of this highly favoured nation.

At a crisis so alarming, when we are threatened with a deprivation of our dearest civil privileges and with the introduction of principles destructive of our still more valuable religious advantages, we feel solicitous that every necessary means of defence may be adopted and such adequate supplies raised as the exigencies of the State may require, assuring your Majesty that, however inconvenient it may prove to ourselves, we will cheerfully contribute our equitable proportion to any plan which the wisdom of the Legislature may deem necessary to the public safety and welfare.

Depending upon the protection and support of the sovereign Disposer of all events, we are determined to stand or fall with the constitution of our country, and to transmit to posterity, unimpaired, the distinguishing blessings we as a nation have the happiness to possess under your Majesty's mild and paternal government."

Inspections. May, 1797.

The King having ordered that all Volunteer corps throughout the kingdom should be inspected, the Huddersfield Volunteers were inspected by Colonel Oswald on the 27th May, 1797, and this inspection was held in a field at Dryclough, Crosland Moor, formerly known as the "Volunteer Field," a name still appearing on old surveys. The field so called was no doubt the drill ground of this corps.

Having set out the names of the original officers of the corps it is not without interest to observe the changes wrought by time in its *personnel* and the changes, too, in rank. The Army List of 1800 gives the following information:—

Officers of Huddersfield Corps, 1800.

RANK.	NAME.	DATE OF COMMISSIONS.
Lieutenant-Colonel	Sir George Armytage, Bart.	11 Jan., 1797.
Major	Northend Nichols,	,, ,,
Captains	Richard H. Beaumont,	18 Nov., 1794.
	Joseph Haigh,	,, ,,
	William Horsfall,	11 Jan., 1797.
Captain-Lieutenant and Captain	Joseph Scott,	11 Jan., 1797.
Lieutenants	Walter Stables,	18 Nov., 1794.
	Bramel Dyson,	,, ,,
	John Hudson,	,, ,,
	Richard Clay,	11 Jan., 1797.
	Spencer Dyson,	,, ,,
	Joseph Atkinson,	,, ,,
	Matthew Mason,	,, ,,
Adjutant	William Horsfall,	,, ,,
Agent	Mr. Croasdaile, Silver Street, Golden Square.	

Before concluding my account of the corps established in 1794 and disbanded on the conclusion of the Treaty of Amiens there remains but to add such particulars as are available as to the strength of this force, which had now, (1798), assumed the title of the *Huddersfield Volunteer Corps* or *Royal Huddersfield Fusilier Volunteer Corps*. The Commandant was still Sir George Armytage and I find in the Record Office the following further details:—

State in 1798 and 1802 of the *Huddersfield Volunteer Corps* or *Royal Huddersfield Fusilier Volunteer Corps*.

State of Corps, 1798 and 1802.

	1798.	1802.
Commandant,	Sir George Armytage.	
No. of Companies,	4	6
Establishment,	No reference	No reference.
Total	Ditto.	Ditto.
Captains	2	4
Lieutenants	4	4
Ensigns	3	6
Staff	1 Adjutant, 1 Colonel, 1 Major.	Ditto.
Sergeants	4 Drill, 8 other.	18
Corporals	With rank and file.	
Drummers	8	20
Efficient rank and file	200	290

Date of service accepted—No reference.

Pay.

		s.	d.	
Colonels	.. ..	15	11	per day
Majors ..	.. ..	14	1	,, ,,
Captains	.. ..	9	5	,, ,,
Lieutenants	.. ..	4	4	,, ,,
Adjutants	.. ..	3	9	,, ,,
Ensigns ..	.. ..	3	3	,, ,,
Sergeants	.. ..	1	6½	,, ,,
Drummers and Privates	..	1	0	,, ,,

Clothing.—No reference.

If we would form a complete conception of the voluntary services rendered by the people of our country at this anxious period to the maintenance of domestic order, we must now turn our attention from the Royal Huddersfield Fusiliers to another body, less military perhaps, in its nature, but still well entitled to be reckoned among the Volunteer forces of the country. I refer to the *Huddersfield Armed Association* and other Armed Associations of its vicinity. I have already, in the preceding part, narrated the genesis of this peculiar species of organization. It remains but to place on record the steps taken in the locality in response to the invitation of the Crown and in compliance with the enabling statute. Armed Associations.

A meeting of the inhabitants of the town and parish of Huddersfield was held at the George Inn on the 23rd of April, 1798, in pursuance of a public advertisement, to take into consideration the propriety of forming an Armed Association for the protection of the town and neighbourhood. Meeting at Huddersfield to form, April 23, 1798.

Sir George Armytage, Bart., in the Chair.

Resolved :—

First—That at the present alarming crisis, when we are threatened with immediate invasion, it is expedient that an Armed Association be formed to assist the magistrates in preserving the peace of this town and neighbourhood, in case the Volunteers who have so nobly offered their services should be ordered away to oppose the landing of the enemy.

Secondly—That the Huddersfield Armed Association do consist of one troop of cavalry and two companies of infantry, to serve without pay, and to be armed and clothed at their own expense, who shall not be subject to martial law, nor be liable to march further than ten miles from Huddersfield.

Thirdly—That, if Government should approve of this measure, the following resolutions be adopted for the regulation and good order of the said Association.

FOURTHLY—That the uniform of the cavalry shall be a plain scarlet hussar jacket, three rows of silver buttons, silver chain to each shoulder, with silver fringe and bullion, helmet cap inscribed, "Huddersfield Volunteer Cavalry," black bear skin on the crest, white plume with red top, white leather breeches, military boots, blue cloak and military horse-furniture. That the uniform for the infantry shall be a blue coat, with scarlet collar and cuffs, and gold epaulets, white waistcoat, white linen pantaloons and black gaiters, a round hat with a feather and a loop, sword hung to a white shoulder belt, pouch to another to cross. That all reasonable economy shall be observed in everything relating to the said Association, The times for learning the exercise shall be regulated by the Committee, so as to interfere as little as possible with the other engagements of this Association.

FIFTHLY—That each member on his entering into this Association be required to take the oath of allegiance.

SIXTHLY—That a Committee be formed for the purpose of regulating the admission of members into this Association conformably to the directions contained in the Circular Letter of the Secretary of State; that they do appoint officers, and make all other necessary regulations respecting the said Association.

SEVENTHLY—That the said Committee do consist of the following gentlemen, who shall meet at the George Inn every Tuesday and Friday evening, at six o'clock, in order to receive the names of such persons as may choose to enter into this Association and to carry into effect the aforesaid resolutions; any five of whom may be competent to act, viz. :—

Names of Committee.

Joseph Radcliffe, Esq.,	Rev. Mr Wickham,
Mr. Thomas Atkinson,	Mr. John Horsfall,
Mr. Jo. Atkinson, sen.,	Mr. John Whitacre,
Mr. Law Atkinson,	Mr. Benjamin Haigh,
Mr. Abraham Horsfall,	Mr. Thomas Holroyd,
Mr. Firth Macauley,	Mr. Henry Stables,
Mr. Thomas Allen,	Mr. Rowland Houghton,
Mr. Robert Scott,	Mr. John Houghton,
Mr. Jonathan Roberts,	Mr. Daniel Crosland,
Mr. William Roberts,	Mr. Shires, Paddock,
Mr. R. R. Batty,	Mr. Armytage, Highroyd,
Mr. John Brook, Flashes,	Mr. Walker, Lassels (sic) Hall,
Mr. William Armytage, Almondbury,	Mr. Harrop, Holmfirth,
Mr. John Roberts, Longwood House,	Mr. John Dobson, Huddersfield,
Mr. Jo. Brook, Huddersfield,	Mr. James Dyson,
Mr. Godfrey Webster,	Mr. dward Hawxby,
Mr. Thomas Nelson,	Mr. Sturges, sen.,
Mr. Jo. Taylor,	Mr. Thomas Houghton,
Rev. Mr. Coates,	Mr. Turner.

"Resolved: That the thanks of the meeting be given to the chairman.

(Signed) G. Armytage, Chairman."

RULES AND REGULATIONS.

Rules and Regulations.

1—That the members of this Association be divided into troops and companies of not less than fifty men each, one captain, one lieutenant, one cornet, two sergeants, one trumpeter, and two corporals to each troop of cavalry; one captain, one lieutenant, one ensign, three sergeants, two corporals, one drummer and one fifer to each company of infantry, and one adjutant to the whole. Such commissioned and non-commissioned officers to be appointed by the committee, and the commissioned officers to be subject to his Majesty's approbation, and to act under his Majesty's commission.

2—That as regularity and discipline are of the utmost consequence we agree to obey our officers, and each officer his superior officer, when on duty, and in order to obtain a knowledge in the use of arms, we will attend the drill every Monday and Thursday evening at 5 o'clock precisely during the first two months after we commence exercise.

3—That as punctuality is essentially necessary in the prosecution of this undertaking, we hereby agree that each officer and non-commissioned officer shall forfeit and pay, on demand, the sum of two shillings, and each private one shilling, to the person appointed to receive the same, in default of their not being present each day of exercise when the roll is called over, unless prevented by illness, or being more than seven miles distant from Huddersfield for the Infantry, and ten miles for the Cavalry; (afterwards it was agreed by the Cavalry to forfeit for absence: the major, seven shillings; captain, six shillings; lieutenant, five shillings; cornet, four shillings; sergeants, three shillings; corporal, two shillings; private, one shilling, each day.

4—That each member of the Cavalry Corps shall be provided with a sabre and one pistol, the sabre to hang from a white waist-belt.

5—That each member of the Cavalry Corps shall deposit ten guineas when sworn in, to the person appointed to receive the same, towards furnishing their clothing and arms &c., &c. and to pay for the remainder of their clothing and arms &c. when they are delivered to them.

6—That each member of the Infantry Corps shall provide himself with clothing, conformable to the 4th resolution, exact in colour and as near as possible in quality, and exact to the pattern dress proposed by the committee. And we also agree to pay for the arms and accoutrements when delivered to us by the committee.

The Present Officers.

Major Commandant of the Association of the Parish of Huddersfield — Officers. Joseph Radcliffe, Esq.

Captain of Cavalry—Law Atkinson, Esq.
Lieutenant—Firth Macauley, Esq., Clough House.
Cornet—Joseph Brook, Huddersfield.
Captain of Infantry—Henry Stables, Esq., Huddersfield.
Lieutenant—William Hirst, New Street.
Ensign—Godfrey Webster, ditto.
Captain—John Roberts, Esq., Longwood House.
Lieutenant—Joseph Taylor, Birkby.
Ensign—Jos. Hudson, Huddersfield.
Adjutant—John Duckworth, Huddersfield.

Commissions dated the 22nd May, 1798.

According to the War Office list of 21st April, 1800, the following appear as the officers of this Infantry Association:—

		COMMISSION DATED.
Major Commanding	Joseph Radcliffe,	22 May, 1798.
Captain	Henry Stables,	,, ,,
Lieutenants	William Hirst,	,, ,,
	Joseph Taylor,	23 May, ,,
Ensigns	Godfrey Webster,	22 May, ,,
	Joseph Hudson,	23 May, ,,

Colours.

"STANDARD FOR THE CAVALRY.—In the centre, the Rose and Thistle, over which is a Crown; at the right corner at the top, and the left corner at the bottom, is an oval, H.A.A.; at the left corner at the top, and the right corner at the bottom, is an oval, the Hanover Horse, on crimson satin, with silver fringe and tassels.

COLOURS FOR THE INFANTRY.—The Union Flag, in the centre of which is the King's Arms."

I am indebted to the courtesy of the Rev. H. H. Rose, the vicar of Slaithwaite, near Huddersfield, for permission to reproduce from documents preserved in the parish chest, certain returns, of considerable antiquarian interest, of men capable of serving in these Armed Associations. These returns are valuable as indicating the strange straits to which government was reduced in its quest for armed forces and the rude machinery then existing for calling forth the manhood of the country.

On April 25th, 1798, R. Beatson, Chief Constable of the West Riding, addressed to (*inter alios*) the Constable of Slaithwaite a mandate in the following terms:—

"TO THE CONSTABLE OF SLAITHWAITE, WITHIN THE SAID RIDING.

West Riding of the County of York.

By virtue of an order from his Majesty's lieutenant and deputy lieutenants of and for the said riding, at their general meeting for that purpose assembled, unto me directed, YOU ARE HEREBY REQUIRED, upon receipt hereof, to make out a true and fair return of the numbers of men residing within your Constabulary who are of the age of fifteen years, and under the age of sixty years, distinguishing how many of them are, by reason of infirmity, incapable of active service and which of them are engaged in any Volunteer corps, and what corps; and which of them are willing to engage themselves to be armed, arrayed, trained and exercised for the defence of the kingdom, and upon what terms, and with what arms they are now furnished, or can furnish themselves; and which of them are willing to engage, in case of emergency, either gratuitously or for hire, as boatmen or bargemen, or as drivers of waggons, carriages, or teams, or as pioneers, or other labourers for any works or labour which may be necessary for the public service; and what implements they can respectively provide or bring for such service—and also distinguishing all aliens and quakers within your said

Constabulary, who, by reason of infancy, age or infirmity, or for other cause, may probably be incapable of removing themselves in case of danger—and likewise a return of all boats, barges, waggons, carts and horses, and of all mills and public ovens within your Constabulary; and which of such boats, barges, waggons, carts and horses, the owners thereof are willing to furnish in case of emergency, for the public service, either gratuitously or for hire; and with what number of boatmen, bargemen, drivers and other necessary attendance, upon what terms and conditions, to enable His Majesty and the persons acting under his authority to give such orders as may be necessary for the removal, in case of danger, of such persons as shall be incapable of removing themselves and for the removal or employment, in His Majesty's service, of all boats, waggons, horses, cattle, corn, hay, meal, flour and other provisions, matters and things aforesaid, as the exigency of the case shall require. Which returns touching the several purposes aforesaid, you are to prepare in writing, conformable to the respective schedule, herewith sent to you, and make and bring the same to the deputy-lieutenants acting in and for the said Riding, at their sub-division meeting, for that purpose to be held on the tenth day of May next, at the White Hart in the said Riding, at ten o'clock in the forenoon, and there verify the same upon your oath. Herein fail not.

GIVEN under my hand the 25th day of April in the Year of our Lord, 1798.

R. BEATSON,

Chief Constable."

Return by the Constable of Slaithwaite in pursuance of the above Order.

Numbered May 1st, 2nd, 3rd, 4th, 5th, by Benj. Bailey.

May 10th, 1798, sent to Wakefield.

	In Slaithwaite.	In Lingarths.	Total.
The whole number of men between the ages of 15 and 60	483	133	616
Will serve on horses	6		6
Will serve on foot	115	15	130
Infirm	31	11	42
Armed Corps	4	1	5
Old people not able to remove themselves, and infants	389	70	459
Horses	81	16	97
Carts	61	17	78
Sword	1		1
Pistol	1		1
Fire-lock	1		1
Pike	1	2	3
Pioneers and labourers..	65	21	86
Felling axes	5		5
Pick axes..	29	2	31
Spades	33	2	35
Shovels	5		5
Bill hook	1		1
Saws	3		3
Fork	1		1
Han	1		1
Servants with cattle	21	2	23
Servants with teams	22	5	27
Drivers	1	1	2
Total	1357	298	1659

One Public Oven can bake one hundredweight of bread in twenty-four hours.

One Corn Mill can grind twenty-four quarters of corn in one week.

The whole number of men in Slaithwaite and Lingarths between 15 and 60 years	616
The number of men infirm and not fit for active service between 15 and 60 years	42
Firm ..	574
The number of men who are willing to be trained and exercised in Slaithwaite for the protection of their own town and neighbourhood, and to enlist their own civil officers provided Government will furnish them with arms	136
The number of armed corps in Yeomanry, Cavalry, Volunteers and Armed Associations	5
The number of men willing to serve as Pioneers and Labourers in case of emergency	86
The number of men willing to serve as servants of cattle, teams, and drivers in case of emergency	52
	279
Firm ..	574
	279
Remains ..	295

Perhaps even more instructive as to the spirit of the times are the notes of the returning-officer anent each name. I reproduce some of them :—

"John Ramsden, Waterside, engineer, two children under three years old. No objection to be enrowled (*sic*) in the Infantry, provided they be trained at Slaithwaite and Government finds arms.

William, Benjamin, and Matthew Sykes, sons of John Sykes, clothier, Brookside, guarantee to serve with pick-axe and shovel which they will themselves provide.

Joel Hoyle, Highfield, clothier, will be a labourer, and hath no implements. Will work hard.

Joseph Bamforth, Inghend, one horse and cart *gratis* in case of emergency; one pick and spade do.

Joseph Richard and Edmund Barrett will serve in Infantry for the defence of the town and neighbourhood.

Samuel Wood, butcher, Town, will furnish himself with arms and stand up for the defence of the town and neighbourhood.

John Bamforth (Mr. Sykes) : 'If Dob go, I go alongside her.'

James Sykes, Cophill, is determined to kill a Frenchman, if possible."

Not so another James Sykes who is described as a "driver with a long whip." This James is distinguished by the note, "will assist all in his power for the French to have their own. Consequently he must be a Jacobin."

To a later date belonged still another return, of like character to the preceding, and equally exemplifying the untiring care the

Government in those times felt it necessary to display, to secure exact information as to all the available resources which it might, at need, summon to its assistance. It has been kindly placed at my disposal by Sir George J. Armytage, Baronet, of Kirklees, and the return and accompanying notice tell their own story :—

Sir George Armytage, Bart.,

Take Notice that you are hereby required, within four days from the date hereof, to prepare and produce a list in writing, to the best of your belief, of the christian and surname of each and every man resident in your dwellinghouse, between the ages of 18 and 45, distinguishing in such list their age and rank or occupation; and also which of the persons so returned labour under any infirmity likely to incapacitate them from serving as militiamen; and which of them (if any) is a peer of this realm, or a commissioned officer in His Majesty's regular forces or in any one of His Majesty's castles or forts or in the Local Militia or an officer on the half-pay of the navy, army or marines, and whether such half-pay officer hath tendered his services to serve as an officer in the Militia, or in any corps of Yeomanry, or Volunteer Cavalry, or is incapable of service; and also which of them is a non-commissioned officer or private man, serving in any of His Majesty's regular forces, or in the Local Militia, or a commissioned officer serving, or who has served four years in the Militia, or an effective member of any of the Universities, or a clergyman, or a teacher, licensed within the Riding to teach in some separate congregation, whose place of meeting shall have been duly registered within twelve months, or a constable or other peace officer, articled clerk, apprentice, seaman or seafaring man, or a poor man who has more than one child born in wedlock, or a person who has served personally or by substitute, or paid a fine for not serving in the Militia or Army or Reserve. And you are to sign such list with your own name, and to deliver or leave the same at my house in Hartshead-with-Clifton.

Dated the 14th day of December, 1815.

Names.	Description.	Age.	Whether any child, and if any, whether under 14.	Exempt or not exempt from Militia.	Grounds of Exemption.	Effective Yeomanry or Volunteer Cavalry.	Licensed Teacher not carrying on Trade, or Medical Practitioner actually practising.
A. B.	Farmer ..	40	1 under 14	Not exempt	..	..	..
C. D.	Gentleman	28	None	Exempt	..	Yeomanry or Volunteer Cavalry	..
E. F.	Surgeon ..	44	2 above 14	Exempt	..	..	Surgeon
G. H.	Grocer ..	30	3 under 14	Not exempt	..	..	..
J. K.	Servant ..	18	None	Exempt	Apprentice	..	..

N.B.—If any house is divided into distinct storeys, or apartments occupied distinctly, each distinct occupier is required to make this return. Neglect of compliance with this notice will subject the party to a penalty of £1 os. od. Non-effective members of yeomanry or volunteer cavalry claiming exemption become liable to a penalty of £30.

TAKE NOTICE, That the seventh day of January, 1815, at the Old Cock Inn, in Halifax, at the hour of Ten in the forenoon, is appointed for hearing appeals within this sub-division, by persons claiming to be exempt from serving in the Militia, who must in such case produce a surgeon's certificate of their inability, and such persons neglecting to appeal at the above time and place and afterwards appealing, become liable to a penalty of £2 os. od.

Constable of Hartshead-with-Clifton.

Robard Fitton and John Woodhead.

A LIST of the Christian and Surnames of each and every man resident in my dwelling-house at Kirklees Hall, in the Division of Morley, in the West Riding of the County of York, between the ages of eighteen and forty-five :—

NAME.	Description.	Age.	Whether Children or not.	Exempt or not Exempt from the Militia.	Ground of Exemption.
Robert Willoughby	Footman ..	34		Has been Sergeant in the Staincross Local Militia.	..
Nathan Firth ..	ditto	30	1		..
Thomas Scott ..	Groom ..	22			..
Edward Cummerson	Gamekeeper	32			..
Richard Cryer ..	Under do.	23		Private Soldier in the Leeds Local Militia.	..
John Armytage ..	Esquire ..	23			..
George Scott ..	Servant to ditto.	21			..

Dated the 21st December, 1815.

For Sir Geo. Armytage, Bart.

Chas. Brooke, Agent.

Delivered a duplicate hereof to John Woodhead, Constable of Clifton, the day and year above.

I have been fortunate enough to see, and in fact, to handle an actual uniform of the *Leeds Armed Association* of 1798. This uniform, which is similar in cut and shape to that of the Huddersfield Fusilier Volunteers (1794), and probably also to that of the Huddersfield Armed Association, consisted of red coat with black velvet collar, cuffs and lappels, edged all round with a narrow piping of white, crimson sash, black shoulder belt and sword, the latter with the regulation gold and crimson sword-knot. Silver epaulettes (on the strap an embroidered "fleece" in gold), flat silver buttons at equidistances (not in pairs), having thereon raised "fleece" with the letter "L" beneath. Silver engraved oval breast plate bearing monogram, "L.A.A.," with Crown engraved above. Silver gorget, quite plain, with the Leeds coat of arms engraved in centre. This ornament had been worn for nearly one hundred years by the officers of Infantry regiments, to denote their position as such. I have thus been enabled to more fully realise what manner of figure our gallant ancestors presented when attired for their military duties. Major Lewis Motley (Leeds Rifles), very kindly procured me the inspection of this uniform, which was temporarily in the care of Ambrose Edmund Butler, Esquire, of Kepstorn, Kirkstall, near Leeds, Lord Mayor of that city in 1902. This uniform was that of Thomas Butler, Esquire, (Mr. A. E. Butler's grandfather), whose commission as lieutenant in the *Leeds Armed Association* bore date 9th July, 1798. He died in 1831. Portions of another uniform, which I have also been privileged to inspect, were in the possession of Major Motley. These consisted of gold epaulettes, touched up with green silk (and hence I conclude the facings of the coat would be green), with gilt buttons, also a red and white feather worn in front of the shako, crimson sash and an oval gilt breast plate of the Leeds Volunteers, and a rectangular breast plate of the Leeds Local Militia. All these are grouped in a military device encircling the miniature of the wearer of the uniform, Mr. Thomas Motley, (the grandfather of Major Lewis Motley), who, I find from the Army Lists of 1807 and 1810, held a commission (dated 6th July, 1804) as ensign in the Leeds Volunteers (1803-8), and afterwards a captain's commission (dated 20th February, 1810), in the 2nd Battalion Leeds Local Militia.

Regiments to denote their position as such.

These fragments appear, therefore, to be partly those of the Leeds Volunteers (1803-8) and partly of the Leeds Local Militia (1808-14). In this view I am fortified by the judgment of my friend, Mr. S. Milne Milne, (late Bradford Rifles), who, along with my old friend, Major Walter Braithwaite (Leeds Rifles), accompanied me on my visit of inspection. Mr. Milne, I need hardly say, is a recognised authority on all questions of military uniform, and is responsible for the description and details of the above-mentioned uniforms.

PART II.

SECTION II.

1803-1859.

I have in the preceding part of this work (section 3), already shewn how the renewal of hostilities after the short-lived Treaty of Amiens led to the hurried passing through Parliament of the Defence Act and the Levy *en masse* Act of 1803. I have quoted, too, the words of Dr. Bright in which he described the spirit with which Englishmen of all parties and all classes resented what they believed to be the perfidy of Napoleon aud hastened to offer their services to the Government against a tyrant whom they were persuaded would know no rest till he had humbled the pride of Britain and ravaged the homes of its people. The present section will shew the steps taken at this crisis by the people of Huddersfield and its vicinity to take their share in the general arming of the nation and add their aid to the movement which, for a time, transformed an industrial country into an armed camp.

The latter of the Acts I have mentioned, the Levy *en masse* Act, received the Royal Assent on July 27th, 1803. No better evidence of the perturbed, one might almost say nervous, state of the public mind need be mentioned than the fact that only two days later, July 29th, a meeting was held at the old George Inn, Huddersfield, then in the Market Place, of the gentlemen and merchants of the town and neighbourhood. Mr., afterwards Sir Joseph Radcliffe, Bart., J.P., D.L., of Milnsbridge House, presided, a gentleman whose many public services, at this and later periods, have been so often recorded and were so conspicuously acknowledged by his Sovereign that I may be excused from their further recital, save so far as his name appears in the Volunteer records with which I am now concerned. At that meeting it was resolved to summon by public announcement a public and more representative gathering of the "gentlemen, clergy, merchants and inhabitants of the several parishes of Huddersfield, Almondbury, Kirkheaton, Kirkburton and the Township of Quick in the Upper Division of Agbrigg." At this meeting, held at the George Inn, on August 1st,

Meeting, July 29th, 1803, in Huddersfield.

1803, Mr. Radcliffe again presided, and the meeting first adopted the following loyal address:—

"To the King's most excellent Majesty:—

May it please your Majesty,

We, your Majesty's dutiful and loyal subjects, the gentlemen, clergy, merchants and inhabitants of the town and neighbourhood of Huddersfield, humbly beg leave to approach the Throne at this momentous crisis, with the strongest assurances of our unalterable attachment to your Majesty's person and Government. We sincerely regret that the wisdom, the justice and the moderation of your Majesty's counsels have proved ineffectual in preserving to us the blessings of peace, and that the boundless ambition of the daring usurper of the Government of France has again involved us in war, and threatens the invasion of this happy land. Proud of the highly valued privileges which Britons enjoy, firm in the justice of our cause, happy in that mutual confidence which results from the exemplary beneficence of the sovereign and the grateful and united affections of the people, and relying on the blessing of Divine providence, we fear not the haughty menaces of our enemies, and behold their preparations with indignation yet without alarm. From a conviction that everything dear and valuable to a free and independent nation is involved in the present contest, we most willingly submit to those privations which the wisdom of your Majesty's counsels may deem necessary, and are determined to support, with our persons and our property, the honour and dignity of your Majesty's Crown and Government, and the rights and independence of our country. May your Majesty be the favoured instrument of Providence, to check the devastating progress of that power, which, hitherto with impunity, has trampled on the rights of humanity, and may He enable you speedily to terminate the war with glory, and to re-establish the blessings of peace.

Loyal Address to the King.

(Signed), JOSEPH RADCLIFFE,

Chairman."

The following resolutions were then adopted, and appeared in the *London Gazette*, of 13th August, 1803. The address was presented by the Honourable Henry Lascelles and William Wilberfore, Esquires, representatives in Parliament for the county of York. It will be observed that some of the resolutions had reference to the Cavalry, the formation of which would naturally be intermixed with that of the Volunteer Infantry:—

"That a corps of Volunteer Infantry be raised in this district on as large a scale as possible, so as to be respectable, and also a corps of Volunteer Cavalry."

"That Sir George Armytage, Bart., be requested to take the command of the corps of Infantry intended to be raised," and "that John Lister Kaye, Esq., be requested to take the command of the corps of Cavalry intended to be raised."

Resolutions adopted.

A canvass of the various districts for the purpose of obtaining the names of Volunteers was decided upon, and the meeting resolved:—

"That books shall be immediately opened in each township within the district for the enrolment of such as may wish to serve in each corps, and that the gentlemen whose names are hereunto subjoined be requested to wait upon the inhabitants of their respective townships for signatures, and be desired to make their returns to Mr. Law Atkinson, of Moldgreen, on or before Wednesday, the 10th day of August, inst., at 10 o'clock in the forenoon:—

HUDDERSFIELD—Mr. Houghton, Mr. Horsfall, Mr. Woolley, Mr. W. Stables, Mr. Josh. Brook and Mr. T. Atkinson, junior.

FARTOWN—Mr. Holroyd, Mr. Whitacre, Mr. Brook and Mr. Roberts.

BRADLEY—Mr. Rawstorne, Mr. Waller and Mr. Ewbank.

MARSH—Mr. Benjamin Haigh.

LINDLEY AND QUARMBY—Mr. Waterhouse, Mr. Fawcett and Mr. Waterhouse of Knowl.

LONGWOOD—Rev. Mr. Robinson and Mr. Sykes.

DEANHEAD AND SCAMMONDEN—Rev. Mr. Falcon.

SLAITHWAITE—Rev. Mr. Wilson and Mr. S. Wood.

MARSDEN—Mr. John Haigh.

GOLCAR—Mr. Joseph Haigh and Mr. Joseph Hall.

DEIGHTON—Mr. Tinker and Mr. Netherwood.

DENBY—John Lister Kaye, Esq.

KIRKBURTON, SHELLEY, SHEPLEY, THURSTONLAND—Rev. Mr. Wickham, Mr. Booth, Mr. Hardy, Mr. R. Turner, Mr. Stocks and Mr. J. Walker.

FOULSTONE, WOOLDALE, HEPWORTH, CARTWORTH—Mr. John Haigh, Mr. Harrop, Mr. John Bates and Mr. George Moorhouse.

KIRKHEATON—Mr. L. Atkinson and Rev. Mr. Sunderland.

DALTON—Mr. Mallinson and Mr. Beaumont.

LOCKWOOD—Mr. Ingham, Mr. North and Mr. J. Horsfall.

ALMONDBURY—Mr. Allen, Mr. John Roberts and Mr. W. Scott.

SOUTH CROSLAND—Mr. W. Beaumont.

NORTH CROSLAND—Mr. J. Roberts and Mr. Lockwood, junior.

HONLEY—Mr. Armitage, Mr. Leigh and Mr. Brooke.

LEPTON AND WHITLEY—Mr. Walker and Mr. Jno. Beaumont.

MELTHAM—Mr. Brooke.

AUSTERLEY—Mr. John Armitage.

HOLME—Mr. C. Green.

THONG—Mr. A. Green.

LINGARTHS—Mr. Shaw.

FARNLEY—Mr. W. Roberts and Mr. Scott.

QUICK—Mr. Harrop, Dobcross; Mr. Jno. Buckley, Upper Mill; Mr. Josh. Harrop, Grasscroft; Mr. Jno. Roberts, Linfits; and Mr. Jno. Radcliffe, Stonebreaks.

A further meeting was held of the gentlemen, clergy, merchants and inhabitants of the parishes aforesaid, and of the townships of Quick, Mirfield and Cumberworth, at the George Inn, on 10th August, 1803, Mr. Radcliffe again presiding, when it was resolved:— Further Meeting, August 10th, 1803.

"That an offer be made to Government to raise a corps of Volunteer Cavalry and a corps of Volunteer Infantry to consist of 1,100 men, or three-fourths of the whole number of men enrolled for military service in the first class of the said parishes and townships under the Act of 43, Geo. III. c. 96, the Cavalry to be commanded by John Lister Kaye, Esquire, and the Infantry by Sir George Armytage, Bart." Further Resolutions.

I have already stated the leading provisions of this statute. It requires to be remembered, for the full understanding of the above resolution, that application of the statute to a district was only to be suspended when three-fourths of the men enrolled in class 1 under that Act took service in a Volunteer Corps; and the zest with which, all over the country, men enrolled themselves in Volunteer corps may, perhaps, be attributed not so much to a desire to shirk military service as to a natural preference to serve under officers resident in their own neighbourhood, whom many of them knew and probably respected as their own landlords or their own employers.

The resolution to form Volunteer corps of Cavalry and Infantry having been adopted, it became necessary to invite subscriptions for the defraying of the necessary expenses, and the following gentlemen were appointed in their respective districts. It will serve to inform or remind those of this generation who were the leading spirits in their several localities a century ago, if I reproduce the names of those appointed to solicit subscriptions:—

HUDDERSFIELD—Mr. Houghton, Mr. Horsfall, Mr. Woolley, Mr. W. Stables, Mr. J. Brook and Mr. S. Dyson.

FARTOWN—Mr. Holroyd, Mr. Whitacre and Mr. Brook.

BRADLEY—Mr. Rawstorne, Mr. Waller and Mr. Ewbank.

MARSH—Mr. B. Haigh, Mr. U. Booth and Mr. J. Dobson, Junr.

LINDLEY AND QUARMBY—Mr. Waterhouse, Mr. Fawcett and Mr. Waterhouse, Knowl.

LONGWOOD—Rev. Mr. Robinson and Mr. W. Dawson.

DEANHEAD AND SCAMMONDEN—Rev. Mr. Falcon and Mr. Walker.

SLAITHWAITE—Rev. Mr. Wilson, Mr. S. Wood and Mr. Schofield.

MARSDEN—Mr. John Haigh and Mr. W. Horsfall.

GOLCAR—Mr. Jo. Haigh, Mr. Jo. Hall and Mr. W. Sykes.

DEIGHTON—Mr. Tinker and Mr. Netherwood.

MIRFIELD—Mr. Joshua Ingham, Junr.

DENBY—Jno. Lister Kaye, Esquire, and Mr. J. Ness, Junr.

KIRKBURTON, SHELLEY, SHEPLEY AND THURSTONLAND—Rev. Mr. Wickham, Mr. Booth, Mr. Smith, Mr. Hardy, Mr. Turner, Mr. Stocks and Mr. Walker.

CUMBERWORTH AND CUMBERWORTH HALL—Rev. Mr. Railton, Mr. S. Senior and Messrs. Jno. and Jo. Wood.

FOULSTONE, WOOLDALE, HEPWORTH, CARTWORTH, HOLMFIRTH—Mr. Harrop, Mr. Stephenson, Mr. Jno. Haigh, Mr. John Bates, Mr. Geo. Moorhouse and Mr. Newton.

KIRKHEATON AND DALTON—Rev. Mr. Sunderland, Mr. Mallinson, Mr. Law Atkinson and Mr. Beaumont of Dalton Green.

LEPTON AND WHITLEY—Mr. Walker and Mr. Jno. Beaumont.

MELTHAM—Mr. Brooke and Mr. Jo. Eastwood.

LOCKWOOD—Mr. Ingham, Mr. North and Mr. Jno. Horsfall.

ALMONDBURY—Mr. Allen, Mr. J. Roberts and Mr. W. Scott.

SOUTH CROSLAND—Mr. W. Beaumont and Mr. D. Harrison.

NORTH CROSLAND—Mr. J. Roberts and Mr. Lockwood, jun.

HONLEY—Mr. Armitage, Mr. Leigh and Mr. Brooke.

AUSTERLEY—Mr. Christopher Green.

HOLME—Mr. Anthony Green.

THONG—Mr. Jno. Armitage.

LINGARTHS—Mr. Shaw.

FARNLEY—Mr. W. Roberts and Mr. J. Scott.

QUICK—Mr. Jno. Harrop, Dobcross, Mr. Jno. Buckley, Uppermill, Mr. Joseph Harrop, Grass-croft, Mr. John Roberts, Linfits, and Mr. Jno. Radcliffe, Stonebreaks.

"That the subscriptions be paid at the bank of Messrs. Perfect, Seaton, Brook & Co."

"That every subscriber of fifty pounds and upwards be a member of the committee, and any three of whom shall be competent to act."

The above resolutions were directed to be forwarded to the Lord Lieutenant, and the meeting was adjourned to the 18th inst. When the meeting reassembled on that day, though but a week had elapsed, it was able, from the returns, to resolve:—

"That a return of 1400 men as Volunteers for the Upper Division of Agbrigg and the townships of Mirfield and Hartshead-cum-Clifton be made to the Lord Lieutenant."

It was also resolved:—

"That £7 be allowed to each member of the Corps of Cavalry from the general fund," and that "Sir George Armytage, Baronet, shall have the nomination of the officers of the Infantry, to be transmitted to the Deputy Lieutenant of the district, who will forward them to the Lord Lieutenant for His Majesty's approbation," and "that every gentleman in the division who is inclined to become an officer in the Infantry be requested to make an offer of his services immediately, addressed to Sir George Armytage, Baronet, Kirklees."

The appointment of officers to the Cavalry was in like manner entrusted to Mr. John Lister Kaye.

It was further agreed :—

That the undermentioned townships be required to produce not less than the annexed number of Volunteers :—

Township	Number	Township	Number
Almondbury	96	Farnley Tyas	24
Honley	72	Meltham	42
Netherthong		Huddersfield	180
South Crosland		Kirkburton	36
Lockwood		Thurstonland	18
Linthwaite		Shelley	30
Longwood	150	Shepley	12
Lindley-cum-Quarmby ..		Wooldale	
Golcar and		Foulstone	
Scammonden		Cartworth	
Slaithwaite and	54	Hepworth	
Lingards		Holme	186
Marsden-in-Almondbury ..	24	Austonley	
Marsden-in-Huddersfield ..		Upperthong and	
Kirkheaton	18	Holmfirth	
Dalton	30	Quick	246
Lepton	30	Mirfield	36
Whitley	24	Hartishead-cum-Clifton ..	42

Meeting, August 29th, 1803.

At an adjourned meeting of the gentlemen, clergy, merchants and inhabitants of the several parishes and townships aforesaid, held at the George Inn, Huddersfield, on Monday, the 29th August, 1803, Mr. Joseph Radcliffe in the chair, it was resolved :—

Resolutions thereat.

"That each township within this division is required to enrol as Volunteers six times the number of men as are balloted to serve in the old militia, and it is recommended to the several townships to select such men as are unmarried, and have the fewest incumbrances. *

"That John Lister Kaye, Esquire, be requested to attend at Huddersfield to enrol the men, and to administer the oath to the corps of Cavalry.

"That Sir George Armytage, Bart., be requested to attend to enrol the men, and to administer the oath to the corps of Infantry in the following townships, viz:—Huddersfield, Kirkheaton, Dalton, Whitley, Lepton, Almondbury, Lockwood, Marsden, Quick, Mirfield and Hartishead-cum-Clifton.

"That Josh. Radcliffe, Esquire, be requested to attend to enrol the men, and to administer the oath to the corps of Infantry in the following townships, viz.:—Longwood, Lindley-cum-Quarmby, Linthwaite, Golcar, Scammonden, Slaithwaite and Lingarths.

* This has doubtless reference to the statutory quota fixed for each county.

"That George Armitage, Esquire, of Highroyd, be requested to attend to enrol the men and to administer the oath to the corps of Infantry in the following townships, viz.:—Honley, Meltham, Netherthong, South Crosland, Farnley Tyas, Kirkburton, Thurstonland, Shelley, Shepley, Wooldale, Foulstone, Cartworth, Holme, Hepworth, Austonley and Upperthong.

"That each of the above-mentioned townships be required to complete their lists with the least possible delay, and that Sir George Armytage, Baronet, Josh. Radcliffe and George Armitage, Esquires, be requested to inform the gentlemen of the respective townships when it will be convenient for them to attend to enrol and to administer the oath.*

"That the several lists of enrolment be returned to the adjourned public meeting, to be held at the George Inn, Huddersfield, on Friday, the 9th September, at 10 o'clock in the forenoon.

"That John Lister Kaye, Esquire, be requested to apply to Government for the allowance for contingencies, and to order the clothing and accoutrements for the corps of Cavalry.

"That Sir George Armytage, Baronet, be requested to apply to Government for arms and other allowances, and to order the clothing and accoutrements for the corps of Infantry and that the expense of clothing each man do not exceed the sum of £2 12s. 6d.

"That the gentlemen in each Township are requested to collect the whole of the subscriptions of Five Guineas and under, and to pay the same into the Bank of Messrs. Perfect, Seaton, Brook and Company on or before Friday, the 9th September.

"That all subscribers of above Five Guineas are requested to pay 25 per cent. on their respective subscriptions into the hands of Messrs. Perfect, Seaton, Brook and Company, on or before Friday, the 9th September.

"That a list of the subscribers to the corps of Volunteer Cavalry and Infantry in the Upper Division of Agbrigg be inserted as soon as completed in both the Leeds papers."

At a meeting of the Committee on the 1st December, 1803, it was resolved:—

"That the sergeants of the Volunteer Infantry be furnished with swords and sashes at the expense of the Committee; and that £21 17s. od. be allowed for quarters for the drummers at 1/- per day."

Committee Meeting, Dec. 29th, 1803.

At another Committee meeting on the 29th December, 1803, it was resolved:—

"That £600 be allowed Sir George Armytage in advance for the pay of privates in the Upper Agbrigg Infantry; and that Sir George Armytage be allowed sergeants' halberts and sword-belts, drummers' swords and belts, and drums with sticks."

---

* I, A. B., do solemnly promise and swear that I will be faithful and bear true allegiance to His Majesty George the Third and I will faithfully serve His Majesty in Great Britain for the defence of the same, against all his enemies and opposers whatsoever. So help me God. 43 George III., c. 96, sec. 58.

As shewing the quantity of clothing, or cloathing, as the word seems to have been occasionally spelt, the following resolution is of interest :—

> "That 1,000 great-coats be furnished for the Volunteer Infantry, and that Mr. Whitacre and Mr. Jo. Haigh be requested to provide the cloth."

The Mr. Whitacre referred to in this resolution was that Mr. John Whitacre, of Sun Woodhouse, who carried on business at Whitacre Mill, Deighton, as a woollen manufacturer. There is a short account of his family, which laid claim to an ancient lineage, in Burke's "Landed Gentry." Mr. Joseph Haigh was, no doubt, Lieutenant-Colonel Joseph Haigh, of Golcar Hill, of whom I have already given some account in the 1st section of Part II. of this work.

I do not propose to extract from the records the minutes *seriatim*. They deal mainly with matters of detail: the pay of the drill-sergeant and subscriptions. One resolution seems to indicate, what was no doubt the case, the existence of a very vague idea of how far the Volunteers must rely on local contributions and how far they could count on Government aid. It is as follows :—

> "May 3rd, 1804. That Sir George Armytage be empowered to order knapsacks for the Upper Agbrigg Volunteer Infantry, *provided they are not allowed by Government*."*

Another refers to a contingent now, alas! though not defunct, yet to some extent shorn of its glory, as the drummers of to-day are not used for the same purposes as aforetimes :—

> "That the Huddersfield Drummers be allowed 6d. per day in addition to 1/. per day for their attendance on Field days."

The Drummers.

In former times, every company according to its strength, had one or two drummers who had duties and required qualifications of a varied character, to the extent of being required to possess a knowledge of languages, as well as having to inflict corporal punishments and execute the sentences of Courts Martial. It is explained by Ralph Smith, in somewhat quaint language, that :—

"All captains must have drommes and ffifes and men to use the same, whoe shoulde be faithfule, secrette, and ingenious, of able personage to use their instruments and office, of sundrie languages; for often times they bee sente to parley with their enemies, to sommon theire fforts or townes, to redeeme and conducte prysoners and dyverse other messages which of necessity requireth language. If such drommes and ffifes shoulde fortune to fall into the handes

* The italics are mine.—R. P. B.

of the enemies noe guifte nor force shoulde cause them to disclose any secrettes that they knowe. They must ofte practise theire instruments, teache the companye the soundes of the marche, allarum, approache, assaulte, battaile, retreate, skirmishe, or any other callinge that of necessity shoulde be knowen. They must be obediente to the commandemente of theyre captain and ensigne whenas they shall commande them to comme, goe, or stande, or sounde their retreate or other callinge. Many things else belong to their office, as in dyverse places of this treatise shall be said."*

The *Leeds Mercury*, of October 29th, 1803, contains a list of the subscribers to the Huddersfield Corps of Cavalry and Infantry, and I exhibit it hereunder.

The resolution to collect these subscriptions was only adopted, it will be remembered, on August 10th, 1803. That, in ten weeks, subscriptions amounting to nearly £7,000 were promised to this fund is as significant an indication of the popular apprehensions and the sense of the urgency of the situation as it is possible to find.

Subscribers to the Huddersfield Corps of Cavalry and Infantry in the Parishes of Huddersfield, Almondbury, Kirkheaton, Kirkburton, and the Township of Quick, in the Upper Division of Agbrigg, with Mirfield and Hartishead-cum-Clifton :—

HUDDERSFIELD

	£	s.	d.		£	s.	d.
Sir George Armytage, Bart.	200	0	0	Joseph Bradley	10	0	0
Sir J. Ramsden, Bart. ..	200	0	0	John Hirst	4	4	0
J L. Kaye, Esq.	200	0	0	Mrs. Crosland	4	4	0
Benj. Haigh	105	0	0	Samuel Lancaster ..	1	1	0
John Whitacre	105	0	0	John Dobson	21	0	0
Thos. Holroyd	100	0	0	George Lockwood ..	10	10	0
Mrs. Nicholls	100	0	0	Frederick Hudson ..	3	3	0
Wm. Fenton	100	0	0	John Hick	3	3	0
A & J. Horsfall	100	0	0	Miss Armitage	5	0	0
G. C. Seaton	50	0	0	John Dyson	1	1	0
Joseph Brook	50	0	0	Thomas Starkey ..	2	2	0
John Houghton	50	0	0	Thomas Hirst	2	2	0
W. W. Stables	50	0	0	Joseph Armitage ..	5	5	0
John Roberts	50	0	0	Ely Eagland	2	2	0
Wm. Horsfall	40	0	0	John Tyne	1	1	0
W. Horsfall, junr. ..	30	0	0	— Lister	1	1	0
Francis Downing ..	20	0	0	Messrs. Tinker	20	0	0
J. Lees	5	0	0	Miles Netherwood ..	5	5	0
John Booth	5	0	0	Wm. Hellawell	5	5	0
Thomas Parkin	1	1	0	George Netherwood ..	5	5	0
James Hayley	5	5	0	Joshua Berry	2	2	0

* Grose's Military Antiquities.

Huddersfield.—*Continued.*

Name	£	s.	d.
John Tavernor	10	10	0
Henry Stables	20	0	0
John Brooke	31	10	0
Wm. Waller	10	10	0
J. Whitaker Lane	15	0	0
George Hirst	10	10	0
Rowland Houghton	25	0	0
William Stocks	10	0	0
William Booth	5	5	0
Ab. Beaumont	2	2	0
Ab. Thewlis	3	3	0
Richard Thewlis	2	2	0
Thos. Depledge	2	2	0
Rev. Mr. Coates	5	5	0
J. Dyson & Co.	21	0	0
Moorhouse & Co.	21	0	0
James Fletcher	3	3	0
John Skilbeck	5	5	0
Richard Clay	5	5	0
Thomas Spencer	1	1	0
John Riley	3	3	0
Thomas Marshall	10	10	0
T. Nelson & Co.	21	0	0
Joseph Blackburn	2	2	0
Thos. Shires	10	0	0
Miss Fenton	6	6	0
W. Styring	2	2	0
John Tasker	1	1	0
Samuel Clay	2	2	0
Priest & Ness	5	5	0
Josiah Lancashire	5	5	0
John Edwards	3	3	0
John Wright	1	1	0
Thomas Vernon	5	5	0
Atherton Rawstorne	20	0	0
Thomas Waller	5	5	0
John Hubank	5	5	0
Samuel Day	2	2	0
Francis Spence	2	2	0
Job Hirst	2	2	0
Wm. Lockwood	2	2	0
Richard Hudson	3	3	0
Daniel Schofield	1	1	0
John Hudson	1	1	0
Joshua Jubb	1	1	0
James Hinchcliffe	1	1	0
William Dyson	1	1	0
John Goldthorp	1	1	0
Jonas Mellor	1	1	0
John Firth	1	1	0
Frank Hirst	1	1	0
John Hinchcliffe	1	1	0
Joseph Dyson	1	1	0
Joseph Pilling	1	1	0
Edward Hinchcliffe	0	10	6
Joshua Brooke	0	10	6
John Gibson	0	10	6
Thos. Murgitroyd	0	7	0
Luke Greenwood	5	5	0
James Midwood	5	5	0
Henry Brooke	2	2	0
Jonas Wood	2	2	0
John Sutcliffe, Junr.	10	10	0
William Wilkes	3	3	0
Samuel Ingledew	5	5	0

Longwood.

Name	£	s.	d.
Jos. Radcliffe, Esq.	200	0	0
Rev. Mr. Robinson	1	1	0
Richard Tredale		5	0
Thomas Schofield		5	0

Scammonden.

Name	£	s.	d.
Rev. Mr. Falcon	10	0	0
J. Walker	10	0	0
Small Subscriptions	13	14	6

Golcar.

Name	£	s.	d.
Joseph Haigh	100	0	0
William Sykes	20	0	0
James Shaw	5	5	0
John Wood	5	5	0
John Eastwood	5	5	0
Edmund Eastwood	5	5	0
James Ramsden	5	5	0
Robert Ramsden	2	2	0
William Lockwood	2	2	0
John Shaw	2	2	0
John Swift	2	2	0
E. & J. Blackburn	2	2	0
James Eastwood	2	2	0
Joseph Horsfall	2	2	0

Golcar.—*Continued.*

Hugh Ramsden	5	5	0	Francis Savill	1	1	0
Charles Turner	5	5	0	John Ainley	1	1	0
Benjamin Hinchcliffe	5	5	0	Jos. & J. Walker	1	1	0
Jos. & Thos. Shaw	5	5	0	Samuel Wood	1	1	0
John Haigh	3	3	0	Samuel Walker	1	1	0
Edward Haigh	2	2	0	John Gledhill	1	1	0
William Hinchcliffe	2	2	0	Benjamin Dyson	1	1	0
William Hall	2	2	0	Joseph Miller	1	1	0

Slaithwaite.

Rev. Mr. Wilson	20	0	0	Joshua Cock	1	1	0
Edmund Eastwood	20	0	0	Benjamin Bailey	1	1	0
J. Dyson	10	0	0	Widow Bamford	1	1	0
Samuel Wood	5	5	0	Thomas Shaw	1	1	0
Thomas Haigh	4	4	0	James Bamforth	1	1	0
Thomas Varley	2	2	0	Nathan Carter	1	1	0
Joshua Dransfield	1	1	0	William Varley	1	1	0
James Eastwood	2	2	0	Samuel Wood	1	1	0
Abraham Taylor	1	1	0	James Pearson	1	1	0
James Bamford	1	1	0				

Almondbury.

Thomas Allen .. 100 0 0

Farnley Tyas.

Earl of Dartmouth	50	0	0	Matthew Hallas	2	2	0
Robert Scott	100	0	0	William Nowell	2	2	0
William Roberts	15	15	0	Jonathan Senior	2	2	0
Thomas Kaye	10	10	0	John Crosley	1	1	0
Joseph Shaw	10	10	0	John & Jonas Kaye	1	1	0
Jonas Kaye	4	4	0	Joseph Smith	1	1	0
Charles Kaye	4	4	0	Matthew Kaye	1	1	0
Charles Kaye, Junr.	2	2	0	Mat. Lockwood	1	1	0

Lockwood.

Benj. Ingham	100	0	0	John Butterworth	4	4	0
John Taylor	50	0	0	James Eastwood	5	5	0
Timothy Bentley	30	0	0	Paul Kinder	5	5	0
William North	20	0	0	John Brook	5	5	0
Joshua Crosland	20	0	0	James Crowther	2	2	0
Joseph Hirst	20	0	0	William Milnes	2	12	6
George Shaw	10	0	0	John Tate	2	2	0
Charles Crowther	5	5	0	Francis Crow	5	5	0
James Shaw	5	5	0	B. & T. Tate	10	10	0
Eli Holmes	2	2	0				

Honley.

George Armitage	50	0	0	Benj. Robinson	5	5	0
W. & J. Brooke	50	0	0	Joshua Robinson	10	0	0
T. & W. Leigh	50	0	0	S. Jessop	5	5	0
James Armitage	21	0	0	Abraham Hanson	1	1	0

South Crosland.

G. & W. Beaumont ..	50	0	0	David Harrison	5	5	0
John Sykes	5	5	0	John Batley	3	3	0

Linthwaite.

Benj. Lockwood.. ..	21	0	0	John Taylor	2	2	0
George Roberts	10	10	0	Joshua Hall	1	1	0
James Roberts	10	10	0	Joseph Parkin	0	10	6
John Haigh	2	12	6				

Meltham and Netherthong.

James Mellor	19	0	0	Richard Bannister ..	2	2	0
John Taylor	1	1	0	Joseph Roberts	2	2	0
Joseph Batley	1	1	0	Edward Bower	1	1	0
John Garlick	1	1	0	James Garlick	1	1	0
William Brooke.. ..	10	10	0	John Gledhill	1	1	0
Tho. Moorhouse ..	20	0	0	James Taylor	2	2	0
B. Wilson	10	0	0	Elihu Hobson	1	1	0
Joshua Woodhead ..	5	5	0	James Rawcliffe	1	1	0
Joseph Eastwood ..	5	5	0	C. Sykes	1	1	0
Jer. Taylor	5	5	0	John Ellis.. .. .	1	1	0
John Siddal	2	2	0	James Bower	0	10	6
W. Woodhead	2	2	0	William Eastwood ..	1	1	0

Lingards.

Rev. Mr. Murgatroyd ..	5	5	0	William Bamford ..	2	2	0
Miss Schofield	5	5	0	James Garside	2	2	0
John Varley	5	5	0	Edw. Kenworthy ..	2	10	0
James Bamforth ..	5	5	0				

Kirkheaton.

General Barnard ..	100	0	0	James Cowgill	5	5	0
Rev. Mr. Smithson ..	10	0	0	John Armitage	5	5	0
Rev. Mr. Sunderland ..	5	5	0	William Bayley.. ..	2	2	0
John Mallinson	5	5	0	Benj. Strickland ..	1	1	0
Richard Beaumont ..	5	5	0	Thomas Dutton.. ..		10	6

Dalton.

Thos. Atkinson	105	0	0	Richard Horsfall ..	1	1	0
Law Atkinson	100	0	0	William Horsfall ..	1	1	0
J. Beaumont & Son ..	6	6	0	Thomas Bray	1	1	0
Joseph Dodson	5	5	0	John Wilson	1	1	0
Benjamin Bray	2	2	0	John Milnes	1	1	0
George Senior	1	1	0				

Lepton.

Samuel Walker	50	0	0	Thomas Hudson ..	1	1	0
W. & F. Pontey	5	5	0	John Moorhouse ..		10	6
John Jessop	2	2	0	George Peaker		10	6
William Whittle.. ..	1	1	0	Valentine Senior ..		10	6
John Jessop	1	1	0	Thomas Poole		10	6
Matthew Broadhead ..	1	1	0	Richard Armitage ..		10	6

Kirkburton.

	£	s.	d.		£	s.	d.
Rev. Mr. Wickham and Sisters	50	0	0	John Haigh	2	2	0
John Booth	10	10	0	J. & A. Hey	2	2	0
Richard Booth	5	5	0	Mrs. Dickinson	2	2	0
William Booth	2	2	0	John Bingley	1	1	0
Joseph Nobles	2	2	0	William Earnshaw ..	1	1	0
				Mrs. Littlewood		10	6

Shelley.

Jonathan Smith	10	10	0	Richard Turner	3	3	0
Benjamin Stocks ..	3	3	0				

Thurstonland.

Miss Horsfall	105	0	0	Charles Jenkinson ..	1	1	0
Thomas Hardy	21	0	0	Mrs. Ellis	1	1	0
Richard Gill	5	5	0	Joseph Heppenstall ..	1	1	0
Amos Airley	3	3	0	John Armitage	1	1	0
— Sedgwick	2	2	0	James Cocker	1	1	0
Jonas Walker, Senior ..	2	2	0	Thomas Savage	1	1	0
Joseph Mitchell	2	2	0	Jos. Armitage, Senior ..	0	10	6

Holmfirth.

James Harrop	50	0	0	John Woodhead	2	2	0
John Bates	20	0	0	John Hinchcliffe ..	2	2	0
Cookson Stephenson ..	20	0	0	David Dixon	2	2	0
Thomas Blythe	5	5	0	John Woodhead	1	1	0
John Dickinson	5	5	0	John Haigh	1	1	0
John Wood	5	5	0	George Dyson	1	1	0
William Garside	5	5	0	Joshua Kirk	1	1	0
Richard Boothroyd ..	5	5	0	Joseph Cuttel	1	1	0
J. K. Wordsworth ..	5	5	0	John Battye	1	1	0
John Napier	5	5	0	George Smith	1	1	0
Jonas Hobson	5	5	0	Ann Womersley	1	1	0
George Hobson	4	4	0	S. & M. Iveson	1	1	0
Joseph Wood	4	4	0	Joshua Cuttel	1	1	0
Joseph Peaker	3	3	0	Joseph Roberts	1	1	0
Jonathan Eastwood ..	3	3	0	Robert Middleton ..	1	1	0
George Heward	3	3	0	Joseph Woodhead ..	1	1	0
James Boothroyd ..	3	3	0	William Senior	1	1	0
Jonathan Brook	3	3	0	James Turner	1	1	0
John Moorhouse	3	3	0	Richard Turner		10	6
John Roberts	2	2	0	Jonathan Wood		2	6

Upperthong.

Joseph Hirst	10	10	0	Ely Wimpenny	6	6	0
Emor Brook	1	1	0	G. & J. Farrar	10	10	0
John Hinchcliffe	1	1	0	J. Charlesworth	5	5	0
Richard Hargreaves ..	1	1	0	Eb. Wimpenny	3	3	0
Ely Hoyle	1	1	0	Thomas Battye	3	3	0
Benjamin Thewlis ..	1	1	0	James Battye	3	3	0
Jonathan Fallas	1	1	0	Joseph Mellor	1	1	0

Upperthong—*Continued.*

Name	£	s.	d.
James Fallas	1	1	0
Jos. Moorhouse	15	15	0
Elizabeth Taylor ..	10	10	0
John Armitage	10	10	0
Richard Woffenden ..	7	7	0
John Hampshire ..	1	1	0
Joshua Woodhead ..	1	1	0
Jonathan Turner ..	1	1	0
Mrs. Wimpenny ..	1	1	0
Thos. Charlesworth ..	1	1	0

Holm.

Name	£	s.	d.
Rev. Mr. Broadhurst ..	5	5	0
Anthony Green	5	5	0
John Haigh	5	5	0
John Green	5	5	0
Ely Broadhead	3	3	0
J. Butterworth	2	12	6
Joseph Leake	1	1	0
John Hayward	1	1	0
James Hattersley ..	1	1	0
J. Hinchcliffe & Co. ..	1	1	0

Cartworth.

Name	£	s.	d.
Math. Butterworth ..	5	5	0
James Hinchcliffe ..	5	5	0
John Littlewood	5	5	0
John Booth	5	5	0
Wm. & E. Leak	6	6	0
John Batty	3	3	0
Joseph Taylor	3	3	0
Joseph Marsden	3	3	0
John Roberts	3	3	0
James Haigh	3	3	0
John Bray	2	12	6
Ab. Littlewood	2	2	0
Joseph Bramah	2	2	0
J. Butterworth	1	11	6
Ely Hinchcliffe	1	1	0
Joseph Barber	1	1	0
John Lockwood	1	1	0
James Haigh	1	1	0
John Hinchcliffe ..	1	1	0
Joseph Hinchcliffe ..	1	1	0
Isaac Cheetham	1	1	0
James Hinchcliffe ..	1	1	0
Lee Greensmith	1	1	0
John Gill	1	1	0
J. Butterworth	1	1	0
Charles Thewlis	0	10	6
J. Castle	0	10	6
George Roebuck	0	10	6

Austonley.

Name	£	s.	d.
Mrs. Shaw	20	0	0
Geo. Charlesworth ..	10	0	0
John Wimpenny	5	0	0
Christ. Green	3	3	0
John Roebuck	2	2	0
Joseph Tinker	2	2	0
Joseph Broadhead ..	2	2	0
J. Charlesworth	2	2	0
Joshua Barber	2	2	0
Joseph Barber	2	2	0
John Goddard	2	2	0
Joseph Woodcock ..	1	1	0
John Woodcock	1	1	0
John Tinker	1	1	0
John Wimpenny	1	1	0
J. Charlesworth	1	1	0
J. Broadhead	1	1	0
John Taylor	1	1	0
Robert France	1	1	0
James Beardsall	1	1	0
Sarah Green	1	1	0
James Sikes	0	10	6

Lord's Meer.

Name	£	s.	d.
J. Harrop, Dobcross ..	50	0	0
Jas. Buckley, Greenfield.	50	0	0
John Buckley, Upper Mill	25	0	0
Henry Whitehead, Dobcross	20	0	0
Joseph Lawton	5	5	0
Edmund Buckley, Tunstead	2	2	0
Ralph Whitehead ..	1	1	0
John Hide	1	1	0
John Marshall	1	1	0
George Marshall ..	1	1	0
John Booth	5	0	0
John Broadbent	5	5	0
Wm. Radcliffe	1	1	0
John Heawood	1	1	0

Lord's Meer.—*Continued.*

S. Collier, Dobcross	5	5	0
Henry Platt	2	2	0
John Wrigley	5	5	0
James Waterhouse	5	5	0
John Smith	3	3	0
James Harrop	4	4	0
Josiah Lawton	5	5	0
John Booth	1	1	0
John Harrop, Sen.	5	5	0
James Platt	1	1	0
Charles Scantair	1	1	0
Joseph Lawton	1	1	0
Wm. Bell, Delph	5	5	0
T. Harrop, Dobcross	20	0	0
T. Shaw, Upper Mill	10	10	0
John Platt	10	10	0
John Platt, Jr.	5	5	0
Wm. Ratcliffe, Cross	10	10	0
G. Shaw, Furlane	10	10	0
Robert Buckley	10	10	0
Ralph Bradbury	5	5	0
James Andrew	2	2	0
Francis Platt	1	1	0
John Andrew	3	3	0
Abram Rhodes	3	3	0
John Radcliffe	2	2	0
John Shaw	3	3	0
Samuel Bentley	2	2	0
Wm. Radcliffe	2	2	0
Joseph Platt, Senr.	1	1	0
John Bottomley	1	1	0
Joseph Whitehead	1	1	0
Joseph Wrigley	1	1	0
James Whitehead	1	1	0
B. Winterbottom	5	5	0
S. Wigginbottom	5	5	0
Edmund Schofield	2	2	0
Mark Windross	1	1	0
Wm. Broadbent	1	1	0
James Wood	1	1	0
W. Rhodes, Whitefoot	1	1	0
Robert Rhodes	1	1	0
Thomas Rhodes	1	1	0
J. & A. Bottomley	3	3	0
John Broadbent	2	2	0
James Broadbent	1	1	0
John Rhodes	1	1	0
J. Platt, Dobcross	1	1	0
J. Andrew, Boardshurst	10	10	0
H. Hyde, Farnlee	3	3	0
Thos. Marshall	3	3	0
J. Buckley, Shaw	1	1	0
James Harrop	1	1	0
James Whitehead	1	1	0
Philip Buckley	1	1	0
N. Lees, Upper Mill	2	2	0
Thomas Brown	2	2	0
Small Subcriptions	5	18	6

Shaw Meer.

J. Lees, Clarkfield	50	0	0
Geo. Buckley	10	0	0
James Harrop	10	10	0
Robert Hadfield	5	5	0
John Platt	5	5	0
John Buckley	5	5	0
J. N. Binning	5	5	0
Wm. Blackburn	5	5	0
John Buckley	2	2	0
Law Fox	2	2	0
Abram Wood	1	1	0
James Garside	1	1	0
Edmund Buckley	5	5	0
James Greaves	1	1	0
James Biswick	2	2	0
William Haigh	5	5	0
John Lawton	1	1	0
R. Winterbottom	1	1	0
Isaac Seville	5	5	0
James Wood	1	1	0
Joseph Buckley	1	1	0
Robert Buckley	6	6	0
Benj. Harrop	5	5	0
Henry Buckley	4	4	0
Edward Harrop	1	1	0
William Greenwood	2	2	0
Joseph Garside	1	1	0
James Scanlan	2	12	6
Thomas Dronsfield	1	1	0
Henry Buckley	1	1	0
J. & W. Buckley	2	2	0
John Schofield	1	1	0
George Schofield	1	1	0
Henry Brierley	1	1	0

Shaw Meer.—*Continued.*

Robert Shaw	1	1	0	William Buckley	1	1	0
Jonathan Wilde	1	1	0	Small Subscriptions	1	16	0
James Mills	1	1	0				

Quick Meer.

J. Radcliffe, Stonebreaks	50	0	0	William Shaw	5	5	0
Jos. Harrop, Grasscroft	50	0	0	John Nield	2	2	0
James Taylor	10	10	0	Wm. Kenworthy	1	1	0
George Bramall	10	10	0	John Hilton	10	10	0
John Thackray	5	5	0	Daniel Woolley	1	1	0
J. & W. Knight	21	0	0	John Buckley	2	2	0
George Knight	2	2	0	John Wrigley	4	0	0
Robert Platt	5	5	0	John Robinson	5	0	0
George Rhodes	5	5	0	John Lees	10	10	0
George Schofield	1	1	0	John Schofield	1	1	0
John Booth	5	5	0	James Saville	2	2	0
J. & S. Lees	5	5	0	Daniel Thackray	5	5	0
Wm. Lees	1	1	0	Henry Swift	2	2	0
Abm. Saville	2	2	0	William Kenworthy	1	1	0
John Shaw	2	2	0	James Wright	15	15	0
George Shaw	1	1	0	John Bostock	4	4	0
Peter Saville	1	1	0	Benj. Wrigley	1	0	0
Samuel Wrigley	5	5	0	Thos. Humphrey	2	2	0
Joseph Taylor	10	10	0	Mary Wrigley	4	4	0
Miles Wrigley	1	1	0	Small Subscriptions	2	2	0

Friar Meer.

John Roberts	50	0	0	Benj. Garside	5	5	0
J. Buckley, junr.	5	5	0	James Mills	2	2	0
James Shaw	5	5	0	Benj. Mills	1	1	0
Jonas Ainley	5	5	0	Thos. Standing	1	1	0
Edmund Buckley	5	5	0	Francis Davenport	2	2	0
John Buckley	5	5	0	James Shaw	2	2	0
Abram Garside	5	5	0	Peter Lowe	2	2	0
Wm. Rhodes	2	2	0	Daniel Wrigley	4	4	0
Benj. Schofield	5	5	0	Abram Whitehead	3	3	0
James Schofield	5	5	0	Joseph Shaw, junr.	5	5	0
John Schofield	5	5	0	J. Lawton, Delph	5	5	0
Joseph Schofield	10	10	0	James Mills	3	3	0
John Kenworthy	2	2	0	John Lees	1	1	0
James Mills, Wood	10	10	0	Nanny Shaw	1	1	0
J. Clifton	2	2	0	Joseph Shaw	1	1	0
John Broadbent	2	2	0	John Buckley	1	1	0
Giles Wood	1	1	0	John Kenworthy	1	1	0
J. Wigginbottom	1	1	0	Jos. Broadbent	1	1	0
Thomas Shaw	2	2	0	James Rhodes	1	1	0
Benj. Garside	1	1	0	Widow Garside	2	0	0
Robert Garside	1	1	0	Small Subscriptions	3	8	0

Mirfield.

Name	£	s.	d.	Name	£	s.	d.
Joshua Ingham	100	0	0	Joshua Hirst	21	0	0
Samuel Brooke	52	10	0	Benjamin Smith ..	21	0	0
Samuel Walker	31	10	0	Benjamin Wilson ..	10	10	0
John Kitson	21	0	0	Mr. Hill	10	10	0
Joseph Marriott	21	0	0	J. & J. Wheatley ..	21	0	0
Josh. Ingham, Jr. ..	21	0	0	W. & T. Dawson ..	10	10	0
Daniel Ledgard	21	0	0	Moravians at Well-house and in the Town of Mirfield ..	48	2	6
Charles Brooke	21	0	0	Sundry Subscriptions ..	113	10	0
William Pilling	21	0	0				
Richard Brooke	21	0	0				
Edward Sykes	21	0	0				

Hartishead-cum-Clifton.

Name	£	s.	d.	Name	£	s.	d.
Sir G. Armytage, Bart.	100	0	0	John Stockwell	2	2	0
Rev. M. Lucas	20	0	0	John Gleadhill	3	3	0
Joshua Goldthorpe ..	10	0	0	Paul Pinder	1	1	0
Henry Wilby	10	0	0	Anthony Brook	2	2	0
James Armitage	5	5	0	Henry Walker	2	2	0
Christopher Brook ..	5	5	0	Richard Denison ..	1	1	0
John Brook	5	5	0	Peter Bedford	2	2	0
J. Goldthorpe & Sons ..	10	10	0	Joshua Woodcock ..	1	1	0
Jeremy Brearley ..	2	2	0	John Davies	2	2	0
George Brearley.. ..	2	2	0	Samuel Middleham ..	1	1	0
James Brearley	2	2	0	James Ogden	1	1	0
John Hargreaves ..	2	2	0	William Capper	2	2	0
Samuel Airson	2	2	0	Samuel Turner	5	5	0
William Briggs	2	2	0	Joseph Adamson ..	1	1	0
Chris. Brook, Senr. ..	1	1	0	Kitt Womersley	1	1	0
Charles Rayner	1	1	0	Crispin Wilkinson ..	2	2	0
Joshua Sinkinson ..	2	2	0	Thomas Greenwood ..	2	2	0
Edward Wright	1	1	0	M. Thomas & Sons ..	10	10	0
William Horsley ..	1	1	0	Henry Hopper	0	10	6
George Wright	1	1	0	John Fearnley	2	2	0
Mrs. Green	2	2	0	John Drake, Clerk ..	2	2	0
John Garlick	1	1	0	William Drake	1	1	0
Robert Ramsden ..	2	2	0	William Furniss.. ..	2	2	0
Samuel Camm	1	1	0	John Charlesworth ..	5	5	0
Thomas Drake	1	1	0	Benj. Barker	2	2	0
Francis Hirst	1	1	0	John Drake	1	1	0
Wm. Saville	2	2	0	Jonathan Wilby	1	1	0
Thomas Pratt	0	10	6	Robert Fitton	2	12	6
Joseph Pratt	1	1	0	Thomas Woodhead ..	4	4	0
Charles Walker	0	10	6	George Jackson	1	12	6
Mark Womersley ..	1	1	0	William Brooke	1	1	0

Total Amount of Subscriptions .. £6,609 19 6

The following account of the state of the corps and details of the pay in 1803 is extracted from the files of the Record Office:—

State and Pay of the Corps.

Colonel	Sir George Armytage.
No. of Companies	12
Lieutenant-Colonels	2
Majors	2
Adjutant	1
Captains	12
Lieutenants	26
Ensigns	8
Sergeants	60
Corporals	60
Drummers	14
Rank and File	1140

PAY.

Colonel	1	1	11	per day.
Lieutenant-Colonel ..		15	11	
Majors		14	1	
Captains		9	5	
Adjutants		6	0	
Lieutenants		5	8	
Ensigns		5	8	
Sergeants		1	6¾	
Corporals		1	2¼	
Drummers		1	1¼	
Rank and File		1	0	

I may here usefully add that according to the Estimates of 1803-4, the large number of 463,000 men were raised for local service as Volunteers.

The Volunteers of 1803 were doubtless more liberally dealt with than their predecessors, for there were the subscriptions as a fund in aid. Thus I find in October, 1803, a resolution that "Thomas Mundell and —— Dickenson," presumably drill-serjeants, "be allowed 10/6 per week for one month past, and that One Guinea per week be allowed to each of them for instructing the drummers and fifers for the future."

The corps whose initiation I have described was called *The Upper Agbrigg Volunteers*, with a strength at one time of 1,333 officers and men. Sir George Armytage was its Lieutenant-Colonel. I gather from a coloured synopsis of the establishment and uniforms of the various corps of Volunteers of Great Britain, published in 1807, that the uniform was a red coat with yellow or buff cuffs and collar. The breeches were white, with gaiters up to the knee buttoned up the side. The dress of the officers differed

Strength of the Upper Agbrigg Volunteers.

from that of the men only by the distinction of silver epaulettes. The head dress was the stove-pipe hat of the period with peak, and a large brass or gilt plate in front from which rose a tuft. The Army List of 1804 enables me to furnish the following particulars as to the officers of this force:—

Lieutenant-Colonel Commanding, Sir George Armytage, Baronet	Aug. 15th,	1803.
Lieutenant-Colonel Northend Nichols ..	"	"
" " Joseph Haigh	Nov. 29th,	1803.
Major Bramhall (or Bramel) Dyson	"	"
" Walter Stables	"	"
Captain Spencer Dyson	Aug. 15th,	"
" William Horsfall	"	"
" Matthew Mason..	"	"
" John Wolley (Woolley)..	"	"
Captain Ganis Seaton (in next year's List called Jervas Charles Seaton)	"	"
Captain John Harrop	"	"
" John Radcliffe	"	"
" Walter Beaumont	"	"
" John Roberts	"	"
" Lewis Fenton	"	"
" George Moorhouse	Nov. 29th,	"
" James Booth	"	"
Lieutenant John Roberts	Aug. 15th,	"
" John Buckley	"	"
" John Lees	"	"
" John Marsden	"	"
" James Roberts	"	"
" Joseph Armitage	"	"
" Henry Nelson	"	"
" Henry Heron	"	"
" John Allison	"	"
" Michael Turner	"	"
" Joseph Hinchliffe	"	"
" James Brook	"	"
" William North	Nov. 29th,	"
" Edward Shaw	"	"
" Richard Tinker	"	"
" Edward Mundle	"	"
" Benjamin Stocks	"	"
" John Schoofield, (Scholefield) ..	"	"
" William Turner	"	"
" Thomas Greenwood	"	"
" John Walker	"	"
" William Shaw	"	"
" James Hall	"	"
" J. Scholes	"	"

Ensign Samuel Knight	Aug. 15th,	1803.
" William Blackburn	"	"
" John Braye	"	"
" John Harrop, junr.	"	"
" John Lodge	"	"
" Joseph Dyson	"	"
" John Blackburn	"	"
" George Tinker	Nov. 29th,	"
" Richard Roberts	"	"
" William Bailey	"	"
Chaplain, Rev. Thomas Wickham, M.A. ..	"	"
Adjutant, James Jenkin	"	"
Quartermaster, John Taylor	"	"
Surgeon, Joseph Bradshaw	"	"

This list gives a total of fifty-five officers and the number of captains, twelve, may be presumed to have corresponded with the number of companies. The number of ensigns, twelve, is also in conformity with the general rule, but the number of lieutenants appears to have been in accordance with the provisions of two lieutenants to every company of 120 men, prescribed by section 30 of the Levy *en masse* Act already referred to. Averaging the companies at a strength of 100 men each, we may arrive at a tolerably accurate conception of the proportions of the force.

Their Commissions.

I have been permitted by Sir George J. Armytage, of Kirklees, the great-grandson of that Sir George whose name so prominently, so honourably and so frequently recurs in the local annals of the days now engaging our attention, to copy from the originals in his possession the commissions of some of the officers. Why these commissions should have been left in the hands of the lieutenant-colonel of the corps I do not know and can offer no surmise. I am clear, however, that many of my readers will care to have preserved the actual text of one at least of these interesting relics of bye-gone times, and I therefore reproduce the words of that of Lieutenant-Colonel Northend Nichols. The batch in Sir George J. Armytage's possession includes those of First-Major Joseph Haigh, Second-Major George Beaumont, Captain Bramall Dyson, Lieutenant Joseph Armytage, Ensign John Braye, Lieutenants John Marsden and William Saunders, and Ensigns John Lodge and John Harrop, all of which, with the necessary changes of name and rank, are in identic terms.

By William Wentworth Fitzwilliam,
Earl Fitzwilliam, Viscount Milton and Baron Fitzwilliam in England;
Earl Fitzwilliam, Viscount Milton and Baron Fitzwilliam in Ireland.

Lord Lieutenant and Custos Rotulorum of the West Riding of the County of York, and of the City of York and County of the same, or Ainsty of York; and one of the Lord's of His Majesty's Most Honourable Privy Council.

Commission of Lieut.-Col Nichols.

To Northend Nichols, Esquire.

By Virtue of the Power and Authority to me given by a Warrant from His Majesty, under his Royal Signet and Sign Manual, bearing date the 22nd day of May, 1804, I, the said Earl Fitzwilliam, Do, in His Majesty's Name, by these Presents, constitute, appoint, and commission you the said Northend Nichols to be Lieutenant-Colonel of the Upper Agbrigg Corps of Volunteer Infantry, but not to take rank in the Army, except during the time of the said Corps being called out into actual service; You are therefore to take the said corps into your care and charge, and duly to exercise, as well the officers as soldiers thereof, in Arms, and to use your best endeavours to keep them in good order and discipline, who are hereby commanded in His Majesty's Name, to obey you as their Lieutenant-Colonel: And you are to observe and follow such orders and directions, from time to time, as you shall receive from His Majesty, your Lieutenant-Colonel Commandant, or any other your superior officer, according to the Rules and Discipline of War, in pursuance of the Trust hereby reposed in you.

Given under my hand and seal the 15th day of August, in the 43rd year of the reign of our Sovereign Lord, George the Third, by the Grace of God of the United Kingdom of Great Britain and Ireland, King, Defender of the Faith, and in the Year of our Lord One thousand Eight hundred and Three.

WENTWORTH FITZWILLIAM. (Seal).

Brief notices of some officers.

Of Captain Fenton.

Of Lieut. Wm. North.

Of Lieut. H. Nelson.

Of Lieut. Allison.

Of Captain Blackburn.

It will be observed that many of the officers appearing in the Army List of 1804 had held commissions in the corps that formed the subject of the previous part. Captain Lewis Fenton contested Huddersfield in the Whig interest on its enfranchisement in 1832. Lieutenant William North lived at North House, Lockwood, and was lessee of the Corn Mills at Shorefoot. Lieutenant Henry Nelson lived at Nelson's Buildings, erected by his father, with whom he was in partnership as a cloth merchant, the firm being Thomas Nelson & Co. He died in 1848. His only son was Lieutenant-Colonel in a regiment of Artillery Militia in the East Riding. Lieutenant Allison was of a Westmoreland family, being educated at St. Bees' College, Cumberland, and was a school fellow of Henry Brougham, afterwards Lord Chancellor. Mr. Allison practised as a solicitor in Huddersfield, he was the Clerk to the County Justices in that town, and in 1812 conducted for the Crown the prosecution of the Luddites. He died in 1847, aged 70. Mr. Blackburn, afterwards successively Lieutenant and Captain, was also a solicitor who practised in New Street, Huddersfield. He was a predecessor of Mr. Whitehead, who subsequently took into partnership the late Mr. Robert Thomas Robinson, the first returning officer for the borough of Huddersfield, to whose practice I succeeded in September, 1869.

It would appear from a statement in the *Leeds Mercury*, of August 13th, 1803, that those anxious to be enrolled as Volunteers at this time could not be or were not all accepted, for it is there alleged that nearly three thousand men had enrolled their names to serve as Volunteers in the Upper Division of Agbrigg, consisting of Huddersfield, Almondbury, Kirkheaton, Kirkburton, and the Township of Quick. It is certain that the corps under Sir George Armytage never, at its strongest, approximated to a strength of 3,000 men.

The enrolment of Volunteers.

On September 5th, 1803, I find from the same journal, Earl Fitzwilliam had the gratification of communicating to a general meeting of the Lieutenancy of the West Riding His Majesty's gracious acceptance of the efforts made for raising the various corps of the Riding, and his Lordship expressed his anxious desire no effort should be spared to bring the corps into a good state of discipline.

Their offers of service accepted, Sep. 5th, 1803.

On November 25th, 1803, the Upper Division of Agbrigg Volunteer Infantry, consisting of 1,200 rank and file, commanded by Sir George Armytage, Lieutenant-Colonel-Commandant, were inspected by Colonel Grayson in Woodsome Park, near Huddersfield. On the same day, the West York Volunteer Cavalry, consisting of five troops, commanded by John Lister Kaye, were inspected at Elland Town Field, also by Colonel Grayson.

Inspection, Nov. 25th, 1803.

Not only were the various companies rapidly filled with their complement of recruits, a fact which the cynic critic might have had some ground for attributing to the general desire to evade the Militia ballot, but the men who assumed voluntary military duty appear to have addressed themselves seriously to the task of learning their drill, a fact which the cynic critic would have some difficulty in explaining. The following extract from the *Leeds Intelligencer*, of January 2nd, 1804, is eloquent alike of the spirit that pervaded the people and of the zest with which those who took up arms endeavoured to make themselves worthy of the cause they had embraced.

"In every town and village within the circuit of this paper the spirit of Volunteering is carried on with the utmost alacrity, and from the information we can obtain, the progress and discipline is equal to the unwearied exercise by which it is attained. The Volunteer Infantry, both officers and privates, who form two battalions of about 700 men each, are, beyond any previous example, zealous to excel in arms and military tactics. The order just received from Government for a new ballot for the Army Reserve, to attach to all men from the age of 18 to 45, whether Volnnteers or not, unless they have attended 24 drills previous to the 1st instant, we are happy to find will lay hold of very few indeed of our officers, many of whom have attended nearly double that number."

One has to put himself back in imagination a hundred years to fully appreciate the prayer which the Rev. Mr. Wickham, chaplain of the corps, offered on the occasion of the presentation of their colours to the *Upper Agbrigg Volunteers* by Lady Armytage, and the speech delivered on the same occasion by her husband. The presentation was made on 19th March, 1804. Twelve companies of the *Upper Agbrigg Volunteer Regiment*, each of 111 men, assembled on Crosland Moor, Huddersfield, the ground being kept by Captain Scott's Troop of West Riding Volunteer Cavalry. My report is from the *Leeds Mercury* :—

Presentation of Colours, March 19th, 1804.

The Chaplain's Prayer.

"O cheerful and omnipotent Lord God, who hast taught us to look up to the throne of Thy mercy in all our necessities and to place our chief confidence in Thy most mightiful protection, hear and accept we beseech Thee the supplications which we offer up to Thee this day. We acknowledge we are sinful men, O Lord, and cannot of our own deservings claim the least of Thy favours; yet inasmuch as Thou hast promised to be the helper of them that flee to Thee for succour, we presume upon the merits of Him who is Himself righteousness and salvation to implore Thy forgiveness and to entreat Thy blessing.

O God! without Thee nothing is strong, nothing is Holy. To Thee, therefore, and to Thy Most Holy name we dedicate these banners, the tokens of our attachment to Thy sacred truth, of our Loyalty to the best of Sovereigns and of our unanimity in that just cause of warfare in which, through the provocations of an imperious and menacing enemy, we are again unhappily involved. The Lord's kind providence watch over them and keep them, ever aiding and furthering the endeavours of these brave men and of all others in the Kingdom who, like them, have willingly offered themselves and are prepared to hazard their lives for the defence and preservation of their native land. Inspire their hearts with such constant courage and magnanimity, with such ardent love of their country, its religion, laws and principles, as may ensure them success in all their enterprises, and, should they be called to the conflict, glorious victory in the day of battle; shield them, Most Mighty Lord of Hosts, with Thy stretched out arm; succour and support them in their trial of strength and when, through Thy effectual assistance, they shall have willingly borne their part in defeating the proud foe and putting to confusion the unjust oppressors of mankind, suffer them, O Father of Mercies, to return to their homes in triumph and peace amid the joyful acclamations of their grateful countrymen, with hearts duly sensible of Thy paternal care and with voices filled by a sense of praise and thanksgiving to Thee, their Refuge and Deliverer.

Uphold, O God! our defender, Thou King of Kings, and look upon the face of Thine anointed, our most gracious Sovereign, restore him we beseech Thee to his health, grant him yet a long and happy life upon earth and after death everlasting felicity and glory in Thy Heavenly Kingdom, incline steadfastly towards Him the hearts of all his people, so that, his counsels and endeavours being always directed to their safety, prosperity, and honour, in this perilous time, none may be found wanting in affectionate regard to his person or in dutiful submission to his authority; but that all of us may, in our several stations and in our whole conduct, manifest that true obedience and loyalty which Thy sacred word hath imposed on Christian subjects as their bounden duty and service. Hear, O Lord, we beseech Thee, from Heaven, Thy dwelling place, maintain our cause and let our prayer enter into Thy presence, through the merits and intercession of Jesus Christ our Mediator and Advocate, after whose profile words we conclude and commend our own imperfect petitions.

Our Father, &c."

Lady Armytage in presenting the colours, said :— Speech of Lady Armytage.

" Sir,

Fully impressed with the sense of the honour conferred on me in being appointed to present you with these colours, I now with pleasure offer them to the acceptance of the respectable corps under your command. Allow me, at the same time, to express my best wishes that that spirit of loyalty by which you have been actuated to take up arms in defence of your country and that resolution in the hour of danger which have been so manifest, may ensure that, should the enemy effect a landing on our coasts, your endeavours to oppose them may be crowned with success and resolvent with victory."

Sir George Armytage, in response, said :— Of Sir George Armytage.

" Madam,

In the name of myself and the corps which I have the honor to command, I beg to return you and the ladies you now represent our sincere thanks for the honour you have this day conferred upon us by presenting us with these splendid colours. The good opinion you have expressed of those by whom they are to be defended will, I trust, excite them to indulge in that noble and patriotic conduct which has this day brought us into the field."

Turning to the corps under his command the gallant baronet continued :—

" Brother Volunteers,

Let us resolve to unite firmly in the gallant cause and rather lose our lives than not defend these ensigns to our utmost. Let them ever be monitors over our conduct in that constitution the duty of which we have pledged ourselves to fulfil. Let them ever remind us of our duty to our King and country and let a sense of those duties stimulate us to join with the great mass of our brothers now in arms and to contribute our full share towards supporting our beloved Monarch on his throne and securing his and our own possessions against the attack of a most rapacious foe.

We are now fully apprised of his sanguinary intentions; but I trust he will not find us tamely disposed to submit, and, on our own soil, become the slaves of a foreign usurper. Do not let the enemy surprise us, heedless of our danger. If we do, we shall become the easy conquest of our invaders.

The history of the world affords no instance of a country united and determined to maintain its freedom that ever was conquered. Disgraceful, indeed, would it be for us to be found wanting by our enemies. Let us prepare to risk our lives in our country's defence rather than they should accomplish its destruction. Let every man, when he returns home, go back to his proper place and determine to do his duty by conducing, with his heart and hand, towards supporting the public cause. I wish not to trespass unnecessarily on your time and attention but I hope before we separate this day we shall come to a unanimous resolution that we have done nothing till we have placed this country in a perfect state of security. I say nothing to you, my brother Volunteers, which I do not feel from the bottom of my heart. I do not call upon you for any exercise in which I myself will not join, to the last farthing of my fortune and the last drop of my blood. It will be my pride to be the foremost in the ranks of my countrymen and to stand or fall in the defence of my country."

Presentation of Colours to Volunteer Cavalry.

The Volunteer Cavalry were not neglected in the presentation of colours—on 12th April, 1804, the Major-Commandant of the West York Volunteer Cavalry received at Woodsome Park a very handsome standard. The ground was kept by a detachment of Colonel Sir George Armytage's Regiment of Upper Agbrigg Volunteers.

Annual Training, May, 1804.

On May 28th, 1804, there is an announcement in the *Leeds Mercury* that the Upper Agbrigg Volunteers, 1,300 strong, would march through Leeds, under the command of Sir George Armytage on their way to York. They remained at York apparently for their twenty eight statutory days of drill and training. They conducted themselves at York, so we are assured by the same journal, "as attentive soldiers and good citizens"; were inspected at Knavesmire by Colonel Lee and received great approbation in their military duty and, on their return to Huddersfield on Tuesday, June 19th, Market-day at Huddersfield by the way, "they were received with the most hearty congratulations." The Volunteer of to-day, accustomed to the not always flattering remarks of the small boy and nursemaid who watch his progress through the street from Drill Hall to Exercise Ground, will read the above extract with mingled feelings.

Annual Training, 1805.

On October 1st, 1805, the Agbrigg Voluteers, under the command of Sir George Armytage, marched to York, but this time for only 21 days' drill and training.

Inspection.

On the 17th October, they were inspected at Knavesmire by General John Hodgson, who, in Brigade Orders, expressed great satisfaction at their steadiness and good appearance in the field and the correct and excellent manner in which the different evolutions were gone through, in the following terms:—

Brigadier-General Hodgson has the honour of expressing to the Lieutenant-Colonel, Sir George Armytage, Commander of the 6th West York, his great satisfaction at their steadiness and good appearance in the Field this day. The very correct and excellent manner in which the different evolutions were performed convinces the Brigadier-General that the most unremitting attention has been paid to the discipline of the regiment.

The regular and soldier-like conduct of the regiment during the time of their being on permanent duty in this City entitles them to the approbation and best thanks of the Brigadier-General.

(Signed) THOMAS WILLIAMS,
Major of Brigade.

The colonel also expressed his approbation of their general good conduct in the most pleasant terms.

On Thursday, the corps marched from Leeds on the way homewards, and a short distance from Huddersfield they were met by a number of inhabitants who welcomed their return, and they were entertained in the most hospitable manner.

March, 1806, Official Return of strength of Corps.

On March 26th, 1806, a Return was made to the House of Commons on the state and efficiency of the Volunteer force from which I extract the following: "The Upper Agbrigg Corps is commanded by Sir George Armytage, Baronet, and there are 12 companies, 2 field officers, 2 captains, 30 subalterns, 4 staff, 44 sergeants, 12 drummers; present on inspection, 584, absent, 421, total establishment on day of inspection being 1,200 strong. The Inspecting officer, Lieutenant-Colonel Balcomb, of York, expressed his opinion that the state of the clothing was good, as also was that of the arms and accoutrements, and, speaking generally, the Inspector was pleased to say "that the corps was a remarkably fine body of young men in a good state of discipline, fit to act with troops of the line. The officers understood their duty and were very attentive." This compares favourably with the Report on other corps of which the appointments were said to be "only indifferent" and the discipline merely "advancing." There were at this time 34 different Volunteer corps in the West Riding alone, composed of all kinds of units from the Upper Agbrigg Volunteers, 1,333 strong to the Addingham Infantry, 67 strong.

Number of Corps in West Riding.

The inspection referred to in the Report was probably held on the "Volunteer Field," Dry Clough, Crosland Moor.

April 17th, 1806, Meeting of County Magistrates.

On April 17th, 1806, I find record of a meeting of the County Magistrates and Deputy Lieutenants at which the following resolutions were passed. I am unable to say what, if any, peculiar emergency had suggested the propriety of the resolutions being adopted at that particular time. It may have been that the Training Act of Mr. Windham, of which an account has already been given, was regarded as sounding the death-knell of the Volunteers and the resolutions of the magistrates of the riding may have been in the nature of the customary expressions of condolence.

Present: -

Bacon Frank, John Beckett, Godfrey Wentworth Wentworth, William Wrightson, Samuel Buck, Joseph Radcliffe, M. A. Taylor, Jos Priestley, Jonathan Walker, Richard Walker and John Naylor, Esquires; Sir Francis Wood; H. W. Colthursts, D.D., William Wood, W. Ray, John Lowe, James Geldard and Jer. Dickson, clerks.

Their Resolutions.

It was resolved :—

"That the thanks of this meeting be given to the various corps of Yeomanry and Volunteers serving in this Riding who, in the hour of danger, stood forth for the security of their country."

Resolved :—

"That this meeting strongly recommend to the serious consideration of this corps the propriety of continuing in their present situations until the plans of His Majesty's Ministers respecting the Volunteer system are fully explicated and ascertained."

The following editorial note in the *Leeds Mercury*, of the 26th April, has evident reference to the same subject :—

"We have authority to state that Earl Spencer, one of His Majesty's principal Secretaries of State, has been pleased to approve of the resolution passed at Pontefract on the 17th instant, by the Magistrates and Deputy-Lieutenants, relative to the Volunteers, and that his Lordship, in his communication to the Vice-Lieutenant, on that subject, has expressed much satisfaction at the moderation with which these resolutions appear to have been framed, and the unanimity which prevailed at so general and respectable a meeting."

In the year 1808 I find, on search in the Record Office, the rank and file had considerably diminished in numbers. At that time there were only 980 as compared with 1,140 in the year 1803. The ensigns were one less, the drummers had increased by one. The sergeants numbered 58, the corporals 59. In other respects the state was the same as in 1803. But the year 1808 saw the rise of a new Force or rather, perhaps, one should say the appearance of the old force under a new name. The establishment of the Local Militia in that year led, as we have seen, to the disbandment of most, though not of all the, Volunteer levies of the county. The Huddersfield Volunteers ceased to exist or continued their existence under new and presumably preferable auspices. Sir George Armytage, who became the Lieutenant-Colonel-Commandant of the Agbrigg Local Militia took over with him to his new command the bulk of his officers and also the bulk of his men. The following table shews the posting of officers, 1803-1807. A comparison of it with the list of officers in 1810 will shew with what unanimity the officers followed the lead of their commander :—

Upper Agbrigg Volunteer Infantry.
Postings of Officers, 1803-1807.

Name.	Ensign.	Lieut.	Captain.	Major.	Lieut.-Colonel.	Remarks.
Sir G. Armytage, Bart.	..	..	..	..	15 Aug. 1803	Lieut-Col. Commandant.
Joseph Haigh	..	..	..	15 Aug. 1803	29 Nov. 1803	
Northend Nichols	..	..	..	.. ..	15 Aug. 1803	
George Beaumont	..	..	..	15 Aug. 1803	..	
Bramel Dyson	..	..	15 Aug. 1803	29 Nov. 1803	..	Vice Haigh promoted.
Walter Stables	..	..	,,	,,	..	Vice Beaumont.
Spencer Dyson	..	..	,,	..	..	
William Horsfall	..	..	,,	..	..	
Matthew Mason	..	..	,,	..	..	
John Woolley	..	..	,,	..	..	
Gervis C. Seaton	..	..	,,	..	..	
John Harrop	..	..	,,	..	..	
John Harrop, junr.	..	..	3 May, 1806	..	..	
John Radcliffe	..	..	,,	..	..	
Walter Beaumont	..	..	,,	..	..	
John Roberts	7 Mar. 1803	..	,,	..	..	
Lewis Fenton	..	..	,,	..	..	
George Moorhouse	..	..	29 Nov. 1803	..	..	Vice Bramel Dyson promoted.
James Booth	..	..	,,	..	..	Vice Stables promoted.
James Roberts	..	15 Aug. 1803	7 Mar. 1805	..	..	
John Roberts	..	,,	..	..	..	There appear to have been two of this name.
John Roberts	7 Mar. 1805	..	..	..	..	
John Buckley	..	15 Aug. 1803	..	..	..	
John Lees	..	,,	..	..	..	
John Marsden	..	,,	..	..	..	
James Roberts	..	..	7 Mar. 1805	..	..	Vice Dyson resigned.
Joseph Armitage	..	15 Aug. 1803	,,	..	..	Vice Beaumont resigned.
Henry Nelson	..	,,	..	..	..	

UPPER AGBRIGG VOLUNTEER INFANTRY—*Continued.*

Name.	Ensign.	Lieut.	Captain.	Major.	Lieut. Colonel.	Remarks.
Henry Heron	..	15 Aug. 1803	..	..	..	Called Henry Francis Heron in some Army Lists.
John Allison	..	"	..	..	..	
Michael Turner	..	"	..	..	..	
Joseph Hinchliffe	..	"	..	..	..	
William Saunders	..	"	..	..	..	
James Brook	..	"	..	..	..	
William North	..	29 Nov. 1803	..	..	..	
Edward Shaw	..	"	..	..	..	
Richard Tinker	..	"	..	..	..	
Edward Mundle	..	"	..	..	..	
Benjamin Stocks	..	"	..	..	..	
John Schofield	..	"	..	..	..	
William Turner	..	"	..	..	..	
Thomas Greenwood	..	"	..	..	..	
John Walker	..	"	..	..	..	
William Shaw	..	"	..	..	..	
James Hall	..	"	..	..	..	
J. Scholes	..	"	..	..	..	
Edward Shaw	..	15 Aug. 1803	..	..	..	
William Blackburn	15 Aug. 1803	7 Mar. 1805	..	..	..	
Robert Wrigley	..	"	..	..	..	
Joseph Blackburn	..	"	..	..	..	
John Beck (or Buck)	..	"	..	..	..	
Samuel Knight	15 Aug. 1803	6 April, 1805	..	..	..	
Robert Wrigley	..	7 Mar. 1805	..	..	..	
Samuel Wrigley	..	6 April, 1805	..	..	..	
John Battye	..	9 Mar. 1805	..	..	..	
Edmund Buckley	15 Aug. 1803	22 Sep. 1806	..	..	..	
William Earnshaw	..	"	..	..	..	
John Braye	15 Aug. 1803	..	..	..	..	

UPPER AGBRIGG VOLUNTEER INFANTRY—*Continued.*

Name.	Ensign.	Lieut.	Captain.	Major.	Lieut.-Colonel.	Remarks.
John Lodge	15 Aug. 1803	..	..	..	..	
Joseph Dyson	"	..	..	..	..	
John Blackburn	"	7 Mar. 1805	..	..	..	
George Tinker	29 Nov. 1803	.. ..	..	..	..	
Richard Roberts	..	22 Sep. 1805	..	..	..	
Joseph Roberts	7 Mar. 1805	..	..	..	..	
William Bailey	"	..	..	..	..	
John Earnshaw	5 Nov. 1805	..	..	..	..	
Robert Tinker	"	..	..	..	..	
R. Drinkwater	6 April, 1805	..	..	..	..	
John Taylor	"	..	..	..	..	Quarter-master Paymaster, 11 July, 1804.
John Schofield	7 Mar. 1805	9 Sep. 1805	..	..	..	
Joseph Scott	22 Sep. 1806	..	..	..	..	
Joseph Hazlegraves (or Hazlegreave)	"	..	..	..	..	
George Wright	"	..	..	..	..	

Chaplain ..	Rev. Thomas Wickham ..	15 August, 1803.
Adjutant	James Jenkins	" "
Quartermaster ..	John Taylor	" "
Paymaster ..	John Taylor	" "
Surgeon	Joseph Bradshaw	" "

In the Army Lists of 1805 and 1807, Benjamin Bradshaw's name appears as surgeon, commission dated 15th August, 1803.

The first appointment of officers appears in the Army List of 1803 as on 29th October, 1803, but the Lord Lieutenant's were dated 15th August, 1803. There are numerous variations between the dates of appointment in the *Gazette* and Army Lists. I have set out the names as closely as possible with the order appearing in the Army Lists, and not alphabetically.

Officers of Local Militia in 1810.

The following is the list of the officers extracted from the Army List of 31st July, 1810, with the dates of their commissions:—

RANK.	NAME.	COMMISSION.
Lieutenant-Colonel Commanding ..	*Sir G. Armytage ..	1808, 24th September.
Lieutenant-Colonel	*Northend Nichols ..	" "

Rank.	Name.	Commission.
Majors	*Bramhall Dyson ..	1808, 24th September.
	*John Woolley	1810, 31st March.
Captains ..	*John Roberts	1808, 24th September.
	*William North	,, ,,
	*Richard Tinker.. ..	,, ,,
	*James Brook	,, ,,
	*Henry Nelson	,, ,,
	*John Allison	,, ,,
	*Joshua Hinchliffe ..	1810, 31st March.
	*Benjamin Stocks ..	,, ,,
	*James Hall	,, ,,
	*Robert Wrigley.. ..	,, ,,
	*Joseph Blackburn ..	,, ,,

Captains John Roberts and William North were promoted majors in 1813; Godfrey Webster appointed captain in April, 1810.

Rank.	Name.	Commission.
Lieutenants ..	*Edmund Shaw (? Edward)..	1808, 24th September.
	*Samuel Knight	,, ,,
	*John Schofield	,, ,,
	*William Earnshaw	,, ,,
	*Joseph Roberts	,, ,,
	*Joseph Hazelgreave	,, ,,
	Robert Dunlop	,, ,,
	Ralph Lawton	,, ,,
	Timothy Bradbury	,, ,,
	John Hurst	,, ,,
	Joseph Moorhouse	,, ,,
	James Bates	,, ,,
	Thomas Clarkson	,, ,,
	*John Buttery (or Buttrey) ..	,, ,,
	George Shaw..	,, ,,
	Thomas Anderson	1810, 31st March.
	John Dickin Whitehead ..	,, ,,
	George Whitehead	,, ,,
	Samuel Gawthorp	,, ,,
	George Wilson Addison ..	,, ,,
	John Bradley..	,, ,,
	John Thomas Morley ..	,, ,,
	G. Shaw	,, ,,
	*W. B. Garside	,, ,,

Lieutenants Edmund Shaw, Samuel Knight, William Earnshaw and John Buttery promoted captains in 1813.

There were no ensigns in 1810, but in 1813 Clarkson was appointed ensign.

Adjutant.. ..	John Littlewood	1808, 24th September.
Quartermaster ..	John Taylor (Lieutenant)..	,, ,,
Surgeon	Benjamin Bradshaw ..	,, ,,

I have prefixed an asterisk to the names of those officers who had served in the Agbrigg Volunteers.

Of Robert Dunlop.

I am glad to be able to furnish some information as to two of the gallant officers whose names appear in the list of officers of the Local Militia in 1810. I refer to Mr. Robert Dunlop and Mr. Thomas Anderson. Both these gentlemen were from the land of the leal. Mr. Dunlop was the fifth son of Walter Dunlop, Esquire, of Whitmuir Hall, Selkirkshire and Agnes Dickson, his wife, eldest daughter of Archibald Dickson, Esquire, of Hassendeanburn, Roxburghshire. He was born at Whitmuir Hall, December 20th, 1781, and at Whitmuir Hall, too, he died, May 4th 1829, whilst on a visit. He was buried in the Church Yard at Ashkirk, Selkirkshire. He came to Huddersfield about 1805 and there engaged in the business of a woollen cloth merchant in partnership with his brother-in-law, Thomas Hastings, under the style of Dunlop and Hastings, the place of business being in King Street, behind the shop of Mr. Hoskin, grocer. Dunlop's residence was next to the Queen Hotel, the building afterwards used as an office by Mr. T. W. Clough. He married Janet, daughter of Robert (qy. John) McMillan of Brocklock, Kirkcudbrightshire. Mr. Walter Dunlop of The Grange, Bingley, is his eldest son, Mr. John McMillan Dunlop, of Holebird, Windermere, his second. There were also three daughters.

The military spirit which led Robert Dunlop to join the Local Militia was shared by other members of his family.

His brother, James Dunlop, was, in 1794, lieutenant in the Rochdale Independent Volunteer Company, being gazetted captain in 1796. Another brother, John, in 1798, received a Lieutenant's commission in the 4th Regiment of Militia of Scotland. In 1800 he was appointed factor to Lady Mary Montgomery and settling at Auchans, Ayrshire, transferred to the Dumfries Regiment of Militia. In 1808 he was appointed Adjutant of the Middle Regiment of Local Militia of the County of Ayr and held that post till the disbandment of the corps. Another brother, William, went in 1801 to India as a cadet in the service of the East India Company. In 1803 he was Ensign in the 11th Bengal Native Infantry; in 1824, Captain of the 26th Native Infantry; he became Major in the same year and being posted to the 52nd Native Infantry, was employed in reduction of native forts during the Aracan War. In 1829, at the request of the Governor-General, he assumed command of the 1st European regiment (afterwards 1st Bengal Fusiliers) which had declined in prestige and required a strong colonel. He was transferred to the 49th B.N.I. in 1832; in the following year was Deputy Commissioner General and Quartermaster General of the Bengal Army; in 1836 one of a special Embassy to Lahore; a Major-General in 1841.

Of Thos. Anderson.

The other officer to whom I have referred, Mr. Thomas Anderson, seems to have come to Huddersfield either along with Robert Dunlop or about the same time. He was a Dumfrieshire man, hailing from Cramilt, near Moffat in that county. He and young Dunlop were in partnership at one time as Anderson and Dunlop, and subsequently the senior partner in that firm appears to have joined Mr. John Tyne in the firm of "Anderson, Tyne and Co." They carried on business at Mark Bottom Mills, Paddock, and had a warehouse in Union Bank Yard. On Mr. Tyne's death Mr. Anderson removed to Manchester, where, in conjunction with his brother John and with Mr. William Thorburn, he carried on business under the style of "Andersons and Thorburn." That firm endures to this day. Mr. Anderson was a Tory, though his must have been a kind of Toryism very similar to latter day Liberalism. He supported the Factory Acts, an extension of the Franchise and a modified Home Rule for Ireland. He resided while in Huddersfield at Newhouse. In 1834 he acted as chairman of the Committee of Mr. Michael Thomas Sadler when he contested Huddersfield against Mr. John Blackburn K.C. and Captain Wood. Lieutenant Anderson was a man of very commanding figure, standing 6 feet 6 inches. He married Miss Betty Kilner, daughter of Mr. Thomas Kilner of Croft Head, behind the Cloth Hall. Croft Head no longer exists having been replaced by Sergeantson Street. Mr. Thomas Kilner was the grandfather of Mr. Jacob Thomas Kilner, our respected townsman, who has kindly given me these particulars.

Strength of Local Militia in 1808.

In 1808, there was only one return of the strength of the Huddersfield Corps of Local Militia, and that a very meagre one, from September to December, when the regiment was not assembled for exercise. There were then one adjutant, one quartermaster, one sergeant-major, ten sergeants and only five drummers. The pay was 6/- per day to adjutants, 3/- per day to quartermasters, 1/10 to the sergeant-major, 1/6 to serjeants, and 1/- to drummers.

Officers in 1812-1813.

The list of officers in the latter period differed from that already set out for the years 1808-1810 in the following particulars:—John Roberts and William North had been promoted captain and the name of Littlewood, the adjutant, appears in the list of captains. The names of Hinchliffe, J. D. Whitehead junior, Littlewood,

85:- Agbrigg (Huddersfield) Local Militia, 1808.

Wilson, Taylor, Thos. Shaw, Batley and Bradshaw appear for the first time in connection with the Local Militia as Lieutenants, though Bradshaw had held a commission in the Volunteers.

Uniform of the Upper Agbrigg Local Militia.

The uniform of the Agbrigg Local Militia was much the same as the old Volunteer uniform of 1803, scarlet coat, with yellow facings and collars. (See plate). As to the colours of this Local Militia, the general regulation for colours dated 1743 as before mentioned still remained in force. A considerable change, however, had been made in the appearance of the "Great Union" by the addition of the red cross of St. Patrick upon a white ground, in consequence of the union with Ireland which took place 1801, the actual wording of the Order in Council being as follows:—"The Union flag shall be azure, the crosses saltire of St. Andrew and St. Patrick, quarterly per saltire, counter-changed, argent and gules, the latter fimbriated of the second, surmounted by the cross of St. George of the third, fimbriated as the saltire." It was further ordered "that the shamrock should be introduced into the Union wreath, wherever that ornament or badge should be used."

Colours.

It will be noticed that the King's Colour, the great Union, contains this newly adopted cross of St. Patrick. The centre is occupied by the Royal Arms, England, Scotland, Ireland, with the arms of Hanover upon an escutcheon of pretence; the *fleur de lys* of France disappeared, as a quartering, from Royal Arms, in accordance with the conditions of the Treaty of Amiens, 1802. The whole within a wide and discursive wreath of laurels, above this wreath the regimental title, "Agbrigg Local Militia." The regimental colour below has the new "Union" in the upper corner, the flag itself being made of yellow silk, the colour of the regimental facing, according to the Regulation. In the centre appear the arms and crest of Sir George Armytage, Bart., the colonel of the regiment, within a trophy of arms, cannons and flags, with the regimental motto, "*pro rege et patriâ*," below. The whole device within a laurel wreath, regimental title above, as in the King's colour. The use of family arms upon regimental colours was absolutely abolished in 1743, but these private distinctions were occasionally placed upon the second colours of Local Militia regiments, and this may be taken as one of the rare cases. These colours have been copied from the working pattern in the books of the London firm who made them.

Regimental Number.

The Huddersfield Local Militia was numbered third in the West-Riding.

ld title unteers ed.

Although the local levies from 1808 were undoubtedly Local Militia they appear to have clung to the old and familiar title of Volunteers, as indeed they had some grounds for doing, for according to the *Leeds Mercury* of 29th April, 1810, in the whole Upper Agbrigg Local Militia Regiment of upwards of 1300 strong the number of balloted men did not exceed six.

The name "Huddersfield Volunteers" is also preserved upon a "Subscription Prize Medal," kindly lent to me by Mr. Samuel Milne Milne of Calverley House, near Leeds. The medal is of silver, circular in form, about 2in. in diameter, and on the rim is the legend "*Huddersfield Volunteers.*" The inscription recorded that the medal was "won by Jos. Jenkinson, May 19th, 1812, for the best shot at ball practice." (See plate.)

There were 11 battalions of Local Militia in the West Riding of Yorkshire and I give the names from the Army List of 1810 of the Lieutenant-Colonel and the number of the other officers of each rank so that the reader may make his own comparison of the position and approximate strength of the Agbrigg Local Militia with the rest of the Local Militia in that division of the county:—

Craven.—Colonel the Lord Ribblesdale, Lieutenant-Colonel Richard Heber, 2 Majors, 12 Captains, 16 Lieutenants, 7 Ensigns.

Halifax.—Lieutenant-Colonel Commandant Thomas Horton, Lieutenant-Colonel Thomas Ramsden, 2 Majors, 10 Captains, 22 Lieutenants, 5 Ensigns.

Sheffield.—Lieutenant-Colonel Francis Fenton, Lieutenant-Colonel Thomas Leader, 2 Majors, 11 Captains, 13 Lieutenants, 6 Ensigns.

Claro.—Lieutenant-Colonel Commanding Richard Wood, 2 Majors, 6 Captains, 7 Lieutenants, 5 Ensigns.

Leeds had two battalions.—1st battalion, Lieutenant-Colonel Commandant William Smithson, Lieutenant-Colonel Thomas Ikin, Major Christopher Beckett, 10 Captains, 11 Lieutenants, 6 Ensigns. 2nd battalion, Lieutenant-Colonel Commandant William Smithson, Lieutenant-Colonel John Hill, Major Henry Hall, 10 Captains, 10 Lieutenants, 3 Ensigns.

Morley.—Lieutenant-Colonel Commandant John Hardy, Lieutenant-Colonel Walker Ferrand, 2 Majors, 10 Captains, 13 Lieutenants, 5 Ensigns.

Staincross.—Lieutenant-Colonel Commandant Sir Francis Lindley Wood, Baronet, Lieutenant-Colonel John Spencer Stanhope, 2 Majors, 12 Captains, 9 Lieutenants, and 4 Ensigns.

Strafforth and Tickhill.—Lieutenant-Colonel Commandant Samuel Walker, Lieutenant-Colonel Henry Walker, 2 Majors, 9 Captains, 10 Lieutenants, and 4 Ensigns.

Wakefield.—Lieutenant-Colonel Commandant George Wroughton, Lieutenant-Colonel John Smyth, 2 Majors, 10 Captains, 12 Lieutenants, 3 Ensigns.

York City (included in the West Riding in the Army List).—Lieutenant-Colonel Commandant, Sir W. M. Milner, Baronet, Lieutenant-Colonel William Milner, 2 Majors, 12 Captains, 24 Lieutenants and 4 Ensigns.

Each of these Battalions had also an Adjutant, Quarter-Master and Surgeon.

The records of the Agbrigg Local Militia, from their formation in 1808 to their dissolution, are not of an exciting nature. "Happy," it has been said, "is the nation that has no history." If that be true also of the Local Militia the Agbrigg corps must have been indeed a happy one. I find, in the *Leeds Mercury* of May 16th, 1812, record of a quarrel between some members of the Agbrigg and the Wakefield Regiments of Local Militia "respecting the superiority of their corps." Words led to blows and "the town was thrown into a good deal of confusion. Sir George Armytage ordered the drums to beat to arms and the streets were scoured by a horse patrol. Shortly after 10 p.m. the streets were cleared and tranquility restored." It is a long time, I imagine, since the streets of Wakefield were clear at 10 p.m. Some men of the Wakefield regiment were confined to barracks for a few hours and then, as the newspapers express it, "the incident closed." Some records of the Corps.

There was also one other little matter which was deemed worthy of report by the excellent journal I have so frequently quoted. It appears that the corps was at Pontefract in April, 1811, for the annual training. "A character of some notoriety of that place charged one of the privates with picking his pocket, but on it being clearly made out that the charge was altogether false, the accuser was placed in a blanket and was regaled with a hearty tossing to the amusement of the whole corps."

With these exceptions the records of the corps, so far as a search in the local papers reveals, appear to have been confined to the annual assemblies for training, and the inspection and reports of Inspecting Officers. It may be of interest to preserve here a copy of the Notice calling up the Local Militiamen for training and exercise. It will be observed that in the Notice subjoined the men are only called up for 20 days and not for the statutory period of 28 days. The explanation probably is that, whilst the statute fixed a limit not to be exceeded, the Executive was at liberty to order assembly for a lesser period.

Local Militia.

Form of notice calling up Corps for annual training.

West Riding County of York, City and County of the City of York.

In pursuance of an Order or Directions from the Right Honourable Earl Fitzwilliam, Lord Lieutenant of the West Riding of the County of York, City and County of the City of York,

I do hereby give notice

That the Local Militiamen enrolled for the said Riding, City and County of the City of York are required, according to His Majesty's commands, transmitted to the said Lord Lieutenant by the Secretary of State, to assemble respectively at the times and places undermentioned to be trained and exercised for 20 days according to the directions of the Local Militia Acts, namely:—

The Morley Regiment at Pontefract on the 9th May next.

The Halifax Regiment at Halifax on the 15th May next.

The Agbrigg Regiment at York on the 28th April inst.

The 1st Battalion of the Leeds Regiment at Pontefract on the 29th May next.

The 2nd Battalion of the Leeds Regiment at Pontefract on the 21st June next.

The Staincross Regiment at Doncaster on the 25th April inst.

The Claro Regiment at Ripon on the 15th May next.

The Wakefield Regiment at Wakefield on the 16th May next.

The Craven Regiment at Harrogate and Knaresborough on the 11th May next.

The Sheffield Regiment at Sheffield on the 2nd May next.

The Strafforth-and-Tickhill Regiment at Doncaster on the 6th June next.

And notice is hereby further given,

That all persons enrolled to serve in the said Regiments and Battalions who shall not attend at the times and places appointed as above mentioned for their assembling respectively as aforesaid, will be liable under and by virtue of the said Acts to be apprehended and punished as deserters.

THOMAS BOLLAND,

Clerk of the General Meetings.

Leeds, 25th April, 1810.

On April 26th, 1810, accordingly, I find it noted in the *Mercury* that the Upper Agbrigg Militia Regiment, upwards of 1,300 strong, under the command of Sir George Armytage, marched into Leeds *en route* for York. The same authority informed the public of their safe return on May 18th. They appear to have been inspected at York on the 16th, by Lieutenant General Vyse, the general of the district, as witness the following order:—

"York, 16th May, 1810.

Parole-Armytage,

Lieutenant-General Vyse requests Lieutenant-Colonel Sir George Armytage, together with the officers, non-commissioned officers and privates of the Regiment under his command, will accept of his best thanks and strongest approbation of their appearance and performance in the Field this day. So much proficiency acquired in so short a time is the surest criterion of that real assiduity and attention which render every expression of praise or approbation unnecessary."

The *Leeds Mercury* seized upon the "exemplary and undeviating" discipline of the Local Militia at this time to point a pretty moral. In its issue of July 14th, 1810, it remarked—

"The whole of the Local Militia having now completed the annual training required by the Act, the present seems a very convenient opportunity for remarking on the exemplary and undeviating subordination to their officers which has been manifested by all the corps of the Yorkshire Local Militia, and particularly those of this Riding. And we believe the reason is, that the common people in this district are in general better informed than in most of the other parts of the Kingdom, for it is an undoubted fact that in proportion as men are ignorant they are rude, disorderly and unmanageable, and the general instruction of the people would do more than 10,000 prosecutions for libels to secure the peace and good order of the country."

Annual Training, 1811.

In March, 1811, the period of training appears to have been still further reduced, for the *Mercury*, March 10th, 1811, records the issue of official orders for assembling the Local Militia in Great Britain for 14 days' training and exercise, exclusive of the days of marching. All the men who had not been trained in any preceding year were to be assembled for 7 extra days preceding the assembling of the rest of the corps. No corps was to be permitted to assemble before April 1st, or subsequent to October 1st. The exercise to be performed at one period. Every corps to be assembled at its own headquarters or as near thereto as circumstances would permit.

Inspection of that year.

The Agbrigg Local Militia, commanded by Sir George Armytage, concluded their annual training at Pontefract for the year 1811, about April 27th. They were inspected on Heath Common, Wakefield, by Colonel Pulleyne, "who expressed his approbation of the steadiness and precision with which they went through their manœuvres." According to the *Mercury*, "they left behind them both at Pontefract and Wakefield an excellent character for regularity and good behaviour."

Annual Training, 1812.

On April 25th, 1812, they were assembled at York for 20 days' annual training.

Annual Training, 1813.

On May 20th, 1813, the Agbrigg Local Militia, described by the *Mercury* as "a remarkable fine body of men," assembled at York for training. They were commanded, as on previous occasions, by Sir George Armytage. They were nearly 1000 strong.

Inspection of that year.

On 4th June, 1813, they were reviewed at Knavesmire, York, by General Grey, who expressed his satisfaction at the proficiency the regiment had attained in their military duties, which he attributed in a great degree to the unremitting assiduity of their officers, and assured them that he should consider it his duty to return to Government the most favourable report of the state of the regiment.

The *Mercury* added, "It affords us pleasure to say that the orderly behaviour of the men in quarters fully equalled their soldierly conduct in the field."

I do not know which of the annual trainings of this corps inspired the local muse nor am I able to state who was the author of the following lines, a print of which has been kindly lent to me by Sir George J. Armytage The author, whoever he may have been, was, like all poets, modest, and contented himself with subscribing his effusions, "G. W., King Street, Huddersfield." There was a Captain Godfrey Webster and a Lieutenant George Whitehead in the corps, but I cannot say if either of those officers was the author of this poetical effusion.

Ode to the Agbrigg Local Militia.

TO THE
UPPER AGBRIGG VOLUNTEERS,
COMMANDED BY
SIR GEORGE ARMYTAGE, BART.,
On their marching to York, to be on permanent duty for three weeks.

——:o:——

When Gallic arrogance met just disdain,
And sons of Albion formed the martial train,
Astonish'd Europe ceased not to admire
Britannia's greatness and her patriots' fire;
The ag'd, the infant, join'd the female's praise,
To valour's worth a monument to raise.

Yes. Volunteers, you, for your native soil,
Acquire experience, and as vet'rans toil;
Leave, for a time, the comforts you have known,
And make e'en foes your bravery to own;
Your grateful countrymen applaud your deeds;
For Britain's cause all others supersedes.

Go, Agbrigg's sons, you'll keep that cause in sight
Which stimulates and fits you for the fight;
Which bids the tyrant rather come than stay;
(For Britons wait impatiently the fray!)—
To merit vict'ry, with your col'nel's word,
Your prompt obedience always will accord;
So shall each officer find due respect,
And discipline be guarded from neglect;
Confining thus the wav'rings of the brain,
No pois'nous rancour dare your conduct stain;
But all shall know, though born near craggy hills,
The soldier's duty every bosom fills;
Thousands will then with emulation burn,
And thankful Agbrigg greet—your bless'd return!

The Agbrigg Volunteers.

——:o:——

Hail! Britons, bold Britons, enroll'd in the cause
Of your fam'd constitution, its freedom and laws!
Old England rejoices—each bosom is charm'd!
Admiring the brave, independently arm'd.
Then practise *Brown Bess*—at Proficiency aim:
Be soldiers in Duty as well as in name.
Huzza! huzza! Volunteers, your oath keep in view;
Your Country's Defence is entrusted to you.

Your commander, whose brav'ry and worth are well known,
In defence of his King has his loyalty shown.
When he gives the command, you will eagerly go
To meet the ambitious, implacable foe!
Then practise &c.

In vain Frenchmen hope that old England has foes
'Mongst men who derive their support from her laws;
Who will fight for their Isle!—it enraptures each heart
That providence favour'd his birth in this part.
Then practise &c.

Old England, now rous'd, lion-like will repel
Invasion's foul monsters, the fav'rites of hell.
Our King is our countryman; Britons, rejoice!
And rally around him with heart and with voice!
Then practise &c.

May George and his Queen shine in history's page!
And, when reaching extreme, highly honour'd old age,
May they, leaving this world, speed to glory their way,
And partake of that crown which can never decay.
Let's practise &c.

G. W.

King Street, Huddersfield.

In May, 1812, of the same year—the year made memorable in our local history by the Luddite depredations—the magistracy appears to have contemplated the necessity of calling out the Local Militia in aid of the civil power. An alternative, or perhaps an additional, course, the establishment of a sort of unofficial constabulary appears to have also found favour with the magistrates. The following proceedings are not without interest to the student of our local annals:—

Calling out of Local Militia contemplated, 1812.

Court House, Wakefield, May 14th, 1812.

At a general meeting of the Lord Lieutenant and of the Deputy Lieutenants and Magistrates of the West Riding of the county of York, convened at the request of the Lord Lieutenant, present, the Earl Fitzwilliam, the Lord Lieutenant, Sir Thomas Turner Slingsby, Bart., High Sheriff, and a great part of the Deputy Lieutenants and Magistrates of the Riding. Resolved:—

"That in case it shall be found necessary on account of any riots or public disturbance to call out the Local Militia to assist in suppressing the same, that they shall be called out in divisions as occasion shall require in the following order, namely:—

1st Division.	2nd Division.	3rd Division.	4th Division.
Sheffield,	City of York,	Wakefield,	Strafforth,
Craven,	1st Leeds,	Claro,	2nd Leeds,
Morley.	Halifax.	Staincross.	Agbrigg."

Resolved:—

"That it is the opinion of this meeting that no measures can contribute more effectually for the preservation of the peace than the voluntary association of individuals, and it is earnestly recommended that every Township in the West Riding do form within itself an Association of every well disposed person therein for the purpose of preventing the committing of any outrages by day or night upon the person or property of any of His Majesty's subjects, and that every Association under this resolution be denominated an Association for the preservation of the peace."

Resolved:—

"That it is the opinion of this meeting that an additional number of sub-constables be appointed in every township and that it is earnestly recommended to the respectable inhabitants to offer themselves for that purpose, not only as giving additional strength to the civil power but as a greater safeguard to themselves."

Resolved:—

"That the above Resolution be published in the provincial newspapers."

The Lord Lieutenant having left the chair

It was resolved:—

"That the thanks of this meeting be given to the Lord Lieutenant for calling the same and for his able and impartial conduct in the chair."

By order of the Committee,

EDMUND BOLLAND,

Clerk of the General Meetings of Lieutenancy.

Offer of services out of their county.

I have already, in Part I. of this work, referred to the Acts 54 Geo. III. c. 19 and 55, Geo. III. c. 76 authorising the Crown to accept from the Local Militia voluntary offers of service out of their counties, for a period not exceeding forty two days in the whole year. In the *Leeds Mercury* of January 1814 it was stated that "The Agbrigg Regiment of Local Militia, both officers and men, had offered their services to do duty in any part of the country which the Crown might require," and the issue of the same journal for February 19th of that year contained the announcement that the Local Militia were to be assembled for one day only to ascertain what number of men might be willing to extend their services out of their respective counties for a period not exceeding 42 days in that year, each man to receive two guineas, one in money and the other in necessaries.

The days of the Local Militia were, however, now already numbered. On April 11th, 1814, Napoleon abdicated his throne, and was shortly afterwards sent to Elba. It was believed the world had done with him for good and all. There is no need to look for further explanation of the following communication addressed to the Commanding Officers of Local Militia :—

"Whitehall, May 2nd, 1814. 1814. Annual Training pretermitted.

Sir,—I am directed by Lord Sidmouth to acquaint you that it is not intended to assemble the Local Militia for training and exercise during the present year.

I am, Sir, your most obedient humble servant,

J. H. ADDINGTON.

To the Officer Commanding the Local Militia.

In July, 1814, the House of Lords voted its thanks to the officers, non-commissioned officers and men of the several corps of Local Militia and of Yeomanry and Volunteer Cavalary and Infantry for the seasonable and eminent services they had rendered their King and country. The resolutions were in these terms :— House of Lords' thanks to Local Militia.

Die Martis, 5° Julij, 1814.

Resolved :—

"*Nemine dissentiente*, by the Lords Spiritual and Temporal, in Parliament assembled, that the thanks of this House be given to the officers of the several corps of Local Militia and of Yeomanry and Volunteer Cavalry and Infantry which have been formed in Great Britain and Ireland, during the course of the war, for the seasonable and eminent services they have rendered their King and country."

Resolved :—

"*Nemine dissentiente*, by the Lords Spiritual and Temporal, in Parliament assembled, that this House doth highly approve and acknowledge the services of the non-commissioned officers and men of the several corps of Local Militia and of Yeomanry and Volunteer Cavalry and Infantry which have been formed in Great Britain and Ireland, during the course of the war; and that the same be communicated to them by the Colonels and other Commanding Officers of the several corps, who are desired to thank them for their meritorious conduct."

Ordered :—

"That the Lord Chancellor do communicate the said resolutions, by letter to the Secretary of State for the Home Department, in order to be by him communicated to His Majesty's Lieutenants of each county, riding and place in Great Britain; and to His Excellency the Lord Lieutenant of that part of the United Kingdom called Ireland."

GEORGE ROSE, Cler' Parliamentor.'

The resolutions were transmitted by the Secretary of State, Lord Sidmouth, to the Lord Lieutenant of the West Riding, and by him to Sir George Armytage, by whom they were communicated to the regiment he had commanded from the day of its formation. The following address from Sir George to his regiment, which accompanied the resolutions, no one can fail to read without full appreciation :—

THE UPPER DIVISION OF AGBRIGG, &c.

"Kirklees, Huddersfield, 29th July, 1814.

Thanks of Sir George Armytage.

R. O.,

Lieutenant-Colonel Sir George Armytage, having received the following honourable testimonial, addressed by the Secretary of State for the Home Department to the Lord Lieutenant of the West Riding of the County of York, with certain resolutions of the House of Lords, cannot let this opportunity pass without congratulating the officers, non-commissioned officers and men of the Agbrigg Regiment of Local Militia and the former Volunteer Corps; wishing it to be distinctly understood that this applies to both services. He requests they will accept his best thanks for their uniform good conduct during the time he has had the honour to command the regiment under its various changes of service, which never changed the disposition of the true *patriot*.

It is one of the most gratifying periods of Sir George's life which enables him thus to congratulate his brother officers, soldiers, and this populous and industrious neighbourhood, on the blessings of peace, now so happily returned. May it be perpetual.

That this Order, with the Circular and Resolutions, be made public, as a lasting mark of the approbation expressed by the country of our united services.

By order of

Lieutenant-Colonel Sir George Armytage, Bart.,
JOHN LITTLEWOOD, Captain and Adjutant.

The House of Commons, also, had placed on record its sense of the patriotic services of the Local Militia, and by the command of the House, Speaker Abbott thus addressed the several Lords Lieutenant :—

"House of Commons, 7th July, 1814.

My Lord,

The Commons' thanks to Local Militia.

By the command of the House of Commons of the United Kingdom of Great Britain and Ireland, I have the honour of transmitting to you their unanimous vote of thanks of the officers of the several corps of Militia, Local Militia and of Yeomanry and Volunteer Cavalry and Infantry, which have been formed in Great Britain and Ireland during the course of the war, for the seasonable and eminent services they have rendered to their King and country.

And also the unanimous resolution of the House signifying their high approbation and acknowledgment of the services of the non-commissioned officers and men of the several corps of Militia, Local Militia and of Yeomanry and Volunteer Cavalry and Infantry, which have been formed in Great Britain and Ireland during the course of the war, and that this resolution of the House be communicated to them by the Colonels and several Commanding Officers of the several corps, who are desired to thank them for their meritorious conduct.

In transmitting this resolution of the House of Commons I have the greatest satisfaction at the same time in bearing testimony to its high sense of the value of those services, by which the regular army has been so largely augmented and enabled to carry on its operations in a manner so glorious to itself and so beneficial to the interests of all Europe.

I have the honour to be, my Lord,

Your Lordship's most obedient servant,

CHARLES ABBOTT, Speaker.

To Earl Fitzwilliam,

His Majesty's Lieutenant of the West Riding of the County of York."

The vote was in these terms:—

6° Die Julii, 1814.

Resolved *Nemine Contradicente*,

"That the thanks of this House be given to the officers of the several corps of Local Militia which have been formed in Great Britain during the course of the war for the seasonable and eminent services which they have rendered to their King and country."

Resolved *Nemine Contradicente*,

"That this House doth highly approve and acknowledge the services of the non-commissioned officers and men of the several corps of Local Militia which have been formed in Great Britain during the course of the war and that the same be communicated to them by the Colonels and other Commanding Officers of the several corps, who are desired to thank them for their meritorious conduct."

Ordered,

"That Mr. Speaker do signify the said Resolutions to His Majesty's Lieutenant of each county, riding and place in Great Britain.

J. DYSON, Cl. D. Dom. Com.

On April 20th, 1816, the *Leeds Mercury* recorded the issue of a circular by the Secretary of War to the Commandants of the Local Militia containing the following arrangements which were immediately to take place. The permanent pay of the staff was to cease on the 24th inst. The arms, drums, clothing and accoutrements were to be sent into the public stores, but should there be any sorts of clothing belonging to men enrolled before the 17th March, 1812, they were to be delivered to the men to whom they belonged. The non-commissioned officers and drummers were to be discharged on the 24th inst., unless the packing, &c., should not be completed in the time, in which case two sergeants might be retained for the completion of the business 14 days, but no longer. The Adjutant was to be the only officer to be placed on the reduced pay of 4/- per diem.

Disposal of surplus funds.

In some corps, funds appear to have existed unappropriated to the purposes for which they were subscribed. Doubtless these funds were dealt with in different ways. Though I may be overstepping strictly local bounds, I imagine more than Leeds readers will be interested by an announcement in the *Leeds Mercury* that "at a meeting of subscribers to the fund of the late Leeds Volunteers it was determined that the surplus in the treasurer's hands, amounting to about £700, should form an accumulating fund in aid of the expense attendant upon the removal of the unsightly pile of buildings between Briggate and Cross Parish, usually called the Middle Row."

This, presumably, was considered to be an application of the *cy prés* doctrine.

ess Book Local ilitia.

I have described the birth of the Local Militia, I have narrated the doings of its lusty youth, I have recorded the complimentary messages that served as its epitaph and I have given at least some information as to the disposal of its worldly assets. A more cheerful topic shall conclude its story. Sir George J. Armytage has kindly lent me the mess book of the regiment. The last entry in it is of a dinner on January 11th, 1815, at the Rose and Crown. This was an old hostlery formerly situate near to Vicar's Croft in Kirkgate. It was a famous house in the old coaching days. It was demolished some years ago to make room for the outlet from what is now known as Venn Street into Kirkgate, and for other improvements. The dinner was possibly the last occasion on which the gallant officers of the Upper Agbrigg Local Militia met—perhaps to drink in solemn silence to the memory of their suspended corps.

The serious reader may feel disposed to resent the frequent entry in the mess book of wagers that seem somewhat frivolous to an age that has almost forgotten how to laugh. But it must be remembered they were often the pretext for indirectly replenishing the coffers of the mess whilst also contributing to its gaiety. I confess for my own part that the devices by which our forefathers varied and enlivened their anxious duties are not without their interest to me and may possibly be indulged by others equally lenient to the foibles of mankind.

Who can restrain a smile at reading, for instance, that (May 12th, 1810) Captain Nelson was fined, for the benefit of the Mess Fund, the sum of 5/- "for making his return in the French language." And by appeal to what written or unwritten code of justice or of honour was Lieutenant Dunlop mulcted in a like amount "for translating same." It is reassuring after this to read that Captain North, "charged with giving a private leave of

absence without the knowledge of Sir George Armytage, was tried and acquitted." Both love and strife seem to have provoked these gallant officers to a wager, for in May of the same year there is an entry, "Captain Nelson wagers with Captain North that Mr. Buttery is married to Miss —— and not Mr. Ratcliffe," whilst Major Woolley "bets Captain Hall a bottle of wine that Bates throws Lieutenant Whitehead." Lieutenant Whitehead appears to have been addicted to the Cumbrian sport, for on May 15th he is fined a bottle of wine "for wrestling with Lieutenant Garside," and paid his 5/- like a man. Another lieutenant is fined a bottle for swearing at the mess table. Captain Blackburn,* on April 13th, bets Captain Allison* five bottles to one that Sir ———— does not invite the officers of the regiment to dinner." The baronet whose name I suppress was not Sir George Armytage. The officers of the Mess of the existing corps may tax their ingenuity in supplying the hiatus and gratifying their love of hazard by a wager as to the result of the bet of 1810. Another bet of the same date must have surely been made when dinner was far advanced, "Lieutenant George Shaw bets Lieutenant George Whitehead thirteen bottles of wine to twelve that he, (Lieutenant Whitehead), does not run round the Racecourse without walking." A few days later Major Dyson is fined 10/-, or more probably two bottles, for not giving the word of command correctly in the manual exercise and Lieutenant Roberts is fined 5/- for dictating to the same gallant Major on the field—presumably in a laudable endeavour to rectify the Major's misdirections. It must have been difficult to escape fining at that merry mess. The Commanding Officer himself is fined and paid 5/6 for sitting down before grace was said. Well! grace was often long drawn out in those days, though less often perhaps by Army Chaplains than other Divines One lieutenant loses a bottle about the spelling of the word "mahogany," another about the age of a lady. Lieutenant Bradley is fined a bottle for "being newly married," and with the sorrows of this hapless Benedict I may reasonably drop the curtain upon the doings of this frolic corps.

Huddersfield Armed Association, 1820.

The early months of the year 1820 were, in the manufacturing districts, marked by great distress and much unrest. Political agitation was very rife, and the leaders of a people maddened by long want incited their credulous dupes to acts of violence as senseless as they were nefarious. The sufferings of the masses were attributed to the supineness, the indifference or the cupidity

* *Arcades ambo*—lawyers both.—R.P.B.

of the governing classes. A march in force upon London was resolved upon. A desperate populace should wrest by force the concessions that were denied to the pleadings of justice and the dictates of reason. A plot was formed by the inhabitants of the small villages and hamlets surrounding Huddersfield to seize that town. The early morning of Wednesday, the 11th April, was fixed upon for the attack. The magistrates, however, had for some time been aware that something unusual and something serious was afoot. A hand bill was issued by the magistrates calling on the inhabitants to "come forward and be sworn as special constables as the only alternative to prevent the Watch and Ward Act being put into force." At a meeting held at the George Inn, on April 8th, it was resolved, if necessary, but certainly not otherwise, to apply to the Lord Lieutenant to put in force the Watch and Ward Act. Mr. Joseph Haigh, who presided, said that "he was persuaded no arguments would be required to obtain the assent of the inhabitants to the above step as such were the diabolical designs of the conspirators that if their plot had not been discovered it is probable not one of those present at the meeting would have houses to go to." The Act referred to was doubtless the statute of March, 1812 (52, George III., c. 17), passed with special reference to the Luddite outrages. It, indeed, recites that "considerable numbers of persons have for some time past assembled themselves together on different occasions, in a riotous and tumultous manner, in several parts of the County of Nottingham and the town and County of the town of Nottingham, and in the adjoining counties, and have had recourse to measures of force and violence." The Luddite riots, the local reader will remember, spread from the county of Nottingham to Yorkshire. Section 11 of the Act authorised the magistrates, if they should be of opinion that the officers ordinarily appointed were insufficient for the preservation of the peace and protection of the inhabitants and the security of their property, to order that every man above 17 years of age and rated to the relief of the poor, should be liable to the duties of watching by night and warding by day. Section 18 defined the duties of the watcher and warder. He should, "during his time of watching and warding, to the utmost of his power, endeavour to prevent all murders, burglaries, robberies, affrays, and all felonies, outrages and disorders";* and for that end he was empowered to

* For an account of the Watch and Ward of very early days see *English Constitutional History* by Taswell-Langmead.

"arrest and apprehend all Nightwalkers, malefactors, rogues, vagabonds, and other loose, idle, disorderly and suspicious persons . . . . . and deliver the same to the constable at the watch house, to be there detained till they could be carried before a Justice." The watchers and warders were to be paid out of the rates and also furnished at the public expense with "rattles, staves, lanterns, and such weapons, arms and accoutrements" as the Justices should direct.

The hours of watching and warding are not specified in this Act but in 1253 they had been fixed at from sunset to sunrise between Ascension Day and Michaelmas.

On April 10th a meeting was held at the George Inn "for the purpose of considering the best means of forming an Armed Association in aid of the civil power and for the permanent and more effectual protection of the town and neighbourhood." It was resolved:—"That an Armed Association shall be formed for the defence of the town." Several gentlemen, we are told, came forward for the purpose, were supplied with arms, and actively co-operated with the civil and military powers. The shops were closed, the streets barricaded and armed patrols traversed the environs. At break of day a mounted messenger, riding in hot haste, galloped into the town with the alarming news that several hundred men, armed with pikes, guns and other weapons, bearing a standard and beating a drum, had been encountered by the patrol in the village of Flockton, and that they were marching on Huddersfield. Another armed force was reported to be assembled on Grange Moor. The small military force in the town was concentrated in the Market Place, which was barricaded. A detachment of the Fourth Irish Dragoons, which had been quartered in the town, was sent out to intercept the advance from Grange Moor. But the insurgents had learned, if somewhat tardily, the value of the precept that discretion is the better part of valour. When their outposts or scouts warned them of the approach of the military they flung away their arms and returned each man to his own home. There were several arrests, a solemn trial at York, on the capital charge of high treason, and twenty-two of the rioters were transported.*

Threatened attack on Huddersfield.

Some days later the *Leeds Mercury* of April 15th contains an account of a further alarm, heightened by an explosion at the barracks of some two hundred ball cartridges. The members of the

---

For a fuller account see Sykes's "*History of Huddersfield and its Vicinity.*"

Armed Association assumed their arms and stood to their posts, but again the night passed and Huddersfield, with the morn, was able again to breathe freely.

There were, I may observe, not wanting those who insinuated that the members of the Armed Association were not entirely disinterested in the zeal with which they offered their services. A correspondent of the *Leeds Mercury*, of May 13th, 1820, makes the sly remark that the *Huddersfield Armed Association* were not pluralists and had no wish to monopolize military honours, as they were sworn in to their new service just before the Militia Ballot took place.

The Armed Association formed in Huddersfield does not appear to have been immediately disbanded. As they were a kind of fencible company, raised for a special purpose and a limited period, the names of their officers found a place in the Army List. In the *Leeds Mercury*, of 5th August, 1820, we find, apparently from the *Gazette*, that Lewis Fenton was captain commandant, Robert Dunlop captain, and Thomas Anderson, J. C. Laycock, John Sunderland Hirst and Tristram Ridgeway, lieutenants. A new title is given to the Association. It is no longer called the *Huddersfield Armed Association*, but the *Huddersfield Independent Association*, and the corps had still other designations. It appears under the title of *Huddersfield Infantry* in the Army List of the "Militia, Yeomanry, Cavalry and Volunteer Infantry," bearing date September 30th, 1820, and its officers, with commissions bearing date May 27th, 1820, were :—

Captain Commandant	Lewis Fenton.
Captain	Robert Dunlop.
Lieutenants	Thomas Anderson.
	James Campey Laycock.
Ensigns	John Sunderland Hirst.
	Tristram Ridgeway.

In 1825, the "Huddersfield Infantry" are, in the Army List, transformed into the "Huddersfield Riflemen." The names of the above officers are repeated, but the ensigns have been promoted to the rank of lieutenant. It is perhaps necessary to caution the reader that the mere fact of the appearance of these names in the Army List in 1825 is not of itself sufficient evidence that any body of Huddersfield Riflemen then existed. It not seldom happened that names once inserted were retained in the list for many years after their owners had passed away.

The uniform of the Armed Association of 1820 was bottle green with black facings on collar and cuffs, green worsted epaulettes, a crimson sash worn round the waist. The jacket was tight fitting, the hat of a high stove-pipe shape, with a thick wooden protection in the crown. It will be seen from a subsequent page that on the formation of the Huddersfield Volunteers in 1859, Mr. James Campey Laycock, one of the Fencibles of 1820, produced his uniform for the inspection and guidance of the officers in their deliberations upon the uniform then to be adopted. Uniform.

Mr. G. W. Tomlinson, in his "Founders of the Huddersfield Subscription Library" publishes sundry extracts from the manuscript diary of Mr. John Hannah. Mr. Hannah was a native of Dumfries. The Hannahs of Hannahfield, near Dumfries, were a family of standing and property in that neighbourhood. He left Dumfries in 1781 to tempt fortune south of the border, doubtless mindful of the Scotchman's motto, *Vestigia nulla retrorsum.* He ultimately settled in Huddersfield, founding the firm of woollen merchants, "John Hannah & Co.," Mr. Thomas Kilner, of Carr House, being one of the partners and Mr. Weale the other. Their warehouse was at the junction of Rosemary Lane and Castlegate, the premises up the Lane being used as cropping shops. John Hannah was the father of that Alexander Hannah whose name will be found in connection with the Local Volunteers of 1859, and who married Miss Brook, the daughter of William Brook Esquire, of Gledholt, whose son, Mr. William Brook, was the first sergeant-major of the Volunteers in 1859. Mr. John Hannah, to revert to the founder of the local branch of the family, appears to have been a considerable person in the town and to have enjoyed the friendship of its leading men. He had the laudable industry to keep a diary and one finds in it mention of "friends dropping in to drink a glass of wine with me." He lodged in his earlier days with Mr. Henry Bradley in King Street, then almost a new street. He mentions the Hastings, the Dunlops, the Andersons, the Alexanders, all, like himself, from beyond the Tweed. The Dunlop and Anderson he mentions would be the Dunlop and Anderson who held respectively a captain's and lieutenant's commission in the Huddersfield Infantry and Fencibles. In 1812 Hannah himself had been a member of a "Voluntary Association" formed in the Luddite time, and the diary contains the words "I was one of the 20 that watched that night," from which it may be surmised the members of these Associations took duty by rotation. Some notices of officers of Armed Association.

There are some members of the Armed Associations of this period whom I am loth to dismiss with a mere record of their names. Of Captain Lewis Fenton, the first member whom Huddersfield returned to Parliament, it is unnecessary to add to what other local records have preserved.

Of J. C. Laycock.

James Campey Laycock was a solicitor and founder of the honoured firm of Laycock, Dyson & Laycock. He was born 4th May, 1796, at Appleton near York, received his education at a Tadcaster school and was originally intended for a commercial career, being apprenticed to the well known firm of Potters, linen bleachers, Manchester. He, however, finally elected for the law, was articled to Messrs. Russell & Co., solicitors, York, and was admitted solicitor in Hilary term 1819. In the following year he opened his office in Huddersfield, fortified by letters of introduction to many of the leading families of the town and neighbourhood. He was appointed clerk to the local justices, December 15th, 1828. He filled with dignity, integrity and ability many other posts of trust. He was a staunch conservative and churchman, and died at the advanced age of 88, on February 17th, 1885. One solitary tombstone there is in England, I believe, with the inscription: "Here lies an honest lawyer." It does not rest above the remains of James Campey Laycock, but no more appropriate epitaph could have been graved upon his tomb.

Of Tristram Ridgeway.

Tristram Ridgeway, a native of Ashton-under-Lyne, was a woolstapler, his warehouse, now pulled down, being in Station Street, his residence then being in West Parade. For a time he traded as "Executor of G. Lawton," afterwards on his own account. On retiring from the woolstapling business he accepted a post in the Huddersfield and Agbrigg Savings Bank. He resided at Bath Buildings. His second wife was a daughter of the Rev. John Coates, M.A., Vicar of Huddersfield 1791-1823. In 1894 Miss Elizabeth Bennett Ridgeway erected a reredos in the Huddersfield Parish Church, in memory of Tristram and Penelope Ridgeway. There was, I find, a Tristram Ridgeway, a surgeon in the Armed Association (Infantry), at Ashton-under-Lyne, his commission being dated November 29th, 1798. He was possibly the father of the subject of this brief notice, who died March 8th, 1870, aged 76 years, and was buried in the Huddersfield Parish Churchyard. Born 1794, he was only 26 years of age when he received his commission in the Huddersfield Armed Association.

Of John S. Hirst.

John Sunderland Hirst was born in August, 1781, probably at The Hurst, Longwood. He married Miss Hannah Brook, the daughter of William Brook, of Meltham Mills. He died December 22nd, 1866, and was buried at Linthwaite Church. He was uncle of the late Joseph Hirst, of Wilshaw, whose mother was a sister of Mr. Charles Brook, of Healey House. He had five sons and three daughters, one of whom, Miss Mary Martha Hirst, of Wood Cottage, who has kindly favoured me with these particulars, still survives. Mr. T. Julius Hirst, J.P., of Meltham Hall, who was a lieutenant in the 44th (Meltham) West York Rifle Volunteers, in 1868, is his grandson.

Complimentary Banquet, 1820.

It will be remembered that when, in 1820, the Armed Association was formed, the seriousness of the emergency had necessitated the quartering in the town of the military. They were the 4th Dragoon Guards and 85th Regiment of Light Infantry, some 200 men in all. When tranquility was restored and the feeling of alarm local events had very naturally excited had subsided, the ladies of the town and neighbourhood started a subscription to reward the men "for their meritorious and exemplary exertions during the late alarm." The amount collected was £74. The men were entertained at dinner at the George Inn and the Rose and Crown Inn. Some £50 was left in hand after defraying the cost of the dinners, from which we may conclude dining and wining was a less costly business then than now. Of this surplus, thirty guineas was given to Mr. George Whitehead, the active deputy constable of Huddersfield, and the rest expended in clothing for the soldiers' wives and children, and for the sick at the hospital. The men, we are told, "conducted themselves with highly praiseworthy decorum, and appeared much gratified at this liberal mark of respect from their fair country-women"; and with so eminently satisfactory a quotation this notice of that troubled period may fitly close.

PART II.

SECTION III.

(A.D. 1859-1874.)

In the 4th Section of Part I. of this work I have described at sufficient length the events that, in 1859, if not absolutely causing certainly quickened the revival of the Volunteer movement. I have set out at large the War Office Circular of the 12th May of that year signifying the readiness of the Crown to accept the services of Volunteer corps. There now remains but to narrate the steps taken in the town and neighbourhood of Huddersfield to raise such corps and the further task of tracing the growth of the local Volunteer force from its birth, through its infancy to its majority, and thenceforward to the year which many considerations constrain me to fix as the limit of this chronicle. It was reasonable to suppose that this part of my labours would be the lightest and involve the least enquiry and research. As a fact it has entailed much labour, from the circumstance that little or no care appears to have been taken to preserve the books, correspondence and other documents essential to the preparation of a connected history such as a reader might be justified in expecting of events comparatively so recent.

A Rifle Club contemplated.

The first idea of those gentlemen who took the initiative in the local Volunteer movement (1859) would seem to have been a very modest one—to establish merely a Rifle Club. I gather that a meeting was held at the office of Mr. Alfred Jessop, probably in the early summer of 1859. Mr. Jessop was a solicitor practising in the town, who appears to have taken little or no part in subsequent proceedings. I have before me a circular sent out, at the inception of the movement, headed "Huddersfield Rifle Club"; but as the body of this circular speaks of a Rifle Club or Corps, it may be that the words club and corps were used either as convertible terms or to suggest for consideration alternative schemes. From this circular I find that it was in contemplation to form a Rifle Club, that some would enrol themselves as "honorary subscribing," others as "acting" members. The following gentlemen are stated in the circular to have consented to support the movement with pecuniary assistance and to enrol themselves as honorary subscribing members :—Messrs. Joseph Armitage, J.P., George Armitage, J.P, John Brooke, J.P., Thomas Pearson Crosland, J.P., Joseph Taylor Armitage, J.P., Thomas Mallinson, J.P., Bentley Shaw, J.P., Lewis Randle Starkey, J.P., Charles Brook, junr., James William Carlile, James Campey Laycock, Henry Robinson, George Dyson, Nicholas Carter, Jabez Brook, Frederick Learoyd, Joseph Wrigley and Joseph Brook. The following gentlemen had agreed to be enrolled as acting members :—Henry Frederick Beaumont, J.P., Bentley Shaw, J.P., (who acted as chairman *pro. temp.* of the organizing committee), Edgar Fenton, Thomas Brooke, junr., James Bradbury, Frederick William Greenwood, Thomas Hudson Battye (honorary secretary *pro. temp.*), John Brooke, junr., Frederick William Jacomb, John Haigh, junr., Joseph Acheson Harrison, Alfred Jessop, Edwin Learoyd, Henry Brook, Thomas Abbey Bottomley and William Fred Crosland. These names seem to exhaust the favourable responses from a total of two hundred residents approached in this manner and from whom promises of £185 were obtained.

Honorary Subscribing Members.

Acting Members.

The meeting at Mr. Jessop's office seems to have arrived at the decision that to establish a Rifle Club would prejudice the formation of a Rifle Corps. But I do not discover that at this meeting any decision was arrived at either to form a club or corps. I learn from Colonel F. Greenwood, J.P., that some weeks after the meeting at Mr. Jessop's office, Mr. Thomas Hudson Battye, also a solicitor, invited a few of those who had interested themselves in the movement to meet at his office in Kirkgate, when it was finally resolved to form a shooting club. This, no doubt, is the meeting consequent upon the circular to which I have already referred. It seems that the gentlemen whose names I have already enumerated offered their services as a Shooting Club to the Government of the day, but the War Office authorities declined the offer in this form. This refusal caused Mr. Greenwood, afterwards Lieutenant-Colonel Greenwood, to wait upon Mr. William Moore, doubtless as a representative of the promoters of the movement, and desire him to call a public Town's Meeting to consider the propriety of establishing a Volunteer Corps. Mr. Moore was the Constable of the town at that time. Huddersfield was not then a corporate borough, and the office of Constable was analogous to that of Mayor. Mr. Moore complied with the requisition and issued the following proclamation :—

1859. The Constable of Huddersfield's Proclamation.

"I do hereby call a public meeting of the inhabitants of the Borough of Huddersfield for the purpose of taking into consideration the propriety of establishing a Volunteer Rifle Corps.

June 9th, 1859, Town's Meeting at Huddersfield.

The meeting will be held in the Gymnasium Hall on Thursday evening, June 9th, 1859, at 7 o'clock, when the attendance of those gentlemen who take an interest in this national movement and of those spirited individuals who will probably manifest their ardour by becoming members of the intended corps is particularly requested.

WILLIAM MOORE, Constable."

The meeting so summoned was largely attended and feeling seems to have run high. It was vehemently alleged by those who opposed the proposal to establish a Volunteer corps that the promoters of the meeting were influenced chiefly by a sinister desire to divert the attention of the people from questions of domestic reform to military pageantry, in fact that the movement was a Tory dodge, an accusation doubtless as hotly resented as it was hotly urged. The meeting broke up in confusion without arriving at the expected conclusions and a claim by the proprietor or lessee of the gymnasium, Mr. Le Blanc, of £5 for compensation for damage to the furniture was admitted and paid.

I extract from the *Huddersfield Examiner* a report of the meeting, at which, as will be seen, the most prominent, as he certainly was the ablest, opponent of the proposed corps was Mr. Joseph Woodhead. Many years have passed since that stormy meeting of June 9th, 1859, and Mr. Woodhead is still with us, full of years and full of honours. He has sate in Parliament for a neighbouring Division, he has occupied with conspicuous ability the Mayoral Chair of Huddersfield, which has conferred upon him the well merited dignity of the freedom of the borough; he has for more than half a century played a conspicuous part in our midst, and however I may dissent from his opinions on many vital questions yet I am pleased here to offer my tribute of respect for those qualities of head, heart and character that have raised him to his present well earned estate. And now for the report of the meeting:—

"On Thursday night, the 9th June, 1859, the meeting convened by Mr. Moore was held in the Gymnasium Hall, for the purpose of taking into consideration the propriety of forming a Rifle Corps for Huddersfield. Mr. Moore occupied the chair, and in introducing the subject said he had called them together, not at the request of a number of individuals in the shape of a requisition, but, having met a great number of individuals in his progress throughout the town (he should say scores), who had intimated a desire for such a meeting for the purpose of establishing a voluntary Rifle Corps, he thought he would not impose upon them the trouble of getting up a requisition, as it was a thing that was general throughout the country. He had not come to make a speech, but merely to introduce the business of the meeting, and for the purpose of hearing any observations which any gentleman might be disposed to make. Every individual had a right to say what he thought and to exercise his own opinion. To expect anything like unanimity in Huddersfield would be a hopeless affair. He did not anticipate it, and he could assure them that whatever might be the result of that meeting it would not break his heart. They were met there for a material purpose. Their object was simply for the defence of this great Empire. There was no party feeling associated with it; it was merely a question of the preservation of the integrity of the Empire. As for himself he had no fear of invasion at all. He believed that there was not the slightest ground for apprehension; but as things were uncertain in this life he thought the best way to secure peace was to be prepared for war. Hence he quite approved of the move that had taken place in the establishment of Rifle Corps. He did not see what harm it would do. He did not see that it would engender any improper feeling, if the thing were carried out in an orderly manner. So many circumstances were daily arising in the world that it was best to be prepared for the worst. It would give him great pleasure if it was the unanimous feeling of the inhabitants to establish a Rifle Corps without any interference with the harmony and goodwill of the neighbourhood. He was once a member of a Rifle Corps himself. He was the ninth man enrolled, and he believed he made a very smart soldier. He knew that it quickened him and did him no harm in a moral point of view; physically it did him a great deal of good, and he believed that would be the effect which it would have on the fine, spirited young men of this neighbourhood. He concluded by reading letters from the following gentlemen, apologising for absence and expressing their sympathy in the object for which the meeting was convened. Captain Nelson, native of Huddersfield, but then in camp in the South, who offered his assistance in the formation of a Rifle corps, and expressed his conviction that Huddersfield ought to be able to give 500 men to such a corps; George Armitage, Esquire, J.P., J. Brook, Stamp Distributor, Mr. Dunderdale, Steward to Mr. Beaumont at Whitley Hall and Chas. Brook, junr., Esquire, Meltham Mills. Mr. Bentley Shaw was then called upon to move a resolution. He said that it was not his intention to speak when he entered the room but when called upon he certainly could not refuse to do what he firmly believed to be his duty. He was certainly surprised on his return from a somewhat lengthened excursion in the South, to find that Huddersfield had done nothing in the way of forming a Rifle Corps. He was not an alarmist, he was not expecting an invasion, at the same time he should be very sorry to lie down in a sort of false security. He thought the aspect of affairs abroad at present was so very serious that it behoved England to look about and take care of herself. They did not know what might happen in the course of a short time. He would not pretend to trouble them with any prophetic announcement of his own views of what might happen, because the most farseeing were sometimes mistaken. However he did sympathise most sincerely with the spirit that had been manifested throughout the length and breadth of the land, for the purpose of forming defensive corps in the shape of Volunteer Rifles. He believed that the corps would be very efficient in case of an invasion. He hoped that these corps might never be required, but at the same time, as the Chairman had very pertinently observed, the best way to keep peace was to be prepared for war. He did not want it to be thought that he was sympathising with war. He had a great dread of war, but at the same time there was no telling what position England might be forced into by circumstances and therefore it was their duty, in connection with other towns of the kingdom, to establish a corps that would be a credit to themselves. He concluded by moving 'That in the present state of the Continent it is desirable that this country be fully prepared for any emergency, and therefore this meeting is of opinion that a Volunteer Rifle Corps for Huddersfield District be immediately formed.' MR. T. MALLINSON seconded the resolution. He admired the spirit which had prompted the young gentlemen of other towns to come forward to form themselves into Volunteer Rifle Corps. He must say he had no idea of becoming a soldier himself or anything that looked like it, at the same time he was glad to see so large a meeting assembled there that evening, he believed for the purpose of forming themselves into a Rifle Corps for the purpose of defending our Queen and country and their own homes and firesides. He was sure he would admire the man who had come there for that purpose. He was too old himself to become a soldier, but he would do everything he could to encourage the young men of the neighbourhood to join, and he was sure a corps so formed would be found as efficient as those in any other part of the country. THE CHAIRMAN observed that from placards posted throughout the town some persons seemed to be afraid to trust the people with arms, and yet, strangely enough, these were the very persons who had the strongest possible confidence in the extension of the franchise. They had no confidence in the patriotism of the people. MR. JOSEPH WOODHEAD then moved an amendment, in doing which he disclaimed all factious motives. The question before them was not a party question. Both the mover and the seconder of the resolution had stated that the way to insure peace was to be always prepared for war. He thought that statement was to be taken with qualifications. Did they mean that they were always to be prepared to plunge into war at a moment's notice? Was that the way to secure peace? He believed it was the continual preparations for war by France and Austria which had resulted in the present struggle. Did they not see that such a state of things fostered a war spirit? They had gathered together large bodies of troops, and those who, in the first instance, had the direction of them often became their slaves and were compelled to act at the behest of the army, whose love of violence they were unable to restrain. Unless they did what they could to keep down this war spirit, the more fear was there of those outbreaks which unhappily they now saw in Europe. The chairman had said he did not fear invasion, the mover and seconder of the resolution had said there was no danger of an invasion. Why, then, in the name of common sense were they there that night?* If they were as secure now as they had been at previous periods of our history why were they assembled? They were told, to form a Rifle Corps for the defence of the country. To defend the country! Why, did not their own admission contradict the statement? Did they not admit that there was no fear of invasion, and therefore, no necessity for special defence? He believed that the notion for the formation of Rifle Corps had been instigated by

---

*The chairman might have retorted on Mr. Woodhead that he did not expect his house to be burned down, but nevertheless, he had insured against that contingency.—R. P. B.

men (he meant originally, he did not charge the promoters of that meeting) with a view to draw the attention of the people of this country from questions of domestic legislation. (Cries of 'No, No,' 'Yes, Yes,' loud cheers and disapprobation.) The Queen in her speech declared neutrality in the present war. The Ministers in their speeches made the same declaration, the people of this country in public meetings assembled, had declared for neutrality, and, by the way, he wondered why, in Huddersfield, there had been no meeting in favour of neutrality. He was glad they all agreed on the impolicy, and he might say, wickedness, of any interference in the struggle now going on between the despots of the Continent. Well, he was saying that the whole nation had agreed for neutrality; and the promoters of the meeting had also declared that there was no need for extra defence and no fear of invasion, and now he wanted to carry this to its logical conclusion, namely, to rest quietly as they had done before, not, however, without a powerful force behind them in the army and navy of the country. If there should be anyone on the Continent insane enough to dream of invading us they had their regular standing army. They knew the vast expense the maintenance of our troops cost the country; and if they were not in an efficient state why was it they paid so much money? There was a reason. If they were not in an efficient state there was a method by which they might be made so, that Government should be made more amenable to the people of this country, that the maladministration of the army and navy should be brought to an end and a system of examination established by which the highest posts should be given to the best men, and by which the private in the ranks might elevate himself to be a General in the field if he had the ability to do so. Mr. Woodhead proceeded to point out the difficulties which an invading army would have to encounter both in landing and in making progress should they succeed. Of whom were they afraid? France? She had enough to do at present. Austria? Where were her ships to bring over her troops? Italy? She was trying to work out her own freedom. Russia? No! they would tell him they were afraid of none of these. Then what were they afraid of? The phantoms which they had conjured up in their own minds. Nothing could be more detrimental to the interests, the peace and prosperity of this country than the fostering of a warlike spirit, and this would be sure to be the consequence of the formation of rifle corps and therefore he opposed the movement. If he had seen a disposition throughout the country to make a national movement he could certainly have regarded it with more favour, although he should still have supposed it ill-timed, and he could have supposed there was no sinister object in view: but, as he had said before, while he acquitted the promoters of that meeting of any sinister object, he did not acquit many of those who had raised the cry for rifle corps; and it was because he believed that it would divert their attention just now from questions of domestic legislation that he felt utterly opposed to their formation, and he should at all times, except in cases of extreme necessity. He therefore moved as an amendment 'That, in the opinion of this meeting, this country does not require the formation of Volunteer Rifle Corps for the purpose of self-defence; that in regard to the war on the Continent our true policy is one of strict neutrality, and that, under existing circumstances, our chief attention ought to be given to representative and administrative reform.' THE CHAIRMAN said that Mr. Woodhead had enquired who was to pay the expense of the Rifle Corps? He (the chairman) was of opinion that Government ought to do it, to provide all necessary clothing and accoutrements and ought also to pay Volunteers during the time they were on service in the corps. MR. JOSEPH BOOTHROYD seconded the amendment on the ground that there was no necessity for the formation of Rifle Corps. If there was a necessity, the necessity would be greater than these Rifle Corps, composed of gentlemen, would meet. They ought to be composed of the working classes, if they were really intended for purposes of defence. Animadverting on the proposed appointment of officers by Government Agents, he said, as a citizen of this country, he looked with jealousy on the increase of officialism throughout the land. They had more to fear from foes of that kind, within, than they had from any foreign foe who might be rash enough to invade our shores. It was because he wished to see the full development of mind and trade and the interests of commerce and the general interests of the country that he expressed, from the bottom of his heart, his strong repugnance for the formation of voluntary rifles. He complimented Mr. Moore on the straightforward course that he had taken in calling a public meeting on the question, observing that had the same course been pursued in other towns the result would have been very different throughout the country from what it had been. It had been said that the way to maintain peace was to prepare for war. Now, he held that the tendency would be the very opposite. To be everlastingly talking about invasion and foreign foes and urging the designs which other Governments had upon us excited dissension and increased the jealousy of other Governments towards us; for if we increased our naval and military power we produced a corresponding increase in our foes. Such had been the consequence on the Continent; and though we were separated somewhat from them did they think that it had not the same effect when the Government of this country added to its naval and military resources? Foreign nations would just look with as much jealousy upon our increased armaments as we did upon theirs; so that the formation of Rifle Corps would have the very opposite effect of preserving peace. MR. WRIGHT MELLOR supported the resolution. He could not agree with the course which had been taken by his friends, Mr. Boothroyd and Mr. Woodhead. He respected the motives which had actuated them; but differed from the views they had advanced. If it were true they were in such close proximity to such dangerous neighbours as Mr. Woodhead had shown the Continental armies to be, then it was quite time that they were looking after themselves. If it were true that the Emperor Napoleon, whatever his intentions, had an army that he could not control, and if it were true that armies in search of plunder and conquest would come to the fairest and richest field, it was not an improbable supposition that, in casting about for such a field, they would look across the English Channel and find there the richest and choicest inheritance on God's earth, where all that was valuable, glorious and good was concentrated. With reference to the complaint that the Rifle Corps was to be constituted of the middle and not the working classes, he maintained that the working classes did their share in the defence of England in the regular army. In a word, he wanted the middle class to do their share. Then, as to their accoutrements, he would not have a single shilling from Government towards payment of the expense; because the expense would ultimately be saddled upon the working classes in the shape of taxes, who already did their share of paying. He would have the middle classes do their share in this too, and furnish themselves with accoutrements at their own expense. He concluded by pointing out that if they had efficient middle class Voluntary Corps throughout the country they would be furnished with the best argument against a military force, and would, therefore, be in a position to press upon Government the propriety of cutting down the Estimates. He could rely upon the corps, though it should be composed exclusively of the middle class, and could trust them for doing right in this matter as in others in which they were concerned. THE CHAIRMAN then put the amendment and motion to the meeting successively, but declared that he was unable to decide. He asked another show of hands, but the same result followed. A third show of hands was taken, the audience keeping their seats, but Mr. Moore again declared that he could not positively say whether the motion or the amendment were carried. In answer to numerous calls from the meeting, which by this time was in an uproarious condition, the room was divided; but for the fourth time, he distinctly declared that he was unable to say how the vote had gone, and they would have to be counted out. He then spoke a word or two with one of the promoters of the resolution, after which he turned round and said to the meeting that if he were compelled conscientiously to give his decision he should say that the resolution was carried. This produced great uproar in the meeting and the proceedings became of the most disorderly character. A great deal of angry squabbling took place on the platform, which was crowded. The supporters of the amendment maintained that it had been carried and the opposite party maintained the same concerning the resolution in the most vociferous manner. Mr. Moore shouted 'It's a matter of no importance, the thing will be carried, whether it be carried here or not.' MR. BENTLEY SHAW said he did not expect when he came to the meeting to find Mr. Woodhead on the non-patriotic side. (Tremendous uproar, which continued for some time). He did not mean anything personally offensive. MR. WOODHEAD asked for the withdrawal of the assertion as an unfair and offensive one, whether intended as such or not. MR. SHAW then expressed his readiness to retract the remark which had been regarded as offensive in consequence of Mr. Woodhead's over-sensitiveness. The matter then dropped. A vote of thanks to the chairman was moved by Mr. Carter and seconded, when Mr. R. M. Sisk moved and several voices were heard to second the following amendment, 'That this meeting is of opinion that the fractious, partial and ungentlemanly conduct of Mr. Moore, as chairman of this meeting, is highly censurable.' This was ultimately carried, the original motion not being submitted to the meeting. Several parties then attempted to speak, but could not proceed; and, as the confusion waxed more complete and the uproar more violent, Mr. Moore abruptly closed the meeting by shouting 'The meeting is now dissolved.' The people then dispersed in the greatest disorder."

The Constable appears to have been a man of prescient mind, for it will be observed that he predicted the scheme, "will be carried, whether it is carried here or not." It seems that those who deemed the movement a wise and patriotic one were not to be daunted by an adverse vote of a Town's Meeting, especially as suspicion was not absent that the meeting had been packed by political partizans. They did not allow the grass to grow under their feet, for, on the 22nd June, 1859, a meeting was held at Mr. Battye's office. There were present at the meeting, Messieurs Joseph Taylor Armitage, J.P., John Brooke, Jun., Thomas Brooke,

June 22nd, 1859. Meeting at Mr. Battye's Office.

Frederick Greenwood, Edgar Fenton and Bentley Shaw, J.P. To these names should doubtless be added that of Mr. T. H. Battye, and these gentlemen are clearly entitled to the honourable distinction of being the

FOUNDERS OF THE HUDDERSFIELD
VOLUNTEER CORPS.

Of these only survive Mr., now Lieutenant-Colonel, Greenwood and Mr. Thomas, now Lieutenant-Colonel Sir Thomas, Brooke, to the latter of whom I have been privileged to dedicate this work.

The meeting adopted the following resolutions:—

"That Bentley Shaw, Esq., J.P., be Chairman of this meeting.

"That it is desirable that a Rifle Club be formed to be called "The Huddersfield Rifle Club."

"That the following gentlemen be a committee to carry out the above resolution, viz:—Bentley Shaw, Esq., the Chairman, J. T. Armitage, Esq, Messrs. John Brooke, Thomas Brooke, F. Greenwood, E. Fenton and James Bradbury, with power to add to their number.

"That Messrs. John Brooke, junr., Thomas Brooke, Frederick Greenwood and Edgar Fenton be a deputation to wait upon others who may be willing to join the club.

"That Bentley Shaw, Esq. and Mr. Thomas Brooke be a deputation to wait upon Joseph Armitage, Esq., the Senior Deputy-Lieutenant, in order to the club obtaining proper legal authority to practise.

"That Mr. Battye be Honorary Secretary.

"That each member pay £1 1s. 0d. per annum subscription, to be paid in advance, and that each member find his own arms and uniform, which are expected to cost not more than £10, and his own ammunition."

Mr. Joseph Armitage lost no time in writing to the Lord Lieutenant of the county enquiring as to the steps to be taken to establish a club, and I have before me Earl Fitzwilliam's reply, dated July 4th, 1859, and written from the Royal Hotel, Deal:—

"Sir.—I have deferred answering your letter in consequence of being led to suppose that the present Government would make some alteration in the rules to be laid down for the control and regulation of Volunteer Rifle Corps.* I have not, as yet, received any official information on the subject from the Secretary for War but, as I made a personal request to him for information, I hope very shortly to be put into possession of complete instructions in regard to Rifle

---

* The Lord Lieutenant's answer refers to corps. It will be observed that the resolution was to form a *Rifle Club*. Earl Fitzwilliam's reply used the word "corps," and if there was, in the minds of the promoters, any distinction between a club and a corps, it is possible the Lord Lieutenant's answer led to an abandonment of the notion of a club and the adoption of the project of a corps.—R. P. B.

Corps. You will probably have seen his answers in the House of Commons to questions put to him on this subject. In the meantime I would suggest the enrolment of all suitable persons anxious to serve, from whom the most eligible should be selected for officers.

I have the honour to be,

Your faithful servant,

FITZWILLIAM.

J. Armitage, Esquire. Birkby Lodge, Huddersfield."

Before the above answer was received the Provisional Committee had convened a meeting by circular for the 5th July, 1859, in the Riding School, Ramsden Street. I have before me Mr. Battye's list of persons or firms to whom the circular was sent. These were not residents of Huddersfield alone, but of the villages around. It is with many a heart-pang I have read that list of those who, half a century ago, were deemed the leading people of this district, for alas! of that long roll most have gone to their long rest, though happily the names of many of these are preserved in descendants now living, honoured, prosperous and useful citizens in our midst. At the meeting so summoned Mr. Joseph Armitage, as senior deputy-lieutenant, presided, and the following resolutions were adopted :— 1859. Inaugural Meeting in Riding School.

1—"That all persons present who are willing to become members of or support the formation of a legally constituted Rifle Corps are invited at once to come forward and give in their names to the Secretary in two lists :— Resolutions thereat.

1st—Of those willing to enrol themselves.

2nd—Of those willing to support by subscription.

2—"That the following gentlemen, with power to add to their number, be a committee to manage the affairs of the corps until officers are elected and its legal organization is completed, and to obtain subscriptions, any three, exclusive of the Secretary and Treasurer, being a quorum, and the committee having power to form any sub-committees and deputations, namely :—Henry F. Beaumont, Esq., Messrs. Edgar Fenton, John Haigh, junr., J. A. Harrison, T. A. Bottomley, Henry Brooke, Matthew Fairlamb and Benjamin Brigg.

3—"That H. F. Beaumont, Esq., be Chairman and Bentley Shaw, Esq., Vice-Chairman of the Committee, and that Mr. J. C. Laycock be Treasurer and Mr. T. H. Battye be Honorary Secretary during the provisional formation of the corps.

4—That the accounts of the corps, shewing in detail the expenditure, especially of monies subscribed, be communicated to each subscriber."

Measures were then taken, by personal communications, to obtain the adhesion of Volunteers, the terms of enrolment being that the Volunteers were "to have the nomination of their own officers and of the times and place for the drill and practice." I have seen the original sheets, with the signatures of those subscribing to the terms of enrolment, and, as many of the names will be familiar, I give them below :—

HUDDERSFIELD RIFLE CORPS.

LIST NO. 1.

First Roll. We, the undersigned, hereby agree to enrol ourselves as members of this corps, on the understanding and condition that we have the nomination of our own officers, and of the times and places for drill and practice :—

Henry F. Beaumont,
Edgar Fenton,
John Haigh, junior,
J. A. Harrison,
Thos. A. Bottomley,
Henry Brooke,
Matthew Fairlamb,
Benjamin Brigg,
Henry B. Dyson,
Alex. Hannah,
Fred Liebreich,
R. H. Butterworth,
William Brook,
Thos. Brooke, junior,
R. Lowenthal,
Edward W. Tarn,
W. H. Charlesworth, 12, East Parade,
John Freeman, junior,
W. H. Prince,
William Abbey,
John Bottomley,
Fred Geo. Mallinson,
M. H. Bradley,
Andrew Thos. Anderson,
Henry Barker,
George Oastler Crowther,
Henry Kilner,
J. E. Eastwood,
Fred Walker (South Parade),
J. W. Brook,
James Prince,
Fred Bradley,
William Hoyle,
Frank G. Abbey,
J. B. Abbey,
Geo. Calvert,
Joseph Batley, junior,
Richard Henry Robinson,
Thos. Robinson,
David Boscovitz,
J. T. Beaumont,
Edward Golden,
Alexr. Brook,
Wm. Heslop,
Jos. Bottomley, junior,
Hector M. Beaumont,
John E. Beaumont,
W. Taylor,
Richard Sissons,
Edward Beaumont,
Frederick Greenwood,
William Hick,
Joseph Brook, Buxton Road,
Arthur Heron,
J. K. Lawton,
P. B. Mullion,
Thos. R. Webb,
Josephus Sykes,
C. J. Graham,
Frederick Ramsden,
Thomas Haigh,
Thomas Haigh Bradbury,
Thomas Hirst,
Sam Learoyd,
James Brook,
Thomas Beardsell,
Richard Bance,
Henry Anders,
Albert Hall,
Ben Lockwood.

Negociations for Exercise Ground &c. Before the gentlemen who had given in their names as Volunteers could be officially accepted as a Volunteer corps many preliminary details required to be adjusted. A Drill Hall must be procured, an Exercise Ground obtained and inspected and approved by the War Office and a decision arrived at upon the important matter of Uniform which, though not truly at this time necessary to be submitted to the authorities at Whitehall, yet called for anxious deliberation and debate among the officers or aspirants for the epaulette themselves. A gentleman may be quite willing to die for his country but he would like to die in a becoming dress. This was before the days of kahki. The foe whom the Volunteers expected to engage was a Frenchman, the mirror of fashion, not a ragged unkempt Boer. On all these questions the secretary, at first temporary, afterwards duly appointed, Mr. J. H. Battye, had much lengthy correspondence. Fragments of this only remain and leave the conscientious chronicler much to conjecture as to the proceedings of the committee. It was apparently hoped to secure the Riding School, better known to us as the Armoury. But though the free use of the Riding School was proffered by Mr. J. T. Armitage, its owner, till August 1st, he was unable to enter into a lengthier engagement. The solution of the question was, for a time, found in the following letter from Sir John William Ramsden, Baronet :—

"London,
August 6th, 1859.

Dear Sir,

I have to acknowledge your letter of July 28th requesting my permission for the use of one of the yards of the Cloth Hall as a place of drill for the Huddersfield Rifle Corps. I shall have much pleasure in complying with your request, subject to certain conditions and regulations which Mr. Hathorne has probably already made known to you.

I am, dear Sir,
Your faithful servant,
J. W. RAMSDEN."

T. H. Battye, Esq.,
Huddersfield.

There was difficulty, and, naturally, no slight difficulty, in procuring a suitable field for exercise and practice. Messrs. E. T. Monk & Co., silk spinners, Lower Aspley Mills, were approached. That firm raised an obvious and apparently insuperable obstacle: "We shall have great pleasure in allowing the Rifle Corps the use of our field, but as we have a great number of workpeople to whom rifle shooting would be a novelty and for some time would give us some trouble to keep them at work during practice time, &c." Messrs. Monk, it may be stated to their honour, were prepared to grant the *free* use of the field, if suggested difficulties could be removed. Apparently the negotiations with that firm fell through, and a field was sought from Messrs. Smith, wood grinders, Aspley.

Ultimately, however, the committee's choice fell upon what was then known as the cricket field in Trinity Street, now the recreation ground adjoining or part of the Greenhead Park. It is, I imagine, to this field that the following letter has reference:—

"Preston, October 9th, 1859.

Sir,

I have the honour to report for the information of the Right Honourable the Secretary for War that in compliance with War Office Letter, $\frac{1907}{\text{Inst. Volrs.}}$ I visited the range selected by the Volunteer Rifle Corps* at Huddersfield in company with Mr. T. H. Battye and found the same unsafe and too near the town. It might, however, be rendered practicable by the erection of butts to protect the public on the right. I have, therefore, advised to that effect, and in the meantime, until the decision of the corps be made known as regards the expense, to look for a more suitable situation.

I have the honour to be, Sir,

Your obedient servant,

(Signed) L. FRANKLIN,

Lieutenant 45th Regiment."

The Under Secretary of State for War.

The field was adapted to the necessities of the corps at an outlay of £309 13s. 2d. It was used at first for both shooting practice and drill, afterwards for shooting only, the drill exercises being conducted in a field in Greenhead Lane, between the Huddersfield Vicarage and Springwood Hall. In 1863 the corps acquired the long range at Ashenhurst, above Longley Hall Park.

Selection of Arm Magazine.

The failure of the negotiations for the use of the Riding School and the necessity of at once procuring an armoury compelled the committee to seek elsewhere for suitable buildings. The use of the County Police Station for the deposit of the arms was granted, but this could obviously not be a permanent arrangement. It should be remembered that the Government issued at first only 25 per cent. of the rifles needed for the companies first raised, other members either learning the use of the rifle when one chanced to be disengaged or providing their own. This latter was largely done, and those who so armed themselves kept their rifles in their own custody, consequently no great accommodation was necessary for arm storage. About the middle of 1860 premises suitable for the purpose were secured in Upperhead Row and adapted as an armoury, orderly room and small offices for the permanent staff. The building was that situate behind the Crown Hotel, facing Oxley's old livery stables.

---

*The gallant officer should have said the proposed or embryo corps.—R. P. B.

Still the question of Drill Hall remained unsettled. The various companies as they were formed had to procure drill-rooms as best they could. The first secured in addition to the Cloth Hall Yard appear to have been St. Paul's School Rooms. There is a letter from the Vicar, the Rev. J. Haigh:— **Selection of Drill Hall**

"My Dear Sir,

I give my consent to the Huddersfield Rifle Corps to drill in St. Paul's Boys' School during the evenings of the ensuing winter, with the understanding that any additional expenses which may be incurred thereby be defrayed by the Rifle Corps. With every wish that the corps may fully serve the purpose of its institution,

I am, my dear Sir,

Yours faithfully,

J. HAIGH.

Thomas Battye, Esquire, Secretary."

This Vicar of St. Paul's was of the same family as Lieutenant-Colonel Joseph Haigh of the Huddersfield Fusiliers of 1794.

Crosland's warehouse in St. George's Square and Senior's school room in Spring Street were also used as temporary drill halls in the winter months of 1859. On November 5th, 1860, there being then 4 companies, a Regimental Order directs all the companies to assemble for drill at the "Rose and Crown," in Kirkgate. In the year 1863 the Riding School in Ramsden Street, later called the Armoury, was obtained, and continued to be used as drill hall and permanent head quarters till, in 1901, the present handsome structure in St. Paul's Street was erected.

The members of the earlier companies used to assemble for drill in the Cloth Hall inclosure from seven to eight o'clock every morning, and long before that hour a bugler paraded Edgerton, New North Road, Newhouse and other select quarters of the town, sounding the *reveillé*.

On December 1st, 1860, Major H. F. Beaumont, on behalf of his wife, presented the corps with a silver bugle, inscribed: "Presented by Mrs. Beaumont to the 6th West Riding of Yorkshire Volunteers." **Presentation of Bugle.**

The corps was, on that occasion, at Woodsome Hall, under the command of Major Beaumont.

The question of uniform and other matters were not probably disposed of until after the official acceptance of the offer of service, which was not till November 3rd, 1859, some delay having doubtless been caused by the difficulty experienced in finding a suitable range for rifle practice. The communication of the acceptance by the Crown of the proffered services was intimated to the Lord Lieutenant in the following letter :—

"War Office, 3rd November, 1859.

Acceptance of the first Company, Nov. 3rd, 1859.

V / Yorkshire. / 84.

My Lord,

With reference to your Lordship's letter of the 24th of September, offering for the Queen's acceptance the service of a company of Rifle Volunteers at Huddersfield, under the Act 44, Geo. III., c. 54, I have the honour to inform you that Her Majesty has been graciously pleased to approve and accept the same.

The company is numbered as the 10th in the West-Riding of Yorkshire and its maximum establishment will consist of one captain, one lieutenant, one ensign, 100 men of all ranks.

I have the honour to be, my Lord,
Your Lordship's obedient servant,
S. HERBERT.

The Earl Fitzwilliam."

Some doubt appears to have existed in the mind of Mr. Battye, and probably still more doubt in the minds of the members of his committee, as to the establishment to be allowed, though the letter of November 3rd appears to be explicit enough. There is a letter from the War Office of December 3rd relating to this point. It is addressed to Messrs. E. T. Monk & Co., but for what reason is not obvious:—

"War Office,
December, 1859.

Correspondence as to the Establishment.

Gentlemen,

I am directed by Mr. Secretary Herbert to acknowledge the receipt of your letter of the 24th ultimo, and to inform you that the Regulations of the service admit of the appointment of a Captain-Lieutenant and Ensign to a company of Rifle Volunteers and of a Captain, 1st Lieutenant and 2nd Lieutenant to a company of Artillery* Volunteers.

I am to add that Mr. Herbert will be prepared to recommend the appointment of an Honorary-Surgeon to any company of Rifle Volunteers upon the recommendation of the Lord Lieutenant of the county, but the appointment can under no possible contingency carry pay, and if the company should hereafter become part of a battalion, the officer holding the appointment would have no claim to the surgeoncy of the battalion and his duties would cease.

Such an officer would rank as junior to Assistant Surgeons in the Army and Militia.

I am, Gentlemen,
Your obedient servant,
DE GREY AND RIPON.

Messrs. E. T. Monk and Company."

---

*It was proposed by some to form an Artillery Company, but this was soon abandoned.

The following is the first list of honorary members:—

Joseph Armitage, J.P., D.L.,	Thomas Pearson Crosland,
Thomas Allen,	Bentley Shaw,
J. C. Laycock,	Chas. Brook. Junior,
Joseph Brook,	James Bradbury,
Robert Cameron, M.D.	Edward Brook, Esquires.

The Crown having accepted the offer through the Lord Lieutenant of the first company and the range been duly inspected and approved, the corps was duly constituted, and the following is the muster roll on its first formation:—

First Muster Roll of first Company.

Officers.	Non-Commissioned Officers.
Captain Henry Frederick Beaumont, Esquire, of Whitley Hall,	Sergeant Alexander Hannah,
Lieutenant Joseph Batley, Junior, Solicitor,	" Wm. Brook, of Wells Mills,
Ensign Joseph Acheson Harrison, Merchant,	" Henry Brook, Ironfounder,
Hon. Surgeon Thos. A. Bottomley.	" Frederick Greenwood, Surgeon,
	Corporal David Boscovitz,
	" H. B. Dyson, Wool Stapler.
	" Joseph Bottomley, Junior, Solicitor,
	" Joseph Tyrrel Beaumont, Greenhead Hall.

The above officers were nominated for the approval of the Lord Lieutenant by the members of the corps at a meeting held September 5th, 1859, at the George Hotel.

Privates.

1—Abbey Frank Goodwin, Surveyor, New Street,*
2—Abbey Joe Burman, Surveyor, New Street,
3—Abbey William, Book-keeper at Mr. Dyson's, Grocer, New Street,
4—Anders Henry, at Messrs. Lowenthal's, King Street,
5—Anderson Andrew Thomas, Canal Office, Aspley,
6—Barker Henry, Solicitor, Market Place,
7—Beaumont Hector M., Cloth Merchant, Railway Street,
8—Beaumont John Edward, Cloth Hall Street and Green Side,
9—Bottomley John, Rose and Crown Yard,
10—Beardsall Thomas, Hagg House, Thongsbridge,
11—Bradley Frederick, Clerk at Messrs. Laycock and Dyson's, Arcade,
12—Bradley Matthew H., Imperial Hotel, New Street,
13—Bradbury Thomas Haigh, Colne Bridge,
14—Brigg Benjamin, Merchant, West Parade,
15—Brook Alexander, Stamp Office, Market Place,
16—Brook Thomas, Colne Villas,
17—Brook J. W., Hillhouse,
18—Brook Joseph, at Mr. Brook's, Registrar, Buxton Road,
19—Brook James, Buxton Road,
20—Brook John, Painter, Spring Street,

* The addresses have been added by me as obtained from various papers connected with the corps.

21—Butterworth Robert H., Market Place.
22—Calvert George, Painter, High Street,
23—Charlesworth W. H., 13, East Parade,
24—Crowther George Oastler, County Court,
25—Eastwood James Edwin, Wool Merchant, Brook's Yard,
26—Eddell James Skelton, Hosier, New Street,
27—Fairlamb Matthew, at Messrs. Stott's, Northumberland Street,
28—Fenton Edgar, Solicitor, New Street,
29—Freeman John, junr., at Messrs. Brook, Freeman and Batley, Solicitors, New Street,
30—Golden Edward, Gunsmith, Cross Church Street,
31—Graham C. J., at Mr. Bentley Shaw's,
32—Haigh John, junr., Merchant, George Street,
33—Haigh Thomas, Colne Bridge House,
34—Hall Alfred, at Henry Hirst, junr. and Co.'s, Beast Market,
35—Hattersley William, Builder, Swan Lane, Lockwood,
36—Heslop William, Silversmith, Market Place,
37—Heron Arthur, Clerk, Huddersfield Banking Company,
38—Herring John, at Henry Hirst junr. & Co's, Beast Market,
39—Hick William, Teazle Merchant, Swan Yard,
40—Hirst Thomas, Sheepridge,
41—Hutchinson Benjamin, Commercial Inn, New Street,
42—Kilner Henry, Canal Office, Spring Street,
43—Lawton J. K., Accountant, near Post Office,
44—Learoyd Samuel, at Messrs. Floyd and Learoyd's, Solicitors,
45—Liebriech Frederick, Wool Merchant, Nelson's Buildings,
46—Lister William, Salesman at Allan and Bowes, Northumberland Street,
47—Lockwood Ben, Merchant, West Parade and John William Street,
48—Lowenthal Robert, Wool Merchant, King Street,
49—Mallinson Frederick George, Newhouse and John William Street,
50—Mullion P. B., Accountant, near Post Office,
51—Prince James Turner, Bookkeeper at Messrs. Ogston and Mathison's Railway Street,
52—Prince William Henry, Clerk, Goods Department, L. and N.W. Railway Station,
53—Ramsden Frederick, Beast Market,
54—Robinson Richard Henry, Merchant, New North Road,
55—Sissons Richard, Surgeon, New North Road,
56—Taylor William, Merchant, John William Street,
57—Webb Thomas Rymer, Merchant, John William Street,

The privates appear to have, at first, paid an annual subscription of half a guinea each to the funds of the corps.

The first drill-sergeant and musketry-instructor was Horatio France. I find a letter from the War Office to Mr. Battye, of date December 8th, 1859, in which Mr. Secretary Herbert disclaims any intention to interfere with the appointment of musketry-instructors permanently engaged and paid by Rifle Volunteer Corps.

Sergeant France was a non-commissioned officer of the 34th Regiment of Foot, and proved himself a highly efficient drill-sergeant and instructor.

The motto adopted by the Huddersfield Volunteers was terse and expressive: "*Arma pacis fulcra.*" It was the same as that revived by warrant of the Privy Council in favour of the Honorable Artillery Company, when, in the year 1611, James I. granted that ancient corporation its armorial ensigns on which the motto was engraved. It figured on the breast-plate of the Huddersfield Rifle Corps and also on the first shako plate. Motto of the Corps.

The reader will have borne in mind that Volunteers, officers and privates alike, were furnished by the Government at this period with but a small proportion of the necessary arms, with no uniform, and with no funds for absolutely indispensable outlay. An appeal to the public to furnish what the Government was not then prepared to afford was inevitable; for willing as officers might be to provide their own outfit and to bear other expenses, they could scarcely be expected to undertake the whole maintenance of a corps. The appeal for help met with a generous response, as the following list will shew:—

DONATIONS AND ANNUAL SUBSCRIPTIONS.

	£	s.	d.		£	s.	d.
Earl of Dartmouth (annually) ..	10	10	0	Jere Riley	10	0	0
Sir J. W. Ramsden ..	50	0	0	Joseph Sykes	10	0	0
J. Brooke & Sons	50	0	0	E. G. Sykes (Moscow) ..	10	0	0
Jonas Brook Brothers ..	50	0	0	E. T. Monk (Aspley) ..	5	5	0
Starkey Brothers	50	0	0	T. Brook, Solicitor ..	5	0	0
Bentley Shaw	25	0	0	Thompson & Dodds ..	5	0	0
Tolson Brothers	25	0	0	Thomas Lockwood ..	5	0	0
James Bradbury	25	0	0	Henry Robinson	5	0	0
Joseph Hirst (Greaves) ..	40	0	0	Day & Watkinson ..	5	0	0
J. Taylor & Sons	21	0	0	E. L. Hesp	5	0	0
W. E. Hirst	21	0	0	William Sykes, junr. ..	5	0	0
C. Brook & Sons	20	0	0	James Nield Sykes ..	5	0	0
George Crosland	20	0	0	M. W. Cliffe	5	0	0
J. W. Crosland	20	0	0	J. Atkinson (Bedale) ..	5	0	0
J. T. Beaumont	15	0	0	C. Atkinson	5	0	0
T. P. Crosland	10	10	0	W. Roberts	4	4	0
Joseph Crosland	10	10	0	W. P. England	2	2	0
Charles Crosland	10	10	0	William Johnson.. ..	1	1	0
John Freeman	10	10	0	P. Thornton	1	1	0
James Hinchcliffe.. ..	10	10	0	J. Hirst	1	1	0
D. A. Cooper	10	10	0	B. Thomson	1	1	0
J. C. Laycock	10	10	0	J. Thornton	1	1	0
				William Robinson, Surgeon	1	0	0

DONATIONS AND ANNUAL SUBSCRIPTIONS.—*Continued.*

	£	s.	d.		£	s.	d.
Jere Kaye	10	10	0	A. Bairstow		10	6
Nicholas Carter	10	10	0	W. Veevers		10	6
Robert J. Bentley.. ..	10	10	0	T. Mills		10	0
Do. (annually)	1	1	0	A. Harrison		10	0
William Learoyd	10	10	0	E. Sykes		10	0
W. W. Greenwood ..	10	10	0	J. Cardno		10	0
Learoyd & Sons	10	10	0	A Friend		10	0
H. B. Taylor	10	10	0	W. Roberts		10	0
John Haigh, Sharebroker	10	10	0	J. Burman..		10	0
Joseph Wrigley	10	0	0	W. Dawson		10	0
Wright Mellor	10	0	0	J. Platts		10	0
Milner & Hale	10	0	0	C. Flockton		10	0
A Friend	10	0	0				
William Kaye & Sons ..	10	0	0				
Huth & Fischer	10	0	0	Total	£754	18	0

When at a later date further subscriptions became necessary, Mr. Thomas Pearson Crosland, by personal solicitation, procured the following list:—

	£	s.	d.		£	s.	d.
Brook Thos., Colne Villa ..	10	10	0	Frome Wm.	1	1	0
Brook Josh., Stamp Office (will equip two men of five Companies)* ..	5	0	0	Crosland James & Son, Paddock	10	10	0
				and annually ..	2	2	0
Moore Wm., Post Office ..	5	0	0	Ramsden J. E., Ramsden Mill	5	5	0
Greenwood Wm., Surgeon	10	10	0	Mellor Godfrey	1	1	0
Jones & Hird, Solicitors ..	10	10	0	Robinson Thos., Solicitor* (and equip one man) ..	2	2	0
Crosland H. & W. & Co. ..	5	5	0				
Clarke Dr. J. W., Surgeon	3	3	0	Marsden David, General Manager, Huddersfield Bank	10	10	0
Berry John Graham, General Manager, West Riding Union Bank ..	3	3	0	Rhodes John T., Finisher, Folly Hall	10	10	0
Harper George, Chronicle Office	2	2	0	Crosland Tyne, Paddock ..	5	5	0
Tolson J. S.	2	2	0	Kilner Wm., Market St. ..	5	5	0
Brooke Mrs. Thos., Honley	10	10	0	Huddersfield Banking Co.	50	0	0
Beaumont A., Honley ..	10	10	0	Dyson George, Solicitor ..	5	5	0
Booth James & John ..	3	0	0	Oakes Samuel, Kirkgate ..	5	5	0
Mallinson Thomas, J.P. ..	10	10	0	Turner Joseph & Sons ..	10	10	0
Rhodes & Sons, Wine Merchants	3	3	0	Brooke Ed., Fieldhouse ..	10	10	0
				Lees Josh., Railway Station	1	1	0
Crossley J. E., Wool Merchant	1	1	0	Burgess John, Seed Hill ..	5	5	0

* Mr. Joseph Brook's offer to equip 10 men was equal to a subscription of £50 in addition to his subscription of £5 0 0 and £1 1 0; so also Mr. Thomas Robinson's offer to equip one man was equivalent to a subscription of £5 in addition to his subscription of £2 2 0.

SUBSCRIPTIONS—*Continued.*

	£	s.	d.
Brook & Crosland.. ..	10	10	0
Haigh Thos. & Sons, Colne Bridge	20	0	0
Kenyon J. & T., Dogley Lane	5	0	0
Ogden John	5	0	0
Bradshaw J., Surgeon ..	5	5	0
Hoerle F. A.	5	5	0
Liddell Jno., Market Place	1	0	0
Hird Robert	1	0	0
Robinson Mr., Tailor, Queen Street	1	0	0
Taylor J., Esq., Fenay Hall	25	0	0
Spivey Chas., Druggist ..	1	1	0
Hey Geo., Kirkburton ..	5	5	0
Jowett D.	1	1	0
Ogston & Matheson ..	5	5	0
Fox Jos., Daisey Lea ..	2	2	0
Brierley F., Corn Factor (annual)	0	10	6
A friend from the West ..	0	5	0
Mallinson H., Lindley ..	1	1	0
Crowther J., (of Timothy Crowther & Sons) ..	1	1	0
Edwards & Roberts, Northumberland Street ..	2	2	0
Thornton C. H.	1	1	0
Brook Josh., Stamp Office (further subscription) ..	1	1	0
Barber & Sons, Josh. ..	1	1	0
Sykes Dan	1	1	0
Hall Geo., Druggist ..	2	2	0
Sykes John, Railway St.	2	2	0
Liebriech Emil, New St.	2	2	0
Crosland Geo. & Sons ..	30	0	0
Thornton Cresswell & Co.	3	3	0
Vickerman Joseph, (annual)	1	1	0
Mellor Jos., Thongsbridge	1	1	0
Sykes Ephraim	1	1	0
Iredale Thos, Linthwaite	1	1	0
Shaw Hy., Marsden ..	2	2	0
Oldroyd G.	1	1	0
Oxley Joseph	1	1	0
Wrigley J. & T. C. ..	1	1	0
Robinson Henry, Dudmanstone..	1	1	0
Mallinson T., extra ..	2	2	0
Saville Geo.	1	1	0
Heslop Richard, Jeweller	1	1	0
Battye Sydney F... ..	1	1	0
Etherington W. F. ..	1	1	0
Pratt William, Printer ..	1	1	0
Bradley Saml., Imperial Hotel	1	1	0
Harper Geo., extra ..	1	1	0
Sykes John	1	1	0
Stocks James	1	1	0
Nelson G. N.	1	1	0
Lockwood Jas.	1	1	0
Crowe John	1	1	0
Beaumont Hy. Kilner ..	1	1	0
Total ..	£305	17	6

The first Uniform.

The uniform of the first company of the Huddersfield Volunteers was adopted at that meeting at the George Hotel, on September 5th, 1859, at which, as I have said, the corps nominated its first officers for the approval of the Lord Lieutenant. The task of selecting an appropriate uniform had been entrusted to a committee, and much correspondence passed between the hard-worked secretary, Mr. Battye, and the Lord Lieutenant, and between Mr. Battye and various contractors on the subject. There is a letter of 18th August, 1859, written by the Earl Fitzwilliam to Mr. Battye. It is addressed from Wentworth Woodhouse, the stately home of the Fitzwilliam family: "With reference to uniform I beg to refer you to Major Briggs, commanding the York Rifle Corps, as it is desirable that all rifle corps uniforms should assimilate as much as possible and I have already given my sanction for a uniform for the corps under his command. Any button or facing I shall be happy to leave to the discretion of the different corps." Whether or not the selection committee accepted this suggestion is of little moment now, as the uniform of the York Rifle Corps, which consisted of a light grey cloth, with buff accoutrements, and cap with horizontal beak, was not accepted by the committee.

It may interest the reader to know that on the question of uniform being discussed the late Mr. James Campey Laycock, treasurer of the corps, brought to the meeting of the committee the Volunteer uniform he had worn about 40 years earlier as a member of the Armed Association of 1820. It consisted, as I have said, of a tight fitting jacket of bottle green colour and turned up with black, with green worsted epaulettes, a crimson sash being worn round the waist. The head-dress was a high stove pipe hat with a thick wooden protection in the crown. Mr. Laycock was not able to produce the breeches, and as he had outgrown the rest of the habiliments, Mr. John Freeman, Junior, afterwards an officer in the corps, now Vicar of Woodkirk, Dewsbury, offered to assume them and pose as a lay figure for the inspection of the committee. When the change of costume was effected Mr. Freeman, the upper man thus martially arrayed, stood before the wondering group in his own black and white check trousers.

The production of Mr. Laycock's former uniform, however interesting it may have been, was not likely to further the deliberations of the uniform selection committee, who, having communicated with the commanding officers of the towns in the vicinity of Huddersfield, discovered that they were about to adopt or had already adopted the general design of the uniform of that corps of Victoria Rifles of which mention has already been made. This, therefore, was adopted also by the committee of the Huddersfield Corps; the only difference between this corps and those of the neighbouring corps being in the facings, some minor details, and possibly in the shade of the dark grey cloth. The uniform of the "Victorias" was a black tunic trimmed with black mohair braid in front, with a large epaulette on each shoulder, and a shako with plumes (worn only on parade), a forage cap being the covering ordinarily worn at drill, black trousers and patent leather accoutrements with ornaments. The members of the "Victorias" being, by birth and position, *armigeri*, and as such entitled to wear a sword when they paraded without rifles and bayonet, were provided with that side arm, although it was not a requisite. The Enfield Rifle, too, of this corps, was better finished than the common regulation arm. A considerable number of gentlemen joined the "Victorias" who were candidates for commissions in the army and militia, and thus laudably took advautage of an admirable opportunity for qualifying themselves for their future regimental duties by acquiring a thorough knowledge of their drill in company with others occupying the same social position.* The first uniform, then, for there were several, of the Huddersfield Rifle Corps of this period was that of the Victoria Rifles with the single, though significant, exception that instead of two epaulettes the coat had merely a strap on the‡ right shoulder only. These epaulettes, military marks of distinction, were formerly worn on the shoulder of commissioned and warrant officers. Those for the sergeants and rank and file were formerly of the colour of the facings with a narrow yellow or white tape round it and worsted fringe; those for officers were made of gold or silver lace, with rich fringe and bullion worn on one or both shoulders. When a sergeant or corporal was publicly reduced it was formerly customary for the drum-major to cut off the shoulder knot in front of the battalion.†

The uniform having been selected there was yet the question of its cost to be considered, a matter of no mean importance when we remember that the uniform and equipment had to be wholly provided by the corps. I find that the cost of the "Victoria" uniform for a private was:— Cost.

	£	s.	d.
Tunic and Trousers	4	10	0
Forage Cap	0	14	0
Shako and Plume	2	2	0
Cross Belt, with Cartouche Box	2	5	0
	£9	11	0

To this had to be added the cost of the well finished Enfield Rifles used by that corps, with sword bayonet and scabbard complete, and also the sword which they were entitled to carry, which together amounted to £9, thus bringing the total cost of the uniform for a private in this superior corps to the respectable sum of £18 11 0. The committee, no doubt aware of this cost, succeeded in obtaining a very different estimate and one much more moderate for the

* This is on the authority of Captain Hans Busk, first lieutenant, Victoria Rifles, who relates these facts in his little book on "Rifle Volunteers," published 1859.

† James's *Military Dictionary*.

‡ Obviously this should be "left" shoulder.—R.P.B.

following uniform and accoutrements, the corps to provide the cloth, 38 yards of 54 inches in width, for each suit. I have before me the estimate and below give a full copy of it:—

"September 7th, 1859.

ESTIMATE FOR HUDDERSFIELD VOLUNTEER RIFLES.

	£	s.	d.
A Grey Cloth Tunic, made up and nicely trimmed with black cord and scarlet facings			
A Pair of Trousers, trimmed with black braid ..			
A Grey Cloth Quilted Shako, with bugle and green plume			
An Oiled Silk Cover for same	4	10	0
Accoutrements.			
A Black Patent Leather Shoulder Belt, with bronzed ornament			
A Black Pouch ornamented with Bugle &c.			
A Black Waist Belt and Frog and Expense Pouch ..			
A Forage Cap and Cover if required	0	7	6
Total	£4	17	6

This estimate, it will be observed, provided for scarlet facings, which were not adopted. I find by reference to a return made out by the honorary secretary that the prices above quoted must have been somewhat modified, as follows:—

ARTICLE.	MATERIAL.	COLOUR.	PATTERN.	COST.
Coat	Woollen Cloth	Grey	Tunic	3 15 6
Trousers ..	Do	Do	Military Pantaloons	
Cap	Do.	Black....	An Officer's Undress Cap	
Shako	Felt Cloth....	Do.	The same as used in the Line	
Gloves	....	White ...	....	

To this was added the following remarks:—

	£	s.	d.
The Tunic, Trousers, Patent Leather Accoutrements and Forage Cap, with bronze ornaments, have been furnished under contract at the sum of ..	3	15	6
The Cloth costs, per man..	1	5	0
The Shako	0	16	0
Knee Cap	0	1	2
Gloves		2	4
	£6	0	0
The Rifle and Appendages as furnished by contract*	4	10	0
Total	£10	10	0

*This estimate was from Hibbert & Co. of 8, Pall Mall, East—estimates from other tailors were obtained but not accepted.

From packing invoices I gather that the shako of the officers was of black felt with plume; the accoutrements, black patent leather pouch and belt with silver or electro-plated ornaments, waist belt with clasp, forage cap and covers.

For type of a captain in the above uniform, see plate.

Summer Uniform.

Company No. 1, which, from the circumstance that from its creation it was self-supporting, always enjoyed a position of proud pre-eminence in the corps, was desirous of adopting a summer uniform. The requisite authority was not obtained without a struggle. The first request, made in June, 1860, to the Lord Lieutenant, was for a summer uniform of the same material as that worn by the Indian Troops. The War Office replied that they had no objection to summer uniform being used by the 1st company *only* if no gold lace, and if approved by the Lord Lieutenant; at the same time the War Office hinted that the band uniforms were to be the same as other uniforms with the exception of scarlet cord and braid and coloured plumes. In a War Office circular of 12th June, 1860, Earl de Grey and Ripon said, "there will be no objection on the part of this office to the adoption of such uniform as may meet with the approval of the Lord Lieutenant, provided no gold lace be worn. Bands of musicians are to be enrolled members of the corps and instructed in the use of arms." Again on the 13th June, 1860, he wrote: "You are quite at liberty to adopt a summer suit of clothing provided the pattern is approved by the Lord Lieutenant." On the 28th June, 1860, the Lord Lieutenant wrote that he did not disapprove of a summer uniform, but was of opinion that "no difference, save the slightest possible, between the uniform of the band and that of the private was very desirable." His lordship was also of opinion that to "ensure the general extension of the Volunteer movement it was necessary to reduce the expense of outfit as much as possible, so as to enable the poorer men to join." On 20th July, after carefully considering the matter, the Lord Lieutenant wrote that he "declined to comply with the request for a second uniform of lighter material, such being undesirable, that its additional expense would deter persons who might otherwise become valuable members of the corps, but he was willing to sanction the uniform proposed for the band with the exception of plumes, which," he stated, "are in no case admissible." Strong representations must have been made to him, for he wrote again on the 26th July that he would offer no objection to lighter dress, but it was not to form part of the acknowledged uniform of the corps, and might be worn or not at the discretion of each Volunteer.

It was evident that, although the Lord Lieutenant had approved of plumes, doubtless in deference to the expressed wish of the commanding officers of the various corps he yet had serious objection, not only to their use, amongst other reasons on the ground of cost, but also to the wearing of sashes by officers, for he issued a circular on the 24th May, 1860, through the clerk to the lieutenancy, stating that it was his wish that sashes should not be worn by the officers of the West Riding Volunteer Rifle Corps, and that it was also his wish "that plumes should not be worn by the members of the West Riding Rifle Corps when on duty."

Finally on 20th December, 1860, the fate of the plumes was sealed, for the clerk to the lieutenancy on that date addressed the following letter to Major H. F. Beaumont:—

"I have to inform you that I have to-day accompanied a deputation from the Leeds Corps to the Lord Lieutenant on the subject of the plumes, which it was understoood his lordship had forbidden to be worn at the review and in consequence of representations made to his lordship he has instructed me to say that he will waive his objection to them being worn at the review, but that this is not to be understood to commit him to an approval of them for the future."

Some members of Company No. 1 took advantage of the Lord Lieutenant's permission to don a lighter uniform, and adopted a khaki or Holland jacket with cover of the same colour for the forage cap. I have not been able to ascertain with any degree of certainty whether or not khaki or Holland trousers were worn, as some of those who were in the corps at the time and whom I have consulted are not by any means agreed on the matter. Whilst on the subject of uniforms, it may be well to add that not only the effective or active members but the honorary members also wore or might wear a uniform—a frock coat braided in front, and cap with horizontal beak, but they were not entitled to carry swords.

It was found that some of the rank and file were in the habit of wearing the black trousers on Sundays and holidays, first removing the black braid stripe. To obviate this a scarlet braid stripe was substituted but even this was removed and the trousers worn when not on parade. At last a scarlet piping was sewn into the seam of the trousers and this being too troublesome to remove and replace it proved an effective stop to the abuse. The men quite believed or affected to believe they had a right to wear the trousers when at work, for it is related that a private, no doubt a joiner, mechanic or mason by trade, on one occasion, whilst undergoing the ordeal of the trying-on process, missed a familiar aperture at the side of the trouser and seriously inquired of the tailor—" wheer's th'hoile for a two-foot rule. ?"

It seems that many corps, on the opportunity arising for the first renewal of clothing, had adopted a new type of uniform. The Huddersfield corps did not escape the general feeling, and in 1863 their first uniform was discarded and, with the approval of the authorities, a smarter and more useful one adopted. It consisted of a tunic much shorter in the skirt, decorated with less elaborate braid, with scarlet facings and collar, and scarlet piping down the outer seam of the trousers, with demi-shako with ball tuft. There was very little alteration in the accoutrements and ornaments. Changes of Uniform.

For type of officer in this uniform see plate.

This uniform was worn until the end of 1874, when scarlet was adopted, and the dark uniform which had been worn for some 15 years with considerable pride disappeared. On May 30th, 1860, a band uniform was adopted. It consisted of steel grey cloth, facings of scarlet cord, the caps of same cloth, with scarlet cords and plumes.

I have already mentioned the fact that No 1 Company of the Huddersfield Rifles, officers and men alike, had from the first resolved to be independent of aid, from any quarter, in the provision of its arms, uniform and accoutrements. How far that determination was based on pure patriotism, how far on a proper respect and how far it may have been tainted by a species of arrogance, I do not care to discuss. It is my duty merely to record and in this connection I may well reproduce two letters addressed by Mr. J. Batley to the honorary secretary. The letters explain themselves. No. 1 Company self-supporting.

" Huddersfield,
16th February, 1860.

My Dear Sir,

Referring to our conversation yesterday on the subject of the assistance received by members of our company from the General Fund I think it proper to state my views to you in writing, requesting you to communicate them to the assisted members of our company at the meeting you will convene for the purpose.

Since the formation of the other Rifle companies in the town it has been assumed and accorded to our No. 1 Company as a distinctive feature that it is self-equipped. When the expenditure account, however, comes to be examined, which must soon be the case, it will be found that we are now in possession of assistance out of these funds to the extent—if I have the figures right—of £36 for uniform &c., and £40 10s. for rifles.

This will surprise many, as the assistance was given very quietly, without public vote of any kind, indeed so quietly that even the officers have never been informed either the names of the members so assisted or the extent of assistance given in each case.

I am sure the assisted members of our company will feel willing, nay even anxious, now to have an opportunity of maintaining the distinctive character of our company referred to, and will feel it a duty to make an effort in that direction, especially when it is borne in mind that in the other companies even a working-man is not admitted who does not find £2 10s. towards his outfit.

If this feeling exists the officers are desirous of rendering their assistance to carry it out in such manner as that we may each and all be able to say that our company *is* in truth self-equipped, and has now no contribution from the public funds for this purpose.

With this view we wish you to ascertain whether the assisted members of our company are now willing to enter into an arrangement for the gradual repayment of such assistance as they have received, 1st in uniforms, 2nd in accoutrements, 3rd in arms, spreading it over one, two or three years as may be the most convenient.

If so, we will at once advance and repay to the general fund the £76 10s. due from us. Then the matter will be between our members and our officers only—and the character of our company will be maintained.

Be good enough to acquaint me with the result of the interview you have with our assisted members, in which you will add to my letter your own views on the subject, which will, I do not doubt, have great weight with them.

I am,

Yours very truly,

J. BATLEY, Junior.

T. H. Battye, Esquire."

"Huddersfield,

16th February, 1860.

Dear Sir,

I forgot to say in mine of this morning that if inconvenient to any of the assisted members of our company to arrange at present for the repayment of both uniforms, accoutrements and arms we shall be content in any case to confine the arrangement to the uniform only, and in such case the parties may retain freely as at present their arms and accoutrements so long as they remain in our company, may use them as their own, and may at any future time buy them or acquire them absolutely on an arrangement then to commence for payment for the same in such manner as will be convenient.

I trust that in coming forward substantially to assist our men to remain in the company on equal terms with the rest, we shall be met with an equal desire and spirit to keep up the position and character of our company.

I am,

Yours truly,

J. BATLEY, Junior.

T. H. Battye, Esquire."

I have mentioned in another part that in the earlier years of the force the Government issue of rifles was in order of the merit of the different corps. It is gratifying to be able to record that according to the Table of the Order of Merit of Corps, set out in the *Reserve Forces Circular* of 1st November, 1870, Clause 25, the 5th Administrative Battalion, West Riding Yorkshire,* had 92·04 percentage of efficients, or was the 71st in order of merit out of a total number of 219 battalions of rifle corps.

Regulations of the Corps.

Under section 56 of 44 Geo. III. c. 54, the statute by which the formation of the corps was authorised, it became necessary to prepare and have duly enrolled what may be termed the company's bye-laws, a matter of no small moment and requiring no little skill and trouble. These rules were prepared in accordance with a memorandum regarding the formation, organization, establishment, instruction &c. of Volunteer Corps in Great Britain to be raised under the said Act, issued by the War Office, and with a circular letter based on that memorandum, dated July 13th, 1859, addressed by the Secretary of State for War, Mr. Sidney Herbert, to the Lord Lieutenant of the Riding. I have already adverted to this memorandum and circular, which will be found in the appendix. The rules drawn up for the government of the Huddersfield corps are set out in the appendix and were in substance as follows:—

The corps was to consist of (1) enrolled members (effective, non-effective and supernumerary), (2) honorary members not liable for service but contributing to the funds of the corps, who were not bound to provide themselves with uniform and not permitted to interfere in the management of the corps. Such subscribers were to pay ten guineas or upwards in one payment or an entrance fee of £2 2s. 0d. and an annual subscription of £2 2s. 0d., and this constituted honorary membership and entitled them to practise on the drill and shooting grounds of the corps for their own personal proficiency.

Enrolled members subscribed annually as under:—

	£	s.	d.
Captain	10	10	0
Lieutenant	5	5	0
Surgeon	4	4	0
Ensign	3	3	0
Sergeant	1	11	6
Corporal	1	1	0
Private	0	10	6

* The 5th A.B. consisted at this time of the 6th (Huddersfield) Corps, 32nd (Holmfirth) Corps, 42nd (Mirfield) Corps and 44th (Meltham) Corps.

So that one sees that from private to captain these Volunteers had the supreme gratification of serving their country not merely at their own expense, but of paying somewhat handsomely for the privilege of doing so, and not only so but, by Article 7, must run the gauntlet of a three-fourths ballot of the members of the corps before being admitted to these privileges. The officer in command submitted the names of gentlemen for commissions to the Lord Lieutenant, with whom, subject to the Queen's approval, the appointment rested. The non-commissioned officers were, however, appointed by the officer in command. Each member was to be provided with the approved uniform and accoutrements and pay the expense of his ammunition. The corps was to drill and practise twice a week during the months of May, June, July and August, and once weekly during the rest of the year. Officers. commissioned and non-commissioned, were liable to fines for the non-performance of their duties, and in cases of grave offence, in some instances to censure, in some to fine, and in others, the most serious, to expulsion from the corps.

The senior officer commanding had power to fine for minor offences:—

	s.	d.
For loading without orders or shooting out of time ..	2	6
For discharging rifle accidentally	5	0
For pointing same, loaded or unloaded, at any person ..	10	0
For talking in the ranks	1	0
For smoking, or drinking wine, beer or spirits, during drill or practice	2	6.

ec. 1st, 359, irst Annual leeting.

The first annual meeting of the corps was held at the George Hotel, on December 1st, 1859, under Article 17, to appoint a committee to assist the Commanding Officer in the management of the finances and non-military affairs of the corps. The committee was to be the commissioned officers, the honorary secretary and treasurer and eight other members, four effective and four honorary. The elective members, on a counting of votes were found to be

Effectives.	Honorary Members.
Sergeant Hannah,	Bentley Shaw, Esquire,
Corporal Bottomley,	T. P. Crosland ,,
Private Sissons,	Chas. Brook, Jun. ,,
Corporal David Boscovitz.	James Bradbury ,,

At this meeting Captain H. F. Beaumont presided, and there were present not only members of the corps but others who had taken an interest in its formation, among them, the Vicar of St. Paul's, the Rev. John Haigh, Messrs. L. R. Starkey, J. C.

Laycock, John Freeman, senr., Joseph Brook, James Hinchliffe, James Bradbury, E. T. Monk, D. A. Cooper and William Roberts.

I find no record of any parade of the corps prior to the end of December, 1859, some eight weeks after its official recognition. An order was issued that "members of the corps will assemble Saturday, December 31st, 1859, at 2-30, at St. George's Square, in full uniform, from whence (*sic*) they will proceed in marching order to the cricket ground." The cricket ground, the finally adopted practice ground of the corps, now forming the upper part of Greenhead Park, was approached from Trinity Street at the base of West Hill. The approach was by a footpath bounded by allotment gardens, and the men had to form two deep on entering the ground. On this field, rifle butts were subsequently erected—for short ranges only—a very extensive and lofty wall being erected at the south end to prevent accidents. Lofty as this wall was, a marksman on one occasion managed to overshoot it. Parade.

To return to the first parade. The report of the *Huddersfield Chronicle*, of January 7th, 1860, states that the members of the corps assembled in the Cloth Hall Yard, for practice there. Then, headed by the Meltham Mills Band,* they proceeded down Cloth Hall Street and along New Street to St. George's Square, where, in the presence of some thousands of persons, they went through a number of military evolutions. Then they marched up New North Road to the old cricket ground, where they had file practice and marching and fired blank cartridges. It is gratifying to learn on the authority of the reporter—all reporters, I understand, are omniscient—"that considering the little field practice the men have hitherto had they went through the whole with remarkable precision." After practising till nearly dusk the corps returned to St. George's Square, fired three rounds of blank cartridge and were then dismissed. On the next day, assembling by St. Paul's Schools, they marched to the Parish Church. The sermon was preached by the vicar, the Rev. Samuel Holmes. A desire was expressed by the corps that the sermon should be published, but the reverend gentleman did not accede to the request.

---

*The Meltham Mills Brass Band was then, if not the best, certainly one of the best, in a county in which musical pre-eminence is only attained by rare excellence.—R. P. B.

State and Establishment of Corps, January 1860.

On 2nd January, 1860, when the corps had been but two months in existence, a return of its state and establishment was furnished by the honorary secretary to the *Volunteer Rifle Corps Almanac* for 1860, and I give the return, as it bears official authority:—

"County—West Riding.
Company—10th.
Date of Establishment—Service was accepted 3rd November, 1859.
Headquarters—Huddersfield.
Staff-Captain—H. F. Beaumont.
Lieutenant—Joseph Batley.
Ensign—J. A. Harrison.
Surgeon—T. A. Bottomley.
Musketry Instructor—Horatio France.
Drill Sergeant— do.
Uniform—Dark grey tunic and pantaloons—facings black.
Arms and accoutrements—Short Enfield Rifle—Sword Bayonet.
Numerical strength—82 members and 4 officers.
Drill Ground—Cloth Hall, Huddersfield.
Practice Ground—not obtained—expected to be the Greenhead Cricket Ground.
Annual Subscription—10/6 for privates."

It was a matter of general regret that the popular captain of the corps, Mr. H. F. Beaumont, was compelled, by the indisposition of his wife in London, to absent himself from the first parade. He was, however, able to take the command a fortnight later, January 14th, 1860, when the corps visited Holmfirth, crowds of people and the Holmfirth Old Band meeting the Volunteers at the Holmfirth Railway Station. The band, we are assured by the local press, played several marches in fine style, conducted by Mr. Bates, veterinary surgeon, on horseback. On the route, past the church, through Hollow Gate, over the Bridge, and along the Huddersfield Road to the Cricket Ground, the Volunteers received a perfect ovation. Every available spot of vantage was occupied by enthusiastic spectators, who witnessed the evolutions with interest and acclaim. Messrs J. Moorhouse and J. Harpin, prominent members of the town on the Holme, expressed to the corps the thanks of the people for their visit and demonstration.

January 14th, 1860, Visit to Holmfirth.

I dwell on incidents like these, incidents with which we are now so familiar that they attract little notice and evoke less enthusiasm, because they serve not only to shew how the Volunteer movement met with the full approval of the people at the time, but because they stimulated others to follow the example so nobly set. Amongst old papers I discovered a muster roll or return, dated

January, 1860, shewing the state of the corps at that period, and although made out apparently only the day after the return I have just given, yet it shews a slight increase in the ranks.

Later Roll, January 1860.

"Muster roll of the Huddersfield Volunteers commanded by Henry Frederick Beaumont, Esq., and consisting of one company, the 10th West York Rifle Volunteers.

Headquarters .. .. Huddersfield, January, 1860.
Officers—Captain, Henry Frederick Beaumont,
Lieutenant, Joseph Batley,
Ensign, Joseph Acheson Harrison.

No. of effectives	None.
Non-effectives	84
Establishment	84
Allowed	100
Wanting to complete	16
Number and date of enrolment of the Volunteers last enrolled ..	84. January 3rd, 1860."

It very soon became apparent to those interested in furthering the Volunteer movement in Huddersfield that one company would not suffice to meet the aspirations of those anxious to offer their services in the cause. The beginning of the year 1860 found Mr. Battye in communication with the Under-Secretary for War, the Earl de Grey and Ripon, on the subject of the formation of a battalion in the event of there being raised sufficient additional companies.

Feb., 1860, Correspondence as to additional Companies and formation of Battalion.

The following letter was received by Mr. Battye from the War Office:—

"War Office,
1st February, 1860.

Sir,—I am directed by Mr. Secretary Herbert to acknowledge the receipt of your letter of the 26th ultimo, and to inform you, in reply, that on the application of the Lord Lieutenant of the county he will be happy to sanction the formation of a Rifle Volunteer Battalion at Huddersfield, consisting of either four companies under the command of a Major or of six companies under the command of a Lieutenant-Colonel.

V
10 York
(W.R.)
8.

Mr. Herbert has no objection to receive the offer of the companies one by one, as they are raised, and to unite the 2nd and 3rd with the 1st under the command of a Captain Commandant until the formation of the fourth entitles the corps to be placed under the command of a Major.

Each company must be of not less than the minimum strength of 60 men, and as new companies are added to the corps there will be no objection to the members being distributed among them in any way which may be most convenient, so long as this principle is maintained. It will not, therefore, be necessary to enrol supernumeraries over the maximum establishment of 100 men in any company, and under these circumstances Mr. Herbert does not consider it would be expedient to sanction such an enrolment.

I am to add that the establishment of commissioned officers allowed by the Regulations to a company of Rifle Volunteers whether with or without supernumeraries is one captain, one lieutenant and one ensign.

Signed, etc."

The second company of Huddersfield Volunteers was accepted on or about February 14th, 1860, and the following letter from the Secretary for War to the Lord Lieutenant is proper to be preserved:—

"War Office,
14th February, 1860.

My Lord,

With reference to your Lordship's letter of the 4th instant offering for the Queen's acceptance the service of a company of Rifle Volunteers at Huddersfield under the Act 44, Geo. III., c. 54, I have the honour to inform you that Her Majesty has been graciously pleased to approve and accept the same.

The company has been incorporated in the 10th West Riding of Yorkshire Rifle Volunteers, the maximum establishment of which will consist of one captain commandant, one captain, two lieutenants, two ensigns, one assistant surgeon, 200 men of all ranks, divided into two companies, the Regulations of the service only admitting of the appointment of one captain, one lieutenant, one ensign to a single company of Rifle Volunteers.

I have the honour to be,
My Lord,
Your Lordship's obedient servant,
S. HERBERT."

The following gentlemen were the first officers of No. 2 company:—

Captain—Thos. Pearson Crosland, Gledholt.
Lieutenant—Thos. Brook, Colne Villa.
Ensign—Thos. Brooke, Northgate House.
Hon. Surgeon—Frederick Greenwood.

In August, 1860, Captain T. P. Crosland was anxious to resign his commission in consequence of ill-health. He was persuaded to continue his services to the corps, and to the day of his death extended to it his help and sympathy in every possible way.

On February 28th, 1860, the first and second companies were inspected by Major G. B. Harman, Her Majesty's Inspector of Volunteers in the northern district, an officer who had seen much service in the Crimea, and who was under General Wyndham in the Indian Mutiny. He arrived in Huddersfield at a few hours' notice to inspect the Volunteer forces of the town and enquire into their organization and efficiency, and was attended by the officers of the local companies. He first inspected No. 1 Company, who were in full uniform and under arms. He expressed himself satisfied with their efficiency in general drill exercises, which, he stated, reflected great credit both upon the men and upon the officers.

He then inspected the members of No. 2 Company, in the Drill Room in East Parade, and expressed himself gratified and surprised at the progress made by the company.

On or about February 25th, 1860, another, the 3rd, company, was accepted by the Crown. The following letter of the Earl de Grey and Ripon to Earl Fitzwilliam announced the acceptance:— Formation of No. 3 Company.

"War Office,
25th February, 1860.

My Lord,

With reference to your Lordship's letter of the 20th instant, offering for the Queen's acceptance the service of a company of Rifle Volunteers at Huddersfield under the Act 44, Geo. 3, c. 54, I have the honour to inform you that Her Majesty has been graciously pleased to approve and accept the same. V 10 York (W.R.) 17.

The corps is numbered as the 27th in the West Riding of Yorkshire, and its maximum establishment will consist of:—

One Captain, one Lieutenant, one Ensign, 100 men of all ranks.

I have the honour to be,
My Lord,
Your Lordship's obedient servant,
DE GREY AND RIPON.
In the absence of the Secretary of State for War."

The following gentlemen were the first officers of this company:—

Captain—William Edwards Hirst, Moldgreen.
Lieutenant—Tom Learoyd, The Grove.
Ensign—Joshua Day, Moldgreen.
Hon. Surgeon—Dr. Gardiner, Moldgreen.

Mr. William Edwards Hirst did not qualify and Mr. Thomas Brooke, of Northgate House, was posted to the vacant command. Formation of No. 4 Company.

A fourth company was formed and its service accepted, March 27th, 1860.

The following gentlemen were its first officers:—

Captain—Bentley Shaw, Lockwood.
Lieutenant—John Haigh, junr., son of J. Haigh, Esq., Lascelles Hall.
Ensign—George Henry Greenwood, Huddersfield.
Hon. Surgeon—John Dow, Lockwood.

It has been asserted that there never was a 27th company in Huddersfield. The letter from the War Office of 25th February would seem to make it clear that the third company formed in Huddersfield was at first officially numbered the 27th in the West Riding.

It is certain that the impression prevailed among the Volunteers of Huddersfield that that company was called, and properly called, the 27th, and clearly for that impression the letter of 25th February, 1860, from the War Office, was abundant justification. I have, however, before me a letter from the War Office to Sir James T. Woodhouse, M.P., who has been most courteous in rendering me every assistance in my communications with that office. The letter is dated the 18th April, 1902, and its closing paragraph is as follows:—"I am to explain that according to the records in this Department, the 27th West York Rifle Volunteer Corps does not appear to have formed part of the Huddersfield Corps but belonged to the 1st Administrative Battalion, West Yorkshire Rifle Volunteers, and was subsequently consolidated with the 1st Volunteer Battalion West Yorkshire Regiment, of which it became H and J Companies."

The following is the muster roll of the four companies from December 1860, to May 1861:—

COMMANDANT, MAJOR HENRY FREDERICK BEAUMONT.

FIRST COMPANY.

Muster Roll, May, 1861.

Captain Joseph Batley
Lieutenant Thomas R. Webb
Ensign Henry B. Dyson
Sergeant-Major William Brook
Sergeant A. Hannah
,, Josh. Bottomley
,, David Boscovitz
,, R. Sissons
Corporal W. Abbey
,, J. Brook
,, A. Anderson
,, E. Golden
Private F. F. Abbey
,, Henry Anders
,, Henry Barker
,, S. Barras
,, Thomas Beardsell
,, Hector M. Beaumont
,, J. E. Beaumont
,, John Bottomley
,, T. H. Bradbury
,, Frederick Bradley
,, Matthew H. Bradley
,, Benjamin Brigg
,, J. W. Brook
,, H. Brook

Private Arthur Heron
,, C. A. Hirst
,, Benjamin Hutchinson
,, J. Ibeson
,, J. H. Kaye
,, H. Kilner
,, J. K. Lawton
,, Samuel Learoyd
,, Frederick Liebriech
,, Robert Lowenthal
,, R. W. L. Long
,, T. T. Lunn
,, T. G. Mallinson
,, J. Newton
,, A. Naylor
,, T. F. Norton
,, C. A. Oldroyd
,, J. T. Prince
,, W. H. Prince
,, F. Ramsden
,, David Robertson
,, G. Roebuck
,, F. Smith
,, G. Spurr
,, T. Starkey
,, E. Simmonds

FIRST COMPANY—*Continued.*

Private J. Brook
,, G. Calvert
,, William Hy. Charlesworth
,, G. O. Crowther
,, G. H. Crowther
,, D. Cocking
,, James Edwin Eastwood
,, J. S. Eddell
,, John Freeman, Junior
,, William Hick
,, Thomas Haigh
,, D. Haigh
,, F. Haigh
,, A. Hall

Private W. Taylor
,, I. Thomas
,, James Tolson
,, J. Walker, Junior
,, F. Walker
,, J. Waller, Junior
,, Warburg
,, William Watkinson
,, Herbert Wigney
,, J. A. Wilson
,, J. H. Wilson
,, J. Wilson

Honorary Surgeon T. A. Bottomley.

In May, 1861, the officers of this company were Captain Batley, Lieutenant Henry Broughton Dyson and Ensign Thomas Haigh Bradbury, with Alexander Hannah as quarter-master sergeant and E. Golden as armourer-sergeant.

SECOND COMPANY.

Captain T. P. Crosland
Lieutenant Thos. Brook (Colne Road)
Ensign F. Greenwood
Sergeant William Lawton
,, Moore
,, Hirst
,, Charles Dransfield
Corporal W. Hanson
,, B. Hall
,, D. Clayton
,, Parton
,, Bickerdike
,, Fawcett
Private T. Armitage
,, A. Armitage
,, J. H. Bradley
,, E. Brayshaw
,, Robert Bean
,, J. Beaumont
,, T. Bickerdike
,, J. Brown
,, J. Baldwin
,, G. H. Broom
,, John Brook
,, J. W. Brook
,, E. Balmforth
,, Joe Binns
,, John Carver

Private Charles Jackson
,, Crosland Kemp
,, W. Kenyon
,, Anthony K. Kaye
,, W. Kaye
,, W. H. Kaye
,, John Leng
,, Alfred Lees
,, John Lowe
,, James May
,, J. Middleton
,, James Megson
,, Joe Marshall
,, L. Muir
,, Joel Mellor
,, W. Moore
,, T. R. Nichol
,, T. A. Nichol
,, Bernhard Peil
,, Squire Pollitt
,, Abraham Pilling
,, John Quarmby
,, A. Radcliffe
,, E. Rothery
,, J. Rushworth
,, T. Robinson
,, J. G. Robinson
,, J. Robinson

SECOND COMPANY—*Continued*.

Private J. W. Clark
„ W. H. B. Conlon
„ J. A. Cookson
„ Walter Clayton
„ George Christie
„ W. Dixon
„ John Dixon
„ John Dalton
„ James Dyson
„ Samuel Dyson
„ Thomas Fox
„ T. Fawcett
„ R. Fawcett
„ Walter Flint
„ J. E. Furness
„ J. Fox
„ George Garton
„ T. Gledhill
„ W. Glossop
„ W. Holdsworth
„ G. Hutchinson
„ John Hollis
„ Joe Haigh
„ James Haigh
„ David Haigh
„ W. Helm
„ W. H. Hanson
„ T. W. Hanson
„ I. Heywood
„ J. Hellawell
„ Henry Howe
„ Daniel Hoyle
„ Joseph Hopkinson
„ S. Ibeson
„ W. Jarratt

Private E. Rothery
„ John Rushworth
„ William Shaw
„ Walter Scott
„ W. Shepherd
„ H. Spencer
„ J. Sykes
„ G. H. Stead
„ A. Sykes
„ W. Swallow
„ Richard Shaw
„ Henry Shaw
„ Edward Sheard
„ W. Sutcliffe
„ Henry Sykes
„ J. W. Thomson
„ W. Thorburn
„ Charles Turner
„ J. H. Taylor
„ J. W. Taylor
„ W. Thomas
„ Jenner Wales
„ John Wilson
„ W. M. Walker
„ Ed. Wear
„ John Lee Walker *
„ William Waring
„ S. Whitehead
„ B. Woodhead
„ W. Whitehead
„ Charles Whiteley
„ Ed. Whiteley
„ B. Whitwam
„ E. White.

THIRD COMPANY.

Captain Thos. Brooke, Northgate House
Lieutenant Tom Learoyd
Ensign Joshua Day
Sergeant Edwin Learoyd
„ J. Richardson
„ A. J. Learoyd
„ Edwin Mills
Bugler Henry Blakey
Corporal Bray
„ Beaumont
„ Moorhouse
„ Sutherland

Private B. Horsfall
„ J. Halstead
„ W. Hanson
„ I. Johnson
„ T. Johnson
„ C. H. Kilner
„ C. Kitson
„ T. Lockwood
„ W. Lockwood
„ W. Moorhouse
„ J. Milnes
„ J. McEvoy

* Mayor of Huddersfield, 1895-1897.

THIRD COMPANY—*Continued*.

Bugler Johnson
Private Aspinall
„ A. Beaumont
„ Tom Binns
„ George Brook
„ Henry Brook
„ J. T. Barras
„ H. Blakey
„ R. H. Bailey
„ Ben Berry
„ Henry Briggs
„ Fred W. Calvert*
„ T. Clayton
„ J. Crawshaw
„ Geo. Cliffe
„ W. Campbell
„ L. Comber
„ A. Driver
„ R. Driver
„ J. T. Dearnley
„ Tom Dyson
„ W. R. Denton
„ W. Dyson
„ J. Edwards
„ Emmerson
„ H. Greenwood
„ W. Gledhill

Private Morris
„ Thomas Oldroyd
„ Joe Pickard
„ James Pearson
„ E. Quarmby
„ T. Rothery
„ S. Richardson
„ Jonas Sykes
„ Henry Shepherd
„ G. Smithson
„ James Sykes
„ B. Stocks
„ S. Swift
„ W. H. Shaw
„ T. H. Sykes
„ R. Taylor
„ G. Taylor
„ J. Thornton
„ G. Thornton
„ W. Thirkell
„ T. Webster
„ Abraham Wood
„ W. Waddington
„ Wadsworth
„ H. White
„ Bill Wadsworth

FOURTH COMPANY.

Captain Bentley Shaw
Lieutenant John Haigh, Lascelles Hall
Ensign George Henry Greenwood
Sergeant C. H. Graham
„ J. Roberts
„ F. G. Abbey
„ W. Hutchinson
Corporal E. Brown
„ J. B. Hirst
„ W. Walker
„ B. Baxter
Private H. Ainley
„ G. Armitage
„ B. Baxter
„ G. H. Beaumont
„ J. T. Beaumont
„ J. Beaumont
„ John Berry

Private J. Hoyle
„ T. Longbottom
„ S. Liversedge
„ C. Mann
„ Mackintosh
„ John Mills
„ W. Mitchell
„ B. Naylor
„ H. Nickols
„ M. Nowell
„ M. Oates
„ John Oxley
„ C. Pickard
„ T. Pinder
„ J. Quarmby
„ J. Rayner
„ W. Rayner
„ S. Roberts

*Mayor of the County Borough of Huddersfield 1902-3.

FOURTH COMPANY—*Continued*.

Private	W. H. Berry	Private	H. Renshaw
,,	R. Boothroyd	,,	J. Renshaw
,,	J. Booth	,,	W. Renshaw
,,	W. Bradley	,,	Edward Revel
,,	T. Brook	,,	B. Rodgers
,,	J. Brownlow	,,	W. Rushworth
,,	W. Brown	,,	H. Saville
,,	W. Burns	,,	J. Senior
,,	James Calvert	,,	E. Shaw
,,	W. Crowther	,,	W. Shaw
,,	A. Clarkson	,,	R. B. Shaw
,,	J. W. Cliff	,,	A. Shaw
,,	John Crowther	,,	J. Senior
,,	T. Crowther	,,	J. Southwell
,,	R. Crowther	,,	R. Southwell
,,	B. Dean	,,	J. W. Spedding
,,	John Dyson	,,	W. Starkey
,,	E. Dutton	,,	C. Stockwell
,,	Edgar Fenton	,,	A. Sykes
,,	L. Greenwood	,,	H. Taylor
,,	Thomas Green	,,	J. Thewlis
,,	S. Haigh	,,	Titus Thewlis
,,	W. Hattersley	,,	Townsend
,,	W. Hardy	,,	I. Upton
,,	James Hepworth	,,	W. Walker
,,	T. Heppenstall	,,	C. Williams
,,	Harding	,,	C. Whiteley
,,	M. Hirst	,,	Jno. Whitehead
,,	H. Hodgson	,,	James Whitehead
,,	G. Hulme	,,	C. Williams
,,	T. Jakeman	,,	T. Waller
,,	H. Jones	,,	James Wood
,,	T. N. Kaye	,,	John Waite
,,	H. Kaye		

From December 1860 to May 1861, the average number appears to be about 380 of all ranks.

The above roll is taken from a drill book in the possession of Sir Thomas Brooke Bart., and used by him when in the corps.

Honorary Secretary to Companies 3 and 4, Mr. Chas. Mills.

Mr. Charles Mills, solicitor, for some years after the formation of the 3rd and 4th companies acted as their honorary secretary. Mr. Mills has held the position of clerk to the Justices of the Borough and County Borough of Huddersfield from the very incorporation of the borough, and with what conspicuous ability he discharges the responsible and trying duties of that position none are more ready to declare than those of his professional brethren whose engagements take them to the Justices' Court.

Curiously enough Mr. Mills, though, as the records of the companies shew, proving a most devoted secretary, and though certainly not lacking in the combative disposition, was never enrolled as a member of any of the Volunteer Corps.

The completion of the four companies on March 29th, 1860, enabled the corps to be constituted a battalion, and Mr. H. F. Beaumont was the first Major Commandant. As early as March 21st, 1860, a meeting had been held at Mr. Battye's office, attended by Captain Bentley Shaw, Lieutenant Thomas Brook, Surgeon Bottomley, Ensign Harrison, Lieutenant Batley, Ensign Day, Lieutenant Learoyd, Surgeon Greenwood, Ensign George Henry Greenwood, Captain T. P. Crosland in the chair; and at this meeting it had been resolved, on the motion of Lieutenant Batley, seconded by Captain Shaw, "that so soon as the corps are in a condition to do so, a recommendation of Captain Commandant H. F. Beaumont to be Major be signed by the officers of the four companies and forwarded to the Lord Lieutenant."

March 29th, 1860, the Battalion constituted.

It now became necessary to secure the services of an Adjutant for the battalion. I find a letter, dated "Leeds, September 20th, 1860," from Mr. John William Atkinson to Major Beaumont, in which occur the words, "I have the honour to inform you that the Lord Lieutenant has received a communication from the Secretary for War that he will be prepared to submit the name of Lieutenant Greer for Her Majesty's approval as Adjutant of the sixth West Riding of Yorkshire Rifle Volunteers, upon the receipt of the resignation by him of the commission he at present holds in the Militia."

The Adjutant.

Lieutenant Greer was an officer of the Tipperary Militia. He was appointed adjutant on 31st June, 1860 and posted captain, 8th October, 1860.

The advertisement of March 28th, 1860, for the services of an adjutant, in the *Army and Navy Gazette* and *Volunteer Service Gazette*, was in these words :—"An adjutant wanted for 10th West Riding of Yorkshire Rifle Volunteers; headquarters, Huddersfield. Applications, stating previous service, to be forwarded to T. H. Battye, Hon. Sec., Huddersfield."

Those who are now in a measure responsible for the administration of the finances of the Volunteer companies of to-day will, I think, peruse with interest an estimate made in 1860 of the annual charges of the Huddersfield Volunteers.

The Annual Charges, 1860.

GENERAL CHARGES.

May, 1860.	£	s.	d.	£	s.	d.
Rents—Shooting Ground				29	0	0
Arms depôt				25	0	0
School rooms				25	0	0
Cloth Hall repairs, &c.				20	0	0
Rates, taxes &c. of shooting ground and arms depôt, say ..				5	0	0
				104	0	0
Salaries—Drill Sergeant	55	0	0			
Assistant Drill Sergeant	25	0	0			
Other assistance at shooting &c. ..	10	0	0	90	0	0
				194	0	0
Repairs in shooting ground and arms depôt, stationery and other incidental expenses, say				26	0	0
				£220	0	0
Company charges.						
Things requiring to be done by company, say 100 strong:						
Repairs and replacement of clothing and accoutrements ..				100	0	0
Do. of arms				5	0	0
Ammunition				18	0	0
Bugler				5	0	0
Travelling, entertainment and other expenses, say				30	0	0
				158	0	0
Share of cost of band, say £230—¼				60	0	0
				£218	0	0
Estimated contributions of officers, thus:—						
Majors, total £120—¼..				30	0	0
Surgeon „ £20—¼..				5	0	0
Captains' subscriptions				100	0	0
Lieutenants' „				50	0	0
Ensigns' „				25	0	0
8 non-commissioned officers'..				10	0	0
				£220	0	0

Remarks on foregoing estimates:—

The £220 charges common to whole corps must be the subject of subscriptions from the public of the neighbourhood generally and subscriptions and annual payments by honorary members must be got to cover this.

The £218 charges common to each company is reckoned on the basis that each company contains 100 members and subject to reduction in case the quota is reduced. Whatever is short on these items the officers will have to find."

Instruction of officers at Hythe.

In the summer of 1861 some of the officers of the Huddersfield Corps underwent the course of musketry instruction at Hythe—notably Mr. Thomas Brooke, of Northgate House, and Mr. Edwin Learoyd, the latter of whom gained a prize in the 6th Section, consisting of a handsome silver single handled tankard with an embossed oval device, and the inscription:—Prize, Colour-Sergeant Edwin Learoyd, 6th West York Rifle Volunteers, School of Musketry, Hythe, July, 1861, 6th Section." Mr. Learoyd never accepted a commission, neither did he remain long in the corps, and thus his valuable qualification as an instructor of musketry was lost to the corps.

The month of March, 1860, was made memorable in the annals of the Volunteer movement by many events. For the first time Volunteer officers as such were commanded to the Court of their Monarch. The levée was followed by a dinner and a ball. The account of these functions I extract from the *Times* newspaper of March 8th, 1860:— Levée and Ball, March, 1860.

"On the 7th March, 1860, the Volunteer Service may be said to have attained its majority. It went through all the ceremonies which English usage prescribes for that critical stage of existence. In the morning it made its obeisance to our gracious Sovereign; in the afternoon it dined together at the St. James's Hall; and in the evening it gave a ball at the Floral Hall, Covent Garden. 1860, March 7th, Levée at St. James's.

Many a Volunteer officer in donning at early dawn his uniform of silver grey or russet brown, must have muttered to himself, in spirit if not in words, the consolation of the miserable Damiens, '*La journée sera dure mais elle finira,*' for the work cut out was a severe trial even for the best trained athlete. But for this and many other days' toil and labour compensation comes in the success which attended these ceremonies, and with the final stamp of approval which it has now received, the Volunteer Service, we may hope, has now taken its place amongst the permament institutions of the country; the last thing wanting in England, to make up a kingdom, mighty and flourishing, advanced and feared.

Levée.

Her Majesty the Queen held a Court on the above date in the afternoon in St. James's Palace for the reception, exclusively, of officers of Volunteer corps.

The officers began to arrive at 12 o'clock and were conducted to the drawing room, Queen Anne's room, guard chamber, banquet room and other apartments of the Palace, and were formed into companies. Her Majesty the Queen and Prince Consort arrived from Buckingham Palace soon after 2 o'clock attended by the ladies and gentlemen in waiting.

The Prince of Wales, Prince Alfred and the Duke of Cambridge, General Commanding-in-Chief, attended the Court.

The officers of Volunteers were joined in the drawing room by the Lords Lieutenant of the counties, who accompanied them to the Throne room and introduced them to the Queen. In the absence of the Lord Lieutenant they were introduced by the Under Secretary of State for the War Department."

The following officers of the Huddersfield Corps were presented :—

No. 1 Company.

Captain-Commandant H. F. Beaumont, Lieutenant J. Batley, Ensign J. A. Harrison, Honorary Surgeon T. A. Bottomley.

No. 2 Company.

Captain T. P. Crosland, Lieutenant Thomas Brook, (Colne Villa), and Ensign T. Brooke (Northgate House).

No. 3 Company.

Lieutenant T. Learoyd, Ensign J. Day.

27th Company (No. 4 Company).

Captain Bentley Shaw, Ensign G. H. Greenwood and Honorary Assistant Surgeon F. Greenwood.

The entire list of presentations occupied six columns of the *Times* and included the names of some 2,700 officers.

After the presentation the officers of the several West Riding companies (with the exception of those of Bradford, who had accepted a prior invitation from H. W. Wickham, Esq.) partook of the hospitality of the Lord Lieutenant of the riding, Earl Fitzwilliam, at his family mansion in Grosvenor Place. One hundred and five guests sat down to one of the most sumptuous repasts ever placed before mortals, so at least a local journal affirms. The family plate was put into requisition for the occasion, and the display of gold and silver, with the choice of rich viands with which the dishes were loaded, was such as to astonish many present who imagined that they had before-time seen something of dinners and the different styles in which these can be served up, but who were compelled to acknowledge that all they had before witnessed would not even bear a comparison. The welcome of the noble lord was such as became a hearty Yorkshireman, and was as heartily accepted and appreciated by his guests.

In the evening the officers of the whole Volunteer service met in the large room, St. James's Hall, Piccadilly. The company was confined exclusively to the members of the class with whom the movement originated, and they all appeared in the uniform of their respective corps. The hall was brilliantly lighted, and was decorated with the flags of the principal nations of the world, mingled with our own national colours; and this bright bordering afforded a somewhat striking contrast to the dark green and the light or dark grey hues in which the gentlemen present were attired. The band of the Grenadier Guards played a variety of airs throughout the evening, and special mention may be made of a polka, composed expressly for the occasion by Mr. Godfrey, the band master, called "The Volunteer United Service."

Covers were laid for 680 gentlemen, and every place was occupied. The Duke of Cambridge presided.

The Duke proposed the toast of the evening, "Success to the Volunteer movement." After congratulating all on the earnest desire "which the meeting proved, that this movement should be continuous," His Royal Highness said :—

"It is essentially necessary that to be of any use the movement should be continuous. There have been objections made on the ground that it is aggressive. I deny that altogether. I say it is entirely a movement of defence. In former times we reckoned it certain that with our wooden walls to defend us no enemy could come across the Channel from any quarter of the globe to attack us, but the scientific improvements of modern times—improvements which come upon us so rapidly that we scarcely know what the next day is going to bring forth—witness the Whitworth gun for instance—lead us to the conviction that for our real comfort it is absolutely necessary that a great Empire like ours should always be in a position of perfect security ; that we should be able to say to all the world, 'Come if you dare.' Even those who are most opposed to this movement agree that we ought to be prepared, and that, gentlemen, is just what we wish to be and just what we are. For my part, I rejoice exceedingly, and I am sure that everybody in this hall and everybody in this country will rejoice, at the proof which this movement affords that when the occasion arises there is not a man amongst us who will not come forward to do the best he can for the defence of his country. But it would be a great error to suppose that because I, the head of the army, appear at a meeting of this kind that the army is in any way deficient for defensive purposes. Your vocation is not to take the place of the regular army but to assist it, and I feel sure the very best supplement of the regular army will be yourselves. There is the militia service for which I have the greatest respect. I go down and inspect regiments of militia, and really, when I see the line and militia regiments together, I do not know one from the other. These I call the first reserve of the army. The Volunteer force, of which you are the officers, I trust will be the second reserve. As to your organization, I may perhaps be permitted to say a few words. Many gentlemen seem to suppose that all you have to do is to become good shots. There is my friend General Hay, one of the best shots in the country, who thinks there is nothing like being a good shot. He is somewhat an enthusiast on this subject, and to a certain extent I go with him ; but after all I have a great idea that to make a good soldier a man must know his drill. If you do not know your drill, shooting, in my opinion, is nearly thrown away. I have heard a good deal of talk about loose drill, but depend upon it that you must first drill steadily. Drill steadily first and then you may afterwards become loose *dégagé* riflemen. I have remarked with great pleasure that this movement is taking root downwards, and that at our schools the youth is taking there his lessons in drill. That is the most likely way in which to make this movement permanent. We are often told that we are not a military nation, and we may not be in the common acceptation of the term. We have no conscription for instance, but produce a country where you can have such a display of military spirit as this Volunteer movement affords. Again, are not our Militia, our Regular army all Volunteers. All, Regulars, Militia and Volunteers come from the same source. Are not all actuated by the same feeling in their coming forward, each in their respective services, for the defence of the country? No man in this country is forced to serve in the military forces—every man who serves at all serves of his own free will. I cannot conclude without again expressing my opinion that no man could perform the duty entrusted to him in connection with the Volunteer movement with more zeal and energy than has been displayed by my noble friend, the Under Secretary for War, and I will conclude by proposing the Earl de Grey and Ripon and the Volunteers."

Earl de Grey and Ripon, in responding, observed that the Volunteer force was already estimated to amount to 80,000 men, and he had no doubt that before the end of the next summer it would reach 100,000. It would depend on Volunteer corps themselves whether the movement was to be worthy of England or whether it was to become a mere laughing stock. It had been proved that a Volunteer force could be raised and it was for them to make it permanent. The great body of the force consisted at present of scattered companies, and the object of the Government was to unite them for military and administrative purposes. In order to secure that object the Government meant to supply them with adjutants, and he hoped the result would be a triumphant answer to the carpings and the feeble ridicule of some persons who criticised the movement. Let the movement be properly directed, and in the hour of danger the country would find an efficient defence in the intelligence, zeal and patriotism of the Volunteers.

To the banquet succeeded a ball. The timed fixed for the ball was half-past nine, but as some 1,500 or 2,000 visitors wished to take time by the forelock, it followed that none made particularly rapid progress. It almost seemed as if the carriages had been accumulating since early evening, and not a few even of the ladies grew impatient of their long exile in Pall Mall and actually ventured forth from their carriages at that distance to walk to the hall. Unfortunately the very many entrances into the hall were not brought into use on this occasion and the result was a rather inconvenient amount of delay and stoppage at the foot of the grand staircase. At last the hall was gained, and within an hour after opening it was inconveniently crowded, so that many were glad to turn into the Opera House itself and rest for a while from the scene of brilliant confusion in the hall below. The first impression produced by the appearance of the hall was not perhaps as brilliant in the matter of light as might have been expected, inasmuch as all the many hundreds of gas jets were placed too high. The effect of this, however, soon passed off or was forgotten in admiring the very beautiful aspect of the interior of the hall which was decorated with such taste and effect as to colour as we do not often find bestowed, in this country at least, upon such accessories.

From the time when the doors were opened until a late hour a stream of visitors continued to arrive steadily until the hall and Opera House were throng with not less than 4,000 to 5,000 ladies and gentlemen, the latter, as usual on these occasions, predominating by nearly three to one.

Nearly all the gentlemen were in uniform, and the regiments generally were complimented by the *Times* on having gentlemanlike, well chosen and serviceable uniforms. There were crowds of officers of the regular service, guardsmen, cavalry, artillery and infantry; the militia, too, mustered strongly, and the handsome, though unpretending, uniform of the naval service was to be seen here and there. Deputy lieutenants, too, were numerous, though, of course, all uniforms gave way before the almost Oriental richness of some members of the diplomatic corps with whom, in this respect, nothing short of fancy dresses competes.

Perhaps a desire that the men in the ranks should not feel themselves left out in the cold suggested to the officers of the local corps the festivities that took place in the following June. Major H. F. Beaumont entertained the 1st company at Whitley Hall; Captain Crosland feasted the 2nd company at the George Hotel; Captain Brooke the 3rd company at the Queen Hotel; and Captain Bentley Shaw also entertained his company.

New Designation.

In July, 1860, the style of the 10th West Riding Rifle Volunteer Corps was altered to the 6th. The following letter from the clerk to the Lieutenancy communicated the decision of the authorities:—

"Leeds, 6th July, 1860.

Sir,

I have the honour to inform you that the 10th West Riding of Yorkshire Rifle Volunteer Corps will in future be styled the 6th West Riding of Yorkshire Rifle Volunteer Corps. This alteration will be gazetted on Friday next.

I have the honour to be, Sir,

Your obedient servant,

JOHN WILLIAM ATKINSON.

Major Beaumont,

10th W. Y. R. V., Huddersfield."

In September of 1860 the Huddersfield Volunteers took part in the proceedings of a brigade field day at Bradford. They were to be reviewed at York on the 28th of that month and the exercises at Bradford on the 15th were doubtless designed to accustom the men, most of whom must necessarily have been raw levies, to act together in great numbers. I utilize a local report :—

Field Day at Bradford, September, 1860.

"The largest body of Rifle Volunteers that has yet been brought together, in Yorkshire, met in Peel Park, Bradford, on Saturday, the 15th inst., to be exercised preparatory to the Grand Review at York on the 28th inst. It was originally intended that this Brigade Field Day of West Riding Battalions should be in Kirklees Park, and Major Harman, the District Inspector, had consented to command the united corps; but Sir George Armytage, the owner, apprehending that the large number of people would do serious damage, objected to its being used for review purposes, and hence the design was abandoned.

The Bradford Corps, however, were determined to have a preliminary review in Peel Park, and invited the other Volunteer Corps of the Riding to assemble with them. The result was the four Battalions, namely the 3rd West Riding (Bradford), the 5th (Wakefield with Dewsbury attached), the 6th, (Huddersfield and Holmfirth), and the 7th, (Leeds), mustered on the occasion, and four companies of the 2nd Royal Cheshire Militia, quartered then at the Bradford Barracks, were permitted to join and take part in the manœuvres. The attendance was large, 10,000 persons being present. The battalions, with the exception of Huddersfield and Holmfirth, which did not arrive until three-quarters of an hour afterwards, formed in the town of Bradford and marched to the Review Ground, reaching it at four o'clock, headed by the Band of the 2nd West York Yeomanry. Each of the Volunteer corps was accompanied by its own band, there being six bands altogether. The four companies of the 2nd Royal Cheshire Militia, about 200 strong, were commanded by Captain Stephens and Adjutant Kelsall; the Bradford Rifle Corps, 311 strong, by Major S. C. Lister; the Wakefield with Dewsbury, together 185 strong, by Major Holdsworth and Captain T. H. Cooke; Huddersfield and Holmfirth, 307 strong, by Major Beaumont of Whitley Beaumont, Captain and Adjutant Greer and Captain Moorhouse; and the Leeds, 200 strong, by Captain Horsfall and Adjutant Hunt. Total effective force, including Militia, upwards of 1,200. The arrival of the battalions was signalled by the discharge of one of the Sebastopol guns which were mounted on an earthwork battery on the rising ground at the eastern extremity of the park and similar salutes were fired at intervals during the proceedings. Just after the four battalions which first arrived had taken up their position a detachment of the 12th Royal Lancers from the Leeds Barracks entered the Park, having been permitted by Lieutenant-Colonel Oakes to attend to keep the ground. The detachment was under the command of Lieutenant Morrant in the inevitable absence of Major Harman. The duties of Acting-Brigadier were undertaken by Captain F. Lepper, Adjutant of the 3rd West Riding Bradford Corps. A number of evolutions were gone through of a character similar to those expected to be undertaken at the York Review, although the programme had slightly to be altered in consequence of the formation of the ground. The movement, however, which most interested the spectators was when the five battalions formed in squares with bayonets fixed to resist cavalry and were charged by the Lancers in double line. These soldiers had only returned a few weeks ago from India. They rode young horses only partially trained and considering that circumstance and the nature of the ground the charge was splendidly made.

Captain Lepper, the Reviewing Officer, made a few remarks on the satisfactory manner in which the Rifle Corps had acquitted themselves. He mentioned a few slight defects which he noticed and gave his brother officers some suggestions which he said Major Harman had desired him to communicate to them in order to ensure the success of the movements to be gone through at York."

From the same paper I extract an account of the York review and the subsequent banquet:—

Sep. 26th, 1860, Review at York.

" Since the inauguration of the great patriotic movement which has provided England with the sinews of defensive strength such as our Volunteer army is daily developing, military spectacles have ceased to excite attention because of their novelty. They have, however, taken a greater hold on the public mind than mere novelty can ever impart. The long-talked-of review at York was one vieing in importance and interest with the grandest which has yet been held in the provinces. It was the exhibition of the defensive strength of the largest county in England. Regiments of Volunteers from north, south, east and west were there concentrated in one united army, all the principal towns of the county being represented by their trained bands of sharpshooters. First in priority of local importance appeared the disciplined cohort of Huddersfield, making a good figure amongst its military compeers. The Volunteer movement in this town has been marked with varied phases of popular feeling. At first a kind of lethargic indifference, if not a positive opposition, was generally manifested. The originators had consequently great difficulties to contend with. Those whose position and influence would have given vitality to the movement stood aloof and for upwards of two months after the first drill commenced, when the corps numbered 36, the muster-roll was scarcely enriched by a single additional name. Subsequently the movement became more popular. The services of Sergeant France, of the 34th Foot, were specially engaged and H. F. Beaumont, Esquire, having accepted the office of captain, the company was placed on a more secure footing. At this time about 50 gentlemen had come forward as Volunteers, many of whom expressed their readiness to equip themselves at their own expense. Soon afterwards, T. P. Crosland, Esquire, warmly espoused the cause and undertook to form a 2nd company. He had no sooner taken the initiative than Volunteers in large numbers willingly came forward. A 2nd company which soon exceeded the other in numerical strength was speedily raised, and Mr. Crosland acceded to the wishes of the members to become their captain. This patriotic example was promptly followed; a 3rd and 4th were rapidly raised, and it is not improbable that a 5th will hereafter be added. The numerical strength of the corps is now about 350. There is a good staff of officers, the men are forward in drill and an efficient band has been raised. Indeed, notwithstanding the apathy at first manifested, there are few towns in the West Riding where the spirited efforts made have resulted more successfully. Knavesmire is eminently fitted for the purposes of a military review, and 60,000 men, according to the estimation of military authorities, may be manœuvred there. This place adjoins the high road between Tadcaster and the City of York and comprises about 271 acres. In the centre of a dead flat, bordered on the sides by green slopes, it is excellently adapted for reviews. The principal entrance is at the north end, and from this gate leads the new carriage road direct to the grand stand used on this occasion as the saluting base. The south end of the plain is skirted by a small wood The grand stand, a building which has been erected and improved at considerable expense, was placed at the disposal of the Lord Lieutenant by the Racing Committee. The Review ground, which was kept by a detachment of the 12th Lancers, under the command of Captain Wombwell, presented an imposing and magnificent sight. The state of the ground, however, was a great drawback. In many places it was so sodden that in marching past the grand stand the men were ankle deep in mud, while in other places they had to wade through pools of water several inches deep. It was computed there were about 40,000 to 50,000 spectators. There were about 500 or 600 policemen on duty."

The following is a summary of the distribution and strength of the corps on the ground :—

1st Brigade—Colonel Wade, C.B., Commanding, Major Tyers, Major of Brigade.

Artillery, 1st Battalion—Major Howarth, Commander, 1st East Riding, Burlington, 2nd East Riding, Filey, 2nd North Riding, Whitby, 1st West Riding, Leeds, strength 293.

2nd Battalion—Lieutenant-Colonel Samuelson, Commander, 1st East Riding, Hull, 354.

3rd Battalion—Lieutenant-Colonel Briggs.

1st Administrative Battalion, comprising York, Harrogate and Wetherby, Knaresboro', Ripon and Tadcaster, 458.

4th Battalion—Major Overend, 2nd Hallamshire, Sheffield.

4th Administrative Battalion—Pontefract, Rotherham, Doncaster, 574. Total strength of Brigade, 1,679.

2nd Brigade—Colonel Smith, Commanding, Captain Ewen, Major of Brigade.

1st Battalion—Major Lister, Commander, 3rd and 24th West Riding, headquarters, Bradford and Eccleshill, and 3rd Administrative Battalion, headquarters, Wakefield, Goole and Dewsbury, 587.

2nd Battalion—Major H. F. Beaumont, Commander, 6th and 32nd West West Riding, Huddersfield and Holmfirth, 332.

3rd Battalion—Major Ackroyd, Halifax, 255.

4th Battalion—Major Armitage, 7th West Riding, Leeds, 400.

5th Battalion—Major Wilson.

22nd Administrative Battalion—Skipton, North Craven, Burley, Guiseley and Ingleton, 326. Total strength of Brigade, 1,900.

3rd Brigade—Lieutenant-Colonel the Earl of Cathcart, Lieutenant-Colonel Crawford, Major of Brigade.

1st Battalion—Lieutenant-Colonel Pease, 1st East Riding, Hull, 258.

2nd Battalion—Major Saltmarshe.

2nd Administrative Battalion—Howden, Bridlington, Beverley, Driffield, Market Weighton, 280.

3rd Battalion, North Riding—Captain-Surgeon George Denys.

1st Administrative Battalion—Swaledale, Startforth, Bedale, Stokeley, Masham, Catterick, Richmond, Northallerton, 359.

4th Battalion—Lieutenant-Colonel the Honourable W. E. Duncombe, North Riding.

2nd Administrative Battalion—Malton, Ovingham, Scarborough, Helmsley, Thirsk, Pickering-Lythe, Pickering-Lythe East.

The Review was to commence at one o'clock. The preliminary evolutions having been gone through the Volunteers took up their position and awaited the arrival of the Reviewing Officer, General Sir George A. Wetherall, K.C.B., K.H., Volunteer Inspector for the northern and eastern district. He arrived on the ground at five minutes past three, accompanied by Earl Fitzwilliam, the Lord Lieutenant of the Riding, and a numerous and distinguished staff of military officers. Among the spectators were Earl de Grey and Ripon, Under Secretary of State for War, the Archbishop of York and others. The General first made an inspection of the arms and accoutrements, after which the other evolutions set down in the programme were proceeded with, but after the companies had gone through the movement of marching past the saluting point, which they did in a very commendable manner, worthy of regular troops, the General brought the review to a close, the ground being in such a state as almost to preclude the possibility of further evolutions being successfully carried out. The General, in addressing the commanding officers of the various regiments, said that he had no hesitation in saying that the Volunteers he had just reviewed were amongst the finest body of men he had seen and he had witnessed few Field days on which troops had drilled better. They were composed of men from agricultural and manufacturing districts combined and they laboured under considerable disadvantage. They deserved, however, great credit for their efficiency and he himself could scarcely imagine how they had acquired it. He was quite satisfied that the Yorkshire Volunteers were peculiarly fortunate in their officers. He did not allude to those in command of Brigades, because they were well known soldiers, but he referred to the regimental officers. "I only hope," he added, "that you will continue these exertions, the beneficial effects of which are now so manifest, and that in the course of this year you will begin to complete your drill by ascertaining the use and full power of the beautiful arm which the men possess. In other counties they have established prizes—probably on too liberal a scale—and I cannot instance a better proof of the zeal which actuates the men than the fact that there were 1,270 competitors for prizes at a recent shooting contest in Lancashire. Every one felt himself a rifleman and many of them fired remarkably well. I hope you will encourage this competition as much as possible. It will give me great pleasure to report favourably to the Secretary for War of the appearance of the troops on this occasion, and I hope on some future occasion I shall have the happiness of meeting you all again."

The cost of refreshments for the men was liberally defrayed by the Lords Lieutenant of the three ridings.

Banquet in the Guildhall, York.

A grand military banquet was held at the Guildhall, in York, after this memorable review. The Archbishop of York, Earl Fitzwilliam, Earl de Grey and Ripon, Earl Cathcart, Lord Teignmouth, Lord Bolton, the Dean of York, Admiral Duncombe, M.P., the Honourable W. E. Duncombe, M.P., were among the guests. The Lord Mayor of the northern capital presided. It will be within the memory of many of my readers that the distinguished statesman who was afterwards so worthily to represent his sovereign as Viceroy of India was at that time Secretary at War, and I make no apology for reproducing the substance of his remarks anent the Volunteer movement. In speaking to the force of Volunteers, he said :—

"If we consider what has been the history and the circumstances of this great movement I think we must all be convinced that it is one of the most remarkable which has ever taken place in this country. Eighteen months ago, or perhaps a little more, with the exception, I think, of two Volunteer Corps that had been formed a year or two before the rush of the war, there was not one of that gallant array, numbering about 150,000 men, which since that time has been created by the patriotism and loyalty of England. We are satisfied with the position and reputation of the country, we do not desire that that position should be lowered or that our reputation should be lost, and therefore, when the conviction seized on the public mind that we were not in that state of defence we should be to ensure our independence, the English people came forward to place the country in an adequate degree of defence. One of these methods was this great Volunteer movement. It is not that we underrate the value of that first line of defence, the navy of England, nor that we underrate the importance of also maintaining at home a sufficient force of Regular troops, but we feel that these forces require to be supplemented. It is therefore necessary to appeal to the patriotism of the people and to ask them to come forward freely, at their own expense, to defend their own homes and nobly answer the appeal. You must recollect that the eyes of all Europe are upon you. If you read the foreign newspapers you will find how this movement is discussed and criticised, sometimes in a friendly, sometimes in a less friendly, spirit. Nevertheless we have ample proof that it is attracting a great amount of attention in other countries. I believe the effect of it has been of importance to the peace of the world, but it would be sad to think that in a year or two other nations would be able to say, 'Oh yes! the English were under the influence of custom; they raised this great army, as they called it, of 150,000 men, but when the fashion had gone it has melted away like the snow before the sun.' Let not that be said. The object before us is the permanence of the force and that permanence depends on the one simple matter, economy. If the movement is to be unnecessarily expensive it cannot be permanent. The Government has done much to afford what assistance it could, but the very essence of the movement is that it should be voluntary and not expensive to the country, because, if it were, it would change its nature and would no longer have those claims on our admiration and respect which it now commands. Whether the Government may be able to do more than it has done for the movement, financially or otherwise, depends on the people and the Volunteers themselves. Therefore the first matter to be looked at, as we in Yorkshire understand the question of finance, is that not a shilling be spent without necessity, that the funds of the corps be husbanded for the times which will come. I will also add that however proud we may be of the series of reviews which have been witnessed in this country, they will miss their object if they do not serve to stimulate our zeal and increase our determination to make the Volunteer force a permanent addition to the military strength of the country."

It must not be supposed that dinners, reviews, Court presentations and drills engrossed the energies of the Huddersfield Corps.

On August 1st, 1860, the first attempt at prize shooting took place. It was not what might be termed an authorised prize shooting meeting, but assumed the shape of a sweepstake. Twenty members of the corps, principally from 1 and 2 companies, subscribed for the purpose of awarding prizes to the three best shots, each competitor being allowed three rounds at three separate ranges of 100, 150 and 300 yards. There were fourteen competitors, the remaining subscribers consenting to forfeit their subscriptions. The firing commenced about three o'clock and lasted till five. The following was the result :— **August 1st, 1860, First Prize Shooting.**

"Private John Bickerdike (1st Company) won the first prize, having scored twelve points.

For the second prize there was a good contest. Sergeant-Major Brook, Corporal Dransfield (2nd Company) and Private William Watkinson (1st Company), each scored eleven points, and, to decide the superiority, each shot off an additional round at a 200 range. The result of this was that Corporal Dransfield headed his opponents by lodging the contents of his rifle in the bull's eye, thus scoring three points.

The contest for the third prize then lay between Private Watkinson and Sergeant-Major Brook, and the result was that Watkinson scored two and Brook one, Watkinson thus obtaining the third prize."

Considering the little practice the men had had the firing was very good, and many of those who did not obtain prizes acquitted themselves very creditably.

The shooting practices of the corps did not always pass without untoward incident. Adjutant Greer, in a letter to the *Huddersfield Chronicle*, of October 20th, 1860, complained that the shooting ground at Gledholt was very unsafe. He considered it so owing to the irregularity of the ground between the shooting point and the target, because the undulations in the ground caused the projectile to ricochet, and that, consequently, the best shot was never sure of striking the target, and, in his opinion, this would account for the wandering propensity of the bullet, which is not the fault of the firer.

Adjutant Greer's letter may have been evoked by an incident reported in the same journal, on September 29th :—

Shooting Casualties

"Another incident occurred this week shewing the extreme danger to life arising from the Rifle practice in the present ground under its present conditions. On Wednesday last about 8 a.m. as a servant of Mr. W. Wrigley, manufacturer, who resides at Springdale, just over the Longroyd Bridge, was proceeding up the kitchen stairs she heard something strike a pane of a window over the kitchen door, which it passed through, and struck the wall of the stair passage about a yard above her head. On examination this was found to be a conical rifle ball which had proceeded from the practice ground, near Gledholt Lane. It had passed clean through the glass, making a hole scarcely larger than itself, travelled a passage 8 or 10 yards long, and indented the wall where it struck to the depth of a quarter of an inch, the ball itself being flattened and grazed on one of its sides. Had the point of entry to Mr. Wrigley's house been a yard lower the ball would have caught the servant as she was passing upstairs and life might have been sacrificed. Within 2 yards of the spot of entry and on the same level were two of Mr. Wrigley's sons, dressing at a window. This is the second instance of a ball from the rifle ground entering dwellings in the neighbourhood of Longroyd Bridge, shewing that the conditions of safety do not exist at the butts."

Another incident gave rise in the corps to a joke that never staled and origin to the saying, "Who shot the lamb?," the poor thing falling a victim to the maladroitness of a Volunteer practising at the butts. "The Bugle," for May 7th, 1901, records the following humorous event that may well serve to enliven pages too full of somewhat tedious details :—

"A Prize Shooting Record.

In the middle sixties of the last century, which, as in the case of 'the days we went a-gipsying,' seems 'a long time ago,' the prize list had been completed for the annual competition of the Huddersfield Volunteers, when a gentleman residing in the Edgerton district, who, alas, has since joined the majority, sent a cheque for three guineas to go to the prize fund. As the list was already made out there was a little cogitation over the matter, and finally it was decided that as a sort of reward for good services, Sergeant-Major Hunnybell, an excellent and popular man, should arrange some kind of a contest whereby the three guineas would go to the three assistants in the armoury, who cleaned the rifles and generally kept the place tidy. Now those of the assistants who had been in the army had shouldered a musket in the days when the authorities believed more in cold steel than in leaden bullets, and the sergeant-major had much doubt as to their shooting capabilities. But as it would not have done to have tossed for the prizes he arranged a shooting contest, with conditions which reduced the chance of mishaps to the lowest possible point. The conditions were one round each, at 400 yards, at the Ashenhurst range. The men were solemnly marched to the range, the contest duly came off, and the names of the winners and the prizes they won were duly recorded in the local papers. But, perhaps from an excess of modesty on the part of the competitors, the scores were not recorded. Now we give them: first score an outer, prize £1 11s. 6d.; second, a ricochet hit, prize £1 10s. od.; third, a miss, prize 10s. 6d. This record has not yet been surpassed."

Up to November, 1860, the inspections by Her Majesty's Inspector had only been of individual companies, and as the corps had never up to this time been inspected as a battalion, I give a full account of what was the first inspection of the corps as a battalion:— Inspection, Nov., 1866.

On the 17th November Major Harman made the first inspection of the battalion consisting of 4 companies.

At half-past three the corps paraded at the Cloth Hall under the command of the Adjutant and marched to the Drill ground at Gledholt, entering it from Trinity Street. The weather, though fine, had been, some days previous to the inspection, very unfavourable, and the ground was in a very bad state and it was evident the men would not be seen to advantage and that, the climatic conditions being unfavourable, the drilling would suffer in consequence.

The Inspecting Officer appeared on the ground at half-past four accompanied by Captain Bentley Shaw, upon whom, as senior officer of the corps, devolved the duties of major in the unavoidable absence of Major H. F. Beaumont. The drill comprised the usual battalion movements and manual and platoon exercises. Before the inspection was over, however, darkness set in and almost obscured the various movements. At the close of the inspection Major Harman addressed congratulatory remarks on the satisfactory manner in which the evolutions had been performed. He reported having inspected the drill ground, and said he was of opinion that if in the firing that took place due care was exercised and precaution taken it was impossible that an accident could happen, and if an accident did happen it would be through the negligence of the firer. He impressed upon the men the necessity for keeping their rifles clean. He had gone through the Armoury and regretted to find that some of the rifles were not in so clean a state as he could desire, but that might possibly occur because they were not under the men's care."

The report of the Inspector may well be supplemented by that of the secretary. It is as follows:— Report of Secretary, Nov., 1860.

"The 1st Company is a self-supporting one, members finding themselves in everything, the officers being thus relieved of all expense but that of their own uniforms and personal expenditure only.

On the first formation some exceptions were made, a few had, more or less, their outfits and rifles found out of the general funds. This is being rectified by the officers advancing money to pay and getting these members gradually to repay them by buying of them their outfit and rifles. Very few remain of this class of assisted members; and no new ones are admitted who do not provide everything. Cost of full outfit, including rifle, is from £10 os. od. to £10 10s. od.

2nd Company, composed partly, in the ratio of one third, of self supporting members of the class of small tradesmen, clerks and higher class of warehousemen and some professional men, the rest are artizans, not from any particular place of business or employer, but from all quarters. The general public funds assist in equipping this company by the grant of £133 6s. 8d.

Each man's equipment and clothing cost him from £4 to £5. They use the Government rifle.

With the half of the £133 6s. 8d. the officers get the whole equipped and are receiving back from the men 50/- each by 1/- per week.

3rd Company, composed almost entirely of artizans, the self supporting members not exceeding above a dozen. The £133 6s. 8d. grant was made to this company and the officers are trying to get refunded by weekly instalments. The members of this company are mostly employees of Messrs. James Learoyd and Sons, manufacturers, Leeds Road, and Messrs. John Day and Sons, manufacturers, and Messrs. E. T. Monk and Company, silk spinners, Moldgreen. They use the Government rifle.

4th Company has a larger number of self supporting members than No. 3; probably from one-fourth to one-third are self supporting. The rest are artizans from all quarters, not the workmen of any particular firm. This company also received £133 6s. 8d. grant, and the officers seek refunding from the artizans by weekly instalments. They use the Government rifle"

Strength of the several companies at this period.

I can find no trace of any records of the strength of the battalion at this inspection. I am, however, able to give an accurate account of the strength of the corps at this time, taken from an old drill book which records the attendances at drill and the names of all the officers, non-commissioned officers and men as on the 30th November, 1860.

I extract from this book the names of the captains, subalterns, sergeants and corporals of each of the four companies at this period, as the information will doubtless prove interesting :—

Major H. F. Beaumont, Commanding.

No. 1 Company—Captain Joseph Batley; Lieutenant Thomas Rymer Webb; Ensign Henry Broughton Dyson; Sergeant-Major William Brooke; Sergeants Alexander Hannah, Joseph Bottomley, junior, David Boscovitz and R. Sissons; Corporals W. Abbey, J. Brook and Andrew Thomas Anderson; and 59 men. Total of all ranks, 70.

No. 2 Company—Captain Thomas Pearson Crosland; Lieutenant Thomas Brook (Colne Villa) and Ensign Frederick Greenwood; Sergeants William Lawton, W. Moore, M. H. Hirst; Corporals William Dransfield, W. Hanson, Benjamin Hall, L. D. Clayton; and 88 men. Total of all ranks, 98.

No. 3 Company—Captain Thomas Brooke (Northgate House); Lieutenant Tom Learoyd and Ensign Joshua Day; Sergeants Edwin Learoyd, Joe B. Richardson, Albert John Learoyd and Edwin Mills; Corporals Edwin Bray, Thomas Beaumont, William Moorhouse and John Sutherland; and 61 men. Total of all ranks, 72.

No. 4 Company—Captain Bentley Shaw; Lieutenant John Haigh (Lascelles Hall) and Ensign George Henry Greenwood; Sergeants C. J. Graham, Joe Roberts, F. G. Abbey and John Jagger; Corporals William Hutchison and Edward Brown; and 54 men. Total of all ranks, 63.

Volunteer Ball, 18th January, 1861.

A new and pleasant experience was enjoyed by the Huddersfield Volunteers in the first month of the year 1861. A military ball was given in the Gymnasium Hall (now the public baths, in Ramsden Street), in aid of the funds of the corps. This was, I imagine, the first ball of the kind ever witnessed in Huddersfield. It was, of course, attended by the officers and the ladies whom they escorted, by many of the men, their wives and sweethearts. That was only natural; but the ball presented to the civilian population also an irresistible attraction, and the daughters of serious business men, of grave divines and of severe doctors and lawyers proved, by the zest with which they trod the mazes of the dance, that not merely when the war's alarms affright the soul but also in our lighter moods the smile of beauty is still the mead of valour. I may mention here that one of the youngest of the guests was Charles Edward Freeman (now Registrar of the Huddersfield County Court), but then, or up to a very short time before, a school boy at St. Peter's School, York. He attended the ball in the uniform of a private of the 4th (St. Peter's) company of the 1st West Yorkshire Rifle Volunteers, a light grey uniform with buff accoutrements, which well became the youthful volunteer. Mr. Freeman was thus from the first identified with the Volunteer movement. On leaving school in July, 1861, to enter upon his legal studies in Huddersfield, he was transferred to the Huddersfield Rifle Corps, of which he became an ensign in 1863, was promoted lieutenant in 1866, captain 1868, major commandant of the 6th corps in 1873, major of the 5th Administrative Battalion in 1874, lieutenant-colonel in 1882 and honorary colonel in 1886. Lieutenant-Colonel Freeman gained his captain's certificate in 1871, the Field Officer's certificate in 1873, and later passed the Tactical Examination and received the Volunteer Decoration. He won golden opinions from all ranks in every office he assumed in the corps. He was popular with the men and respected by them. He was zealous in the discharge of his duties, knowing how to secure discipline without severity. His geniality and his ability won the ready co-operation of his brother officers and his devotion to his duty stimulated them to friendly rivalry. At the time he assumed the chief command the corps was in a but languishing condition, it seemed to be under a sinister blight. The vigour of Lieutenant-Colonel Freeman's administration galvanized the corps

Lieut.-Col. Freeman's first connection with Corps.

to new life and rescued it from the dissolution which seemed to overhang it. The battalion gradually attained its full strength of 1,006 officers and men and a very high state of efficiency. More than once during his command it gained the first position in the Government Musketry Returns for England and Wales and on one occasion was second on the list for Great Britain. When Lieutenant-Colonel Freeman retired from the service he carried with him the affectionate goodwill and sincere esteem of all who had been associated with him, alike officers and men, as well as that of the public.

Presentation to Mr. Battye.

To another event of the year 1861 I allude with peculiar pleasure—the presentation of a substantial recognition to Mr. T. H. Battye, the honorary secretary of the corps, of his great and unwearying services. It has been my duty, in collecting and collating the materials for this work, to peruse the correspondence entailed upon Mr. Battye in the inception and furtherance of the work in which he engaged as honorary secretary, and I can therefore appreciate, as few others could, the value and extent of his labours. The presentation was made on Saturday, March 31st, 1861, in St. George's Square, Captain T. P. Crosland, in the absence of Major H. F. Beaumont, having the gratification of handing to Mr. Battye a handsome silver cup containing a purse of fifty sovereigns. The cup was elegantly chased and upon its bowl was engraved a representation of volunteers in practice. A rifleman in full dress was moulded on the lid of the cup, which was inscribed: "Presented, with a purse of fifty sovereigns, to T. H. Battye, Esq., by the honorary and effective members of the 6th West York Volunteer Rifles as a testimonial to his valuable services as honorary secretary during the formation and progress of the corps." The corps and a large body of other spectators witnessed the presentation, in making which Captain Crosland said:—

"Volunteers of the 6th West Riding of Yorkshire, I have to-day a very pleasing though somewhat difficult duty to perform. I had hoped this duty would have fallen into other hands; but the absence through necessity of our Commanding Officer devolves on me the duty which I now proceed to discharge. I can assure you that although I feel some difficulty adequately to express the feelings of Major Beaumont, the officers, non-commissioned officers and Volunteers of the 6th West, I am not aware that ever I had a duty to perform more in accordance with my own inclination. The object for which we are met together is to do honour to whom honour is due. In our honorary secretary, Thomas Hudson Battye, Esquire, we found an early friend, a firm and steadfast adherent and one who, through good report and evil report, has stood firmly by the Volunteers. At the commencement of this movement, when it had taken very little hold on the feelings and the affections of the people of Huddersfield, we found our honorary secretary labouring early and late to place this Huddersfield of ours in as proud a position as that of any of the neighbouring towns; and I must say that to his indefatigable efforts is mainly owing the spectacle we are able to present to-day. There are none but those who have worked with him that can possibly form any estimate of the time and trouble that gentleman has given to the affairs of this corps; and I believe that I merely express the earnest wish of every Volunteer connected with us when I say that I hope he may long be spared to continue his exertions in this good and national cause; that he may long be spared to live in our estimation and affections as he does this day. I may safely say that that small token of our regard (pointing to the cup), lined as it is with 50 sovereigns, is only a very inadequate expression of what our feelings towards him really are. And now, sir, (continued the gallant Captain, addressing Mr. Battye), I am commanded by Major Beaumont on his behalf specially to thank you for the efforts you have made. As I have already said, this corps owes you a lasting debt of gratitude for the services you have rendered, which I hope they will endeavour in some measure to repay by allowing you the pleasing satisfaction of seeing the corps grow in strength, in solidity, in everything that will give to it a martial bearing, so that your great hopes and earnest wishes will be accomplished and Huddersfield placed amongst those towns of our country ready at any moment to defend their fatherland. I have the greatest possible pleasure in presenting to you this cup, beautiful in design, but accompanied by that which I am sure will be regarded by you as a higher recompense, the thanks not only of the Volunteers but of the population of this district."

Mr. Battye, in response, said: -

"Captain Crosland and Volunteers of the 6th West Yorkshire Rifles, the Rifle Volunteers are becoming an organized institution of the British nation. To a large extent they have accomplished the great desideratum of an inexpensive plan of keeping a large proportion of the population constantly instructed in the use of arms without taking them from the productive and ordinary occupations of life. Under it Great Britain has made advance in all the arts and pursuits of peace, with honest frankness and manly bearing among her neighbours, free from all fear of aggression, knowing she is always prepared for defence. That Great Britain may fearlessly progress in all the blessings of peace, may continue to glow as the bright western star of Europe, and by the clear and steady light of tried freedom, founded on tried institutions and the practice and diffusion of real Christianity, may be enabled to afford fostering aid and true guidance to the hundreds of millions of her East Indian subjects who own her sway in Asia; to her Colonies in the great continent of Australasia; her colony at the Cape in Africa; her kindred and other colonies in America and to her many island possessions in every ocean of this globe; and if, in evil times, aggressive wars should reach these shores, that all who are possessed of able hands and willing hearts may be prepared and instructed how to defend our gracious Queen, her Royal family, and this our Great Britain, are the aim and objects of the organization of the Rifle Volunteers. These objects are noble, they are grand, and the Volunteers who act in carrying them out are a noble band of patriots. The 6th West Yorkshire Rifle Volunteers form a worthy portion of this noble band; your ranks comprise much of the flower, the pride and promise of this my native town. I know that enterprise, endurance, perseverance and courage are characteristic qualities of my fellow townsmen. I doubt not you inherit and possess them. They are splendid qualities in all pursuits, whether in peace or war, they are sure leaders to success and victory; and if hostile aggression shall ever call you out to war I am confident that no corps of the Rifle Volunteers will acquit themselves with more heroic fortitude and bravery than the Huddersfield or 6th West Riding of Yorkshire. Captain Crosland and Volunteers of the 6th West Yorkshire Rifles, you have done me the honour to say that I have been largely instrumental in the first raising and forming you as a Rifle Corps; and you present me this handsome silver vase as a memorial of the kindly estimate you put upon my exertions. Your present includes also a sum of £50 with which you had intended to purchase other plate, but which it was suggested should be left to my own selection. The present is a very handsome one, worthy of you as the givers of it. It is very gratifying to me that you thus estimate and acknowledge my services. I accept your present with great pleasure; I shall always associate it with a proud and pleasant remembrance of you. I thank you heartily and as heartily I wish you all long and happy lives and a permanent and honourable career to the 6th West Riding of Yorkshire Rifle Volunteers."

General Annual Meeting, 1861.

At the general annual meeting for this year, held at the George Hotel, on Wednesday, May 8th, 1861, Captain Crosland in the chair, the following resolutions were passed:—

On the motion of Nicholas Carter, Esquire, seconded by Lieutenant Haigh:—

1—"That the accounts as presented up to 1st December, 1860, shewing a balance in hand of £19 7s. 1d., are satisfactory and passed.

On the motion of Captain Brooke, seconded by Lieutenant Brook:—

2—"That from 1st December, 1860, only one fund be recognised for all receipts and payments in relation to the battalion or regiment.

On the motion of Captain Batley, seconded by Lieutenant Brook:—

3—"That the following gentlemen, in addition to the captains of the four companies, are elected as the members of the Finance Committee for the year from 1st December, 1860, to 1st December, 1861, namely:—Mr. Joseph Brook, Mr. Nicholas Carter, Mr. Edward Stavenhagen and Mr. Frederick Learoyd.

On the motion of Captain and Adjutant Greer, seconded by Lieutenant Dyson:—

4—"That the thanks of this meeting are given to Mr. Laycock and Mr. Battye for their past services, and they are requested to continue them as Honorary Treasurer and Secretary for the current year, and that the same are accorded to the Finance Committee of the past year.

On the motion of J. C. Laycock, Esquire, seconded by Edward Stavenhagen, Esquire :—

> 5—"A further outlay being necessary for the completion of the present shooting ground and rendering it safe to the public and to procure and prepare another shooting ground of a much longer range, that this meeting considers these requirements are a good ground for another appeal to the public to contribute the necessary funds."

In speaking to the report, Captain Crosland said the public had subscribed £1,164 1s. 5d. ; expenditure amounted to £816 13s. 9d. He wished it to be understood that in that sum was comprised £400, which was very kindly voted by the committee to aid and assist the formation of artizan companies. £133 6s. 8d. to each of the three* companies was granted by the committee for that purpose. Without this aid it was admitted that three companies, consisting chiefly of artizans, could not have been constituted. It was rather suggested that other places did not like this method of procedure, but Huddersfield was about the first to set the example of practically carrying into effect artizan companies, and the corps had reason to be proud, not only of the attendance of the working classes for drill, but of the progress made and their efficiency. £216 16s. 6d. had been paid for current expenses, such as drill expenses, rent, drill room, &c. Total expenses, £1,033 10s. 3d. Estimates had been made in the year as to the probable expense attendant on keeping up the corps on a respectable footing, a meeting of officers had been called, and it was shewn that £600 at least would be required. This sum was soon raised. The Major handsomely contributed £135 towards it, being one-fifth of the whole, the officers of each of the four companies undertook to raise an equal sum, making £625, and another officer in connection with the corps had promised £30, thus making £655.

In July of this year instructions were received from the War Office for all long Enfield Rifles to be forwarded to the Armoury for the purpose of having them sent to the Tower in substitution for short Enfields.

Changes in commissions to end of 1861.

The following changes in commissions, from the inauguration of the corps to the end of 1861, are to be noticed :—

* No. 1 Company did not require any grant in aid, the privates subscribing, as I have said, 10/6 yearly to its fund, the officers subscribing sums that increased with their rank.

No. 1 Company.

Name.	Rank.	
Greer W. H.	Captain and Adjutant	Retired.
Chichester H. B.	Adjutant	
Beaumont H. F.	Captain—Captain Commandant—Major	
Batley Joseph	Lieutenant—Captain	
Harrison J. A.	Ensign	Retired.
Webb T. R.	Lieutenant	Retired.
Dyson H. B.	Ensign—Lieutenant	
Bradbury Thomas Haigh	Ensign	
Bottomley T. A.	Hon. Assistant-Surgeon—Surgeon	

No. 2 Company.

Crosland T. P.	Captain	
Brook Thomas, Colne Villa	Lieutenant	
Brooke Thomas, Northgate Mount	Ensign	Retired to be Captain of 3rd Co.
Greenwood F.	Ensign	Retired to be Lieutenant of 4th Co.
Kaye Anthony K.	Ensign	

No. 3 Company.

Brooke Thomas	Captain	
Learoyd Tom	Lieutenant	
Day Joshua	Ensign—Lieutenant	
Learoyd Albert John	Ensign	

No. 4 Company.

Shaw Bentley	Captain	Retired.
Haigh John	Lieutenant—Captain	Retired.
Greenwood G. H.	Ensign	Retired.
Greenwood F.	Lieutenant—Captain	
Tolson James	Ensign	
Beaumont Joseph Tyrrel	Lieutenant	
Greenwood F.	Honorary Assistant-Surgeon	Retired on appointment as Ensign.

Review at Knavesmire, Sep., 1861.

On September 25th, there was a great Review at Knavesmire, York, under great difficulties, the ground having been deluged with rain. About 5,000 men were present in the following order:—

1st Brigade consisted of Artillery and Engineers to the number of 500 and 400 respectively.

The 2nd Brigade consisted of Rifles, Colonel Smyth Commanding, Major H. Van Straubenzee, Major of Brigade.

1st Battalion—Lieutenant-Colonel Briggs, 1st W. R. Battalion, York, Harrogate, Knaresboro', Ripon, Tadcaster, 550.

2nd Battalion—Lieutenant-Colonel Holdsworth, 3rd W. R. Battalion, Wakefield, Goole, Dewsbury, Birstal and Selby, 370.

3rd Battalion—Major Saltmarshe, 1st E. R. Battalion, Howden, Bridlington, Beverley, Driffield, Market Weighton and Hedon, 260.

4th Battalion—Lieutenant-Colonel Earl of Cathcart, 1st N. R Battalion, Swaledale, Leyburn, Forcett, Bedale, Stokesley, Catterick, Richmond, Skelton, Northallerton, 300.

5th Battalion—Lieutenant-Colonel W. E. Duncombe, 2nd N. R. Battalion, Malton, Hovingham, Scarboro', Helmsley, Thirsk, Pickering, Lythe, Wydale, Brompton, 470.

6th Battalion—Major Cookson, 12th W. R. Battalion, Skipton, 18th Pontefract, 19th Rotherham, 25th Guiseley, 35th Keighley, 36th Rotherham, 37th Barnsley, 39th Bingley, 450.

3rd Brigade Rifles—Colonel Wade, C. B., Commanding, Major Dowker, Major of Brigade.

1st Battalion—Lieutenant-Colonel the Lord Wharncliffe, 2nd Hallamshire (Sheffield), 300.

2nd Battalion—Lieutenant-Colonel Akroyd, 4th W. R. Halifax, 360.

3rd Battalion—Major Beaumont, 6th W. R. Huddersfield (no number recorded) and 32nd W. R. Holmfirth, 80.

4th Battalion—Lieutenant-Colonel Markham, 7th W. R. Leeds, 450.

5th Battalion—Lieutenant-Colonel Peace, 1st E. R. Hull, 250.

6th Battalion—Lieutenant-Colonel Lister, 3rd W. R. Bradford, 320.

The 10th Royal Hussars, under Lieutenant-Colonel Baker, were present and took part in the Review.

The reviewing officer was Colonel McMurdo, C.B., Inspector General of Volunteers, assisted by Major Harman.

The closing months of the year 1861 and those of the beginning of the year 1862 were full of incidents and fraught with changes of grave moment for the Huddersfield Corps. On the 24th or 25th of November of the former year, Major Beaumont had intimated his desire to retire from the command, his reason being that he could not devote the time necessary for the proper performance of the duties of that office. This led the officers to hold a meeting on the 26th November, whereat it was resolved that Major Beaumont should be requested to delay sending in his resignation for a month to enable the officers to arrange, if possible, for the formation of an Administrative Battalion and so retain Major Beaumont with the rank of lieutenant-colonel, the idea being that his connection with the corps might be preserved without making those demands upon his time and personal attention which his frequent absence from home on public affairs prevented him giving. With this object, a scheme was propounded for the union of the rural companies of Rifle Volunteers at Holmfirth and Saddleworth with the Urban Battalion of the Huddersfield Rifle Corps. It was apprehended difficulties would present themselves in attaining the object in view through a supposed apprehension on the part of the Holmfirth and Saddleworth corps that their union with the Huddersfield corps might in some degree affect their independent local management and position. The suggestion of the formation of an Administrative Battalion was not new to the Huddersfield Corps for, as far back as July, 1859, it had been suggested to them by the Lord Lieutenant of the county that the formation of a battalion in connection with Halifax, Bradford, Wakefield, Leeds and other neighbouring places would be acceptable to the Government, who would sanction such an arrangement, but this suggestion fell through, now to be re-opened in a somewhat different manner or for a different reason.

Retirement of Major Beaumont.

The Holmfirth Corps was prepared to fall in with the suggestion, but Saddleworth was coy; the result being that an Administrative Battalion was not formed, and Major Beaumont, whose many and onerous duties prevented him giving to the work of his regiment that attention he felt it required, resigned his command and retired with the rank of Colonel, but he is on the strength of the battalion to this day.

Appointment of Major T. P. Crosland.

Captain Thomas Pearson Crosland was appointed Major-Commandant *vice* Major Beaumont promoted, his commission being dated the 8th of January, 1862. The officers could not have appointed a more popular or more deserving officer, and the corps was to be congratulated upon succeeding in securing such a popular commander. At one time there had been danger of his services and influence being lost to the corps, as I find on the 27th August, 1860, he wrote to Mr. T. H. Battye, the secretary, tendering his resignation as captain of the 2nd Company of the 6th Corps, alleging as his reason that he "was painfully forced to acknowledge that rest was absolutely necessary, not only for his own sake but for those who had a right to his first and most anxious consideration." Fortunately, however, other counsels prevailed, and he was persuaded to reconsider his decision and retain his captaincy.

The annual meeting of the corps for the year 1862 was held on January 22nd, at the George Hotel, Major Crosland presiding. The financial report for the year 1861 shewed a cash balance of £209 9s. od. A letter from Mr. Bentley Shaw—a constant and generous supporter of the movement from its inception—expressed the belief that it was the best "hearth and home insurance" the country ever subscribed to. The chairman referred to the anticipations entertained by some that the Volunteer movement would be the means of promoting loose habits among young men. That anticipation had not been realized in the slightest degree. The effect had been the reverse. There was nothing that could have had, in his opinion, a more moralizing effect upon the youth of the district than the Volunteer movement. After drill, there was no visiting public houses, no indulgence in loose habits, the conduct of the Volunteers generally had been such that the officers had good reason to be proud of them.

Annual Meeting, 1862.

In April of this year Captain J. Batley, junior, addressed to the members of No. 1 Company a very spirited reprimand for the laxity of their attendance at drill and on parade, Major Crosland in the same month having refused to take the battalion out for battalion drill on account of the very small number present. "If," said Captain Batley, "the young gentlemen who form a large proportion of this company cannot make up their minds to sacrifice, for only a couple of hours on a Saturday afternoon, billiards or other engagements of pleasure, they had better take their names from the roll and let us know how we stand and on whom we can depend. Better admit at once that they have made a mistake in joining the corps; that their self-denial and sense of duty to the movement are not strong enough to resist the little temptations that constantly arise to indulgence and pleasure."

Letter of Captain Batley to his Corps, April, 1862.

In April, 1862, the corps acquired on a yearly tenancy for drill purposes and field manœuvres a large field on the south side of Greenhead Lane, the shooting ground at Gledholt being still retained.

In March of the same year, the Cadet Corps, commanded by Colour-Sergeant Thomas Marshall Tolson, had been inaugurated, and 30 cadets, uniformed in red jackets and grey trousers, accompanied the Huddersfield Battalion to the Doncaster Review in August, 1862, but without taking any part in it. The following are the names and approximate strength of the various corps

March, 1862, Cadet Corps formed.

Doncaster Review, August, 1862.

represented at that Review, the reviewing officer being Colonel McMurdo, C.B., accompanied by Lieutenant-Colonel Harman, Assistant Inspector :—

First Brigade.

Lieutenant-Colonel Hardy, 11th Depôt Battalion, Commanding.

Artillery—Major Sir J. W. Ramsden, Bart., and Captain Commandant Creswick, Commanders, 1st Leeds, 250; 4th Sheffield, 140.

Engineers—Lieutenant-Colonel Child, Commander, 1st Sheffield, 60; 2nd Leeds, 300.

Rifles—1st, Lieutenant-Colonel Lord Wharncliffe, Commander, 2nd Sheffield, 300.

2nd, Lieutenant-Colonel Lister, Commander, 3rd Bradford, 270; 35th Keighley, 80; 39th Bingley, 50.

4th, Lieutenant-Colonel Akroyd, Commander, 4th Halifax, 300.

4th, Lieutenant-Colonel Markham, Commander, 7th Leeds, 300.

Second Brigade.

Lieutenant-Colonel Adams, 49th Regiment, Commanding.

Rifles—1st, Lieutenant-Colonel Briggs, Commander, 1st York, 200; 16th Harrogate, 50; 17th Knaresborough, 50; 27th Ripon, 50; 81st Tadcaster, 36; 33rd Wetherby, 50.

2nd, Lieutenant-Colonel Holdsworth, Commander, 5th Wakefield, 150; 28th Goole, 45; 29th Dewsbury, 60; 30th Birstal, 25; 37th Barnsley, 60; 38th Selby, 50.

3rd, Lieutenant-Colonel Perkins, Commander, 18th Pontefract, 60; 19th Rotherham, 50; 20th Doncaster, 50; 21st Doncaster, 60; 36th Rotherham, 55.

4th, Major Crosland, Commander, 6th Huddersfield, 200; 12th Skipton, 60; 26th Guiseley, 65; 32nd Holmfirth, 60; 34th Saddleworth, 63; altogether about 3,500 Volunteers present.

September, 1862, Review at Huddersfield.

A further Review was held before Lieutenant Colonel Harman on September 6th, 1862, at Springwood Park, Huddersfield. On the morning of the Review, Bentley Shaw, Esquire, of Woodfield House, presented the corps with a magnificent silver cup, handsomely chased, of the value of 40 guineas, as the gift of himself and Mrs. Bentley Shaw to the Rifle Corps. It bore the following inscription, "Challenge Cup presented by Mr. and Mrs. Bentley Shaw of Woodfield House, near Huddersfield, to the 6th West York Rifle Volunteers for annual competition, September 6th, 1862."

The number and distribution and force on the ground were as follows:—

Commander—Lieutenant-Colonel Harman.

Cavalry.	1st Squadron	Major Edwards, Commander	100
	2nd ,,	Captain Armitage, ,,	
Artillery.	Brigade	Captain W. M. Selwyn, ,,	176
Rifles.	1st Battalion, Bradford,	Captain H. S. Hirst, ,,	299
	2nd Battalion, Halifax,	Lieut.-Colonel Akroyd, ,,	297
	3rd Battalion, Huddersfield, Holmfirth and Saddleworth,	Major Crosland, ,,	400
Cadets, Huddersfield.		Colour-Sergeant Tolson.	65.

Total (exclusive of commissioned officers, 1,337.

The year 1862 saw the first authorised prize shooting meeting.

The following prizes were presented to the winners by Mrs. T. P. Crosland, wife of the major:—

H. F. Beaumont's Challenge Medal, with £5 added, to Private Wilson.

Charles Brook's Prize of £10—Corporal Haigh, 1st; Sergeant-Major Brooks, 2nd; Private David Robertson, 3rd.

Bentley Shaw Challenge Cup. The winner of the cup also to take £5 added to it by Major Crosland and be entitled to wear a medal, to be approved of by the major. Winner, Corporal Haigh.

Adjutant's Cup, value £5. Shooting was from an unknown distance, targets twelve inches, bull's eye four inches, one shot each. Won by Private Richardson.

Constable's Prize of £10—Private Robertson, winner.

Mrs. H. F. Beaumont's Prize for Long Enfield Rifle. Best shot at 100, 200 and 300 yards. Winner, Corporal Haigh.

All-comers' Prize, Silver Cup, value £10 and half the entrance fees. Private David Robertson took the Cup.

Samuel Wood Haigh's Prize of £5, divided between Sergeant-Major William Brook and Corporal Haigh.

The year 1863 is memorable in the history of the Huddersfield Volunteers for several reasons. In that year the corps entered upon possession of the new Drill Hall and Armoury in Ramsden Street, and the dark facings of the uniform were replaced by scarlet. A more melancholy interest attaches to the circumstance that on the 3rd June of this year died at his residence at Mount Edgerton, Sergeant Major William Brook, who had been a non-commissioned officer of the corps from its formation. He was connected by marriage with Mr. Alexander Hannah and Mr. Dunlop, of whose

First military interment.

association with earlier levies mention has been made. Sergeant Major Brook was the first Huddersfield Volunteer interred with military honours.

The expense of accommodating the former Riding School in Ramsden Street to the purposes of a Drill Hall and Armoury necessitated a fresh appeal for public assistance, and the following is the list of subscribers :—

Subscriptions towards fitting of the Armoury.

Mr. J. C. Laycock and Mr. Jere Kaye had exerted themselves greatly in canvassing for these subscriptions :—

	£	s.	d.
Charles Brook, junior ..	100	0	0
George Crosland & Sons	100	0	0
Starkey Brothers ..	100	0	0
Sir J. W. Ramsden, Bart.	50	0	0
Bentley & Shaw	50	0	0
J. C. Laycock	50	0	0
Jere Kaye	50	0	0
Joseph Hirst, of Wilshaw	50	0	0
J. & T. C. Wrigley & Co.	25	0	0
Fred Learoyd	25	0	0
William Brooke, Northgate House	20	0	0
Wm. Willans Greenwood	20	0	0
Nehemiah Learoyd ..	20	0	0
John Taylor & Sons, Queen Street South ..	20	0	0
Samuel Wood Haigh, Colne Bridge	20	0	0
Jonathan Haigh, Colne Bridge	20	0	0
James William Carlile, Meltham Mills	20	0	0
F. R. Jones, junior ..	20	0	0
Wright Mellor	10	10	0
Charles William Learoyd	10	10	0
Henry Crowther & Sons	10	10	0
John Sykes, Chairman of Improvement Commissioners	10	0	0
William Keighley ..	10	0	0
Huth & Fischer	10	0	0
David Marsden	10	0	0
Lowenthal Brothers ..	10	0	0
Joseph Sykes, Marsh House	10	0	0
Wm. Learoyd & Sons ..	10	0	0
John Day, Moldgreen ..	10	0	0
Carried forward	£871	10	0

	£	s.	d.
Brought forward	871	10	0
Jos. Senior Tolson, Dalton	10	0	0
Anonymous	10	0	0
Robt. Hy. Tolson, Dalton	10	0	0
Ed. Brooke, Fieldhouse..	10	0	0
Edward Lake Hesp ..	10	0	0
James Wrigley, Netherton	10	0	0
Wm. & Hy. Crosland ..	5	0	0
John Brooke, junr., Spring Vale	5	0	0
Thomson & Dodds ..	5	0	0
Charles William Sikes ..	5	0	0
William Milner	5	0	0
Thomas Brook, Solicitor	5	0	0
Thomas Denham.. ..	5	0	0
G. Holroyd	5	0	0
Jas. Nield Sykes, Lindley	5	0	0
William Sykes, junior ..	5	0	0
George Walker	5	0	0
Ben Lockwood & Co. ..	5	0	0
W. R. Haigh (A. & S. Henry & Co.)	5	0	0
Robert Townend Denton	5	0	0
Law Dyson	5	0	0
Edward G. Sykes, Lindley	5	0	0
F. Hoerle	3	3	0
Thomas Jennings Wigney	3	3	0
Abraham Hopkinson ..	2	10	0
James Burman & Co. ..	2	2	0
Samuel Bradley	2	2	0
E. H. Walker	2	2	0
Benjamin Thornton ..	2	2	0
William Henry Aston ..	2	2	0
Prince of Wales Ball Committee	2	2	0
Samuel Oakes	2	2	0
Total..	£1,035	0	0

On March 2nd, 1864, Major T. P. Crosland was promoted lieutenant-colonel of the 5th Administrative Battalion, consisting at this time of the Huddersfield and Holmfirth Corps. Captain Thomas Brooke, of Armitage Bridge, captain of No. 3 Company, was promoted major of the 6th corps. 1864.

On June 20th of this year 7,800 Volunteers were reviewed in the presence of an immense concourse of spectators at Doncaster, by Colonel McMurdo, who was accompanied by his principal staff officers, Colonel Harman and Captain Lonstaff. There were also present Earl Fitzwilliam, in the uniform of the lord lieutenant, his son, Lord Milton, Colonel Gascoigne, Lieutenant-Colonel Prothero and Sir John William Ramsden, Baronet. The troops reviewed were not drawn exclusively from the West Riding Corps, there being included those from the West and East Ridings, from Lincolnshire, Nottinghamshire and Leicestershire. Doncaster Review, 1864.

The field state of the Huddersfield and Holmfirth contingents was as follows :—

Corps.	Officers.	Sergeants, buglers, band and pioneers.	Rank and file.	Total.
6th West York Rifles	20	44	307	371
32nd West Riding (Holmfirth)	4	26	60	90
Huddersfield Cadets	1	25	60	86
			Total	547

A 5th Company was added to the 6th Corps on 1st March of this year, commanded by Captain James William Carlile, of Thickhollins Park, near Huddersfield, with Lieutenant Thomas Walker Brooke and Ensign Charles William Keighley as subalterns.

In March of this year also a concert was held for the purpose of providing uniforms for the drum and fife band of the Cadet Corps.

On April 8th, 1865, took place simultaneously throughout England, Scotland and Wales, Enfield rifle contests. In that competition over 5,000 Volunteers took part. 111 battalion squads furnished 20 members each, 298 companies 10 members each. Eight prizes of the aggregate value of £138 were awarded to those company squads making the highest scores—the team of the 6th West Yorkshire (Huddersfield) were amongst the first eight highest scorers in company teams and won a money prize of £5 with a total score of 515. The Huddersfield team were Lieutenant Simultaneous National Rifle Contests, 1865.

H. W. Haigh, Sergeant John Brook, Corporal F. Haigh, Corporal James Eddell, Corporal Herbert Wigney, Privates Alexander Brook, G. H. Crowther, F. R. Crowther, J. H. Wilson and A. Hoyle. The winning Huddersfield team expended the £5 in the purchase of a silver cup, on which the names and score of the ten Huddersfield representatives were inscribed. It was presented to Captain Batley as an expression of the esteem in which he was held by his comrades in arms.

Presentation to Captain Batley.

Committee of enquiry into Corps Finances, 1865.

Other proceedings in this year were not so satisfactory. It became necessary to appoint a committee to investigate the accounts of the corps with a view to making expenditure square with income. The committee reported that whilst the officers had, in the preceding year, paid to the battalion fund £525 16s. 8d, the 400 men composing the battalion had earned in capitation grant only £194 10s. od. The committee suggested as a remedy for this anything but creditable state of affairs that every member of the corps be compelled to earn the capitation grant of 20/- by attendance at the requisite number of drills or to pay the amount of the same to the funds of the corps or be expelled, such expulsion and its cause to be announced in Orders. Every member was also to attempt to earn the capitation grant of 10/- for period shooting, with the alternative of paying it himself or being expelled.

It was stated by the committee that the amount paid by the Huddersfield Corps to the Battalion Fund was higher than that paid by the officers of any other corps of Volunteers.

In April, also of this year, Mr. F. K. Crook was appointed to the command of the Cadet Corps on the resignation of Mr. Thomas Marshall Tolson.

Review at York, August, 1866.

On 11th August, 1866, the 6th West Yorkshire joined in a grand Review at York, on which occasion were present the Prince and Princess of Wales, who were accompanied by the Archbishop of York and a select company. The Prince of Wales was dressed in uniform and surrounded by a brilliant staff. Immediately on the arrival of the rest of the party the Reviewing Officer, His Royal Highness the Duke of Cambridge, accompanied by his staff, including many officers of military distinction, and the Right Honourable the Earl of Fitzwilliam, Lord Lieutenant of the West Riding, took up their positions in front of the saluting flag, and the field operations commenced at once with a march of the artillery. The engineers and rifles then followed. Marching past was creditably performed. The Robin Hood Corps, which had, from its commencement, enjoyed a reputation for the precision of its movements, fully sustained its character, and was the only corps on the ground which was honoured with a cheer as it passed the saluting flag. The march past occupied three-quarters of an hour.

The field strength of the 5th A.B. was as follows:—

Corps.	Officers.	Sergeants, Buglers and Band.	Rank and File.	Total.
6th West York, Staff ..	1	25	..	26
Ditto—No. 1 Company	1	5	44	50
No. 2 Company	3	6	74	83
No. 3 Company	3	6	63	72
No. 4 Company	3	5	53	61
No. 5 Company	3	5	50	58
6th West York	14	52	284	350
32nd West York (Holmfirth)	3	30	62	95
41st West York (Mirfield)	4	35	52	91
5th A.B., Staff	2	4	..	6
Total, 5th A.B.	23	121	398	542

The Duke of Cambridge wrote to the Secretary of War the following letter:—

"Grimiston, Tadcaster,
August 12th, 1866.

Sir,

I have the honour to report to you that I inspected yesterday at York 20,000 Volunteers there assembled under the orders of Lieutenant-General Sir Sidney Cotton, K.C.B., and composed of corps belonging to the northern and midland counties of England. Nothing could be more satisfactory than the general appearance and efficiency of these corps. Several batteries of Field Artillery were on the ground, all in creditable order, and the general efficiency of the battalion of Garrison Artillery and Infantry was very striking, reflecting the greatest credit on the commanding officers of regiments and on the officers and rank and file of the several corps reviewed. There was an excellent march past and subsequently a few evolutions were performed with as much steadiness and precision as could be expected from so large a body of men suddenly brought together.

Every credit is due to the Inspector-General of Volunteers, Colonel Erskine, and his assistants for the manner in which the several corps coming from various parts of the country were brought on the ground by the appointed time.

I was enabled at the end of the day's proceedings to express my entire satisfaction to the assembled commanding officers at the result of their exertions and I feel satisfied that the volunteer organization of the country is progressing in such a manner as to justify the most perfect confidence in its continued success and for their extension.

I have the honour to be, Sir,
Your obedient servant,
GEORGE.

The Right Honourable the Secretary of State for War."

The Secretary of State briefly replied:—

"War Office, August 15th, 1866.

Sir,

I have the honour to acknowledge the receipt of your Royal Highness' letter of the 12th instant relative to the Review of Volunteers which took place at York on the 11th instant, and, in reply, to express my gratification at receiving the very favourable account which your Royal Highness has given of the efficiency of the Volunteer corps which took part in the Review.

I have the honour to be, Sir,

Your Royal Highness' most obedient servant,

(Signed), J. PEEL.

Field Marshal His Royal Highness the Duke of Cambridge, K.G."

The 5th Administrative Battalion present at this Review was constituted, it will be observed, of five companies of the 6th West York, one company of the 32nd West York (Holmfirth) and one company of the 41st West York (Mirfield), which had then recently been attached to the Huddersfield Corps.

Resignation of Lieut-Col. Crosland.

In September of the same year, Lieutenant-Colonel T. P. Crosland felt himself constrained to resign his position owing to the great strain upon him caused by his election to the parliamentary representation of Huddersfield. He retired with the rank of Honorary Colonel, and Major Thomas Brooke, of Northgate House, was promoted Lieutenant-Colonel of the 5th Administrative Battalion.

Appointment of Major Thos. Brooke as Lieut.-Col.

Lieutenant-Colonel Brooke was eminently qualified to assume the chief command. He had been one of the first officers of the corps, though at one time his connection with it threatened to be but short-lived. As early as January 18th, 1860, when the 1st Company was but a few months old, Mr. Brooke had desired to sever his connection with the Volunteers but was persuaded to continue his services. He rose rapidly from rank to rank. He spared no pains to qualify himself for the duties of his post. Though probably one of the hardest worked men in the district, filling many public positions exacting time and labour, he yet contrived to undergo the course of musketry instruction at Hythe. As an officer he was an exemplary disciplinarian. His most intimate friend among the officers must not presume upon that intimacy to omit one jot or one tittle of any, the least, of his duties, in the expectation that it would secure him from reproof. Exacting in the performance of every duty, he went the best way to assure it by himself being assiduous in the discharge of his own. Every officer and every private felt that what their commanding officer insisted upon from others was what he himself rendered, and there is no need to seek further explanation of that efficiency in all branches of the corps which marked Colonel Brooke's administration. It is only necessary to add that Colonel Brooke had the rare gift of combining with strictness a winning geniality and consideration that made his subordinate officers his eager assistants and made, too, every private feel that he had in the colonel a personal friend.

Resignation of Captain Batley.

The autumn of 1866 witnessed a well-merited recognition by his company of the services Captain Batley had rendered to the company, the corps and the movement generally. In October, Mr. Batley felt constrained, probably by the increasing demands of his profession, to resign his commission, and No. 1 Company presented to him a silver claret jug and six silver drinking cups. The jug was inscribed: "Presented to Captain Batley, on his retirement from the command of No. 1 Company of the 6th West York Rifle Volunteers, by its present and late members in recognition of his long and valuable services. Huddersfield, October, 1866."

Promotion of and Presentation to Captain Greenwood.

In this same year, Captain Frederick Greenwood (No. 4 Company) also received a well-deserved recognition. Consequent on Major Thomas Brooke's promotion to the command of the 5th A.B., Captain Greenwood was promoted Major of the 6th corps, and on taking leave of his company Colour Sergeant Dixon presented him, on its behalf, with a sword bearing the following inscription: "Presented by the non-commissioned officers of the 6th West York Rifles and privates of No. 4 Company to Major Greenwood, their late Captain, as a mark of respect and esteem. Huddersfield, November, 1866."

1867. Two new Companies, the 6th & 7th.

The year 1867 was signalized by the addition of two new companies to the corps, the 6th and 7th. The first of these was mainly recruited from Outlane and the parts adjacent. The members of that company had the satisfaction of knowing that hard by their own dwellings lay hidden in and preserved by the kindly earth the remains of the first camp known to have been established in this neighbourhood, the camp of the third Cohort of the Breuci auxiliaries of the all-conquering legions of ancient Rome. Major Greenwood had been very active in the formation of the Outlane Company, as indeed he was of others, and I should do violence to my own feelings were I to omit here an expression of the high sense entertained by all the gallant Major's brother officers of his great zeal and untiring labours in the furtherance of the Volunteer movement in general and his constant devotion to the duties of

The services of Major Greenwood in their formation.

every rank he held in the corps with which he was connected. It may not be improper to mention here that the late Colonel Bradbury of the 34th West Riding (Saddleworth) Corps had, not unnaturally, regarded Outlane as a likely recruiting sphere for his own corps and had taken steps to enrol members from that district, but the preference displayed for alliance with the Huddersfield Corps was so manifest and so intelligible that Colonel Bradbury ceased his endeavours.

6th Company officially sanctioned, 8th January, 1868

The first and only officers of this Company, which was numbered 6th in the Huddersfield corps, and officially sanctioned in January, 1868, were Captain James Walker Sykes, of Gosport Mills; Lieutenant Benjamin Casson, high bailiff, Huddersfield County Court; Ensign James Cooper; and Dr. J. E. Crowther, of Stainland, as surgeon.

Captain Sykes bore the sole cost both of drill field and drill room. This company usually marched from Outlane to Huddersfield and back again for battalion drill, a distance of some eight miles. The company drilled in John Ainley's field in fine weather and in the Outlane National School in wet weather, and had their shooting ground on Johnny Brook's Common, Outlane Moor.

On the 25th January of this year the style, "Huddersfield Rifle Volunteer Corps," was sanctioned.

Dec., 1868, 7th Company formed.

In December of the same year was formed the Lindley Company (No. 7), largely from the employees of the great manufacturing firms of Messrs. Joseph Sykes & Sons, Messrs. Joseph Walker & Sons and Messrs. Liddell, Bennett & Martin (now Martin, Sons & Company, Limited).

The first officers of this company were Captain C. E. Freeman, Lieutenant George Henry Crowther and Ensign Robert Mellor.

Formation of No. 8 Company, Mar., 1868.

In March the Lockwood Company was formed (No. 8).

Captain R. Lowenthal was first in command, with Lieutenant James Priestley and Ensign Joe Roberts as subalterns, and in 1871 Mr. James Priestley became captain on the transference of Captain Lowenthal to the command of one of the town companies.

1868, Major Greenwood Lieut.-Col. of the 6th Corps.

The year 1868 was, for the Volunteers of Huddersfield and its vicinity, fraught with events of great pith and moment. In January the gallant officer to whose services I have paid a perhaps inadequate tribute received the official recognition that was their due, and Major Greenwood was in January gazetted lieutenant-colonel of the 6th corps. A gloom was cast over the corps in the following March by the death of Colonel T. P. Crosland. The most careless perusal of these records must have impressed the reader with a sense of the devotion of Colonel Crosland to the Volunteer movement. From the first he embraced that cause with ardour and with that dogged determination to achieve success which, sparing no effort and no sacrifice, ensures the consummation sought. In 1865 Mr. Crosland had been returned to Parliament, and it is more than probable that his transfer, somewhat late in life, to a new and unaccustomed sphere of effort, hastened his end. Colonel Crosland was a man of robust sense, shrewd practicality and great endeavour. His general *bonhommie* was of more effective service to him than much laboured argument to his political opponents, whilst it secured for him the attachment of those among whom he lived. He was interred with military honours in the Cemetery at Huddersfield, 550 Volunteers of all ranks from the 6th West York (Huddersfield), 32nd West York (Holmfirth) and 41st (Mirfield) Corps, accompanying the sad procession, their new lieutenant-colonel at their head. **Death of Col Crosland.**

The ladies of Huddersfield, their committee being Mesdames Tom Learoyd, Edwin Learoyd, John Day, Lawton, Hartley and Bradley, presented to the band of the Huddersfield Corps a set of instruments, with cases, purchased at a cost of some £115, raised by subscription. **1868. Presentation of Band Instruments.**

Not content with this the ladies determined to solicit subscriptions to enable them to purchase two elegant flags. Their exertions to this end were as successful as their previous effort, and a Queen's and Regimental Colour were purchased at a cost of about 40 guineas. These colours are in strict conformity with the Regulations issued in September, 1858. The Queen's Colour is the "Union" throughout, bearing in the centre of the red cross of St. George an embroidered Royal Crown; below it, a long label or scroll of yellow silk, with the words, "VI. West York Rifle Volunteers." The Regimental Colour is of white silk with a red cross, having a small "Union" in the upper corner, next the head of the colour pole. In the centre of the red cross of St. George is a white embroidered heraldic rose, within a small girdle of yellow silk bearing the words, "Huddersfield, 1859." An embroidered wreath of roses, thistles and shamrocks surrounds the girdle, whilst below the wreath again is a long label or scroll of yellow silk, with the motto, "*Arma Pacis Fulcra.*" The Queen's Colours are surrounded or edged with red and gold fringe, the Regimental Colours with a gold and silver fringe; the poles themselves being surmounted with gilt ornaments, a lion and crown, representing the crest of England, and have crimson and gold cords and tassels.

868, March 28th, Presentation Colours. The colours were presented on Saturday, March 28th, by Mrs. Charles Brook, of Enderby Hall, in St. George's Square, in the presence of a large concourse of people. Colonel Bradbury, in command of the 34th West York Rifle Volunteers, also attended to form a line on the upper side of the Square near the two cannons, trophies of the Russian War, which then stood on the spot now occupied by the statue of Sir Robert Peel. Colonel Greenwood was in command of the Huddersfield Rifle Corps. They made three sides of the Square. Mrs. Charles Brook said: "Lieutenant-Colonel Greenwood, officers and privates of the Huddersfield Rifles, as a token of the high regard which Mrs. Captain Learoyd and the ladies of Huddersfield have towards your noble corps, I am requested to present for your acceptance these colours. In doing so we are quite sure that in your hands they will never be dishonoured. For myself, I feel greatly the honour conferred upon me in being selected by the ladies to present them to your battalion, for I am sure it is done in compliment to my husband, knowing, as we all do, the warm interest he ever takes in the prosperity and success of the Volunteers of our native town." Major Brook handed the Queen's colours to Mrs. Charles Brook, who, in passing them to Ensign C. W. Keighley, said:—"With heartfelt pleasure we present the Queen's colours to the Huddersfield Rifles." Captain J. W. Carlile then gave Mrs Brook the Huddersfield regimental colour, and in handing it to Ensign Cooper, Mrs. Brook said:—"With heartfelt pleasure we present the battalion colour to the Huddersfield Rifles. May they belong to our Queen and country." Lieutenant-Colonel Greenwood acknowledged the compliment which Mrs. Brook paid to the corps, to which Mr. Charles Brook replied, and a general salute having been given the band played, "Rule, Britannia," when the standard bearers, accompanied by Colour-Sergeants Cliffe, Golden, Anderson and Ware, marched in slow time down the Square, the band the while playing "God save the Queen," and took up a position in the centre of the line. Afterwards the Huddersfield battalion marched past in open column of companies in quick time and proceeded to the Armoury, where in the evening a Volunteer Ball fitly closed a pleasing ceremony.

1868, Huddersfield Enfield Rifle Club formed. In the early part of 1868, the "Huddersfield Enfield Rifle Club" was established in connection with the 5th Administrative Battalion—the principal objects being the general improvement in shooting of the members, the promotion of a more kindly feeling amongst the various companies and the better representation of the battalion at the County and All Comers' Meetings. This club was in addition to the various company shooting clubs which had been established with marked success since the formation of the corps. The president was :—

Lieutenant-Colonel Brooke.

Vice-Presidents—Lieutenant-Colonel Greenwood and Major Brook.

Captains—Morehouse, Carlile, Joshua Day, J. T. Beaumont, Tom Learoyd, Walker Sykes, William Lawton, Charles E. Freeman and Robert Lowenthal, with a committee consisting of Surgeon T. A. Bottomley, Assistant Surgeon John Dow, Honorary Quartermaster William Eddison, Lieutenants Thomas Walker Brooke, George Henry Crowther, Ensigns Thomas Green Beaumont, J. Dyson and Herbert Wigney, Sergeant-Major Hunneybell, Quartermaster Sergeant John Brook, Colour-Sergeants Avison, David Dixon, Golden and Jaggar, Sergeants J. Hirst and Thewlis, Corporals Beardsell, Pilling and Rhodes and Private Garthwaite, Honorary Treasurer, Private T. S. Yates and Honorary Secretary, Sergeant F. R. Crowther.

This club undoubtedly strengthened the *esprit de corps* amongst the members of the 5th Administrative Battalion, and thus accomplished the chief object sought by the promoters in its establishment.

In May of this year Major Henry Frederick Beaumont was promoted honorary colonel of the 6th corps, and is on the strength of the corps to this day.

Captain J. W. Carlile, of No. 5 Company, was in June promoted major of the 6th corps.

Strength of Corps, 1869.

The Government return of the strength, efficiency and earnings of capitation grant of the corps for the year 1869 was as follows:—

	Extra efficients, each claim 30/-.	Amount entitled, 20/-.	Non-efficients.	Total enrolled strength.
Huddersfield,	406	203	39	648
	Total capitation grant, £812.			
Holmfirth	75	16	19	110
	Total capitation grant, £128 10s.			
Mirfield	110	11	10	131
	Total capitation grant, £176.			
Meltham	45	2	7	54
	Total capitation grant, £67 10s.			

With the exception of the Review on Heath Common, Wakefield, the year 1870 was marked by few events calling for chronicle in these pages.

[illegible] Presentation to Lieut. William Laycock.

On 22nd April, 1870, Lieutenant William Laycock, the son of Mr. James Campey Laycock, who held a commission, it will be remembered, in the "Huddersfield Independent Association" in 1820, was compelled, through pressure of professional work, to discontinue his duties as a Volunteer, and on his taking leave of his company (No. 4) he was presented by the officers of that company, Captain J. Tyrrel Beaumont and Ensign Robert Potter Berry, and the non-commissioned officers and men comprising it, with a silver inkstand, suitably inscribed, as a testimony of the high esteem in which he was held.

1870, May 23rd. Death of Sergt. Major Hunneybell

On May 23rd, Sergeant-Major Hunneybell died. He received his appointment in October, 1861, when Honorary Colonel H. F. Beaumont was in command. He had been formerly Sergeant-Major in the 98th Regiment, and had served 18 years in China and the East Indies, and received two medals for service in the Punjab and China. He was succeeded as Sergeant-Major by Sergeant Wood, who had been Sergeant Instructor under him. Sergeant George Cliffe was appointed Staff Sergeant-Major. Cliffe had joined, as a Volunteer, No. 3 Company, February 2nd, 1860, and was discharged at the age limit on 11th January, 1886, having been Volunteer Sergeant-Major for 16 years. He had been returned as an efficient 27 times, viz., each year from 1860 to 1886, inclusive, and received the Long Service Medal. On Wood's resignation, Sergeant James Anderson, of the 15th Regiment of Foot, was appointed Sergeant-Major of the Battalion.

Nov 19th, And of Hon. Quarter-master Eddison.

Honorary Quartermaster William Eddison died November 17th, aged 69 years. He was one of the most ardent and zealous supporters of the Volunteer movement, and almost from the formation of the corps was Honorary Quartermaster. A strong contingent of the 6th Corps, with band, attended his funeral at Rastrick Church. Mr. Eddison was succeeded by Honorary Quartermaster John Brook on 6th January, 1871.

Review on Heath Common, July, 1870.

At the Review to which I have referred, held on July 30th, on Heath Common, 3,000 Volunteers of the West Riding were present.

The Huddersfield Regiment paraded nearly 800 strong, and were early on the scene, Captain Lewis Randle Starkey, a member of a family long intimately and honourably identified with the town of Huddersfield, then residing at Heath Hall, having invited the battalion to partake of his hospitality. The force taking part and their strength were as follows :—

	Officers.	Rank and File.	Total.
Wakefield Troop of Yeomanry Cavalry (Captain Taylor)	3	46	49
Bradford Corps (Lieutenant-Colonel Hurst)	25	506	531
Huddersfield Corps (Lieutenant-Colonel Greenwood and Major Brook) ..	31	752	783
Wakefield Corps (Lieutenant-Colonel Mackie)	17	417	434
Leeds Corps (Major Robinson) ..	18	449	467
Dewsbury Corps (Lieutenant-Colonel Ed. Day)	11	315	326

The Reviewing Officer was Colonel Anderson, 22nd Regiment, then stationed at Sheffield. He was accompanied by Brigade-Major Lieutenant Stratton, 22nd Regiment, Aides-de-camp, Lieutenants Gully and Davies, also 22nd Regiment, and Captain L. R. Starkey, 2nd West York Yeomanry Cavalry.

The troops marched past in open and close column with great steadiness and precision and then engaged in a sham fight. Colonel Anderson expressed himself highly satisfied with all he had seen.

Officers' Examination, March, 1876.

On 11th March, 1871, Colonel Nason, Assistant Adjutant-General of the District and Inspector of Reserve Forces for the Northern Counties, held an examination of Volunteer officers under the new regulations This was the first examination of officers of the Huddersfield Corps by an Examining Board under the new regulations.

He was assisted by Major E. B. Cook, Adjutant of the Doncaster Rifle Corps, Major W. M. Coopson, Adjutant of the Skipton Corps and Captain Chichester, Adjutant of the Huddersfield Corps.

The examination was a "stiff" one and occupied a great deal of time. Altogether 15 officers presented themselves for examination, including representatives of the Bradford, Keighley, Mirfield and Huddersfield Rifle Corps. The first part of the examination took place at the Armoury, about half-past eleven in the morning and lasted until three, during which time the officers were occupied in answering questions in writing with reference to drill. At four o'clock, a company of the Huddersfield Corps had assembled in Mr. T. W. Clough's meadow near St. Paul's Church, and were put through the new drill by the different officers, to test the latter in the practical part of their duty. The examination was not completed until about seven o'clock in the evening, and at its close the Assistant Adjutant General expressed his satisfaction with the way in which both officers and men had undertaken the out-door drill, and expressed the hope that when he inspected the whole of the regiment he should find it as proficient as that company, in which case he should have great pleasure in reporting in a most satisfactory manner to the War Office.

The following officers and non-commissioned officers of the corps satisfied the examiners and received their certificates of proficiency and thus became entitled to the extra capitation grant of £2 10s. od.; Lieutenant-Colonels Brooke and Greenwood passed the School at Aldershot. The rest passed before the Examining Board:—Captain Joseph Tyrrel Beaumont, Charles Edward Freeman, Thomas Walker Brooke, James Priestley, Albert Williamson, 41st (Mirfield) Corps, Lieutenants Joseph Bottomley, Thomas Kilner Mellor, George Henry Crowther, Thos. Green Beaumont (41st), W. G. Lockwood (41st), Ensign Robert Mellor, and, I may add with modest pride, the author. Of these officers it is gratifying to note that Lieutenant Crowther was promoted Captain in 1873, Major in the 16th Corps in 1880 and Honorary Lieutenant-Colonel in 1886.

The following non-commissioned officers were examined at Huddersfield and Mirfield by Captain and Adjutant Chichester:—Sergeant-Major G. Cliffe; Colour-Sergeants David Dixon, D. Haigh, D. Kaye Rhodes, E. Wear; Sergeants G. Bottomley, J. Bradbury, C. Brotherton, W. B. Clayton, B. Eastwood, F. Hirst, J. W. Hirst, W. Hopley, J. Johnson, John Liddell, A. North, J. North, J. Shiels, J. Smith, J. Wright, Barlow, Avison, Horsfall, Ledgard and Priestley.

Sergeant John Liddell, I may say without derogating from the merits and the services of the other non-commissioned officers, had a volunteer record of long and distinguished service. He received his commission as Ensign in 1873, was promoted Captain in 1875, Major of the 6th Corps in 1882 and Honorary Lieutenant-Colonel in 1893.

Sept., 1871, Review at Doncaster.

On 23rd September of this year a Review was held at Town Moor, Doncaster, of the Huddersfield, Saddleworth, Leeds, Dewsbury, Bradford, Halifax, Skipton, Craven, Doncaster, Barnsley and other corps, numbering about 4,000 strong, before

Colonel Nason, Assistant Adjutant General of the 3rd Northern District. The strength of the battalions was as follows :—

5th A. B., including Huddersfield, Holmfirth and Mirfield, Lieutenant-Colonel Greenwood Commanding, Major Brook and Major Day, Captain and Adjutant Chichester, Surgeon Marsden, Mirfield, and Assistant Surgeon Foster, Huddersfield. Total, about 550.

Dewsbury, 29th W. Y. R. V., Major Wormald in command, Captain and Adjutant Stewart, 254 of all ranks.

Saddleworth, 34th W. Y. R. V., Major Collins commanding, Hon. C. G. Legge, Adjutant. Total of all ranks, 356.

Bradford, 3rd W. Y. R. V., Major Mullar commanding, Captain and Adjutant Nield, Total on field, 400.

Leeds, 7th W. Y. R. V., Major Robinson commanding, Captain and Adjutant Hunt, Surgeon-Major Loe and Lieutenant Joy, Aide-de-camp. Total, 563.

Halifax, 4th W. Y. R. V., Colonel Holdsworth commanding, Major Emmett, Major Ridgway, Captain and Adjutant Coates. Total, 443.

Doncaster, 37th A. B., including Doncaster, Rotherham, Barnsley, Wath and Pontefract, Colonel Stanhope commanding and Major Cook. Total, 600.

Leeds Engineers, Lieutenant-Colonel Child, Major Moore, Captain and Adjutant Longbottom, Surgeon-Major Nunnelly and Assistant Surgeon Hayward. Total, 550.

The battalions were divided into two brigades. The 1st brigade under the command of Colonel Brooke of the 5th A.B. with the following staff:—Captain Pointz, Royal Marine Light Infantry Brigade, Aide-de-camp; Captain and Adjutant Shields, Leeds Artillery Volunteers.

The 2nd brigade was under the command of Lieutenant-Colonel Hirst of the 3rd W.Y.R.V., Captain Benwell, 2nd West York Militia and Aide-de-camp, Captain Townley, Wakefield.

The march past at quarter distance commenced at half-past three, and the report said that the Huddersfield and neighbouring corps executed the movement with a preciseness and soldierly bearing which, especially considering the lumpy state of the ground, deserved a word of recognition and praise. Afterwards a sham fight took place. Colonel Nason then addressed the officers as follows :—

"Gentlemen, I have to thank you for the attention you have shewn to-day, and I trust that, considering the shortness of the time, what has been done may be instructive. The regiments moved steadily and well, and I am happy to say that as far as I can judge there was very little fault. I am delighted to see that there is that true soldier-like spirit amongst Volunteers, that when they are wanted for any position they are ready to come forward."

Oct., 1871, Memorandum of Lieut.-Col. Brooke to the Officers.

In October, 1871, Lieutenant-Colonel Brooke, as the result of suggestions made to him by Colonel Nason, addressed a memorandum to the officers of the corps, in which he urged the organization of a "close and accurate instruction amongst the officers themselves." To that end a class had been arranged, to meet weekly, half the time on each occasion to be occupied in reading and explanation of the drill-books, under the direction of the adjutant, with catechetical instruction therein, the remainder of the time to be devoted to drill in the Armoury, the drill to be conducted either by the adjutant, sergeant instructors, or one of the officers. No officer, whatever his rank, to be present merely as a spectator, but to fall in under the orders of the instructor of the day. The series of drill and instruction was to begin with the rudiments of recruit drill and to be progressive at the discretion of the adjutant. The strictest conformity with the authorised words of command was to be enforced. The memorandum concluded with the suggestion that each officer should consider it a matter of personal honour to attend the classes, unless unavoidably prevented. A table prepared at this time in connection with the memorandum and the classes formed in pursuance of its suggestions shewed that of the West Riding Volunteers, Huddersfield (6th West York) had the greatest number of proficient officers, in number 25, of whom two had been passed by the School of Instruction and nine by the Board; Dewsbury (29th) had 18 officers, eight of whom had been passed by the Board; Holmfirth (32nd) had three officers, none of whom had obtained certificates; Saddleworth (34th) had 21 officers, one of whom had been passed by the Board; Mirfield (41st), five officers, three of whom had been passed by the Board; and Meltham (44th), two officers, and no certificates obtained.

Classes formed.

Jan., 1872, Circular of Lieut.-Col. Brooke to the men.

The memorandum addressed by Lieutenant-Colonel Brooke to the officers was supplemented on January 22nd, 1872, by a circular letter of the same gallant officer, issued, by Colonel Greenwood's permission, to the men. Colonel Brooke reminded those members of the corps that the duties of a Volunteer could not be discharged without a certain amount of sacrifice and self-denial, and it would therefore be well for every man who regarded those duties as a mere matter of amusement or indifference to immediately send in his resignation, bearing in mind that every Volunteer had bound himself to strict conformity with the Regulations and Orders of his corps by the solemn sanction of his oath. He begged each Volunteer to support the credit of his corps by a punctual and regular attention to the Orders; if unable or unwilling to give the careful attention which was necessary, to remove his name from the roll as early as possible.

In December of this year, Colonel Brooke, to the regret of officers, non-commissioned officers and men, and to the regret also of the many friends and supporters of the Volunteers who were not themselves members of the corps, felt himself compelled to resign his commission, other public duties, which he conceived to have a more imperative claim upon his attention, rendering his discharge of the duties of his command beyond his strength. Dec., 1872, Resignation of Col. Brooke.

On the 20th March, 1873, Honorary Surgeon John Dow, of Lockwood, died. He had taken a life interest in the Rifle Corps and was known as an excellent athlete. His funeral was attended by about 100 of the Huddersfield Rifle Corps, under the command of Captain Freeman. Death of Hon-Surgeon John Dow.

The resignation of Lieutenant-Colonel Brooke was quickly followed by that of Lieutenant-Colonel Greenwood, and on May 27th Major Joshua Day was gazetted Lieutenant-Colonel of the 5th A.B., and on the same day the promotion of Captain C. E. Freeman to be Major of the 6th Corps was notified, and Lieutenant P. Bingham Schreiber, late Lieutenant 1st Foot and Captain and Adjutant of the 1st Tower Hamlets Rifle Volunteers, was appointed Adjutant, *vice* Captain and Adjutant Chichester resigned. Resignation of Lieut.-Col. Greenwood. Major Day gazetted Lieut.-Col., May 27th, 1873.

The corps at this time consisted of eight companies, viz.:—the five original companies and the Outlane, Lindley and Lockwood companies.

The diminution in the membership which marked this critical period of the corps history suggested the advisability of reducing the number of companies. On January 20th, 1873, a Regimental Order announced the change as follows:— Jan. 20th, 1873, Reduction of No. of Companies.

"No. 1 Company to stand unchanged.
No. 8 Company to join No. 2.
No. 5 Company to join No. 3.
No. 7 Company to join No. 4.
Non-commissioned officers to take rank according to seniority and retain their stripes."

By an Order of the Secretary of State dated 8th April, 1873, forming clause 22 of the Auxiliary and Reserve Forces Circular of 21st April, 1873, whereby the Infantry Auxiliary forces were attached to the sub-district brigades of the army, the 5th Administrative Battalion was attached to the 10th Sub-district Brigade. The Brigade Depôt was stationed at Bradford, the Militia Regiment being the 4th West York and the other Rifle Volunteer Battalions being the 29th and 34th West York R.V. Corps.

By an Order of the Secretary of State dated 20th December, 1873, forming clause 1 of the Auxiliary and Reserve Forces Circular of 1st January, 1874, the Administrative Battalions of the Rifle Volunteers of the 10th Sub-district Brigade, instead of being attached to and forming part of the brigade mentioned in the above order of 8th April, 1873, were re-distributed and attached to the 9th Sub-district Brigade, the Brigade Depôt being Halifax, the other Rifle Volunteer Battalions being the 4th and 34th West York R.V.'s.

It was inevitable that the retirement of two such officers as Lieutenant-Colonel Brooke and Lieutenant-Colonel Greenwood should seriously affect the stability and threaten the future of the Huddersfield Corps. Lieutenant-Colonel Day and Major Freeman were confronted by no mean task when they entered upon the duties of their new commands. They addressed themselves to the work before them undismayed by its difficulties and had the satisfaction of seeing their efforts rewarded by no little success. On the occasion of the Prize Distribution by Mrs. Thomas Brooke, the wife of Colonel Brooke, the late Commandant of the 5th A.B., on October 11th, 1873, Major Freeman reviewed the situation of the corps very aptly. He said:—

"At the beginning of the Volunteer movement in 1859, the Volunteer Corps only had one company, but had increased so rapidly that in 1868 there were five companies in the town itself and three out-lying companies at Lindley, Lockwood and Outlane. At that time the Volunteer forces of the town were at their greatest strength. Since then from one cause and another the corps had declined a great deal, until, at the end of last year, although there were eight companies nominally on the Register, there were only 278 men on the books. He did not think they need be altogether surprised, for there were many ways in which they might account for it. Firstly, the panic which caused the rise of the Volunteer movement had passed away. The novelty of the movement had worn off, and times were very prosperous in a commercial sense. Many who joined the corps in the earlier years found there was not so much obligation as formerly for them to give their time to volunteering, and they had therefore gradually left the corps. Some time ago Lieutenant-Colonel Brooke, Colonel Greenwood and other officers resigned, and they were left almost at their wits' end. It then became necessary to consider whether the corps should be continued or not. He was happy to say it ultimately resulted in Colonel Day being induced to accept the command of the Administrative Battalion whilst he, Major Freeman, took the command of the town corps. They found that out of 298 men who were on the books at the end of October, 40 had resigned, leaving a strength only of 258 men. Last year they found it necessary to reduce the nominal strength from eight companies to four, so as to consolidate the corps. The Huddersfield Corps had, at the Annual Inspection of 1872, a strength of 288 men, exclusive of Meltham, Mirfield and Holmfirth. When they came to look at the returns of the present year they found in the four companies 288 men on parade, exactly the same number as there were last year before the number of companies had been reduced. He thought that highly satisfactory. They had tided over very difficult times and he hoped they would have still more men connected with the corps at the end of that month, which was the close of the volunteer year. He thought they would have 10 or 20 more effective men than they had last year. He believed the corps had now got into good working order and that the result had been brought about by all working together. He believed it was now worked by the hearty co-operation of all. Everyone had an opportunity at the officers' meeting of expressing anything which he thought would be to the welfare of the corps. They would all know that Colonel Hibbert was of opinion that they were very much improved in drill and were now in very good order. The strength of the four companies might be raised without any difficulty to 100 each and if they raised it to that he hoped they would not attempt to increase it beyond that strength. He had very great pleasure in seeing once more among them their late Colonel, Mr. T. Brooke, who continued to take a great interest in the battalion."

Colonel Brooke, in responding on behalf of his wife, who had presented the prizes, after giving the men some very wholesome advice on prize shooting, stated he had spent many pleasant years in connection with the battalion. Some of his best friends had been gained in his service there, and he hoped and thought he had still many friends there. As far as his own leaving was concerned, it was a positive duty, but it was a very painful wrench to sever his connection with so many friends; still he hoped, although they were not officially connected, they might many a long year be connected on such occasions as the present.

He congratulated Colonel Day and Major Freeman on the excellent form in which the men appeared before them. He had lost what little power he had of criticising military movements; at the same time, he could not help saying the men looked well set up. He trusted that harmony and good feeling would ever be preserved among the members of the battalion, and it would be, to his dying day, a pride to him to have been connected with it."

On the transfer of Captain and Adjutant Schreiber on the 1st July, 1873, to the 1st Administrative Battalion Cambridge Rifle Volunteers, Captain W. S. Hardinge was appointed Adjutant of the 5th A.B.

On the 23rd May, the first camp in connection with the corps was pitched in the Drill Field, Greenhead Road, and the Huddersfield, Holmfirth, Mirfield and Meltham Corps, 475 strong,

May, 1874. Camp in Greenhead Park.

under the command of Lieutenant-Colonel Day and Major Freeman, marched into camp.

The Huddersfield Corps consisted of:—

No. 1 Company, commanded by Captain Joseph Bottomley, with Lieutenant Thomson and Sub-Lieutenant Pilling.

No. 2 Company, commanded by Lieutenants Rhodes and John Liddell.

No. 3 Company, commanded by Captain G. H. Crowther and Lieutenant Robert Mellor.

No. 4 Company, commanded by Lieutenants James Dunderdale and George Lewis Batley.

Holmfirth (32nd), commanded by Lieutenants Beardsell and J. R. Mellor.

Mirfield (41st), commanded by Captain Albert Williamson and Lieutenant Crowther.

Meltham (44th), commanded by Captain E. C. Gooddy and Lieutenant T. Julius Hirst.

The battalion was encamped for seven days. The total strength of the battalion was 591. The staff consisted of Lieutenant-Colonel Day, Major Freeman, Captain and Adjutant Hardinge, Quartermaster Brooke, Sergeant-Major Anderson, four instructors, and band and buglers consisting of one sergeant and 35 men. The parade state as follows:—20 officers, 43 sergeants, 38 band and buglers and 430 rank and file, total 531.

The battalion was inspected in camp by Colonel Hibbert, who complimented Colonel Day on the steadiness of the men and the excellent manner in which they had executed the various movements and also upon the way the battalion had acquitted itself whilst under canvas.

The following report was received from Sir G. J. Wolseley, Inspector-General of Reserve forces:—"His Royal Highness the Field Marshal Commander-in-Chief is glad to find that the regimental camp of the battalion was in admirable order; that every arrangement was good and that the attendance was large. His Royal Highness considers the report (of the inspecting officer) very satisfactory and the improvement since last year most marked."

Subscriptions for new Uniforms, 1874.

In consequence of the union of the corps in brigade, it was considered desirable, in the year 1874, to adopt scarlet jackets. A subscription list was opened to meet the cost of this change and a sum of about £800 was obtained in this way. The following list of subscribers is interesting as shewing how unvarying in their assistance some of the supporters of the corps proved themselves in the hour of need.

SPECIAL FUND raised by subscription in Huddersfield for the purpose of providing great coats and new uniforms and of assisting in paying the expenses of a week's encampment:—

	£	s.	d.
Thomas Brooke, Armitage Bridge, £50 this year and £50 next year ..	100	0	0
J. W. Carlile	100	0	0
Starkey Brothers.. ..	52	10	0
Edward Brook, Meltham Hall	50	0	0
J. Taylor & Sons	50	0	0
Sir J. W. Ramsden, Bart.	50	0	0
H. F. Beaumont	50	0	0
E. A. Leatham, M.P. ..	10	0	0
Ed. Brooke & Sons ..	25	0	0
John Day & Sons ..	50	0	0
John Brooke, Dunstable..	10	0	0
J. C. Laycock	5	0	0
John Freeman	10	0	0
Anonymous	15	0	0
J. Batley	5	0	0
Robert Dewhirst	40	0	0
William Brooke	10	10	0
Thomas Brook	10	0	0
— Sykes	5	0	0
J. Crowther & Sons ..	10	0	0
C. W. Sikes	5	0	0
W. R. Haigh	5	0	0
John Liddell	5	0	0
Qr. Mr. Brook's Ball ..	10	10	0
G. W. Tomlinson.. ..	1	1	0
Mrs. Brook, Enderby ..	10	0	0
And several others,			

Amounting in all to between £600 and £700.

The corps was inspected by Major Harman, August 10th, 1861, and by the same gallant officer, now lieutenant-colonel, on June 21st, 1862, but on neither occasion was the field state or the strength recorded. The only record I can find is that at the Inspection in 1862 four companies of the 6th corps and one company of Holmfirth were on parade. It was inspected again on June 27th, 1863, when the total strength on parade was 414, including 82 from Holmfirth. There was also a Cadet Corps under the command of Colour Sergeant Thomas Marshall Tolson. It was again inspected by Colonel Harman, in June, 1864, when the battalion mustered in full strength and formed eight companies, exclusive of cadets; by Lieutenant-Colonel Wombwell, on 26th August, 1865, when the battalion, comprising the 6th (Huddersfield), 32nd (Holmfirth), and 41st (Mirfield) Corps, had a strength of one lieutenant-colonel, one adjutant, four sergeants of the staff, one major, four captains, three lieutenants, five ensigns, 19 sergeants, four buglers, 261 rank and file, total 293 of the 6th corps; 92 of all ranks for the 32nd corps; and a total of all ranks of 72 for the 41st corps, altogether 457. Colonel Wombwell again, on 7th July, 1866, inspected the battalion comprising the 6th, 32nd, and 41st corps. The field state of the 6th was 347, the total strength on the books 393; the field state of the 32nd, 95, total

Corps Inspections and strengths.

strength 100; the field state of the 41st, 82, total strength 103. On parade there were 524 out of a total of 596. Colonel Wombwell again inspected the Administrative Battalion in June, 1867, consisting of five Huddersfield, one Holmfirth and one Mirfield companies. The total strength of the Huddersfield Corps was 445, of the Holmfirth, 113, and the Mirfield, 96, the total strength of the battalion being 654. At the inspection by Colonel Wombwell, on June 27th, 1868, the strength of the Huddersfield Corps was 672 on parade out of a total strength of 741, that of the Holmfirth parade strength, 110, total strength 115, of the Mirfield parade strength 106, total strength 125, making on parade a total of all ranks of 888 out of a total strength of 981 for the 5th A.B. The battalion was inspected on 10th July, 1869, by Colonel Wombwell, the regimental state of the constituent corps being:—Huddersfield (including staff), 655; Holmfirth (32nd), 113; Mirfield (41st), 137; Meltham (44th), 57; 5th Administrative Battalion Staff, 7; total enrolled strength, 969. At the annual inspection by Colonel Wombwell, on July 2nd, 1870, held at Armitage Bridge, in the grounds of Lieutenant-Colonel Brooke, the commandant of the battalion, the parade state of the 6th Corps was 595 of all ranks; of the 32nd, 101; of the 41st, 114; and of the 44th, 55; total parade state, 865. The total strength of the Huddersfield Battalion, including officers, staff, buglers and band, at this time was 699.

The Inspection on July 29th, 1871, was by Colonel Nason, formerly of the 49th Regiment, and the total strength of the eight companies of the 6th West York was stated at 617; of Mirfield, 74; of the Meltham, 47; and of the Holmfirth, 57: the total strength of the 5th A.B. being 795. The strength of the Huddersfield Corps had fallen from 660 on November 30th, 1870, to 592 on November 30th, 1871, a decrease of 68. In 1871, the efficients were 469, non-efficients 123, none passing into the second class.

Colonel Nason again, on 13th July, 1872, inspected the Battalion, consisting of six Huddersfield, one Holmfirth, one Mirfield, one Meltham, companies. The total strength of all ranks was stated at 625, the parade strength being 476, the small number on parade being accounted for by the inclemency of the weather. The inspecting officer on July 19th, 1873, was Colonel Hibbert, Assistant Adjutant General, when the parade strength of the Battalion was, the 6th (Huddersfield), 288; 32nd (Holmfirth), 48; 41st (Mirfield), 88; 44th (Meltham), 41. Total, 465; and absent with and without leave, 39. In 1874, the Battalion was inspected in camp, the total strength being 591 and the parade strength being 531.

Government Capitation Allowances.

It will be remembered that until the passing of the Volunteer Act of 1863 and the issue, pursuant to section 11 of that Act, of the Order in Council on 27th July in that year as to the requisites of efficiency, no monetary assistance whatever had been received by the Volunteers from Government. There are no records of the capitation allowances to the Huddersfield Corps up to 1867. In that year the corps received £587; in 1868, £993 10s. 0d.; in 1869, £803 10s. 0d.; in 1870, £786 10s. 0d.; in 1871, £670 10s. 0d.; in 1872, there is no record; in 1873, £477; in 1874, £623.

Summary of the Commandants and Staff of the 5th A. B.

The following is a summary of the commandants and staff of the 5th Administrative Battalion and of the increase of establishment:—

The 5th Administrative Battalion was formed on the 18th of September, 1862, and at that time consisted of the 6th and 32nd (Holmfirth) Corps, with a staff consisting of Major Thomas Pearson Crosland and Captain and Adjutant H. B. Chichester.

A 5th Company having been added to the 6th Corps Major Crosland was appointed Lieutenant-Colonel on the 2nd March, 1864, and on the same date Captain Thomas Brooke was appointed Major.

Alexander Hannah was appointed Honorary Quartermaster of the 5th A.B., 20th October, 1863.

The (41st) Mirfield Corps was added to the Administrative Battalion on its formation in 1864.

On the 21st September, 1866, Lieutenant-Colonel Crosland retired and was appointed Honorary Colonel, and Major Thomas Brooke was appointed Lieutenant-Colonel *vice* Colonel Crosland retired. Major Greenwood of the 6th Corps was appointed Major of the 5th A.B. on the 18th April, 1867, and William Eddison, Honorary Quartermaster, on 14th May, 1866.

On further increase of establishment of the 6th Corps by three additional companies and by the inclusion of the 44th Corps (Meltham) from its formation, Major Thomas Brook (Colne Villa) was appointed Second Major in the 5th A.B. on the 19th February, 1868.

Major Beaumont was appointed Honorary Colonel of the Battalion on 28th April, 1868.

John Brook, of High Street, was appointed Honorary Quartermaster on 6th January, 1871, in succession to William Eddison, deceased.

On the retirement of Colonel Thomas Brooke and Major Greenwood in January, 1873, Major Joshua Day of the 6th Corps was appointed Lieutenant-Colonel of the 5th A.B. and Captain Freeman, Major, on the 28th May, 1873.

Captain and Adjutant Chichester resigned 17th May, 1873, and Captain Percy Bingham Schreiber was appointed Adjutant on 28th May, 1873, but only served for a few weeks, when, on the 1st July following, Captain William Sheffield Hardinge was appointed Adjutant.

Dr. John Edwin Foster was appointed Surgeon on 31st December, 1873.

Prizes and winners.

BEAUMONT GOLD MEDAL.

Presented by H. F. Beaumont, Esq. It was to be worn by the highest scorer in five shots each at 150, 200, 250 and 300 yards and to be competed for by those only who made eight points and upwards in shooting for company medals.

YEAR.	PRIZES. By whom distributed.	NAMES OF WINNERS.
1861	Mrs. H. F. Beaumont	Private David Robertson, No. 1 Company.
1862	Mrs. T. P. Crosland	Private Wilson.
1863	Major T. P. Crosland	Corporal F. Haigh, No. 1 Company.
1864	Charles Brook, junior, Esq., Meltham Hall	Private Muir, No. 2 Company.
1865	Mrs. T. P. Crosland	Private F. R. Crowther, No. 1 Company.
1866	Mrs. Thomas Brooke, Armitage Bridge	ditto.
1867	Mrs. J. W. Carlile, Thick Hollins	Corporal F. R. Crowther.
1868	Mrs. H. F. Beaumont	Corporal Geo. Garthwaite, No. 2 Company.
1869	Mrs. Bentley Shaw	ditto.
1870	Rev. W. B. Calvert, M.A.	Assistant-Surgeon J. E. Foster, No. 6 Company.
1871	Colonel Greenwood (in the absence of the Mayor of Huddersfield)	Lieutenant G. H. Crowther, No. 7 Company.
1872	Wright Mellor, Esq., Mayor	Colour-Sergeant David Dixon, No. 4 Company.
1873	Mrs. Thomas Brooke, Armitage Bridge	Private George Rhodes, No. 1 Company.
1874	Mrs. Joseph Crosland, Royds Wood	Private J. C. Woodhouse.

This medal at the present time (1903) is held by Quartermaster Sergeant C. H. Wood.

Bentley-Shaw Silver Challenge Cup.

Presented by Mr. and Mrs. Bentley Shaw, of Woodfield House, Lockwood, to be competed for by 12 volunteers from each company who made the highest score for shooting for company medals. The cup to be held by the captain of the company whose average score was the highest.

Year.	Number of Company.	Name of Badge Winner.
1862	1	Corporal Haigh.
1863	2	Corporal F. Haigh.
1864	2	Private Muir.
1865	1	Corporal Herbert Wigney.
1866	1	Sergeant Herbert Wigney.
1867	1	Sergeant A. Radcliffe.
1868	2	Private Yates.
1869	1	Ensign Herbert Wigney.
1870	2	Colour-Sergeant Wear.
1871	2	Sergeant Radcliffe.
1872	1	Private George Lewis Batley.
1873	1	Private George Lewis Batley.
1874	3	Captain G. H. Crowther.

Field Officers' Silver Challenge Cup.

(Value £15 15s. 0d.)

Presented in 1868 to the 6th Corps by Lieutenant-Colonel Greenwood, Major T. Brook (Colne Villa) and Major J. W. Carlile, for the highest aggregate prize throughout each annual competition. The cup to be held by the captain of the company to which the winner belonged, and to become the property of the member winning it three times.

Year.	Number of Company.	Name of Winner.
1868	2	Bugler Tindall.
1869	2	Sergeant Radcliffe.
1870	1	Corporal Spurr.
1871	2	Corporal George Rhodes.
1872	1	Corporal C. S. Stewart.
1873	4	Private T. Ward.
1874	1	Corporal E. Beevers.

In 1891, the cup became the property of Sergeant (now Quartermaster Sergeant) C. H. Wood, he having won it three times, viz.: in 1875, 1884 and 1891.

War Office Return.

The following War Office return may appropriately be included:—

Huddersfield Volunteers.

Formed as 10th West Riding of Yorkshire Rifle Volunteer Corps on the 3rd November, 1859, with an establishment of two companies.

A company was added on 3rd March, 1860.

On the 3rd July, 1860, the corps was styled the 6th West Riding of Yorkshire Rifle Volunteer Corps,* with an establishment of four companies, and in 1862 it was included in the 5th Administrative Battalion, West Riding of Yorkshire Rifle Volunteers.

The establishment was raised to six companies on the 10th December, 1867, and on the 25th January, 1868, the designation of the "Huddersfield Rifle Volunteer Corps" was sanctioned.

On the 31st January, 1868, the establishment was raised to seven companies, but was reduced to four companies on the 14th December, 1873.

When the Administrative Battalion was consolidated in 1880, the Huddersfield Corps became the four headquarter companies of the 6th West Riding of Yorkshire Rifle Volunteer Corps.

In 1883 the territorial title of 2nd Volunteer Battalion West Riding Regiment was assumed.

There are no records in this Department shewing the strength of the Huddersfield Volunteers prior to 1867. The strength from that date to 1881 is as follows:—

1867	..	6th West Yorkshire R. V. C.	.. 560 all ranks.
1868	..	" "	.. 732 "
1869	..	" "	.. 648 "
1870	..	" "	.. 660 "
1871	..	" "	.. 593 "
1872	..	" "	.. 278 "
1873	..	" "	.. 313 "
1874	..	" "	.. 378 "
1875	..	" "	.. 400 "
1876	..	" "	.. 400 "
1877	..	" "	.. 401 "
1878	..	" "	.. 393 "
1879	..	" "	.. 400 "
1880	..	No record of the strength of the four companies at Huddersfield which were included in the Consolidated Corps.	
1881	..		

---

*If the reader will refer to p. 354 he will observe that the levies of 1803 were also styled the 6th West York, a coincidence at once curious and happy.

Postings of officers of 6th West Riding Yorkshire Rifle Volunteers and 5th Administrative Battalion, as supplied by the Clerk to the Lieutenancy, from the raising of the corps to the time when the jurisdiction of the Lord Lieutenant was abolished and provision made that commissions in the Volunteer Force should be granted by Her Majesty, Section 6 of the Regulation of the Forces Act, 1871, chapter 86. **Postings of Officers.**

Tenth Company (Huddersfield).

Date of Commission.	Names.	Rank.	
Nov. 18th, 1859.	Hy. Fredk. Beaumont ..	Captain ..	
	Joseph Batley, Junior ..	Lieutenant..	
	Joseph Acheson Harrison	Ensign ..	Resignation accepted 11th Sept., 1860.
Dec. 12th, 1859.	Thomas A. Bottomley ..	Honorary Surgeon ..	
Feb. 24th, 1860.	Thos. Pearson Crosland	Captain ..	
	Thomas Brook	Lieutenant..	
	Thomas Brooke	Ensign ..	
Feb. 28th, 1860.	Bentley Shaw	Captain ..	
	John Haigh, Junior ..	Lieutenant..	
	George Hy. Greenwood	Ensign ..	Resignation accepted 5th July, 1861.
Mar. 3rd, 1860.	Thomas A. Bottomley ..	Surgeon ..	
Mar. 5th, 1860.	Captain Henry Frederick Beaumont	Captain Commandant	
	Tom Learoyd	Lieutenant..	
	Joshua Day	Ensign ..	
	Frederick Greenwood ..	Assistant Surgeon ..	Resignation accepted 22nd June, 1860.

April 13th, 1860.—The 10th and 27th West Riding of Yorkshire Rifle Volunteers have, with an additional company, been incorporated, and the whole corps is numbered as the 10th.

April 13th, 1860.	Frederick Greenwood ..	Ensign ..
May 2nd, 1860.	Captain Commandant H. F. Beaumont.. ..	Major ..
May 14th, 1860.	Thomas Brooke	Captain ..

July 10th, 1860.—This corps in future to hold the 6th place in the West Riding Volunteer Force.

Sixth West Riding of Yorkshire Rifle Volunteers.

Date of Commission.	Names.	Rank.	
Sept. 4th, 1860.	Lieutenant Joseph Batley, Junior	Captain ..	
	Thomas Rymer Webb ..	Lieutenant ..	Resignation accepted 19th April, 1861.
	Henry Broughton Dyson	Ensign ..	
Feb. 21st, 1861.	Lieutenant and Adjutant Wm. Henry Greer ..	Captain ..	Resignation accepted 5th Dec., 1861.
May 13th, 1861.	Ensign Henry Broughton Dyson *vice* Webb resigned	Lieutenant ..	
	Thomas Haigh Bradbury *vice* Dyson promoted	Ensign ..	Resignation accepted 24th July, 1863.
June 12th, 1861.	Lieutenant John Haigh *vice* Shaw who retires	Captain ..	Resignation accepted 5th Dec., 1861.
	Ensign Frederick Greenwood *vice* Haigh promoted	Lieutenant ..	
	James Tolson *vice* Greenwood promoted ..	Ensign ..	
Aug. 15th, 1861.	Anthony Knowles Kaye	Ensign ..	
Nov. 26th, 1861.	Lieutenant Fredk. Greenwood, *vice* Haigh who retires	Captain ..	
Nov. 29th, 1861.	Joseph Tyrrel Beaumont, *vice* Greenwood promoted	Lieutenant ..	
Dec. 24th, 1861.	Adjutant Harry B. Chichester, to serve with the rank of	Captain ..	
Jan. 8th, 1862.	Captain Thomas Pearson Crosland, *vice* Beaumont who retires ..	Major ..	
Jan. 23rd, 1862.	Lieutenant Thos. Brook, *vice* Crosland promoted	Captain ..	
	Ensign Joshua Day, *vice* Brook promoted ..	Lieutenant ..	
	Albert John Learoyd, *vice* Day promoted ..	Ensign ..	
April 16th, 1862.	John Freeman, Junior, *vice* Tolson who retires	Ensign ..	Resignation accepted 3rd Nov., 1863.
July 22nd, 1863.	Joseph Bottomley ..	Ensign ..	
Oct. 23rd, 1863.	Charles Edward Freeman	Ensign ..	

SIXTH WEST RIDING OF YORKSHIRE RIFLE VOLUNTEERS.—*Continued.*

DATE OF COMMISSION.	NAMES.	RANK.	
Mar. 2nd, 1864.	Lieutenant Tom Learoyd, *vice* Brooke who retires	Captain ..	
	James William Carlile ..	Captain ..	
	Ensign Anthony Knowles Kaye	Lieutenant..	
	Ensign Albert John Learoyd, *vice* Tom Learoyd promoted ..	Lieutenant..	
	Geo. Wm. Crosland, *vice* Kaye promoted ..	Ensign ..	
	Robert Bentley Shaw ..	Ensign ..	
Mar. 7th, 1864.	Thomas Brooke, *vice* Crosland who retires	Major ..	
Mar. 24th, 1864.	Robert Lowenthal ..	Ensign ..	
Feb. 28th, 1865.	Henry William Haigh, *vice* Dyson resigned..	Lieutenant..	
May 5th, 1865.	Lieutenant Joshua Day, *vice* T. Learoyd resigned	Captain ..	
	Ensign Robt. Lowenthal, *vice* A. J. Learoyd resigned	Lieutenant..	
	William Lawton, *vice* Day promoted ..	Lieutenant..	
	Thomas Kilner Mellor, *vice* Robert Bentley Shaw resigned ..	Ensign ..	
May 14th, 1866.	Thomas Walter Brooke, *vice* Lowenthal promoted	Ensign ..	
Sep. 14th, 1866.	Lieutenant Henry William Haigh, *vice* Batley resigned	Captain ..	
	Ensign Joseph Bottomley, *vice* Haigh promoted	Lieutenant..	
Oct. 4th, 1866.	Captain Frederick Greenwood, *vice* Brooke resigned	Major ..	
	Lieutenant Joseph Tyrrel Beaumont, *vice* Greenwood promoted ..	Captain ..	
	Ensign Charles Edward Freeman, *vice* Beaumont promoted ..	Lieutenant..	

SIXTH WEST RIDING OF YORKSHIRE RIFLE VOLUNTEERS.—*Continued.*

DATE OF COMMISSION.	NAMES.	RANK.	
Oct. 29th, 1866.	The Rev. William Bainbridge Calvert ..	Honorary Chaplain ..	
Dec. 22nd, 1866.	Ensign Thomas Kilner Mellor, *vice* A. K. Kaye who retires ..	Lieutenant..	
	George Henry Crowther, *vice* Bottomley promoted	Ensign ..	
	Charles William Keighley, *vice* Mellor promoted	Ensign ..	
Mar. 5th, 1867.	John Freeman, junior ..	Ensign ..	
Oct. 29th, 1867.	Tom Learoyd, *vice* Haigh resigned	Captain ..	
Dec. 26th, 1867.	Major Frederick Greenwood	Lieutenant-Colonel ..	
Jan. 20th, 1868.	James Walker Sykes ..	Captain ..	
Feb. 18th, 1868.	Lieutenant William Lawton	Captain ..	
Jan. 20th, 1868.	Benjamin Casson ..	Lieutenant..	
Feb. 18th, 1868.	Ensign George William Crosland	Lieutenant..	
Jan. 20th, 1868.	James Cooper, *vice* J. Freeman resigned ..	Ensign ..	
Feb. 18th, 1868.	Robert Ellis Dewhirst ..	Ensign ..	
Jan. 20th, 1868.	John Dow	Assistant Surgeon ..	
Feb. 20th, 1868.	Captain Thomas Brook, *vice* Greenwood promoted	Major ..	
	Lieutenant Charles Edward Freeman, *vice* Brook promoted ..	Captain ..	
	Ensign George Henry Crowther, *vice* Freeman promoted ..	Lieutenant..	
	Ensign Thomas Walker Brooke	Lieutenant..	
	Robert Mellor, *vice* Brooke promoted ..	Ensign ..	
	Herbert Wigney ..	Ensign ..	
Mar. 7th, 1868.	William Laycock ..	Ensign ..	
Mar. 12th, 1868.	James Brook	Ensign ..	

SIXTH WEST RIDING OF YORKSHIRE RIFLE VOLUNTEERS.—*Continued.*

DATE OF COMMISSION.	NAMES.	RANK.	
Mar. 19th, 1868.	Lieutenant Robert Lowenthal	Captain ..	
	James Priestley ..	Lieutenant..	
	Joe Roberts	Ensign ..	
Apl. 28th, 1868.	Henry Frederick Beaumont	Honorary Colonel ..	
June 5th, 1868.	Captain James William Carlile	Major ..	
Jan. 13th, 1869.	Lieutenant Thomas Walker Brooke, *vice* Carlile promoted ..	Captain ..	
	Ensign William Lay cock, *vice* Freeman promoted	Lieutenant..	
July 12th, 1869.	Ensign Robert Ellis Dewhirst, *vice* Crosland resigned ..	Lieutenant..	
	Arthur Moore, *vice* Dewhirst promoted ..	Ensign ..	
Aug. 30th, 1869.	Ensign James Brook, *vice* T. W. Brooke promoted	Lieutenant..	
	Albert Mallinson, *vice* James Brook, promoted	Ensign ..	
Oct. 13th, 1869.	Robert Potter Berry, *vice* William Laycock promoted	Ensign ..	
Oct. 30th, 1869.	Assistant Surgeon John Dow, *vice* Bottomley deceased	Surgeon ..	
	John Edwin Foster, *vice* Dow promoted ..	Assistant Surgeon ..	
Dec. 1st, 1869.	Henry John Terry, *vice* Moore resigned ..	Ensign ..	
Apl. 2nd, 1870.	Charles Albert Berry, *vice* Roberts resigned	Ensign ..	
June 9th, 1870.	Ensign Robert Potter Berry, *vice* Laycock who retires	Lieutenant..	
Feb. 3rd, 1871.	Captain Joshua Day, *vice* Carlile who retires	Major ..	
	Lieutenant James Priestley, *vice* Day promoted	Captain ..	

Sixth West Riding of Yorkshire Rifle Volunteers.—Continued.

Date of Commission	Names	Rank	
	Ensign Henry John Terry, vice Dewhurst who retires	Lieutenant..	
	William James Dunderdale, vice Robert Potter Berry promoted	Ensign ..	

Holmfirth 32nd West Riding Rifle Volunteers.

Date of Commission	Names	Rank	
January 2nd 1860	John Earnshaw Morehouse	Captain ..	
	John Harpin	Lieutenant..	
	George Henry Hinchliff	Ensign ..	Resignation accepted Sept 2nd, 1862
	Charles John Trotter ..	Honorary Assistant Surgeon ..	
	John Morehouse Dyson	Ensign ..	
	The Rev. John Fearon ..	Honorary Chaplain ..	

Fifth Administrative Battalion West Riding Yorkshire Rifle Volunteers.

Sept. 1862.—The 6th and 32nd Corps formed into the 5th Administrative Battalion with a staff consisting of one major and one adjutant and the corps composing it will retain their present Nos. in the county force.

Date	Names	Rank
Sep. 22nd, 1862.	Thos. Pearson Crosland	Major ..
Oct. 20th, 1862.	Alexander Hannah ..	Honorary Quarter-master ..
Mar. 2nd, 1864.	Major Thomas Pearson Crosland	Lieutenant-Colonel ..
	Thomas Brooke, *vice* Crosland promoted ..	Major ..
May 14th, 1866.	William Eddison, *vice* Hannah resigned ..	Honorary Quarter-master ..
Sep. 21st, 1866.	Thos. Pearson Crosland	Honorary Colonel ..
	Major Thomas Brooke, *vice* Crosland resigned	Lieutenant-Colonel ..
April 18th, 1867.	Frederick Greenwood, *vice* Brooke promoted	Major ..
Feb. 19th, 1868.	Thomas Brook	Major ..
July 13th, 1868.	Hy. Frederick Beaumont, *vice* Crosland deceased	Honorary Colonel ..
Jan. 6th, 1871.	John Brook, *vice* William Eddison deceased ..	Honorary Quarter-master ..

Mirfield 41st West Riding Rifle Volunteers.

Date of Commission.	Names.	Rank.
Nov. 23rd, 1864.	Edward Day	Captain ..
	John Stancliffe Hurst ..	Lieutenant..
	Thomas Wade	Ensign ..
Jan. 7th, 1865.	William Marsden ..	Honorary Assistant-Surgeon ..
Aug. 1st, 1865.	James Howgate, Junior, *vice* Wade resigned ..	Ensign ..
Mar. 17th, 1866.	Lieutenant Jas. Howgate, Junior, *vice* Hurst resigned	Lieutenant..
	Albert Williamson, *vice* Howgate promoted ..	Ensign ..
May 1st, 1867.	Ensign Albert Williamson, *vice* Howgate resigned	Lieutenant..
	Thos. Green Beaumont, *vice* Williamson promoted	Ensign ..
Mar. 15th, 1869.	Lieutenant Albert Williamson, *vice* Day resigned	Captain ..
	Ensign Thomas Green Beaumont, *vice* Williamson promoted ..	Lieutenant..
	Joseph Barker	Lieutenant..
	Alfred Barraclough, *vice* Beaumont promoted..	Ensign ..
	John Crowther	Ensign ..
	William Marsden ..	Assistant Surgeon ..
April 5th, 1870.	William Greenwood Lockwood, *vice* Barker deceased	Lieutenant..

Meltham 44th West Riding Rifle Volunteers.

Date of Commission.	Names.	Rank.
Aug. 29th, 1868.	Edward Coleman Gooddy	Captain ..
	Thomas Julius Hirst ..	Lieutenant..
	The Rev. Edward Collis Watson	Honorary Chaplain ..

10TH AND 6TH WEST RIDING YORKSHIRE RIFLE VOLUNTEERS.

THE HUDDERSFIELD VOLUNTEERS.

Postings of Officers from the War Office Returns.

RANK.	NAMES.	DATE APPOINTED.	
Honorary Colonel ..	Henry Fredk. Beaumont	28th April, 1868	Still serving
Lieutenant-Colonel ..	F. Greenwood	26th Dec., 1867	Resigned 1st Jan., 1873
	C. E. Freeman .. Honorary Colonel ..	5th Aug., 1882 24th Mar., 1886	Resigned 9th Oct., 1895, retaining rank
	Thomas Edward Hirst, Honorary Colonel ..	20th Nov., 1895 8th Jan., 1896	Resigned, retaining rank, 1st Jan., 1898
Majors ..	Henry Fredk. Beaumont	28th April, 1860	Resigned 7th Jan., 1862
	Thos. Pearson Crosland	7th Jan., 1862	Resigned 5th Mar., 1864
	Thomas Brooke	5th Mar., 1864	Resigned 3rd Oct., 1866
	Frederick Greenwood ..	3rd Oct., 1866	Promoted
	Thomas Brook	28th Feb., 1868	Resigned 7th Dec., 1872
	James William Carlile ..	5th June, 1868	Resigned 3rd Feb., 1871
	Joshua Day	3rd Feb,, 1871	Resigned 26th Mar., 1873
	Chas. Edward Freeman	28th May, 1873	Promoted
	George Henry Crowther, Honorary Lieutenant-Colonel	7th Aug., 1880 3rd April, 1886	Resigned, retaining rank, 17th Jan., 1891
	John Liddell, ... Honorary Lieutenant-Colonel	28th Oct., 1882 4th Mar., 1893	Resigned, retaining rank, 20th Nov., 1895
	Thomas Edward Hirst ..	7th Feb., 1891	Promoted
Captains ..	Henry Fredk. Beaumont	19th Nov., 1859	Promoted
	Thos. Pearson Crosland	23rd Feb., 1860	Promoted
	Thomas Brooke	15th May, 1860	Resigned 1st Mar., 1864
	Bentley Shaw	27th Feb., 1860	Resigned 11th June, 1861
	Joseph Batley	3rd Sep., 1860	Resigned 13th Sep., 1866
	John Haigh	11th June, 1861	Resigned 22nd Nov., 1861
	Frederick Greenwood ..	25th Nov., 1861	Promoted
	Thomas Brook	23rd Jan., 1862	Promoted
	James William Carlile ..	1st Mar., 1864	Promoted
	Albert John Learoyd ..	1st Mar., 1864	Resigned 4th May, 1866

10TH & 6TH WEST RIDING OF YORKSHIRE RIFLE VOLUNTEERS.—*Continued.*

RANK.	NAMES.	DATE APPOINTED.	
Captains (continued)	Joshua Day	4th May, 1866	Promoted
	Henry William Haigh ..	13th Sep., 1866	Resigned 29th Oct., 1867
	Joseph Tyrrel Beaumont	3rd Oct., 1866	Resigned 1st Feb., 1873
	Tom Learoyd	29th Oct., 1867	Resigned 11th Sep., 1872
	James Walker Sykes ..	20th Jan., 1868	Resigned 7th June, 1873
	William Lawton.. ..	18th Feb., 1868	Resigned 14th Aug., 1872
	Charles Edward Freeman	28th Feb., 1868	
	Commandant Major 5th Administrative Battalion	28th Jan., 1874	Promoted
	Robert Lowenthal ..	19th Mar., 1868	Resigned 8th July, 1874
	Thomas Walker Brooke	13th Jan., 1869	Resigned 26th Dec., 1871
	James Priestley	3rd Feb., 1871	Resigned 7th Dec., 1872
	Joseph Bottomley ..	1st Jan., 1873	Resigned, retaining rank, 18th Mar., 1882
	George Henry Crowther	24th Dec., 1873	Promoted
	Robert Mellor	8th July, 1874	Resigned 19th May, 1875
	John Liddell	22nd Dec., 1875	Promoted
	George Lewis Batley, Honorary Major ..	24th July, 1880 11th Aug., 1888	Resigned, retaining rank, 7th Feb., 1891
	Edward Herbert Armitage	7th Aug., 1880	Resigned 21st Dec., 1881
	George Ernest Lowenthal	18th Feb., 1882	Resigned 18th Nov., 1882
	Thomas Edward Hirst..	3rd May, 1882	Promoted Major 7th Feb., 1891
	Henry Watkinson .. Honorary Major ..	16th Dec., 1882 3rd Feb., 1894	Resigned, retaining rank, 27th Nov., 1895
	Robert Welsh .. .. Honorary Major ..	16th Dec., 1882 28th Apl., 1894	Resigned, retaining rank, 17th April, 1895
	Frederick William Brook	21st Jan., 1888	Deceased 23rd July, 1889
Lieutenants ..	Joseph Batley	15th Nov., 1859	Promoted
	Thomas Brooke	23rd Feb., 1860	Promoted
	John Haigh	27th Feb., 1860	Promoted
	Tom Learoyd	6th Mar., 1860	Promoted
	Thomas Brook	23rd Apl., 1860	Promoted
	Thomas Rymer Webb ..	3rd Sept., 1860	Resigned 4th April, 1861

10TH & 6TH WEST RIDING OF YORKSHIRE RIFLE VOLUNTEERS.—*Continued.*

RANK	NAMES.	DATE APPOINTED.	
Ensigns (continued)	Herbert Wigney ..	28th Feb., 1868	Promoted
	William Laycock ..	7th Mar., 1868	Promoted
	James Brook	12th Mar., 1868	Promoted
	Joe Roberts	19th Mar., 1868	Resigned 2nd April, 1870
	Arthur Moore	12th July, 1869	Resigned 1st Dec., 1869
	Albert Mallinson ..	30th Aug., 1869	Resigned 5th June, 1872
	Robert Potter Berry ..	13th Oct., 1869	Promoted
	Henry John Terry ..	1st Dec., 1869	Promoted
	Charles Albert Berry ..	2nd April, 1870	Resigned 5th June, 1872
	Wm. James Dunderdale	3rd Feb., 1871	Resigned 31st Mar., 1875
	John William Rhodes ..	5th June, 1872	Promoted
	Alfred France	20th July, 1872	Promoted
	William Thomson ..	1st Feb. 1873	Promoted
	John Liddell	28th May., 1873	Promoted captain
Sub-Lieutenants ..	Edward James Pilling ..	28th Jan., 1874	Promoted
	George Lewis Batley ..	21st Feb., 1874	Promoted
	Ed. Herbert Armitage ..	1st July, 1874	Promoted
	G. Ernest Lowenthal ..	14th April, 1875	Promoted
	S. Mellor	22nd Dec., 1875	Promoted
	Thomas Edward Hirst ..	22nd Dec., 1875	Promoted
	Thos. Pearson Crosland	5th July, 1876	Promoted
2nd Lieutenants ..	Albert Ernest Learoyd ..	27th Feb., 1878	Promoted
	Harry Watkinson ..	15th Mar., 1879	Promoted
	Robert Welsh	19th May, 1880	Promoted
	Frederick William Brook	19th May, 1880	Promoted
Adjutants ..	Captain W. H. Greer ..	? 28th Oct., 1860 9th Nov., 1860	Resigned 23rd Nov., 1861
	Captain Harry B. Chichester	24th Dec., 1861	
	Captain P. B. Schreiber	28th May, 1873	Transferred 1st July, 1873 to 1st Administrative Battalion, Cambridge Rifle Volunteers
	Captain W. S. Hardinge	1st July, 1873	Died 26th Oct., 1875

RANK.	NAMES.	DATE APPOINTED.	
Adjutants (continued)	Captain C. E. Croker-King	18th Mar., 1876	to 21st Aug., 1878
	H. L. Brett	22nd Aug., 1878	to 1st Sep., 1883
Honorary Surgeon ..	Frederick Greenwood ..	23rd Feb., 1860	Cancelled 18th June, 1860 (see Ensign above)
Surgeon ..	Thos. Abbey Bottomley	3rd Nov., 1860	Deceased (no date recorded)
	John Dow	30th Oct., 1869	Deceased 20th Mar., 1873
	John Edwin Foster ..	31st Dec., 1873	Promoted
	Honorary Surgeon-Major	3rd April, 1886	
	Surgeon-Major ..	1st Feb., 1889	Resigned, retaining rank, 27th Nov., 1895
	Surgeon Lieutenant-Colonel	1st Dec., 1891	
Assistant Surgeon ..	John Dow	20th Jan., 1868	Promoted Surgeon
	John Edwin Foster (Surgeon to Administrative Battalion) ..	30th Oct., 1869	Promoted Surgeon
Honorary Chaplain ..	Rev. W. B. Calvert, M.A.	27th Oct., 1866	Resigned and appointed Acting Chaplain 20th March, 1875
Acting Chaplain ..	Rev. W. B. Calvert, M.A.	20th Mar., 1875	Resigned 30th April, 1884

HOLMFIRTH.

32nd West Riding of Yorkshire Rifle Volunteer Corps.

Formed 26th May, 1860.

One Company.

Headquarters, Holmfirth.

Included in 5th Administrative Battalion West Riding of Yorkshire Rifle Volunteers from 18th September, 1862.

On consolidation became part (E Company) of the 6th West Riding of Yorkshire Rifle Volunteer Corps, 1st June, 1880.

Title of 6th West Riding of Yorkshire Rifle Volunteer Corps changed to 2nd Volunteer Battalion West Riding Regiment by General Order dated 1st February, 1883.

Officers.

Rank.	Names.	Date of Appointment.	
Captains ..	J. Earnshaw Morehouse	1st June, 1860	Resigned 11th Sept., 1872
	John Morehouse Dyson	11th Sep., 1872	Resigned, retaining rank, 24th July, 1878
	Thomas Beardsell ..	7th Aug., 1878	Resigned 23rd May, 1885
	G. E. Nelson	27th May, 1885	Died 28th Nov., 1887
Lieutenants ..	John Harpin	1st June, 1860	Died (no date recorded)
	Thomas Beardsell ..	16th Oct., 1872	Promoted
	Joseph Ramsden Mellor	1st June, 1873	Resigned 7th June, 1876
	G. E. Nelson	7th June, 1876	Promoted
Ensigns ..	Geo. Henry Hinchliff ..	1st June, 1860	Resigned 20th Aug., 1862
	John Morehouse Dyson	20th Aug., 1862	Promoted captain
	Joseph Ramsden Mellor	16th Oct., 1872	Promoted
Sub-Lieutenant.. ..	G. E. Nelson	7th June, 1876	Promoted
Honorary Assistant Surgeon ..	Charles James Trotter ..	1st June, 1860	Resigned 20th Mar., 1875
Honorary Chaplain ..	Rev. J. Fearon	20th Aug., 1862	Resigned 20th Mar., 1875
Acting Chaplain ..	Rev. J. Fearon	20th Mar., 1875	Died in 1877

Posting of Officers not recorded in the War Office since consolidation.

Strength of all Ranks.

There are no records in the War Office which shew the strength prior to 1867 nor after consolidation.

Holmfirth (32nd West Yorkshire).

1867 ..	105	1872 ..	62	1876 ..	73
1868 ..	120	1873 ..	50	1877 ..	61
1869 ..	110	1874 ..	63	1878 ..	72
1870 ..	104	1875 ..	73	1879 ..	71
1871 ..	74				

Mirfield.

41st West Riding of Yorkshire Rifle Volunteer Corps.

Headquarters, Mirfield.

One company and one sub-division.

Formed 15th November, 1864.

One sub-division added 2nd February, 1869.

Included in 5th Administrative Battalion from formation.

On consolidation became K Company of 6th West York Rifle Volunteer Corps, 1st June, 1880.

Title of 6th West Riding of Yorkshire Rifle Volunteer Corps changed to 2nd Volunteer Battalion West Riding Regiment, by General Order of 1st February, 1883.

Officers.

Rank	Names.	Date of Appointment.	
Captains ..	Edward Day	22nd Nov., 1864	Resigned 18th Feb., 1868
	Albert Williamson ..	15th Mar., 1869	Resigned. Honorary rank of Major, 10th April, 1886
	John Crowther, Honorary Major ..	8th May, 1886 29th May, 1886	Promoted Major 11th Dec., 1895; Honorary Lieutenant-Colonel 15th Jan., 1896; resigned, retaining rank, &c., 1st Jan., 1898
Lieutenants ..	John Staincliffe Hurst ..	22nd Nov., 1864	Resigned 16th Mar., 1866
	James Howgate, Junior..	16th Mar., 1866	Resigned 30th April, 1867
	Albert Williamson ..	30th Apl., 1867	Promoted
	Thos. Green Beaumont..	15th Mar., 1869	Resigned 24th June, 1874
	Joseph Barker	15th Mar., 1869	Deceased 23rd Mar., 1870
	William Greenwood Lockwood	5th April, 1870	Resigned 22nd Nov., 1873
	J. Crowther	1st June, 1873	Promoted
	W. J. F. Dandison ..	3rd May, 1876	Resigned 7th Feb., 1879
Ensigns ..	Thomas Wade	22nd Nov., 1864	Resigned 31st July, 1865
	James Howgate	31st July, 1865	Promoted
	Albert Williamson ..	16th Mar., 1866	Promoted
	Thos. Green Beaumont..	30th Apl., 1867	Promoted
	Alfred Barrowclough ..	15th Mar., 1869	Resigned 22nd Nov., 1873
	John Crowther	15th Mar., 1869	Promoted
Sub-Lieutenant ..	W. J. F. Dandison ..	3rd May, 1876	Promoted
Honorary Assistant Surgeon ..	William Marsden ..	6th Jan., 1865	Resigned 15th Mar., 1869
Assistant Surgeon ..	William Marsden ..	15th Mar., 1869	Resigned 24th June, 1874

Strength of all Ranks.

No records in the War Office shewing strength prior to 1867 nor after consolidation.

1867 .. 98	1872 .. 100	1876 .. 108
1868 .. 124	1873 .. 95	1877 .. 104
1869 .. 131	1874 .. 85	1878 .. 108
1870 .. 126	1875 .. 98	1879 .. 103
1871 .. 118		

Meltham.

44th West Riding of Yorkshire Rifle Volunteer Corps.

Headquarters, Meltham.

One Company.

Formed 10th July, 1868

Included in the 5th Administrative Battalion.

Disbanded 11th January, 1876.

Rank.	Names.	Date of Appointment.	
Captain ..	Edward Coleman Gooddy	29th Aug. 1868	Resigned 8th Jan., 1876 on disbandment
Lieutenant ..	Thomas Julius Hirst ..	29th Aug. 1868	Resigned 8th Jan., 1876 on disbandment
Honorary Chaplain ..	Rev. Edward Collis Watson	29th Aug 1868	Resigned 20th Mar., 1875 on appointment as Acting Chaplain

Strength of all Ranks.

No records in the War Office shewing strength prior to 1867.

1867 .. 70	1870 .. 62	1873 .. 37
1868 .. 54	1871 .. 56	1874 .. 36
1869 .. 71	1872 .. 74	

Disbanded 11th January, 1876.

The period I have traversed in this the final section of this work embraces the years between 1793 and 1875, a term of eighty years. Not least striking of the many changes I have had to record have been those of uniform. The Volunteer levies have been true to the adage, *on revient toujours à ses premiers amours*. The year 1794 found the local levies with a uniform in which scarlet was the predominant hue. The year 1874 saw them clad in a garb that had at least so much in common with the uniform of their predecessors; and with that year I must conclude my labours.

The later history of the corps whose fortunes I have followed with so much interest, and whose welfare will always be near to my heart, is an attractive theme; but I must leave its treatment to other and abler hands, rejoicing for my own part that I have been enabled to furnish this contribution to the annals of my native town, and to preserve to posterity records that otherwise might easily have perished, and which I am persuaded many will care to see rescued from the oblivion that might have befallen them.

FINIS.

APPENDICES.

APPENDIX A.

War Office, Pall Mall,

May 12th, 1859.

Her Majesty's Government having had under consideration the propriety of permitting the formation of Volunteer Rifle Corps under the provisions of the Act of 44 George, III. cap. 54 as well as of Artillery Corps and Companies in maritime towns in which there may be forts and batteries, I have the honour to inform you that I shall be prepared to receive through you and consider any proposal with that object which may emanate from the county under your charge.

The principal and most important provisions of the Act are:—

44 Geo. III. 54 Section 3. "That the corps be formed under officers bearing the commission of the Lieutenant of the county.

Section 20. That its members must take the oath of allegiance before a Deputy Lieutenant or Justice of the Peace or a Commissioned Officer of the corps.

Section 22. That it be liable to be called out in case of actual invasion or appearance of an enemy in force on the coast or in case of a rebellion arising out of either of those emergencies.

Section 23. That while thus under arms, its members are subject to military law and entitled to be billeted and to receive pay in like manner as the regular Army.

Section 40. That all Commissioned Officers disabled in actual service are entitled to half pay, and Non-commissioned Officers and Privates to the benefit of Chelsea Hospital, and widows of commissioned officers killed in service to such pensions for life as are given to widows of Officers of Her Majesty's Regular Forces.

Sections 30 and 31. That members cannot quit the corps when on actual service but may do so at any other time by giving 14 days' notice.

Section 5 That members who have attended 8 days' in each 4 months or a total of 24 days' drill and exercise in the year are entitled to be returned as effective.

Section 4. That members so returned are exempt from Militia ballot or from being called upon to serve in any other levy.

Section 50. That all property of the corps is legally vested in the Commanding Officer and subscriptions and fines under the rules and regulations are recoverable by him before a magistrate."

---

* The marginal references to the Statute are mine.—R.P.B.

The conditions on which Her Majesty's Government will recommend to Her Majesty the acceptance of any proposal are :—

"That the formation of the corps be recommended by the Lord Lieutenant of the county.

That the corps be subject to the provisions of the Act already quoted.

That its members undertake to provide their own arms and equipments and to defray all expenses attending the corps except in the event of its being assembled for actual service.

That the rules and regulations which may be thought necessary be submitted to me in accordance with the 56th section of the Act.

The uniform and equipments of the corps may be settled by the members subject to your approval, but the arms, though provided at the expense of the members, must be furnished under the superintendence and according to the Regulations of the Department in order to secure a a perfect uniformity of gauge.

The establishment of officers and non-commissioned officers will be fixed by me and recorded in the books of this office, and, in order that I may be enabled to determine the proportion, you will be pleased to specify the precise number of private men which you will recommend and into how many companies you propose to divide them."

I have only to add that I shall look to you as Her Majesty's Lieutenant for the nomination of proper persons to be appointed officers subject to the Queen's approval.

I have the honour to be, &c.,

Your most obedient servant,

J. PEEL.

Her Majesty's Lieutenant for the County of

The War Office Circular of 25th May, 1859, is fully set out on pp. 125-128 inclusive.

APPENDIX B.

War Office,

13th July, 1859.

My Lord,

Her Majesty's Government are fully sensible of the public spirit displayed by large numbers of Her Majesty's subjects who have offered to form Volunteer Artillery or Rifle Corps under the Act 44 Geo. 3, cap. 54. Though engaged in important and often lucrative occupations, they have expressed their willingness, at their own cost and at a considerable sacrifice of time, to instruct themselves in drill and in the use of the arm, whether rifle or great gun, which they propose to adopt, with a view to fit themseves to act as auxiliaries to Her Majesty's Regular Forces in case of public danger.

But though the very essence of a Volunteer Force consists in their undertaking themselves to bear, without any cost to the public, the whole charges of their training and practice previous to being called out for actual service, Her Majesty's Government are of opinion, that it will be but fair to the Volunteers, as a just acknowledgment of the spirit in which their services are tendered, to relieve them, in some degree, of the expense which their first outfit will entail upon them, and of which the purchase of arms is necessarily the heaviest item.

It is not necessary for the purpose of instruction that each individual of a corps should be provided with a rifle, since a Musketry Instructor cannot superintend a larger class than about 30 men. It is proposed, therefore, to issue in the first instance to each corps Enfield Rifles at the rate of 25 per cent. of the effective members for the purpose of instruction, the Government undertaking [illegible] the whole effectives of the force, whenever it may be called out for active service [illegible] the enemy.

[illegible] necessary however before these arms can be issued, or indeed before [illegible] any Corps can, for the future, be accepted, that certain precautions [illegible] a view to ensure the public safety, and the efficiency of the [illegible].

[illegible] Government entertain no objection to the members of any [illegible] Corps providing themselves with breech loaders, or any other [illegible] Rifle for purposes of ball practice, upon the understanding that, [illegible] regulation gauge in barrel and nipple, no practice ammunition can [illegible] the Government for such arms.

[illegible] the Corps will, however, under all circumstances, be furnished [illegible] of the Enfield Rifle, with the use of which weapon the members [illegible] acquaint themselves, as in case of the active services of the [illegible] Force being required, it must be exclusively armed with the rifle [illegible] the regular Forces of Her Majesty.

[illegible] Secretary of State must be satisfied by the report of competent [illegible], who will be sent down for the purpose, that a sufficient and safe [illegible] can be obtained within a reasonable distance of the Head [illegible] there no such range can be found, a Rifle Corps would clearly be [illegible] for want of practice, or dangerous, if attempting it where the [illegible] country affords no sufficient security against accident, which would [illegible] upon the Volunteer Force in general, and would tend to indispose [illegible] wards them.

[illegible] Lord Lieutenant must satisfy himself, and must certify to the [illegible] State, that a secure place of custody for the arms, and a competent [illegible] take charge of them, have been provided at the expense of the [illegible].

[illegible] Militia County Stores or Police Stations might, no doubt, in some [illegible] be made available for this purpose.

[illegible] The Rules and Regulations for the government of Volunteer Corps [illegible] submitted to and approved by the Secretary of State.

[illegible] The Corps must be subject to periodical inspection by a Military Officer [illegible] for that purpose.

[illegible] Royal Highness the General Commanding-in-Chief, with a view to [illegible] facility for the musketry instruction of the Volunteer Force, has [illegible] the reception of two Officers or members of each Company, at their [illegible] or that of the corps, at the School of Musketry at Hythe, to [illegible] modified course of instruction, which shall enable them to conduct the [illegible] of their Companies upon the general principles adopted in the regular Army with such signal success. A large Musketry Class of Sergeants of the

Disembodied Militia will, moreover, soon be formed at Hythe, so that within the course of a few months there will be a vast increase in the number of Musketry Instructors, who will be available for the instruction of the Volunteer Force.

But Her Majesty's Government are especially anxious to direct the attention of the Lords Lieutenant of maritime counties in which our commercial ports and chief arsenals are situated, to the desirability of forming Artillery rather than Rifle Corps.

In case of war the vast number of guns mounted in our coast defences will require a large Artillery force to work them, and the Volunteers can in no way be so useful to the public service as when formed in Artillery Corps to man the batteries, and thus release a proportionate force of Royal Artillery for service in the field.

Her Majesty's Government will, therefore, in all cases where coast batteries are available for practice, give a preference to the formation of Artillery Corps. At places on the sea coast at which batteries do not now exist, but where the Military Authorities may deem it advisable to place guns hereafter, Artillery Corps may usefully be formed, if the members, aided by the residents in their vicinity, would take upon themselves the erection of earth works.

In that case guns would be provided by the Government for training and practice, and for arming the works in case of necessity.

Should the Lords Lieutenant of maritime counties be of opinion that these suggestions can be carried out, Her Majesty's Government will request the Military Authorities to afford competent professional advice as to the selection of proper sites for such coast defences, and as to their construction and armament.

With a view to the formation of Volunteer Associations in our commercial ports and open rivers, for manning and working boats or ship's launches, armed with single guns to be supplied by the Government as recommended in the 17th paragraph of the Circular of the 25th of May last, the Board of Admiralty will be requested, on application from the Lords Lieutenant, to send down a competent Officer to give his advice to these Associations in regard to their organization and equipment, and to aid them in the gunnery instruction.

Misconceptions having apparently arisen with regard to the selection of individuals to fill the position of Officers in the Volunteer Force and of their responsibilities, I can only repeat, that while I shall not be disposed to question the grounds upon which a Lord Lieutenant may recommend any person for a Commission for Her Majesty's approval, I cannot recognize the principle of the election of their Officers by any body possessing, in any sense, a military organization.

With the view of facilitating the early development of the Volunteer system, I transmit, for general information and guidance, the accompanying memorandum, shortly recapitulating the conditions upon which Her Majesty's Government have determined to sanction the formation of Corps, showing their proposed organization and establishment, and the nature of the aid which it is proposed to afford them, and indicating a course of proceeding which, by obviating in a great degree necessity of reference to this office, will afford the means of a more speedy and effectual realization of the loyal and patriotic desire so widely manifested throughout the country by Her Majesty's subjects, to place their services graciously at the Queen's command, for the general defence of the nation.

I have the honour to be,
My Lord,
Your obedient Servant,
SIDNEY HERBERT

To the Lord Lieutenant
Of the West Riding of Yorkshire.

APPENDIX C.

MEMORANDUM regarding the Formation, Organization, Establishment, Instruction, &c., of Volunteer Corps in Great Britain, to be raised under the Act 44 Geo. III., cap. 54.

CONDITIONS OF ACCEPTANCE OF OFFERS OF SERVICE.

1—In all cases of actual invasion, or appearance of any enemy in force on the coast of Great Britain, or of rebellion or insurrection arising or existing within the same, or the appearance of any enemy in force on the coast, or during any invasion, but not otherwise, the services of the Volunteer Force will extend to any part of Great Britain.

2—Before giving his sanction for the formation of any Rifle Corps, the Secretary of State will require that safe ranges for rifle practice be obtained, of not less than 200 yards, this being the minimum range of any practical utility. An Officer will be sent, upon the requisition of the Lord Lieutenant, to assist the Volunteers in selecting a practice-ground, and to report upon its sufficiency or otherwise. For this purpose it should be stated to whom the officer should address himself, and when it will be convenient to receive him for this duty.

3—That accommodation for the safe custody of the arms (at police stations, county militia stores, or elsewhere), and a competent person to keep them in good order be provided, at the cost of the corps; and that the expense of keeping the same in repair be borne by the funds of the Corps.

4—Rules and regulations for the government of the force and for its discipline, when not subject to martial law under the provisions of sections 22 and 23 of the Act 44 George III., cap 54, shall be submitted to and approved by the Secretary of State for War.

When so approved, these will, under section 56, be valid and binding upon the members of the force, and the penalties will be recoverable before a Magistrate.

It is proposed to assemble a Committee, composed of five members of the Volunteer Force, aided by one Military Officer to be nominated by the Secretary of State, to compile a code of rules and regulations to serve as a model or guide which will greatly assist the Volunteer Corps in drawing up their Rules.

5—That Corps be subject to periodical inspection by a Military Officer deputed for that purpose.

The uniform and equipments of all the Corps must be approved by the Lord Lieutenant, and should be as far as possible similar for Corps of Artillery and Rifles respectively within the same county in order to enable the Government at any time to form the corps into battalions.

Preliminary Course to be adopted with a view to the sanction of a Volunteer Corps.

7—In order to facilitate the formation of Corps, the Lord Lieutenant, before transmitting any offer of service, should ascertain and report to the Secretary of State that the members clearly understand that if their offer be accepted, they thereby become amenable to the general provisions of the Act 44 George III., cap 54, as well as to the six foregoing conditions. It is necessary to observe that no proposals for the formation of Corps, nor application connected with the organization, equipment, or government of the Force, can be entertained by the Secretary of State for War, unless they be recommended by the Lord Lieutenant of the county, or in the Cinque Ports and Stanneries, by the Lords Warden, and in the Isle of Wight, by the Governor.

Organization.

8—In order to render available the services of individuals residing in places not capable of raising so large a body as a Company, and more especially with the view of encouraging, as largely as possible, the formation of small bodies of artillery at the smaller maritime places, Her Majesty's Government have determined, in such cases, to sanction the formation of sub-divisions and sections of Artillery and of sub-divisions of Rifle Companies, with a proportionate number of Officers.

Establishment Artillery.

9—A Company of Artillery will consist of

not less than 50 } effectives,
nor more than 80 }

with 1 Captain,
1 Lieutenant,
1 2nd Lieutenant,

A sub-division to be not less than 30 effectives,
with 1 Lieutenant,
1 2nd Lieutenant.

A section, not less than 20 effectives,
with 1 Lieutenant.

Establishment Rifles.

10—A Company will consist of

not less than 60 } effectives,
nor more than 100 }

with 1 Captain,
1 Lieutenant,
1 Ensign.

A sub division of not less than 30 effectives,
with 1 Lieutenant,
1 Ensign.

11.—It is to be understood that the formation of Companies, sub-divisions, or sections will not be sanctioned for a less number of effectives than the establishments herein assigned to these bodies respectively, but that they may exceed [illegible] that number.

In places in which, from their large population as well as [illegible], several companies, whether of Artillery or Rifles, are likely to be raised, the Secretary of State will be prepared, with a view as far as possible to increase the efficiency of the Volunteers by enabling them to accommodate their arms in a common storehouse and to secure a practice range for the whole number of companies instead of for each company separately, to accept their services as a Battalion, on the recommendation of the Lord Lieutenant, provided that a sufficient number of companies and of men be raised to justify such an organization. When therefore as many as eight companies or a force not less than [illegible] 500 strong, though with fewer companies, can be raised, the Government [illegible] sanction the appointment of a Lieutenant-Colonel, a Major and Adjutant, to be paid by the Corps.

For the rural districts of a county, in which, from the distance from each other of the several companies, it may be inconvenient to unite them in battalions, the Secretary of State will be prepared, on the application of the Lord Lieutenant, to recommend to Her Majesty the appointment of a Field Officer of the rank suited to the amount of the Force in each district, to superintend the whole of the several companies and sub-divisions not forming a part of any battalion.

SUPERNUMERARIES.

12.—The sanction of the Secretary of State for War must be obtained for the enrolment of any supernumeraries beyond the establishment, whether as effective members for general service, or of individuals who, desirous to contribute by their influence and means to the formation of volunteer corps, may be unequal to greater physical exertion than the mere attendance at the stipulated drills and the performance of local duties.

NON-EFFECTIVES.

13.—The admission of honorary members or non-effectives, willing to contribute towards the expenses of the corps, will also be sanctioned by the Secretary of State. For these members a separate column is set apart in the Return, Schedule A in the Volunteer Act.

PRECEDENCE OF COMPANIES &C. OF VOLUNTEERS AND OF OFFICERS.

14—Artillery Corps will, as in the regular service, rank before the Rifle Corps. The whole volunteer force of a county will take precedence throughout Great Britain, according to the date of the formation of the first company of their respective arms in a county. The several companies will rank, as Artillery and Rifles respectively, within their own counties in the order of their formation. The whole county force and the several companies, sub-divisions, and sections will be numbered and entered in the Army List.

In order to the assignment of precedence, the sub-divisions will rank after the companies, as Artillery and Rifles respectively, according to the dates of their formation, and the sections after the sub-divisions.

Volunteers for manning Gun-Boats, &c.

15—Volunteers associated for the manning of gun-boats, launches, &c., will be subject to the rules for the organization, establishment, and precedence of Artillery Volunteers, and will be allowed the same advantages as regards instructions and practice as those which will be found in Article 25 for the Artillery Force.

Rank of Officers.

16—Officers will, of course, take precedence according to the dates of their commissions.

Officers holding similar commissions, bearing the same date, will rank according to the precedence of the force of their respective counties, or, if belonging to separate companies in the same county, then, according to the precedence of their respective companies, and if belonging to the same corps they will take precedence according to the order in which their names are inserted in the Army List.

Equipment Artillery.

17—Artillery Corps will not be required to have small arms.

Each Volunteer will provide himself with a waist-belt of black or brown leather, for the reception of side-arms.

N.B.—Gold lace is not to be worn, that being the special distinction for Officers in the Regular Forces.

Equipment of Rifles. Arms.

18—Upon the conditions stated in Article 4, rifles to the extent of 25 per cent. of the effectives will be supplied by the Government, for purposes of instruction, upon requisition according to a prescribed form, which will be furnished on application to the War Office. In case of being called out for active service in the field the whole force will be armed by the Government.

Her Majesty's Government entertain no objection to the members of any Volunteer Rifle Corps providing themselves with breach loaders, or any other description of rifle, for purposes of ball practice, upon the understanding that, if not of the regulation gauge in barrel and nipple, no practice ammunition can be issued by the Government for such arms.

Every Rifle Corps will, however, under all circumstances, be furnished with 25 per cent. of the Enfield rifle, with the use of which weapon the members are expected to acquaint themselves, as in case of the active services of the Volunteer Force being required, it must be exclusively armed with the rifle common to all the regular forces of Her Majesty.

Accoutrements.

19—Accoutrements, to be provided at the expense of the members, will consist of waist-belt of black or brown leather, sliding frog for bayonet, ball-bag containing cap-pocket, and twenty-round pouch.

Patterns may be seen, on application at the pattern-room, War Department, Pimlico.

Ammunition Artillery.

20—The supply for practice will be issued, free of cost, from the local magazines in charge of the Royal Artillery, in such quantities as shall be hereafter determined

Ammunition and Targets. Rifles.

21—Article 8 of the Circular of 25th May last is revised as follows:—

There will be no special allowance of ammunition for training recruits, but the following uniform annual issues, at the cost price, will be sanctioned for the duly qualified effectives (See sections 5, 6, 7, 8 of the Volunteer Act),

Viz: 100 Rounds ball per man.
60 ,, blank .
176 Percussion caps.
20 Ditto for snapping practice.

The application for ammunition must be made by the officer commanding to the Secretary of State for War, according to forms which will be furnished by the War Office

22—Targets will be issued at cost price, as stated in the Circular of 25th May, not exceeding five per Company. Forms of requisition will be furnished by the War Office.

Returns to be rendered.

23—The attention of Officers commanding is particularly called to the necessity of the utmost regularity in rendering the several Returns, of which forms are annexed, specified in the Volunteer Act. These provide a check upon all the contemplated issues, and the necessary intimation for the regular inspection of the Force.

Attendance at Drill.

24—It is to be understood, with reference to the 5th, 6th, 7th sections of the Volunteer Act, that the number of days' attendance at muster, stipulated by the Act, viz.: eight days at least, in the course of four months, need not be continuous; but in order to entitle any Volunteer to be returned as an effective, it is necessary that he should have attended on the prescribed number of days the ordinary drills established by the Officer commanding, whose duty it will be to consult the convenience of the members in so far as the efficiency of the force will permit.

Drill and means of Instruction. Artillery.

25—The Artillery Volunteers will be taught the garrison gun drill by instructors from the Royal Artillery.

They will be appointed to certain batteries or guns in the nearest possible vicinity to their homes, and when they shall have become sufficiently instructed, they will be told off and permanently attached to particular guns to undertake its general service.

As the Royal Artillery have the charge of all batteries, magazines, and ordnance stores, no responsibility or charge will devolve on the Volunteer Corps in respect to them.

When any Company of Artillery, or portion thereof, shall have been actually enrolled, the Officer commanding will notify to the Secretary of State for War when the Volunteers are ready to commence drill, whereupon the necessary arrangement will be immediately made for giving effect to the above provisions.

26—At places on the sea coast at which batteries do not now exist, but where the military authorities may deem it advisable to place guns hereafter, Artillery corps may usefully be formed, if the members, aided by the residents in their vicinity, would take upon themselves the erection of earth-works.

In that case guns would be provided by the Government for training and practice, and for arming the works in case of necessity.

Should the Lords Lieutenant of maritime counties be of opinion that these suggestions can be carried out, Her Majesty's Government will request the military authorities to afford competent professional advice as to the selection of proper sites for such coast defences, and as to their construction and armament.

Volunteer Artillery Manual.

27—It will materially facilitate the progress of this course of Instruction if each Volunteer will provide himself with, and carefully study the small Volunteer Artilleryman's Manual, now in course of preparation, and shortly to be published at a moderate price, by Boddy and Son, Wellington Street, Woolwich.

Drill Instruction. Rifles.

28—A similar inexpensive Manual for the use of the Volunteer Rifles, is in course of publication by W. Clowes and Son, No. 14, Charing Cross and every Volunteer Rifleman should make himself master of its contents.

The aid of Drill Instructors from the Disembodied Militia will be afforded to the Volunteer Corps, to facilitate which, the Lords-Lieutenant have been requested to empower Officers commanding regiments of disembodied Militia to grant, without further reference to the War Office, the aid of two sergeants of the Permanent Staff, for a period not exceeding three months, to any Volunteer Company (or one sergeant for a sub-division) belonging to the county, or to any such Company (or sub-division respectively) of an adjacent county, should the Militia force of the county to which the Corps belongs be embodied; provided the application be recommended by the Lord-Lieutenant of such adjacent county.

Should there be no sergeants of disembodied Militia available as drill instructors for a Volunteer Corps within the limits of its own or of an adjacent county, application must be made by the Lord-Lieutenant to the Secretary of State for War.

It is most desirable that any irregularity of conduct on the part of any sergeants thus employed be immediately reported to the Officer commanding.

The sergeants of the Permanent Staff cannot be employed upon this duty without their consent; and it is necessary that the Volunteer Corps afford them remuneration of 1s. a day, and a billet or lodging, or 4d. a day in lieu thereof.

This ought not to be in any respect a permanent charge upon the members, since it may reasonably be expected, that intelligent and zealous individuals will be found in every corps, who will, in a comparatively short time, qualify themselves to act as non-commissioned officers and drill instructors.

Musketry Instructors.

29—It is of the greatest moment that the musketry instruction of the Volunteer Force be carried out on the sound principles which are followed in the regular service These are given in a condensed form in the before-mentioned Manual

When a Corps shall have become well acquainted with the ordinary recruit drill, and sufficiently handy with their arms to undertake with advantage the more advanced instructions of the musketry course, the aid of musketry instructors will be afforded, to as great an extent as possible, upon the same terms of remuneration as before stated for drill instructors.

Instruction of Volunteers at the School of Musketry.

30—H.R.H. the General Commanding-in-Chief has been pleased to sanction the reception of a limited number of Officers or Members of Rifle Companies, at their own expense or that of the corps, at the School of Musketry, at Hythe, to undergo a modified course of instruction, which, with due attention on their part, will qualify them to act as the chief instructors of their companies.

The first class will assemble on Saturday, 23rd July, and the course will last about 14 days.

Any members, in the proportion of two per Company, desiring to avail themselves of these means of instruction, are requested to make immediate application to this effect, through their Commanding Officer, to the Secretary of State for War, in order that timely intimation may be made to the Military Authorities.

Forms of Return referred to in Article 22.

To *A. B.*, Her Majesty's Lieutenant for the of

Muster Roll of the persons enrolled and serving in the

of commanded by

[illegible] [illegible] exemption, say) [illegible] Exemption.				Effective Supernumeraries (if any) not entitled to Exemptions.				Non-Effectives.			
No.	[illegible]	Name	When Enrolled.	No.	Parish.	Name.	When Enrolled.	No.	Parish.	Name.	When Enrolled.
1		A. B.									
[illegible]		C. D.									
[illegible]		E. F.									
[illegible]		G. H.									
				Effective Members entitled to Exemption, absent on Leave.							
				No.	Parish.	Name.	When Enrolled.				
[illegible]		L. M.									
[illegible]		N. O.									
11		P. Q.									
12											
13											

N.B.—Discharged or quitted since the date of the last Muster Roll :
A. B.,
C. D. &c.

Establishment allowed -

Supernumeraries allowed

Total number -

Total number in the corps exempt under this Act from serving in the Militia or other additional force - - - -

Ditto—not exempt from serving in the Militia or other additional force - -

Total number of men enrolled in the corps -

I do hereby certify, that the above Corps [*or* Company, *as the case may be*] was inspected on the day of by *or* has been ready and willing to be inspected in the last four months.

Signed, *A. B.*,
Commanding Officer.

I, *K. L.*, Commanding Officer of the do hereby certify upon my Honour, in pursuance of the Act of Parliament, 44 Geo. III, cap. 54, that I have not, to the best of my knowledge and belief, inserted or caused to be inserted in the above Muster Roll, as an effective man, the name of any person who has not duly attended at the muster and exercise of the said corps [*or* company, *as the case may be*], as required by the said Act, and who has not taken the Oath of Allegiance, or been absent on leave given in pursuance of the said Act, or prevented by actual sickness, as has been certified to me by a Medical Practitioner, or has been otherwise proved to my satisfaction, and who is not an effective man.

Signed, *K. L.*,
Commanding Officer.

Dated the

To *A. B.*, Her Majesty's Lieutenant for the of
I. *K. L.*, Commanding Officer of the
[*as the case may be*], serving in the County of
or City of [*as the case may be*], do hereby certify,
That *C. D.* of [*his Description and Parish*] is an effective Member of the said Corps *or* Company [*as the case may be*] within the provisions of an Act passed in the forty-fourth year of the reign of his Majesty Geo. III., cap. 54.

Signed, *K. L.*,
Commanding Officer.

Dated the

Form of Certificate.

Commanding Officer of the

Do hereby certify, in pursuance of an Act passed in the forty-fourth year of the reign of his Majesty Geo. III., cap. 54, that the several persons herein named and described are severally enrolled and serving in the said corps as effective members thereof, and were effective members up to the date of this certificate.

Signed,
Commanding Officer.

Dated the day of

APPENDIX [illegible]

[illegible] West Riding of Yorkshire Rifle Volunteers.

Officers.

Captain [illegible].

Lieutenant [illegible]. Ensign [illegible].

Committee of Management

Under Rule [illegible].

FOR THE YEAR 1859-1860.

Effective Members.	Honorary Members.
Sergeant Mr. [illegible].	T. P. Crosland, Esquire.
Corporal [illegible].	Bentley Shaw, Esquire.
Corporal [illegible].	Charles Brook, Junior, Esquire.
Private [illegible].	[illegible] Bradbury, Esquire.

Honorary Secretary—Mr. [illegible].

Honorary Treasurer—Mr. Laycock.

Bankers—The Huddersfield Banking Company.

Rules and Regulations.

Article I.

Corps under 44 Geo. III. c. 54.

The Corps having been raised under the Act 44 Geo. III., c. 54, the Members are consequently subject to the provisions of that Act, and to all the regulations which have been or shall be issued under the authority of the Secretary of State for War.

Article II.

Effective and Honorary Members.

The Corps shall consist of two classes, (1) ENROLLED MEMBERS, consisting of effectives, non-effectives, and supernumeraries; (2) HONORARY MEMBERS, the latter contributing to the funds of the Corps, but not being enrolled for service.

Article III.

Honorary members not to interfere, and need not have uniform or enrol.

Honorary Members shall not interfere in any way with the military duties of the Corps; neither shall it be obligatory on them to provide themselves with uniform nor to enrol themselves.

Article IV.

Annual Subscriptions, as follows:—of Effectives.

The Annual Subscriptions of the enrolled Members of the Corps shall be as

	£	s.	d.		£	s.	d.
Captain	10	10	0	Sergeants ..	1	11	6
Lieutenant ..	5	5	0	Corporals ..	1	1	0
Surgeon	4	4	0	Privates	0	10	6
Ensign	3	3	0				

Article V.

All subscribers of £10 10s. od. or upwards, in one payment, or of an entrance fee of £2 2s. od., and of £2 2s. od. annually, to the funds of the Corps, shall be admitted as Honorary Members, and entitled (subject to rules and regulations to be made or sanctioned by the Committee) to practise on the drill and shooting grounds when not required by the effective Members

Subscriptions and Life Payments of Honorary Members.

Article VI.

All Subscriptions shall fall due on the first of the month succeeding that in which the Queen shall have signified her acceptance of the service of the Corps; and on the same day in each succeeding year, viz.:—1st December.

Subscriptions fall due.

Article VII.

All future candidates for membership of the Corps shall be proposed by a member, in writing, sent to the Honorary Secretary; who shall summon a general meeting of the Corps, to ballot for the admission of such candidate, who must be approved by three-fourths of the members present at that meeting.

Election of Members.

Article VIII.

The Officer in command will propose gentlemen to the Lord Lieutenant for commissions as Officers; but the appointment of all Officers is vested by Act of Parliament in the Lord Lieutenant, subject to the Queen's approval.

Appointment of Officers.

Article IX.

The Non-commissioned Officers shall be appointed by the Officer in command.

Appointment of Non-commissioned Officers.

Article X.

Each member must be provided with uniform and accoutrements of the pattern approved by the Lord Lieutenant of the Riding.

Members to provide Uniform and Accoutrements.

Article XI.

Each member shall pay the expense of his ammunition.

Members to pay for Ammunition.

Article XII.

The corps will assemble for drill and practice, twice a week, during the months of May, June, July, and August; and once a week, during the remainder of the year: but the opportunity for attending instruction drill and rifle practice shall be afforded to the Volunteers at least three times a week at convenient hours.

Drill and Practice times.

Article XIII.

The commanding Officer shall fix the time and place for parades, drills, and rifle practice, having regard to the convenience of the members.

Drill and Practice times to be fixed by Commanding Officer.

Article XIV.

The expression "Property of the Corps" shall include all articles which have been purchased out of the funds of the Corps, or given or presented to it.

Property of Corps to include Articles purchased, &c.

ARTICLE XV.

Each member shall be responsible for the due preservation of all articles issued to him, which are the property of Her Majesty's Government, or of the Corps, fair wear and tear only excepted.

ARTICLE XVI.

The property of the Corps is, by 50th Section of Act 44 Geo III. c. 54, legally vested in the commanding Officer but a committee to aid him in the management of its finances and other non-military affairs shall be appointed annually This committee shall consist of the commissioned Officers and Honorary Treasurer, and Honorary Secretary of the Corps, and eight members, to be elected annually by ballot—four from the effectives and four from the honorary members of the Corps; the first election to take place within one calendar month from the services of the Corps being accepted.

ARTICLE XVII.

Annual General Meeting.

That there shall be an Annual General Meeting of the Corps on or about the first day of December, at which the Committee shall make a statement of the proceedings during the past year; and the election of the Committee for the ensuing year shall then take place.

ARTICLE XVIII.

Abstract of Accounts to be made out annually.

The commanding Officer shall cause an abstract of the accounts to be annually prepared for the information of every member of the Corps.

ARTICLE XIX.

Fines on Commissioned Officers failing to attend Drills, &c.

The commissioned Officers shall, with the approval of the Officer commanding, make such arrangements that one of them, at least, shall be present at the weekly parades, or whenever a special parade shall be ordered. In case of this arrangement being broken, all the commissioned Officers of the Corps shall be subject to a fine of five shillings each, unless it be proved to the satisfaction of the Officer commanding that the non-observance has been occasioned by the neglect of the Officer whose turn it was to be present; in which case that Officer shall be fined ten shillings.

ARTICLE XX.

Fines on Non-Commissioned Officers failing to attend Drills, &c.

The Non-commissioned Officers shall, with the approval of the Officer commanding, make such arrangements that at least two sergeants and two corporals shall be present with the Corps as often as it shall assemble. In the event of this arrangement being broken, all the Non-commissioned Officers shall be subject to be fined two shillings and sixpence each, unless it be proved to the satisfaction of the Officer commanding which of them is to blame; in which case the offending person shall be fined five shillings.

Article XXI.

The senior Officer commanding shall have power, subject to the approval of the commanding Officer, to inflict fines for minor offences as follows:—

Commanding Officer to have power to inflict Fines.

	s.	d
For loading without orders, or shooting out of time ..	2	6
For discharging rifle accidentally	5	0
For pointing the same, loaded or unloaded, at any person	10	0
For talking in the ranks	1	0
For smoking, or drinking wine, beer, or spirit, during drill, or practice	2	6

Article XXII.

All fines imposed on members of the Corps shall become due on the first day of the month succeeding that in which they have been incurred, and shall be collected by the Company's Sergeant, and paid by him to the Captain, who shall enter the same in a book kept by him or his nominee for that purpose.

Fines to be collected by Sergeant, &c.

Article XXIII.

When the Corps is not assembled for actual service, the commanding Officer, by the general provision of Act 44, Geo. III., c 54, is solely responsible for the discipline of the Corps, but it shall be lawful for him at any time to assemble a Court of Enquiry, consisting of two Officers and two enrolled members of the Corps, to be appointed by rolster, for the purpose of investigating any irregularity, or assisting him in coming to a conclusion upon it; and any enquiry in reference to a commissioned Officer shall be made by a court composed of officers of the volunteer establishment within the Riding of the County, convened under the authority of the Lord Lieutenant.

Court of Enquiry to investigate irregularities.

Article XXIV.

That any member who shall commit any act or offence which may injuriously affect the honour, peace, or prosperity of the Corps, shall, on proof thereof before a court of enquiry, convened by order of the Commanding Officer, consisting of two officers and two enrolled members, according to rolster, be liable to be censured or fined by the commanding Officer, from whose decision there shall be no appeal, and, if not a commissioned Officer, shall further be liable to be expelled and to forfeit any interest that he may have in the Corps; but any court of enquiry in reference to commissioned Officers shall be composed of commissioned Officers only of the volunteer establishment, convened under the authority of the Lord Lieutenant.

Court of Enquiry may censure or expel Members.

Article XXV.

Style of Musketry Instruction to be adhered to.

The system of musketry instruction recommended for volunteers by the Commandant of the School of Musketry, at Hythe, must be adhered to.

Article XXVI.

Members to provide themselves with the Volunteer's Rifle Manual and copy of the Rules.

Every volunteer is expected to provide himself with "The Volunteer's Rifle Manual," and with a copy of the Rules of the Corps.

Memorandum.—*The acceptance of the Services of the Corps was announced by letter, dated the 3rd of November, 1859.*

APPENDIX E.

THE REGULATIONS OF 1861 FOR THE VOLUNTEER FORCE SO FAR AS RELATES TO THE INFANTRY.

Dated, War Office, 19th January, 1861

The following Regulations published by the authority of the Secretary of State for War supersede all Circulars and Orders hitherto issued relative to the Volunteer force, and are to be strictly observed until altered by proper authority.

Any alteration which may become necessary hereafter will be notified to all Commanding Officers by a Circular Memorandum embodying the new Regulation, and referring to the part of these Regulations which is modified or cancelled thereby.

DE GREY AND RIPON.

CONSTITUTION AND ESTABLISHMENTS.

1—Volunteer Corps are raised under the Act 44 Geo. III. c. 54 They are subject to the provisions of that Act and of the Statutes by which it has been amended, and to all Regulations which have been or shall be made with regard to them by the authority of Her Majesty's Principal Secretary of State for War

2—In all cases of actual invasion, or appearance of an enemy in force on the coast of Great Britain, or of rebellion or insurrection arising or existing within the same or on the appearance of an enemy in force on the coast or during an invasion, Volunteer corps may be assembled for actual service; and whenever they are so assembled, they will be liable to serve in any part of Great Britain, unless a special arrangement to the contrary has been sanctioned at the time of Her Majesty's acceptance of their service

3—The members of a Volunteer corps are either enrolled or honorary.

4—Enrolled members are persons of every grade, whose names are duly entered for service in the muster roll of a corps.

5—Honorary members are persons who contribute to the funds of a corps, but are not enrolled for service.

6—The Volunteer force is composed of the following arms:—

Light Horse Volunteers,
Artillery Volunteers,
Engineer Volunteers,
Mounted Rifle Volunteers,
Rifle Volunteers.

7—The general object of the force, when on actual service, is to supplement the Regular, Militia, and other forces in the country.

* * * * * * * * *

8—The following Tables contain the authorized establishments of the different arms of which the Volunteer force is composed.

In these Tables, two numbers divided by a line signify the maximum and minimum strength; thus, 100—60 means not more than 100 nor less than 60.

Table of Establishments for Rifles.

Sub-division—One lieutenant, one ensign, one quartermaster-sergeant, 3—2 sergeants, 3—2 corporals, one bugler, 49—22 privates ; total, 59—30.

Company.—One captain, one lieutenant, one ensign, one quartermaster-sergeant, one colour-sergeant, 4—2 sergeants, 5—3 corporals, two buglers, 84—48 privates ; total, 100—60.

Battalion of four companies.—One major, four captains, four lieutenants, four ensigns, one adjutant, one surgeon, one sergeant-major, one quartermaster-sergeant, one armourer, one orderly-room clerk, one bugle-major, four colour-sergeants, 16—8 sergeants, 20—12 corporals, eight buglers, 332—188 privates ; total, 400—240.

Battalion of six companies.—One lieutenant-colonel, six captains, six lieutenants, six ensigns, one adjutant, one surgeon, one assistant-surgeon, one sergeant-major, one quartermaster-sergeant, one armourer, one orderly-room clerk, one bugle-major, six colour-sergeants, 24—12 sergeants, 30—18 corporals, twelve buglers, 501—285 privates ; total, 600—360.

Battalion of eight companies.—One lieutenant-colonel, one major, eight captains, eight lieutenants, eight ensigns, one adjutant, one surgeon, two assistant-surgeons, one sergeant-major, one quartermaster-sergeant, one armourer, one orderly-room clerk, one bugle-major, eight colour-sergeants, 32—16 sergeants, 40—24 corporals, sixteen buglers, 669—381 privates ; total, 800—480.

Battalion of twelve companies.—One lieutenant-colonel, two majors, twelve captains, twelve lieutenants, twelve ensigns, one adjutant, one surgeon, two assistant-surgeons, one sergeant-major, one quartermaster-sergeant, one armourer, one orderly-room clerk, one bugle-major, twelve colour-sergeants, 48—24 sergeants, 60—36 corporals, twenty-four buglers, 1,008—576 privates ; total, 1,200—720.

(Note).—When over twelve companies, a Rifle Corps will be divided into two battalions, each with field officers and staff in the above proportions.

A company and a sub-division, or two or more companies of Engineers, Mounted Rifles, or Rifles, may be formed into one corps, under the command of a captain-commandant, in accordance with Article 42 ; and such a corps would be entitled to an assistant-surgeon, in addition to the establishment due to the number of companies, &c. of which it is composed.

Formation of Corps.

9—Persons wishing to form a Volunteer corps should place themselves in communication with the Lord Lieutenant of their county, with whom it rests to offer their services for Her Majesty's acceptance through the Secretary of State for War.

10—An establishment is alloted to every Volunteer corps on its formation.

The Commissioned Officers of a corps are to be reckoned towards the number of enrolled members required to complete the establishment.

11—In offering the service of a * * * * Rifle Volunteer Corps for Her Majesty's acceptance, it is desirable that the Lord Lieutenant should state—

(a)—The place proposed for the head-quarters of the corps.

(b)—The number of Volunteers who are prepared to enroll themselves.

(c)—The proposed establishment of the corps—that is to say, of how many divisions, sub-divisions, troops, companies, squadrons, or battalions, as laid down in the tables given in Article 8, it is intended to consist.

(d)—That the Volunteers have secured the use of a rifle practice ground, and have provided a safe store house, and a competent guardian, for any Government arms which may be issued to them.

(e)—The name and address of some person with whom the officer sent to inspect the practice ground may communicate.

The form in which this information should be given is stated in Appendix A.

12—The Secretary of State for War, on receiving the Lord Lieutenant's offer, will, when the proposed practice-range has not previously been approved, appoint a competent officer to visit the locality, and to communicate with the person mentioned by the Lord Lieutenant. It will be the duty of the officer thus appointed to inspect the rifle practice ground or grounds proposed for the use of the corps, and to report, for the information of the Secretary of State for War:—

(a)—The situation of the ground proposed.

(b)—The extent of range afforded, which must not be less than 200 yards.

(c)—What arrangements are required to secure the safety and convenience of the public.

(d)—The nature and dimensions of the butts which are to be erected.

(e)—Whether the Volunteers have obtained the consent of the owners and occupiers of the ground for its being used as a range

13—If the Inspecting Officer's report is satisfactory, and the other information detailed in article 11 has been duly furnished, the Secretary of State will then lay before the Queen the Lord Lieutenant's offer of the services of the corps; and, should Her Majesty be pleased to accept it, he will signify Her Majesty's pleasure to the Lord Lieutenant, with whom it will rest to communicate it to the corps.

14 to 19—Refer to Engineers and Volunteer Artillery, omitted.

20—When any increase is proposed in the establishment of a corps, the Commanding Officer is to certify to the Lord Lieutenant in accordance with the form given in Appendix C, that the number of Volunteers enrolled and ready to be enrolled in the corps, exclusive of those who are non-effectives under the Act, amounts to the minimum number of the enrolled members required for the proposed establishment. The Lord Lieutenant will forward this certificate to the Secretary of State, together with the additional offer of service for Her Majesty's acceptance.

21—The establishment of a corps is liable to be reduced if the effective strength of the corps should at any time fall below the minimum establishment assigned to it, and if there should be no reasonable hope of its speedily regaining its proper strength.

PRECEDENCE.

22—The Volunteer force, in which general term the Yeomanry are included, takes precedence immediately after the Militia.

23—In the Volunteer force, the different arms rank in the following order, viz.:—

Light Horse Volunteers,
Artillery Volunteers,
Engineer Volunteers,
Mounted Rifle Volunteers,
Rifle Volunteers.

The relative precedence of a county in any one of these arms does not affect its precedence in any of the others.

24—In every arm, the relative precedence of a county is determined by the date on which the Secretary of State has first received a letter from the lord-lieutenant of that county, offering the service of the corps of that arm for Her Majesty's acceptance.

25—In every county, the relative precedence of the different corps of any one arm is determined by the date on which the Secretary of State has, in each case, received the lord-lieutenant's offer of service.

26—The relative precedence of officers in the entire Volunteer force is determined solely by the rank and date of their commissions in that force.

27—The relative precedence of officers of different corps, holding commissions of the same rank and date, is determined by the relative precedence of the corps to which they respectively belong.

28—The relative precedence of officers of one corps, bearing commissions of the same rank and date, is determined by the order in which their names appear in the Army List. This order is the same as that in which the appointments are inserted in the "London Gazette."

29—Every corps on its formation receives a number indicating its relative precedence with regard to the other corps of the same arm in the county within which the head-quarters of the corps are situated, *e.g.*, "10th Lancashire Rifle Volunteer Corps."

30—The corps under the command of a field-officer are allowed, in addition, to receive special designations, *e.g.*, "The Bristol Rifle Volunteer Corps." Other corps are allowed to style themselves by special titles but only in conjunction with their authorised number and general county designation, *e.g.*, "24th Devonshire (Bicton) Rifle Volunteer Corps."

All applications for leave to bear special designations or titles must be made through the Lord Lieutenant of the county; and no corps is permitted to bear any designation or title except in accordance with this regulation.

31—When the authorised number of any Volunteer corps becomes vacant by the disbanding of the corps, or by its amalgamation with others, the numbers borne by the remaining corps of the same arm in the county are not altered in consequence, except with the consent of the corps concerned.

Commissioned Officers.

32—The Commissioned Officers of the Volunteer force, except Adjutants, are appointed by the Lord Lieutenant of the county to which their corps belongs.

33—All proposed appointments and promotions of Commissioned Officers, except Adjutants, are submitted for the Queen's approval by the Lord Lieutenant through the Secretary of State for War.

34—All proposed resignations of Commissioned Officers are submitted for the Queen's acceptance by the Lord Lieutenant through the Secretary of State for War.

35—When any Commissioned Officer resigns his Commission, and at the same time receives another of the same rank in a different corps, he is allowed to retain, in the general service, the date of his former commission.

36—The commission of any Commissioned Officer of substantive rank cannot be vacated except by promotion, resignation, deprivation or death.

37—The fee due on any commission is to be paid by the officer receiving the commission.

The amount of the fee is left, in each county, to the discretion of the Lord Lieutenant; but it is desirable that it should not exceed £2 2s. on the commission of a Field Officer and £1 1s. each on the commission of officers of all other ranks.

The commissions of all Volunteer Officers, except Adjutants, are exempt from stamp duty.

38—The appointments, promotions and resignations of Commissioned Officers are inserted in the "London Gazette," free of charge, on being duly notified to the Editor, by the direction of the Lord Lieutenant.

Such notification should be framed strictly in the terms of the Secretary of State's letter conveying Her Majesty's approval or acceptance of the appointment, promotion or resignation concerned.

39—Officers on full pay of Her Majesty's army or navy are not eligible for other than honorary commissions.

40—An officer cannot ordinarily hold two substantive commissions at once in the Volunteer force.

41—When two corps are raised by the influence of one person, this person may, if the Lord Lieutenant considers it necessary, be appointed Commanding Officer of both the corps; but whenever the force is called out for actual service, he will be required to resign the command of one of them.

42—When a corps consists of more than one troop, battery, or company, and is not under the command of a Field Officer, the senior captain is allowed, on the recommendation of the Lord Lieutenant, to bear the designation of "Captain Commandant." This title does not require a separate commission, or confer any additional rank.

43—No quartermaster or paymaster is allowed on the establishment of a corps when the force is not called out for actual service; but instead of such officers the Secretary of State will be prepared, on the application of the Lord Lieutenant of the county, to sanction the appointment of two supernumerary lieutenants to every corps under the command of a Field Officer.

44—The appointment of musketry instructor does not carry a separate commission; but when an officer who has obtained a 1st class certificate at the School of Musketry is recommended by the Lord Lieutenant to act as instructor to his corps, the appointment, on being approved by the Secretary of State, will be noted in the Army List, without causing any alteration in the establishment of the corps.

45—When the musketry instruction of a corps is carried on by an officer not possessing a 1st class certificate from the School of Musketry, he can only be designated as Acting Musketry Instructor, and his appointment need not be submitted to the Secretary of State.

46—The appointment of an honorary colonel to corps under the command of a Lieutenant-Colonel is permitted, when recommended by the Lord Lieutenant.

47—The appointment of Honorary Chaplains is allowed on the recommendation of the Lord Lieutenant, but it can under no contingency carry pay, and will cease whenever the corps is called out for actual service.

48—The appointment of an Honorary Assistant Surgeon is allowed to every corps which is not entitled to a Medical Officer of substantive rank, but it can under no contingency carry pay, and will cease whenever the corps is called out for actual service, or becomes entitled to a Medical Officer of substantive rank, unless, in the latter case, the Lord Lieutenant should recommend the appointment of Honorary Assistant Surgeons, in the proportion of one for every troop, battery, or company, on the express ground that they are necessary in order to ensure the attendance of a Medical Officer whenever the corps is practising with ball or blank ammunition, and on the distinct understanding that such attendance will be really given by the officers appointed.

49—Appointment of Honorary Veterinary Surgeon—omitted.

50—No officer holding an Honorary Commission can in virtue of it take precedence of any officer holding a substantive commission of the same rank.

51—It will be required that substantive officers should be effective members of their corps, unless it should be represented by the Lord Lieutenant to the Secretary of State that there are, in any particular case, special reasons for a relaxation of this regulation.

Non-Commissioned Officers.

52—The non-commissioned officers of a corps are appointed by the Commanding Officer from among the enrolled members.

53—Lance-Sergeants and Lance-Corporals may be appointed by the Commanding Officer.

54—A non-commissioned officer may be reduced by the Commanding Officer of his corps, for any sufficient cause, after the circumstances have been duly investigated and recorded by a Court of Enquiry.

Enrolled Members.

55—No person below the age of seventeen should be enrolled in a Volunteer corps.

56—Any out-pensioner of Her Majesty's Regular forces, not belonging to, or required for, the force of enrolled pensioners, may be enrolled as a Volunteer, with the consent of the Secretary of State for War, applied for and notified through the Staff Officer of Pensioners of the district in which the out-pensioner resides.

57—Apprentices may be enrolled with the consent of their masters.

58—Enrolled members are classed as effectives or non-effectives.

59—In order to be reckoned as effective, an enrolled member must have (*a*) taken the oath of allegiance after his enrolment; and (*b*) attended the authorised drills of the corps, properly armed and accoutred, on the number of days prescribed by the law, unless he has been absent with leave, or prevented by recognized sickness.

60—The authorised drills in virtue of which an enrolled member is reckoned as effective need not take place on consecutive days. One-half of them must be musters of the whole corps; the remaining half may consist (*a*) in the case of a corps of more than one troop, or company, of troop or company drill, or instruction in musketry, ordered by the Commanding Officer, under the command of one of the company officers; (*b*) in the case of a scattered rural corps, of squad drills ordered by the Commanding Officer, and attended by an officer of the corps, provided that authority for such an arrangement has been previously obtained from the Lord Lieutenant of the county, who should be guided, in granting it, by the local difficulties experienced by the Volunteers in assembling for drill.

In all these cases the Volunteers must be properly armed and accoutred.

61—All enrolled members who do not fulfil the conditions stated in Articles 59 and 60 are to be reckoned as non-effectives.

62—Supernumerary members are members enrolled beyond the maximum establishment of the corps. They cannot be enrolled without the special authority of the Secretary of State for War, given on the recommendation of the Lord Lieutenant; and they are not entitled to the exemptions granted by the Act of Parliament.

Honorary Members.

63—The number of honorary members attached to any corps is not regulated by the Secretary of State for War, and such members are not included in the muster roll of the corps to which they are attached.

They are not subject to military discipline, nor allowed to interfere with the military duties of the corps; but they are permitted to wear its uniform unless a special provision to the contrary is contained in the authorised rules of the corps.

They are not, under any circumstances, liable to be assembled for actual service.

Rules.

64—The Commanding Officer of every corps is required to transmit to the Lord Lieutenant for submission to Her Majesty as soon as may be after his appointment, the rules proposed for the government and discipline for the corps when not on actual service.

For this purpose he will be furnished, on application to the War Office, with a copy of the Model Rules drawn up by a committee of Volunteer officers assembled at the War Office, on 10th August, 1859. The Secretary of State has approved these Rules, subject to such modifications as the circumstances of each corps may render necessary or desirable; but he will not object to consider any body of Rules drawn up in a different manner, which may be duly submitted for Her Majesty's approval by the Lord Lieutenant of the county.

The Model Rules are substantially the same as those of the Huddersfield Corps. *Vide Supra.*

Volunteer Corps should be careful to retain a copy of the Rules submitted to the Secretary of State for Her Majesty's approval, as the Draft Rules forwarded to the War Office must be retained there.

65—In order that a corps may be able to prove, in a Court of Justice, the authenticity of the Rules approved for it by Her Majesty, it is desirable that it should possess a copy of them certified both by order of the Secretary of State and by the Lord Lieutenant.

To effect this, the Lord Lieutenant, on receiving from the Secretary of State for War a letter signifying Her Majesty's approval of the Rules of a corps, should cause any modification which may be specified therein to be at once incorporated in the Rules, and should then forward a copy of them to the War Office. The copy so forwarded will be examined there, and, if found correct, will be certified, and returned to the Lord Lieutenant, to be deposited, after having received his signature, among the records of the corps.

The document forwarded to the War Office for certification must be a fair copy, without interlineation or erasure, and must contain nothing more than the approved Rules of the Corps, under their authorised heading. Space must be allowed for the necessary certificates, which are to be appended immediately after the last rule, and be in the following form:—

"I hereby certify that Her Majesty does not disallow the foregoing Rules as those of the Volunteer Corps.

....

for the Secretary of State for War."

"War Office,

186 ,

"I hereby certify that I have received the foregoing Rules from the Secretary of State for War, and that they are approved and confirmed by Her Majesty for the Volunteer Corps.

....

Her Majesty's Lieutenant
for the County of ."

186 .

Courts of Enquiry.

66—It is competent for the Lord Lieutenant of a county, or the Commanding Officer of a corps, to order a Court of Enquiry to assemble for the investigation of any subject.

The duties of a Court of Enquiry depend on the instructions which the authority convening the court may think proper to give.

A Court of Enquiry is not a judicial body; it has no power to administer an oath; but it is to be considered as a council of which the Lord Lieutenant or any officer in command may take advantage, to assist him in arriving at a correct conclusion on any subject on which it may be expedient for him to be thoroughly informed. If, however, the enquiry has reference to a Commissioned Officer, the court can only be convened under the authority of the Lord Lieutenant, to whom it will report, and must be composed of officers of the Volunteer establishment within the county.

Administrative Organization.

Administrative Organization.

67—It is desirable that the small corps of Light Horse, Artillery, Mounted Rifle and Rifle Volunteers, in the several counties, should, when of sufficient numbers, be united respectively in administrative regiments, brigades or battalions, if it is not practicable to form them into corps having a more compact organization.

Its Object.

68—The object of this administrative organization is to unite separate corps under a common head, to secure uniformity of drill among them, and to afford them the advantage of the instruction and assistance of an adjutant; but it is not intended to interfere with their constitution or financial arrangements, with the operation of their respective rules, or with the powers specially conferred on their Commanding Officers by the Act 44 Geo, III, c. 54, or to require them to meet together for united drill in ordinary times, except with their own consent.

Proposal for Administrative Union.

69—All proposals for the administrative union of corps must be submitted by the Lord Lieutenant of the county to the Secretary of State for War; and any representations from the corps concerned relating to their administrative organization, are to be addressed to the Lord Lieutenant, who, if he deems it necessary, will communicate with the Secretary of State for War on the subject.

70—In effecting the formation of administrative regiments, brigades or battalions, the union of corps is to be considered with reference to locality, and not to their numerical standing in the Army List.

71—The following is the administrative staff allowed;—For four * * * * * * companies, one major and one adjutant. Administrative Staff.

For not less than six * * * * * * * companies, one lieutenant-colonel and one adjutant.

For not less than eight * * * * * * companies, one lieutenant-colonel, one major and one adjutant.

For not less than twelve * * * * * * companies:—one lieutenant-colonel, two majors, and one adjutant.

72—The Administrative Regiments, Brigades, or Battalions, in any County, are numbered consecutively, for the sake of distinction, according to the dates of their formation. Their precedence, however, is not determined by the numbers so assigned to them, but by the county number of the senior corps belonging to each.

73—Head-quarters are fixed for each Administrative Regiment, Brigade, or Battalion, in addition to those of the different corps of which it is composed.

74—In sanctioning the formation of an administrative body, composed of four * * * * * * companies, it is intended to provide only for cases where no more than that number can be formed in a county, or in a town where it is not considered advisable to bring in any Rural Corps; and no two such bodies, of this strength, can be formed in one place.

75—When any corps, the establishment of which entitles it to an adjutant, is administratively united with others, the appointment of adjutant of the corps will not be filled up; and when any corps to which an adjutant has been already appointed is so united with others, the adjutant of the corps will be re-commissioned as Adjutant of the Administrative Regiment, Brigade, or Battalion.

76—Corps in two or more adjoining counties may be administratively united, on the joint recommendation of the Lords Lieutenant of the counties concerned.

77—Subject to the powers conferred by the law upon the Commanding Officer of each corps, the Field Officer commanding an Administrative Regiment, Brigade, or Battalion, will have the general charge of the drill and discipline of the several corps composing it. He will inspect them from time to time, and will take notice of, and, if necessary, report, any infraction of the provisions of the law, or of the orders of the Secretary of State for War relating to the use of the arms, the regulations about clothing, distinctive marks of rank &c. He will also be responsible that uniformity in drill is preserved throughout the Force under his command. When present at the drill or parade of any of the corps, he will invariably be in command, and if two or more of them should wish to meet together, for united drill, his permission must first be obtained, and the movements &c., will be subject to his approval. If any of the corps should desire to attend the field day of any corps not under his command, his permission must also be obtained in the first instance.

78—No officer of a corps forming part of an administrative body has any authority over the other corps of which it is composed in consequence of their administrative union, but whenever the several corps, or any number of them, meet together for drill, the senior officer present assumes the command.

79—Whenever the temporary absence of the Field Officer commanding an Administrative Regiment, Brigade, or Battalion, may render it necessary to appoint another officer to discharge his duties, the command will devolve upon the next senior officer present, provided the authority of the Secretary of State shall have been obtained, through the Lord Lieutenant, for the exercise of such command.

80—The Commanding Officer of a corps forming part of an administrative body is allowed to hold at the same time a commission as a Field Officer on the Administrative Staff in special cases in which the Lord Lieutenant is of opinion that there are strong local reasons for recommending such an arrangement.

81—When the establishment of a corps forming part of an administrative body entitles it to a major, the appointment can only be filled up on the understanding that, in the event of the administrative regiment, brigade or battalion, becoming afterwards entitled to a second field officer, the major of the corps will be selected for that appointment, to which he may be commissioned without resigning his commission in the corps.

82—When a corps already under the command of a major becomes part of an administrative body, a second field officer will not be allowed on the administrative staff unless the Lord Lieutenant should consider it expedient to recommend the major of the corps for that appointment.

83—An administrative regiment, brigade or battalion cannot have rules having legal force under the Act 44 Geo. III, c. 54, distinct from those of the several corps of which it is composed.

Attachment of Corps.

84—Under special circumstances, small corps may be temporarily attached to other corps of the same arm, for the purposes of drill, and the officer commanding the larger corps may direct his Adjutant to afford assistance in the instruction of the corps so attached.

85—Upon the special recommendation of the Lord Lieutenant, small corps may be attached to other corps, or to administrative bodies of a different arm.

86—In both these cases the application for the sanction of the arrangement is to be made to the Secretary of State for War through the Lord Lieutenant.

Assemblies for Drill, Review or Rifle Shooting.

87—When corps of any arm or arms, not exceeding, in the aggregate, the force of one brigade, wish to assemble together for drill, a joint notification of their desire to do so should be sent by the several commanding officers, through the Lords Lieutenant of their counties, to the Secretary of State for War, who, if he approves the proposed arrangement, will signify his sanction of it to the Lord Lieutenant.

88—The command of the brigade, while drilling, will devolve upon the senior officer present.

It may, however, be necessary, with a view to the inspection of the corps, or for the purpose of affording instruction to such brigades as may require it, that an inspecting officer should be appointed by the Secretary of State for War. Such an officer, when appointed, will superintend the movements of the brigade, but will not, unless specially ordered, take the command.

89—It is not intended that a separate application should be made on every occasion when two or more battalions of Volunteers propose to meet regularly for brigade drill. In such cases, if the times and places of meetings are specified in the application, a general permission, extending over several weeks, will be given at one time.

90—Articles 87 and 89 are not intended to apply to the case of one battalion of Volunteers keeping the ground while another is being drilled or inspected, or to the united drill of the corps of smaller size than battalions. In such cases, no preliminary sanction from the Secretary of State is required.

91—When it is proposed to assemble for drill a force exceeding one brigade, an application for permission to do so, stating the place, time, and probable number of Volunteers, must in the first instance be sent in to the Lord Lieutenant of the county in which it is intended to hold the field day, who, if he approves of the proposal, will forward it to the Secretary of State for his sanction.

If this sanction be given, each corps wishing to be present will then apply through its own Lord Lieutenant for permission to attend; the manœuvres to be performed must be submitted to the Secretary of State for his sanction at least one week before the time appointed for the field day by the senior Volunteer officer intending to be present, and the Secretary of State for War will appoint an officer to command.

92—Reviews of large bodies of Volunteers may be held from time to time by the general officers commanding districts, or other officers of high rank and position in the Army, and the regulations to be observed in such cases are laid down in the correspondence which is given in Appendix E.

It should, however, be distinctly understood that no Volunteer corps can be compelled to attend any such review in time of peace.

93—Volunteer corps may, when circumstances permit, be brigaded with other forces. Any application on this subject is to be addressed to the Secretary of State for War, through the Lord Lieutenant of the county.

94—When Volunteers belonging to one or more corps are brought together under arms at rifle shooting matches, or on other occasions, the senior officer present is to be considered as in command of all the Volunteers upon the ground; and, although his position in this respect does not involve any authority for his interference in the arrangements of the meeting, yet he is held responsible for the due maintenance of order and discipline among the Volunteers under arms.

Uniform, Clothing and Accoutrements.

95—Every Volunteer corps is allowed to choose its own uniform and accoutrements, subject to the approval of the Lord Lieutenant of the county, and provided no gold lace is introduced.

96—It is desirable that a uniform colour should be chosen for the clothing of corps of each arm within the same county. This is most important in the case of corps which are likely to be united together in Administrative Regiments, Brigades, or Battalions.

97—The distinctions in uniform and appointments which are prescribed in the Regular Service and Militia to denote the rank of the wearer should be observed strictly by Volunteers of the various grades, as far as they are applicable to the Volunteer force. In this respect the dress regulations for the Army are to be taken as a guide.

98—As the force should at all times be prepared for actual service, it is recommended that every Volunteer should, in addition to the articles worn on his person, be provided with the undermentioned kit, which is calculated on his minimum requirements in the field.

(a)—Refers to Light Horse or Mounted Rifles—omitted.

(b)—For a member of a * * * * * * Rifle Volunteer Corps:—

Knapsack; great-coat or cloak of the pattern approved for the corps; one flannel shirt; one pair of flannel or serge trousers; one pair of worsted socks; one pair of boots; one hold-all, containing knife, fork, spoon and comb &c.; one towel; soap; one tin of grease; one mess-tin and cover.

A model valise, saddle-bag and knapsack, containing the above mentioned articles, are deposited for inspection at the Military Store Department, Grosvenor Road, Pimlico.

99—The pouches should be capable of containing sixty rounds of ammunition, and should be so fixed as not to interfere with the arrangement of the knapsack.

A model set of accoutrements, calculated to meet these requirements, is deposited for inspection at the Military Store Department, Grosvenor Road, Pimlico.

100—Commissioned Officers and Sergeants alone are permitted to wear side-arms when off duty, and then only the authorised weapons of their respective ranks.

101—Neither standards nor colours are to be carried by corps on parade, as the Volunteer Force is composed of arms to which their use is not appropriate.

N.B.—Volunteers when in mourning will wear a piece of black crape three inches wide round the left arm above the elbow.

Stores.

102—Every Volunteer Corps is supplied gratuitously with arms from the Government Stores, to the full number of its enrolled members if required.

103—The arms at present supplied to each description of Volunteer Corps are detailed in Appendix F.

104—Before any Government arms can be issued to a corps, it is necessary for the Lord Lieutenant to satisfy himself, and notify to the Secretary of State, in accordance with articles 11 and 17, that one or more places of security for the custody of the arms, and competent persons to take charge of them have been provided at the expense of the Volunteers. The stores should be thoroughly dry and well-aired buildings, free from worm eaten timber, and should be kept well whitewashed and clean. The Militia County Stores or Police Stations will probably be available in some places for the purpose.

105—Commanding Officers of Volunteer Corps are to apply for the arms required, on the prescribed form of requisition given in Appendix G.

106—Every rifle issued to a corps is to bear engraved upon the heel-plate the letter V, and the letters denoting the county, according to the arrangements shown in Appendix H, the number of the corps should also be added and the rifles should be numbered consecutively from 1 upwards, in the manner shown in Appendix J. Care is to be taken that the arms are, in all cases, marked by engraving and not by stamping.

In addition to the letter V. no letters, except those indicating the county, need be engraved on the rifle issued to Rifle Volunteer Corps.

107—An allowance for marking the arms is granted by the Government; and all claims on account of it are to be forwarded to the War Office, accompanied by a certificate from the Commanding Officer of the corps, showing the number of arms marked, and that they have been marked in strict accordance with Article 106. The allowance is as follows:—

For rifle, rammer, bayonet, and scabbard, and fitting the scabbard to the bayonet	Threepence for the stand complete, with a further allowance of a half-penny for the muzzle-stopper.
For a private's pattern wrench ..	Three half-pence.
For a sergeant's ,, ..	Twopence half-penny.

When a rifle, bayonet, rammer, scabbard, or muzzle-stopper requires to be re-placed and re-marked, a charge of one penny each will be allowed for the rifle, bayonet, rammer, or scabbard, and a half-penny for the muzzle-stopper.

108—The arms of a corps will be marked by the Government, previous to their issue, in any case in which a request to that effect is inserted in the requisition on which the arms are demanded.

109—All arms issued to a Volunteer Corps remain the property of Her Majesty's Government; and the Commanding Officer for the time being is held responsible for their being at all times in a serviceable state, and for their being returned into store when required, in good condition, fair wear and tear excepted.

110—Great attention should be paid to the proper cleaning and care of the arms entrusted to the Volunteers; and the Commanding Officers are to point out to those under their command, that the barrel of a rifle is so delicately finished that, should rust be permitted to accumulate inside, it must inevitably destroy the integrity of the grooves, and, consequently, impair the accuracy of the weapon.

The establishment of officers and non-commissioned officers for a Volunteer Corps is amply sufficient to ensure a proper supervision of the arms, consistently with other occupations. Neglect of duty must, therefore, always exist in a corps where the arms are in bad order.

The cleaning a rifle constitutes an important part of the drill of a recruit, and is explained in the Field Exercises and Evolutions of Infantry, part 6, section 33.

The locks of the rifles, when in use, should be taken to pieces and thoroughly cleaned and oiled, at least once every two months, by properly qualified persons. In wet weather the rifles should invariably be cleaned immediately after use.

111—Volunteers must not, under any circumstances, tamper with the locks of their rifles, and any rifles which, on inspection, may be found to have had their locks improperly altered, will be at once returned into store, and repaired at the expense of the corps.

112—The arms are to be deposited, after drill, in the armouries of the corps, except when the Commanding Officer may judge it expedient to permit members of the corps to keep their arms at their own houses, in which case a written permission is to be given by him to each member who is allowed to take his arms home. As the Commanding Officer is responsible to the Government for the condition of the arms issued to the corps, it will be his duty to give these permissions with care, and any of them may be withdrawn by him whenever he may consider it necessary. The arms retained in private custody will be subject to inspection at any time by the assistant inspector of the division, and the Field Officer commanding any administrative regiment, brigade or battalion to which the corps may belong; and they are to be examined at least once a month by the Commanding Officer of the corps, or by some officer or officers appointed by him for that duty.

Every Commanding Officer is required to cause the number of arms in the custody of individual members to be inserted in the periodical return furnished by the adjutant.

In any case in which the arms are neglected, the discretionary power granted to the Commanding Officer in this article will be withdrawn.

Ammunition. 113—Ammunition in the following annual proportions, to be reckoned from the 1st April in each year, is allowed to Volunteer corps of the several arms, viz.:—

RIFLE.

For every enrolled member, for his first year of service, gratis, 110 rounds ball, 20 rounds blank, 163 caps; allowed to be purchased, 110 rounds ball,* 100 rounds blank, 231 caps; total 220 rounds ball, 120 rounds blank, 394 caps. After his first year of service, gratis, 90 rounds ball, 60 rounds blank, 165 caps; allowed to be purchased, 130 rounds ball,* 60 rounds blank, 209 caps; total 220 rounds ball, 120 rounds blank, 374 caps.

---

* Including 20 rounds for prize shooting.

114--Every corps is required to provide a secure place for the custody of its small-arm ammunition; but in cases where the store of ammunition is sufficiently large to make it desirable that military magazines in barracks should be used for its custody, barrack-masters are instructed to afford facilities for its reception provided there is sufficient room for it in the magazines under their charge.

115—When ammunition is forwarded by Government for the use of a corps, careful arrangements should be made by the Commanding Officer for its conveyance from the railway station or port to which it may have been transmitted. Should the arrangements be of an ordinary character, they are left to the discretion of the Commanding Officer, who is to take due precautions for the security of the ammunition, and for the safety of the public. But in cases in which it may be deemed expedient to employ members of the Volunteer Corps in taking charge of the ammunition in its transit from a railway station or store, the duty is to be discharged in a strictly military manner.

116—When ammunition is packed in metal cylinders, the cylinders are to be returned without delay to the station from which the ammunition is sent.

117—The small-arm ammunition supplied to corps gratuitously is to be applied for separately from that allowed to be purchased, and as much of it as the magazines of the corps will accommodate is to be applied for at one time. It will be forwarded free of cost to the headquarters of the corps, if the whole annual allowance is included in one demand, otherwise the carriage of only the first portion issued will be paid by the public. The carriage of ammunition supplied on payment must in all cases be paid for by the Volunteers on delivery.

Requisitions for small-arm ammunition are to be forwarded to the War Office on the forms given in Appendix K.

118 to 120—Refer to Artillery Volunteer Corps—omitted.

121—The articles for musketry instruction enumerated in the forms of Requisition given in Appendix N are supplied to corps by the Government at cost price.

122—Volunteer corps should provide themselves with the undermentioned articles, viz.:—Brushes, large, for colouring targets (1lb. brushes), ditto, small, for colouring targets (sash tools); whiting, lampblack, glue (to make size), twelve files (to retain documents), sponge, chalk (common).

123—Volunteer corps may be supplied with certain books, which are included in the form of requisition given in Appendix O, at the prices stated therein.

124—Claims for payment for stores supplied by the Government at cost price are forwarded from the War Office to the corps concerned, with instructions for the payment of the amount due, either into the Bank of England, to the credit of army funds, by means of receivable orders which will be enclosed for the purpose, or to some local accountant of the War Office.

In the case of ammunition supplied on payment, the Commanding Officer is, in the first instance, to notify to the War Office his acquiescence in the correctness of the claim, as in some cases the barrels and other packages charged for in the claim are returned into store, and the amount to be paid is thus reduced. In the case of ammunition supplied gratis, the barrels and other packages are invariably to be returned.

125 to 126 refer to Artillery—omitted.

ADJUTANTS.

127—The Lord Lieutenant of the county recommends officers to the Secretary of State for War for appointment as adjutants; and the Secretary of State for War, after having satisfied himself as to the qualifications of a candidate, submits his appointment for the Queen's approval. The appointment is held under the Queen's Commission.

128—The Lord Lieutenant in recommending any candidate for appointment, should state (*a*) his age, and military service; (*b*) if any of this service has been in a Militia Regiment, the period or periods during which the regiment has been embodied; (*c*) whether he still holds a commission, and if so, of what rank, and in what corps. This statement should be accompanied by testimonials as to the character and professional ability of the candidate, given, if possible, by one of his former Commanding Officers. The testimonials should be forwarded in original, with copies which will be retained at the War Office. The address of the candidate should also be given.

129—No officer whose age exceeds fifty years is eligible for the appointment of adjutant.

130—The military service necessary to qualify a candidate for appointment in the several arms is as follows:—

* * * * * * * * * *

In the Rifle Arms:—Four years' service in Her Majesty's Imperial or Indian Armies, or in that of the East India Company, or in the Royal Marines, or in the Embodied Militia; or three years' such service in the case of any candidate who is in possession of 1st class certificate from the School of Musketry.

131—The fitness of every candidate for appointment will be tested by an examination conducted by a Board of Officers appointed by the General Commanding-in-Chief, at the request of the Secretary of State for War.

The subjects of examination for the several arms are given in Appendix Q.

132—Every adjutant is required, before receiving his commission, to transmit to the Secretary of State for War the following declaration:—

"I do hereby declare, upon my honour as an officer and a gentleman, that in order to obtain the appointment of an Adjutant in the
, I have not given, paid, received or promised and that I do not believe that anyone for me has given, paid, received or promised directly or indirectly, any recompense, reward or gratuity to any person or persons whatever.

Witness (C. D.)   Signed (A. B.)"

133—The appointment of every adjutant is notified by the Secretary of State for War to the Lord Lieutenant of the county, who will then direct the Adjutant to assume his duties.

134—The appointment is inserted in the "London Gazette" free of charge, on being duly notified to the Editor, by the direction of the Lord Lieutenant, and the commission, when duly signed, is forwarded from the War Office to the Adjutant.

135—The amount of the stamp duty on an Adjutant's commission viz:—£1 10s., is deducted from the first issue of his pay, but no fee is chargeable on his commission as Adjutant.

136—As the public services of an Adjutant are to be available at all times, he will not be allowed to follow any other profession or to hold any other appointment, public or private.

137—The pay and general allowances granted by the Government to an Adjutant are:—

Pay: at the rate of eight shillings a day.

Allowances: (*a*) to cover the cost of forage for a horse; or if the Commanding Officer should have exempted him, for the time being, from the obligation of keeping a horse, to provide for travelling expenses, at the rate of two shillings a day; (*b*) to cover contingent expenses in connection with correspondence &c., with the War Office; at the rate of £4 a year for every troop, battery or company; and at the rate of £2 a year for any sub-division or section not forming part of a company.

138—A special additional allowance of two shillings a day, in lieu of travelling expenses, is granted to the adjutant (*a*) of every Administrative Regiment, Brigade, or Battalion containing a corps, of which the headquarters are situated at a distance of more than five miles from the Administrative Headquarters; (*b*) of every corps in which the regular places of assembly for drill of two or more of the troops, batteries, or companies, are at a greater distance than five miles, or that of one troop, battery, or company, at a greater distance than seven miles from the headquarters of the corps.

139—Claims for the pay and allowances due to adjutants are to be transmitted to the War Office, as soon as possible after the expiration of each quarter, in order that the necessary authority may be given for the issue of the amount due, through the Paymaster General.

All such claims are to be made on War Office Form No. 1615, which is given in Appendix R, and are to be forwarded through the officer commanding the corps, or Administrative Regiment, Brigade, or Battalion, as the case may be.

140—When an adjutant proceeds to the School of Musketry, by order of the Secretary of State for War, for the purpose of receiving instruction, he will be granted (*a*) an allowance of five shillings a day during the period of instruction, and (*b*) his actual and necessary travelling expenses in proceeding from and returning to his headquarters.

The adjutant, on [illegible] to his headquarters, [illegible] forward to the War Office through [illegible] Commanding Officer a claim for the allowance and expenses on War Office Form No. [illegible], which is given in Appendix S.

141—An Adjutant of Volunteers is purely a staff officer, and is not allowed to hold a regimental commission as Field Officer, Captain or Subaltern.

If he has served as a commissioned officer in Her Majesty's Imperial or Indian forces, or in the army of the East India Company, or has held the rank of Captain in the Embodied Militia, he may be appointed by the Lord Lieutenant of the county, subject to the Queen's approval, to serve with the rank of captain.

In all other cases he must have served five years as an officer, either in the Militia or Volunteers, in order to become eligible for the rank of captain.

Except for the purposes of instruction, no Adjutant is entitled, by virtue of his superior rank, to take the command of any force of Volunteers, when an officer of the corps to which they belong is present.

142—A Commanding Officer may grant leave of absence to his adjutant for any period not exceeding one month.

Any application for leave of absence for a longer period than one month is to be made, through the Commanding Officer, to the Secretary of State for War. The application must state whether proper provision has been made for the performance of the adjutant's duties during his proposed absence, and give the name of the officer who is to supply his place.

The leave of absence should not exceed, in the aggregate, two months during the year.

143—Every adjutant is subject to the general provisions of the Mutiny Act and Articles of War, and is liable to be tried by court-martial for any crime committed against such Act or Articles of War.

144—An adjutant is appointed to give instructions to the Volunteers, and to assist his Commanding Officer in carrying on the military duties of the Corps, or Administrative Regiment, Brigade, or Battalion, as the case may be; but he is not to take any part in the non-military or financial affairs of the corps. He is under the orders of his Commanding Officer, and is also bound to conform to all instructions which he may receive from the War Office through his Commanding Officer. It is his duty to visit the component parts of the corps or administrative body, as often as may be practicable consistently with local circumstances, and in accordance with the orders of his Commanding Officer.

The adjutant of a corps is to keep the muster roll. The adjutant of an administrative body is to have access to the muster rolls of all the corps composing it.

145—Every adjutant is required to keep a diary of the instruction imparted by him to the Volunteers, according to the War Office Form, No. 1,617, which is given in Appendix T. This diary is to be certified by the Commanding Officer, and transmitted to the War Office, through the Assistant-Inspector of the Division, on the 1st of every month.

He is also to prepare and furnish, under the direction of his Commanding Officer, all such returns as may, from time to time, be called for by the Secretary of State for War.

146—In accordance with Her Majesty's Warrant of 19th June, 1860, retired pay will be granted to adjutants after they have completed the undermentioned periods of service in the Imperial or Indian Forces, Royal Marines, Embodied Militia, or the army of the East India Company, and in the Volunteer force, viz. ;—

Fifteen years, five years of which as adjutant of Volunteers,				3s. per diem.	
Twenty years, seven	"	"	"	4s.	"
Twenty-five years, ten	"	"	"	5s.	"
Thirty years, fifteen	"	"	"	5s.	"

Such pay will be granted to those adjutants only who may, through age or infirmity, become unfit for the performance of the duties of their commissions, or whose services may cease to be required by reason of reduction by order of Her Majesty; but no adjutant of Volunteers will have any title to retired pay, in consequence of the portion of the force to which he is appointed dissolving of its own accord, or otherwise falling below the establishment entitling it to an adjutant.

No adjutant on the Retired List, who may accept any military office or employment of profit under Government, will be entitled, for the period during which he holds such office, to claim any portion of this Retired Pay.

Every adjutant who may claim the Retired Pay to which he may become entitled under this Article, must, previously to receiving it, produce to the Paymaster General of Her Majesty's Forces, a declaration taken and subscribed before a Justice of the Peace or some other person authorised by law to administer such declaration, in the words or to the effect following, viz:—

I, A. B., do solemnly and sincerely declare that I was serving as adjutant in the from the to the , and that I now claim to receive Retired Pay at the rate of a day from the to the , during which period I did not hold or enjoy any office or employment of profit, civil or military, under the Crown or any other Government, besides the Retired Pay of a day now claimed, except my half pay as .

(Articles 147 to 167 of the Regulations, as originally published, have been cancelled, and are omitted. The following Articles, 147 to 167 inclusive, were substituted for those so cancelled.

Memorandum.

War Office, August 22nd, 1861.

With a view to afford increased aid to Volunteer corps in obtaining properly qualified drill instructors, the Secretary of State for War has cancelled Articles 147 to 167 of the Volunteer Regulations, and the following Articles are to be substituted for them, from the 1st of September next.

De GREY and RIPON,

Sergeant-Instructors.

[illegible]—Sergeant-instructors will be provided at the public expense to . . . . . Rifle Volunteer Corps in the proportion of one to each corps of from one to three companies, two to each corps of from four to seven companies, three to each corps of from eight to twelve companies or upwards. Second or subsequent battalions will receive sergeant-instructors in the same proportion as corps of the same number of companies. Administrative Battalions composed of corps whose head-quarters lie within a circle having a radius of one mile, will only be allowed the proportion of sergeant-instructors to which they would be entitled if they were consolidated corps, unless an increased number cannot be allowed in very special cases represented to the Secretary of State by the Lord Lieutenant.

148—Light Horse or Mounted Rifle Volunteers—omitted.

149—One of the sergeant-instructors in each battalion may be appointed sergeant-major. The appointment, which is to be considered temporary, rests with the Commanding Officer of the corps, who for any sufficient reason may deprive a sergeant of it.

150—The qualifications required for candidates for the appointment of sergeant instructors for . . . . . . Rifle Volunteer Corps, are as follows —

. . . .

For Rifle Corps.

Five years service three of which as a non-commissioned officer) in the Imperial or Indian Armies. A competent knowledge of Infantry drill. A good character established by satisfactory testimonials. Age not to exceed fifty years.

151—Applications for the appointment of sergeant-instructors are in every case to be submitted for the approval of the Secretary of State for War by the Commanding Officer of the Volunteer Corps to which it is proposed that the sergeant should be attached. The application is to be accompanied by testimonials of character, and a certified copy of the non-commissioned officer's record of service, and to be forwarded through the Assistant-Inspector of the District. If the corps belongs to an Administrative Battalion, the application must be transmitted to the Assistant-Inspector through the Field Officer commanding.

152—A sergeant-instructor will receive, from the date of his appointment, consolidated pay at the following rates:—If in receipt of pension, 2s. 4d. per day; if not in receipt of pension, 2s. 7d. If he is appointed sergeant-major of a battalion, he will receive an additional allowance of 6d. per day. This pay is to be issued by and charged in the accounts of the staff officer of pensioners of the pensioner district in which the head-quarters of the corps are situated.

153—Sergeant-instructors who have not previously gone through a course of instruction at the School of Musketry, must be prepared to do so if required.

154—omitted.

155—Sergeant-instructors to Volunteer Corps may be obtained from the Regular army in the following manner:—Non-commissioned officers of eighteen or more years' service in the Infantry, and twenty-one or more years' service in the Cavalry, who are, in the opinion of their Commanding Officers, qualified to act as sergeant-instructors of Volunteer Corps, and who are desirous of obtaining those appointments, will be reported to the Adjutant-General, and noted as candidates. Commanding Officers of Volunteer Corps wishing to obtain the services of one of them will make application in the manner directed in Article 151, to the Secretary of State for War, who will direct the application, if approved, to be forwarded to the General Commanding-in-Chief, with a view to a sergeant being posted to the corps as soon as possible.

156—Such non-commissioned officers employed as sergeant-instructors will be borne on the rolls of their respective regiments as supernumeraries for service with Volunteer Corps until the completion of their period of service for discharge to pension or otherwise, and will receive the consolidated pay named in Article 152, in lieu of all other pay and allowances whatever. On their discharge they will be allowed to renew their engagements as sergeant-instructors on the terms laid down in the above-named Article.

157—If the Volunteer corps to which non-commissioned officer of the Regular Forces is attached as sergeant-instructor should, from any sufficient cause, cease to require his services before he has completed the period of service entitling him to be discharged, he will return to his regiment, if he is not posted to another Volunteer corps.

158—If a non-commissioned officer transferred from the regular forces is guilty of misconduct before his discharge from the army, he may be sent back to his regiment on the representation of the Commanding Officer to the Secretary of State for War.

159—Every sergeant-instructor to a Volunteer corps is subject to the general provisions of the Mutiny Act and Articles of War, and is liable to be tried by court-martial for any crime committed against such Act or Articles of War.

160—All sergeant-instructors are to be considered as under the supervision of the adjutant, who is required to report to the officer commanding the corps any irregularity of conduct, incompetence, or want of attention which he may observe on the part of any instructor; and the Commanding Officer, when necessary, will report the circumstances of the case to the Secretary of State. In the case of an Administrative Regiment, Brigade, or Battalion, the adjutant will also report such instances of irregularity to the field officer commanding.

Sergeant-instructors of such Volunteer corps as may not have at present the services of an adjutant will be placed under the supervision of the nearest Volunteer adjutant or other officer, according to the directions of the Secretary of State for War.

In the event of a sergeant-instructor being guilty of any offence of a sufficiently grave nature to induce his Commanding Officer to refer the case for the consideration of the Secretary of State, he is to be placed in arrest until orders are received as to his disposal.

[illegible]

[illegible]

[illegible]

[illegible]

165—A [illegible] [illegible] from the Militia under the foregoing Articles may be attached to a Volunteer Corps for any period not exceeding three months, and his engagement may be renewed at the expiration of such period, with the consent of the Commanding Officer of the Militia Regiment; but no sergeant of the permanent staff of the Militia can be permitted to remain with a Volunteer Corps during the embodiment or annual training of his Militia regiment.

166—Volunteer Corps are not to make direct offers to non-commissioned officers serving in the Regular Army to become their sergeant-instructors, nor to attempt to induce sergeants of the Militia, or sergeant-instructors attached to, or engaged by, other Volunteer Corps, to quit their regiments or corps without the consent of the Commanding Officer of the Militia Regiment or Volunteer Corps. In any case in which it may be proved that offers of this kind have been made, the Secretary of State will refuse his consent to the appointment of the non-commissioned officer concerned.

167—The principal duty of a sergeant-instructor is to attend to the drill and instruction of the corps to which he is attached; but the Commanding Officer of the corps may employ him to take charge of the arms of the corps, or to discharge other similar duties of a military character, provided they do not interfere with his special functions. He will not be permitted to engage in any trade or business.

168 to 170 relate to Artillery and Engineer Corps—omitted.

Instruction in Musketry.

171—Classes for the Musketry Instruction of Volunteers are periodically formed at the School of Musketry. The course of instruction extends over about fourteen working days; and the lodgings and all other personal expenses of the Volunteers admitted to it must be provided for by themselves, or by the corps to which they belong. They are not required to pay any fees, and ammunition is issued to them gratuitously.

Every Volunteer admitted to the course should take his uniform with him, and also the rifle which he is in the habit of using with his own corps.

172—The various corps are permitted, in succession, to nominate one member each to a Volunteer class at the School of Musketry.

Before any class is assembled, the Secretary of State will cause due notice of its assembly to be given to the Commanding Officer of every corps entitled to send a member to it; and it will be necessary for the Commanding Officer, in submitting his nomination, to annex:—

(*a*)—A certificate that the member concerned is thoroughly acquainted with the Manual and Platoon Exercises.

(*b*)—A statement from the Volunteer expressing his willingness not to quit the School of Musketry till the termination of the course of instruction, without the special sanction of the commandant, and also to impart instruction in the authorised system of musketry on his return to his corps.

The forms in accordance with which this certificate and statement should be drawn up are given in Appendix V.

173—Volunteers attending the modified course of instruction in musketry, who may wish to obtain certificates of qualification to act as sergeant-instructors to their corps, will be permitted to remain at the School of Musketry for six or eight days after the termination of the course, and will then be examined as to their ability to impart instruction.

174—The rifle practice-ground of a Volunteer Corps must afford a range of at least 200 yards, but it is desirable that the range should extend to 900 yards.

175—Corps which are without duly appointed Adjutants are not permitted to exercise with either blank or ball ammunition when in military formation, until such time as the assistant-inspector of the division pronounces the members to be qualified for so doing.

176—The Enfield Rifle having been constructed solely with a view to being used with Government ammunition, such ammunition only should be employed in testing the sight of it.

177—Those Volunteers only who have attained the proficiency prescribed in part 5 of the Regulations for conducting the musketry instruction of the army are permitted to wear the cross-muskets upon the sleeve of the tunic.

This particular badge represents, in the regular army, a prescribed standard of qualification in musketry, which cannot ordinarily be attained by Volunteers, whose course of instruction is necessarily limited, and who are, in many instances, unable to procure the length of range required for shooting in the 1st class, from which alone marksmen having the other qualifications required by the Regulations are taken.

As it is very desirable, however, that some marks of distinction should be worn by the best shots among the Volunteers of such corps as are not in position to practise at ranges between 650 and 900 yards, and to be exercised in judging distance, practice &c. as prescribed in the Musketry Regulations, page 73, paragraph 7, special badges should be adopted to denote proficiency of firing at various ranges, viz:—

(*a*)—When the range available extends to 300 yards only, the Volunteer who obtains the greatest number of points over fifteen in the 2nd class may wear a rifle embroidered horizontally.

(*b*)—When the range is between 350 and 600 yards, the Volunteer who obtains the greatest number of points over twelve in the 2nd class may wear a rifle embroidered horizontally with a star immediately above it.

(*c*)—When a range available extends to 900 yards, every Volunteer who obtains seven points and upwards in the 1st class may wear a rifle embroidered horizontally with two stars immediately above it.

(*d*)—When the range is between 650 and 900 yards, the Volunteer who obtains the greatest number of points above seven in the 1st class may wear a rifle embroidered horizontally with three stars immediately above it.

A Volunteer cannot wear the Cross Muskets, under Paragraph 1 of this Article, without the authority of the Secretary of State, which is to be obtained through his Commanding Officer, whose recommendation is, in every case, to be accompanied by the Return given in Appendix W, duly certified by himself and the Musketry Instructor.

The other badges referred to in this Article may be worn on the authority of the Commanding Officer.

178—The badge of a sergeant instructor in musketry to a Volunteer Corps should be Cross Muskets and a Crown, but this badge can only be worn by a Volunteer who holds a certificate from the School of Musketry that he is capable of imparting instruction in musketry.

179—The badge marking efficiency in shooting is to be worn on the left arm, immediately above the cuff of the sleeve; that for a sergeant-instructor in musketry on the right arm, midway between the elbow and the shoulder. The badge should be worked on cloth the colour of the facings, and is in no case to be worked in gold.

180—The following details the practice :—

When the ranges only extend to 300 yards, the following practices are to be performed :—1st period, 20 rounds; 2nd period, 20 rounds; file-firing, 10 rounds; volley-firing, 10 rounds; skirmishing, 10 rounds; total number of rounds to be fired, 70. The second class to repeat the practice of the third class; firing at a single target. Volleys to be fired at 300 yards standing, and skirmishing between 300 and 200 yards.

When the ranges only extend to 400 yards.—1st period, 20 rounds; 2nd period, 20 rounds; file-firing, 10 rounds; volley-firing, 10 rounds; skirmishing, 10 rounds; total number of rounds to be fired, 70. The second class to fire 10 rounds at 350 yards, and 10 at 400 yards, one distance a day.

When the ranges only extend to 450 yards :—1st period, 20 rounds; 2nd period, 20 rounds; file-firing, 10 rounds; volley-firing, 10 rounds; skirmishing, 10 rounds: total number of rounds to be fired, 70. The second class to fire 5 rounds at 350, 5 at 400, and 10 at 450 yards, but not more than 10 rounds a day.

When the ranges only extend to 500 yards :—1st period, 20 rounds; 2nd period 20 rounds; file-firing, 10 rounds; volley-firing, 10 rounds; skirmishing, 10 rounds; total number of rounds to be fired, 70. The second class to fire 5 rounds at 400, 5 at 450, and 10 at 500 yards, but not more than 10 rounds a day.

When the ranges only extend to 550 yards :—1st period, 20 rounds; 2nd period, 20 rounds; file-firing, 10 rounds; volley-firing, 10 rounds; skirmishing, 10 rounds; total number of rounds to be fired, 70. The second class to fire 5 rounds at 400, 5 at 500 and 10 at 550 yards, but not more than 10 rounds a day. (Should a range of the full extent become available, the third period to be executed in this instance only, and 90 rounds expended).

When the ranges only extend to 600 and under 900 yards, 1st period 20 rounds; 2nd period 20 rounds; 3rd period 20 rounds; file-firing 10 rounds; volley-firing 10 rounds; skirmishing 10 rounds; total number of rounds to be fired, 90. The first class men are not to fire at any distance until an opportunity of a range of 900 yards offers.

Books of Instruction &c.

181—The following works are to be used in conducting the instruction of Volunteers :—

Field exercises and evolutions of Infantry; with the Circular Memorandum dated 1st May, 1860, addressed to the Infantry of the line, by order of the General Commanding-in-Chief, which is given in Appendix X.

Regulations for conducting the musketry instruction of the army.

Attaching Officers to other Forces for Instruction.

182—Any commissioned officer may be temporarily attached, for the purpose of receiving instruction :—

To Infantry regiments of the Regular Army, or to Infantry regiments of the Militia, for any period not exceeding one month.

183—Any officer wishing to be attached to a portion of the Regular or Militia Force, under article 182, is to apply to the War Office, through the Commanding Officer, and to specify in his application the particular corps to which he wishes to be attached, and the period for which he desires to remain with it.

184—During the period for which an officer is attached to a portion of the Regular or Militia Force, under article 182, he is required to attend regularly the drills prescribed, and in other respects to conform to the arrangements made for his instruction.

Correspondence and Returns.

185—All official correspondence from Volunteer Corps is to proceed from the Commanding Officer, or to pass through him.

186—All letters on questions of drill, and questions arising out of inspections, are to be addressed to the assistant-inspector of divisions, who, when necessary, will refer them to the War Office.

187—All letters on questions relating to the constitution of a corps, or to any breach of discipline in it, are to be addressed to the Lord Lieutenant, who, when necessary, will communicate with the Secretary of State for War on the subject.

188—Letters on subjects of finance are to be addressed to the Lord Lieutenant, or to the War Office, as the case may require.

189—Letters on all subjects not enumerated in articles 186, 187 and 188 may be addressed to the War Office.

190—When a corps forms part of an administrative regiment, brigade or battalion, the official correspondence of the officer commanding the corps, on military subjects, is to pass through the officer commanding the administrative regiment, brigade or battalion.

On matters of finance, and the issue and account of stores, it is to be addressed direct, either to the Lord Lieutenant or the War Office as the case may require.

191—Artillery Volunteers—omitted.

192—Correspondence and rules for conducting the same—omitted.

193—Postage of letters—omitted.

194—Forms of returns, requisitions &c., bearing War Office numbers—omitted.

195—The following returns are to be rendered :—

Returns. Annual return by Commanding Officers of corps to Lords Lieutenant through the clerks of general meetings of Lieutenancy, due 1st August; form given in Appendix Y.

Annual return by Commanding Officers of corps to Secretary of State for War, due 1st August; form given in Appendix Z.

Annual return by Commanding Officers of corps to General Officers commanding districts, through the assistant inspector of divisions, due 1st August, form given in Appendix Z.

Abstract of Muster Roll by clerks of general meetings of Lieutenancy to the Secretary of State for War, due 1st August. Form given in Appendix AA.

Adjutant's Quarterly Return (in duplicate) by adjutants, through their Commanding Officers, to Assistant-Inspectors of Divisions, due 1st January, 1st April, 1st July and 1st October; Form given in Appendix BB.

Artillery Volunteers—omitted.

Diary of adjutant's duties by adjutants, through their Commanding Officers, to the Secretary of State for War, through the Assistant-Inspectors, due 1st of every month: Form given in Appendix T.

Annual certificate of effective membership by Commanding Officers of corps to District Surveyors of Taxes, due between 1st April and 5th May; Form given in Appendix FF.

196—For the Military Inspection of the Volunteer Force, Great Britain is divided as follows:— Districts for Military Inspection.

1st Division; London—containing Kensington; Chelsea; St. George's, Hanover Square; Westminster; St. Martin-in-the-Fields; St. James's, Westminster; Marylebone; Hampstead; St. Pancras; Islington; Hackney; St. Giles's; Strand; Holborn; Clerkenwell; St. Luke's; East London; West London; London City; Shoreditch; Bethnal Green; Whitechapel; St. George's-in-the-East; Stepney; Poplar; St. Saviour, Southwark; St. Olave, Bermondsey; St. George's, Southwark; Newington; Lambeth: Wandsworth; Camberwell; Rotherhithe: Greenwich; Woolwich; Lewisham.

2nd Division; South-Eastern—containing the rural parts of Surrey and Kent; Sussex; Hampshire; Berkshire; Cinque Ports; Isle of Wight.

3rd Division; East-Midland—containing the rural parts of Middlesex; Hertford; Buckingham; Oxford; Northampton; Huntingdon; Bedford; Cambridge; Essex; Suffolk; Norfolk.

4th Division; South-Western—containing Wiltshire; Dorset; Devonshire; Cornwall; Somerset.

5th Division, Midland—containing Gloucester; Hereford; Salop; Stafford; Worcester; Warwick; Leicester; Rutland; Lincoln; Nottingham; Derby.

6th Division; North-Western—containing Chester; Lancaster; Isle of Man.

7th Division; Northern—containing York; Durham: Northumberland; Cumberland; Westmoreland.

8th Division; Welsh—containing Monmouth; Glamorgan; Carmarthen; Pembroke; Cardigan; Brecon; Radnor; Montgomery; Flint; Denbigh; Merioneth; Carnarvon; Anglesey.

9th Division; Scotland, North-Eastern—containing Haddington; Berwick; Roxburgh; Selkirk; Peebles; Edinburgh; Linlithgow; Stirling; Fife; Kinross; Clackmannan; Perth; Forfar; Kincardine; Aberdeen; Banff; Elgin; Nairn; Inverness; Ross and Cromarty; Sutherland; Caithness; Orkney and Shetland Islands.

10th Division: Scotland, South-Western—containing Dumfries; Kirkcudbright; Wigton; Ayr; Bute; Renfrew; Lanark; Argyll; Dumbarton.

197—Every division is placed under an Assistant-Inspector, who is a Field Officer, appointed accordance with the Act 44 Geo. III., c. 54, s. 12, and whose duty it is (a) to assist the Inspector General of Volunteers in carrying out the annual or other inspections of the several corps in his division, and in dealing with such military questions as may arise out of them; (b) to regulate the transmission of all returns which Commanding Officers are directed to forward to the War Office through him; and (c) to see that the regulations regarding the storage of arms, drill, and other military matters, are duly observed by the Volunteers in his division.

198—After every inspection of a corps, the Assistant-Inspector will make a Return on the Form GG, and furnish a confidential report to the Secretary of State on the Form HH, as given in the Appendix.

(Signed) HERBERT.

Information to accompany proposals for formation of Volunteer Corps.

(a)—What is the place proposed for the headquarters of the Corps? (b) How many members are ready to be enrolled? (c) What is the proposed establishment of the corps? (d) Have the members provided a rifle practice ground for inspection? (e) Have they provided a safe place of custody for the arms? (f) Have they provided a proper person to take care of the arms? (g) With whom is the inspecting officer to communicate on arriving at the locality?

(Signature of the Lord Lieutenant)

Dated

Artillery Volunteers—omitted.

Note.—I have not thought it necessary to reproduce the Appendices of Forms annexed to the above Regulations.—R.P B.

LIST OF AUTHORITIES.

Acklom, Captain J. E.—"England for ever safe from the Invader."
Do. Origin of the present Volunteer movement (1862).
Alison—History of Europe.
Annual Register, The.
Army Lists 1794-1825.
Army List, Local Militia, 1810-1811.
Army Orders relating to the Volunteers.
Army Regulations.
Bacon, Lord—Essays.
Barrett, C. R. B.—Battles and Battle Fields in England.
Besant, Sir Walter—Life of Whittington.
Blackwood's Magazine.
Bright, Dr.—History of England.
British Army, The—By a Lieutenant-Colonel in the British Army.
British Volunteer, The, 1799.
British Military Library, 1799.
Burrows, Montagu—Historic Towns.
Busk, Hans Captain—The Rifle Volunteer.
Cannon—Historical Records of the British Army.
Capern, David—"Principal Events of the Volunteer Force, 1859-71."
Carey, Captain C. W., and others—"The Volunteer Question."
Census Returns, Registrar General's Report on.
Clarendon, Lord—History of the Civil War.
Clay, J. W.—Account of Monuments of Elland Church.
Clode—Military Forces of the Crown.
Common Council, City of London, Journals of.
Commons, House of, Journal.
Cope, Sir W. H.—History of the Rifle Brigade.
Council, Orders in.
Digest of the Law relating to Volunteer Corps, 1803 (pamphlet anon:).
Encyclopædia Britannica.
Evans, E. T.—Records of the 3rd Middlesex Rifles.
Ferrars—History of Limerick.
Froude—History of England.
Fry, T. H.—Volunteer Statistics.
Gardiner—History of the Great Civil War.
Gazette, Army and Navy, The
Gazette, London, The
Gazette, Volunteer Service, The
Gentleman's Magazine.
Goodenough and Dalton—Army Book of the British Empire.
Grant, James—British Battles on Land and Sea.
Green—History of the English people.
Grose—Military Antiquities.

LIST OF AUTHORITIES.—*Continued.*

Hallam—Constitutional History of England.
Hamerton, Lucy—Reminiscences of Olde Eland.
Hansard—Parliamentary History.
Hardiman—History of Galway.
Haydn—Dictionary of Dates.
Hicks, Colonel J. C.—Records of the Percy Artillery.
Historical Records of the 3rd Buffs, the 80th, 81st, 82nd, 85th and 90th Regiments.
History of the origin and formation of our Volunteer Army, 1867.—Collection of pamphlets.
Holinshed, Chronicles.
Howe, David—The Volunteer Question.
Howells—State Trials.
Hume—History of England.
James—Military Dictionary.
Journals of the Royal United Service Institution.
King Cooper—Story of the British Army.
Leadman—Battles fought in Yorkshire.
Macaulay—History of England.
MacNevin—History of the Volunteers of 1782.
Do. History of Belfast.
MacNevin and de Beaumont, Ireland.
Marga du, Géographie Militaire
Martial Biography or Memoirs with Glossary, 1806.
Maurice, Baron: *De la Défense Nationale en Angleterre.*
Military Extracts (Newspaper Cuttings, 1800-1816).
Moore, Captain A. T., R.E., Essay by.
Orders in Council.
Parliamentary Returns.
Pepy's Diary
Preston, Lieutenant Thomas—Patriot in Arms.
Rapin's History of England.
Raikes—History of Honourable Artillery Company.
Raikes—First Regiment of Militia.
Records, Parish (Slaithwaite).
Regulations, The Volunteer, 1859-1901.
Reports of Royal Commissions and Departmental Committees.
Revue des Deux Mondes.
Scott, Sir S.—The British Army.
Sharpe—London and the Kingdom.
Statutes at large.
Stuart—History of Armagh.
Sykes—History of Huddersfield and its Vicinity.
Taswell-Langmead—English Constitutional History.
Telfer, Major C. E. D., Essay by.
Terry, Captain H. Astley (60th Rifles)—Historical Records of the 5th A.B. Cheshire Rifles.

LIST OF AUTHORITIES.—*Continued.*

Tomlinson, G. W.—"Some of the Founders of the Huddersfield Subscription Library."

Trail—Social England.

Venn's Military Observations.

Walter, Major James—The Volunteer Force: History and Manual, 1881.

Ward's Animadversions of Warre.

Watson, Lieutenant Duncan, Essay by.

Whitelocke.

White, Major J. G.—Records of the Doneraile Rangers.

Wilde, Colonel Rodney—History of the Tower Hamlets Volunteer Brigade.

Woodburne—The Story of our Volunteers.

LIST OF SUBSCRIBERS.

[illegible], Joe E., New Street, Huddersfield.

Addington, The Right Honourable Lord, Addington Manor, Winslow, Bucks.

Armitage, Major Arthur C., Kirroughtree, Newton Stewart, N.B.

Armitage, Sir George J., Bart., F.S.A., Kirklees Park, Yorkshire.

Armitage, W. H., J.P., Banney Royd, Huddersfield.

[illegible], Major Frederick W., Longley Hall, Huddersfield.

Beaumont, Councillor E. A., Huddersfield.

Beaumont, Colonel Henry Frederick, V.D., Whitley Beaumont, Huddersfield.

Beaumont, T. G. (late Lieutenant 41st (Mirfield) West York Rifles), Dewsbury Mills, Dewsbury.

Beaumont, J. Tyrrel (late Captain 6th West York Rifles), Bilton, Harrogate.

Bentley, F. W., J.P., Rosewood, Huddersfield.

Berry, Mrs., Broomfield, Fixby, Huddersfield.

Berry, Miss, Broomfield, Fixby, Huddersfield.

Berry, Mrs. Robert Porter, Edgerton, Huddersfield.

Booth, James J., Whitegates, Netherton, Huddersfield.

Booth, John James, High Street, Huddersfield.

Boothroyd, Jonas, King Street, Huddersfield.

Braithwaite, Major Walter, V.D., Headingley, Leeds.

Brook, Major Charles, J.P., Burghwallis Hall, Doncaster.

Brooke, George, Christ Church Vicarage, Mirfield.

Brooke, J. A., J.P., Fenay Hall, Huddersfield.

Brooke, Lieutenant-Colonel Sir Thomas, Bart., J.P., Armitage Bridge.

Brooks, Samuel H., J.P. (late Captain 4th Volunteer Battalion Manchester Regiment).

Buckley, Arthur, Tunstead, Greenfield, near Oldham.

Cadman, His Honour Judge J., Heaton, Ackworth, Pontefract.

Calvert, Alderman Fred, J.P., Wakefield Road, Moldgreen, Huddersfield.

Carlile, Lieutenant-Colonel E. Hildred, J.P., Helme Hall, near Huddersfield.

Chadwick, S. J., F.S.A. (late Captain 7th West Yorkshire Artillery Volunteers), Lyndhurst, Dewsbury.

Chichester, Mrs. H. B.,

Clay, John W., F.S.A., J.P., Rastrick House, Brighouse.

Cooper, Captain J. E., Assistant Editor Volunteer Service Gazette.

Crosland, Thomas Pearson (late Lieutenant 6th West York Rifles and 2nd West York Yeomanry Cavalry), Birkby Grange, Huddersfield.

Crosland, John Pearson, 15, Prince of Wales Terrace, Scarborough.

Crowther, Elon, J.P., Brockholes, Huddersfield.

Crowther, Lieutenant-Colonel G. H., Thorn Hill, Edgerton, Huddersfield.

Dartmouth, The Rt. Hon. the Earl of, Patshull, Wolverhampton.

Dean, Edwin, J.P., Lewisham House, Slaithwaite.

Demetriadi, Surgeon-Captain L., The Oakes, Huddersfield.

Dickens, James Norton, Park Drive, Heaton, Bradford.

Drake, James, J.P., 9, Cedars Road, Clapham Common, S.W.

Dyson, Thomas J., B.A., Hartley, Kirkburton.

Finlinson, Arthur, Westfield House, Huddersfield.

Firth, T. F., J.P., The Flush, Heckmondwike.

Fletcher, Archibald H. J., M.A., Crow Trees House, Rastrick.

Fox, Major George W., V.D., Staincliffe Hall, Dewsbury.

Freeman, Colonel Charles Edward, J.P., V.D., Oakwood House, Edgerton, Huddersfield.

Freeman, Rev. John (late Ensign 6th West York Rifles), Woodkirk Vicarage, Dewsbury.

Fry, T. H., The Elms, Belmont Hill, Blackheath, S.E.

Gamble, Colonel Sir D., Bart., C.B., V.D. (2nd Volunteer Battalion South Lancashire Regiment). St. Helens.

Gratwicke, Major G. F., Exeter.

Greenwood, Arthur, Greenholme, Burley-in-Wharfedale, Yorkshire.

Greenwood, Lieutenant-Colonel F., J.P., Edgerton Lodge, Huddersfield.

Haigh, C. T. E., Colne Bridge House, near Huddersfield.

Hall, Charles, Huddersfield.

Hamerton, Miss Lucy, Elland.

Hanson, John H., Holmwood, Edgerton, Huddersfield.

Hartley, Robert Bramwell, Cleckheaton.

Hastings, Captain John H., Eaton Road, Ilkley.

Hastings, Major W. H., Hillhead, Sidmouth.

Hicks, Colonel John George, V.D. (formerly Commanding 2nd North (Percy) Volunteer Artillery), Oakfield, Benwell, Newcastle-on-Tyne.

Higginson, Mrs. Theoph :—Colonel Theoph. Higginson, C.B., deceased.

Higginson, Miss Gertrude A., 19, Prince's Square, Bayswater, W.

Hill, Miss E. Winifred, Liverpool.

Hirst, A. Brook, Myrtle Grove, Quarmby, Huddersfield.

Hirst, Miss M. M., Wood Cottage, Meltham Mills, Huddersfield.

Hirst, Colonel T. E., Bramham Gardens, S.W.

Hirst, T. Julius, J.P. (late Lieutenant 44th (Meltham) West York Rifles), Meltham Hall, Huddersfield.

Hoerle, George F., Hatfield House, East Twickenham.

Hopkinson, Captain A. H., Cleveland House, Edgerton, Huddersfield.

Huddersfield Free Library (A. G. Lockett, Librarian).

Jones, J. Edmund (late Captain 1st West York Rifles), Clifton Terrace, York.

Kaye, Anthony Knowles, Westfield House, Moldgreen, Huddersfield.

Keighley, C. W., J.P. (late Lieutenant 6th West York Rifles), Newhouse Hall, Huddersfield.

Kitson, Colonel Sir James, Bart., M.P., Gledhow Hall, Leeds.

Knaggs, R. Lawford, M.D., 27, Park Square, Leeds.

Knaggs, Samuel, Bradley Lane, Huddersfield.

Last, E. Walter, Finthorpe, Almondbury.

Laycock, William, St. Michael's, Newton Abbot.

Learoyd, Edwin, Ellerslie, Huddersfield.

Lee, P. H., Halifax Old Road, Huddersfield.

Leeds City Library (Thomas W. Hand, City Librarian).

Leeds Subscription Library (D. A. Cruse, Librarian).

Leslie, Lieutenant-Colonel G. F. (4th Batt. Rifle Brigade, Depôt, Gosport, *temp.*)

Sykes, D. F. E., LL.B., Meltham.

Sykes, Lieutenant-Colonel W. A., I.M.S., Peshawur, India.

Taylor, Mrs. James Eastwood, Fitzwilliam Street West, Huddersfield.

Taylor, Henry, Woodville, Edgerton, Huddersfield.

Taylor, L. W., Brier Hall, Gomersall, Leeds.

Taylor, Rev. R. Fetzer, Hedenham Rectory, Bungay.

Thornhill, Thomas Bryan Clarke-, Rushton Hall; Northamptonshire.

Tinker, A. L., Market Street, Huddersfield.

Tinker, Harold, Market Street, Huddersfield.

Terry, Henry (late Lieutenant 6th West York Rifles), 72, Avenue du Bois de Boulogne, Paris

Volunteer Service Gazette, The, Fleet Street, E.C. (per Captain J. E. Cooper, Assistant Editor).

Walker, Captain P. B., Lees House, Dewsbury.

War Office, The.

Watkinson, T. B., Rawthorpe Hall, Huddersfield.

Wheatley, Joseph, J.P., Woodlands, Mirfield.

Wilson, Captain H. (*Hon. Lieut. in Army*), Moorlands, Mirfield.

Wood, T. Outterson, M.D., F.R.C.P., 40, Margaret Street, Cavendish Square, W.

Woodhouse, Sir James T., Knt., M.P., Brough House, Brough, Yorkshire.

Yerburgh, Robert, M.P., 25, Kensington Gore, S.W.

INDEX A.—*Continued*

B.

INDEX B.—*Continued.*

INDEX F.—*Continued.* PAGE

G.

H.

P.

INDEX S.—*Continued.*

INDEX S.—*Continued.*

T.

U.

W.

J. BROADBENT AND CO., PRINTERS, HIGH STREET AND ALBION STREET, HUDDERSFIELD

Lightning Source UK Ltd.
Milton Keynes UK
UKOW07f2138150415

249685UK00009B/591/P